SPAIN
A Modern History

SPAIN
A MODERN HISTORY

Salvador de Madariaga

Frederick A. Praeger, *Publishers*

NEW YORK, N. Y.

BOOKS THAT MATTER

Published in the United States of America in 1958
by Frederick A. Praeger, Inc., Publishers
15 West 47th Street, New York 36, N. Y.

© 1958 in the United States of America
by Frederick A. Praeger, Inc.

Library of Congress catalog card number 58-9695
Type set at The Polyglot Press, New York
Printed in the United States of America

PREFACE

Since the first edition of this work was published in 1930, Spain has undergone deep changes through the cruel Civil War which, from 1936 till 1939, raged on her soil. These events must be recorded. This book must be written.

It is not the kind of book one writes for—or with—pleasure. It *had* to be written. Spain is one of the key countries in the world, owing both to her geographical position and to her close ties with the people of half the American continent. It was important that when at last the day has come to lay down the weapons of war and to begin rebuilding, an objective examination of the events of 1931-41 should be available, written with the inside knowledge which only consanguinity can provide.

The peculiar circumstances in which the Republic lived and died made it most difficult for nationals and foreigners to attain such an objectivity. Only a handful of Spaniards politically unattached, physically free (which meant, exiled from the beginning of the war) and ready to undergo the ostracism with which public opinion penalizes those who do not follow its meanderings, could keep a steady hold over the general line of events

v

without swerving either way more than the weight of the events themselves and the deficiencies of information now and then impelled them to do. If in these conditions, this handful of middle-of-the-way Spaniards kept their heads, it was not without difficulty. Right and left (physically and politically speaking) their friends fell victims to the fascination, the passion, the abhorrence or the enthusiasm of this or that extreme. A, who in 1931, as an old and staunch Monarchist, had been perturbed at the fall of the crown, burned with holy Communist zeal in 1936; P, an old Republican, ever in an uncompromising opposition under the Monarchy, an opposition to which he had sacrificed his military profession, was in 1936 a convinced Nationalist or Francoist out of his deep disappointment with the mistakes of the Republic. Information was confused, biased both ways, hardly ever objective. Within one hour and one hundred yards, one could hear in Paris the effectives of the International Brigades put at 70,000 and at 5,000 by men who had both been present when the Brigades had saved Madrid. Guernica was bombed by the Germans and burned by the Revolutionists in the columns of the same New York paper which one searched for objective news. Still, one had to keep one's head and above all one's heart in the midst of the turmoil.

This could only be done by refusing to budge from the bedrock of the deepest facts—the facts of human character, and in this case, of the national character of Spain. But, needless to say, when referring to the Spanish character in order to explain one of the most tragic follies a nation ever committed against herself, we are not likely to bring out its most attractive features. We shall constantly have to refer to the failings of Spanish psychology, as in all honesty we are bound to do. This by no means implies that Spaniards are in any way inferior to other peoples. It merely means that in the variegated picture of their qualities and defects, a certain number of shortcomings bear heavily on their political life. I have set them down objectively.

One is ashamed to have to write such things. It sounds almost old-fashioned to claim to base one's conclusions on an implicit belief in an objective reality independent of our mental whims and our unruly emotions. When Einstein, perhaps unwisely, described as the *"Theory of Relativity"* his mightly step forward on the road toward that immutable reality around us, every hasty, aesthetic thinker, too lazy to hammer on into the stubborn block of the unknown, every political zealot, too shaky as to the mental bases of his particular "ism," hailed relativism as salvation; so that, argue as honestly as one may and as carefully as one's mental integrity dictates, there will always be a polite shelving of one's argument with a seemingly openminded "Mr. So-and-So speaks from the point of view of the middle-class liberal," or some such meaningless device for refusing to think and more generally even for refusing to give up what one has held as thought. The world has thus been mapped out into thought-tight zones of relative thinking, and the implication is that these zones produce thought which is equally good or equally bad, all explicable by the class or nation or religion to which one belongs. That way lies anarchy, and while this dreadful mental relativism and nihilism prevails, reconstruction, order and peace are bound to remain beyond the reach of men.

The fact is that here is such a thing as nature and that it has its laws. Einstein's discovery has corrected but not invalidated Newton's laws; even if it had superseded them, it would have put a better known image of the laws of the stars in place of the old: but the laws of the stars would be there all the time. So it is with human life. It has its laws, and the challenge of our modern world to us, individual human beings, can only be met, and our way of life can only be saved, if we can try to regulate our collective life by doing less violence to its inherent laws—as yet undiscovered—than we have so far done. There is only one way thereto, the way of science, which may be described with a time-honored phrase, *trial and error*. No bias for or against any nation, class, religion, is permissible in this endeavor, which above all requires an unswerving loyalty to truth.

This is the spirit in which the following pages are written. It meant of course the pursuit of truth even when, as is often the case, truth is not simple. The democratic spirit of our age leads many minds to the demagogic temptation of oversimplifying matters to suit the lazy general. It is the easiest road to popularity, but not the most honest—nor perhaps the safest in the end. It is by no means certain that the oversimplifier, the put-that-in-words-of-one-syllable sort of man is the man simple people will follow, for after all the people do not turn out to be simple. Under their minds, even when undeveloped (perhaps particularly when undeveloped in the shallow way of our machine-made schools) the lives of the people are rich with the complexity of the spirit, and they are ready to understand that the things of life should be complex and therefore that their analysis should be complicated. It is only a certain type of limited, mechanized intellectual who will mistake the complicated for the obscure. Things should be clear or made clear by hard work if need be, but they are generally complicated in themselves. The history of the Spanish Civil War is clear but by no means simple.

I have tried to disentangle it and to make it clear. If here and there the result is not up to the level of my ambition, the error is sure to be one of mere fact, easily corrected. I trust it will never be found to be one of faith.

I feel bound to add one word. In my narrative of the events which led to the Civil War, as well as in that of the war itself, it may at times seem as if I stressed the errors and shortcomings of the Left more heavily than those of the Right. This was inevitable for two reasons. The first is that in the countries for which I am writing this study, it is about what actually happened in the Left that new light is particularly needed. The second is that it is from the Left rather than from the Right that we expect our future. It is the Left, therefore, which stands in need of criticism.

I hardly know the men of the Right. I lunched once with General Franco and a common friend, in 1934. I had never met him before and have not seen him since. My single conversation with Sr. Gil Robles did not last five minutes. I used to see Calvo Sotelo often when we both were in our early twenties, but lost sight of him before he reached the summits with Primo de Rivera; I met Señor Lerroux for the first time in May 1931.

On the other hand, every one of the leaders of the Left—Largo Caballero, Prieto, Azaña, Besteiro, Fernando de los Ríos, Araquistain, Negrín, Alvarez del Vayo—were old acquaintances or friends of a lifetime. It was in these men I, like every other liberal or Socialist Spaniard, had put my trust. This may also explain why I have been led to concentrate on their doings rather than on those of the other side.

S. DE M.

CONTENTS

CONTENTS xiii

BOOK 1

LAND,

PEOPLE, and

MONARCHY

PART 1

LAND, PEOPLE, and HISTORY

CHAPTER 1

THE LAND

The main fact about the land is its inaccessibility. Spain is a castle. The Iberian Peninsula stands at a higher mean altitude than any other part of Europe save Switzerland, and, if it be borne in mind that Switzerland rises on a pedestal of high lands while Spain rises from the sea, the average altitude of Spain (2000 feet approximately) will appear as more impressive than the average altitude of Switzerland (3600 feet). Mont Blanc is in the center of Europe, far from the sea; the Iberian Peninsula can show peaks comparable with, though not as high as, Mont Blanc on its four coasts: north, the Cantabric range; west, the Sierra de la Estrella; south, the range of the Andalusian coast; and east, the knot of mountains behind Valencia. Save for the valley of the Guadalquivir, which penetrates in a gradual ascent to the very heart of the peninsular labyrinth, the whole territory is thus surrounded by high walls, leaving between them and the ocean only narrow strips of land inter-

5

sected by torrents, short valleys soon abruptly walled by rising
lands (as the Tagus valley) or narrow passages through which
the river winds its way from its inner valley to the sea (as in the
case of the Ebro). Thus closed in behind the high walls of its
several coastal cordilleras and the towering Pyrenees, the Peninsula stretches as a vast tableland, broken up, however, into
several compartments both by ranges of mountains and by
deep depressions.

The citadel of this castle is the Central Tableland or *Meseta
Central,* an archaic formation stretching over two-thirds of the
territory at an average altitude of about 2000 feet, and generally considered as the geological nucleus and the oldest constituent of the Peninsula. This tableland gives the country its
most typical features: loftiness, bareness, space. It lies, slightly
tilted in a southwesterly direction, leaning on the Cantabric
range to the north, and on the Iberian cordillera to the northeast. It is bounded on the west by the depression which separates
it from the Atlantic plain on which Portugal lies; to the southwest by a sheer drop forming a wall at the foot of which falls
the Guadalquivir. The meseta is thus a true citadel surrounded
by walls and waters. The valley of the Guadalquivir, which
bounds it on the south, explains Andalusia. Beyond the western
edge the Tagus spreads out in a low-lying plain which accounts
for Portugal. North of the Cantabric range, Galicia, Asturias
and Santander lie and thrive on the seashore with their backs
leaning on the borders of the Central Tableland. From the
Basque depression to the Catalan coastal chain, the Ebro flows
in a deep ditch wedged in between the Pyrenees and the Iberian
range, in a kind of triangle which contains the lands of the
old crown of Aragon; Valencia is wedged in between the sea
and the formidable walls which bound the tableland on the east;
while Murcia, on the northeastern slope of the Andalusian
range, communicates with Castile through the steppes of La
Mancha immortalized by Don Quixote. Nor is the Meseta itself a mere flat tableland. A range of high mountains, perpen-
dicular to the Iberian range, cuts it from northeast to southwest
into two portions: Old Castile, the land of the Duero, known in

English-speaking countries under its Portuguese name of Douro; and New Castile (with La Mancha), the land of the Tagus or Tajo, which the Toledo range separates in its turn from the Guadiana valley. It is now maintained that the Central Tableland has (in relatively recent times) undergone an upward movement which contributes toward increasing its isolation from the surrounding parts of the peninsular territory.

A geographical survey reveals, therefore, the centrifugal character of the peninsula. Madrid, the capital of the kingdom, communicates with the north through three mountain passes, the lowest of which rises to 4700 feet. The two main railways connecting Madrid with the north have to ascend about 1500 to 1600 feet in their first 60 miles. The towns on the northern coast, Bilbao, Santander, Gijón, Coruña, are reached by railway from the Central Tableland through regular strings of tunnels coiled in inextricable knots in and around the high valleys of the north and northwest. The railway to Málaga crosses the Andalusian range very much as an Alpine climber ventures on unexplored ground, always on the edge of precipices, and almost to this day Madrid has been unconnected directly with Valencia, its nearest seaport (as the crow flies), through the sheer power of natural obstacles. The northwestern territory, the four Atlantic valleys, the Ebro valley and the southeastern territories are mutually inaccessible and point in different directions; moreover, the tableland is also separated from the Portuguese plains by a sudden drop in altitude. The general inaccessibility of the peninsula is thus prolonged inward, and walls and battlements divide within itself the territory which walls and battlements separate from other countries.

From such a topography considerable variety is to be anticipated. In point of climate, however, the Peninsula may be classified into two main regions: wet and dry. The frontier between them starts on the Catalan coast, north of the Ebro, running westward past the point where the Iberian and the Catalonian ranges meet; then, circling round south of the Cantabric range, it turns southward, following the Portuguese frontier though advancing into Spanish territory on the high lands stretching north and south of the Tagus, and leaving on dry territory the whole of southern Portugal. This line divides the Peninsula into two parts: north and west of it lies a soft, temperate, and rainy climate; south and east of it a country with a hard, extreme and dry climate. Of the 226,590 square miles of the Peninsula, 101,790 belong to the northern and western temperate and wet region, while 124,800 belong to the extreme dry southeast. Portugal partakes of both, though in unequal proportions, most of it belonging to the temperate wet zone. If Portuguese territory be excluded, the representative figures are 69,420 for the rainy Northwest and 122,460 for the dry Southeast. Temperate and rainy Spain represents, therefore, about 36 per cent, or slightly over one-third of the Peninsula. Yet these figures must be carefully interpreted. A large proportion of the temperate part of Spain is made up of high, uninhabitable regions, and, though the valleys which they hide away in their labyrinths are rich and thickly populated, there is in their very isolation an inherent element of weakness from the point of view of their contribution to the spirit and character of the country as a whole. Both Spains make Spain, the temperate and the extreme; but there is little doubt that the extreme is the more important of the two. Lofty, bare and spacious, this Spain impresses the mind with a sense of primitive strength. Whether in summer, when it receives on its "monk-colored" mantle the fierce caress of an overpowering sun; or in autumn, when deep purple clouds drag their mysterious shadows across its unlimited plains in silence; or in the thin, clear winter, when the sunlight seems to lend its cold gleams to the sharp knives of the Sierra winds; or in its fleeting spring; the Castilian tableland is a country with a grandeur and a majesty which make it the worthy companion of the great scenes of nature—seas and skies—and of the great moods of the spirit—poetry and contemplation.

North, south, east and west of the Central Tableland, and in deep contrast with its vast monotony, Spain presents to the traveler every possible landscape. Portugal is a sunnier Normandy. Norway has no more picturesque fjords than Galicia, nor Switzerland more impressive peaks than the snowy moun-

tains of Asturias and Santander; the Scot, winding his way up
the industrial valley of the Nervion, may well imagine himself
traveling toward Glasgow along his busy Clyde; the wooded
slopes of Navarra are a match to those of the Black Forest;
the Ebro valley, with its alternation of dry, broken, reddish
cliffs and fertile oases is, perhaps, purely Spanish; but lower
Catalonia is a Mediterranean country, and could be either
Italian or Greek; Valencia and Murcia, whose rivers run dry
so that their checkered plains may flourish, are still Moorish,
with now and then a Palestinian touch in the landscape—the
palm tree and the Biblical well. Andalusia, again, is purely
Spanish, though it might be dreamed of in Persia or in the
pages of the *Thousand and One Nights*. And yet all this variety
is, so to speak, shrouded in an atmosphere of unity. From soft,
moody Galicia to parched, clear Murcia, glowing under its hot
sun; from the snowy pines of Asturias to the dusty palm trees
of Alicante; from the puritanical narrow valleys of grey Guipuz-
coa to the blossoming *vegas* of western Andalusia, the same air,
the same mood seems to be suggested by nature. Spain is one
under all her Spains, and this is the first mystery which has to be
solved. What is this one quality which unifies the several qualities, this deeper impression which covers and colors all other
impressions? A kind of primitive strength, static, unexpressed. A
kind of passive vigor. It is best understood, perhaps, in the wild
vegetation of its dry, uncultivated lands, particularly those broken territories which the more enterprising traveler is apt to
discover for his gratification in the higher recesses of its mountainous knots. The earth is often but that rough sand which
results from decomposing granite. For the greater part of the
year it is dry, now baked by a merciless sun, now contracted
by the severe frosts of a luminous winter. Yet this rough earth
clings to its mountain side and brings forth sturdy, vigorous
plants, small wiry twigs covered with tiny flowers which no dew
ever comes to refresh—little flowers of infinite variety and so
strong in aroma that, once it has been scented, all other country
walks seem flat to the most imaginative of senses. Botanists say
that of the ten thousand flowers known in Europe more than half

are to be found only in Spain; navigators, that the scent of Spain is perceptible from the seas before her coasts are in sight. Such is the primitive fertility of the Peninsula, a fertility which is but a sign, a symbol of that quality which makes it one in its variety. Its quiet strength, its permanent vitality, is the source of that impression which the traveler finds everywhere as the Spanish essence under the Catalonian, Aragonese, Castilian and Andalusian forms. Rough, primitive, dry, but rich in spontaneous scent, in wild vegetation, in uncultivated grace, the Peninsula is, in itself, apart from the people who inhabit it, a great power and a great presence.

CHAPTER 2

THE PEOPLE

Varied but one is the land; varied but one the people. Recent anthropological studies show the complex mixture of physical types which can be found in Spain. A center of round-headed types seems well established on the Cantabric coast, stretching from Santander to Coruña, while a similar center of long-headed races would appear to exist on the southeastern coast, between Alicante and Almería. Yet long-headed types are also the rule in Castile, Teruel, Alava and even Orense and Portugal, while round-headed ones are to be found in Cáceres and in the south-ernmost part of the Peninsula, i.e. the district of Málaga, as well as among the women of the Guadalquivir valley. This blend of types becomes still more apparent when types are defined, not merely by the usual proportion between the two diameters generally adopted to discriminate between so-called long-headed and so-called short-headed races, but by a higher number of cranial indexes. By adopting a three-dimensional method a contemporary Spanish anthropologist has outlined a map of racial regions which illustrates the intimate blending of the purely racial elements in the Peninsula. An endeavor to establish a certain amount of order in this chaos of data would lead to dividing the Peninsula into the following regions:

1st Region—Inhabited by a long-headed type. Can be subdivided into two zones:

(*a*) The Aragonese Iberian zone, with a long, high, narrow skull and a fairly high proportion of light-colored eyes and fair or red hair (about 35 per cent).

(*b*) The Valencian zone, which occupies the eastern coast from the Ebro mouth to the Cape of Gata. Here the face is even narrower than in the preceding zone and the proportion of blue and gray-eyed and fair and red-headed types is much smaller.

These two types have been related to an African-Iberian or Berber race.

2nd Region—Inhabited by a round-headed type. May be subdivided as follows:

(*a*) Cantabrian zone (Santander to Coruña). The skull is wide and somewhat low, yet the face is apt to be narrow; the nose sharp and the eyes low but wide-set; a colorful complexion, frequently red or fair hair, clear hazel eyes.

(*b*) The Estremadura zone. A less robust race with more angular features and darker eyes, though blue eyes are not rare.

These two zones have been traced to Celtic origins, though the second is sometimes considered as Ligurian.

3rd Region—A middle type, also subdivided into two zones, closely related, however:

(*a*) The Basque zone. The skull has a shape intermediate between the two extreme types mentioned in Regions 1 and

2; the face is long and narrow, the nose sharp and aquiline, the eyes low. Light-colored eyes are found in a proportion of about 40 per cent.

(*b*) The Castilian zone. Still within the middle group, yet with a tendency toward the long-headed type. The name Castilian should not be taken literally here, as this region includes provinces which are not politically Castilian (such as León), while it leaves out Santander (politically Castilian, but belonging to the second or round-headed region) and Soria and Logroño (belonging to the first region, Aragonese variety). Its most constant feature is the absence of fair hair and light-colored eyes.

Other less marked types are:

4th Region—The Manchegan type, with a high and narrow skull, often short, a low forehead, a heavy jaw, long nose and wide-set eyes. It is believed to represent an old prehistoric Peninsular stock.

5th Region—The round-headed Andalusian. A dark-colored type inhabiting the provinces of western Andalusia.

Finally, there are two considerable regions, namely, eastern Andalusia and Catalonia, the study of which has led to no further conclusion than the extreme complexity of their physical characteristics and, therefore, the probable mixed character of their inhabitants. Such a conclusion can evidently be generalized to cover the whole Peninsula. A physical study of the Spanish race confirms the view that the Spaniard results from a mixture of several races, the clearest types of which would appear to be a long-headed Iberian, settled, roughly, along the Ebro valley and the eastern coast, and a round-headed Celt occupying the north coast from Santander to Cape Finisterre.

The earliest settlers of the Peninsula were Ligurians. The Iberians, probably of North African origin, began to enter Spain and to settle in the East and South possibly before Europe and Africa were torn asunder. Between 2500 and 1700 B.C. there were already contacts between the Iberians of southern Spain and Brittany, the British Isles, Scandinavia and Germany; later, toward 1200, contacts began between Iberian Spain and southern Italy. The Celts, a more or less Nordic people, began to invade northeastern Spain toward 900 B.C., while a century later, the Phoenicians founded Cádiz and Málaga. Toward 600 B.C. the Northwest and West were overrun by the second Celtic invasion. Despite this fact, the two different stocks which had shared the Peninsula did not mix in any measurable degree. The formidable natural obstacles which the country raises on the traveler's path kept them apart, and while the Celts developed in the cold and damp Northwest along the general lines of the European Iron Age, the Iberians flourished in the pleasant, warm climates of the East and South where for about two or three centuries their inherent talents, stimulated by foreign, Eastern influences, maintained a brilliant civilization.

The first of these foreign settlers were the Phoenicians and the Greeks. They had settlements on the southeastern and eastern coasts, and were isolated factors with but a small connection with the hinterland. Carthage had a deeper influence. Two great towns were founded by the Carthaginians: Cartagena and Barcelona. But the hold of Carthage lasted but a third of a century, and it was succeeded by the sway of Rome, which was to leave on Spain the deepest racial and social influence before that of the Arabs. The Romanization of the country was extremely quick once the military resistance was broken. By the end of the Augustan period Rome had conquered Spain with her arms, and Spain Rome with her letters. The literature of the Silver Age is Spanish. The two great Antonine Emperors, Trajan and Hadrian, were Spanish. Such a swift adaptation suggests not so much an educational as a colonizing effort on the part of Rome. Roman soldiers, ex-soldiers, civil servants mixed with the aboriginal population and contributed to Romanization.

The several hordes of barbarians which overran the country from the first half of the fifth century on cannot be said to have left in Spain either a racial or a social influence comparable with that of the Romans. They disrupted Roman civilization and plunged the country into anarchy, out of which in the course of time the Visigothic Kingdom was gradually evolved. It cannot be said that the Visigothic period contributed much to the social and racial characteristics of the Spaniards. Most of what was institutional in it had been left over from the Roman period, whether it was actually Roman or Iberian. The only important event which occurred during the Visigothic era was the adoption of the Christian religion as the religion of the state; first in its Arian form, then in the orthodox Catholic form, thanks to King Recared (586-601). But the very inadequacy of the Visigothic military state enabled the South of Spain to settle down to its usual task of evolving a culture and a civilization. During this period St. Isidore shines in Seville, a beacon not only for Spain, but for the whole of Christendom.

The Visigothic sway fell at the hands of the people who, with the Romans, were to exert the deepest influence over the Spaniards. The Arabs, or the Moors as they are called, with a truly impartial inaccuracy, invaded Spain in 711. Almost instantly they covered the whole Peninsula, with the exception of the inaccessible valleys of the high Cantabric and Pyrenean ranges. From 711 till the fall of Granada in 1492, they lived on the most intimate terms with the people they found in the Peninsula, both in peace and in war—two forms of intimacy. The Reconquista is not so much a war as a historical period, the true meaning of which can only be grasped when medieval Spain is seen as the frontier between the Islamic and the European civilizations of the time.[1] From the ninth to the eleventh century the civilization of our world is Islamic. Christendom is in the dark while Islam shines in Baghdad and in Córdoba with all the lights of science, art, politics, culture and refinement. Northern Spain is divided up into petty barbarian kingdoms on whom the mighty and refined Khalif of Córdoba looks down very much as the French President was later to look down upon Moroccan tribes. Islamic Spain gives the world her philosophers, astronomers, mathematicians, mystics, poets, historians. In one of the smallest courts of El Andalus, in Almería, there were five

---

[1] *See* on this point the scholarly book of Don Ramón Menéndez Pidal, *La España del Cid,* 1929.

thousand looms weaving all kinds of cloth from brocade and silk to wool and cotton, and the Prime Minister of a small state (a kind of Islamic Goethe in his Spanish Weimar) had four hundred thousand books in his library, while the "great" and famous library of the monastery of Ripoll in Christian Catalonia boasted of its paltry 192 volumes. During this period the Christian kingdoms of northern Spain were the tributaries of the Khalif of Córdoba, i.e. of the monarch of "Spain," in financial, political and cultural matters, and it was to Córdoba that they sent their ministers, or that they repaired themselves, to seek the help of the Khalif, to ask for his protection, to beg him to arbitrate between their rival claims. Toward the end of the tenth century Almanzor, a Napoleonic dictator, arose in the khalifate and in a series of swift campaigns reduced the Christian kingdoms to complete subjection, from Catalonia to Galicia, carrying numberless trophies to Córdoba, in the mosque of which he hung as lamps the bells of St. James of Compostela.

But the Islamic civilization entered a period of decadence. The khalifate of Córdoba fell into weak hands, and disintegrated into smaller kingdoms, while Christian civilization was rising in Europe under the leadership of high-principled kings (Robert the Pious of France, St. Henry of Germany, St. Stephen of Hungary and, later, Ferdinand I of Castile-Leon). Seven years after Almanzor's death (1009) Sancho García, Count of Castile, entered Córdoba at the head of his knights. The wheel had turned full circle. El Andalus was going to break up and its petty kingdoms were to fall vassals to the northern king—to "Spain." The body, Spain, was the same, but the spirit which it was to house was going to change, within the eleventh century, from the spirit of Islam to that of Christianity. The North produced its representative hero in El Cid, just as the South had produced Almanzor, and almost exactly one hundred years later. But just as Almanzor was no longer exactly the khalifate, but in reality the beginning of its disintegration, so El Cid was not yet exactly the king of Spain, but the herald, the precursor of the king.

The struggle, however, is much less one of nations and peo-

ples than of religions and civilizations. Señor Menéndez Pidal
has shown that the North was more Christian than the South
was Islamic. El Andalus contained:

1. Moslems of Eastern origin, many of whom had married
Christian women.

2. Moslems of Spanish origin (Gothic or Hispano Roman)—
numerically far stronger than the first group—who had been
converted to Islam in the course of time, and who also had often
married Northern women;

3. A considerable Christian population (Mozárabes) who
lived amidst the Moors, under their Christian faith and Visigothic laws, ruled by Christian bishops and counts;

4. Isolated Christian lords who had succeeded in retaining a
kind of independence in the midst of Islam.

El Andalus was bilingual. Both Arabic and *Romance* were
spoken, and the line between the two languages was not one
of religion, but one of culture. Arabic was spoken in the higher
ranks of society, *Romance* by the lower classes. There were
Moslems in Spain who knew no other language than *Romance*.

This picturesque constitution of El Andalus explains the progress of the Reconquista after the second half of the eleventh
century. Beneath the religious difference the people were very
much the same, north and south. The drive southward was led
less by a feeling of foreignness toward the inhabitants of El
Andalus than by a tradition which felt Spain as one, and which,
therefore, led the most powerful of the Spanish states to recon-
stitute the unity of Spain. This tradition had been handed down
from the Roman and Visigothic periods through the kingdom of
León to the king of Castile. By 1276, the date of James of Aragon's death, the whole Peninsula was under Christian control.
James' states bordered on the south those of Alfonso the Sage.
Ferdinand III (St. Ferdinand), Alfonso's father, had reduced the
Moorish possessions to the kingdom of Granada, which had
become one of his tributaries.

Much as the temper of the Spanish people toward the Moors
and Jews changed after the eleventh century, until it led them
to the wholesale expulsions of a later date, there is no doubt

that in their four hundred years of cordial intimacy in peace and war the racial intermixture must have been deep. Not only the Moor but the Jew was bound to become an important element in the Spanish people as at present constituted. The typically Oriental characteristics of the Spaniard, though they may have preexisted, must have been reinforced by these four centuries of familiarity with two typically Oriental races.

The Peninsula acts as a sounding board for Oriental races, who usually give their richest sounds in it. Thus Spain brought to a high degree of excellence no less than three Oriental races: the Arab, the Jew, and the Gypsy. It was in Spain that Arab civilization rose to its highest brilliancy; Spanish Jews were the greatest luminaries of Hebrew civilization since Biblical times; and as for the Gypsy, the superiority of the Spanish type over any other is not to be proved by books, but by the observation of the living specimens which may be found in Andalusia.

Such are the influences, racial, historical and local, which, in the course of ages, have fashioned the Spanish people, as we find it, on the threshold of modern history at the beginning of the sixteenth century.

A direct observation of this people leads to the same conclusion to which we were led by the survey of the land it inhabits; outward variety and inward unity. There are in Spain several well-defined types:

The Gallegan, in the northwestern corner of the Peninsula, shrewd, intelligent, hard-working, thrifty, physically strong, provides Spain with lawyers, politicians, stevedores, policemen and the famous gangs of mowers who, in the early summer, travel southward and return home, scythe in hand, harvesting the whole peninsular crop. The inhabitant of a soft, gray land, the Gallegan is of a dreamy disposition, poetical and imaginative, superstitious, apt to believe in apparitions and to feel the presence of the supernatural world. His mind and life have been admirably rendered by the most distinguished of modern Gallegan men of letters, Don Ramón María del Valle-Inclán.

The Asturian, a close neighbor of the Gallegan, is less reserved and more consciously intelligent, less cautious and more vivacious. He is still deeply poetical, but the faith, at times naïve, of the Gallegan, is here undermined by a quiet yet keen sense of humor. These natural gifts are expressed in a popular poetry which ranks with the best to be found in a country so rich in popular poetry as Spain. Asturias has given Spain several of her enlightened statesmen. Its spirit is fitly represented in contemporary literature by Ramón Pérez de Ayala.

If, following the northern coast eastward, we skip the province of Santander, a purely Castilian province in spirit, we come next to the Basque country, a labyrinth of narrow valleys, green as befits a land generously watered by skies too often gray. The Basques are forestmen, fishermen, peasants; they are strong, healthy and simple. In recent years their inherent spirit of enterprise has blossomed out to such an extent that the Basque has become the chief capitalist of modern Spain. The Basque is apt to hold fast to his opinion, as people who have not many opinions to spare are wont to do. He is stern, loyal, uncompromising and narrow. It is in the Basque valleys that the narrow-minded clerical Catholic movement finds its mainspring and its fastest strongholds. Loyola was a Basque. There are Basques of a different school of thought, more amenable to compromise, as the great name of Unamuno suffices to prove.

At the other, the Mediterranean, end of the Pyrenees, the Catalans occupy a symmetrical position.[2] Aslant south of Basques and Catalans, the valley of the Ebro may be considered as the geographic definition of the kingdom of Aragon. The Aragonese is the most primitive, perhaps the most genuine, representative of the distinctly Spanish features. Spontaneous, frank, he is apt to form extreme opinions; he is uncompromising, stubborn, richer in intuition than in conscious intellect, independent, proud and individualistic. Goya was an Aragonese, and his genius conveys the genius of Aragon better than any works of literature.

South of the Ebro the kingdom of Valencia, linguistically connected with Catalonia, is Mediterranean and expressive like Catalonia, but spontaneous and primitive like Aragon; more

---

[2] For Catalan psychology, *see* Chapter 16.

peasant than *bourgeois*. The passions of the Valencian are stronger and more easily aroused than is the case with his northern cousin. His love of pleasure is not so keen, nor is he so fond of thrift and comfort. Though as gifted as Catalonia in artistic tendencies, Valencia manifests herself in color rather than in eloquence. The best exponents of her spirit are two well-known artists recently lost by her: Blasco Ibáñez the novelist, and Sorolla the painter.

If the Basques bring to the Spanish character force rather than grace, the Andalusians provide it with grace rather than force. The Andalusian is richer, no doubt, in aesthetic gifts, which he manifests freely in his daily life. Flowers and songs are his constant companions and an innate wisdom his principal virtue. The genius of Andalusia has been most felicitously expressed by two Sevillian authors, the brothers Serafín, and Joaquín Alvarez Quintero.

In the midst of all these varieties of Spain stands the central and normal type of country, Castile. The Castilian spirit has been best expressed, and for all time, by the greatest of Castilians and of Spaniards—Cervantes. Don Quixote and Sancho are, strictly speaking, Manchegan, but the differences between La Mancha and Castile are not easily discernible, particularly at the psychological depth to which the great Castilian takes us. Castile, moreover, provides the best specific example of Spanish character in general, i.e. that character which constitutes the unity under their variety and binds together the several types of Spaniards by means of an inner link.

As with the land, so with the men. The sense of unity under the variety comes from an impression of primitive strength, of all-round synthetic vigor. It may be first observed when dealing with the people. It will be noticed that the people, i.e. the popular classes, north or south, east or west, possess qualities of wisdom, of heart, of manners, which the visitor is used to connect with the cultured or well-to-do levels of society. The usual test—illiteracy—breaks down in Spain. Illiterates speak like Seneca, sing like Blake, and behave like Louis XIV. A composure, a quiet assurance, covered with respect but not oiled with subservience, a genuine fellow feeling, a quick sense of dignity yet free from susceptibility, suggest that the Spanish people are endowed with a natural notion of equality springing from a deep sense of fraternity. A sense rather than a feeling; for rather than a definite movement, or manifestation, or even mood, it is an atmosphere in which moods and movements manifest themselves.

Such a sense of the inherent equality of all men springs from a religious substratum. Whether consciously or not, the Spaniard lives against a background of eternity, and his outlook is more religious than philosophic. Hence it is that the two poles of his psychology are the individual and the universe; the subject and the Whole; and that life for him should consist in the absorbing of the universe by the individual, the *assimilation* of the Whole by the subject.

The individual thus becomes the standard of all life—an individual voluntarily stripped of all but essential tendencies. Instinctively at home in essential things, the Spaniard is therefore apt to evade the grasp of things which are less high up in the scale—things merely necessary or useful or advisable. The Spaniard is therefore unfettered by any sense of social pressure or intellectual standard. He is spontaneous, "all-around," always entirely present and wholly engaged wherever he happens to be. He shuns abstractions as much as any Englishman and is as free from inhibitions as any Frenchman can be. He is neither a citizen of an equalitarian state, nor a partner in a national society, nor a subject in an empire. He is a man.

This individualist is an egoist. His person is the channel through which the life-stream is made to pass, thus acquiring a personality polarized along a definite individual direction. The Spaniard therefore feels patriotism as he feels love—in the form of a passion whereby he absorbs the object of his love and assimilates it; that is to say, makes it his own. He does not belong to his country so much as his country belongs to him, and as his perspective is concrete and individualistic it follows that he is apt to feel his patriotism with an intensity in inverse proportion to the area of the regions which surround him.

Moreover, the instinct for preserving his own liberty makes him eschew all forms of social cooperation, since all collective work tends to enslave the individual and to reduce him to the status of a piece, of machinery. His anti-cooperative instinct comes to reinforce his tendency to dwell on the two poles of his psychology—man and the universe—leaving uncultivated the middle stretches in which social and political communities lie.

These middle stretches are precisely those which can be at best governed by ethical and political principles. But the Spaniard, however interested he may be in such principles, governs his life by an individual sense of direction which works in him precisely by virtue of the passive character of his inward attitude toward life. In what concerns collective, and particularly political, life, the Spaniard is apt to judge events according to a dramatic criterion, singularly free from any practical considerations or intellectual prepossessions. It follows that in Spain, liberty, justice, and free trade matter less than the particular Smith or Jones who is to incarnate them for the time being. Nor, be it said in passing, is such a point of view quite at variance with the experience of countries more politically minded than Spain. In this dramatic criterion of the Spaniard, his sense of man may be observed. His sense of the universe manifests itself in his tendency to found his political institutions on the widest and most universal basis, i.e. the religious basis. Thus his patriotism, considered as a mere manifestation of group consciousness, is weakened both ways: at the individual end, because the individual tends to absorb the nation rather than allow himself to be absorbed by it; at the universal end, because the Spaniard who widens his outlook does not stop at the borders of the nation, and seeks to embrace the whole world.

This oscillation between the two extremes, man and the universe, is the rhythm that underlies the history of Spain.

It is easy to see how these psychological premises lead to the two constant features of Spanish political life which may be symbolized in the words: *dictatorship* and *separatism*. The individual, moved by stronger vertical than horizontal impulses, i.e. by natural forces expressed directly in him rather than by forces transmitted by tradition or absorbed from the environment, tends to assert his personality and (like a bottle already full of its own contents) to refuse other influences. This leads to dictatorship, observable not merely in the public man, statesman, general, cardinal, or king at the head of the state, but in every one of the men at the head (or on the way thereto) of every village, city, region, business firm, or even family in the country.

The dictator is most averse to separatism in others, since it limits the area of his own dictatorship; but he is a separatist himself, for he separates himself from others in what concerns the usual collective functions of study, discussion, give-and-take, and agreement. The strong individual, vertical pattern of the Spaniard and the weakness of his horizontal tendencies, those of course which weave men together in a social tissue, explain the separatism of Spaniards and the ease with which, at the slightest shock, regions, cities, political parties, classes, services of the state, are torn asunder and fall away from each other. Needless to say, there will always be topical causes to determine the cracks in the collective texture of the country; but the facility with which such causes produce the cracks and the depth of the cracks themselves are due to the quality of the texture and not to the circumstances which act upon it. Nothing in fact is more characteristic of the Spanish nature than this *brittle* quality of its collective self which, by the way, we find exemplified in the Disunited States of Spanish America (the fruit of dictatorship and separatism) as opposed to the United States of Anglo-Saxon America.

Separatism and dictatorship, however, are passions of the Spaniard; they are not his sense. When in the realm of sense, the Spaniard is unusually creative and realistic. But for him to attain this plane, he needs a higher passion strong enough to raise him to a unity from the dispersive level in which he is wont to dwell. Such a high passion was the faith which he once attained in the sixteenth and seventeenth centuries and which gave Spain a strength in unity such as she has never known since and may perhaps never know again.

CHAPTER 3

THE SPANISH EMPIRE

The modern history of Spain may be divided into the following periods of approximately the same duration:

1. Rise and fall of the Spanish Empire (1492-1700).

2. (a) Restoration, new rise and new fall of Spain, as a world power under the Bourbon dynasty (1701-1800).
   (b) Rise of modern Spain as a self-contained nation (1800 to the present date).

In 1479, Isabel became queen of Castile, and Ferdinand king of Aragon. In 1492, they conquered Granada from the last of the Moorish kings in Spain and Christopher Columbus discovered America. Spain's career as a world power had begun.

Spain is thus the first great nation to attain full stature. The reign of Ferdinand and Isabel may be considered as symbolical of the forces which we are to observe at work in Spanish history.

These forces may be reduced to three: the two extreme tendencies, individualism and universalism, both typical of the Spanish character; and a middle force then strongly active everywhere in Europe: state consciousness. Anarchy, religion, politics. The individual, the Church, the state. The first of these three forces was at play throughout the Middle Ages both in Castile and in Aragon. Isabel owed her crown at least in part to the disorders which the turbulent Castilian nobility maintained against her predecessor and brother, the wretched Henry IV. Religion and politics may be seen incarnated respectively in Isabel and Ferdinand. It is not through sheer accident that Isabel was the queen of the Central Tableland, slanting away from the Mediterranean, rising above the Atlantic coast, isolated in its austere and primitive simplicity; while Ferdinand was the king of the Ebro valley, sloping toward the Mediterranean, open to the winds of Italy and to the temptations of wealth and conquest.

Isabel, daughter of a mad princess and mother of a mad queen, was herself a highly strung woman, earnest, firm, conscientious, deeply possessed by the sense of her responsibility as the minister of God on earth. Every one of her actions was taken on this background of eternity. Her reign was inspired by the necessity of making Spain one in spirit. Her mind was religious and her vision essentially universal.

Ferdinand was a politician. He was the Politician: the model on which Machiavelli outlined his ideal *Prince*. Astuteness was his method as much as or more than force.. His aim was not spiritual, but political. His mind was positive and his vision national. Isabel and Ferdinand reigned on a footing of equality. Under their common rule the Spanish anarchy became a state and the Spanish state became a church.

Not, be it understood, The Church; least of all, the Roman Church. The expulsion of the Jews was not a Roman but a Spanish idea. The Inquisition was conceived and founded as a department of state, outside the jurisdiction of the Church and its bishops; and though in later years Rome sought to regain control over it, and did in part, the royal tendency to yield as little as possible to papal pressure remained as active as ever.

Nor was Queen Isabel less firm in handling the Church at home. She resisted with great energy all attempts made by the ecclesiastical jurisdiction to encroach on the state jurisdiction. With the help of her confessor, Ximénez de Cisneros, Archbishop of Toledo, she undertook a strict reform of the Spanish Church. The Crown secured from Rome considerable control over the Church in America. Thus the Spanish state, while identifying itself with the spiritual interests of the Catholic faith, did not submit to the Roman Church. It was itself a church in that for it nationality and religion became one and its official interests were religious, i.e. the spiritual welfare of its subjects..

As was to be expected, the essential and permanent element of this policy, i.e. its religious character, is stronger than its political aspect. It explains why the standard by which the state is unified should be not political nor linguistic, but religious. Thus this royal couple, who insisted on the conversion of all their new subjects to the Catholic faith, mantained a strict separation between the political institutions of their two kingdoms, with the significant exception of the Inquisition. The Catalans, subjects of the Crown of Aragon, maintained their consuls in Castilian ports as in other foreign ports after the union of the two crowns. The Cortes, the judiciary, remained distinct. As to language, the kingdom of Aragon was bilingual; for Aragon proper spoke Castilian while the Catalans, who began then to speak Castilian through mere social causes, such as the natural prestige of the language spoken at court, were the object of no official action to stimulate this evolution. Political and cultural unity was not found essential. What was essential was a unity of faith. Hence the expulsion of the Jews. Ferdinand and Isabel have been severely criticized by learned economists and historians for having overlooked the disastrous economic consequences of such a measure. We might as well criticize Mahatma Gandhi for disregarding the political philosophy of Henry Ford. The Decree was sanctioned on March 31, 1492. Granada had been taken from the last Moor on January 2. All royal work was not, of course, so directly inspired by religious zeal. Unruly nobles were reduced to obedience with an iron hand; legislation was unified; municipal liberties, while respected in outward forms, were gradually brought under royal supervision and authority; the value of money was accurately defined and maintained uniformly throughout the kingdom; a protectionist policy was pursued with remarkable perseverance.

If the religious inspiration of the Castilian queen prevailed in home affairs, Ferdinand's political genius and the Mediterranean traditions of Aragon gained the upper hand in foreign policy. The Ebro valley looked toward the southeast. Catalonia was the natural rival of the King of France in a common claim over the Roussillon—Catalan by race and language, French by geographical necessity. The duel was thus against the French king and the battlefield Italy. After many episodes the rivalry ended in the victory of the Spanish king, who, at his death in 1516, left to his heir the islands of Sardinia and Sicily, more than half the Italian Peninsula, and the Roussillon.

Nor was war his only method for securing Spanish supremacy. He had woven a net of princely marriages which, even though often torn by the ruthless hand of death, caught untold political wealth in its remaining meshes for the house of Spain. All his daughters were politically married: Isabel to the Duke of Beja, heir to the Portuguese throne; Katherine to Henry VIII of England; Joan to Philip the Handsome, head of the house of Burgundy. Thus on the death of Ferdinand, who survived Isabel by twelve years, Charles, Joan's son, found himself king of Spain, of half the Italian Peninsula, the Low Countries and a fair portion of the northeast and southeast of what is now known as France.

Such was the political basis which Ferdinand prepared for the spirit of Isabel to rise above national limitations toward universal aims. The man who was destined to inaugurate a universal policy in Europe was half-Spanish, half-Flemish by birth and wholly Flemish by education. Distant and contemptuous at first toward his mother's country, he became the instrument of her historical destiny and, when exhausted by the struggle he sought relief from the burden of his crown, he chose a Spanish monastery for his retreat.

Three historical lines intertwine in the history of the Spanish Empire under the Austrian dynasty: the natural evolution of Spain herself; the evolution of Spain as the leading factor in European politics; the development of discovery and colonization in America. During this period Spain was the foremost power in the world. Her territories comprised the south of Italy, Holland, Belgium, Spain, Portugal and considerable parts of France; the whole of South and Central America with most of the western and southern portions of the United States, the Philippine Islands, Madeira, the Azores and Cape Verde Islands, Guinea, Congo, Angola, Ceylon, Borneo, Sumatra, the Moluccas, and a number of settlements in other Asiatic lands. During the reign of Charles I Portugal was a separate nation, but the Central European territories under the imperial crown were also to all intents and purposes a part of the Spanish Empire. Nor was this empire great in size only. It was great also in the prestige gained by the adventurous and romantic character of its discoveries and by the varied emotions which the stores of precious metal Spain was supposed to obtain from her El Dorado awoke in other lands.

Spain was thrust on the world stage by an impulse directed toward religious unity. Such an impulse was to dominate all her policy, at home, in Europe and overseas. At home, it explains the Inquisition, the decay of the university, the drying up of sources of intellectual leadership in her middle classes, the impoverishment of her civil service, and, in the end, the lamentable weakness of the state at the death of Charles II, the incapable king. In Europe it accounts for the tragic efforts which Charles V (Charles I of Spain) made to heal the wound of the Reformation and to save the unity of Europe, his decision to leave the Low Countries to the Crown of Spain (Philip II) and not to the German Imperial Crown (his brother Ferdinand), the struggles between Philip II and the Netherlands, and the final exhaustion of the Spanish Monarchy in the hopeless task of retaining the Low Countries within the fold of the Church. In America, the impulse of the Spanish people toward religious unity accounts for the proselytizing ardor of many a conquistador, whose zeal had to be tempered by the wiser friar at his elbow; and it explains the basis of racial equality which distinguishes Spanish colonization and the prodigious effort for the religious and general education of the Indians which makes it an exceptional enterprise in those times and a worthy model even in our own.

The net result of these efforts was that Spain became at that time the enemy, though for different reasons, of practically every nation that counted in the world. If we want to bring about a better understanding of history, we must endeavor to write under the steady light of this principle—that Europe is fundamentally one and that her wars were civil wars. The key period of Spanish history cannot be understood unless the motive which animates it is appraised at its true value. The Austrian dynasty, worthy heirs of Ferdinand and Isabel, was always alive to the capital distinction between purity of faith and dogma and submission to Rome. The Spanish state was a church, but it was not The Church. Spain was the soldier of God, but she did not allow the Pope to define her duties. Far from it. As the history of the Counter Reformation shows, Spain was the chief factor in the reformation and purification of the Church from within. Charles and Philip, moreover, were the moving forces which led to the Council of Trent, the intellectual and moral leadership of which was also, to a considerable extent, Spanish.

Both Charles and Philip had to fight the "King of Rome." Charles' (Spanish) ambassador in Rome advised him to profit by his troubles with Clement VII in order to abolish the Pope's temporal power. Philip II set up a council presided over by the Archbishop of Toledo to act in lieu of the Pope at the time when the King of Spain was not on speaking terms with him. The brilliant school of theologians and lawyers which Spain produced in this period, practically all churchmen, sided with the king in these matters. Their stand was firmly religious, and they were therefore the more disposed to argue down the merely ecclesiastical point of view of Rome. The same reason, i.e. a profound freedom of mind within the bounds of dogma, explains why, although they were with the king against the Pope, they were

with the people against the king. The king is "God's minister on
earth"; therefore he must behave or bear the penalty of misbehavior. Father Mariana, the Jesuit historian, justifies regicide
against a king who betrays God's trust. He was not the only
jurist to think so boldly in those days of absolute monarchy.
Fox Morcillo, whom Philip II esteemed so much that he made
him the tutor of his son and heir, was of opinion that no obedience was due to the king who transgressed the laws, and he
declared that the form of government—monarchy or republic—
mattered little. The greatest of Spanish jurists, Father Vitoria,
one of the precursors of the League of Nations, in a discussion
on war, limits the power of the king to what is right and the duty
of his subects to what they think is right. Father Vitoria was no
irresponsible intellectual. He was the chief authority of the land
in matters of law and theology; his advice was sought by the
king on questions of moment. Father Vitoria laid down the
theory of the conscientious objector in unmistakable terms: "If
a subject is convinced of the injustice of a war, he ought not to
serve in it, even on the command of his prince . . . hence follows
the corollary that subjects whose conscience is against the justice
of war may not engage in it whether they be right or wrong.
This is clear, for *whatever is not of faith is sin*." A position
equally individualistic, over and above the duty owed to the
king, appears in *The Mayor of Zalamea,* the best perhaps, certainly the most popular, of the plays of Calderón. The mayor,
a wealthy peasant, has had a daughter dishonored by the captain
of the king's infantry billeted in his house. He has the captain
hanged. The king in person (Philip II) upbraids him for his
high-handed behavior, and the mayor answers in four lines which
have won deserved fame in Spain: "To the king we owe our
life and fortune, but honor is the patrimony of the soul, and the
soul belongs to God."

We are now in a position to understand what was the spirit
which animated the Spanish nation. It was no Romish bigotry,
no abject submission to a tyrannical king, but a subtler, nobler
and higher spirit. Uncompromising in matters of religious unity,
stern in matters of duty and conscience, yet sufficiently free to

stand up with the king against the Pope and with the people against the king. As Father Vitoria puts it, "The prince derives his authority from the republic": "[*Princeps*] *habet auctoritatem a republica.*" Such a spirit, it will be seen, combines the tendency to religious unity which several centuries of religious preaching and crusading had at last kindled in the Spanish breast with the individualistic turn of character of the race; the synthesis of these tendencies intensified by the discovery of America and by the dramatic events of the Reformation—such is the force which drove Spain during two centuries from glory to ruin.

CHAPTER 4

THE SPANISH EMPIRE
——(CONTINUED)——

The kings of the Austrian dynasty are, above all, in the pregnant image of Oliveira Martins, Pharaohs. Their main idea is the religious unity of the country. After the revolt of the *Comuneros* (1519-20), caused by the inexperience of Charles V, who tried to govern Spain through his Flemish favorites, the power of the monarchy was well established. The King of Spain reigned over not one but many kingdoms, each with its administration, its Cortes, its laws and *fueros,* or local rights. Had the Austrian dynasty been a tyrannical institution, it would have undertaken the political unification of the Peninsula. The spirit of the time, however, did not aim at political but at religious unity; while the Austrian kings closely watched the Inquisition and expelled the unconverted Moors from Spain, they allowed every part of their dominions to maintain its local liberties. Nor was the task as easy as might be imagined. Erasmus was in great favor in

Spain. When directly attacked in the rest of Europe, he sought the help of his Spanish friends—perhaps in the hope of "turning" what for him would have been the formidable opposition of Charles V. Vitoria was on the side of Erasmus; the anti-Erasmus campaign made but little headway in Spain until the death of the inquisitor general Manrique (1538), who had forbidden all attacks on Erasmus' works. While Erasmus' Dutch friends suggested that the right to criticize him should be restricted to the Pope and to the Spanish inquisitor general, and a Spanish canon of Salamanca coined the witticism, "He who doth Erasmus harass is a friar or an ass," the campaign against Erasmus was actively stimulated in Spain by no less a bigot of the Catholic cause than the English ambassador, Edward Lee. The Erasmian current prepared the way for the Lutheran movement, led in Spain by a chaplain of Charles and Philip, and in Naples, then Spanish, by Juan de Valdés, brother of Charles' private secretary and one of the masters, indeed founders, of modern Spanish prose. The movement cost his See to the Archbishop of Toledo, Carranza, who, despite his record as Mary Tudor's adviser in England, was suspected of Lutheran leanings, and despite his austere life, was removed. The Inquisition dealt with this "pest," applying its powerful prophylactic methods to it, and Charles was not remiss in urging severity on the inquisitor general.

Purged from the foreign danger, the monarchy turned to its own home ills. The Jews had already been dealt with by Ferdinand and Isabel. There remained the Moors, two classes of them: the Moriscos, converted to the Christian religion, and the Mudéjares, who had remained faithful to Islam. The clergy and the king entertained grave misgivings as to the existence of so strong a mass of religious aliens in the nation. The idea of their forced conversion was bound to come to the fore. It is useless to condemn a sixteenth-century idea with our twentieth-century minds. That subjects should follow the religion of their sovereign was then an accepted proposition in practically the whole of Europe, Protestant as well as Catholic. It found its staunchest opponents . . . in Spain. Yet they were overruled. Charles had the matter so much at heart that he asked the Pope to release him from the oath which he had given to the Cortes of Aragon (in the territory of which most of the Mudéjares lived), pledging himself not to convert the Mudéjar population by force; and this done, despite the opposition of the Cortes and nobility of Aragon (less bent on religious unity than Castile), the decree of forced conversion was promulgated (September 1525). As a measure of relief, the Valencian converted Mudéjares (who thus became Moriscos) were granted exemption from all interference by the Inquisition for forty years.

But the Morisco was not very much safer than the Mudéjar in a nation determined to achieve religious unity. The forced conversion of the latter added a considerable contingent of Christians of doubtful loyalty to a mass which, at best, was but lukewarm in its Christian faith. Philip II had to listen to all kinds of advice on the matter. Military chiefs, such as Mondéjar, Captain General of Granada, were for leniency. Ecclesiastics, such as Inquisitor Deza, were for ruthlessness. The king gave way to Deza, whom he even (logically) made both cardinal and captain general, and thereby got what Mondéjar had prophesied —a rebellion. The rebellion was crushed by Don Juan of Austria. During the first years of Philip III's reign the Moriscos were expelled. Such is the power of attraction of the Peninsula that, despite the inhumanity of the measure, numerous Moriscos stole back into Spain.

While the Monarchy endeavored thus to ensure the religious unity of the country, the several kingdoms continued to live an autonomous life. Despite the obvious advantages of centralization for a monarchy continuously engaged in war, the old division into separate kingdoms, which had been inherited from Ferdinand and Isabel, was maintained. The kingdoms other than Castile had their own viceroys, Cortes, troops, civil services, taxes. The difficulties which this autonomy entailed fell ultimately on long-suffering Castile, whose Cortes were more easily convened and convinced (not always by means as pure as the end). Portugal, which belonged to the Crown of Spain during the better part of the sixteeth and seventeenth centuries.

was left in complete possession of its local liberties—a fact which would have been unthinkable in a centralistic country such as France. Aragon gave a splendid opportunity to Philip II in connection with the flight of Antonio Pérez, one of the king's secretaries, whose influence at court came partly from his talents, partly from his friendship with Ruy Gómez, Philip's minister, an advocate of conciliatory policy in the Netherlands and an enemy of the Duke of Alba. Pérez had acted in Madrid in support of Don Juan of Austria's policy in the Netherlands, and this activity had brought him into close touch with one of Don Juan's secretaries, Escobedo. In March 1578 Escobedo, who had come to Madrid on a mission, was found dead in the street. Pérez was accused by Escobedo's family and friends. The king acted with his usual hesitation and remissness, but in the end had Pérez arrested. Pérez fled to Aragon. There existed in Aragon a dignitary, the Justice, whose powers included the custody and protection of all alleged criminals until their guilt had been proved. This protection the Justice extended by locking up the men concerned in a special prison, the Cárcel de Manifestados. Pérez put himself under the custody of his country's Justice. Philip II bethought himself of the Inquisition and had Pérez accused of heresy. Pérez was transferred from the prison for *manifestados* to the prison for heretics, for such was the wealth and variety of prisons Spain enjoyed in those times. Meanwhile, Pérez had rashly countered the king's attack with a "memorial," in which he asserted that the death of Escobedo had been decided upon by His Majesty in person. The people of Aragon rose as one man against the violation of their *fueros* or liberties. Philip's attitude towards Aragon was curious. He was ruthless with the rebels and unnecessarily cruel with the Justice, who was beheaded. But he did not profit by the circumstances, as a French king would certainly have done, to reduce Aragon to the common law of Castile. All he did was to obtain from the Cortes of Aragon (1592) that the Justice should no longer be immune to recall by the king. The case of Catalonia is still more striking. When Catalonia was beaten to submission after a rebellion which lasted twelve years (1640-52), the king did not abolish the *fueros*. On the contrary, he deliberately confirmed them in 1653.[1]

The tendency of the age is therefore clear. Religious unity yes, but no excessive political unity. Absolutism, yes, but no despotism. Similarly, in matters of the mind, a severe discipline of books and teachings in all that concerned dogma, but the most liberal help granted to education and the arts. Spain was already famous for her universities. Along with Salamanca, specializing in law and theology, Alcalá, founded by Cisneros, became the center of learning and the seat of the highest authorities on Chaldean, Hebrew and Greek. During this period, no less than thirty-four universities flourished in Spain, most of them founded by private initiative.

The rhythm of culture and the arts follows the political rhythm. Thus, if the period of greatest power corresponds to the end of the reign of Charles V and the beginning of that of Philip II, the period of greatest intellectual splendor comes a little later, covering almost exactly the reigns of Philip III and Philip IV. Spain, which under Ferdinand and Isabel had already produced a work of truly Shakespearian greatness in *La Celestina,* gave then to the world a literary wealth which only England could rival though not surpass. From the theater to lyrical poetry, from mystical experience to applied psychology, from education to the novel, from wit and criticism to pamphleteering and satire, Spain invades and explores every area of the creative mind with admirable vigor, everywhere a pioneer. This was the period, to cite but the very greatest, of Cervantes, Lope de Vega, Calderón and St. John of the Cross.

A similar activity was at work in the arts. This is the period when Spain absorbed the Flemish Charles V, of whom she made a Spaniard, and the Greek Theotocopuli, who became, also, a Spaniard known as El Greco. This is the time of Ribera, Zurbarán and Velázquez, of the great Spanish musicians, Morales, Guerrero, Cabezón and Victoria. In all the fields of culture and

[1] *See* Chapter 17.

polite society Spain was then the leader and model, and Spanish was a language which no man or woman of good birth could afford to disregard. Spanish was, in fact, the language spoken at the German imperial court for at least a century. The printing presses of Spain, Italy, France, the Netherlands and Germany turned out Spanish books to satisfy a world demand, and Spanish intellectuals spread over all Europe, partly through the natural expansive force of the races at that time, partly through the powerful stimulus which impelled toward emigration many free minds who had felt too close to the Inquisition.

It has become customary to sum up the history of Spanish creative effort in America in three hasty generalizations: cupidity, cruelty and ignorance. Were they justified, the picture would still have to be completed with the astounding fact of the discovery itself, the long list of almost incredible feats of imagination and endurance which gradually revealed to the world the extent, wealth and splendor of its new acquisition.

The four voyages of Columbus took place in 1492, 1493, 1498 and 1502. On the first and second of these voyages he discovered lands which, under threat of severe punishment, he made his companions accept as Japan, but which we nowadays believe to be Cuba and the other Antilles; on the third voyage he discovered one of the rivers of the Garden of Eden, which we now believe to be the Orinoco, the main river of a country which Spaniards in later years renamed Little Venice or Venezuela. On his last voyage Columbus discovered the country known as Honduras. In 1506 he died, still full of fantastic delusions as to the lands he had discovered, his last days overcast by difficulties which arose partly from the cumbrousness and niggardliness of the Spanish state, partly from the action of envious rivals, partly from his own difficult nature.

Simultaneously, Vicente Yáñez Pinzón, one of the three brothers who had accompanied Christopher Columbus on his first voyage, and a host of other navigators and explorers sallied forth from Spain and took up the new sport. Their expeditions were individual enterprises. If they lost limb, health, or wealth or even life, theirs was the loss. If they discovered or conquered territories, the gain was the crown's. A curious fact, and one which shows the strength which the crown had acquired, even in so individualistic a country as Spain, is that, while all these conquerors conquered by themselves, none conquered for himself. The land was no sooner trodden than they planted the cross on it, and took possession of it in the name of the Queen of Castile.

The discovery was made by Castile and not by Aragon. We are again confronted with the consequences of the peculiar shape of the Peninsula. The Crown of Aragon rules over the valley of the Ebro, falling towards Italy; the Crown of Castile seeks the sea through the valley of the Guadalquivir, which flows southwest and through the northern and northwestern ports. Thus, while Ferdinand, and later, Charles V, are busy in Europe, their Castilian, Andalusian and northern subjects swarm over the ocean and, turning their backs on Europe, open out a new world.

There was another kingdom equally well placed for exploring the world. The Portuguese were early in the field. Many, some of the best of them, worked under the Spanish Crown. Magellan left the Spanish shores on September 20, 1519, and, after marvelous adventures, discovered the Straits to which he left his name, and was killed in an obscure fight with the natives near the Philippines; his chief surviving officer, Elcano, a Basque, arrived in San Lúcar, on the Guadalquivir (September 6, 1522), the first captain to circumnavigate the earth, in a ship which deserved her name of *Victoria*.

By this time the Spaniards, with some Portuguese and Italians, had discovered every island in the Caribbean Sea and the Gulf of Mexico, Florida, most of Central America on both sides of the Isthmus; the Pacific Ocean, first seen from the Isthmus by Balboa, whom Keats immortalized in a sonnet under the name of Cortéz; and the whole of South America. Panama was founded in 1519; Nicaragua discovered in 1521. In 1519 Hernán Cortés, at the head of 11 ships, 400 soldiers, 200 Indians, 32 horsemen and 11 pieces of artillery, conquered New Spain (Mexico). In 1523 he began to look for the channel between the two oceans, the existence of which Charles V had assumed on the assumption that good strategic principles were part and parcel of the Creator's plan. Cortés and his successors devoted infinite patience, endurance and resources to the search for this channel. Meanwhile Florida was explored, and Pineda discovered the Mississippi. In 1527 Narváez ventured inland. Cabeza de Vaca with three other survivors of his expedition walked through the territories which separate Florida from New Orleans. Nothing daunted by this disastrous attempt, other Spaniards followed in the quest northward, and discovered Georgia, Arizona with its Grand Canyon, Arkansas and Missouri. One of these explorers made bold to assert that California, which he had crossed and explored, was *not* an island. But he was not believed by sober-minded people.

In 1524, Pizarro, financed by a priest who lived in Panama, tried his hand at the conquest of Peru. He tried again in 1526. Finding it too hard a nut to crack, he sailed for Spain and sought the help of the king, with whom he signed a treaty, which enabled him to leave Panama for Peru, in 1531, at the head of no less than 227 men. Such were the armies which conquered empires in those days. Mendoza, at the head of 14 ships, sailed for the Plata in 1534, and founded Our Lady of the Good Winds, now shortened to Buenos Aires. Ayolas, whom he left in charge on his return to Spain, thought he might as well do a bit of exploring meanwhile, and, having discovered Paraguay, founded its present capital Asunción. In 1541, Cabeza de Vaca sent an expedition which, through Brazil, arrived in Asunción. By the middle of the century the whole of the territory irrigated by the Paraguay and Parana rivers was in Spanish hands. The activity of sailors and explorers passed then to the Pacific Ocean. The Philippine Islands were explored, and Manila founded in 1570.

The islands in the Caribbean Sea had been promptly colonized by the Spaniards. The first elements were brought from Spain. Horses, oxen, sheep, pigs, hens, dogs, unknown in America before the discovery, were abundant a few years later to the point that in many cases cattle were killed merely for the hides.

The Spaniards introduced sugar mills. Cortés, having pacified Mexico in 1521, introduced the cultivation of sugar, silk, and the vine in his new country. In a few years the Spaniards had tried to acclimatize most of the home plants and animals, succeeding in most cases, failing in some. It is said that wheat was first sowed on American soil by Inés Muñoz, Pizarro's sister-in-law, who, as she was sorting a barrel of rice from Spain, came upon a few grains of wheat which she carefully put aside and tried in a flower pot. Others attribute the same providential role to Cortés' Negro servant. Nor was mining neglected. The attention bestowed on the methods for extracting metals from their ore, and the numerous writings on techniques and inventions published both in the metropolis and overseas at the time, show that this branch of economic development had not been overlooked. In every economic direction the Spaniards set their new possessions in motion with remarkable celerity.

But their main effort was in the realm of enlightenment. The Church, which from the first had taken a leading part in the colonization and government of the New World, as it did in the governments of the metropolis, was deeply imbued with the idea that the basis of the right of the Spaniards to be in America was their capacity to bring the Indian within the fold of the Faith. Sinned against—as what principle is not?—forgotten, at times prostituted, the principle remained in force and consciously or unconsciously governed the actions of responsible Spaniards in America for three centuries to come. It explains the absence of color bar in Spanish America. The first Bishop of Mexico, Juan de Zumárraga, founded a college for Indian noblemen in order that they should be in a position to teach the native language and ways to Spanish monks and priests who came over to catechize the New World—an example of the spirit in which the immense civilizing work of the Spaniards in America was carried out. When the University of Mexico was founded (1533), there were already several colleges standing in New Spain. The Spaniards founded and maintained universities in New Spain (Mexico, the capital; Mérida; Chiapas and Guadalajara); Santo Domingo (the capital of the islands, same name); Cuba (Havana); New

Granada, now Colombia (Santa Fe, where there are two universities); Peru (Lima); Chile (Santiago); the viceroyalty of La Plata, now Argentina and part of Bolivia (Córdoba, Charcas). It must be noticed that these universities organized the study of the native languages. Numerous colleges, generally founded by religious orders, contributed to this educational work. Finally more attention was paid to elementary schools than was the case in the metropolis (a clear case in which religious zeal had happy effects). The missions, still a familiar sight in California, testify to this special creative power of the Spanish Church in America.

Much of this civilizing effort was made in the language of the Indians themselves, which shows both its eagerness and its disinterestedness from the national point of view. Compared with present-day colonization, generally understood from the point of view of the colonizer, who brings (and generally imposes) his language, Spanish colonization was singularly free from self-seeking. The friars preached in Aztec, Quechua and the other languages of the land; they wrote grammars, vocabularies, catechisms, in these languages, as mere tools for their catechizing mission. They studied the history and customs of the Indians. Many historians and specialists of the American pre-Columbian world devoted themselves to this work. They were all eclipsed by the name of Father Sahagún, whose whole existence was consecrated to the study of Mexican life, art and society, and who may be considered not merely as the greatest authority on Mexican history, but as the founder of the modern school of history, with its wide curiosity open to all the ways of private and collective life. It is curious to note that Father Sahagún wrote his monumental work in the Mexican language. Efforts of a similar nature were made in other parts of the Spanish domains, and particularly in Peru, Central America, the Plata and Chile.

This attitude of the monks and clergy on the spot had its parallel in the Peninsula, and exerted a strong influence on the government, and on the general attitude of the crown. Much bitter ink has been spent in denouncing Spanish conduct toward the Indians. In actual fact, both in theory and in practice, Spain was in advance of the times. Had the Spanish monarchy conformed to the ideas prevailing at the time, the Indians would have been reduced to legal and practical slavery and the cruelest methods—current even in Europe—would have been used against them. As it was, the crown established legal freedom for all Indians, and allowed slavery only in the case of cannibals and natives who resisted evangelization. The position gradually became worse for several reasons: much cruelty was caused by wars, then barbarous everywhere; the cupidity and callousness of many a settler often made miserable the lot of Indian workers, both free and slave; the reluctance of the Indians to perform any work whatsoever produced difficulties similar to those which have been met with in our own times by twentieth-century colonizers. In 1503 orders were given that free Indians should be obliged to work for a salary, though stress was laid on the fact that their status remained that of free men—a decision which, though perhaps inevitable at the time, was bound to open the way to practical slavery. Before the death of Ferdinand, the pressure of economic conditions and of the ideas prevailing at the time had overruled the generous innovations of Queen Isabel. Her spirit, however, lived again in the famous Bishop of Chiapas, Father Las Casas, whose admirable life was spent in unremitting endeavor to put the case of the persecuted Indians before the emperor. Nor was he alone in such a task. Many an eminent man—Zumárraga, Palafox, Ruiz Montoya—took up the cudgels for the native race, and this must be said for their efforts: that though they were unable to stop the evil in the Antilles, where the Indian population rapidly dwindled down and disappeared, the Indian population of all continental Spanish America, far from diminishing, increased and prospered, and to this day constitutes the most important stock in a number of Spanish American countries (Mexico, Peru, Bolivia and others).[2]

[2] "Unfortunately, the exceptional opportunities for study which had been offered by surviving primitive people had been largely neglected. Civilization had been more concerned with exterminating these than with collecting information from their manners and customs. The native Tasmanians might have thrown a flood of light upon the problems of the

In Europe the policy of Spain was inspired with the same religious principle which animated her home and her colonial life by Charles V, emperor of Germany as well as king of Spain. He had to engage in a long struggle with Francis I, which was partly a chapter in the long-drawn duel between Austria and Spain. Francis I was defeated and taken prisoner (1526); but the Peace of Madrid, which he signed then, was not and could not be final. The duel was, in a sense, a permanent historical necessity, yet, as we shall see anon, it was in Charles' own mind an indispensable preliminary to the work of unity which he had planned. A similar necessity explained his expedition to Tunis (1535) against Barbarossa, the pirate whom the Turkish Sultan had put at the head of his fleet. Charles, the conqueror of Tunis, and the deliverer of twenty thousand Christians enslaved by the pirates, appeared then before the whole Christian world as its true leader, worthy of the imperial crown, the only sovereign crown of Christendom.

Charles V was the greatest monarch of the Austrian dynasty. His very hesitations toward the Reformation should be read in relation to the high and noble dream which animated him. He heard on the one hand the Duke of Brunswick, in the name of the Catholic princes, and the prelates at Mainz, urging him to take strong action; on the other the wise and generous advice of his Spanish secretary, Valdés, whose leanings were not unfavorable to the Reformation. His policy was not definite, but it was clear. He wished to save the unity of Christendom while remaining faithful to the purity of his faith; hence, while uncompromising as to dogma, he tried to compromise as much as he could in every other way.

His mind is nowhere more clearly expressed than in the ad-

Middle and Late Palaeolithic culture phases, but seventy years from the date of the first European settlement they had been wiped out."

Thus, Mr. Henry Balfour, curator of the Pitt Rivers Museum at Oxford, speaking—as reported in the London *Times*—to the British Association in Johannesburg (August 1, 1929), condemns a colonizing enterprise neither Spanish nor old. The reader may compare these remarks with the admirable work of Father Sahagún in Mexico in the sixteenth century.

mirable speech which he delivered on Easter Monday, 1536, before the Pope Paul I, his cardinals and ambassadors. This document should be read in full. It is one of the great pages of European history. It is an act of accusation against the King of France (Francis I) for having been the main obstacle in the way of the fulfillment of the emperor's dearest wish, in his own words, "the peace and calm of Christendom." Having offered to give Milan to one of Francis' sons, Charles ends up in truly knightly fashion by proposing to the King of France to settle the matter between them in what Don Quixote would have called a singular fight:

> Therefore, I promise your Holiness, in the presence of this sacred college and of all these knights here present, if the king of France wishes to meet me in arms, man to man, I promise to meet him armed or unarmed, in my shirt, with sword and dagger, on land or sea, on a bridge or an island, in a closed field, or in front of our armies or wherever and however he may wish and it be fair.

In this speech he is a worthy grandson of the great queen. He reveals himself full of his dream of peace and unity. "I say it once and three times: I want peace; I want peace; I want peace." Such are the last words of his address. And more than once in the text he refers to the peace and unity of Christendom, but does not say one single word as to the Reformation. The enemy he wants to fight is the infidel, the Turk. In his mind, the unity of Christendom comprises the whole of Europe. He is a truly great emperor and perhaps the first great European.

His successors mark with the descending curve of their capacities the slope of Spain's downfall. Philip II, the most intelligent, was hampered by a mistrustful nature which prevented him from delegating the smallest portion of his enormous powers. From the cell which he had built for himself in the Escorial, the palace which he had built for God, he tried to govern his immense dominions down to the minutest details. His policy was essentially religious unity and war on the infidel; but he lacked his father's political vision, and with him the religious ideal of Isabel and Charles V degenerated into bigotry. He continued his father's policy in the Mediterranean by entering into an alliance with Venice and with the Pope against the Turk, who was beaten at Lepanto (1571) by an allied fleet commanded by Philip's brother, Don Juan of Austria, but the king's mistrustful and vacillating policy robbed him of the fruits of victory. In the Netherlands the king's policy was even less fortunate. Though his methods varied—first ruthlessness with the Duke of Alba (1567-73), then moderation with Requesens (1573-75), then half-and-half mixtures with his brother Don Juan and with Alexander Farnese—his principle remained the same: no compromise on dogma. He lost the Southern Netherlands, which he handed over to his daughter and to her husband, the Archduke Albert. But the crucial moment in this reign, and indeed in the history of Spain, came when the Armada sent by Philip II against England was defeated in 1588. One hundred and sixty vessels, two thousand six hundred guns, eight thousand sailors and twenty-two thousand men—such was the force which was at last to avenge the insults received by the Lord, as understood by Philip, at the hands of the Lord, as understood by Queen Elizabeth. The man who had organized and armed this formidable fleet was, perhaps, the greatest sailor of the time—Don Alvaro de Bazán, Marqués de Santa Cruz. He died shortly before the date appointed for the departure of the fleet. In his stead Philip chose the Duke of Medina Sidonia, who entreated the king to relieve him of the post, for, he said, he knew nothing of the things of the sea and was, moreover, what is known as a bad sailor. Philip explained that the true admiral was the Lord. The year 1588 is the date which marks the turning point in the history of the sea. From that date the Spanish command of the sea begins to weaken and that of England to rise.

Philip III, a man of honest mediocrity sunk in unintelligent bigotry, and Philip IV, a selfish, brilliant man of the world, were mere figureheads. The Spanish Empire under their rule continued an evolution already determined by a century of masterful errors. The wars in the Netherlands flared up again now and then; France, under the strong hand of Richelieu, became the protagonist of the enemies of Spain—mostly the Protestant nations of the north. Though at first victorious on land and sea, Spain was finally beaten in the battle of Rocroy (1643). The Treaty of Westphalia put an end to the European war, but not to the Franco-Spanish war. Spain had still ten years of hard fighting to live through in Flanders, Italy and Portugal.

When Philip IV died, in 1665, he had lost Portugal and many of the territories of present-day France which he had inherited. He left a son feeble of mind and will and aged four. Charles II's reign was all chaos and disorder at home, wars and disasters abroad. The dismemberment of the vast, but now almost inert, body of the Hispano-Austrian dominions continued, actively aided by the King of France, Louis XIV. In actual fact, the foreign adventures (rather than policy) of this reign were the last act in the century-long duel between the French monarchy and the House of Austria. The denouement of this duel came as a triumph for France when Charles, who died in 1700, left his throne to Philip of Anjou, grandson of Louis XIV. A war ensued in which Austria, England and Holland upheld the rights of the Austrian archduke to the throne of Spain. Philip remained king, but of a kingdom which in 1714 had lost Flanders, Minorca and Gibraltar.

The role of Spain as a leading Great Power ends here. Leaving aside for the present other reasons of a more matter-of-fact character, the main cause of Spain's failure lay in the very task which she had dreamed of achieving. Universality was then impossible, even within the restricted limits of Christendom. The faith which Spain wanted pure and intact was not susceptible of a universal appeal. Her policy cost her untold sacrifices of money abroad, and of liberty, particularly liberty of thought, at home. In 1700 began the century which was to burn much that Spain had worshiped and to worship much that Spain had burned.

CHAPTER 5

A NEW CENTURY, A NEW DYNASTY,
AND A NEW SPAIN

The nation has lost her own call or vocation. The religious atmosphere in which such a vocation manifested itself has vanished. The century is called an intellectual one, and the court, once frequented by ardent monks and bishops, is now in the hands of intelligent Frenchmen.

If the spirit of old Spain has vanished, the cumbrous machinery which it had gradually evolved is either rusty or altogether paralyzed. The Frenchmen are bewildered by the multitude of councils and boards, *fueros* and local liberties.. They miss the unity of the French monarchy and the clarity of French administration. The century dominated by French thought shifts the stress from the religious to the political, and the Spanish crown ceases to worry about religious unity, but seeks to reduce Catalonia to the laws of Castile. Gradually the Inquisition relaxes its hold over the people. Catalonia lost her liberties in 1714. As a compensation, and in consonance with this policy of centralization, commerce with the New World, reserved till then to the subjects of the Crown of Castile, and to the two ports of Seville (and later Cádiz) and Coruña, was opened to all Spaniards. Several hindrances to internal trade, such as customs barriers, were also removed. These modest measures, with now and then a short period of peace, sufficed to bring about a recovery. Commerce, both internal and foreign, flourished once again, and under the able leadership of an efficient minister, Ensenada, the navy was resuscitated. The monarchy was happy in its ministers, at least in those in charge of home affairs. The chaotic finances left by the disastrous regime of the Austrian dynasty were put on a sound basis. Municipal, sanitary, transport reforms were introduced; a new impulse was given to manufacturing; technical education was fostered; plans for internal colonization were prepared and even carried out; and the Bank of San Carlos, forerunner of the Bank of Spain, was founded by Charles III.

Spain tried to get on with the business of this world. Her relations with Rome reflected this change. Even in the height of its religious phase, the Spanish monarchy had never, as we know, abdicated its religious rights. Charles V's relations with some of the Popes had been cold and Philip II's frigid. Philip V actually broke with Rome, which had backed his rival in the War of Succession, and the negotiations for an agreement, though begun in 1714, dragged on till 1754, when a concordat was signed which, in fact, put the Church of Spain under the authority of the king. As the ideas of the century penetrated in Spain, more and more drastic measures were adopted to curtail the power of the Church to amass wealth, and the privileges of the Inquisition were severely regulated. This evolution culminated in the expulsion of the Jesuits (1767).

The age was particularly favorable to culture, and both official and private initiative stimulated the creation of all kinds of institutions for the fostering of education, art, science and letters. A typical Spanish entity should be mentioned: the Economic

Societies of Friends of the Country, free associations formed
by well-to-do persons in various provinces, and having for their
object the education of the people in all matters connected with
agriculture, industry and commerce. But the tone of the century
is not typically Spanish. It is, therefore, a period during which
Spain produces many men of first-rate talent but no real genius.
The best men of the period are critics like Father Feijóo or
statesmen such as Jovellanos. Art, like letters, though estimable,
is pale after the glories of the seventeenth cntury—until, toward
the end of the eighteenth, Goya enters the stage, not only of
Spanish, but of universal art. Goya, however, lives beyond this
period, and some of his best works are like flames surging above
the fire which consumed old Spain and from which new Spain
arose like a phoenix.

The foreign affairs of the House of Bourbon were no more
typically Spanish than their home policy, and were, moreover,
less successful. The War of the Spanish Succesion had pretty
well achieved the ruin which the later Austrias had prepared
and, though all the allies on either side were supposed to have
fought for the good of Spain, the Peace of Utrecht was like the
sale by auction of a grandee's house. England kept Gibraltar and
Minorca, which she had occupied in the name of the archduke,
presumably for Spain. Italy and Flanders went the way of nature.
England gained also the right of *asiento,* equivalent to a monopoly of the Negro slave trade with Spanish America and the
right to keep a 500-ton ship filled with merchandise off New
Cartagena.

But as a set-off against so many losses, Spain had got rid
of her religious preoccupation. Leaving the Lord to take care
of Himself, she was now free to devote a little attention to her
own affairs. Philip V's first administration understood this and
acted in consequence, by abstaining from adventures and giving
the country a much needed rest. Unfortunately, the queen died
and Philip married Elizabeth Farnese, a lady whose passionate
maternal love proved nearly as devastating for Spain as Philip
II's religious dreams, for it would not be satisfied with anything
short of a throne for each of her children. In 1746 the king

died, when negotiations were beginning toward the Treaty of Aix-la-Chapelle (1748).

Ferdinand VI, his successor, was a peace-loving man. In his reign, Spain made a significant decision which she was often to repeat in later years, indeed to establish as one of the cardinal principles of her foreign policy: solicited as a prospective ally by both France and England, about to engage in a war (which was to be known as the Seven Years' War), Spain decided to remain neutral. When in agreement, with both; when in disagreement, with neither: this was to be for a long time and still is Spain's policy toward the two great western nations. Ferdinand's decision, taken in the face of such tempting offers as the restitution of Gibraltar, shows both the wisdom of the monarch and the love of political passivity to which Spain had by now resigned herself.

Ferdinand VI died at the age of forty-six, and Charles III, his half-brother, who succeeded him, though a most enterprising and enlightened despot in home politics, proved a worthy heir of his loving mother, Elizabeth Farnese, in his somewhat unwise conduct of foreign affairs. England, it must be owned, was not helpful. When Charles III, in the Family Pact which he signed with France (1761), claimed that England sought the control of the sea, he was leveling an accusation which events were by no means to belie. The Family Pact opened a period of wars between England and Portugal on the one hand and Spain and France on the other, the main episode of which was the cooperation of French and Spanish troops in the War of American Independence—a fact generally unknown, and mentioned here with no intention of belittling the glory of Lafayette. The Treaty of Versailles (1783) gave back Minorca and Florida to Spain. But Florida went the way of nature in later years, when the infant, godmothered by France and Spain, had grown his teeth.

There seems to be a kind of law that Spain devours the wit of dynasties. After the shining lights of Ferdinand, Isabel, Charles V, and even Philip II, the intellect of the Austrian dynasty degenerated rapidly down to the paltry level of Charles II. After Philip V, Ferdinand VI and Charles III, none of them a genius, yet still acceptable kings, the Bourbon dynasty gave Spain Charles IV, whose mental powers were of the most touching modesty. He reigned, at first, with the ministers whom he had inherited from his father—Floridablanca, Campomanes, Aranda, the instruments of enlightened despotism—then with the minister whom his wife had chosen for him, on grounds best known to herself and to everybody else but her husband. Godoy, whom the queen made Duke of Alcudia, and whom, later, the king made Prince of Peace, sent an expedition against the French Revolutionary Government, which had just beheaded Louis XVI. But meanwhile England again was not helpful and carried on her lonely and profitable game—colony hunting. Spain fell into the hands of France, and with France suffered the defeat of St. Vincent. Further cooperation with Napoleon brought about the destruction of the Spanish fleet at Trafalgar. Napoleon rewarded Spain with a regular invasion, begun under the guise of an expedition against Portugal. Charles IV went to see Napoleon at Bayonne, and abdicated.

The fool was succeeded by the knave. Ferdinand VII is easily the most contemptible king that Spain has had to put up with. He also went to Bayonne, was forced to abdicate, and was kept under strict watch in a French château while Napoleon gave the crown of Spain to his brother Joseph. The Spanish people called Joseph Bonaparte by the picturesque—if unmerited—name of "Pepe Botellas," which amounts to Joe Bottles. Here the Spanish people entered the political stage. A new period of Spanish life had begun.

The Spanish monarchy organized the "kingdoms" overseas as images of its European kingdoms. The aim of the Spanish monarchy was, therefore, to seek the welfare of the two commonwealths *(las dos repúblicas),* namely, that of the Spaniards and that of the Indians. This welfare comprised, for the Whites, a "clean" faith and sound prosperity; for the Indians, conversion, *policía,* i.e. civilization, fair treatment and the preservation of their rights. The towns, or *pueblos,* were conceived as either Spanish or native, and though the natives were allowed to settle in Spanish towns, no Spaniard, except the priest, was allowed to settle in Indian *pueblos*. The colonization began, of necessity, by a kind of trust system: each of the first settlers received an *encomienda* or trust whereby he was to protect, civilize and convert a certain number of Indians, while the Indians were to work for him for a remuneration. Municipal institutions, analogous to those of Spain, completed the local arrangements. To preside over all, the dominions were divided into viceroyalties, the number and importance of which varied considerably with time, while two remained constant in their wealth, power and majesty: that of New Spain with its capital in Mexico and that of Peru with its capital in Lima. The viceroys were images of the king, save that their authority was limited both by frequent instructions and by the encroaching power of more unwieldy bodies, the *audiencias*.

The streams of commerce converged upon the Gulf of Mexico and the Caribbean Sea. The goods and precious metals gathered at regular intervals were conveyed to Spain in fleets or convoys owing to the insecure state of the seas; for even when Spain was not actually at war (which was rare) piracy was not then as disreputable a profession as it became when England sided with the police. In spite of commercial legislation singularly rich in economic mistakes, the colonies made fair progress, mostly through breaches of the law on the part of nationals and foreigners, and sometimes through unexpected help from Heaven. Thus when Seville, with an eye on its trade monopoly, protested against the rich trade which had developed between Peru and China through the Philippine Islands, the crown refused to intervene on the ground that the suppression of such trade relations across the Pacific would ruin any chances of evangelizing the Chinese.

The development—commercial, political and intellectual—of the Spanish dominions was as quick and successful as might be expected in the circumstances. Account should be taken of the fact that the initial generation of settlers were after all soldiers and adventurers, a type nowhere particularly gifted in the virtues of peace, precisely because they are gifted in the virtues of war. The immense courage, endurance, hardiness and imagin-

ation which went to the discovery and to the conquest could not
but start the work of settlement rather tumultuously. And yet,
this work was achieved quickly and well. It often called forth
criticism and even eloquent condemnation in the sixteenth century from exalted and idealistic Spaniards such as Las Casas,
and, two centuries later, from intelligent and efficient Spaniards
such as Ulloa and Jorge Juan. But foreign critics, provided they
were well informed, and not merely copying Spanish denunciations, have always been free in appraising and even admiring
the work of Spain in America. The subject has suffered from its
vastness. While great hardship was the rule in the Caribbean
region at the beginning of the conquest and in certain Peruvian
districts, and in occasional and more or less isolated places at
nearly all times, the system as a whole worked well and hu-
manely. From the economic point of view, Humboldt found the
Indian worker in Mexico better off than the European peasant.
Biologically, the Indian has survived and even thrived in the
greater part of the Spanish possessions; even from the religious
point of view, the Spanish sway over the Indian was milder than
might have been expected, for, considering them as minors, the
crown had them exempted from the Inquisition.

No better illustration could be found of the spirit which animated the Spanish Empire than the way it solved the problem of
its frontiers. Practically all of its settlements had frontiers adja-
cent to savage tribes; it had to ensure its peace and security; it
had to convert the heathen. Philip III embodied these principles
in his instructions to his viceroys. The result was the truly Christian system of the missions, by which the catechizer took over
most of the dangers and most of the work. The work of the
missions cannot be described or judged by generalization. The
Jesuit establishments in Paraguay bear little resemblance to the
missions in California or to those in the Orinoco valley. In many
cases, reality forced the priests, the monks and the state to strike
a compromise between sword and cross. But, on the whole, it
is fair to say with an English historian that "it may safely be alleged that so vast a region of savagery has never elsewhere been
pacified with so much patience and so little violence, and that

an immense, indefensible frontier has never won comparative security at so little cost of life and treasure" (F. A. Kirkpatrick in *Cambridge History*).

But what about the other *República,* the Commonwealth of Whites? Insistence on the welfare of the two commonwealths implied severe limitations on the liberty of these whites. Emigration was restricted and controlled, settlement carefully watched. So much for the principle. Then came the defects inherent in Spanish rule at the time, whether at home or overseas. Crushing taxation, cumbrous and slow administration; fitful justice, at times severe and just, at times corrupt and lax; overregulation of life and movements even to trifling details; meddlesomeness of the Inquisition—in fine, all the ills of a priestly and paternal administration which takes itself seriously, multiplied and at times alleviated by all the exceptions, loopholes and irregularities to be expected from a people of individualists.

The Spanish Empire lasted three centuries. During this time it held a whole continent and many nations beyond it in the longest period of peace which they, or indeed any region of their size, has known. It introduced Christendom and civilization, the sciences and the arts. It explored the possibilities of building canals through Panama, Nicaragua and the Patagonian Straits. As Humboldt handsomely acknowledges, it spent more money than any government of its time for the advancement of knowledge. And this mighty effort was carried out under continuous attacks both by war and by piracy on the part of numerous and strong enemies. Yet the Spanish Empire held on and finally gave rise to a number of nations which keep its language and its traditions. In short, so far as America is concerned, the Spanish Empire presents. a normal three-century evolution ending, in true biological fashion, in the creation of new and independent offshoots.

In its wider aspect, the Spanish Empire embodies the idea of religious unity predominant in the sixteenth century. Though the effect of the political shortcomings of the Spanish people should not be overlooked, there is no doubt that the very greatness of the cause which they espoused contributed not a little to

Spain's ultimate downfall. Such a cause demanded great sacrifices both at home and abroad. The loss of liberty of thought and a disastrous financial burden were the two prominent ones. But it would be unfair to forget that the cause exacted and obtained a higher level of international behavior, particularly in naval warfare, than was then the rule among the enemies of Spain.

The greatest loss, perhaps, was the unavoidable break in national tradition which Spain had to undergo when the world outstripped its views of universal unity. The defeat of the Armada was a mortal blow. Death was slow and took more than a century. The French dynasty brought the eighteenth century into Spain. While the old tendencies still lived deep in the national consciousness, the statesmen of the Bourbon period endeavored to rationalize Spain. The aim was new, but the methods remained the same, for reason and efficiency were enforced on authority and from above. Thus, of the two characteristics of the Austrian Empire, religious unity and absolutism, both cosubstantial with Spain in the sixteenth and seventeenth centuries, the eighteenth century eliminated the first, while the second, absolutism, remained alive until the nineteenth century. Spain worked hard during this century to outlive it, i.e. to evolve something else in its place. She is still trying.

CHAPTER 6

THE NINETEENTH CENTURY

The nineteenth century in Spain can only appear as a turbulent
and chaotic period without any meaning whatever unless it be
realized that, in the history of Spain, it stands as an era of
reconstruction *from the very ground upward*. The collapse of
the Bourbon dynasty under Napoleon's combined strength and
perfidy meant more than a mere change in regime for Spain.
It meant a revolution in her outlook. Spain had always been
a deeply monarchial country, in which the king was the incarnation of the state and the minister of God on earth. The king
was the fountain of honor and authority, as the incarnation of
the state; but he was the first servant of the community, the first
slave of duty as the minister of God. When the Bourbon dynasty
came to occupy the Spanish throne, the religious absolutism of
the Spanish monarchy took on a strong dose of French despotism. Charles III, with all his good intentions, governed more
despotically than Charles V or Philip II. There is in the Bourbon

56

kings more of the personal master, less of the symbolical institution, than there was in the Austrian dynasty. It follows that
the absolutism of the Bourbons was at bottom less in harmony
with the natural tendencies of the Spanish people than the Austrian rule. After all, the political turn of mind of a people is
rooted in the subsoil of its psychology, and no history which fails
to penetrate thither can ever convey the true sense of its life.
The strong "sense of man" which animates the Spanish character
leads the Spaniard to incarnate abstract political ideas as well
as institutions. Not Liberty, Equality and Fraternity, but the
particular Tom, Dick or Harry who is to pull the strings of
these three inert deities. Not Judiciary, Executive and Delibera-
tive, but the Harry, Dick or Tom who is to act for them. This
is one of the dominant factors in Spanish political life. The
other is the individual's resistance to all social pressure, a resistance which acts in two ways: by preventing the Spaniard
from taking full advantage of cooperation, and by making him
particularly sensitive to all superiority assumed by any man not
hallowed by an authority either inherent or symbolical. The
king, that is, would be the object of reverence and obedience so
long as he did his duty, i.e. so long as he was a Christian king.
Nor was this a mere doctrine to be stowed away in books. It was
taught in theological schools, and formulated in unmistakable
terms in one of the most famous plays of Calderón:

> "En lo que no es justa ley
> No ha de obedecer al Rey."

"He should not obey the king in commands against the law."
Nostre bon plaisir is not, therefore, the ultimate fount of law.
It is possible for the king's commands to run counter to the
justa ley. There is, in other words, a natural or just law which
is dictated by his reason to every good and true man, what Father
Vitoria calls the wise man's judgment *(judicium sapientis)*.

Such is the point on which the Bourbon dynasty failed to
understand the Spanish genius. Philip V imported the solar
system of his grandfather, Louis XIV, *le roi soleil*. Had Ferdinand VI left direct descendants it is just possible that the dynasty

would have found its roots in the national psychology. But his successor was Charles III, who came from Italy at an age when men's ideas are set. He was one of the prototypes of the enlightened despot which the century produced. His reign, fruitful as it was in "reforms," may be considered as the period during which the winds were sown which brought about the harvest of storms of the nineteenth century.

Firstly, the ruin of the monarchical sense of the Spanish people. This all-important change in the history of Spain began when the dynasty finally adopted the tone of personal power and the man-king asserted himself through the kingly symbol. Charles III could afford the risk. His half-witted son Charles IV and his treacherous and cruel grandson Ferdinand VII dishonored the crown by identifying it with their own unworthy heads. Much blood was to flow in Spain as a consequence of this deep-lying transformation of Peninsular life.

Then Charles III's reign saw the invasion of Spain by French eighteenth-century ideas. Spanish intellectual leadership, which had been homogeneous under the Austrian dynasty—whatever the methods used for obtaining such a result—split into two parts: one faithful to an ideal which, though rooted in the Spanish people, had become obsolete; the other committed to a view which, though in the full glory of its new-born light, was strangely out of harmony with the Spanish genius. The first belief was the old ideal of the symbolical monarchy, inherited from the Austrian days. The men who remained faithful to it failed to realize that such an ideal, even if workable under the Austrian dynasty, was utterly unworkable under the Bourbons, whose religion was either an affair of state (as with Charles III) or a benighted superstition (as with Charles IV and some of his successors), but no longer a leading beacon. The second school were too fascinated by the new philosophy to realize that under the phrase "sovereignty of the people" they had swallowed the principle of *nostre bon plaisir* dressed in a new garb which was no more acceptable to the Spanish people than the old. French centralization, French State despotism, was in reality the only alternative which the new men opposed to the obsolete Spanish absolutism of the Austrian theocratic brand.

Finally, this reign removed all obstacles to the unrestricted liberty of the sovereign. By establishing the king as the fountain of law, this reign prepared the downfall of such later monarchs as were unable to bear the weight of so much liberty.

The history of the nineteenth century—and of what is past of the twentieth—is the history of the endeavor of the Spanish people to erect new institutions on the ruins of the old. This endeavor was thwarted by a succession of monarchs singularly unfitted for the discharge of their high responsibilities or singularly unfortunate in their preparation therefor; by the division of the intellectual classes into two irreconcilable camps, neither of which advanced a practical solution consonant with the people's character; by the dispersive tendencies inherent in the character of the people and even in the soil of the country. It was gradually helped by the growing prosperity which the country owed to its inherent virtues and particularly to the sobriety and capacity for hard work of its inhabitants; and by the steady growth of culture and wisdom which the country owed chiefly to the devotion and genius of a handful of men working with little or no help from the state and at times under its inimical threats or actions.

The people begin the century by rising against the French. This rising was a spontaneous movement of loyalty and affection toward the royal house. In 1808 the people were still profoundly imbued with the monarchist ideal. But that king whom the people acclaimed was groveling before Napoleon in Bayonne, where he was putting the crown of Ferdinand and Isabel, of Charles V and Philip II, at the feet of a Corsican upstart. The people of Spain created *Juntas* or committees, which took upon themselves the defense and government of the country abandoned by the king. The monarchy had fallen and broken itself to pieces, and in Madrid and Coruña, Asturias and Valencia, these broken pieces of the monarchy were taking in hand the affairs of the nation. Such an experience was to have far-reaching effects.

In 1812 the Cortes met in Cádiz, convened not by the king but by the people. They were controlled by the Liberals. Spain was given a constitution. It was the first round of the long match between the two beliefs. The Liberal victory was not to be long-lived. The people had to turn against the invader. Much obloquy has been cast on the *Juntas* and on their armies for not showing as much effective discipline and organization as Wellington's redcoats. Wellington was England, a prosperous and organized country. The *Juntas* were the Spanish people. And yet it was an army of this people which inflicted the first defeat on the dreaded troops of the invincible Napoleon, at Bailén, where Dupont, with twenty thousand Frenchmen, capitulated before General Castaños. England came to the rescue, though the beginning of her intervention was not conspicuous for its efficiency. Three generals, Wellington, Burrard and Dalrymple, succeeded each other at the head of the English army in Portugal in less than forty-eight hours, all duly accredited. The result was that Wellington's first successes against the French were nullified by the Convention of Cintra. The combined efforts of the English force and of the Spanish guerrillas succeeded in driving Napoleon out of Spain. Ferdinand, till then a prisoner in France, came back to occupy the throne which his people had reconquered for him.

He had forgotten nothing and learned nothing. He flouted the Cortes, and started to govern in the worst possible taste as a personal despot, surrounded by a camarilla of worthless and low individuals.

The Liberal leaders, unable to count on popular support, sought the help of a few army officers who, holding liberal views, could be expected to bring about a system of reason and liberty through methods of force and coercion. On the collapse of the old system, Spain found herself with practically no political institutions of any kind. The old municipal institutions which the nation had spontaneously created *pari passu* with the reconquest, had gradually been absorbed by the crown. There was no basis on which to build up a political opinion. Of the two schools into which the Spanish leading classes had split, one, the traditional school, was well content with this state of affairs. It was indeed a confirmation of the theories which the traditional school maintained. The other school was bound to take the historical or evolutionistic attitude: "The people are indifferent because they are unenlightened; they have been left in the dark by centuries of obscurantism; but wait and see what happens when we enlighten them." The Liberal hotheads lacked the wisdom to wait. They were impatient. They wished to see a Liberal Spain during their lifetime, even at the risk of their life. They called on the soldiers. Honor to their memory, but we are still suffering the consequences of their intemperate action. And nowadays, moreover, the soldiers are on the other side of the barricade.

Riego, the military leader whose forces brought back the Constitution—how strange the word becomes when tossed about to and fro amidst cannon and bayonets—has left a name in the history of Spain, for till recent years, in fact, till the urban masses went practically over to socialism and changed their music accordingly, the *"Himno de Riego,"* written in his honor, has rung in Spanish cities wherever there was Liberal blood to spill.[1] From 1820 till 1823 the Liberals tried to govern constitutionally. The Liberals had to contend with the lack of loyalty of the king, who hated the constitution and was an artist in matters of perjury; and, finally, with the enmity of the foreign powers which, alarmed at the success of the Liberal revolution in Spain, sent a hundred thousand Frenchman to quell it. They were known as the hundred thousand sons of St. Louis. King Ferdinand was able to indulge in his favorite pastime—manhunting. Though he did his very best, he did not satisfy the right wing of his absolutist supporters, who, under the name of *apostólicos,* gathered around Ferdinand's younger brother, Carlos. Thus began the evolution whereby the division between two political tendencies became a dynastic division and then a civil war.

Ferdinand had no sons. He left two daughters by his fourth wife, María Christina of Naples. Spanish law permitted women

[1] It was the official National Anthem from 1931 till 1938.

to be heirs to the throne. Salic law, which the Bourbon dynasty had brought over from France, debarred them from such a right. The last years of King Ferdinand, while worse than sterile for the nation, were seething with intrigues, whereby Don Carlos on the one hand and the queen on the other endeavored to secure the throne. As the *apostólicos* had chosen Don Carlos for their leader. Doña María Cristina smiled her best Neapolitan brands on the good-natured Liberals who, moreover, found a mother and a little girl an appropriate idyllic combination to crown their Liberal arcadia. The queen won the last round, and her daughter, Isabel, was crowned on her father's death.

Following a precedent which her deceased husband had established, and which her daughter was to raise to the status of a dynastic tradition, the queen regent immediately proceeded to betray the party which had given her support in time of need. She had, however, to compromise at first with Liberal ideas, for Don Carlos had taken the field in the north, and the times were not propitious for throwing away any support which might be forthcoming. Given the attachment of the Spanish people to civil war, there seems no reason why the Carlist struggle should have ended. A Liberal leader, Mendizábal, who owed perhaps to his Jewish blood a measure of practical shrewdness uncommon in Spain, succeeded in forcing the bigoted queen to adopt the measure which was to deprive the war of much of its popularity with the pious upper middle classes. He secularized the immense lands of the Church and put them on sale at prices so tempting that the well-to-do had to choose between the two worlds. They took the lands and became Liberals. The state took over their good money, and the Carlist war ended in reconciliation on the field of Vergara (1839). But the struggle in the field was but a symptom. The real struggle was—and still is—inherent in the body politic of the country. María Cristina, with the cooperation of the moderate section of the Liberals, had contrived a law restricting the municipal liberties of the towns. The advanced Liberals objected in the name of Liberty, and manifested their opposition in a pronunciamiento which forced the queen to revoke the law on her own authority—surely a step not to be expected from such staunch enemies of absolutism. The head of the rising, Espartero, became regent in 1841, and had to leave office in 1843, a victim of the same method which had enabled him to attain it—another pronunciamento also made in the name of Liberal principles. Queen Isabel, then thirteen years old, was declared of age.

This was, of course, a pure constitutional fiction. Queen Isabel was never of age, though she died a grandmother. The best that can be said on her behalf is that she could plead effective extenuating circumstances. Her father was a contemptible person and her mother a mediocre and sensuous woman; she herself was put in charge of one of the most exacting tasks in Europe at the tender age of thirteen. Her mother was by then discredited and remarried. She was surrounded by men of all kinds, every one of them superlatively full of his own particular self. Institutions and traditions were weak, and as a result of protracted intrigues between Paris and London, she was deliberately married to her cousin, Don Francisco, who was notoriously unable to gain any ascendancy whatsoever over his wife and queen.

These were the circumstances which in part, at any rate—for the queen embroidered on their canvas with a genuine zest for which credit must be given her—explain the scandalous reign of Isabel II. In private life she created her own standards of queenly behavior. In public life she conformed to the traditions of her worthy parents. She betrayed her first prime minister, Olózaga. She then gave power to González Bravo, a converted radical, who tried to convince his new friends that a mere civilian could gag the nation as effectively as any general; but the camarilla were not impressed and General Narváez took office in 1844.

The new prime minister was a perfect example of the military politician, a type which has been the curse of Spain in modern times. It is a type not altogether devoid of genuine national precedents in the history of old Spain, and some of its features recall well-known figures of the Spanish past, not excluding the Cid himself. But in the nineteenth century the type takes on new forms. We find it now on the Liberal side (Riego), now on the reactionary side (Narváez), now in a dubious zone hesitating between Liberal leanings and friendships and a reactionary temperament (O'Donnell); but in every case the soldier politician is built on a pattern which it may be useful to outline here.

To begin with, he is a patriot. He does not come to politics through the intellectual roads of the university and in his tender years. He arrives late, when he has already made his mark in the army, when, both from the material and from the social point of view, his position is sure and his situation is made. His first attitude, therefore, is apt to be that of a natural observer who finds fault with "the whole lot of talkers" and feels sure that he can put everything right if he is only left free to apply decent military methods.

In this attitude he is strengthened by his ignorance and by the tendency to think in simple categories, which is one of the features of the mere soldier. His idea of law is less an idea than a feeling of irritation akin to that which arises in a determined walker trying to beat his steady record across a field netted with barbed wire. He knows what is good. He sees what is good. He wants to go there direct. An argument is an obstacle.

Whether liberal or reactionary in his ideas, the Spanish military politician is a reactionary by temperament. He wants to have his way, not to pool his ideas or wishes. At his best he belongs to the category of the benevolent despot of the eighteenth century; at his worst, to that of the Oriental despot when honorable. For it is a characteristic of this interesting genus that their sense of honor is strong—a fact not always recognized by their adversaries, mainly because honor is a subjective criterion which may counsel different and even opposite actions to different men. For the military politician is, of course, a strong individualist. The native individualism which every Spaniard brings to the world is made more acute in him by his ambition —since, *ex hypothesi,* he is ambitious—and by the military temperament. This last element of his individualistic nature explains why the soldier-politician contributes so much to developing the worst feature of Spanish political life: the excessive influence of personal ambitions. Moreover, military education has disastrous effects on Spanish psychology. The Spanish character has an innate tendency to become overbearing. The military law of obedience from below and orders from above encourages such a tendency. What the Spanish character needs is the education and the strengthening of the tendency to give and take and to cooperate. Now, given the pride and stiffness of the Spaniard, such an education can only be attempted by appealing to objective tasks in view, and not by exacting submission to a chief. The military politician is unable to realize either this fact, or any of the essential facts of Spanish life, for he is only concerned with externals.

And of such externals the first which strikes him is order. The military idea of order is purely mechanical. When men are arranged as pawns in threes or fours, that is order. If they could be ranged in order of sizes, that would be heavenly order. All the military leaders Spain has had were obsessed with this idea of external order—oblivious of the fact that the most shocking example of disorder a nation can give the world is to keep a general at the head of its civil government. And as their idea of order is purely material, so are their methods to obtain it. *Palo y tente tieso,* which means "a blow with my stick and keep erect." [2]

Naturally, the military politician objects to freedom of the press. Free discussion is the true way toward true order. But the military politician does not know what true order is. All military politicians, even those who entered politics through the Liberal gates, have revealed themselves unable to govern without the censor. Instinctively, they limit the political field to the arena of material forces, in which they feel stronger.

In the history of modern Spain the military politician, however, incarnates a tendency which is not without both theoretical justification and practical importance. The Spanish people cannot acquire political experience without considerable disorder

[2] The English language needs five words to the Spanish single and eloquent *palo,* because, in Spain, the mere mention of the weapon suggests not merely the use but the action.

and unrest. This disorder and this unrest are detrimental to the growth of both wealth and institutions, which in their turn are indispensable for political experience. Thus the country finds itself now and then in a mood of political weariness ready to sacrifice many of its political ideals for a crust of bread eaten in peace. Such are the moods in which the military politician can hope, not merely to be obeyed, but to be heard. Peace and prosperity are not in themselves ideals wherewith to appeal to the Spanish nation; but they may become so through force of circumstances. The trouble comes when the military politician, having secured peace and prosperity by exceptional methods, fails to realize that such methods are detrimental to the higher aims which every country must set before herself. That man shall not live by bread alone is a Gospel truth which military politicians do not often appraise in its true import.

For, as a matter of fact, Spanish military politicians are not particularly rich in religious gifts. Most of them, if not all, have been matter-of-course Catholics without concerning themselves much about it, except on great occasions. There is a deathbed story about Narváez which, true or not, is significant in this connection. "Does Your Excellency forgive all his enemies?" the priest asked him. And the dying man, in a determined voice: "I have no enemies. I have had them all shot." Discount Narváez's particular resoluteness and what remains is common to all Spanish military politicians. They are believers because they "don't bother their heads about that kind of stuff," but they are not bigoted clerics. They are, in fact, generally well disposed toward education and toward a reasonable policy of religious liberty— only . . .

In actual fact, whatever their personal attitude may have been, Spanish military politicians have always ended in countenancing, tolerating, or even fostering clerical reaction. There are several reasons for this constantly recurring fact of modern Spanish history. Like seeks like and clerical reaction is too closely akin to political reaction not to benefit by it. Moreover, the administrations led by military politicians erect a wall of censorship between them and the public so that clerical pressure over the civil service can increase in a thousand little ways without fear of protest from the intellectual leaders of opinion; finally, in such periods the crown, though less influential than under civilian administration, was generally given a freer hand in purely religious questions, and the crown in Spain—nowadays— is always clerical.

Thus, on the whole, it will be found that when military politicians appear on the Spanish stage the permanent difficulties which beset political life are increased by their rivalries and ambitions, though simplified at times if there happens to be among them an outstanding personality with sufficient power to oust all others; that even then, though the country is able to benefit from a period of peace and prosperity, the political education of the people suffers from the methods of force adopted; and, finally, that a clerical reaction usually sets in, with disastrous effects in all walks of life, politics and education.

Queen Isabel's reign had to suffer not one, but five military politicians: Espartero, Narváez, O'Donnell, Serrano and Prim. Its history is but a succession of periods of resolute government (Narváez) with the acquiescence and help of the queen and her clericals cut short by Liberal pronunciamentos (Espartero, O'Donnell), which brought in cabinets of a mild democratic tendency working under an inimical and intriguing court. Incidentally, the country was involved in two external adventures —a war in Morocco (1859), in which O'Donnell's victories remained sterile, owing mostly to British intervention, and the ill-fated expedition in Mexico in collaboration with France and England. Gradually, however, the absolutist tendencies of the queen had taken on the worst features of her father's reign, and the popularity of the once beloved child-monarch had vanished. Her repeated disloyalties toward some of her advisers led many of them to the conclusion that the root of the evil was in the queen herself. Liberals decided that the next pronunciamento should aim at a change in the occupant of the throne. In the autumn of 1868 the army and the navy revolted. Queen Isabel crossed the frontier and her reign was over.

Now or never. Did we not say that the root of the evil was

in the crown? Was not the queen expelled under posters bearing the inscription: "Down with the spurious race of the Bourbons. A condign punishment of their perversity"? The Spaniards were free and left to themselves. Now they would show what they could do.

What could they do? They had lost half a century fighting: fighting against the French; fighting among themselves; fighting the hostility of a despicable court; fighting—the hardest fight, perhaps, of all—against their own political shortcomings. And so, when the time came to act, they found the masses either wrong-headed or indifferent and the leaders both inexperienced and intransigent.

This experimental period opens and closes with two names: Serrano and Prim. Both generals, of course. Serrano, the head of the Provisional Government, and Prim, his right-hand man, more popular and more intelligent than his chief, were unable to bring the remaining political leaders to agree as to the form of government to be adopted, and left the matter to the Cortes, in which a majority declared for a monarchy. This vote brought about a Republican revolt in Aragon which Serrano had to quell. A monarch was sought in Europe—incidentally providing the reason or the pretext for the Franco-Prussian War—and was finally found in the person of Amadeo of Savoy. Prim, who had negotiated his election, was murdered on the very day the king landed in Cartagena. The disappearance of his magnetic personality precipitated a political confusion which the king would have been unable to master even if he had known the Spanish language, but which, through his ignorance of Spanish, became a nightmare. The gentleman-king, as he was called by the Spaniards—whom adversity had led to think such a conjunction rare enough to be emphasized—abdicated in 1872. The Cortes voted a republic in February, 1873, but split hopelessly as to procedure and were dissolved by a *coup d'état*. The new Cortes, convened in May, voted a federal system, but split again as to the particular unit to be adopted as the basis of the federation (old kingdoms, new provinces, small cantons). In less than one year the republic knew four presidents. The last of them, Castelar, allowed himself to be ousted by a military pronunciamento. Serrano took power again, but this time not as the godfather of a new era of liberty, but as the military dictator who came to relieve the country of the weight of liberty which it was unable to carry. On December 29, 1874, a brigade of soldiers proclaimed Isabel's son king of Spain.

The main fact about Alfonso XII is that he had known adversity, and, therefore, his education was less incomplete than had been the rule with Spanish kings. He was a man who knew his mind, and he seems to have had a true sense of the responsibilities of his position. He had also a good minister; but, unfortunately, not a great one. Cánovas consolidated the monarchy for a generation, but he was not the man to provide it with a basis solid enough to last for a century. He relied on force and fiction. A constitution was voted with the clear intention of governing under, over, around, and even through it, but never honestly with it. And so this man, personally honest and honorable, even devoted, was the greatest corrupter of political life which modern Spain has known.

He was effectively helped by his compeer, Sagasta, an exradical ex-revolutionist, who took the leadership of the Liberal party. "Time and I against everybody" was his motto, and he lived up to it. What in Cánovas was, at bottom, pessimism over his countrymen, in Sagasta was pessimism over things. The Restoration rests thus on two symmetrical figures, the stern pessimist and the smiling pessimist.

And yet they found a nation ready to build up a normal and healthy political life, a king of free and independent mind, for once unfettered by a camarilla, and not in the least disposed to allow one to gather round him. A Carlist outburst disposed of, Cánovas and Sagasta carried on a policy of make-believe. Instead of developing poltical habits in the people by enforcing a clean electoral law and seeking the opinion of the electorate (however restricted it might be), Cánovas and Sagasta chose to invert in practice the system which had been outlined theoretically in the Constitution. The consequences of such a step were bound to be disastrous, and Spain is still suffering from them.

The system evolved may be summed up as follows. A general election was managed from Madrid. The Director of Politics of the Home Office, which by an irony of fate is known in Spain as *Ministerio de la Gobernación,* was the expert who saw to it that in each district the government candidate was returned. The Government had its majority. The opposition was granted an adequate number of votes to keep it well disposed to carry on the game. Naturally enough, political life, thus deprived of its healthy source of power, sought to obtain it where it could be found. The obvious alternative was the king. It is a deplorable yet a transparent paradox that these two men who were obsessed with the idea of the crown, should have evolved a system which, through sheer mistrust of the people, ended in exposing the crown to the odium of party politics. Cánovas, at the beginning of the Restoration, had genuine power. Had he chosen the right path, i.e. the creation of a restricted but effective electorate in which to deposit it, he would have put the Bourbon monarchy on an unassailable basis, and we should see in him the greatest Spanish statesman. As it is, he advised the king to play a constitutional game, and while he corrupted the electorate from the Home Office, he corrupted the crown from the premiership. The crown learned from its prime minister to consider itself as the true source of power. The seed fell on ground which had been prepared of old. But the source of power is not in kings. What of Spanish generals?

Life, however, went on around all these pretenses. Industrial progress, education, communications, greater intimacy with foreign movements, the advent of Socialism—in short, all the several aspects which in Spain, as everywhere, modern life was taking on—brought about not so much unrest as activity in the people. Gradually the system was led to enlarge the basis on which it rested: a few politicians and the king could not suffice. New sources of power had to be called into play. The Restoration developed two allies: the Church and the army.

Strictly speaking, the allies were not new. The army had impatiently proclaimed King Alfonso without waiting for the Cortes to do it. The Church had been won over by Cánovas during the first years of Alfonso's reign. But the Restoration came gradually to feel the power that the two institutions wielded in Spain, as the deplorable policy of its two protagonists gradually elbowed the people out of the constitution through the dismal door of disillusionment, and as all other institutions in the country, notably Parliament and the Judiciary, lost authority and prestige in the process. This evolution was favored by the queen regent. Alfonso XII unfortunately died young. His wife, María Cristina of Hapsburg, a lady of the highest moral standing, took over the regency with remarkable dignity and devotion. In true quixotic fashion, Castelar, the Republican leader, refused to rise against a "lady and a cradle." The queen showed pronounced clerical leanings and a disposition to listen willingly to the swarm of generals who fluttered about the plums of office.

Spain could still offer its soldiers of fortune enviable posts overseas. Cuba, Puerto Rico and the Philippine Islands had to be governed. The army had practically monopolized the three governor-generalships and, so far as Cuba and the Philippines were concerned, at any rate, it had misgoverned them effectively enough to make a military governor indispensable. Just as nations take a good deal of ruining, colonies take a good deal of misgovernment. But in Cuba there was a third party. The United States of America is known to be particularly anxious to ensure a high level of peace, happiness and good government in every nation whose territory happens to be strategically placed from the point of view of the Panama Canal. The peace and happiness of the Cubans became thus a matter of great concern for statesmen in Washington, and interference, both official and unofficial, in Cuban matters gradually became the rule. Negotiations went from bad to worse, partly because the Spanish Government was afraid of putting the gravity of the situation before public opinion and was by nature inclined to be unyielding; partly because, as events were to prove, there were strong forces in America working for war. Fate was on the side of the yellow press, and an American cruiser, the *Maine,* was blown into Havana harbor when the two governments were still pursuing conversations.

Despite the efforts of the American ambassador in Spain and

of many truly peace-loving Americans, the American warlike party, ably helped by one or two Napoleons of the press, won the day, and Spain had to embark on the last of her imperial wars. The people were left in the dark as to the most important events, misled as to the true power of the potential enemy, sacrificed to the fetish of the period—the dynasty. A fleet of disciplined sailors sacrificed itself twice to this senseless policy. Admiral Cervera agreed to sail for America knowing that he had at his disposal none of the elementary conditions for holding the seas, and having succeeded in reaching Santiago, thus immobilizing the American fleet there, he again agreed to come out and fight, obeying superior orders because it was decided that for the good of the dynasty there was to be a sea fight. The American army off Santiago, on the brink of withdrawing before the spirited resistance of the Spaniards, was relieved to find that the Spanish commander in Havana thus came to their rescue by ordering the fleet out to sea. Indeed in this picturesque war it looked much as if the chiefs on either side were, of course unwittingly, the best allies of their adversaries. But the United States had a greater margin to spare, and the war soon came to an end. By the Treaty of Paris, 1898, Spain wound up her colonial empire: Cuba was made nominally independent, while Puerto Rico and the Philippine Islands passed over to the United States.

Four years later, on May 17, King Alfonso was declared of age, and took charge of the destinies of the country as constitutional king. These two events contribute to give the end of the century a particular significance in the history of Spain. The loss of the last remnants of her empire forced Spain to recoil on herself and to find herself. The reign of Alfonso XIII must be understood in this light. Spain has behind her a closed imperial cycle, a closed world mission and a century of political turmoil. The twentieth century must show the new Spain emerging from the ruins of the past. How far is this Spain new? How far is she the old Spain under new forms? What are her hopes, what her possibilities, what her message?

PART 2

"SCHOOL and LARDER"

CHAPTER 7

"SCHOOL"

Though the importance of material factors should not be over-looked, the true source of the Spanish Renaissance is of a spirit-ual character. The most pressing need was, of course, a new spirit in education. But foreign observers have often gone astray owing to the ready-made idea that a nation's education must be measured solely by the index of illiteracy. A Scotch university professor, while staying in a boarding-house in Seville, observed once how rudely a Spanish commercial traveler was behaving toward an Englishman with whom he had entered into an argu-ment. The maid in attendance was also shocked at the behavior of her countryman. She was a peasant girl from one of the valleys around Seville, and could neither read nor write. When at last, to everybody's relief, the commercial traveler left the room with a bang, the maid turned to the Englishman and, with that respectful familiarity which is the gift of the Spanish people, said soothingly: "Never mind him, sir, he is a man without

75

education." "What an admirable thing to say," added the Scotch professor, out to discover Spain. A Spaniard would not have found it admirable at all, but merely matter-of-course. Instinctively he knows that education and letters go no more necessarily together than holiness and prayers.

The argument based on education in all its theoretical perfection is, of course, unanswerable. Take any human being, act on him in such a way as to draw out (educate) his inherent powers, and you must perforce enrich his personality. This is not an argument, it is a truism. But when, the point being granted on the assumption of an education theoretically perfect, we are asked to agree to an education reduced to a grotesque makeshift consisting mostly in communicating ability to read ready-made trash, we grow cold and cautious.

That this caution is justified no one can deny who has glanced at nine-tenths of the printed material which circulates in countries proud of their level of literacy. Books and newspapers are very largely goods belonging to the stimulant or stupefying group, such as alcohol, tobacco, or even opium and cocaine, and it is doubtful whether, in at least 50 per cent of the cases, the schoolmaster does more than enable human beings to have access to a kind of mental drug. But in a country like Spain the question takes on an even greater complexity. If our reading is correct, the Spanish nation is, above all, a nation of men of passion whose main characteristic is spontaneity; we may expect the people of Spain to be particularly gifted. And that is what experience shows. All observers of Spain, national or foreign, bear witness to the innate distinction, dignity, originality and creative power of the people of Spain. Spanish folk poetry is, in its simplicity, one of the finest known to man, worthy to be quoted along with the most beautiful creations of individual poets. A nation whose untutored people can manifest itself with so much beauty and power may well pause before deciding whether so-called education is, or is not, an unmixed blessing. Not that Spain has ever hesitated. No one but benighted clericals has ever suggested that elementary schools should be curtailed. The problem of education in Spain is not most urgent at the base but at the top, for the people are better qualified to fulfill their functions than the leaders to fulfill theirs; and in order to educate such a people without spoiling its wonderful gifts, the education of the teachers must be particularly careful and exacting —which in its turn implies that education must be taken in hand first at the top.

On the threshold of our age Spain found herself confronted with the necessity to restock her culture, most of the wealth of which had been dilapidated or badly depreciated by a shift in world values. Despite the brilliance of individuals, the atmosphere of collective ideas was thin. The middle classes had turned away from the Catholic religious culture which had animated them and given them character and personality. Part of them had fallen into devout Philistinism of the kind fostered by the Jesuits, particularly among the well-to-do classes; others lived on ready-made ideas imported from France. Culture at the top is what Spain had to evolve, and of course she had to evolve it out of her own substance, for she is far too original to borrow or even to adapt.

Fortunately, she found the men at hand—a small group of men who, just at the moment when the Liberals thought their millennium had set in with the Revolution of 1868, gathered the harvest of experience which the century had yielded and, turning away from politics, decided to start on the long path of education. The leader of this band of pioneers was perhaps the noblest Spanish figure of the nineteenth century: Don Francisco Giner de los Ríos.

In order to understand such a man one must go back to that fleeting period in the sixteenth century when Spain fell in love with Erasmus and produced Vives, when Juan de Valdés in Naples attained so fascinating a combination of true saintliness, intellectual distinction and worldly grace.

Francisco Giner was born in 1839 in Ronda, that most picturesque of Andalusian towns, and early migrated to Madrid, where his uncle, Don Antonio de los Ríos Rosas, was a prominent politician. In 1866 he won the Chair of Jurisprudence and International Law in the University of Madrid. The University

was then intellectually led by Sanz del Río, a follower of the
new educational and philosophical opinions preached at the
time in Germany by Krause. In 1867 the Minister of Education,
Orovio, tried to force Professor Sanz del Río to sign a profession
of fidelity to the crown, to the dynasty and to the Catholic
religion. He refused and was deprived of his chair. Don Francisco Giner resigned his own chair as a protest, though the
deprivation of his salary implied then a serious sacrifice for him.
The Revolution of 1868 reinstated all the persecuted professors
in their chairs. But the Restoration brought back Orovio to the
Ministry of Education and the same oppressive measure was
enacted against the liberty of the chair. Giner, who after Sanz
del Río's death was the recognized leader of the group, led
the protest, but the government had him and his colleagues
prosecuted, exiled and deprived of their chairs. Cánovas, then
prime minister, sent Giner a message begging him to withdraw
his protest and giving him every assurance that the decree,
though officially promulgated, would remain unapplied. Giner
refused to compromise on so dubious a basis and Cánovas had
him removed at four in the morning from his sickbed and sent
under custody to a fortress in Cádiz. English public opinion
was deeply stirred. The English consul visited the prisoner and
offered to enlist English sympathy on his behalf, but Giner
politely declined. His dignified attitude only increased English
sympathy. Offers were made to him which amounted to the
creation of a free Spanish university in Gibraltar. Soon afterward, Don Francisco and his friends were set at liberty, but
deprived of their chairs.

Fortunately, this time, the men who were persecuted had a
leader worthy of the attentions of adversity. Don Francisco
realized that the time had come for carrying the fight into its
true field. Instead of pitting Liberal against Reactionary in the
often bloody and always sterile game of politics, the time had
come for directing the energies of enlightened leaders toward
action and private initiative. Don Francisco preached by example. There they were, a handful of professors without a university: let them found a school. And thus was born the true

nursery of contemporary Spain: the *Institución Libre de Enseñanza*.

If, for some of them, this change in their activity was a kind of exile from the romantic lands of politics, for Don Francisco it was a return to the fatherland. He was a born teacher. His spirit was not so much in his books as in his living and personal communication, in the indefinable charm and quiet authority of his nature, his sweet persuasiveness, his endless patience, enlivened here and there by a subtle vein of irony, his sure taste, his genuine friendliness, his unfailing loyalty and his total lack of self-seeking. Naturally, while realizing that a thorough-going evolution in educational methods was indispensable as a preliminary to any political progress in the country, he took up the task for its own sake, seeing in education a self-contained art the aim of which is to create men.

The *Institución* was born as a kind of private university. But Don Francisco Giner had other ideas. He was bent on education, not on mere instruction. He knew that the work had to be begun at the beginning. Gradually, he made the *Institución* concentrate on the young until it became an elementary and secondary school. First and foremost, he understood the school not as a teaching factory, but as an environment. The school conceived of as life on the threshold of life was not only his doctrine, but his instinct and his behavior. Tuition was made to cover the arts and the knowledge of civilizations. Games, excursions, seashore holidays were organized as a part of school life. And when, in 1884, Giner and Cossío came to the London International Conference on Education, in the course of which they paid a high tribute to the educational value of English games for the formation of character, they were able to show the world a flourishing example of a school founded and maintained by private initiative, "the first institution in Spain that has introduced manual work throughout the whole course of elementary education, perhaps the first in Europe to have made it compulsory in the secondary course, on the ground of its being an absolutely indispensable element not only of technical education but, within certain limits, of all education that is rational and human." The *Institución* had also adopted coeducation, though in this it followed a practice traditional in Spain.

The *Institución* stimulated other educational establishments, both friendly and unfriendly. Its influence began to make itself felt on official centers. Most of the staff of the *Institución* belonged also to the University of Madrid, or to other state educational establishments. The phase of persecution had passed and the sacrifice of Giner and of his friends had at least secured for the Spanish Chair a freedom equal to that which university professors enjoy in the freest nation.[1] Giner had been reinstated in 1881 and he spread his quiet but penetrating light into the darkest recesses of the old-fashioned university. The wide humanism and the alert curiosity of his mind were stimulating; all branches of knowledge seemed to blossom and to bear fruit wherever he passed.

The *Institución* thus acted as a leaven in the educational and general life of the country. The universities had fallen from the days of their splendor. In the old days they had lived a life of their own, each according to its traditions. Salamanca, the most famous of them, had seen times when more than six thousand students congregated from all parts of the world, attracted by the learning of its sixty professors. It was a democratic institution, the professors being elected by the students, while the rector was not only elected by the students but was a student himself. The universities were, in fact, institutions evolved by the nation and not set up by the state. Professors were not officials, but workers whom their co-workers in other walks of life trusted to perform their job properly. The state, of course, absorbed this spontaneous national life as it was to absorb all national life, particularly under the Bourbon dynasty. The universities rapidly decayed while simultaneously the state increased its hold over them. The two evolutions were parallel, and it would be a mistake to interpret the first as the cause of the second. The brief period of enlightened despotism of the eighteenth century had done much to start university life in the direction required by

[1] This does not of course refer to either General Primo de Rivera's or General Franco's dictatorship.

the times. When Torres Villarroel applied for the Chair of Mathematics and Astrology in Salamanca it had been vacant for thirty years. By the end of the eighteenth century good scientific work was being done in a few of the universities; but, though Charles IV and Godoy endeavored to stimulate their life, the general policy of the king and of his minister was bound to be fatal to Spanish culture as it was to every other form of Spanish life. As for Ferdinand VII, he was definitely hostile to learning. The Carlist influence which controlled the actual springs of power during most of the years of the nineteenth century did its best to thwart the free evolution of the universities. Nowhere was the struggle between Reactionaries and Liberals keener than in the field of education.

In Giner's time the universities were mere government establishments for the granting of official diplomas. In a sense all universities tend fatally to become degree factories. But in Spain, when Giner first began to observe them, they were nothing else. In a sense the evil was less than might appear on the surface, since the very soullessness of the university made it innocuous to the young men and women who came to it with souls of their own. Self-reliance, the help provided by the *Institución* and the presence of some trusted and loved masters (Giner himself one of them) did much to ease matters. Giner, moreover, stimulated studies abroad by all means in his power.

At this juncture the effects of Spain's return on herself as a consequence of the Spanish-American War began to be felt. What Don Francisco Giner had realized in 1876 was rapidly sinking into the consciousness of the nation, home from her last adventure with the seed of wisdom in her heart, like Don Quixote after his defeat at the hands of the Knight of the Mirrors. Abroad—abroad. Spontaneously, parents began to send their boys and girls to be educated in France, in England, in Switzerland, in Belgium, in Germany. The feeling was in the air and the men were at hand who could capture it and turn it to account. The *Junta para Ampliación de Estudios* was created in 1907.

The new organization was a significant proof of the far-reaching effects of Giner's creative genius, not only in its aims, but in its inception and methods. The state had come to realize that it was incompetent to deal directly with the most delicate national problems—a result of the subtly penetrating atmosphere, the tacit criticism, the quiet work of Giner and his followers, as well as of a general rise in the level of public opinion. Yet it was obvious that the authority and the funds for any educational work of national scope had to come from the state. A formula was found which met these two apparently conflicting requirements: the government handed over a grant and certain powers to an autonomous body, a committee of prominent scholars. As if clearly to signify that the new institution was to be run under strict scientific inspiration untainted by politics, the committee was presided over by Dr. Ramón y Cajal, the great physiologist to whom modern neurology owes its main inspiration. As for the actual work of the committee, by one of those generosities of Fate which nations cannot expect very often, Spain, who had produced a Giner at the time of inspiration, found a Castillejo at the time of execution.

He was a man with a lofty brow which (as Rostand remarked of his own) stretched from the eyebrows to the back of the head, a bald head, a long and narrow skull, a face of inconspicuous features, a cropped, fair mustache and a complexion burned by frequent exposure to the cold and hot winds of the Sierra; the mouth of a shrewd peasant and eyes like gimlets—but gimlets alive. The Spanish language, in spite of its rich vocabulary, having broken down under the strain of his requirements, Señor Castillejo drew on several other languages as well, all of which he spoke with fluency, a rapidity and a frequency which reminded the listener of one of those smoke screens which modern warships emit in order to move at ease behind their dense atmosphere. The suggestion is haunting, for Señor Castillejo obviously combined the purity of the dove with the guile of the serpent. Many an entertaining tale might be told—were it wise to do so—of the ways whereby he succeeded now and then in making a cabinet minister sign the right decree when his natural inclination would have led him to sign the wrong one.

Señor Castillejo's genius was revealed to the wary when the new institution, which was to revolutionize Spanish education in a few years, appeared before the world under an unassuming name: *Junta para Ampliación de Estudios;* great things could be expected from a man with such a gift for misnomers.

The expectations thus raised were met. A regular crop of students and graduates were sent every year properly chosen and prepared for their stay abroad, and stimulated with the certainty that the result of their work would, if found worthy of it, be published in an adequate setting. Laboratories and centers of research were organized and kept going with both technical ability and admirable devotion; a model secondary school was set up in Madrid, an establishment which vied with the best and most up-to-date to be found in any country; finally, residential colleges for men and women were founded in Madrid with conspicuous success.

The *Junta* endeavored to maintain the strictest impartiality in confessional matters, sometimes in most trying circumstances. This was one of the factors in the situation which its enemies found most embarrassing. Thus, when the bigoted clerical enemies who, more or less shamefacedly, tried to represent the *Junta* as an element of denationalization, directed an attack on the secondary school which it had created in Madrid, the *Junta* was able to show that the (Catholic) religious instruction provided in the school to all but those who did not desire it was more complete than that available in any ordinary government establishment. The *Junta's* success, moreover, depended to a great extent on the exceptional powers of self-denial of those whom it employed. Like Caesar's wife, the *Junta,* not content to be honest, looked it as well, and, as it was closely scrutinized, many were the cases in which the workers who had devoted their lives to it deprived themselves of salaries or emoluments not only allowed in law, but legitimate in equity.

The effects of this activity soon began to be felt. Gradually, the young men sent abroad returned home ripened by their experience and settled either in business, in government departments, or in the universities. The gain was always certain. But the greatest gain came from those who took up educational work. The leaven of the *Junta,* and therefore of the *Institución,* began to act in the universities. There is nothing more striking than the change in tone which could be observed in every Spanish university during these years: the vitality, the eagerness, the organizing ability, the sense of solidarity which had been developed in all of them in a varying degree. This movement owed much to the *Junta.* Directly or indirectly it may be traced back to Giner.

CHAPTER 8

GALDÓS AND THE 1898 GENERATION

While, to indulge for once in contemporary jargon, Giner built
up the *ethos* of the nation, Galdós was vigorously rebuilding
its *epos*. Spain has not produced a greater novelist since Cervantes. Born in the Canary Islands in 1839, he soon evinced
an artistic turn of mind in music and in drawing, then was
made to study law. The young student arrived in Madrid when
the storm of 1868 was brewing. The unpopularity of Isabel II
was reaching its apex; political clubs were boiling over with
enthusiasm for freedom and eloquence, and the barracks were
hearing the call. His eyes, though inexperienced, began to see
through and below this political activity, perceiving the genuine
movements of national psychology on both sides of the bar-
ricades already discernible to the imagination. When these barri-
cades actually took shape in substance, cutting the nation into
two camps, Galdós we may presume, threw in his lot with the
revolutionaries, for, though at heart impartial and neutral, his

85

neutrality and impartiality presupposed liberty, and he was bound to be for the time being on the side of light. In those early days he wrote his first work, *La Fontana de Oro,* a novel in which, under a title suggestive of the age (a name of one of the political clubs in which he saw the ferment of the revolution gradually rise), the type of his later productions was already emerging; for this novel may be considered as belonging to both the great series of works which he was to create: his *Episodios Nacionales* and his contemporary novels. The former are in themselves a true history of nineteenth-century Spain seen, not from the scholar's window, but from the curbstone and at times from the top of a tree, the exposed street corner just fought over by rival factions, the private house of a politician, the darkest recess of a café seething with conspirators, the country orchard turned into a battlefield by a skirmish between Liberals and Carlists. Characteristically enough, the *Episodios Nacionales* begin with Trafalgar the title of the first of them—and constitute an imposing collection of five series (the last unfinished) of ten novels each, in which the Spanish nineteenth century is felt alive. In a sense the contemporary novels show an equal attention to the actual life of Spain as it flowed under his eyes. But here his creative imagination was freer, and he was soon able to show the breadth and depth of his conception of life. His main theme is, of course, that of the greatest artists: the relations between man and the forces of the universe, Life Death, Love. He is fascinated by the problem of Christianity and of the possibility of absorbing its ideals in our Western societies. Such is the theme of *Nazarín,* and particularly of his masterpiece, *Angel Guerra.* He shows love at work under all its complex aspects. His marvelous impartiality—only temporarily veiled during an anticlerical phase covering but three or four of his works—his intellectual honesty and the truly magnificent gift for conveying a sense of vigorous optimism even when relating stories of death and despair are some of the more relevant features which make him, while an unmistakable Spaniard, a novelist with a universal appeal.

Hence the all-important role which must be assigned to Galdós as one of the spirits who molded contemporary Spain. He brought out the true nineteenth century from a truly national (i.e. non-party) point of view, dwelling on its history as a Spaniard without bias; and he let fall on the Spanish character a flood of universal light, achieving a work which is one of the treasures of European literature while it incidentally fortifies and clarifies the Spanish consciousness of Spain.

Despite its inherent virtues and its vitality, the movement initiated by Don Francisco Giner and continued by his disciples would probably have petered out in an empty atmosphere of indifference had it been an isolated manifestation of private activity. As for Galdós, his influence would perhaps also have vanished with time. But both Giner and Galdós were more than mere isolated men. They were the signs of a general renascence, so that when their influence began to gather momentum it merged with other movements of an altogether different origin and character, yet springing from the same wave of new power. The most important of these movements was that known by the rather inaccurate name of "the Generation of 1898."

The date, of course, refers to the Spanish-American War. The men then young were able to observe at close quarters the hollow insincerity, the incompetence and the pompous frivolity of most of the figureheads of the Restoration. The nation had been kept in the dark and deceived; she knew neither the gravity of the Cuban revolt nor the strength of the powerful country which had come to the rescue of the insurgents; she had not been informed of the most important steps in the negotiations which led to the rupture; she knew nothing, of course, of the state of blissful unreadiness in which both army and navy had been allowed to stand by while the conversations with the United States went from bad to worse; she was ignorant of the conditions under which Admiral Cervera had sailed to his doom knowing that he would have neither base, nor coaling station, nor transport ships, nor any of the most elementary requisites for a fleet to exist, let alone fight. The nation had received from the government nothing but stimulants. When the repatriation of the army began and the Spanish towns saw the processions of yellow ghosts landing from the ships, the Islands gone, the warships lost, the men given over to yellow fever, there was a healthy reaction, the healthier for its quiet intensity. This was the mood of the nation when the generation of 1898 wrote.

Four men stand out as the leaders of this movement: Joaquín Costa, Angel Ganivet, Miguel de Unamuno and José Ortega y Gasset. There were others. Moreover, the movement had nothing of an organized drive. It was a spontaneous and natural mood which manifested itself in seemingly independent activities, just as a natural season, though an unmistakable fact of nature, can only be deduced from a number of separate events. It was not considered as a definite historical unit at the time, but only later, when a new generation began to look at their elders with some perspective and realized the striking unity of the spirit which animated them. The very character of the movement was complex, extending from politics to literature, so that amongst the men who were later seen as within the group there were some who distinguished themselves in the field of pure letters— such as Azorín; some even who never wrote a line in a political mood, being artists and nothing else—such as Valle-Inclán.

Joaquín Costa was one of those many-sided minds which are typical of a country so rebellious to specialization as Spain. A notary by profession, he was a scholar by vocation and had studied with equal industry the laws, customs and religion of the early inhabitants of the Peninsula, the political and social ideas underlying Spanish popular poetry and folklore, the methods whereby his own legal profession could be made more useful and effective, the features of agrarian collectivism in Spain and many more nondescript problems of a political, social, technical and even philological character. He was not a popular, not even indeed a well-known, man beyond a circle of friends and admirers when, in the critical years at the beginning of the century, he challenged Spain to a new life in his famous polemical works: *Reconstitución y Europeización de España* (1900), *Crisis Política de España* (1901), and particularly his contribution to the inquiry organized by the *Ateneo de Madrid* on the evils of Spanish public life under the significant title of *Oligarquía y Caci-*

quismo como la forma actual de Gobierno de España. Don Joaquín Costa was an Aragonese with a strong individualistic temperament, which not infrequently showed itself in the form of strong temper, a fierce and fiery patriotism, and all the impatience and the intolerance of a man whose whole life had been spent in pure and disinterested service for his country and for knowledge. His outburst, for it was somewhat in the manner of an outburst, aimed at raising the people from their lethargy and bidding them shake off the artificial system which the Restoration had evolved in lieu of government. He was loud in his denunciation of the rhetorical appeals to the past made by men unable to deal with the present. His message was to look things sternly in the face, to cease gilding the bare present with the glories borrowed from a bygone past. "Lock up the Cid's sepulcher under a treble key," he advised Spain, and attend to the needs of the day. What were those needs? He defined them with his usual thoroughness and precision, but also with his power for striking formulas which circulated afterward like coins: "School and Larder" was the slogan which he invented. It will be seen that Costa saw the primary needs of the day. An educational and an economic evolution were necessary before the Spanish people could develop the virtue without which all political communities are bound to live a precarious life— solidarity.

In deep contrast with this powerful voice resounding in the political arena, Angel Ganivet's quiet disquisitions might sound almost detached, yet the impression would be erroneous. Ganivet was a man of deep feeling, as shown by his suicide, which deprived Spain of one of her most brilliant hopes at a relatively early age. But he was a philosopher by vocation and a Granadino by birth, and a mind formed by Granada is bound to learn serenity from the alleys of cypress trees which make her a favorite haunt for poets. His first grown-up years were spent in the company of a small group of men of his meditative turn of mind, discussing philosophical problems in one or other of the gardens of Granada, eminently fitted for so noble a purpose. An ornamental fountain with his effigy in a pleasant corner of the

Alhambra Park still groups in welcome harmony his pensive
features, the quiet leafy shadows of the park and the ever-present
murmur of running water which keeps company with the mind
and tunes it to hear the permanent in the fleeting. In 1896,
Ganivet published his *Idearium Español,* a classic of restricted
utterance, originality, ponderation; a searching and penetrating
analysis of the Spanish soul and of the permanent features which
have resisted all the changes brought about by influences and
events even as deep as the advent of Christianity and the discovery of America. There was between Costa and Ganivet a
contrast of matter as well as manner. While Costa insisted mostly
on the negative characteristics of the Spaniards and with the
voice and gesture of a Bible prophet urged them to mend their
ways and to Europeanize themselves, Ganivet laid stress on the
positive features of Spain, on the qualities and ways whereby
she brings an original contribution to civilization; his message,
suggested rather than actually expressed, is that such positive
qualities must be cultivated and refined. And, as if to illustrate
the paradoxical turn which things are wont to take in Spain, it
happened that while Costa shouted forth "Europe, Europe,"
with the unsociable and ultra-individualistic way of an uncompromising Iberian, Ganivet wrote his Iberian Essays with the
polish of a true European.

A similar contrast, though with an altogether different grouping of qualities, will be found by comparing the other two
leaders of the generation of 1898: Miguel de Unamuno and
José Ortega y Gasset. The one a Basque, the other born in
Madrid, these two men were destined to take over the dialogue
initiated by Costa and Ganivet, and to drive it into the Spanish
conscience.

English-speaking people interested in Spain have no excuse
for wondering what sort of a man and mind Unamuno may be,
for his best and most typical work has been translated in so
admirable a fashion as to justify the view that great translators,
like great poets, are born. *The Tragic Sense of Life in Men and
Peoples*[1] is a discussion on the relations between the immortality

[1] New York: Dover.

of the soul, the existence of God, and man's own views and wishes, conscious and unconscious, on these all-important matters. From the outset Unamuno boldly puts man, man concrete and complete, "the man of flesh and bones," at the center of his inquiry. He does not neglect philosophy, indeed there is no philosophy that he has not read, but behind it he goes in search of the philosopher whose "flesh and bones" we get in his books devitalized into syllogisms. The man Kant, the man Spinoza, are for Unamuno the true key to their systems. Instead of a search into older books he seeks the sources of books in the secret places of the author's heart. He is, of course, fully aware of the fact that in thus searching the vital sources of thought he destroys its objectivtiy, or, as he would put it, he forces thought to drop the mask of objectivity which it is wont to wear. But he is not equally ready to grant that we are the worse for it. Truth, for him, is in the struggle ever alive in men's hearts. Truth, in fact, is that struggle. And, possessed by this idea, Unamuno endeavors to free man from all intellectual veils and trappings, to accustom him to the contemplation of his own naked self standing before the Lord. Such was the message which Unamuno brought with burning conviction to the Spanish nation at the beginning of the twentieth century. A universal message, essentially of a religious character, it was of course, neither national nor political. Yet, precisely because of its inherent universality and also because it lays so much stress on the individual and on his relation to God, Unamuno's message was bound to appeal deeply to Spain. Virtually, it amounted to a restatement of the theme of Christian unity in a modern and a liberal setting. It implied also an affirmation of Spanish values as, not antagonistic to, but certainly original and independent of, European values.

The opposite view was taken by Ortega y Gasset, who, though strictly speaking, can hardly be counted as one of the "Generation" in point of age, reached fame and leadership early enough to be considered as one of its undisputed prophets. Ortega was frankly on the side of Europe. His antagonism to Unamuno—a purely intellectual antagonism of course—springs from natural causes and may be explained by circumstances of race, education and personality. Unamuno was a pure Basque, in so far as racial purity is attainable even by Basques. He was, therefore, more inclined to grow in depth than in width and more gifted in force than in grace. He was apt to be a man of one idea. A professor of Greek in the University of Salamanca, of which he was rector until a petty political intrigue deprived him of his post, he formed his mind in Spain and rarely came to Madrid, which he found too poor in Spanish character for his taste. Though not a nationalist—in fact, rather an anti-nationalist— he was intensely national. His strong temper, moreover, led him to express his views in a forcible manner. His headstrong, independent personality was admirably expressed in his face and figure—a healthy complexion and a vigorously structured head in which every bone demanded and obtained its full share of attention despite the attraction of two aggressive eyes and the poise of the whole face challenging all comers. Unamuno was essentially unsocial. Nature, interminable walks alone or with a friend readier to listen than to speak, were his main pleasures, and his themes were primitive and essential. In society he was apt to wield a heavy hammer. The stories attributed to him, even if inaccurate in fact, are significant. In a circle of friends he has just explained how he needs a considerable amount of sleep every twenty-four hours; an unfortunate mortal, who does not know his ways, ventures to doubt the necessity of such a waste of time. "Five hours a day are all I need." "Ah"—comes the hammer—"but when I am awake I am far more awake than you."

Ortega was a Castilian. He was born in Madrid and, as he himself has pleasantly said, on a printing press. *"Yo que nací sobre una rotativa . . ."* He refers to *El Imparcial,* the (then) leading newspaper in the country, owned by his mother's family (Gasset) and edited by his father (Ortega Munilla). Ortega was thus born a journalist, and from his early days acquired the instinct to look at things *sub specie publicitatis.* Hence, perhaps, one of the strongest influences in the shaping of his political and even philosophical personality; for there is *public* in *publicity,* and every force of a kind to strengthen the none too keen collective tendency of the Spaniard should be welcome whatever its origin. Ortega matured this predisposition to think collectively by his education in Germany. He was sent (a sign of the times) to study philosophy with Cohen in Marburg. We may well imagine the effect of the neat, quiet, German little town on the youthful sensibility of our Spanish student; the revelation of its order, cleanliness, method, social discipline, on this Iberian born in the bustle of the newspaper office of the most individualistic capital in the world, a city of absolute kings. Then in the town of order and method, the sanctuary of thought; the Jewish spirit clarified and intellectualized by German *kultur;* the Oriental yearning purified into Western research. No. The Iberian must not be allowed to go to seed in his unruly anarchy; he must learn to curb his instincts and impulses to the civic order, his inspiration and imagination to the order of science which is method. And so Ortega, who, had Giner and his "abroad" movement never existed, might have become a mere brilliant journalist, developed into a philosopher and Europe was the richer by one of her most original minds.

But though by natural genius and training Ortega became a stimulating philosopher and interpreter of life, he kept a connection with the newspaper world in that his main interest was in the events of the day—the intellectual events, of course; that is, the latest ideas. A further contrast with Unamuno. While the Basque prophet is always theoretical, even when dealing with the latest murder case or *coup d'état,* Ortega is always "in the news," even when dealing with eternal things. The very question which burns constantly in Unamuno's heart—Does God exist? Has He made us? Must we make Him?—a question to which he leads, whatever may be the starting point of his writing or conversation, is turned by Ortega into a piece of sensational news. One morning he casts a glance over the horizon, strains his eyes for a while, then advancing to the forefront of his newspaper he announces the tidings to all whom it may concern in big block capitals: "GOD IS IN SIGHT." The voice is eminently social.

Thus taste and conviction determined in Ortega a European attitude, for is not Europe the incarnation of the social model which the traditional individualism of Spain has for ever before it in the generation of 1898? Ortega represents the voice of European Spain. His tendency is critical of pure Spanish values. He advocates science, philosophy, method, technique, the study of foreign books, first-hand knowledge of foreign universities. He preaches with deeds. He becomes a professor of philosophy in the University of Madrid and devotes his time to the study of contemporary currents of German philosophy; he endeavors to evolve his own doctrines, particularly with regard to Spain and her character *(Meditaciones del Quijote, España inverte-brada)*, or, to present-day ways of thinking, such as relativity *(El tema de nuestro tiempo)*.

Ortega and Unamuno, then, even more definitely than Costa and Ganivet, are the protagonists of the two trends of thought which the generation of 1898 brings to light: one stands for the salvation of Spain within her own substance; the other for her renovation by European influence and example. In a sense, Spain, which, like England and Russia, is a country on the borders of Europe and therefore not purely European, had in these two men a pair similar to that which Russia evolved in Dostoevski and Turgenev; the one intensely Russian and indifferent, if not hostile, to Europe, the other a convinced European and critical of Russia as such. But the case of the two Spaniards is even more complicated. Unamuno, in his unchecked spontaneity, was a voracious consumer of European values and showed readiness to assume every kind of tendency, save, perhaps, the fastidious aestheticism of a d'Annunzio, or the smiling Parisian indifference of Anatole France; this ever ready curiosity for things human, combined with the permanent appeal of his main theme, make him, while intensely Spanish, a universal author. Ortega, on the other hand, more exacting and intellectualized, showed a far less hospitable mind; there was, moreover, in his temperament a curious imperviousness to the Anglo-Saxon world; and these limitations, combined with his tendency to ride on the top of the wave of fashion, make him less universal though more abstract and general in his thought than Unamuno.

These four men lead the generation of 1898. The message of

this generation springs from a critical mood prepared by a long century of trial and error (with a stress on error), and determined by the defeat of 1898. What are we? What have we done? What are the Spanish values which circulate in the world? What is the trace which Spain has left in history, in thought, in European civilization? Why all this disorder at home? Why this sham and pretense? A Constitution flouted, a Parliament which is a comedy, general elections which are but markets for votes or else free fights, corruption and incompetence. Whither are we to turn? Such is the tone of the generation. At its lowest, doubt, and in many cases, negation. To the president of an *audiencia* (provincial law court) who ranted against the incompetence of the navy, Costa retorted with his usual directness: "If *audiencias* had to navigate!" The first mood of the generation is, therefore, fiercely negative and critical. Nothing. There is nothing but sham and hollowness. We must begin afresh. And then, as soon as the new men turn their faces toward the morrow, the split occurs. Though all belong inherently to free Spain, that Spain in which the old religious earnestness had been delivered from its dogmatic shackles by the same Europe which she had fought in bygone days, the New Spaniards broke asunder as to their estimate of what New Spain was to be. Some of them, with Costa and with Ortega, carried forward their European position; we must, they said, make Spain a European people; others, with Ganivet and Unamuno, hesitated to accept all that Europe means: sons of Europe, no doubt, but all the sons of Europe are not identical. We have our message for the world. Europe is economic, scientific and mechanistic. We are . . . what we are. Our main concern still is the salvation of our soul. And to a reproach that Spain has brought but little to European civilization (in its mechanistic sense) Unamuno will answer: "Let them invent." Not in vain did Ortega describe him as "the brother and the enemy."

But this very duel within the new generation was salutary and stimulating. A touch of civil war is always necessary in order to catch the eye and ear of the self-absorbed Spaniard, whose interest in his neighbor is aroused if and when there is a reasonable prospect of breaking his head (of course to help him save his soul). Civil war, moreover, as Unamuno has pointed out, is the cleanest and purest of wars, for it is less likely to be infected by sordid and material motives than a war against strangers, and is generally waged for spiritual reasons. The split in the generation of 1898 led to no spilling of blood, though ink did run freely, but in so far as different voices argued the points at issue the Spaniard's attention was caught and held and the voices were heard.

A further fact which contributed to the success of the generation was the character of the Spanish press. This is hardly the place for a technical history of the press in Spain. For our purpose it will suffice to draw attention to the peculiar conditions under which papers had to live and prosper in a century in which dictators, under several names of a more or less constitutional character, were always ready to ride roughshod over whatever liberties were granted, on paper, for the circulation of opinions. There is still a newspaper in Barcelona whose title bears witness to the difficulties with which the press had to contend in the nineteenth century, and to its vitality to resist them. This paper was suspended and it reappeared the next day under a new name. Suspended again, it again reappeared under a third name. And the game went on, the editor inventing every night the name under which it was to appear the next morning, till one day, his imagination exhausted, he christened his paper *The Deluge*. The name remained, for it so happened that the paper was no longer suspended, and Barcelona is, perhaps, the only town which rejoices in a deluge a day. On the whole, however, the Restoration was favorable to the growth of a fairly prosperous and free press, and, save in exceptional circumstances such as general strikes and revolutionary risings, its liberty to print whatever came into its hands was not curtailed. Gradually, the period of relative peace and prosperity which Cánovas and Sagasta secured for the country allowed the press to develop and to evolve a definite national type. Even the most prosperous newspapers have a relatively moderate circulation. This is due partly to the individualism of the Spaniard, which, by preventing amalgamation and stimulating individual initiative, leads to a large number of small newspapers—Madrid has a considerably larger number of newspapers than London—partly also the fact is due to the lack of those enormous centers of population which powerful industries tend to create. Another feature of the Spanish press is that it is practically always under the direct inspiration and control of one leading personality, generally the founder and owner. This remains the case even after the appearance of newspapers owned by limited liability companies, or what are known in Spain as *periódicos de empresa*. It follows, of course, that the Spanish newspaper is apt to reflect the personality of its leading spirit and that the qualities and defects of Spanish newspapers differ profoundly from those of press organizations understood as commercial firms. Spanish newspapers are far more independent of business than is the case in other countries. Moreover, the national proclivity to put the stress on man rather than on things carries, as its corollary, that the newspaper reader in Spain is more interested in views than in news. His stand is, that since there is no getting away from man, at bottom all news is views, and therefore views pure and simple are better than views parading as news. Moreover, news is ephemeral and its bloom goes with the day; views have a more permanent value and allow the reader to scent the fragrance of a human mind. This simplifies journalism, and eases the budget of many a newspaper. The saving in telegrams permits a generous list of contributors, who sign, of course, for the reader wants to know with whom he is conversing.

Newspapers act, in Spain, not only as newspapers, but also as weeklies and monthlies, and even as books. They are the main organs of intellectual distribution and exchange, by far the most important link between the nation and its intellectual leaders. In this capacity the Spanish press has shown its originality and a deep insight into the nation's peculiarities. The old newspapers carried, perhaps, somewhat too far the individualistic liberty which they granted their contributors. Later, until the Franco regime killed the Spanish press, a better balance was generally reached between the claims of the contributor and the claims of the newspaper as a whole.

A press thus understood was bound to be of great assistance at a time when Spain began to feel herself again. The themes raised by the generation of 1898 were all in that zone extending over literature, politics and history, which has always interested Spanish readers. The columns of the daily press were gradually opened to the new men, most of whom had acquired celebrity in a short-lived "daily" which, characteristically enough, had chosen for its name the word *España*. The preoccupation with the fact, the historical phenomenon "Spain," was apparent in the name of this orginal newspaper, as it was to be in later years in the weekly founded by Ortega y Gasset, with the same name.

Some of the newcomers worked almost exclusively in the literary field. Azorín, for instance, though later he dabbled in politics, was then a pure word-artist applying his wonderful gifts for vivid description to the discovery of out-of-the-way Spain for the Spaniards. He revealed an admirable faculty for rendering Spanish scenes which no Spaniard had ever observed before precisely because they were sights to be enjoyed every day. He made Castile live for the Castilians. Valle-Inclán brought to Spanish letters the poetical gifts of the Northwest so closely allied to the lyrical vein of Portugal. Benavente began to write his plays of Spanish bourgeois life. And, along with the men of letters, the generation evolved its own political philosopher in Don Ramiro de Maeztu. An Anglo-Basque, born in Biscay, Maeztu won distinction in the press from an early age. His success may be traced to a fund of experience due to an adventurous youth which led him among other occupations to work as a laborer in Cuba; a gift for expressing general things in striking terms of a noble simplicity; and an exceptional sensibility toward new ideas which made him adopt with equal intensity and sincerity the latest view which happened to impress him. A man of strong convictions withal, whose mind moved along a steady line of evolution, beginning in intellectual anarchism and passing through liberalism, Nietzschean ideas and Guild Socialism, ended in Roman Catholic orthodoxy, intellectual absolutism, and the acceptance of the post of Spanish ambassador in Buenos Aires, under General Primo de Rivera's dictatorship. Maeztu was, in the 1898 group, the representative of Anglo-Saxon ideas. Whether he owed this role to his English blood or not, the fact is that, from the first years of the century, he settled in London and began to provide the Spanish papers with a running commentary on English manners of thinking and living, which he maintained at a high level of intellectual distinction for a considerable number of years.

He was the first prominent Spaniard to settle in England for that purpose. Till then the Spanish press had relied on their Paris correspondents for news and views of the outside world. The result was obvious. The vision of the world which the average newspaper reader obtained had to undergo the simplifying processes by which complex and irrational things become clear, simple, rational and universal through the filter of the French mind. The importance of this fact on the life of Spain could hardly be exaggerated. French ways of living and thinking have a fascination which conquers at once. France wears all her charms on her neat face. The Spanish nation, in her nineteenth-century rebirth, was but too prone to take her cue from her perfect neighbor. But we know that the genius of France differs profoundly from the genius of Spain. This apparently simple model was singularly difficult to emulate. The feeling that Spain was but a France which had missed fire was the natural outcome of such a state of affairs.

With the arrival of Maeztu, the attention of Spain was turned toward England. The field of influence and observation suddenly widened out, and Spanish public opinion began to absorb new ideas, new standards and a new outlook on the world, and therefore on Spain herself. This transformation may be compared to that of the scientific opinion of Europe when Copernicus put forward his views and made men realize that the center of the heavens was not the earth, but the sun. Such a change prepared the ground for the dethronement of the sun itself and for the ultimate disappearance of any center of the heavens whatsoever. Similarly, by transferring the center of attention from Paris to London, Maeztu prepared the Spanish mind for a truer understanding of the world and of Spain herself by objective standards independent of both French and English points of view. There is an ingrained tendency in France to consider Paris as the center of the world. London is too wide in its interests and perspective to make that mistake, and, moreover, the English mind is not geometrical and abstract like the French, but empirical and organic; so that while France sees the world as a geometric figure, a kind of Place de l'Etoile, with Paris in the middle, England sees it like a forest in which each tree stands on its own stem.

Ramiro de Maeztu was well prepared to realize all these facts and to convey their import to his readers. The first of a series of men of letters who devoted their youth to an interpretation of Anglo-Saxon values in terms of Spanish civilization, he had the merit of converting public opinion to the importance of Anglo-Saxon civilization. It became necessary for a respectable newspaper to have a London correspondent, by which, of course, was meant not a mere telegraphic correspondent in charge of a news service, but a racy writer and thinker in charge of a *views* service, a mind alert enough to catch the light of English life and ways and to cast it in vivid colors over Spanish public opinion. This was the period which saw the rise of Ramón Pérez de Ayala and of Luis Araquistain, both men formed in London in the school of English life.

Nor was the change welcome merely because it brought English views and ways to bear on the development of modern Spain. The main point was that the educational effect of the daily press had been strengthened by the access of a new civilization to be observed and criticized, and that, therefore, further acquisitions were bound to be sought in similar fields. By a natural process of development the newspapers established touch with German public life. Some of the men who had lived in London, and had realized there the value of their experience, went to Germany and learned the language. Maeztu and Araquistain settled in Berlin. Ortega had, from the very beginning of his intellectual life, shown a strong attachment to German ways of thinking. Though less widely felt than the Anglo-Saxon influence, the German influence was, perhaps, deeper owing to the growing number of students who, through the *Junta para Ampliación de Estudios,* were constantly flowing into the German universities and returning to Spain enriched with a new mental discipline.

Thus the period that stretches between the end of the Spanish-American War and the beginning of World War I is one of intense intellectual activity during which Spain develops her university life and educates her public opinion. In the first case the main instrument in the change is the *junta;* in the second, the *press.* In both cases the method is the same: an increasing intimate contact with the outside world.

CHAPTER 9

ECONOMIC DEVELOPMENT

AGRICULTURE

The spiritual and intellectual awakening outlined in the preceding pages was, of course, the continuation of a movement begun in the nineteenth century, yet its quickening at the beginning of the twentieth must undoubtedly be interpreted as one of the effects of the pruning of the old Iberian oak, the last branches of which had just been somewhat ruthlessly plucked by the United States. No better proof could be found than the sudden rise in economic vitality which Spain experienced simultaneously. Whether we turn our attention to agriculture or industry, to commerce or to banking, to mining or to the harnessing of electric power, to railways or roads, or to any other manifestation of what is pleasantly described as material progress, the period of 1898-1914 was an exceptional, and at times even an epoch-making one, in Spanish economic history.

102

It is a clear case in which the economic interpretation of history is, if not belied, at any rate considerably sobered by events. The economic factors were not the cause but rather the effect of the moral and spiritual adaptations which the loss of the colonies made necessary. By no stretch of the imagination can it be said that the stimulus then felt in Spain was due to the fact that the capital which Spain used to place in her colonies was repatriated—for it was not; nor that capital ceased to go to the lost colonies—for it did not; nor that men of ability and enterprise formerly lost by the metropolis remained at home—for the loss of Cuba and the Philippines brought no other change in the distribution of Spanish manhood than the reabsorption by the metropolis of the host of officials, good and bad, which she had sent overseas. The true import of what then happened was far deeper, far more fraught with enduring consequences, than any such outward material event. Spain felt then that the era of overseas adventures had gone, and that henceforth her future was at home. Her eyes, which for centuries had wandered to the ends of the world, were at last turned on her own home estate. The first thing to do was to take stock of her situation. What were her assets?

Spain is fundamentally an agricultural country. Opinions as to her soil and climate have fluctuated, as opinions about Spain are apt to do, between extremes of extravagant optimism and of exaggerated pessimism. For a time it was customary to initiate any discussion of Spanish soil by quoting Lucas de Mallada's famous dictum on the distribution of Spanish lands from the point of view of their fertility:

1. Lands totally bare, 10 per cent.
2. Lands with but a small capacity for producing, either because of excessive altitude or owing to a bad constitution or to drought, 35 per cent.
3. Lands moderately productive, lacking in water or unfavorably placed or with a defective constitution, 45 per cent.
4. Lands which make us think that we were born in a privileged country, 10 per cent.

The authority of the writer contributed not a little to the prevailing pessimism on the subject of the Spanish soil. Contemporary writers take a somewhat soberer view of the matter and, while refusing to see Spain as a Garden of Eden, tend to react from Mallada's pessimism, and to provide fairly acceptable reasons for their opinion. The latest calculations, based on official figures, duly corrected to take account of the excessive discretion which taxpayers are apt to evince in matters of land statistics, would put the proportion of cultivated lands at rather less than half the area of the national territory, i.e. somewhere between 50 and 60 million acres (Spain's total area approximates 125 million acres). This does not include, of course, land used as pasture and underbrush, which amounts to a figure between 50 and 60 million acres, leaving rather less than 15 million acres for totally sterile lands and urban or industrial areas.

The unusually high proportion of pasture and wood is explained, for the most part, by the broken nature of the country, which does not allow normal methods of cultivation to be used. Visitors to some particularly well cultivated parts of Spain, such as Majorca, may recall that even particularly unpromising lands placed on steep hillsides are, by dint of ingenuity and labor, transformed into fertile gardens by the inhabitants. But such a work can only be undertaken in exceptional circumstances, and for the most part the high lands of Spain are bound to remain fallow. If it be added that the centuries-long wars which the country has undergone have thoroughly depopulated her forests, thereby denuding the hills of their earth and depriving the lands of water, further reasons may be found, for the unusually high proportion of low-producing districts in Spain. Moreover, in the dry part of the country which covers nearly two-thirds of the Peninsula, water is extremely scarce, and in certain regions almost entirely lacking. The productivity of the regions known as the *Huertas of* Valencia and Murcia is entirely due to the ingenuity of its inhabitants, who have succeeded in husbanding their scanty resources of water with admirable skill and perseverance.[1] The agricultural production of Spain increased in value from 81⅓ million pounds (2440 million pesetas[2]) between 1897 and 1901 to 127⅓ million pounds (3824 million pesetas) between 1903-7, which, even if due allowance is made for the decrease in the purchasing capacity of the peseta, shows a considerable advance. This advance had been not merely maintained but considerably improved upon, since the yearly production of Spanish agriculture was in 1930 as high as 306⅔ million pounds (9201 million pesetas), an average of rather more than 6 pounds per acre of national territory (cultivated or not) and of about 15 pounds per head of the population.[2]

[1] The usual comment here on the part of unfriendly observers is that the irrigation system of these regions was due to the Moors, and that the Spaniards have no merit in it. But even if we admit that the irrigation system originated with the Moors, a debatable point which the greatest Spanish expert on Arabic culture and civilization, Professor Rivera, answers in the negative, the present-day inhabitants of these regions *are* "Moors," as anyone who cares to look at them may find out for himself. Moreover, the Moors were officially expelled under Philip III. Are we to count for nothing the skill and perseverance wherewith the system has been preserved and considerably developed since? Nor is the system a mere feat of rural engineering. The important point is its social and traditional aspect. Without the vigorous tradition behind the irrigation system of Valencia and Murcia, such an institution as the *Tribunal de las Aguas* would not have resisted the wear and tear of centuries. Whatever the actual origin of this original institution, it has succeeded in perpetuating itself entirely on tradition, and its vitality is rooted in the people who compose it and live it. The Tribunal is a judiciary and administrative body on which the whole irrigation system rests. Every Thursday, under the porch of the Apostles of the Cathedral, the Tribunal sits in the open, on a level with the street. It is composed of seven syndics, representing the water users of the seven main canals of the *Huerta,* water users themselves, belonging to the hard-workng peasantry which elects them and maybe tomorrow will pass judgment on them. The Tribunal, despite this democratic origin and composition, this modest and simple make-up, seems shrouded in a strange majesty and never sees its authority challenged or flouted by any of the men over whose interests it has so considerable a power. The *Tribunal de las Aguas* is a most eloquent proof of the capacity of the Spaniard for evolving and vitalizing institutions when the necessary basis exists, i.e. the complete recognition of the individual as an autonomous unit.

[2] At par, £1=25 pesetas 22. The exchange has fluctuated during the period discussed. Figures in the text are calculated at the rate of 30 pesetas to the pound, the then rate of exchange.

The progress of Spanish agriculture during the present century is a well-established fact due to progress in a number of the factors which bear upon agricultural production. The most important of these factors is water. Practically the whole of the area of arid Spain would, of course, benefit by irrigation. A fair proportion of it has been cultivated under an irrigation system dating from at least Moorish days. In the nineteenth century there were sporadic attempts to develop the irrigated area. But the movement did not acquire true impetus till the beginning of the twentieth century. Two men must be mentioned in this connection: Joaquín Costa, who made irrigation one of the constantly recurring themes in his "School and Larder" campaign, and Rafael Gasset, one of the typical politicians of the Alfonsine period who, though indistinguishable in many ways from the other political figures of his time, devoted most of his public life to the study and execution of irrigation schemes.

The first attempts were perhaps too optimistic. It was calculated that about 10,000,000 acres could be reached by irrigation. Present-day experts do not care to go beyond more modest figures ranging from 6,000,000 to 7,000,000. Of this area of what might be described as potential irrigation, 3,385,000 was already being irrigated in 1918, according to the estimates of the *Junta Consultiva Agronómica*. The efforts made by the government comprise:

1. Construction. A general plan of canals and reservoirs approved in 1902. It included new reservoirs, such as the Pantano de la Peña in North Aragon, which completely transformed about 40,000 acres of land; the development of existing works; the building of new canals and the adaptation of certain navigable waterways, such as the Canal de Castilla, to irrigation purposes.

2. Legislation granting special subsidies to irrigation enterprises in order that landowners should be able to face the cost of adapting the land from dry to irrigated culture. Long-term loans at low rates of interest have been granted, but here the question borders on political problems. Broadly speaking, the economic efficiency of irrigation schemes is in inverse proportion

to the size of the holdings. The intensive culture to which irrigated lands can be put in a country where sunlight is plentiful thrives best with a system of small holdings. More often than not the areas benefited by public works are to be found in provinces in which enormous latifundia are the rule. The government here made perhaps the gravest error of the last fifty years—the failure to tackle and solve the problem of land ownership.

Next to irrigation, dry farming is one of the typical features of the modernizing tendency observable in Spanish agriculture. Under the old system, applied nearly everywhere in dry Spain, only one-third of the land was tilled every year, leaving two-thirds fallow in order to restock the soil and to retain the scanty water which Heaven granted from year to year. This system is gradually disappearing everywhere except in the large *cortijos* of Andalusia, in which irrigation is somewhat hindered by difficulties connected with the capital outlay which the change of cultivation would require in tenures of this vast size. Everywhere else the land is put to a better use. Several causes are contributing to this development. First, the increase in the use of fertilizers, both home-manufactured and imported. Secondly, the increasing use of agricultural machinery. For years the taunt that the Spanish peasant still scratched his arid soil with the Roman plow was sure to be found in every book of travel. In 1898 there was only one firm of agricultural machine manufacturers in Spain; in 1930 there were numbers of them, and at least nine important ones, while agricultural machinery of all kinds was imported in growing quantities. A third cause of agricultural progress was an increasing solicitude on the part of the state. Here, again, the origin of the progress must be traced to Rafael Gasset, and the date (1903) must be noted, as it corresponds with that period of Spanish introspection which has been analyzed in previous pages. *Granjas* (experimental farms) managed by government experts were set up in the thirteen agricultural regions into which the country was divided at the time, and a number of specialized institutions were organized with a view to educating both peasants and experts in the agricultural art, such as the *Instituto Agronómico de Alfonso XII,* a kind of agricultural college housed in Madrid, and schools for agricultural workers specialized in vine, olive, silk and other agricultural produce. The *granjas,* moreover, carried on "agricultural missions," i.e. circuits of lectures on such things as the use of agricultural machinery, of fertilizers, of irrigation, choice of seeds and particular points arising out of local conditions.[3] Experiments made in cotton and tobacco, the introduction of hops, the fostering of the silkworm and a number of other developments tend to show that the reawakening of Spanish agriculture had reached even the generally unpromising regions of officialdom.

INDUSTRY AND COMMERCE

MINERAL INDUSTRIES—Though much less important than its agricultural wealth, the richness of the Spanish subsoil has, perhaps, attracted more attention. Practically every invasion in the history of Spain—with the exception of the Moorish—was determined by the lure of the mineral treasures which the Peninsula concealed. Spain possesses almost every mineral, some in exceptional abundance, so that, until the arrival of the United States in the field, Spain was the most important producer in the world of many precious ores, and particularly of copper, lead, and mercury. Finally, though not in such liberal quantities, Spain owns important coal deposits. And yet it can hardly be said that the development of all this mineral wealth had come up to what might be expected, given the generosity of nature. Several factors account for this.

The first is the tendency to consider mines as adventures rather than business enterprises. The law itself, (December 28, 1868), which, until 1900, regulated the ownership of the sub-

---

[3] The director of one of these *granjas,* Señor Arana (*Granja* of Zamora) was the originator of the new dry farming method which reclaimed vast areas of fallow land. Señor Arana claimed that the fallow system can be avoided altogether by a judicious use of agricultural machinery, whereby the moisture usually lost by evaporation when the surface of the soil is allowed to crack, as the effect of drought, can be retained.

soil, seemed to have been drafted by and for mine speculators. It provided that the ownership of a deposit should be vested in the person who should have officially discovered it, *denunciado*. A *denuncia* became thus a kind of letter patent with which quickwitted penniless amateur geologists stood at the gates of the future, claiming toll money for the right to develop the land. This law no doubt helped to discover the wealth of the country, but not to develop it.

Then, the country does not lend itself easily to the development of its ore and coal deposits, owing to the obstacles with which the road and rail engineer has to contend. Many a seam of excellent coal, many a mount of sterling hematite, awaits in idleness the railway or the road which will actualize its potential wealth. Though slackness has, no doubt, its part of responsibility, most of the stones thrown at Spain by irate or supercilious strangers come from citizens of countries admirably fitted for inland transport.

Finally, Spain lacked the capital and the political stability for sinking considerable sums in enterprises which live and thrive in continuity, while, though possessing a considerable number of distinguished engineers, she had not applied her mind to the building of great technical and business enterprises.

Here, again, the beginning of the twentieth century is the crucial date. The law amending the more objectionable aspects of concession-hunting dates from 1900; and another law, amending the first was enacted in 1910. Under the new system, the concessionaire must pay a tax per unit of surface, whether he works the mine or not. A commission was set up to study an adequate mining code, and although the draft had not passed through the slow mills of Parliament before General Primo de Rivera stopped them from working with his sword, much of what it contained has passed into actual official practice by way of decress and regulations. The trend was frankly nationalistic. The nineteenth century had, in fact, allowed foreign holdings of mines to a somewhat dangerous extent—dangerous not so much from the point of view of defense and economic independence as from that of the relative power of big business and of the national government. The royal decree of June 14, 1921, actually limited mining concessions or transfers to Spaniards and Spanish-controlled firms.

Progress in legislation and organization in a period of relative stability, and when a new spirit of application and study was abroad, culminated in a general rise in mining production.

One of the most remarkable features in the mining position is that the rate of progress has been quicker in transformation than in extraction. Progress in this field began with the century. In 1901 there were 138 factories working coal and minerals; in 1909 they had increased to 189. As for the particular materials produced, it may be said that Spanish metallurgy is one of the most varied, for, though not as to quantity, Spain produces practically every metal and important chemical raw material.

The most important of Spain's metallurgical industries is the production of steel and iron. It is an industry with deep historical roots in the country, since the medieval *forja catalana* provided the world model for pig-iron production until the discovery of modern methods.

The progress in Spanish metallurgy since the beginning of the century, both in quantity and in quality, is evident, though the position of the country does not yet correspond to her natural wealth in ore and fuel. Yet, despite the moral handicap of protection, and possibly helped by its material advantages, Spanish manufacturers were growing alive to the possibility of conquering foreign markets for their iron and steel, notably in the Mediterranean, while national markets have been steadily expanding since 1898.

Similar progress was shown by the industries based on other metallic ores, in which Spain is singularly rich. Copper is exploited in the district of Huelva, mostly by British capital; lead in the provinces of Jaén in northern Andalusia, and also in Murcia. The first of these two districts, in particular, is one of the most important lead-producing regions in the world. Zinc is extracted in both Murcia and Santander. The famous Almadén mines and works are still one of the chief sources of world supply for mercury. Tin, tungsten, silver and gold are also extracted in smaller quantities as well as bismuth, antimony, sulphur and practically every other mineral. Considerable deposits of potash exist in the whole Pyrenean region, but the corresponding industrial development has been hampered by foreign vested interests.

The manufacture of machines of all kinds is perhaps one of the industrial activities for which Spain was tradionally and psychologically least prepared. Yet this branch of industry shows unprecedented progress during our period.

CHEMICAL INDUSTRIES—The mineral wealth of the country, and particularly the existence within the territory of abundant pyrites, rich potash deposits and excellent sources (both sea and mineral) of common salt, with, moreover, easily available electrical power, should have enabled Spain to build up a powerful chemical industry. Here again, though the position is by no means what might be expected in view of the natural resources of the country, the keynote of the present century is rapid progress, hampered perhaps by an insufficient coordination of efforts. The most important firms specialized either in the distillation of wood or in fertilizers, pharmaceutical products, or perfumes—this last an industry particularly favored by an almost unlimited supply of excellent olive oil on the spot.

THE TEXTILE INDUSTRY is also of very old standing in Spain. Wool was, of course, a famous Spanish product from the early days of Spanish history; the silk industry, notably during the Moorish period, reached a degree of exceptional splendor, and cotton was grown and manufactured in Andalusia long before the modern age. These industries, particularly cotton-weaving, suffered a severe setback after the Spanish-American War, which cut off a safe market. Yet the recovery that ensued, due almost entirely to the expansion of the home market, was relatively swift, and had a steady and permanent effect. As a typical example of the growth of this industry during the present century we may quote the cotton figures for 1903, 1912, and 1920, respectively: 1.7, 2.2, and 2.5 million spindles. By far the most important center for textile industries was the region of Barcelona—this choice being determined partly by a local proclivity to this kind of industry, partly by the commercial advantages of a great port, partly by the possibility of hydroelectrical development afforded by the Pyrenean valleys. Cotton, in its turn, contributed to the development of wool, though this industry flourished in places as far apart as Béjar (in the province of Salamanca) and Alcoy (in the kingdom of Valencia). Silk was manufactured in the Southeast and South, notably in Valencia and Murcia. A number of other textiles were also produced, and in particular the excellent esparto grass for which Spain is famous. Signs were not lacking of a tendency to develop the cotton industry in Seville, a region in which certain types of cotton may be grown under good conditions, and which, moreover, abounds in electrical power.

POWER—Spain can draw on two abundant supplies of power: her coal and lignite mines, and her waterfalls. Both have been considerably developed since the beginning of the present century.

1. *Coal and Lignite*—Though not one of the great coal centers, Spain has enough coal deposits to meet her own requirements, at least, if the matter be considered on a merely statistical basis. In actual fact, a variety of reasons (the three most important of which are quality, price and communications) force her to import about one-third of her normal consumption. Coal districts are to be found in practically every region.

2. *Hydroelectric Power*—A somewhat theoretical calculation, on the basis of a 10 per cent exploitation of the annual rainfall, estimates the possibilities of hydroelectric power in Spain at rather more than five million h.p. Other calculations, based on the total volume of water flowing in Spanish rivers—estimated at 1500 cubic meters per second, with an average flow of 600 meters—would put Spanish hydroelectric power at eight million h.p. Estimates are bound to be vague, owing to the irregular and extreme character of the climate.

The most moderate estimate, however, is optimistic enough, and everything in recent years tends to show that Spain is definitely aware of her possibilities in this field. Curiously enough, though the beginning of electricity in Spain dates as far back as 1888, on the occasion of the Barcelona Exhibition, the first plant for transmitting electric power at a high voltage, a kind of work in which Spain was to become a pioneer in Europe, was installed near Madrid in that historic year—1898. A force of 3000 h.p. drawn from the Manzanares River was transmitted to Madrid at a voltage of 15,000 volts. It was quickly followed by plants for bigger and bigger distances and voltages: 26,000 volts (*Hidro-eléctrica Ibérica*), 50,000 volts (*Bolarque*), 65,000 and 130,000 volts (*Hidro-eléctrica Española*). The most vigorous effort was made between 1898 and 1910, the period which saw the electrification of practically every watermill in the country and when a kind of electrical *fiat lux* lit up the secular darkness of villages which had known no other light than the tallow candle and the oil lamp. By 1917 there were 881,884 h.p. of hydroelectric power available; by 1922 the figure had risen to 1,202,-280 h.p., while the proportion of the power actually utilized to the available power had passed from 42 per cent in 1917 to 65 per cent in 1922.

The electrical harnessing of the country's water resources has continued to attract the attention of the public, the authorities and the business community. Schemes of growing importance are in course of execution or in study—notably the systematic exploitation of the Guadalquivir valley and the long-discussed Duero scheme, protracted owing to the complications involved in its international character (Portugal holding somewhat different views from Spain). The total capital of the firms engaged in the production and distribution of electricity was estimated at $413,278,500 in 1930.

The main problem to be faced for further development is, of course, that of regularity and reliability. As firms market a higher proportion of their available power the necessity of securing a regular supply becomes more and more pressing. Two solutions are in sight: the control of rivers by means of appropriate dams; the use of poor or unfavorably placed fuel in reserve steam stations.

The first of these two solutions offers particular advantages in a country in which there are many demands on water and there is only a fitful and scanty supply thereof. Irrigation, town water supply, sanitation, power, are the four main uses to which rivers are put. They are not irreconcilable, but they may be conflicting if no one takes the trouble to coordinate their claims. Spain has evolved an original and fertile idea toward the solution of this problem, the *Confederaciones Hidrológicas* or chartered associations of all the municipal, provincial and business entities interested in a particular river and its affluents. The idea arose in Zaragoza, the main town on the main river of Spain. The *Confederación del Ebro* proved so successful that the Duero, Guadalquivir and other rivers soon followed suit, and in 1926 (March 5) a royal decree gave an official assent and a charter to these spontaneous creations of the nation. The decree stipulated that such confederations must be set up in the river basins in which the state considered them necessary, or else when 70 per cent of the agricultural and industrial concerns interested in the river demanded it. Once the confederation had been recognized as necessary by the state, affiliation and cooperation became compulsory for all official bodies (such as municipalities and county councils), irrigation associations, water users, private and public enterprises dependent on the river or its tributaries. The main tasks of the confederations were to study general schemes and, in general, to administer and husband the water available in the whole basin. The idea met with a ready response everywhere.

The second remedy available in order to meet the irregularity of water power in the Peninsula is the use of fuel for electrical purposes as auxiliary to waterfall production. As it happens, Spain possesses abundant supplies of fuel, either too poor in quality or too inaccessible to be marketable after transport charges have been added to cost of extraction. The ideal solution for all such deposits is transportation in the form of electrical power. Important plants have been set up on this principle. A more general system of electrical supply based on a network of hydroelectric and steam-generating plants has been under consideration for some time.

In conclusion, Spain's supply of natural power is abundant, and only requires enterprise and coordination to put it to a good use. In recent years there have been considerable developments both in the use of power and in the ability to develop it in the best possible way.

COMMUNICATIONS—Nature has treated Spain with niggardliness in what concerns communications. A rugged surface, brittle material and an extreme climate, all the conditions for bad roads and difficult and expensive railways are to be found in the Peninsula. Road-building did not begin till the middle of the eighteenth century, though the work had an illustrious precedent in that medieval saint, Dominic of the Causeway (Santo Domingo de la Calzada), who, in the eleventh century, improved the pilgrims' road to Compostela and dotted it with hostelries. In this, as in many other aspects of Spanish life, the leading monarch was Charles III, though the plans for his road-building enterprises had been prepared in the reign of his predecessor Ferdinand VI. By 1802 the road system covered 388 leagues. A document dated 1856 calculates that Spain had the equivalent of 2,850 miles of roads in 1833. In 1856 the figure was 4,100 miles. But, in 1868, when Queen Isabel II left the throne, her reign had raised the figure to 10,800; and it is only fair to record that this reign, in many respects so deplorable, left an honorable trace in road-building. Nor were her successors—with the exception of the revolutionary period—less active, for by 1900 the road system of Spain had reached a total of 22,200 miles.

Here, as in other fields, the first years of the present century proved exceptionally fertile. By 1919 the figure of 1900 had been more than doubled (47,800 miles). This figure was far from adequate. Much remained to be done both in quality and quantity. But consideration should be given, when comparing these figures with those of other lands, to the high cost of construction due to the broken nature of the country and to its sparsely distributed population. Road-building and maintenance made enormous strides, and both commercial and pleasure traffic were adequately served. Several *auto-pistas,* or special roads for fast motor traffic, were constructed.

For all its steel rails and signals and stations and uniformed officials, a railroad is a road, and Spanish railways had to contend with difficulties similar to those which prevented the swift development of roads, i.e. a broken country and an extreme climate. They had also to contend with difficulties of their own, the first of which was that, while road-building had a tradition and official dignity dating from the Roman Empire, railway business abounded in adventurers, speculative men claiming full freedom to do what they liked with their money. Spain did not suffer from the more frantic pranks of railway speculation and on the whole the capital to which she owes her railways (French, and to a lesser extent Belgian and British) worked honorably and conscientiously. Yet there was a certain amount of watering, or overcapitalization, which was to remain one of the difficulties in a situation already burdened by excessive natural costs. Then politics stepped in. Lines were not always built along the economic but along the political route, and subsidies may at times have been proportioned to political services rather than to geographical difficulties or economic handicaps.

On the whole, however, the railway system was built expeditiously and efficiently, though natural difficulties made it somewhat expensive. By 1920 the total state subsidy to construction was estimated at 800 million pesetas ($97,726,881), while the average cost per kilometer was put at 375,000 pesetas ($45,804). The "virtual" length of the Spanish mile of railway (i.e. the length of straight flat line equivalent to an average Spanish railway mile from the point of view of speed and haulage) is about 2.1. It will be seen therefore that nature had made transport in Spain more than twice as difficult as in the flat countries of north and central Europe. It is calculated that the transport of coal from the collieries to Madrid more than doubles its price.

Such unfavorable circumstances explain why Spain's railway system is relatively small. In 1896 it measured 7,800 miles. But though it had risen only to 9,200 in 1911, that year saw traffic exactly doubled, the number of passengers increasing from 25.7 to 50.3 millions and that of goods from 14.3 to 29 million tons. It will be seen how the end of the century is here again a critical date, marking a clear difference in the rhythm of development. The system was over 9,900 miles long in 1930. Progress was in the following directions:

1. The building of new main lines, much needed, particularly in a number of central districts.

2. The construction of secondary and so-called "strategic" lines (the word "strategic" in Spanish railway jargon means little more than a label to allow higher subsidies in partciularly diffi- cult regions).

3. Electrification, much to be desired for reasons of general national economy, and quickly developed in recent years. Main lines in Asturias, Catalonia, the Basque region and Castile are already electrified.

4. The conversion of the whole of the "normal" system of the Peninsula to the European gauge. The Spanish railways were built on a gauge of 1.674 meters, i.e. 239 millimeters wider than European lines. The conversion to the European width is con- sidered important both economically and politically by the best observers. It has been held up so far owing to the high estimated cost (which varies from 800 to 3000 million pesetas according to whether experts are favorable or hostile to the idea). A further argument in favor of this scheme is that it would allow Spain better to fulfill her natural role as the transit route between Europe and Africa. A Spanish engineer, Colonel Jevenois, has been at work for some time on a scheme for a railway tunnel under the Straits of Gibraltar.

Nothing could better illustrate the growing demand for com- munications than the rapid development of road transport.

Though the Spanish road system is hardly more adequate than the railroads in proportion to the area and population of the country, the total length of regular motor bus lines was in 1930 nearly double that of railways, i.e. 18,600 miles. Regular airlines exist also between the main towns (Madrid-Barcelona, Madrid-Seville, Madrid-Lisbon and Seville-Lisbon), apart, of course, from the regular French line connecting Paris with French Africa via the eastern coast of Spain.

A first glance at the map might lead one to expect that Spain should have developed a flourishing merchant marine, for few European nations have a longer coastline and a greater variety of seas to serve. Yet Spain seldom rose above the eighth rank in merchant marine statistics, lagging behind smaller countries, such as Norway and the Netherlands. Several factors account for this, the most important being precisely her geographical position on the main line to South America and the East, which makes it possible for other flags to offer cheap freight rates from Spanish ports. It should be added that the hinterland conditions of Spanish ports are far from favorable, owing to the broken character of the land and to the high cost and low speed which it entails in land transport. Finally, Spanish rivers do not lend themselves easily to navigation, and the best of them flow out of Spain into Portugal.

The crucial date in the development of the merchant marine is also 1898. At this date the total merchant tonnage of Spain was 552,000. It was 816,000 in 1903; 877,000 in 1913; 1,106,000 in 1923. In so far as the prosperity of shipping lines is determined by their capital expenditure, the protectionist tendency to have the ships built in the country somewhat cuts across the equally protectionistic tendency to develop the merchant marine.

COMMERCE—There is a special difficulty when discussing foreign commerce. Figures do not work, or rather they work too well in the hands of those who use them. Nations, with an eye on commercial treaty negotiations, and exporters with an eye on foreign customs, find it to their interest to overstate their exports. Import figures tend, therefore, to produce what might be described as *over-statistics,* and export figures *under-statistics.* It happens, of course, that as between two nations A and B, what is an import for A is an export for B, so that by a patient study of foreign statistics one may, perhaps, hope to come as near the truth as this elusive lady will consent. But such a study would lead but to uncertain results, since it would be difficult to strike an accurate middle course between the under-statistics of one side and the over-statistics of the other.

The above remarks apply to Spanish foreign trade as to the trade of other nations. The revaluation of goods which took place in 1922 was of so drastic a nature that the total value of imports for 1921 was put at 1,261,000,000 pesetas or at 2,834,000,000 pesetas according to whether the old or the new system were applied; while, for exports, the figures would be 812,000,000 and 1,584,000,000 pesetas. New evaluations raise import values by 124 per cent, and they raise export values by only 95 per cent. Total figures, however, pass from 2074 to 4418 million pesetas, i.e. from $265,972,810 to $528,096,520.

With the reservations which these statistical peculiarities suggest to the wary reader, it may be gathered that the trade of Spain shows a development parallel to all the other signs of economic development which we have observed. Total yearly trade up to 1894 oscillated within 200 million pesetas of the 1500 million, i.e. within 6.7 million pounds of 50 million. In the period between 1898 and the outbreak of the First World War the total trade oscillated within 10 million sterling of 60 million pounds. Disregarding the official revaluation, the postwar figure tends to settle round about 80 million pounds. If official revaluations be considered—and they cannot be altogether disregarded, since values have altered—the figure would have to be about doubled.

The official figures for the balance of trade for the period 1900-1924 would amount to a deficit of rather more than 6,000,000,000 pesetas (£200,000,000). Nearly all of this deficit (5,500,000,000 pesetas) would be due to the years 1921-1924, precisely those years during which new values were in operation.

The trend of the foreign trade of Spain seemed to be unfavorable to the country. Even after the readjustment of values effected in the reverse direction by the Council of National Economy in 1925, the figures for 1926 and 1927 showed deficits as high as 543 and 688 million pesetas respectively. The deficit of the Spanish balance of trade could not, however, have been very alarming, or its effects would have been felt in the economic life of the country.

CONCLUSION

This rapid survey of Spain's economy should be completed with a few observations of a more organic character. Spain is an exception in the Western world with regard to economic sovereignty. Britain, France, Belgium, Germany, the United States, Switzerland and Italy have invaded her with capital and experts, and while they have up to a point contributed to Spain's development, they have on the whole, as might be expected, rather prevented than fostered the growth of her industries to the limit which the country's possibilities warranted. Fifty per cent of the pyrites of the world come out of Spain, but the British capitalists who control the mines have seen to it that practically none of the industries which might be founded on this untold wealth flourish on Spanish soil. The potash deposits of the Catalan Pyrenees are rich and vast, but the European capitalists who control this market have seen to it that they remain sterile. The country with richest copper deposits in Europe must buy its copper from England; the country which produces the iron ore of Bilbao pays for iron utensils five times what they cost in Portugal.

Not all the fault lies with the foreigner. An organic study of Spanish economy has never been attempted. Why cannot Basque ironmasters and Catalan textile manufacturers do without such high tariff walls? Is it—as some of them allege—because Castilian bread and Gallegan meat are too expensive? Or is it the other way about? Is the agricultural life of the country what it should be? Is there an intelligent policy with regard to power?

Can Spain reach an internal peace without industrializing herself boldly in places such as the Rio Tinto valley left starving by the foreign capitalists? Or should she first grow peaceful habits before hoping to grow an industry?

These questions are theoretical. In practice, everything happens at the same time. But it is plain that the main need here for Spain was at the beginning of King Alfonso's reign—and still is now after the Civil War—a steady effort to gain self-knowledge and to foster the growth of a body of skilled people to take charge of her affairs objectively. Foreign capitalists had a strong hold over many of Spain's industries because the Spanish banker put but little trust in the Spanish technician and the Spanish investor put but little trust in either. This is the hard fact. The number of Spanish technicians with an objective capacity to do things well was growing rapidly at the beginning of the century. This was one of the leading avenues toward better days, and during the reign of Alfonso XIII everything which was to block it—political and social disorder in particular—would inevitably work against the best interests of the country. The beginning of the twentieth century should have marked for Spain the end of passion and struggle and the beginning of study and common sense.

PART 3

THE ELEMENTS OF THE REIGN OF ALFONSO XIII

CHAPTER 10

THE KING

The reign of Alfonso XIII sees the struggle to drive into the consciousness of the Spanish people the lessons of the intellectual and economic awakening which has been outlined in the preceding chapters. The nineteenth century, full of romantic, unrestrained individualism, rich in inchoate enterprises, resounding with the clash of civil wars, lit up still with far-off visions (the last conflagrations of a dying empire), uplifted by short-lived hopes of constitutional perfection and free development, followed by no less agitating periods of reaction and dictatorship; creative withal, witness how, in the midst of the Peninsular agitation, a few bold, optimistic public men, with the help of foreigners, imported the strong impulses of material civilization—a century of strife and transition, imagination and emotion, unlimited hopes and unrestrained activity, is over. The Restoration did much to appease its feverish rhythm, yet twenty-five years are not enough to calm down the echoes of such stormy times, and Cánovas and Sagasta felt now and then that not even their opiates could put to sleep this nation, forever young though heavy with experience. The true remedy was not to come from the palliatives which they devised—military measures, the suspension of constitutional guarantees. It was slowly evolving under their eyes, thanks to the twenty-five years of relative peace which they gave the country. The national will was taking in the ballast of economic solidarity, the national mind was beginning to feel the brakes of a universal culture. The reign of Alfonso XIII was destined to gather in the benefit of this double progress. The Spanish monarchy had once again a great task before it. A great nation was to come of age. The monarchy had to grow accordingly or to risk its life. Such was the dilemma which Fate had laid on the cradle of the man who was born a king.

With stubborn relentlessness Fate still pursued Spain in her kings. Alfonso XII had died in the prime of youth. And when the times demanded that the crown should be worn by an experienced head, preferably an heir well-seasoned by long and patient waiting on the steps of an illustrious and long reign, Spain began her twentieth century under a boy king. Alfonso XIII was sixteen when, in 1902, he took up his heavy responsibilities.

He was then an attractive prince in whose open and immature features eagerness, good will and wonder were revealed with charming spontaneity. A quick intellect, but of rather the active than the speculative kind, impulsiveness, love of action, a certain imperiousness covering, perhaps, the fear of opposite wills, and an earnest desire to perform his royal duties to the best of his ability and to be of service to his country though unmistakably at the head of it—such were the main elements in his personality. But, as time was to show, the main thing was the personality itself. The new king was somebody. He soon felt the ambition to play his part in the life of the nation, and who would blame him for thinking that it was to be a leading part? Outside circumstances as well as the inner voice of his ambition pointed the same way. He was the summit of civil life; he was the heir to a long tradition of absolute monarchs never wholly and sincerely converted to the half measures of constitutionalism. He was, in practice, through the short-sighted policy of Cánovas, the true source of political power, the pivot of all government, the *de facto* ruler of parliaments and cabinets. Political leaders, neglecting the "sovereign people," came to him for the authority which they would not seek in the public opinion they were supposed to lead. He was the center of all adulation and intrigue; the polestar of all political hopes; the sphinx of the political future. And he was sixteen, twenty, twenty-five, thirty. Are we to wonder that he tried to rule?

Rather should we wonder at his restraint during those first years of his reign—when more impetuous youth might have come to grief. But, despite appearances to the contrary, there were in this impulsive man folds and counterfolds of cautiousness, treasures of patience, a marvelous capacity for circling obstacles and for taking the long way about. And it must be laid down as a tribute to his political sagacity—to that practical intelligence which was perhaps his chief characteristic—that he gave himself time to find his bearings and to feel where his true course lay.

There is a criticism easy to formulate from the standpoint of principles. It is true that, strictly speaking, the king had a constitution to go by and that, moreover, he had sworn it on the gospels. But we know by now that the constitution was deliberately used as a tool by Cánovas and Sagasta—and considerably soiled in the process. Moreover, while by ancestry and tradition the king could not be expected to feel much attachment toward a constitution having for its official object the limitation of his powers, by training the king belonged to that school of Spanish thought which accepts neither liberalism nor democracy. The crux of the matter is here. It is in the fact, so unpalatable to Spanish liberals as to be repressed by them into oblivion, that the doctrines of liberal democracy have conquered but a small proportion of the Spanish nation, including perhaps the majority, though by no means the whole, of its intellectuals. It is convenient to attribute much resistance to the "backwardness" of Spain. The explanation satisfiies the foreigner and excuses the national from any mental exertion. But the matter is much more complex than that. When the Rousseau-Voltaire-Godwin-Franklin ideas spread over Europe, Spain had behind her a whole era of imperial experience, rich in political thought. She had, moreover, in her veins a blood of strong originality, an unyielding national spirit, character which had resisted centuries of foreign intercourse. The new universal ideas, so attractive in their abstract perfection, so taking in their optimism, could not convince the Spanish mind nor conquer the Spanish temperament. They were delicate seeds, requiring the soft, moist lands of milder climates. The dry, parched, extreme soil of Spain must yield a sterner philosophy. Its creeds could not be so easygoing and debonair. The Spaniards still lingering in the traditions of old would be content with the political and religious faiths of the past. The Spaniards whose intellect had succumbed to the new ideas were beginning to despair of ever seeing them take root in the soil of Spain. But the Spanish political philosophy of the day was not—is not—yet born.

Not that the king was ever likely to fill the gap. His mind, though keen, was not bent on philosophy. But the absence of a clear set of faiths, though it may not be felt by the person, makes itself felt in his acts. The king was a first-rate politician; he was not a statesman. Had he been a statesman, he might have evolved that Spanish political philosophy which we still miss in the renascence of Spain. Had he found such a philosophy in his environment, he might have risen to statesmanship. The good will and even the ability—all but a decided disinclination for the things of the mind—were there. As it happened, neither the man nor the philosophy were what the situation required, and the king had to remain what he was: the acutest politician of his reign.

This reign was to be the most important, the richest in historical meaning since that of Charles III. Under Alfonso XIII, Spain became an industrial nation, reached the highest level of population since her pre-Roman days, returned to full membership in the world of culture which she had all but led in the sixteenth century; was thrown back into full participation in international politics by the Great War and by the reopening of the Moroccan question; reconquered spiritually that America which she had discovered, populated, civilized and lost; and saw grave problems of industrialism and nationalism rise in her home life and stimulate her political thought.

In the midst of this activity, the king grew to maturer years in a school of mere politics. Most of the men who surrounded him took the short view; he did not take a much longer one. Most of them saw the historical movements of their great nation merely as they affected their own political position; he saw them in relation to the crown and to its power. The king's political position being the highest, and his political interest the most permanent, his actions were generally the least divergent from the true national interest. Thus it is that the royal politician strikes the detached observer not merely as the most acute, but often as the most patriotic of the public men with whom he had to cooperate. Nor is this view to be lightly dismissed. In the absence of an objective standard on which to base his actions, the king could not but choose the stability of the throne as the main principle of his policy. And it must be added, in all fairness, that not one of the political leaders who surrounded him —whatever they may have said or written—acted on any other assumption.

If the royal policy is open to criticism it is not so much, therefore, in that it sought the stability of the throne rather than that of constitutional principles and peaceful development of a contented democracy, as in that it failed to perceive the true lines along which such stability was to be sought. It is at this point, perhaps, that we touch on the weakest spot of King Alfonso— a weakness which makes him, it must be owned, a typically Spanish king. It is a kind of tacit pessimism which makes him rely on force. The liberal who seeks stability in the interest of the greater number is an optimist—a modest optimist, perhaps— in that he believes that men will know their interest when they see it, and will act accordingly. But there is a kind of pessimism which does not credit men with enough sense to be enlightened egoists, and believes that they are always ready to do the foolish

thing unless there are soldiers and policemen to hold them back.
By temperament, King Alfonso belonged to this school; by training, he was confirmed in it. His education was in the hands of
men of austere frame who were no democrats, no optimists.
Priests and artillery officers are not an appropriate ground for
the development of Rousseau's views. Had King Alfonso been
entrusted in his tender years to Don Francisco Giner, Spain
would probably have become a peaceful and contented nation
with a monarchy well grounded in a prosperous peasantry. As
it was, peasant risings were countered by an increase in the
numbers and salary of the Civil Guards, and the king, while
playing the game of outward politics with liberals and conservatives, came gradually to recognize but two parties in the real
politics of the nation: the Church and the Army.

The tale of political events is but the canvas on which real
events were being woven by Fate. A tedious sequence of cabinets, crises and elections; the gradual disintegration of the old
parties, owing partly to the rivalry between the several leaders
competing, not for the votes of the electorate, but for the royal
signature which would enable the winner to fake them, partly
to the king's own use of this tool; and, while the system was
rapidly decaying at the top, a new political vitality attacking its
very roots, for the electorate was awakening, so that it was
becoming more and more difficult for governments to "make"
an election and, therefore, to "win" it. Real decisions were made
difficult either by royal veto or by Church obstruction or by
military bullying; at times also by the selfish opposition of a
limited but active section of public opinion. In the rising com-
plication of national life, the king, whose taste for personal
power had by now become pronounced, sought help in the army.
From his earliest days he had felt attracted by parades and
uniforms. Had not the war tragedy ruined the reputation of
William II, King Alfonso would have been well on the way to
emulate many of his more theatrical habits. As it is, the Spanish
king took up his personal role in the army with a style all his
own, a youthful dash combined with a kind of popular zest
reminiscent of the plebeian tendencies of Ferdinand VII and

Isabel II, yet with a touch of distinction. The fashion of using the second person singular in talking to persons whom he meant thereby to honor—a fashion to which his nineteenth-century ancestors were also addicted—shows him again inclined to that mixing of personal and official atmospheres typically Spanish, yet perhaps not without danger for a modern king. His temperament, his tradition, his surroundings, all tended to involve him in the turmoils of events which were to shake the country, then the world, then the country again.

CHAPTER 11

THE AGRARIAN QUESTION

The basis of Spain's national life is, we know, her agriculture. It follows that the basis of her social life is her agrarian organization. A study of the obstacles which a defective agrarian organization, in inextricable combination with a defective political system, have put across the path of Spain would be one of the most instructive illustrations of the complexity of collective life. There is little in the general situation of the Spanish countryside which was not already known and denounced more than a century ago. "The situation in the northwest of Spain," writes Professor de los Rios, "is the same as that described in the Report of 1763 on Seignorial Rights fortunately preserved in the Record Office, while the position in the rest of Spain is still reflected in the Memorials presented to the Economic Society of Madrid and published in 1780." We are touching here one of the key facts in Spanish history. Much has been written, and much may still be waiting to be written, in the inkpots of the

world, on Spanish conservatism. But how much of this conservatism is due to the fact that, once an agrarian system goes
wrong, it becomes so hopelessly entangled with a wrong political
evolution that centuries may elapse before the nation evolves out
of the meshes or breaks through them toward a new freedom?

Spain, with her area of 195,000 square miles, had then a
population of about 22,000,000 people. She was and still is an
exception in Western Europe, where the density of the population is everywhere more than twice, and in some places more
than three times, as great. She was, in a remote past, under the
favorable social and political conditions, a densely populated
country. The reason for this heavy decline in population is not
merely to be sought in the fact that she remained faithful to
the old European sport of civil war longer than the other nations
of Western Europe, with the single exception of her northern
cousin, Ireland; but in deeper and more permanent causes: i.e.
her agricultural production, nay, the very fertility of her land
and her very climate have been allowed to deteriorate through
a defective handling of her agrarian problems.

There are parts of Spain, notably in the Northwest, the province of Pontevedra for instance, the population of which is as
dense as in Belgium; others, such as certain regions of the Ebro
and Guadalquivir valleys, as well as a few privileged districts
on the eastern coast, in which the cooperation of sun and water
have created true paradises; but by the side of these developed
and wealthy regions, vast deserts of uncultivated lands, true
steppes such as can only be found in certain Hungarian or
Russian zones, waste on their barren plains the light and heat
of a bounteous sun. In four provinces of that Andalusia, whose
very name evokes riches and fertility, the area of steppe land
is put at no less than 1,650,000 hectares (rather more than
4,100,000 acres). For the whole of Spain the waste of uncultivated land was estimated at 5,478,000 hectares (about 13,-
500,000 acres) by Señor Flores de Lemus just before the First
World War. The figures are certainly smaller today. But on a
conservative estimate it is safe to say that "wild and forest land,"
including the above figure plus the figures for pastures, meadows

and forests, covers an area equivalent to, or slightly bigger than, that of cultivated lands. The latter, moreover, do not yield as much as they might. Here again, certain districts of good climate and abundant water, intensely and intelligently cultivated, present enviable results; but the immense majority of the lands under cultivation show a production below that of other countries. Much is sometimes made of this fact in order to show the inferiority of the Spaniard, an impression one usually brings to the subject; and the striking difference between the figures for wheat produced in Spain and in Denmark is occasionally used in such a way as to suggest that, if only the Spaniard abjured popery, his bushels per acre would rise accordingly in the statistical columns which measure national prestige. Though the religious tenets of the tiller may influence the yield of his soil—who knows how much of the quality and quantity of the faith passes from the heart to the arm and from the arm to the plow and the furrow?—it seems safer to stick to the soil itself and to the climate in which the soil lives. Now, the majority of the cultivated lands of Spain are poor; so poor indeed that nobody but specialists in poor soils would care to waste their time in scratching them for corn or vine; and the climate is so dry that none but a race used to goatlike sobriety would hope to see crops break through its hard crust.

Yet, even here, progress is possible. A distinguished expert, Don José Gascón, asserts that, in the course of an experiment carried out on extremely poor soil in Palencia, he obtained an average crop of 2,695 kilograms per hectare, i.e. as high as any in Europe and more than 2½ times the average yield of Spanish corn lands. Indeed, both Señor Gascón and Señor Carrión, an equally experienced authority, hold the view that, but for a few southeastern districts, the whole of dry Spain could, if properly cultivated, yield as high an average crop as the best average obtainable in the rainy area of Europe. This optimistic view is perhaps unduly influenced by the excellent results obtained under exceptionally skillful cultivation. The fact remains that there is room for improvement in the yield of Spanish lands. Agricultural progress in Spain may then take place in two directions:

by settlement and development of "wild and forest land," and by improved cultivation of tilled land. Both these lines of evolution would tend to increase the population of the country and to widen the basis of its economic wealth. In both directions, state action had been more or less timidly initiated under the monarchy. Schemes of afforestation appeared regularly in the budget. Now and again one would manage to escape and would be put into effect in the particular district which was wanting it. A Committee of Internal Colonization endeavored to settle agriculturists on lands requiring labor. Finally the *granjas agrícolas* acted as centers of instruction and stimulation to their respective neighborhoods. Progress was evident, yet not sufficient to stir an old situation out of its impressive inertia. For, in its essence, the problem was not so much one of cultivation as one of law.[1]

From the point of view of the size of the estates, Spain may be roughly divided into two areas: an area of small holdings and long leases, and an area of large holdings and short leases. The agrarian problems of these two districts are entirely different and, toward 1930, could be described in the following terms.

The line between the two is not unlike that which separates rainy Spain from dry Spain, for undoubtedly a wet climate—all other things being equal— favors intensive cultivation and permanency. This is confirmed by the fact that the area of small holdings, covering roughly the northern third of the Peninsula, extends southward along the eastern coast and even westerly along the south coast, following the zone of irrigation. There are, of course, a few exceptions, such as the rich Vega, or plain of Granada, which, though abounding in water, is a land of large holdings.

The first difference between these two areas is that, while the

[1] A British critic writes that my criticism, against Spanish agriculture particularly, is not fair, since, compared with countries of similar climate and soil, the yield per acre is on the whole better. Thus the figures for wheat in quintals per ha. for 1935 were: Spain, 9.4; U.S.S.R., 8.3; U.S.A., 8.2. He also points out that the average yearly figure for the Positos (cf. p. 140-41) for 1929-1933 was 73 million pesetas.

problems in the large holdings zone are fairly uniform, those in the districts of small holdings vary according to the regions considered. On the whole, the eastern part of this area is composed of small holdings sufficiently large and productive to support a family. Often, as in the case of the irrigated districts of Valencia, Murcia and Aragon, their very fertility demands an amount of work and attention which absorbs the activities of the family in a healthy endeavor. Conditions along the northern coast are also well balanced. But in the northwest part of León and Asturias, as well as the whole of Galicia, the situation is far from satisfactory. These districts are afflicted with an antiquated system of *fueros* or seignorial rights which weigh heavily on the produce of a generally overworked farmer. The rights are a part of the estate and in no way depend on the legal relations which may otherwise be arranged between the landlord and his tenants. It follows that the certainty of a comfortable income from his estate enables the landlord to neglect its possibilities altogether, and, in fact, to become an absentee. The *fuero* stands in very much the same relation to the economy of the Gallegan land as the royalty to that of the British mine, save that it weighs on it more heavily.

Both zones present the most objectionable feature of Spanish agrarian life, i.e. the totally unrestricted right of the landlord to arrange the terms of the lease as he wishes. In the short-lease area this liberty of the landlord may be offset, up to a point, by the liberty similarly granted by law to the tenant. The difference in economic conditions is often, of course, sufficient to destroy this legal symmetry, and nowhere more so than in Galicia. For here, not only is the tenant often in debt to his landlord, owing to the operation of the *fuero,* but the high density of the population maintains an endemic land famine which puts the peasant at the mercy of the landlord. Galicia is thus the nursery of Spanish emigrants, and the expatriated *Gallego* is a familar figure in the rest of the Peninsula, as well as in the whole of South America.

Nor is the picture rosier in the area of large holdings and short leases. This description is hardly accurate, for what really happens in this zone is that a small number of owners possess a disproportionate amount of the land, leaving the remainder to be distributed in very small holdings of very little value. Thus in the last years of the monarchy the official data of the province of Avila show that, out of 13,530 land-tax payers, no less than 11,452 had a daily income of less than a peseta (about 8d.); 1758 had an income of less than 5 pesetas a day; and there remained 155 with incomes between 5 and 8 pesetas daily. It may therefore be said that in this fairly representative Spanish province more than 91 per cent of the landowners earn less than the average urban industrial worker. The figures for that part of the territory which was reassessed—about one-third of the national area—lead to exactly the same conclusions. Out of 1,026,412 landowners paying tax 1,007,616 "enjoyed" incomes below 8 pesetas a day; and, of these, 847,548 landowners had incomes below 1 peseta. It follows that the landowning system of this part of Spain results in maintaining a class of proletariat landowners who differ in no way from agricultural workers at the mercy of the wage market.

Two legal features aggravate the situation. The first is that no law limits the liberty of the landlord to cultivate his large estates or not. The small farmer or landowner-worker, bound by dire necessity, lives on the soil and makes it produce; the big landowner, in practically every case an absentee, may choose to hand over a few spaces for cultivation and, living on the produce of them, to reserve the rest for hunting, the raising of bulls for bull-fighting, or merely the adornment of his ducal coronet. Furthermore, the big landowner is free to cultivate his land as he wishes and to decide as to the labor he will apply to it. If for economic or other reasons—political, for instance,—he thinks it better to employ a couple of hundred men, he need but send his steward to the market place of the next township and they will sign on without looking closely into the salary; if, perchance, it suits him best to drive the men back to want and the subsequent submission which it breeds, he may do so, even though knowing it means so much per cent less in his crop yield. Such things are not mere speculation: they actually happen.

The second legal feature which contributes to make the position worse is the above mentioned liberty of the landlord to arrange the terms of his lease. The liberty is, of course, symmetrical in theory; not so, however, in practice, for the tenant must have his land while the landlord need not lease it. The exploitation of estates by a system of tenant-farming which divides and subdivides them to the benefit of all but the unfortunate man who does actually scratch the soil must be considered as a kind of disease of the body politic of the country. The law does nothing to remedy it. Rather the reverse, for it allows the landlord to increase the rent whenever he wishes and to evict the tenant with so much facility that the tenant is never sure of his land and has no guarantee that the money he may spend on it will not go to fatten his landlord's pockets under another tenant, or even be used as an excuse for raising his own rent.

It will be readily understood that, under such conditions, a class of agricultural workers entirely dependent on landlords is a permanent feature of the social situation of the country. This mass of workers lives in an endemic state of unemployment and tends, of course, to gravitate toward districts with large and prosperous estates. Naturally enough, this situation gives rise to uneconomic features. The workers are fully aware of the obvious advantages of ca'canny when the number of men far exceeds the number of jobs; the landlord is led to decrease wages accordingly, and a kind of race away from economic soundness sets in. Andalusia is the typical region in this respect. Though wages are extremely low—ranging in 1930 from one peseta and meals to five pesetas, with a fairly general average of two and a half to three and a half—there are long periods of unemployment of from 90 days (in up-to-date districts) to 150 days in the year. Married workers seek to better their miserable position by renting small plots of land and by using the work of their wives and children. School attendance under these conditions is precarious, and the school authorities cannot enforce the law without doing violence to their better feelings.

The existence of a vast agricultural population which the

governing classes had proved unable to save from misery was perhaps the most serious evil in Spanish life. It was an economic evil, for it is evident that the wealth of the country would benefit by a more adequate relationship between the land and its tillers, and that, through land law reform, Spain would certainly succeed in raising her food supply and a substantial surplus for export at export prices.

It was a social and political evil owing to the social ferments which it developed in the mass of agricultural laborers. Ill-fed, ill-clothed, lacking in instruction, with no stake in the land, the best of them combed out by emigration, the agricultural laborers of Andalusia in particular were a ready ground for all kinds of violent propaganda. By temperament and psychology the Andalusian tends to the philosophical anarchy of Kropotkin; environment and experience tempt him to follow the violent path of Bakhunin. Blasco Ibáñez, who studied them at close quarters, has given a vivid description of the sudden illumination wherewith the passage of an inspired apostle of anarchism may light up the wretched and miserable lands of southern Spain. Observers of Spanish political life are well aware of the curious relationship between the active anarchist ferment which is endemic in Barcelona and the passive anarchist attitude which lies in waiting in the Andalusian fields. This attitude was fostered by some unwise landlords and estate managers, too overbearing and too stupid to read the signs of the times; but, worse still, it was often fostered by the government itself. The Socialist party worked admirably for years to convert these miserable populations to the constitutional and parliamentary way of salvation. It was a Herculean task with an old, skeptical and individualistic race, kept in subjection for centuries in the name of law and order; but, when the masses, at last converted, came to vote, all means, fair and foul, and particularly the foul ones, were put in operation to defeat the legitimate use of the vote; candidates imprisoned or forbidden access to parts of their constituency; faked counting of votes; no recourse was too low or too unfair for the so-called Conservative and the so-called Liberal governments which "made" the election from Madrid. As for wage difficulties, the South has not forgotten how a Conservative Home Secretary met a strike of wage-earners by raising the wages of the constabulary.

What were the remedies? The problems which required urgent attention were two: on the one hand, land ownership and land tenure; on the other, credit.

Efforts were made in both directions. With regard to land ownership the difficulty was twofold: at one end the latifundia, or wide areas under a single ownership; at the other end, the small holdings, too small for economic exploitation. Public opinion was stimulated by a series of inquiries, particularly those undertaken in 1912, on the land situation in the South and Southeast, and that of 1919, on the central and eastern provinces. In a bill presented to Parliament in 1921, latifundia were compulsorily made available for internal colonization. Ideas have been bold and numerous, but, even though at times they went as far as Parliament, they seldom reached the realm of actual fact. Still, a Central Committee of Internal Colonization was set up in 1907 and became, in 1917, the *Instituto de Colonización Interior*, a semi-autonomous body entrusted with the administration of the funds devoted by the state to the acquisition of land and its distribution among smaller settlers. Similar efforts were made to limit the excessive parceling of land, notably suggestions for amending the law of inheritance in this respect. Though not aiming at exactly the same ends, the Homestead Law of 1907 acts in a similar direction in that it limits to the state, municipality, conjoint, and sons, the entities in whose favor the settler's land can be mortgaged, the produce of the land remaining, in any case, free from all charges. This modest beginning was criticized, and efforts toward completing the measure in a more liberal way were attempted, notably in 1921. But while study and preparation were excellent, execution and legislation were poor, partly owing to the political influence of landed proprietors, partly to the instability of Spanish politics.

As for credit, the country had in its *pósitos* an old traditional institution of national rural credit. The *pósito* was originally municipal in character and based, not on money, but on grain.

Its existence has to a certain extent rather hindered than helped the development of more modern state methods. Nevertheless, the *pósitos* themselves were modernized and their credit operations reached a level of about $3,079,000 yearly. Later a national organization of agricultural credit was set up under the name of *Junta del Crédito Agrícola,* which worked for several years with signal success, not only as the provider of credit for the small farmer, but also as the *deus ex machina* which in times of crisis in a particular commodity—be it wine, oil or fruit—stepped in and saved the producer from the exhaustive greed of the trade intermediary.

The only agency which could rival the state in its activities in this field was the Church. Early in the century some enlightened members of the clergy realized the social and political possibilities of this field. A campaign of the clergy, fostered by bishops and priests, led to the creation of not a few rural associations termed "syndicates," having for their main object the organization of rural credit. This was achieved by means of banks based on joint and limited liability, a system which, in the small social area of a village, seems to work satisfactorily. The movement met with considerable success, and the sketch of a federation was first attempted in 1912, when the federation of Old Castile and León syndicates came into being. Others followed, until the whole country was covered by the *Confederación Nacional Católico-Agraria.*

This organization has ambitious aims, and what is more, it attains them. It arranges for the collective purchase of fertilizers and machinery; it organizes collective sales of the produce as well as the collective working of not a few industrial-agricultural operations such as wine, flour and oil production, the organization of slaughter houses and electric plants, etc. The value of its buildings was estimated in 1926 at about 20,000,000 pesetas, while the deposits and loans of its credit banks were calculated respectively at 250,000,000 and 200,000,000 pesetas. Extensive operations of internal colonization were carried out under the auspices of this organism, and valuable work was also done in irrigation.

It will be noted that the word *Católico* is prominently aired on the very title of the federation. At first sight it may appear strange that such care should be taken to insist on the Catholic character of an institution not precisely religious in its activities in a country in which—particularly according to the Church— everybody is a Catholic. The institution thus realized the tremendous political importance of the countryside in Spain, and the federation spent freely in propaganda. It owned seventy periodicals and five dailies in 1930.

CHAPTER 12

LABOR

For Spain, the keynote of the twentieth century has been a rapid development of her economic life and, in particular, of powerful industrial centers in the Basque, Catalan, Asturian, Valencian and other districts, such as Seville and Zaragoza. We also know that, through a defective legal and social organization, her countryside is populated by a peasantry which, in the greater part of the country, and especially of the South, lives in precarious and often in miserable circumstances. We have here some of the elements for a difficult labor situation. On the one hand, centers of industrial attraction, in which wages have a rising tendency, drawing men from poverty-stricken country districts toward the glittering towns, either under the pressure of economic necessity or by an act of industrial warfare; on the other, a mass of urban workers under a permanent threat of dispossession owing to the unlimited reserves of potential blacklegs swarming unfed in the untilled fields. Add to these objective and

143

economic elements the subjective and psychological features supplied by national character, and many of the somewhat bewildering complications of contemporary labor history in Spain will become clear.

There is, perhaps, no other aspect of national life which better lends itself to a comparative study of the local varieties of character within the Peninsula. The matter is of some importance, particularly in connection with not a few of the more extreme and less grounded claims of Catalan nationalists. Labor conditions suggest two definite leading regions—Catalonia and Castile —or perhaps more accurately, two leading cities, Barcelona and Madrid; the fields of influence of which would be: for Barcelona, Andalusia and to a lesser extent Murcia, Valencia and Aragon; for Madrid, the rest of the Peninsula. This geographical distribution is highly significant in that it is wholly spontaneous and natural, not in the least the result of deliberate effort and organization, or of pre-existing lines of communication or administration, but, on the contrary, a fact of nature which, from the outset, determines events. Furthermore, this dualism is not due to a mere opposition between rival men or institutions, nor can it be explained by state or local intervention; still less by the existence of a Catalan nationalism, for labor questions cut across Catalanism at every turn. Here again we are in the presence of a spontaneous fact of nature, the springs of which are in character. For the keynote of Barcelona labor movements is individualistic, while that of the movements led by Madrid is institutional, a contrast which ultimately resides in character and on which it is necessary to insist.

Generally speaking, Barcelona is anarchist and Madrid socialist. It is safe to say that when the European labor movement, which inspired the First International, split in 1879, Marx and Bakhunin parting in different directions never to meet again, the temperaments which underlay their respective doctrines corresponded to the temperaments which underlie Madrid and Barcelona. Thus in this unexpected field of labor evolution, we meet also the institutional instinct and the sense of authority which, in the Iberian Peninsula, are uppermost in Castile. That both sides are aware of what is at stake may be seen in this significant detail: when, in 1870, as a result of the Hague split between Marx and Bakhunin, the Spanish movement divided its forces accordingly (in a congress held at Zaragoza), the Marxian party styled themselves *autoritarios,* while the followers of Bakhunin were known as *anti-autoritarios.* This detail shows the difference which separates the Castilian from the Catalan conception.

The ways of the spirit are not altogether inscrutable, but they are often picturesquely devious. Though Castilian socialism prides itself on its freedom from all religious tenets and considers itself as a natural adversary of the Catholic faith, its policy springs from an attitude toward life which is strongly influenced by the profound traditions of Catholic Spain. That sense of authority, that instinct for government from above, firm leadership, the responsibility and power of the man at the helm, the weight and dignity of institutions, all the subconscious tendencies of Castilian socialism—which it has, of course, in common with every other manifestation of Castilian public life—all may be traced to the Catholic sense of man's weakness and tendency to err, to that profound conviction that it is neither prudent for the community, nor charitable to the individual, to let anyone feel the weight of too much liberty. The *autoritarios* of the nineteenth century were but the worthy descendants of the sixteenth-century Spaniards who had conceived and lived the Spanish Empire as a vast institution based on authority and aiming at the good of man. The faith has changed, and the "other world" has moved from an ever receding eternity to an ever receding ideal; but the gravity, the stern political outlook, and the creative institutional sense are the same. The socialist movement of Madrid is thus the only truly historical entity in Spanish modern politics, i.e. the only feature endowed with an inner life which gives it a permanent, growing and formative value in the life of the country.

In deep contrast to this contemporary version of an old-standing feature of Spanish life, the labor movement of Catalonia appears as a series of fitful agitations, more often than not violent and even terrible, springing from an unrestricted individualism—both theoretical and practical. The socialism of Madrid, though coming from Marx, calls forth the old orthodox pessimism from the depths of the Castilian soul, and becomes thus quickly nationalized. The anarchism of Barcelona, inspired in the teachings of Bakhunin, hails from the inscrutable optimism of Jean Jacques Rousseau, and stirs all the unlit enthusiasm of the Mediterranean romantic. If men are naturally bad, or, in Sancho's words, "as God made them and sometimes worse," institutions are needed to bind them together in mutual help. But if men are naturally good, the evils of collective life must needs come from institutions and tyrants—so the sooner we get rid of them the better for natural man. This creed was bound to appeal to a people as strongly individualistic as the Catalan; it was bound to be received with enthusiasm by a race of poverty-stricken Andalusians who had never seen the right side of an institution. The evolution of the labor movement in Spain is determined by the interaction of these two poles: Madrid and Barcelona; socialism and anarchism; institutions and agitations; political action and direct action.

The historical roots of the movement are old, and legal authorities can go as far back as Alfonso the Sage, in whose juridical masterpiece, *Las Siete Partidas,* there are provisions which, while directed against the *cofradías* or confraternities of workers prejudicial to the land or to the king's sovereignty, are by no means opposed to association. The distinction becomes clearer in later centuries, and a line is drawn between the *cofradías* proper, aiming at class organization, and the *gremios,* based on industry and not on class, the first foreign, the second fostered by old Castilian, Catalan and Valencian laws. Yet, toward 1770, the Superior Council of Castile estimated that there were in Spain 25,927 *cofradías* with a yearly expenditure of 11,687,618 reales and ample landed property. The eighteenth century was unfavorable to both *gremios* and *cofradías,* and the political leaders and thinkers of the period, such as Ward, Campomanes and Jovellanos, attacked them in the name of industrial freedom. Charles III and Charles IV legislated against them, and the Cortes of Cádiz, opening wide all doors to liberty, decreed full industrial freedom in 1813. Ferdinand VII, however, was bent on closing all the doors which the Cortes of Cádiz had opened, and he went back even beyond the relatively liberal days of his father and grandfather. His narrow absolutism did not survive him; before his daughter and successor was of age, the queen regent granted the decrees of 1834, one on *gremios,* which were only permitted if aiming at industrial progress and not "contrary to the liberty of manufacture, the circulation of goods and produce within the national territory or the unlimited competition of capital and labor"; the other laying down that "all those who exercise mechanical arts and trades directly or through other persons are worthy of honor and esteem, for they serve the state in a useful capacity," and, as a logical sequence to this magnanimous principle, the decree recognized that such people engaged in work would have access to state posts, honors, and dignities on a level with idle persons. By such bold steps the Spanish monarchy prepared the resurrection of the liberal principles of Cádiz, which it actually achieved in 1836.

But a labor movement in the modern sense of the word is not merely industrial; it has to breathe the free air of public opinion and, therefore, it must possess political organs and a political life The Spanish labor movement could not develop until the right of associating and meeting was recognized by the state and no longer considered seditious. The gradual conquest of this right is closely interwoven with the political vicissitudes of the nineteenth century. As was to be expected, little progress was made under Ferdinand .VII, a king for whom thinking was a *funesta manía.* Despite a short-lived law of 1822, timidly liberal, official opinion in 1848 still declared illicit all associations "in which newspapers are read and political questions are debated." Not till 1862 do we see a glimpse of what was to come. In that year, 15,000 workers of Barcelona presented a petition to the Congress of Deputies, asking for "freedom of association in order to struggle against capital nobly and peacefully." In 1864 pressure of liberal opinion forced Cánovas to take a step forward by a law so conservative in spirit that public meetings were defined as meetings of more than twenty persons in the domicile of any of them. But the Revolution of 1868 precipitated matters, and by a decree of November 28 the right of meeting and association was established with no other restriction than that of being dependent on no foreign country.

The system under which the labor movement developed in recent years dates from 1876. The Constitution of that year was destined to live for the relatively long period of forty-seven years. This longevity it owed perhaps to a provision which allowed it to go to sleep now and then. Article 17 authorized the suspension of constitutional guarantees by means of a law when the security of the state so demanded it and "in extraordinary circumstances." If Parliament was not in session the government might, nevertheless, suspend the guarantees, submitting its decision to the approval of the Cortes as soon as possible. This provision allowed the authors of the Constitution to be pretty free-handed in granting constitutional guarantees, among which we find in Article 13 the right to meet peacefully, the right to express one's thoughts and the right of "association toward the ends of human life." But if the system did help the Constitution to attain the age of forty-seven—honorably long, given the average expectation of life in Spanish constitutions—it drove the labor movement to live on the frontiers of legality, now "guaranteed" by the Constitution, now persecuted when, as was frequently the case, circumstances were found "extraordinary" by the government, and the guarantees accordingly suspended. This hot-and-cold treatment at the hands of the state was, on the whole, stimulating for the movement, but contributed not a little to encourage the individualistic, anarchist tendencies of Barcelona at the expense of the more statesmanlike and constructive tendency of Madrid.

The first symptoms of a new spirit appear toward 1840. In this year Munts, a Catalan weaver, founded the Association of Handweavers; while in Casabermeja, in the province of Málaga, a peasant rising seized several estates and organized a kind of rebel state which was energetically suppressed by the central authorities. Munts' initiative met with success and, imitated by other trades, it led to a confederation of labor unions which was

created in 1854 under the name of *Unión de Clases*. Both features—the tendency to peaceful association and the tendency
to high-handed direct action—appear, therefore, from the outset.
The third and most unfortunate tendency which the labor movement brings out, that of the state to meddle unsympatheically and
mostly by means of soldiers, was soon to reveal itself. In 1855,
the tactless intervention of General Zapatero, Captain-General of
Catalonia, called forth the first general strike which Spain was to
know, and in which no less than 40,000 workers were involved.
The conflict gave occasion to not a few criminal outbursts, but
better counsels prevailed and the strike was terminated by a compromise in which the workers were moderate enough to waive
their demand for a ten-hour day, and to agree that a mixed
jury should settle their differences. This period was one of labor
trouble all over Spain: secret societies; risings in Zaragoza and
Valencia (1855); incendiarism in Valladolid, Palencia and Zamora (1856); disorders in Olivenza and Badajoz in 1859; a
serious rebellion in Loja, in the name of "the rights of man,
respect for property, a domestic home and all opinions." This
was the period of moderate claims and violent methods.

The ferment operated also in other fields. The same year,
1840, is generally given as the date when the cooperative movement began, with a Cooperative Association of Consumers
founded by a hundred families in Barcelona. Cooperative associations of consumers spread relatively quickly on the eastern
coast, notably in Catalonia. The first cooperative association of
producers appeared in Valencia in 1856 with the significant
name, *La Proletaria*. It had for its object the manufacture of silk.
The movement spread and even won a certain semi-permanent
prosperity. The example of Valencia was followed by Barcelona
and Madrid, where, in 1871, a printing cooperative association
was formed.

Intellectual socialism began toward the same date with Joaquín Abreu, who introduced Fourier's doctrines into Spain, and
was later with Fernando Garrido, founder of the first socialistic
journal of Spain, *La Atracción* (1845), and inspirer of the first
socialist nucleus in Madrid. It is significant that the foundation

of the first socialist newspaper of Spain should have taken place in Madrid at about the same time that Munts founded the first trade union in Barcelona; thus Barcelona and Madrid took up their positions as the industrial and the intellectual leaders of the movement. The tone in Madrid at the beginning was distinctly moderate, particularly under Garrido's successor, Ordax Avecilla, while in Barcelona Abdón Terradas and Monturiol (in the weekly paper *La Fraternidad*) took a definite communistic and revolutionary line.

The year 1868, in which a liberal revolution drove out Isabel II, brought to Spain the first emissary of the "International" in the person of Farinelli, of the Bakhunin brand, soon followed by Lafargue, Marx's son-in-law. The International made quick progress in the generous years when Spain experimented with political liberty (1868-74). The *Manifesto of the International Workers of the Madrid Section to the Workers of Spain* (December 1869) went as far as could be desired by the wildest believer in immediate Marxism. Two labor congresses took place in Barcelona, one in 1870, the other in 1872, attended by 150 labor associations. Some conservative-minded people, who did not like the look of the French commune, asked the government what it meant to do in the circumstances; the debate (October 1871) in the Cortes may still be consulted as a repertory of all the ideas which it is possible to connect with the freedom of association—not excluding those of the immanence and the transcendence of God, which were abundantly discussed by Salmerón. In spite of its all-embracing scope, or perhaps because of it, the debate resulted in nothing but a free hand granted to the government to curtail the activities of the association born with so much nonsensical gas in its head. In this brief period the Spanish branch of the International had gathered 25,000 members, 149 local federations, 361 sections, 12 regional unions. It was declared illegal by the provisional government formed after the *coup d'état* of 1874, which closed the revolutionary period. But this first experiment had been more useful to the labor movement than most of its followers could see at the time, for during those five years the movement had lived down not a little of the folly which it will have to eliminate before it can contribute permanent values to the life of the country.

The era of wisdom was announced by the appearance of the desire to know. After the Restoration of 1875, a few clear heads began to wonder whether the time had not come for finding out the facts about industrial difficulties. The idea was not altogether new. Attempts had been made, in 1855 by Luxán, in 1869 and 1871 by the Cortes. Not till 1883 did the scheme materialize, thanks to Moret, who set up a *Comisión para el estudio de las Cuestiones que interesan a la mejora o bienestar de las Clases Obreras, tanto agrícolas como industriales, y que afectan a las relaciones entre el capital y el trabajo.* Cánovas was appointed chairman. The desire to learn was stimulated by the disorders and crimes produced by the Black Hand, a secret society comprising 150 federations and 50,000 members, which at the time held the whole of Andalusia in terror.

While the commission worked and slowly gathered up a monumental amount of material, the publication of which lasted from 1889 till 1894, the movement went ahead in its two branches, the anarchist and the socialist. The anarchists formed the *Federación de Trabajadores de la Región Española,* which met in congress in Barcelona, 1881; Seville, 1882; Valencia, 1883; Madrid, 1887; and Valencia again, 1888, when it was dissolved; though it left behind a considerable number of adepts and active newspapers such as *Tierra y Libertad,* published in Barcelona. Meanwhile the two forces which were to constitute the socialist movement of Spain were bringing forth the political and the industrial organizations which, to this day, have maintained their hold on labor events in Madrid. The first was represented by the small band of *autoritarios* who had sided with Marx when the Zaragoza split had occurred. They had founded, in 1879, the *Partido Democrático Socialista Obrero,* which came out into the open in 1884, and, in 1886, founded its daily, *El Socialista,* still the leading socialist paper in the country.[1] In 1888 the first congress of the party took place in Barcelona. Most of its leaders, particularly Pablo Iglesias the apostle and

[1] Published in Toulouse (France) during Franco's dictatorship.

founder of Spanish socialism, were also the driving element in
the industrial organization which proceeded apace, for 1888
saw also the creation of the *Unión General de Trabajadores,* the
trade union organization of Spain.

We know that the minority of King Alfonso was a period of
preparation for the industrial development of the twentieth century. In this period both the anarchist and the socialist branch
of the labor movement showed signs of activity. The government
was at times enlightened and well disposed, at times in excessive
sympathy with a class of employers, who were still wholly unable
to see the advantages of a constructive trade union movement,
and who added fuel to the fires of reaction.

Much of the responsibility for the troubles of this time lies
at the door of the anarchists. Bombs, assassinations and other
outrages can hardly be considered good weapons for propaganda, and the inexperienced public could not be expected to
draw a fine distinction between socialists and anarchists, particularly when there were so many interests against such a distinction being made. Though the Congress of Valencia had
dissolved the anarchist federation, a Commission of Relations
and Statistics which it left behind acted as a clearing-house and
leading committee for local branches and endeavored to attract
converts by means of congresses and "federations of resistance
to capital." The movement frankly appealed to the passions of
the crowd and sought to stimulate risings and direct action. In
1889 a petard exploded in the Royal Palace and an employer
was murdered in Barcelona; an epidemic of bombs made numerous victims in Barcelona in 1893 and 1896. Andalusia, always
in tune with Barcelona, saw the peasant rebellion of Jerez in
1892, an aftermath of the Black Hand movement, during which
many an ugly crime was committed. From 1890 to 1902 there
was a series of strikes in practically every part of the country,
often accompanied by violent excesses and followed at times by
excessive government repression. The origin of these troubles, or
at any rate of their disorderly and revolutionary features, was
practically always due to anarchist action or inspiration. The
Socialist Party and the General Union of Workers, though active

and sympathetic in every case of industrial hardship, concentrated their effort on the development of their organization, on peaceful propaganda and on a certain number of political campaigns of a liberal character. Their industrial activities were always inspired by strictly industrial aims and they prudently measured their cooperation whenever anarchist risings were contemplated by the other school. The anarchists, however, succeeded in scaring the nation, and Cánovas, following a Liberal example, passed a law to defend civilized society against the terrorism of those who were in too great a hurry to make it perfect. Cánovas paid with his life. In 1895 he was assassinated by an Italian anarchist.

The period that followed, with the frank development of industrial activity which set in, lent itself particularly well to the advance of the labor movement in all its branches. The Socialist Party and the General Union of Workers consolidated their hold over the masses in North and Central Spain, the General Union passing from 15,000 members in 1899 to 147,000 in 1913, while, what is perhaps more important, the number of its sections grew from 65 to 351. Two important new factors made their appearance. On the one hand, the revolutionary wing of the movement found in the syndicalist ideas brought over from France an adequate compromise between its own anarchist conception and the need of some sort of organization for a collective effort to express itself at all. The general lines of this new philosophy had been formulated by Georges Sorel in his famous book, *Réflexions sur la Violence*. The world was to be organized for the producers by the producers; the method to be purely industrial, since politics were but economics masquerading as the art of government; policy was to be identical with war; the troops were to be the associations of men of the same industry, i.e. the syndicates; the weapons, the class struggle, incidents, strikes, violence. In so far as ideas are dictated by temperament, there was much in this philosophy to appeal to the Barcelona school of labor adepts, and it mattered little that Sorel came forth as a Mohamed whose Allah was Marx and not Bakhunin; for, as the Castilian saying goes, "Let the miracle be done even though the devil do it." The framework, moreover, was at hand; for the idea of uniting the men of one industry was too obvious to be missed in an epoch so rich in labor activity, and there already existed in Madrid, Barcelona and other towns various federations which united the men engaged in the same trade under one central leadership. All that was needed was to instill into them the appropriate *apolitical* views. This was tried, not without success, by centralizing leadership and organization, first in what was known as *La Confederación Nacional del Trabajo,* which, of course, settled in Barcelona, a rival to the politically minded and socialist General Union of Workers settled in Madrid; and then by the *Sindicato Unico,* which was to become famous in the annals of contemporary Spanish history as one of the chief factors in the tragic years of Barcelona.

Much of what was to come, much indeed of what was happening, could be explained also by the shortcomings of the Spanish employer. Nowhere, as a rule, conspicuous for his moderation or his sense of the spirit of the times, the employer is generally more exacting and less tractable in the Catalan region. There is no better wedge than that of the same wood, and the Catalan employer, usually on a small scale, is more often than not a foreman who has succeeded in crossing the line. Much of the peculiar bitterness and at times violence of Catalan labor conflicts becomes sadly clear when viewed in this light. Spanish employers, scared at the success of the more lively labor organizations, decided to take for once a leaf out of the syndicalist book, and met in a Congress of Employers' Federations in 1914. Till then they had followed an oblique line of attack consisting mostly in organizing blackleg syndicates or unions, which, significantly enough, often took the Catholic label. The *Centros Católicos de Obreros* sought to maintain a certain social discipline among the working classes. The Jesuit Father Vicente lent the movement his organizing ability and linked the *Centros* up with the international Catholic labor movement led by Belgium. The national organization was centralized in a *Consejo Nacional de las Corporaciones Católicas Obreras,* founded in 1910 under the

Archibishop of Toledo as chairman. The movement gathered considerable momentum, no doubt helped by the fact that it could draw financial help from wider sources than a wage fund. The number of Catholic labor clubs grew from 160 in 1906 to 376 in 1913. The activities of the movement were of a somewhat complex nature, for the clubs sought to provide illness, unemployment, old age and accident benefits. A more strictly industrial type of Catholic association was developed under the leadership of Dominican specialists, such as Father Gerard and Father Gafo.

When, in the turmoil produced by the First World War, the several movements which agitated the country—among them the labor movement—converged toward the crisis of 1917-21, the labor organizations of the country were progressing, each along its own line, however divergent. The events of the First World War period are of so complex a nature that they can hardly be interpreted under a strictly labor label. All we can do here is to point out that, when King Alfonso took on his heavy responsibilities as nominally irresponsible king of a nominally constitutional monarchy, Labor was no longer the shadowy spirit of a foreign Utopia hovering over a dispersed and ignorant mass of poverty-stricken workers, but a relatively powerful movement evolving toward a conscious republican state-socialism in Madrid, toward religious social institutions in its Catholic organizations, and toward a deliberately violent subversion of society, as at present understood, in the ever-seething caldron of Barcelona and the dissatisfied plains of Andalusia.

CHAPTER 13

THE CHURCH—CLERICALISM

Clericalism is an evil unknown in Protestant countries. In Catholic countries it is sometimes mild, as in Belgium, or even in France, where the evil is perhaps rather anti-clericalism. But it would be difficult to find a country in which clericalism is more rigidly inimical to all reasonable compromise with the *Zeitgeist* than contemporary Spain. The history of the nineteenth century in Spain would have been much quieter and much richer in results had the evolution of the Spanish people taken place in the absence of clericalism and militarism. As it is, the almost chronic civil war, the outward form of that evolution in the nineteenth century, though beginning as a conflict between absolutism and liberalism, gradually degenerates into a conflict between clericalism and militarism and, what is worse, ends in a tacit but efficient treaty of peace and cooperation between the two, so that the arms of the Restoration might well be described

as a sword and a cross (considered as a weapon) surmounted by
the royal crown.

That the once glorious and liberal Spanish Church, the church
which, with Vitoria and Suárez, had founded international law
and, with Mariana, had defined the democratic prince, should
have degenerated to the level of the *curas guerrilleros,* or fighting
priests, and the bogus mystics such as Sor Patrocinio, who, by
simulating stigmata and heavenly visions, brought about cabinet
crises, may be counted as one of the trials which Providence as
history put in the path of a people given to the sin of pride.
Those persons who prefer rationalistic explanations may note
that the Spanish Church was great while it lived on the culture
of the great universities of the sixteenth century, and that its
decadence followed that of the celebrated seats of learning. Ignorant and stubborn monks led the resistance to progressive
measures during the nineteenth century. Larra has left us, in
Nadie pase sin hablar con el portero, a vivid picture of the customs line against books established on the frontier between Liberals and Carlists by monks in the Carlist army. "Recherches?"
asks the monk, scrutinizing a French book found in the baggage
of one of the unfortunate travelers going south. "I suppose this
fellow Recherches must be a heretic. To the fire with it." Larra
is, of course, writing fiction, but the elements of his fiction were
but too real, and in the very month when the present lines were
written, a local priest and a local mayor in a small Spanish
town made a bonfire of all the books of Galdós which had been
purchased by the municipal librarian.

Such persistence in error must correspond to permanent features in the country as a disease does to health. And, of course,
there is no doubt that the Spanish people are profoundly religious. Their inherent religion, moreover, harmonizes in many
points with the Catholic faith. The synthetic and spontaneous
nature of Spanish thought, for instance, is readily attracted by
the doctrine of a revealed dogma, and there are obvious lines of
sympathy between the transcendental pessimism of the Catholic
and the experimental pessimism of the stoic—stoicism being at

bottom the natural attitude of the Spanish soul. Such an attitude places the subject in the mood of a contemplative spectator who sees the world as drama, a point again on which the stoic Spaniard can find himself at home in the Roman faith. Add the Spanish tendency to lay stress on synthetic human standards rather than on ethical values, and we shall see how deeply the Catholic roots have struck ready earth in the Spanish race.

This fact explains the strength of Spanish clericalism. For clericalism, though a disease of Catholic societies, is natural to them, being a diseased growth along the lines of their healthy development; it is, therefore, extremely difficult to attack clerical abuses without seeming to attack Catholic institutions, or even without being naturally drawn actually to attack them. Now a criticism of Catholic institutions, implying as it does a criticism of the faith which they incarnate, is always sure to provoke a strong reaction in Spain. There is, after all, no impregnable ground for such an attack. Moreover, the strength of the Spanish clerical is but the weakness of the Spanish anti-clerical, for, in the immense majority of cases, the anti-clerical brings forward no substitute for the religion which he would displace. The Catholic religion has now been for twenty centuries perhaps the central element in Spanish culture and civilization, and, though fallen on evil ways, mostly under the action of historical causes which have influenced to an equal extent other forms of national life, though fallen even forever from its predominant position in Spanish life, it still is and must remain for a long time to come one of the chief features of the spirit of Spain. The believer, whether a clerical or only an anti-anti-clerical, stands therefore on stronger historical ground than the newcomer, whose ideas are more often than not a heady acquisition without roots even in his own soul.

It is useles to offer the Spaniard that rationalism which, in the form of intelligent doubt, is such a "soft cushion for the well-made head" of the Frenchman. The pendulum of the Spanish soul oscillates between the two extremes, self and the universe. To such a type religion is a necessity even if it be no more than the passive religious attitude of the stoic. It is true that, when he drops out of the Catholic faith, he does not become a Protestant. It is true that the established religion is not, as in England, surrounded by a number of smaller denominations into which the stray people are gathered, forming smaller groups. But the explanation is not, as superficial foreign observers have been led to believe, that all religious preoccupation goes with the dogma which had held it. Far from it. The explanation is to be found in the uncompromising individualism of the Spaniard, who, when ceasing to go to church, makes of his religion a strictly personal affair. We are again in the presence of the now familiar rhythm of the Spanish spirit, oscillating from extreme to extreme without a position of equilibrium in the middle term. Either the religion of authority or that of the solitary individual, the religion of absolute certainty or that of isolated search. All or nothing. It may be worth noticing here that the Catholic religion, by worshiping in Latin and by giving the faithful but a passive role in the worship, reduces to the very minimum the gregarious elements of the service, another feature which explains its success in individualistic Spain.

He remains himself but he is held within an institution, and this fact is also important in a country in which institutions are few and weak. A country, moreover, attached to a tradition of simplicity and even austerity which no amount of familiarity with the civilization of the North has succeeded in breaking. In no sense puritan, it is nevertheless sparing in its pleasures and inclined to look askance at the general loosening of the family ties, the lowering of the standards of feminine modesty, the cheapening of the pursuits of life, which a general emancipation from church worships brings in its train. It is very difficult to discriminate between religious and moral issues, and the fact that cabarets and anti-clericalism both come from France, though in essence perhaps irrelevant, influences the situation far more directly than might be imagined.

The story of Eve and the apple—the fruit, be it remembered, of the tree of knowledge—is a marvelous basis for a crusade against education, and in a country in which husbands do not trifle with feminine slips, the Church is bound to find many an ally—avowed and unavowed—in its efforts to keep Eve away from apples and serpents. There is thus a plausible origin to the obscurantist tendency of the Spanish Church. It comes from Spanish pessimism. Let us keep the children out of mischief. The less they know the less they will want to have. The less they will want to have, the less harm they will want to do. As it happens—as it *would* happen—this philosophy runs along the natural line of the Spanish stoic: let the river of life flow past my window. The decadence of the Spanish Church is then a decadence of inertia.

But times of activity were at hand. Partly, at any rate, the passivity of the Church could be explained by the absence of a methodical and persistent opposition endowed with institutions. Though the history of the nineteenth century may be interpreted as the fight between liberalism and clericalism, the *Isabelinos* and *Alfonsinos* who fought on the liberal side were let down royally by Isabels and Alfonsos as soon a the fights were over; and Alfonsos and Isabels reigned with Carlist principles and tendencies, and, therefore, with the help and sympathy of clerical Spain. Thus, backed by the state and the crown, the Church let itself live, and lacking outside stimulus, did little or nothing to foster the spiritual interests of its flock. Ganivet, writing in 1896, humorously suggested that if a few freethinkers and Protestants could be hired to live in Spain, matters might be improved. He was convinced of the inherent Catholicism of the Spanish nation, but he believed that dissidence was indispensable as a stimulant. We know that his humorous suggestion would have failed, for dissidence, without the resistance which institutions can give it, cannot withstand the formidable weight of the Church. However, dissidence embodied in institutions was to come.

The danger approached from the two quarters whence came the renovating influences in contemporary Spain: the increased complexity of material life and the development of Spanish culture. The first led to the Canalejas reforms in the law of associations; the second to the institutions for enlightenment created by the Committee for the Development of Studies. The charter of the Spanish Church is the Concordat of 1851, signed after an interval of fourteen years, during which the Vatican remained aloof in protest against the anti-clerical measures of Mendizábal. This Concordat is, of course, very favorable to Rome and, particularly in the matter of the religious orders to be admitted into the country, it goes as far as can be desired, mostly through vague and even misleading wording. Though dissolved and expelled a few years earlier, orders of all kinds soon invaded the country again, a fact less harmful than is sometimes imagined; but what was harmful was that these orders, through their inveterate policy of acquiring and accumulating wealth, rapidly succeeded in nullifying themselves as spiritual forces, while interfering with the sound economic and political development of the nation. The right of religious orders to freedom from all government regulation and inspection, a right which, given the general trend of Spanish legislation, constitutes a privilege, was one of the issues between liberals and clericals. The conflict came to a head owing to the development of workers' unions, which made it necessary for the government to reconsider the law of associations in force since 1887. Difficulties, in fact, had begun earlier, when, in 1901, the government decided to apply the law of 1887 to the religious orders, which till then had quietly ignored it in tacit agreement with the bureaucracy. The change meant mere registration with the local authorities for all but the three orders authorized by the Concordat to reside in Spain. All the government wanted, therefore, was that the considerable number of orders, whose very right to reside in Spain at all was, to put it at its lowest, doubtful, should comply with a law which had been in force for fourteen years. Modest as the claim was, it drew protest from the Vatican which proved too strong for the government. The outcome of this struggle is related in a subsequent chapter.

Another point on which battles were fought by the liberals was that of Article 11 of the Constitution of the Monarchy. In virtue of this Article the Catholic religion was declared to be the state religion, and no others were recognized, though they were "tolerated." In point of fact, the clericals were perhaps entitled to their view that the situation created no hardship for any considerable group of people. It is evident, however, to anyone not blinded by bigotry, that if there was but one Protestant, foreign or national, in the country against whom the article implied spiritual discomfort, the situation would be indefensible. There were, however, in Spain, though very few, enough non-Catholics to render a narrow interpretation of Article 11 most unjust and even intolerable. Thus, though Protestant churches and chapels were erected here and there, the law, interpreted as narrowly in their case as it was widely interpreted in that of the congregations, refused them the right to show by any outward signs the use to which they were put. Canalejas made a move toward liberalism in this direction, but the spirit of the Church was so uncompromising that his decree (June 1910), mild and respectful as it was, provoked another protest from the episcopate. The prime minister held his ground, backed by a powerful current of public opinion, and seized the opportunity to reform the law concerning oaths before Parliament and the courts, so as to enable persons of no definite religious views to promise instead of swearing.

Article 11 was also responsible for difficulties in connection with the marriage laws. In theory, Spanish law was based on civil marriage, but it had to take place in church, in the presence of an officer representing civil authority except when the participants had explicitly declared that they did not belong to the Catholic faith. The intention to block civil marriages in an indirect way was obvious. Many more stratagems were applied to the same end. A clerical minister, in 1900, issued a decree whereby civil marriages contracted without the parish priest's opinion being heard as to the religious faith of the participants were to be declared void. Thus not only were the participants put in the position of having to declare that they did not belong to the Catholic fold before they were allowed the benefit of the law in favor of civil marriage, but, according to this decree, their opinion was not to be taken as final, and the parish priest was to be called in to say whether they did or did not belong to his flock. This monstrosity was abrogated by Count Romanones when Minister of Justice and Worship in 1906, but not without a most violent protest on the part of the episcopate.

The efforts of the clerical faction were, however, most pertinacious in the field of education. The policy of the Church rested on two rules: to seek material power by "cultivating" the rich, thereby obtaining legacies for its institutions and, through political and social influences, to block all state developments in education. The result was that, as late as 1923, a leading Spanish expert calculated that fifty per cent of the juvenile population of Spain was not being educated at all; twenty-five per cent was educated by the state and twenty-five per cent by the Church. The state budget for education was then still inadequate by at least one hundred per cent to meet the requirements of the nation, though it had progressed in proportion to the freedom from Church interference which political circumstances had warranted. Elementary schools had increased at the rate of about one thousand teachers a year. Even so the number of state teachers hardly exceeded that of priests and nuns engaged in education, and the amount of money at the disposal of the Church was about equal to that spent by the state. It may be argued that it is no matter who educates so long as there is education. But the question is too serious to be so lightly dismissed. When confronting state with Church education we are not raising a religious issue but an educational issue. Spanish state education was not lay in the French sense of the word; it was religious, orthodox, Catholic, unless of course the family explicitly wished it not to be, an extremely rare occurrence. The true opposition lies in this, that state education is both tolerant and, in non-dogmatic matters, intellectually neutral, whereas the Church educates with *a tendency*, and gives all its teachings a pronounced bias and an intolerant turn. Hence the persistence of a rift in the nation, a state of mutual intolerance born of the intolerance of the Church, since one cannot be tolerant towards intolerance. It should be added that, technically, the methods of the Catholic schools of all kinds are nearly always inadequate.

The Church, however, was threatened with another rival which embodied no mere anti-clericalism. Of necessity, anti-clericalism, even when generous as that of Canalejas was, is negative and combative. The clericals found their stranglehold over the education of the country threatened by a work of deep and far-reaching significance, for, without in the least attacking the Church, still less religion, this work was constructive, peaceful and liberally open to co-operation with sincere believers. We refer, of course, to the movement which began with Don Francisco Giner and the *Institución* and which finally led to the admirable activities of the Committee for the Development of Studies. The clerical faction tried all kinds of weapons to combat the danger. Its first attempts were directed to accusing the committee's activities of anti-Catholic sectarianism. This the committee was able to prove unfounded, for it had always taken great care to number amongst its leaders a good proportion of Catholics and to bestow particular attention on the religious education given on strictly orthodox lines to those who wished to receive it. The trouble, of course, was precisely here, in the fact that orthodox religious education was not compulsory. For compulsion is the key tendency of Spanish clericalism.

A detailed narrative of the tribulations which the Committee had to undergo at the hands of the clericals would be out of place here. Two points must, however, be emphasized. The first is that the clerical faction had always to seek help by dark intrigues in ministerial corridors and even in royal antechambers; the second, that despite the precarious conditions under which the Committee had to live, with this sword of Damocles hanging over its head, it did live and perform its valuable work for the country, owing to the immense prestige and authority which it had gained over high and low alike.

These two significant facts should put us on the way to a right estimate of the power of the Church in Spain. The country is profoundly religious with a religion of its own which for all practical purposes coincides with Catholicism. But the people are profoundly opposed to clericalism. They are not militant anti-clericals, because militant anti-clericalism is a political attitude, and the Spanish people are *apolitical,* but the potential antagonism which underlies their attitude toward clerical matters is definite and precise; it may, in fact, be closely analyzed. With their clear intuitive perception of spiritual facts the Spanish people feel respect and deference toward truly spiritual religious orders: men and women who give themselves to charity or who, in real poverty, devote their lives to contemplation, are safe. But orders which amass wealth and try to influence social life by providing clothes, education or other advantages in exchange for religious liberty do so at their own risk. In 1909 the populace of Barcelona let loose years of accumulated anti-clerical passion. The result was terrible.

Anti-clerical measures have always been popular in Spain, despite what superficial observers say to the contrary. The famous Ubao case, a scandal in which a clerical family was proved to have conspired to lock up a young woman in a convent, under cover of a non-existent religious vocation, in order to secure her money, produced a political agitation not yet forgotten. And when, by a curious coincidence which seems to have been wholly fortuitous, Galdós's play *Electra,* built on exactly the same theme, appeared on the stage at the same moment, its instant success all over the Peninsula and the enthusiastic popularity which it earned for its author plainly showed where the feelings of the Spanish people lay.

There was, no doubt, much strength in the clerical position. It came from the following quarters:

In the first place the clerical tendency of the crown, due to the tradition which entrusted the education of the heir to thoroughly tried clerical men, whether lay or in orders. King Alfonso had been educated by men whose pedagogic, constitutional and philosophical outlook on life would have struck the great Spanish churchmen of the sixteenth century as unenlightened and medieval. It is only fair to add that the clericalism of the crown, rooted in miseducation, was strengthened by political prudence which, even if shortsighted, can hardly be condemned as foolish. This observation implies the existence of other substancial causes of power in the clerical position.

A good proportion of the middle classes are strongly influenced by clerical views. They do not necessarily coincide with the proportion of the nation which is devoutly religious. To take the women, for instance, the majority of middle-class women are devout Catholics, but the majority of this majority give no thought whatsoever to Church politics and are even fairly passive when, in an anti-clerical crisis, the clergy endeavor to mobilize them against the government. The reverse may be said to be the rule with men. Only a minority of middle-class men can be said to be devout Catholics. But of this minority the majority are clericals as well, men being more inclined than women to mix their religion with their politics. Many of these "lay Jesuits" used to move actively in government offices, the universities, the law, provincial and charity administrations. They constituted one of the most secure tentacles of the clerical octopus.

There are regions of Spain in which the people are traditionally clerical, in particular the higher regions of the Spanish Pyrenees from the mountainous districts of Catalonia to the strongholds of Navarra, and beyond to the hills and high valleys of the Basque provinces. These are the districts on which Carlism could always count for raising its civil wars against the accursed liberals who fought for Isabel and later for Alfonso XII. The specter of civil war in the North used to be conjured up to do yeoman service in frightening off liberal reforms. It is, to say the least, doubtful whether the exploits of the *curas guerrilleros* of the nineteenth century could be repeated in the twentieth. The northern peasant is nowadays more sophisticated than his grandfather was, and would probably look closely into the agricultural consequences of a war before indulging in it. Moreover, the big towns such as Bilbao, Zaragoza and Barcelona are thoroughly industrialized and the workers care nothing for the Church and still less for Carlism. Nevertheless, the bogey is there, and it has been efficient enough to frighten liberal governments and the crown with genuine or simulated fears every time bold liberal reforms have been contemplated.[1]

But the most substantial cause of clerical strength in the Church is that it is an institution in the midst of a people whose fanatical love of liberty prevents the development of institutions. Its immemorial roots, its stern discipline, the abundance and, in the lower ranks, the cheapness of its personnel, its intimate, yet autonomous, connection with the state, make of it a vigorous organism within the national organism itself. A typical example of what this implied was the power which the Church was able to wield in education. The fact that it had developed its educational system under a regime of freedom (slightly privileged by state subsidies) is in itself a proof of its value as an institution and a condemnation of the sterility of Spanish liberalism. But let us not be too hard on Spanish liberals. They could not rely—as could the clericals—on the splendid foundation of a historical institution like the Church, always sure of state protection. They had, moreover, in spite of many handicaps, produced the best educational establishments in Spain. But when their precious seed grew and new plantations had to be made, the liberal movement had to call at the state gates and seek its financial help in order to build up the Committee for the Development of Studies with all the inestimable institutions which it implied. Why were there no great and powerful institutions of learning with a liberal spirit in the free zone outside the shadow of the state in which the Church had thriven? Because rich Spaniards give no money for education. The public-spirited rich man, that type to which England and America owe so much intelligent and efficient social work in all spheres, is rare in Spain.[2] The Church, more familiar with the

---

[1] I have left these lines as they stood in the first edition (1930). They reveal some of the historical roots of the somewhat paradoxical attitude of the Basques in the 1936-38 Civil War. Carlism in its most reactionary form is the strongest origin of Basque separatism.

[2] As these words were written announcement was made of a handsome legacy left by the Count of Cartagena to the various Spanish academies and the Prado Gallery. It is significant that this enlightened member of the Spanish aristocracy lived mainly in Lausanne.

usual type of Spanish potentate, makes him open his purse by standing at the gates of paradise and asking for an entrance fee. The rich bigot who keeps Spanish Church schools going is but an egoist who prolongs his selfishness beyond the Bourne. The rich liberal, generally an unbeliever, or, what amounts to the same, a believer in his own individual way, has no such motives for endowing foundations and his name dies forevermore. It is important that this fact should be realized, for it serves to emphasize the value of the Church as an institution in the midst of an ultra-individualistic people such as that of Spain.

A similar remark applies to other social activities. Nursing, for instance, is in Spain overwhelmingly in the incompetent but devoted hands of nuns, despite the sporadic efforts of liberal medical men, such as Dr. Rubio, to foster schools for lay nurses. The matter of agricultural credit is a typical case in point. The intimate connection between Spanish politics and the miserable state of the peasant in the clutches of local usurers is a familiar subject in political books, articles and speeches. The liberal-minded people of Spain are fully aware of its central position with regard to the political evolution of the country. Yet what had been done on the liberal side? What associations, banks, propaganda, help had been forthcoming? None. Meanwhile we know with what intelligent attention the Church had followed up its discovery of the opportunities of agricultural life. A comparison of the educational and the agricultural problem of the country will lead to the same conclusion: i.e. that while the liberal development of the country, through lack of voluntary work and attention, had to rely on state aid, enlightened in its inspiration but slow and fitful in its legislation and inefficient in its working, the Church was able to set to work at once owing to its wealth, to its collective institutional character and also to the influence which it wielded in the higher and middle spheres of official Spain.

But then it may again be asked why not let the Church do its work? It is difficult for anyone not familiar with Spanish life to understand why there should still be in Spain any fuss about clericalism. But the facts of the case are clear. Much as one may wish to stand aloof from the somewhat cheap, radical anti-clericalism which afflicts a certain type of Spanish politician, one cannot be indifferent to the dangers of Church power in Spain. It is obvious that clerical education is thoroughly bad by any standard, as shown in the efforts of Church schools to escape objective examinations; and that, far from checking the tendency to superstition, the Church sedulously encourages it. Worse still, the Catholic Church of Spain is strongly intolerant, and, if it could, it would prevent all development of independent thought in the country. The Church has always applauded measures of a coercive character with regard to the free expression of opinion, and in all its activities there is a tendency to militancy, an aggresive attitude and a self-assertion which are as un-Christian as uncooperative. However deserving of praise some of its work in the realm of rural economy and in certain fields of scholarship may be, its influence on the country is essentially of a retarding and irritating nature. It adds one more problem to those which already burden the conscience and intellect of Spanish leaders. Instead of being, as of old, one of the most powerful instruments of government, it has become an element of strife and division, always ready to abuse its power by oppressing those who do not bow before its narrowly conceived authority. Cases might be told of excellent, useful men broken and lost to the nation by the relentless persecution of hard-headed and hard-hearted bishops with an undue and, generally, an illegal influence on the state. And the pity of it is that, through the unintelligent intolerance of its attitude, the Church blocks the way toward a real solution of the spiritual life of the country, which cannot be a bigoted Roman Catholicism, but which is certainly not to be found in an equally limited rationalism unsuited to the Spanish genius. The only hope is in a movement within the Church itself which may turn inward its overzealous activities for the education of others. The Spanish Church stands in great and urgent need of self-education.

CHAPTER 14

THE ARMY—MILITARISM

Militarism is hardly a correct word in the case of Spain. It is used here only in order to conform with the now traditional misuse of it. The position in Spain bears no resemblance to that of countries—such as prewar Prussia—in which a military caste controlled the national policy, particularly in matters of defense and foreign affairs, with a warlike spirit and intention. In Spain there is no such thing, and the evil would be better described as *praetorianism*. For a body of officers, by no means a caste, controls the political life of the nation, giving but little thought to foreign affairs and intent on the preservation of power and on the administration and enjoyment of a disproportionate amount of the budget.

The evil is relatively new in Spain, yet not without roots both in the old tradition and in the national character. Generals begin to loom large in Spanish history during the Spanish struggle against Napoleon. There is, indeed, food for thought in the fact that praetorianism appears in Spanish politics as Spain begins her free life. Castaños, the conqueror of Bailén, Riego, the first successful conspirator, are the two first names in a list that was to fill up the whole nineteenth century and which has been unexpectedly but dramatically lengthened in the twentieth. Civil war which, with fits of precarious peace, was the chief occupation of Spaniards from 1800 to 1876, and the colonial wars provided a plausible pretext for the maintenance of a military establishment enabling many an officer to climb up the military ladder to the highest official posts. Men like Espartero and Serrano, who became regents of the realm by a combination of military dash and courage with cheap field successes, would never have risen beyond obscure positions in any walk of life requiring a moderate amount of brain power. The army, moreover, by establishing the custom, which it turned into a necessity, of entrusting the governor-generalship of overseas possessions to military men, obtained a number of enviable posts, and by intervening in politics often laid hands also on the high offices of state. This fact made of the military profesion a kind of lottery which all pushing and ambitious men with no excessive love of books were eager to pursue. It would be erroneous to imagine the Spanish army as a huge military machine powerfully organized to obtain the highest possible fighting efficiency out of the large portion of the budget which it consumes. The army is a bureaucratic machine which spends most of the money paid to it in salaries for generals and officers, a lesser amount in war material, and a still lesser sum in preparing for war. The army, in fact, is more important as an instrument of home politics than as a weapon of war.

During most of the nineteenth century the army was, on the whole, a force in favor of liberalism. It has been shrewdly said that the intermittent Civil War of the nineteenth century may be interpreted as a struggle for supremacy between the army and the Church, ending in a compromise. This would explain the army's change of front, during the Restoration, from its liberalism of old to its present reactionary attitude. But this change has more complex causes behind it. Cánovas, who saw the evil of praetorianism, struggled to keep generals out of politics, but, lacking in the constructive statesmanship which was necessary to provide the throne with an alternative basis, he left the country in danger of a relapse. Circumstances made it fatal. The Church was no longer a rival to the army, for the Church in Spain, though a strong prop of the structure, granted the structure, would collapse with it if it went. Danger came from other forces, and in particular from the growth of the spirit of citizenship.

There are at least two reasons for this. The first is that the growth of a spirit of citizenship tended gradually to create a national community standing on its own basis and therefore able to do without the somewhat surgical appliance of the army (or for that matter of the Church). The army instinctively realized that the new force, if allowed to grow, would tend to check the political activities of the military institution and therefore to reduce it to the modest proportion required in a nation as secure from foreign attack as Spain. The second is that, while the new spirit of citizenship stimulated healthy forms of political life and even of agitation, it led also to unfortunate outbursts, not perhaps worse or graver than those which have at times afflicted other democracies, but certainly as bad. New social forces are not always tactful nor even sensible, and at times it was difficult to disentangle the actions of those who endeavored to make a new Spain from the agitation of those who attempted to destroy the old. Armies are seldom credited with much psychological penetration. By a process of natural selection they draw to their ranks a large number of men richer in blood than in judgment. The body of officers, moreover, felt somewhat sensitive after the close of the 1898 war, when the army behaved with its usual courage and spirit of sacrifice but when even its hottest advocates dared not stand up for the efficiency of its administration or for the competence of its leadership. It so happened, moreover, that the spirit of citizenship moved in directions athwart the army's most cherished tendencies. It is only natural that an army should tend to consider itself as an incarnation of the fatherland, and thus the Spanish army felt offended by the nationalist forms which progress took in Catalonia, in which it saw, at times not without cause, a danger to the unity of Spain. Then the political movements of the masses often took a republican-socialist turn, and the army, deeply monarchical, was disposed to feel directly interested in the matter. All these tendencies and feelings were strongly polarized by a vigorous *esprit de corps*. The Spanish army came from all classes. In its social composition it was as open and democratic as the French. There was no reason why a gulf should separate the army and the people. The army, at any rate the body of 20,000 officers which led it, was in direct touch with the middle classes who, along with a sprinkling of aristocrats, filled up its ranks. But there is the *esprit de corps*, the collective form of that strong individualism which is both the gift and the bane of the Spanish nation. Finally the army wielded force, and force, a temptation for all peoples, is the most irresistible of temptations for the Spaniard.

Trouble began in Catalonia when, in 1905, a somewhat scurrilous caricature in a Catalanist satirical paper roused the wrath of some spirited officers, who invaded the paper's premises and destroyed all they found. No disciplinary measures were taken. Far from it. The military agitation which ensued culminated—after one or two ministerial crises—in the so-called Law of Jurisdictions, whereby attacks on officers and military institutions were to be judged before military tribunals.

The government and Parliament which voted it under compulsion, or rather for fear of worse evils, were of "liberal" extraction. They voted with their eyes open. They knew that the battle which civil institutions had just lost was but the first in a long campaign, and several of the men then beaten no doubt realized what the end was to be. From that day, the power of the military class in the state—a power which had always been uppermost, in fact unique, in purely military affairs—overstepped the professional limits and began to intervene in civil life. The progress of citizenship was then severely checked. But the danger was to threaten the older and higher institutions, and this law, which the crown had helped the army to wring from a reluctant Parliament, was to strengthen the army against the true interests, perhaps the safety, certainly the prestige, of the crown itself.

Always prominent in Spanish politics since the Restoration, the army became predominant. The king chose to rest on it against the onward movement of civil life. Now he claimed the right to communicate directly with commanders over the head of his Cabinet ministers, a thoroughly unconstitutional practice which was weakly tolerated by his political advisers; now he organized *audiencias militares,* days on which all his visitors were military and naval officers; now he ostentatiously showed his royal favor by visiting barracks, attending banquets, making speeches, with other stage effects. The army budget became untouchable by civil hands. Money was lavished on military laboratories, schools, health establishments, which was sadly lacking in their civilian counterparts. The posts of Secretary and Under-Secretary for War became military sinecures, not to be entrusted to any civilian. Control of military expenditure disappeared altogether in actual practice. The army and its administration became a state within the state.

Two consequences followed. This huge administration, free from all Treasury control, became as cumbrous as inefficient. It developed a disproportionate head, while it starved its body, so that there were, in 1927, 19,906 officers (including 219 generals) for 207,000 troops, while the habit of sending a considerable number of the men back home instead of keeping them in actual service made this proportion of officers still higher. As it is, and even accepting these figures at their face value, the proportion of officers to soldiers was about one in ten, while in France it was just below one in twenty at the same date (30,622 officers for 606,917 men). This abundantly shows that the administration of the Spanish army was overburdened with a military bureaucracy insufficiently occupied in professional activities precisely because the object of its administration, defense, was starved in order to fatten the subject of it.

As a natural outcome of this state of affairs the body of officers—for that is what in reality stirred behind and usurped the name of the army—turned their attention to civilian affairs. A potential antagonism was implicit in the very conditions under which political life in Spain had to develop. This antagonism was seen acutely every time civilian opinion crossed one of the military dogmas. Whether it were an attempt at reducing extravagant expenses in personnel, or a concession made to Catalan home-rulers, or a decision on Moroccan affairs which reduced the possibilities of that costly adventure from the point of view of military officers ready to gamble their life for promotion and prestige, Parliamentary Cabinets and statesmen were sure of having to go through a Calvary of the most unruly acts—protests, meetings, outspoken declarations by military members of Parliament, or even by the war secretary, a general of course, who, if necessary, did not hesitate to declare that he spoke in the name of the army. The crown invariably stood behind "its" officers.

Gradually this antagonism between the state and the army brought about an organization of the army officers, not, be it understood, aiming at the fulfillment of their professional duties nor along lines of hierarchy and discipline, but on openly trade-union lines for the defense of their rights. This episode of Spanish praetorianism is so closely dovetailed with the historical events determined by the First World War that it had better be left for a later chapter. We would merely point out here that the movement known as the Committees of Defense *(Juntas de Defensa)* was one of the most monstrous aberrations which the history of Spanish institutions can register. The army officers took a weapon from the arsenal of syndicalist labor and turned against the state the force which the state had entrusted to them. The moral effect of this truly anarchist attack on the very source of authority and of institutions was to be so deep that institutions have been falling ever since.

And yet . . . experience shows that an army is an indispensable element in the *internal* life of Spain. It would indeed be difficult to explain how an utterly useless public body could gain such an ascendancy over the nation. The army provides that minimum of outer and mechanical order without which the evolution toward inner and spiritual order, which is the true meaning of progress, cannot take place. The tendency toward disorder springs in the Spanish people from the interplay of certain essential features of its character. Normally passive and quiescent, the Spaniard is given to outbursts of activity and expression when roused by events. Political leaders know this well, for phrases such as "It is necessary to heat up passions" *(Hay que calentar las pasiones)* or "The atmosphere is heated up" *(El ambiente está caldeado),* which in an English political environment would sound incomprehensible, are a matter of course in Spanish life. Then the extreme character of Spanish idealism, that swing between the *nothing* of pessimistic depression and the *all* of optimistic exaltation which typifies it, multiplies in the Spaniard the energies of his energetic moments. Finally, there is in Spain a tendency to split and form separate antagonistic groups always apt to solve their differences in civil strife.

An army in the midst of such a people is an indispensable organ of State. It keeps order and provides a neutral national environment in which all particular tendencies are merged and mixed. Incidentally it performs a certain amount of service as an adult school, giving elementary education to those recruits who come to it in an illiterate condition. This detail suggests a curious parallel between the army and the Church. Both are useful as institutions in a country in which institutions are scarce and precarious owing to the excessive vigor of individualism; the one is the main agent of spiritual development, the other the main agent of order and stability. Yet, mark the tragic inversion of the normal ways of life: while the Church, by its bigoted and superstitious outlook, turns its tremendous strength against the spiritual development of the country, the army by its overbearing and undisciplined attitude toward civil law saps the very roots of order and precipitates the decay of institutions beginning with that of the army itself.

Thus during the first part of the reign of Alfonso XIII there were already discernible the main lines of modern Spain's perennial problem: how to create institutions under the "protection" of the two existing ones, both of which were neglecting, misunderstanding or tragically inverting their own duties and aims.

CHAPTER 15

THE CATALAN QUESTION

THE PSYCHOLOGICAL BACKGROUND

The Catalan question, and in a lesser degree the questions raised by the movements of local consciousness in the Basque provinces and in Galicia, are among the most difficult yet also the most fertile in Spanish contemporary public life. They have been complicated to an incredible extent by the admixture of half-baked notions from the realms of anthropology, art, literature, history and economics. Thus the question whether Catalonia is, or is not, a separate *nation,* the question whether the Catalans are, or are not, a separate *race,* and other disquisitions equally puerile on both sides have been allowed to befog an issue which circumstances make difficult and character makes thorny, but which, on the whole, is clear.

In the opening chapters we had occasion to see how the Peninsula strongly asserts a fundamental unity comprising considerable variety, and how these two same features observable in nature apply also to man. We found in the Peninsula a common general feature, the keynote of which was a lofty inaccessibility, and along with it a variety of environments separated by such obstacles to communications as to constitute a kind of inner inaccessibility between the parts, analogous to the inaccessibility of the whole. Similarly we found that the Spanish character stood out with a vigorous individualism which puts it in a class by itself in the Western world, while within the nation, regional characters stood distinctly separate with a mutual differentiation, a mutual assertion of individualism which drove inward, into the very soul of the nation, the vigorous individualism wherewith the nation confronted the outward world.

Such is the true origin of the centrifugal movements to be observed in certain parts of Spain. And it is not by mere accident that these movements occur in Catalonia, the Basque provinces and Galicia, for it is precisely in these regions of Spain that we may observe the clearest indication of a distinctive individualized genius. A language, in so far as it is the creation of a people, is like a signal to show that there is a people there. That Spanish and French are alike does not mean that the Spanish and the French peoples are alike, since the likeness of the two languages is not due to the two peoples, but to the common historical factor of the Roman conquest. That French and Spanish are different does mean that Spain and France are psychologically different, for the differences between the two languages born of the same stock are obviously due to the difference between the genius of the two peoples.

The claim of Catalonia to be considered as something more than a mere region arises therefore, quite clearly from the fact that she speaks a language of her own. (The attempts of some Castilians to describe Catalan as a dialect of Castilian are too silly to deserve more than contemptuous mention.) Even here, arguments and discussions are seriously wasted on such questions as to whether Catalan comes from Provençal or from somewhere else. Surely the case is clear. Catalan comes from Catalonia.

But what is Catalan and what is Catalonia? For Catalanists

of the nationalistic school the answer is clear: Catalonia proper, or the county or earldom, as it is called, plus the kingdom of Valencia and the Balearic Islands. Some, carrying their enthusiastic logic beyond the frontiers, go as far north as the Roussillon, and, if they do not add to the map the town of Alghero, in Sardinia, in which Catalan is still spoken, they do not forget to mention it in their inventory. Such is in actual fact the *philological* Catalonia. Valencia, however, thoroughly dislikes to be considered as anything else than Valencia. Her language differs sufficiently from Catalan to be entitled to a separate grammar and vocabulary, if her literati cared to build them up as the Catalans have done. But, despite their proud assertions to the contrary, it is doubtful whether Valencian would have remained a separate dialect if there had been a few centuries of Catalan culture in Barcelona. It certainly differs less from Catalan than French dialects from Paris French or Yorkshire English from king's English. Yet, in so far as Valencian can be explained historically by the repopulation of the Valencian lands with Catalan settlers after their conquest by James I of Aragon and Catalonia, the existence of such a language in Valencia may not be so strong a justification of the "Catalanity" of the Valencian peoples. The phenomenon here would be at least partly similar to the common Latinity of French, Spanish and Italian due to the accident of a common Roman conquest.

Leaving aside for the present the Basque language, there exist then in the Peninsula three main lanuages: Castilian in the center; Portuguese in the Southwest (with the Gallegan dialect in the Northwest), and Catalan in the Northeast (with the Valencian dialect in the Southeast). This fact has been interpreted as follows in another of the author's books:

> Seen in its entirety, above the historical and political contingencies which have obscured its intrinsic unity, the Spanish Peninsula appears as one well-defined spiritual entity. This fact the Portuguese critics are beginning to realize and the Catalan critics to forget. Both movements are historically logical, for, while Portugal has outlived the period

of her affirmation as a separate sub-entity within the Spanish wider unity, Catalonia is, on the contrary, but beginning a struggle for asserting her own personality within the Peninsula and putting it beyond reach of attack from political prejudice. Strife psychology is never the ideal atmosphere for thought, and so it will be found that Catalan critics do not always realize the true strength of the ties which bind them to the Peninsula, nay, of the roots which make them part and essence of the spirit of the Peninsula as the land they inhabit is part of its body. But the spiritual unity of Spain does not depend on the vagaries of critics, being grounded on deeper realities. Yet these vagaries do serve a useful purpose, since they bring into relief a fact no less important than that which they tend to obscure, namely, that Spain is not a simple, but a complex unity, a trinity composed of a Western, a Central, and an Eastern modality, the norms of which respectively are Portugal, Castile and Catalonia.

Three languages (or groups of languages) embody these three spiritual modalities of the Spanish race. In the West, the Atlantic modality finds its expression in the Portuguese, of Latin languages the most tender and melodious. In the Centre, the Continental modality inspires that stately Castilian in which strength and grace are as harmoniously combined as tragedy and comedy in good drama. To the East, the Mediterranean modality shapes Catalan and its dialects, languages as supple and soft as clay, as vivid as painter's palettes, as receptive as the still waters of the clean sea which bathes the shores where they are spoken.

In literature and the arts the character of each of these three varieties of Spain may be defined by the predominance of a purely aesthetic tendency. This predominant or specific tendency is in the West lyrical, epic-dramatic in the Centre, and plastic in the East. The lyrical attitude is personal and has for its object the artist himself. The artist sees life as a flow and listens to the murmurs which rise as this flow falls on his own soul. The dramatic attitude is passive and has for its object the world of men. The artist conceives life as an endless drama between character and destiny The plastic tendency is active. The hand stretches towards matter, eager to impress upon it the form obscurely felt in the artist's soul. Matter is therefore the object of the plastic creator, and his way of approach is through the outer crust towards the inner meaning of things. Thus we find in the Eastern modality of the Spanish race the qualities and the defects of the plastic tendency. The Catalan possesses a firm hold on the material aspects of things and a determination to stamp his own personality on the clay of life which can be felt, for instance, in certain cadences of his language. Let the sounds be compared of the words *génie* and *seny*, and the difference will be perceived between a geometric line drawn on a white paper by a mathematician and the heavy impress of a sculptor's thumb on a piece of soft clay. There is always in the Catalan an implicit form which demands as its right some matter in which to become embodied, thus passing from mind into space. Hence a certain sense of order which has misled some people, amongst them many Catalans, into believing Catalonia to be a kind of French spiritual *enclave* in Spain. But the French sense of order is the outcome of a logical type of mind, while the Catalan sense of order is due to a plastic feeling. The French sense of order can be put on paper, is successive, and has but two dimensions, and is felt instantaneously; while the Catalan sense of order is three-dimensional, like the feelings of up and down, back and front, top, middle, and base, symmetry, and, most of all, the feeling that guides the arrangement of useless objects on a mantelpiece.

Yet this feeling of order, though plastic and not logical, does give Catalonia the position of a *liaison* country between Europe and the rest of Spain. Europe, that is the West-Central-European nucleus which more consciously and intelligently represents the ideals of the white race, has chosen the Apollinian rather than the Dionysian path for its way up to the Temple of Mysteries, and, though careful not to reject Dionysian testimonies, yet looks on them with Apollonian eyes. Both the Western and Central types of the Spanish genius partake of the Dionysian rather than of the Apollonian nature. Not so Catalonia. If not always in actual life, at least in her ideals, she is Greek; Greek in that "classic" sense which corresponds to a literary rather than to a truly historical view of the Hellenic nature, Greek not as Aeschylus, but as Goethe. The most original and vigorous of modern Catalan minds, Eugenio d'Ors, has expressed this ideal in a striking little passage:

It is impossible to speak about Goethe coolly. We are troubled by something which is difficult to confess yet impossible to disown. We are troubled by *envy.*

The worst kind of envy, for it does not aim at attributes, but at the substance. Usually we envy great figures some one of their properties or qualities. We should like to possess their eminent gift or their priceless booty, but without ceasing to be ourselves. . . . But our passion towards Goethe is more grave, for its tempts us to the blasphemy of renouncing our own personality.

We should like to *speak* like Demosthenes, to *write* like Boccaccio, to *know* as much as Leibniz, to *possess,* like Napoleon, a vast empire, or like Ruelbeck, a Botanic Garden . . . We should like to *be* Goethe.

All Olympian souls see in this Olympian the image of their own selves elevated to its maximum power, glory and serenity.

Here, the Central European ideal of Catalonia is asserted with all the ingenuity and, be it noted, the "three-dimensional" precision of the Catalan plastic mind. This choice of Goethe as a model is typical, for neither Castile nor Portugal could ever consider Goethe as their ideal. Rather they would turn to Shakespeare, despite his lack of "Olympian" manners. And the reason is that while Western and Central Spain aim at character, Catalonia aims at culture.

Catalonia is determined to plod on the road to progress. Leaving the contemplation of Eternity to the Castilian, she is well content with Time, and particularly with the present time as manifest in the sundry objects of everyday life. The Mediterranean Spaniard is no ascetic. He feels the *joie de vivre* and lives. He does not seek the high summits of speculation, and finds enough grounds for intellectual enjoyment in the many sights of the valley below. He approaches these sights precisely as sights, not as symbols of some higher or deeper significance, but merely as objects the shape and colour of which are in themelves a sufficient attraction. The Catalan is sensuous.

A Spaniard he still is, in that his nature is synthetic rather than analytic. But he differs from the two other types in that he develops along the line of talent and intellect rather than along that of genius and spirit. Thus Catalonia is—mentally—a land of plains at a good medium level, below which and above which fall and rise the inequalities of Castilian genius. The Catalan talent is hard-working and purposeful. It knows the use of the file and of that literary instrument which Flaubert called *gueuloir*. Spanish still in that it improvises, it is no longer so in that it tries to refine the material thrown up by improvisation—a sculptor endeavouring to chisel Greek statuettes in lava.

As it moves south, the Catalan genius, without losing its main plastic tendency, changes considerably in every other respect. Valencia is a land of flame and colour, painted in vivid tones—the gold and green of its orange-groves, the ochre of its earth, the pale blue of its skies, the dazzling white of its low houses over which now and then towers an eastern-looking cupola covered with dark-blue glazed tiles. Here beauty is so abundant on the surface of the world that men forget how to seek for it below. Anyone is an artist, anything a work of art. Thus Valencia disperses its genius and gains in surface what it loses in depth. It is a land of painters, with a decorative talent and a fine feeling for the values of light and quality over the surface of things. When power is added, work of great descriptive value may result. Thus, Blasco Ibáñez.

There is to the south of Valencia a land historically within the kingdom, but spiritually a thing apart. It is the province of Alicante. North of it stretch the colour and flame of Valencia proper; east, the Latin sea; north-west, La Mancha, the very lands in which Don Quixote was born. Just as Galicia is the transition between lyrical Portugal and dramatic Castile, so Alicante is the transition between dramatic Castile and the plastic East. Here, the spirit of the Center touches the spirit of the East; Castile looks on the Mediterranean. The dramatic feeling of man emerges from its depths of concentration and meets on the surface the plastic sense of things. This delicately poised zone of the Spanish spirit is represented in Spanish letters by two contemporary authors: Azorín and Gabriel Miró.[1]

So much for first facts and their obvious conclusions. The Catalan nationalists have endeavored to draw from them other inferences of a somewhat bolder kind. At a time when a minority of Catalanists believed that, by pouring abuse and contempt on Castilian history, character, politics and administration, Catalan progressive ways would stand out more clearly before the world, a time which coincided with much European nonsense about races and progress, a famous Dr. Robert, who became mayor of Barcelona, made a stir by declaring that the Catalan skull was bigger than that of the mere Spaniard. There was an uproar in the Castilian press—in all save a small minority of good-humored people who realized that this difference in size might be merely momentary. But as a matter of fact the eminent doctor was talking through his skull. If there is one thing which recent anthropological studies have shown beyond dispute it is that there is no difference whatsoever between the Catalan "race" and the remaining "races" of Spain. The reader is referred to the second chapter, in which the data available on this point

[1] *The Genius of Spain.* Oxford University Press, 1923.

have been analyzed. He may choose to observe for himself or to register the observations that have been made as to language, sayings, habits and events, and he will certainly come to the same conclusion.

Since language is, after all, the starting point of our opinions, we may as well turn to it for further findings on the matter of character and race in the Peninsula.[2] Now, at first sight, there is no doubt that Catalan does differ profoundly from Castilian and that it suggests a certain outward likeness to French. Gone the poise and balance which Castilian owes to the normal place of the accent on the center of gravity of its words. Catalan drops those final vowels which give their roundness to Castilian and thus provides a linguistic suggestion of shortness, a clipped feeling which, as with French, we are at liberty to connect with the closeness in matters of money by common consent attributed to Catalans in the Spanish world. Yet while French distributes its accent evenly on every syllable of the word, Catalan, like the remaining Spanish languages, possesses a strong tonic accent. It is a language with a definite beating rhythm in direct contradiction to the subtle and soft rhythm which the French language derives from the evenness of its stresses. Moreover, the Catalan dominant vowel is typically different from the French, and makes of Catalan an unmistakably Spanish language. In French, as we know, the dominant vowel is *e*, the moderate and middle vowel *par excellence,* as distinct from the over-subtle and intentional *i* (ee) typical of Italian as from the full and sonorous *a* and *o* typical of Castilian. The characteristic Catalan vowel is an open *ae*, not a pure vowel but a sound with a definite movement in it and with that characteristic sense of fling which we know to be one of the most direct manifestations of the Spanish genius. Spontaneous, integral, personal, this Catalan *ae* is like an ever recurring, nay an almost permanent diphthong. Now a diphthong is the most un-French linguistic feature, the most characteristically Spanish. No one who has heard Catalan spoken, even by the choice minority which endeavors to submit

[2] *Cf.* chapter on languages, in *Englishmen, Frenchmen, Spaniards.* Oxford University Press, 1928.

it to a severe discipline, can doubt that Catalan is a Spanish language, direct, spontaneous, vigorous, fully manifested and popular—that it is, in fact, the language of a man of passion.

This is further confirmed by the fact that Catalan presents that exclusively Spanish feature: the double translation of the verb "to be," one meaning "to be in essence," and the other "to be in state." Now this feature corresponds closely to the most profound characteristic of the Spanish nation, namely, the distinction between that which is essential and that which is passing, between being itself, which is permanent; and circumstances, which are merely ephemeral. The existence of this distinction in the Catalan language would suffice to establish it as one of the languages of the Spanish family, as Spanish indeed as Castilian, Gallegan or Portuguese. Another feature which confirms this solidarity is the fact that the differences which, taken altogether, constitute the two separate languages, Catalan and Castilian, do not occur abruptly, but by a gradual merging of Castilian into Catalan through Aragonese, which can be studied in philological maps. Indeed, the matter is self-evident, and is only mentioned here in view of the somewhat rash statements that have been made now and then when, for political reasons—and not very wise at that—an excessive distinction is drawn between the Catalan character and nature and the character and nature of the other Spanish peoples.

But what then about that "clipped" feeling? It does constitute the most distinctive feature of the Catalan language. It must be coupled with the open *ae* in order to be appraised in its right value, for while it suggests that sense of thrift and even parsimony which corresponds in French psychology to the French *e*, the Catalan *ae* reminds us that there is a certain openness in Catalan psychology, a readiness to live and to enjoy life as it comes without an excessive consideration for the future, without that foresight which is typical of the French nation. It is true that Spain is full of stories in which the Catalan does the wrong thing in matters of money. At first sight they suggest Scotch stories; yet Catalan stories and Scotch stories are, for all their superficial likeness, as far apart as Sabadell and Aberdeen.

Scotch stories are tales of niggardliness, or at any rate of nearness. They suggest a people naturally led to think of economy by a miserly nature.[3] Catalonia, though, is plentiful. She has a splendid sun; she has water. She is industrious. Life is easy for the Catalan who cares to work. The stories told against him are not precisely stories of niggardliness, but of self-interest, inclined to be uncompromising and self-assertive. The typical Catalan story is that of the Barcelona shopkeeper who was a communist, for, he said, "With what I shall get on the day all wealth is distributed equally *plus* the house I have in the country, I shall be quite comfortably off."

Absurd caricatures, no doubt, but let us not undervalue caricatures. *When the river roars it carries water,* says a Spanish proverb, typical of a country in which rivers are not expected to carry water as a matter of course. When *vox populi* insists on a particular feature of a whole people we may suspect *Vox Dei* speaks in it. These stories, however, do not say that the Catalan is mean, thrifty or miserly. They say two things: that, like all Mediterraneans, he has an eye for material things, for the pleasures of life and for the means whereby they can be enjoyed; and that the Catalan is very much alive to the claims of his own self, that he is an individualist. Now the first of these judgments was to be expected from the Castilian, whose outlook on life is more spartan even in the midst of enchanting Andalusia; but the second is startling. Here is a people of fierce individualists witnessing to the individualism of another people living in their midst. The individualism of the Catalan towers, therefore, even above the individualism of the remaining Spaniards. Our conclusion is that the Catalan is an ultra-individualist.

Such a conclusion, based on the indirect and spontaneous signs detected in Spanish life, is, of course, implicit in our interpretation of the language. "The language of a man of passion," we said. And, of course, for the fact is evident, a man of passion living by the Mediterranean. In our opinion, then, the key

[3] But by no means a miserly people. The thrift of the Scotch is saving of *things,* it has a social inspiration. It is utilitarianism, not egoism. It can be most generous.

factors of the Catalan question may be drawn from this statement which at the beginning of the chapter would have been
a truism, but which now is—we hope—an ascertained truth:
that the Catalan is a Spaniard living on the shores of the Mediterranean. It follows that his substantial features are Spanish
while some of his secondary characteristics differ from those
of his co-Spaniards, thereby constituting a sub-type within the
Spanish family. We shall see that this inherent Spanishness of
the Catalan, far from being a favorable factor, is one of the
most serious obstacles toward a solution of Catalanism.

Curiously enough, the Catalan out-Spaniards the Spaniard in
many ways, and far from being, as some of the theoreticians of
Catalanisms fondly imagine, a European exiled in an African
Spain, he is an Iberian showing some of the typical Iberian
features more markedly than the other Peninsular peoples. Thus,
while we know all Spaniards to be essentially men of passion,
we also know that in most of the Peninsular types this "pathetic"
life which flows in them is kept normally in a quiescent state
by a kind of stoic reserve and a sense of balance. But in the
Mediterranean type the man of passion is more given to letting
out, and he easily becomes passionate as well. Reserve is not
so typical of the Catalan as of the Iberian in general. In a
sense, that criticism of the Catalan which one can feel implicitly
in Spanish stories about him means, precisely, that he is lacking in reserve and does not hold life in as well as the other
Iberians do.

The Catalan is as prone as the Castilian, if not more so,
to mix the whole of his personality with his thought, so that
his ideas are apt to be synthetic, personal, disconnected in time
and space and dictated by his passionate sense of life to an
equal, nay, to a greater extent than is the case with the other
Spaniards. Of this we shall have abundant proof when studying the intellectual history of the Catalan movement. But,
though essentially a Spaniard, the Catalan is a Mediterranean.
He lives plastically, he lives in the realm of movements and
forms. And he breathes from his birth the atmosphere of commerce, trade and exchange, which makes of the Latin Sea a

kind of market place surrounded with busy shops on all its
shores. The Spaniard who lives in such a market place must
surely differ from him who lives facing the deserts of mid-
Castile, or on the shores of the immense Atlantic Ocean. He
is more given to rationalizing his passions and intuitions, and
since he is rich in them, as all true Spaniards are, his intellect
has a tougher task to perform and he becomes ingenious. The
Catalan is, therefore, more inclined to use his mind than the
Castilian; he is a more acute contriver of intellectual systems,
a more felicitous artist of words, a better orator. For all his
intellectual application, however, the Catalan is no intellectualist
in the French sense. He is intuitive, as are all Spaniards, and
no more methodical than the rest. The stimulus of the Catalan
intellect comes from his desire to rationalize passion and intuition. It often leads him to wild flights of imagination, characteristic of a passionate type and inconceivable in the moderate
genuine intellectual. We shall see some effects of his ingenious
imagination when dealing with the political aspects of the Catalan movement.

Finally, in the realm of action, we shall find the Catalan a
typical Spaniard in his individualism. For instance, a glance
at the statistics of limited liability companies founded in Barcelona, Madrid and Bilbao in any one year will prove that in
Barcelona the average capital per company is much smaller
than in the Castilian or the Basque city, for the Catalan limited
liability company generally represents the efforts of one man or,
at best, of a very small number of friends. This remark applies
particularly to the average capital per bank, which is distinctly
smaller in Catalonia than in the Basque country or in Castile or
in other provinces, such as Coruña. A sidelight to very much
the same effect comes from the most authoritative of quarters
Señor Cambó, undoubtedly the greatest modern political talent
of Catalonia and perhaps of all Spain. In the course of a
masterly study of the Catalan question Señor Cambó says:
"When it is a matter of managing a private business it would
be difficult to find more gifted men than Catalans. For the
management of enterprises in which interests of many persons

are concerned the leader will very rarely be found in Catalonia. That is why, among us, limited liability companies live so precarious a life." Evidently the Catalan can throw no stones at the other Spaniards on the score of individualism. This is borne out again by the fact that, contrary to what is generally believed, the hold of foreign capital and enterprise on Catalonia is much bigger than on Castile, the Basque country or Andalusia; and, what is more significant still, that there are more Basque and Castilian enterprises in Catalonia than Catalan enterprises in Castile or the Basque country. While on this matter of the comparative progressiveness of the Catalan and the other Spanish types, it may be as well to point out that Catalonia is not at the head of Spain in education. In the list of provinces drawn up according to the number of inhabitants who can read and write, the first is so typically Castilian a country as Santander; the second, a Basque country, Alava; the third, Madrid; the fourth, no less Castilian a province than Palencia (notorious, by the way, as one of the provinces in which political bosses are all-powerful in electioneering); the fifth, another Castilian province, Burgos; the sixth, Segovia, also typically Castilian; the seventh, a Basque province, Guipúzcoa; the eighth, another Basque province, Vizcaya; and we meet with the first Catalan province, Barcelona, in the ninth place on the list; the other three Catalan provinces are seventeenth (Gerona), twenty-first (Lérida), and twenty-second (Tarragona). It cannot be argued that Catalonia is not free to develop her education as she wishes, because the matter of primary education is entirely regulated by municipal law, and the municipalities in Catalonia are as free as those of the remainder of Spain to develop their educational policy as they wish.

It seems clear, therefore, that no *substantial* difference singles out the variety of Spaniard to be found in the northeast of the Peninsula. We discern, of course, in him the dispersive element which is characteristic of the individualistic type. It is most noticeable in Catalan life as between persons. It constitutes the mainspring of the Catalan movement itself, when, transferred to the group, it gives rise to Catalanism from its regionalistic to its nationalistic forms. Separateness, a strong consciousness of the distinctive and differential existence of the self, is the truly Spanish tendency which we find in Catalanism. And thus we are led to the paradoxical yet inescapable conclusion that the purest types of "Spanishhood" to be found in Catalonia are precisely those who, carrying to the extreme, deny that they are Spaniards at all and dream of Catalonia as a separate independent nation.

We may test some of the conclusions by consulting our Catalan friends themselves. Señor Rovira y Virgili is the undisputed theoretician of Catalan nationalism. It would be difficult to find in the whole Peninsula a more Spanish type than this man who sincerely believes he is not a Spaniard at all. A Spaniard in his qualities, his almost puritan disinterestedness in the service of ideas (i.e. his quixotic love of his Dulcinea), his uncompromising faith, his extreme views, his intellectual honesty; a Spaniard in his defects also, in that way of thinking which alters the shape of facts under the heat of intellectual passion, in the lack of political sense, the inability to see any incoherence in his reasoning, the eruption of disconnected ideas as from a volcano. Señor Rovira y Virgili is explaining how the Catalans, under the Crown of Aragon, felt foreign to the Aragonese, in order to draw the conclusion that Catalonia was already a nation with a strong national consciousness. He forgets that exactly the same feeling prevailed between Leonese and Castilians, nay, a keener feeling still, for, after all, Aragon and Catalonia never came to blows, while the rivalry between León and Castile caused much bloodshed. That the Catalans felt the Aragonese to be strangers, that they even felt a national consciousness in that period, proves, therefore, absolutely nothing. What does prove something is the historical detail which Señor Rovira y Virgili enlists in his service: "James I, for example, says in his chronicle that the Castilians *son de molta ufana e erguylloses* (are proud and haughty people)." And in the same work, describing one of the nineteenth-century theoreticians of the movement, our author says: "Almirall was an all-round Catalan, a Catalan on his four sides, a *catalanísimo* spirit. His temperament, his virtues, his very defects are those of our people. He is a magnificent paragon of our race. He was, above all, rich in that sense of dignity, in that haughtiness (*orgullo*), if you prefer, which is the marrow of the Catalan character." We would point out not only the obvious conclusion from the two texts, i.e. that the feature which Señor Rovira y Virgili considers as characteristic of the Catalans is that which struck King James in the Castilians; but also, what is still more telling, the profoundly Spanish character of the style and of the mental attitude of Señor Rovira y Virgili as revealed in this quotation. That attitude of haughtiness and defiance which swells it—and all the page from which it is taken—is at the core of the problem on both sides, tragically preventing unity of thought precisely because of the underlying unity of temperament. Let us give yet another example, if only because it enriches the discussion of the subject itself. The ambition of the Catalanists is to round off Greater Catalonia by including Valencia and the Balearic Islands in it. But so Spanish is the Catalan race that Catalonia, as a center of unity, meets in Valencia with the same centrifugal force wherewith Castile meets in Catalonia. The Valencians do not want to hear any "Greater Catalonia" nonsense. Just as a few silly Castilians claim that Catalan is but a dialect of Spanish, a few Catalans claim, on better grounds, that Valencian is a dialect of Castilian. This, however, Valencia stoutly denies. The librarian of the University of Valencia said to Mr. J. B. Trend (in Castilian, of course): "It is as grave a heresy to Catalanize Valencian as to Castilianize it." Note the word *heresy*. And a young Valencian writer, Señor Durán, who endeavored to espouse the Catalanist cause in Valencia, had to leave his country and settle in Barcelona "in view of the hostility of his countrymen," says Señor Rovira y Virgili himself, too blind, however, to see the strong Spanish spirit which pervades all these facts.

Naturally enough, similar conditions prevail on the other side, i.e. on the Castilian side. The bulk of the nation feels the Catalan problem obscurely, but the two old kingdoms of Castile and Aragon feel it definitely. Historical factors will be considered later, but we may anticipate here that Aragon and Castile were the two stages in the process by which Catalonia was absorbed into a higher, i.e. a more universal, nationhood. Castile, in particular, has within her a conception of imperium not unlike that of old Rome, nearer perhaps to the Roman genius in this respect than anything Europe has produced with the single exception of Great Britain. The psychological situation thus developed may be compared to a kind of tug-of-war. Catalonia pulls away from the group; Castile pulls toward the group in order to hold her in. And as there is much temperament on both sides, this pulling goes on accompanied with a good deal of recrimination.

Generally speaking, there is more mind in Catalonia and more will in Castile. The fertile and subtle wits of the Mediterranean break their successive frothy waves against the cliffs of the stubborn tableland. The somewhat stolid and steady Castilian looks upon the brilliant Easterner with very much the same dogged-puzzled-suspicious determination wherewith the Englishman meets the onslaughts of an over-clever Frenchman. But the Catalan is no more a Frenchman than the Castilian is an Englishman, and temperament makes him now rise into fury, now sink into pessimism, now let himself go to a kind of quiescent and brooding patience. At bottom the difficulty comes from lack of mutual confidence; the Catalan mistrusts the Castilian's sense of imperium and is convinced of the Castilian's inability to understand freedom; while the Castilian suspects that the Catalan is essentially uncooperative and dispersive, and that therefore he will use whatever freedom is granted him to break up that national unity which Castile built up by centuries of hard work, enlightened now and then by fits of statesmanship. Conflicts of confidence can only be cured by time. The objective solution toward which time can work, and probably is working, must be inspired by that formula, somewhat obvious in appearance yet significant if every word in it be granted its full meaning: the Catalan is a Spaniard who lives on the shores of the Mediterranean.

CHAPTER 16

THE CATALAN QUESTION

THE HISTORICAL BACKGROUND

History is a common meadow where everyone can make hay, says a Spanish dictum. The history of Catalonia is no exception to the rule. Yet here, it must be owned, the Catalanist hay is more strongly flavored than the Castilian, for Castilian historians, including the Catalans and even some Portuguese (such as Melo), who wrote histories of Spain never saw that there was anything to prove or disprove by history; and the achievements of Catalonia were never minimized or passed over by them; for the simple reason that they naturally considered them as their own. Not so with those Catalans who have been led by their apostolate to use history on behalf of the Catalanist cause. No serious progress can be made in the Catalan question without a sound historical approach. We hold that even the sympathetic approach of most Castilian historians is not satisfactory, for

194

Catalanists are entitled to miss in it a sufficient (subconscious) recognition of the distinctive national spirit of the Catalan nation. What is required is an outlook which, while avoiding the quiet subconscious absorption of Catalonia by Castilian history, should also keep its head above the clouds of passion which have obscured the most obvious facts in the eyes of extreme Catalanists.

Catalonia does not seem to emerge clearly from the mass of Spain with any definite outline of her own, either under the Roman Empire or during the Visigothic period. Her destinies were identical to those of other parts of Spain. Under the Romans she belonged to the Tarraconensis, a province the capital of which was Tarragona, now that of one of the provinces of Catalonia. However, this Roman province included not merely the present Catalonia, but a considerable proportion of non-Catalan Spain, which varied from time to time; while Valencia never belonged to this Roman province, being part of the Carthaginensis. This period has left many traces, not the least of which is the wealth of Roman remains found in Tarragona and far from fully explored yet. Some Catalan authors have endeavored to take the Roman connection as a basis for special claims to a superior Latinity. Such claims would not appear to amount to much. In the turbulent period of the Visigoths the Catalan region was not differentiated in any way from the rest of Spain. Catalonia, as a word, began in the twelfth century. When, toward the end of the eighth century, the Moors invaded the Peninsula, Catalonia fell to them. But, as in the case of Asturias and Navarra, she soon became one of the centers of Christian recovery, with this notable difference, that having in her Pyrenees several fairly easy ways of access from France, the Christian recovery in Catalonia began under French stimulation. After an unsuccessful attempt by Charlemagne in 785, Louis le Débonnaire took Barcelona in 801 and made it the chief town of a mark which, be it noted, was styled the Spanish Mark without the slightest regard for the feelings of present-day separatists. In 809 the earl in charge of the mark, Wilfred, rebelled against the French king and Catalonia started on her historical career as an independent unit.

She became, that is, one of the small independent units through which the national spirit of Spain was emerging from the Moorish invasion, even as submerged land reappears here and there as seemingly separated islands when the waters begin to recede. There was, properly speaking, no Catalonia then. There was a congeries of counties, i.e. districts under the sway of counts or earls, the most powerful of whom was the count of Barcelona, for he held an ancient city (it had been founded by Hamilcar Barca, the Carthaginese general) rich in the arts of industry and commerce. Gradually the Count of Barcelona absorbed the other counties of the land, mostly by marriage and inheritance. Still he remained Count of Barcelona, even when his sway extended over practically the whole of what is now known as Catalonia and over extensive lands in what is now known as France. With Ramón Berenguer I (1035-76) the true history of Catalonia may be said to begin. In actual fact Catalonia was not conscious of her name and he endeavored to develop unity through order by bringing the customs of the country into some kind of expressed form. This was the origin of the famous *Usatges,* or usages, a systematic codification of feudal customs. The *Usatges* codified and legislated also on political questions, such as the duties and rights of the Count of Barcelona and the obligation laid on every man to participate in military defense in case of danger; on civil matters, such as the protection of strangers; on matters of penal law and of procedure.

This time saw also the development of seafaring activity which was to make the Catalans familiar figures throughout the Mediterranean Sea, eastern as well as western. The successors of Ramón Berenguer I, his twin sons Ramón Berenguer II and Berenguer Ramón II, must be mentioned, if only because they were brought into close relationship with Castile in ways which deserve to be noticed. They inherited the country *pro indiviso,* but soon decided to divide it, a provision by which Ramón Berenguer II, a brave, though kindly and well-disposed person, failed to appease the jealousy and ambition of his brother, so that when he was murdered public opinion had strong suspicions of a fratricide. This did not prevent Berenguer Ramón from remaining the sole possessor of the crown. His dealings with the Moorish kings who surrounded his estate and held many of the lands of what is now Catalonia, brought him into conflict with El Cid, that noble and picturesque hero of the Castilian Middle Ages who enters history through the decorative gates of literary epic. The Cid, exiled by the King of Castile, Alfonso VI (for the habit of exiling good citizens is an early one with Spanish kings), lived the life of a free-lance magnate, conquering Spain from the Moors by means of that curious technique, a combination of raiding, settling, warring and establishing protectorates over weak Moslem princes, which is only now beginning to be fully understood, thanks to the unrivaled scholarship of Señor Menéndez Pidal. In the course of their respective operations, the Cid and Berenguer Ramón came to blows and the Catalan count had the worst of the fight, was taken prisoner and then left free with that mixture of political shrewdness and personal generosity which the contemporary poet saw, and historians confirm in the Castilian hero. Moreover, the Cid, as the medieval poet makes him say in truly magnificent words:

> Contra la mar salada conpezó de guerrear
> A oriente exe el sol e tornós a esa part.

(Toward the salty sea he began to carry war; in the orient rises the sun and he turned toward that part.) Castile, represented by her free-lance, conquered Valencia from the Moors. The King of Castile, Alfonso VI, had been her *de facto* ruler for years through one of his lieutenants whose name is often met with in the *Poema del Cid*—Alfar Hañez. It will be seen how Castile in her all-embracing policy did not neglect the eastern borders. Alfonso VI was active in all the directions of the compass and his efforts were to be seen also toward Aragon, still under Moorish occupation. Valencia was held by the Cid, and later by his widow, till 1109, when it fell to the Moors again. It was not till 1156 that the kings of Castile and Aragon, Alfonso VII and Ramón Berenguer IV, agreed that the conquest of Valencia should be left to the Crown of Aragon—an agreement which did not prevent St. Ferdinand (of Castile) from accepting the homage of vassalage from the Moorish King of Valencia in 1225. This contradiction may be merely superficial, for from the times of Ferdinand I (father of Alfonso VI) the King of Castile claimed a kind of sovereignity over all the princes, Christian or Moslem, of the Peninsula, the traditional motive power for which came from the Visigothic Crown through the Crown of León. This interesting point is made abundantly clear in Señor Menéndez Pidal's book on the Cid; for Alfonso VI, the Cid's sovereign, paid particular attention to it, styling himself Emperor, *Constitutus Imperator Super Omnes Hispanie Nationes.* The other Spanish princes acknowledged this claim and—to come back to our count of Barcelona—it is significant that, when the followers of his murdered brother challenged Count Berenguer Ramón II to a judicial duel, they did so before the King of Castile, Alfonso VI. For anyone aware of the close relationship which existed then in Spain between dueling and the judicial authority of the king—a kind of umpireship in an actual duel of words, arguments or arms—this fact could not be more telling, and it explains other events of equal import which occurred later.

With Ramón Berenguer III the Great and Ramón Berenguer IV, Catalonia became an important Mediterranean power, maybe the most important, and spread considerably beyond the Pyrenees. The Count of Barcelona felt that order at sea as well as on land was necessary for the prosperity of his country, and the Mediterranean was then infested with Norman and Saracen pirates. Ramón Berenguer III was active at sea, and tried, though without success, to settle in the Balearic Islands. His successor, Ramón Berenguer IV, followed the same policy.

Meanwhile, by the joint efforts of the kings of Navarra and of Castile, a new center of Christian expansion had been set up in Aragon. The Crown of Aragon was then on a head unwilling to wear it. Ramiro II had been taken out of the monastery in order to reign. He came, married, had a daughter, married her to Ramón Berenguer IV of Barcelona at the early age of two, and went back to his monastery, leaving the crown in the hands of his Catalan son-in-law, who took the title of Prince and Dominator of Aragon. But at his death (1162) Ramón V, his son, became King of Aragon under the name of Alfonso II (I of Catalonia). This is the moment when Catalonia becomes Aragon. It is but natural that Catalan historians should deplore the change in name. "Catalonia and Aragon now united under the government of the same monarchs," says a contemporary Catalan historian, "maintained their complete autonomy. For Aragon the union with Catalonia was advantageous; it meant the advent of her name to cosmopolitan and imperialistic life. On the other hand, for Catalonia the union with Aragon meant a constant fight against the Aragonese tendencies inimical to all Mediterranean expansion, particularistic and inclined to privilege, as well as the possibility of union with Castile. It meant also through a mere superiority in hierarchy [i.e. the superiority of the title of King over the title of Count] the disappearance of the name of Catalonia from international politics under the name of Aragon, i.e. the disappearance of the name of the principality under the name of the Kingdom." But is that all? Was it a mere reason of verbal hierarchy that made the count of Barcelona become King of Aragon? We believe that this matter should be treated with a keener sense of the value of words at the time when they were used. Some hot-headed Catalanists—not certainly the historian quoted—insist on the fact that Catalonia comes first as being the real driving force in the federation. But the point is that though Catalonia was the driving force in the federation, though till 1410 the Kings of Aragon felt at least as much Catalan as Aragonese and probably more, they were known as Kings of Aragon; their house was no longer the house of Barcelona (they never were the house of Catalonia), and when in later years the Sicilian, Roger de Lauria, declared (in Catalan) that "the fishes [in the Mediterranean] would not dare to appear above water unless they could show on their backs the bars of Aragon," he plainly showed that, for the Catalans of the time, Catalonia had been absorbed in Aragon, for the bars were the arms of the house of Barcelona.

What had happened? A thing both very simple and very complex. The count had naturally changed his name on becoming king. Catalonia did not exist as a name. He was Count of Barcelona. As the nation which a count or king ruled was not at the time clearly distinguished from the private estate which he owned, Barcelona became "Aragon" as a matter of course. So far it is quite simple. But there are subtler forces at play. The more we hear of the power, the civilizing and organizing force, the leadership, the expansion of Barcelona, as compared with the poor Aragonese, who do not come out of Catalanist hands under a very flattering light, the more we must suspect the existence of strangely powerful influences which, robbing Catalonia of all the glory and the fame of the events of which she was the main inspirer, handed them to Aragon. The count who became king was also a Ramón who became Alfonso, that is to say a prince who dropped a Catalan name in order to adopt an Aragonese name recently borrowed by Aragon from León and Castile. The Catalan dynasty linked itself up with the very center of the Castilian dynasty in this choice of the typically central patronymic. True, the change and choice were due to Petronila, mother of the child-king; but the queen was far from all-powerful, for under the nominal supervision of the king's tutor, Henry II of England, the real control of affairs was in the hands of typical Catalans, Guillém Ramón de Montcada and Guillém de Torroja, Bishop of Barcelona. How could such men have allowed the change had it not been in the spirit of the times?

We are, in fact, in the presence of the inherent unity of Spain, drawing all the Spanish nations like a magnet toward the pre-destined center—Castile. The phenomena which pass before our eyes are symmetrical in their movement toward the center: Asturias→Leon→Castile and Catalonia→Aragon→Castile. Under the turbulence and disorganization of the Middle Ages, though broken up into a regular jig-saw puzzle of petty princedoms, the old unified Spain of Roman and of late Visigothic times was acting on history with the magnetic fascination of a historical fate. In fact, the history of the late Middle Ages, during which a unified Spain emerges from the Oriental jig-saw puzzle of the Moorish invasion, is but a repetition of the history of the late barbarian period during which a unified Visigothic and Christian Spain emerges from the Occidental jig-saw puzzle of the Germanic invasion.

The merging of Catalonia into Aragon is thus but another case of a well-known phenomenon of Spanish life. Asturias and Galicia merged separately into León. León, though the true heir of Visigothic unity, after a long epoch of antagonism against Castile, merged with the Castilian Crown. But, though this Castilian Crown was only that of the latest newcomer, an upstart, a mere count who had rebelled against León, just as the Count of Barcelona had rebelled against the King of France, an even more modern count than that of Barcelona and, moreover, poor, the colonizer of a deserted land, without a sea, without a navy, without foreign prestige, without money, *it was León, the Visigothic, the aristocratic, the rich and refined León that merged into Castile and not Castile into León; just as it was the richer, the international, the maritime, the commercial and civilized Catalonia that merged into Aragon and not Aragon into Catalonia.* For this Castilian upstart had before him the prospect, soon to be realized, of conquering Toledo, the imperial city, the center of medieval civilization, the depository of Visigothic tradition, the symbol of Spanish continuity and unity. So, just as Galicia and Asturias merged with León and then all of them with Castile, so Catalonia and Valencia merged separately with Aragon, thence with that Greater Castile which was to be Spain.[1]

The problem is, therefore, not one of mere puerile hierarchy as between count and king. The real reason of the events which puzzle and sadden some Catalan historians is to be found in the magnetic effect of the center of the Peninsula, which sets up a scale of power far more real and important than that of count and king, ascending toward the center and which, in a process

---

[1] I am supported in these views by a penetrating remark of Señor Menéndez Pidal. Just as in France, the North, the country of custom law, gave the language and the center of unity to the nation, imposing them on the South, the country of written law; so in Spain, Castile, the country of custom law, imposed its language and unity on the countries of written law—Catalonia and León (*La España del Cid*).

of unswerving directness, was to culminate in a centralized empire with a capital in Madrid.

Catalonia then entered a phase of her history, in which she acted as the leading member of a bilingual confederation with Aragon. Being on the seaboard, used to foreign enterprise, she was bound to have wider views than the kingdom proper, recently reconquered from the Moors and still busy with its internal reconstruction which, as in every other part of Spain or, for that matter, of Europe, took the form of a struggle between the crown and the more hot-headed and powerful nobles. Yet the situation is apt to be exaggerated as in the passage quoted above. That the Aragonese nobility was a thorn in the flesh of the monarchs and did not always understand what they were after is the truth, but not the whole truth, for incomprehension was not limited to the Aragonese; it was a pure matter of feudal indiscipline, independent of nationality, and the Kings of Aragon had at times as much trouble with the Catalans as with the Aragonese. The great James I was much hampered in his enterprises by combinations of Catalan and Aragonese magnates. Here, again, a hasty or a biased interpretation of a general fact has sometimes been used to justify *a posteriori* the features of separateness and progressiveness which some modern Catalans want to emphasize in Catalonia. This period, from the reign of Alfonso II till the death of Martín I in 1410, is that in which the star of Catalonia shines brightest. The kingdom produced a series of active, efficient and at times admirable kings. Their policy had been outlined in the main by the counts of Barcelona and by the Kings of Aragon. It had three possibilities: France, and in particular the Catalan-speaking lands thereof; the Peninsula; the sea. Much energy was wasted in France, where Peter I took up the cause of the Albi heretics against the French armies of Simon de Montfort. But the Spanish king lost the Battle of Muret and his life; and his successor, James the Conqueror, proved his wisdom by giving up his claims to French territory in exchange for a similar self-denial on the part of the French king over Spanish territory. This act of obvious good sense is deplored by some Catalanist enthusiasts who still cast melancholy eyes on the parts of the philological map of Catalonia which lie beyond the Pyrenees.

The peninsular policy of the Kings of Aragon was unimpeachable. They cooperated bravely and loyally in freeing Spain from the Moors. Peter I, in alliance with the kings of Castile and Navarra, was present at the battle of Las Navas de Tolosa (1212) with a strong contingent of Catalan and Aragonese knights. James the Conqueror took the Balearic Islands, then conquered Murcia, farther south, but, in fulfillment of the pledges of his house toward Castile, he handed over his Murcian conquests to the Castilian king, Alfonso the Sage, his son-in-law. The great King of Aragon showed thereby that prudence which, in strong men, is the crown of courage. It was a typical virtue with him, as revealed in a curious episode of his career worth recording, for it illustrates the drive inward of the eastern Spanish monarchy. James had seen the King of Navarra, Sancho, in 1231. As a result of this interview, both monarchs had made wills declaring each other heirs to their respective kingdoms, an obvious move toward extending the domains of the Crown of Aragon in a northwesterly direction, for Sancho was well advanced in years. But, at Sancho's death in 1234, the Navarrese refused to accept a "foreign" king and James wisely refrained from pressing his claims. By this expedition to and conquest of the Balearic Islands, James put the sea policy of the Catalan-Aragonese federation on a solid basis. He laid the foundations of further enterprises by marrying his son Peter to the daughter of the King of Sicily. Peter the Great, the maritime king, conquered Corsica, Sardinia, Sicily and the coast of Africa. Under his son, James II, a host of Catalans and Aragonese commanded by Roger de Lauria, who were at a loose end in Sicily, were sent to the rescue of the Emperor of Constantinople, and having settled in the Greek Peninsula they founded the duchy of Athens (1326-88), a curious offshoot of Catalan civilization which lasted for a considerable time until it gradually disintegrated through strife and civil war.

Barcelona had by then become a rival of Genoa and Venice in trade and shipping. The Aragonese fleet was a prominent factor in the fight against piracy and in the colonization and trade of the Mediterranean shores. Led by their juristic sense, of which they had given an early proof in the *Usatges,* the Catalans produced, under James I, the famous *Lleys del Consulat de Mar,* the first code of maritime law attempted by Europe and one which was to regulate sea life for a long time amongst seafaring nations. Cultural life was made illustrious by such lights as Francesc Eximeniç, Arnau de Vilanova and, above all, Ramón Lull (1235-1315), the Majorcan mystic, a link between Eastern and Western civilizations, whose picturesque life, from his birth in Majorca to his matyrdom in Tunis, stoned to death by a fanatical Moslem crowd, is so Mediterranean. To that great period which saw the expansion of Catalonia and Aragon the eyes of contemporary Catalans are turned with love and admiration; and to the date 1410 with a sense of regret deeper even than that which seizes them when recalling how the Counts of Barcelona became Kings of Aragon.

For in that year Martín I died without succession and the Catalan dynasty of the kings of Aragon became extinct. The three Cortes of the three nations (Aragon, Catalonia, Valencia) sent delegates to Caspe in order to find a way out. The Catalans preferred James of Urgel, a Catalan candidate; the Aragonese preferred Ferdinand of Antequera, the Infant-Regent of Castile. The Valencians were divided. The influence of an eminent representative of Valencia, Father Vincent Ferrer (since canonized by the Church), turned the scales in favor of the Castilian prince. Catalonia acquiesced, and the revolt of the evicted candidate was easily put down by Ferdinand. He had, however, to learn that Catalonia had by then become a genuinely democratic country. Having refused to pay the tax called *Vectigal* which a Barcelonese custom imposed on king and all, the Barcelona Council sent him a delegate to insist on the city rights. The king, with much mortification of his Castilian pride, surrendered.

The reign of his successor, Alfonso V, was spent almost entirely in Naples, which he had conquered, faithful to the old Catalan policy of expansion in Italy and of rivalry between the Pope and the House of Aragon. In 1447 he further enlarged his

Italian territories by his inheritance of the Duchy of Milan. The King of Aragon became thus the most important potentate in Italy. On his death, however, he gave Naples to his natural son Ferdinand, and his Spanish crowns, together with the Italian islands, to his brother John, King of Navarra. A conflict between John of Navarra and his son Don Carlos, Prince of Viana, degenerated into a civil war in which Catalonia, Aragon and Navarra took part, and Catalonia in particular as a hot partisan of Don Carlos. An agreement made in Villafranca between the Catalans and the king, stipulated that Don Carlos should be his heir (for the king had disinherited him) and that meanwhile he would be sole governor of Catalonia, even during his father's lifetime. Soon afterward Don Carlos died and the *Diputació* of Barcelona entered the path of open rebellion. This story is not found in some of the most extreme Catalanist books, perhaps because when the Catalans, in the ardor of civil war, sought whom they should elect as Count of Barcelona, they landed on Henry IV of Castile without the slightest regard for the pet theories of twentieth-century Catalanists. It is true that after their offer to Castile they made other offers farther afield in the Peninsula and outside it, but the incident is typical of the fact which underlies all Catalan history—namely that the particularist tendency of Catalonia was not due to a sense of national separate existence, but was merely a Catalan psychological feature which exerted itself somewhat blindly by tearing away from the nearest link, then represented by the King of Aragon and Navarra. The present *a posteriori* explanations of Catalan nationalists, if true, would make the offer of the Crown of Barcelona to the King of Castile unthinkable. After years of wasteful war between the old king and Catalonia a compromise was patched up. The king died in 1479. His son, heir to Navarra, Aragon, Valencia, Catalonia, the Balearic and the Italian Islands, was already King of Castile by his marriage to Isabel. The unity of Spain was at last achieved.

Thus ended the period of Catalan history in which the Catalan-Aragonese confederation is ruled by a dynasty of Castilian kings. Catalonia, if the Catalan nationalistic theory of our present day has any meaning, should then have shown signs of decadence, being governed by kings foreign to her spirit and unable to understand her. And yet this is the period which saw Catalan literature and civilization at its highest. The University of Lérida dated from the preceding era (1300), but that of Valencia was founded in 1441 and that of Barcelona in 1450. Catalonia, or more exactly Valencia, contributed the greatest poet of the language, Auzias March (1379-1459); her great prose writer, Roïç de Corella (1430-1500); she (or again more exactly Valencia), produced the romance of chivalry, *Tirant lo Blanch,* known because Cervantes praised it; Bernat Metge, the quiet, smiling philosopher of *Lo Sompni;* Dalmau, the great painter. The epoch is unmistakably one of literary and artistic liveliness, if not of actual splendor (which, in the letters and arts, Catalonia never attained in a degree comparable with Castile and the other leading European nations). Yet the present-day Catalan authors who speak of decadence are not altogether wrong. The Castilian language penetrated into Catalonia, not through legislation, but by the sheer force of Castilian culture and because the virtues inherent in it were beginning to make themselves felt. Before Boscán, the Catalan poets of the court of Alfonso V in Naples wrote in Castilian. Not very much later, Castilian was to be the language of Luis Vives, the great Valencian philosopher who, with Erasmus and Bude, led the renaissance of thought in Europe.

With Ferdinand of Aragon, Catalonia entered the wider unity of Spain. There is, of course, "a difference" in this unity. The fact that Castile did not allow Catalonia to trade with the newly discovered Indies has often been cited. But it has not always been adequately interpreted. The exclusion was not without plausible causes, such as the fear of increased danger for the Spanish fleet passing into the Mediterranean, then infested by pirates. The exclusion, moreover, was not a discrimination against Catalonia only. It applied to all the subjects of the Crown of Aragon. It is but a reminder that the same Ferdinand and Isabel who made the union were, of course, monarchs of a disunited Spain. This distinction between the Spaniards who discovered America and those who did not is the last which preserves the old grouping between the lands of the Crown of Aragon on the one hand, and those of Castile on the other. Spain was to remain for centuries a congeries of separate kingdoms, but the kingdoms of Valencia, Aragon and Catalonia were henceforth considered as individually attached to the crown not through the subentity of the Aragonese federation, but direct, without any intermediate link.

What had occurred? Simply that a people with the gift of unity and of imperium had absorbed into a higher unity a group of three peoples, Catalonia, Valencia, Aragon, which, despite a long personal union, had failed to amalgamate constitutionally.

There followed a period in which Spain, as a whole, ascended to the summit of world power while the county of Barcelona saw her medieval prosperity on the wane. The coincidence of these two movements is not merely casual. Certain facts are obvious: the above-mentioned prohibition of trade with the Indies is one. But need this have stopped Catalan prosperity? The Spanish monarchy forbade the Indies no less severely to trade with Flanders and France, yet both these countries minted money through the discovery of America, not merely by illicit means, but by skillfully adapting themselves to the situation. It is, perhaps, more objectively true to say that the discovery of America disorganized the old economy of the Mediterranean on which Catalan life was founded, and that Barcelona suffered thereby along with other Mediterranean ports.

But the main point, though one which is generally overlooked, is that the Catalan nation failed to realize the immense opportunities which lay in a partnership with the greatest empire which history had known. Here was the age of navigation, and the Catalans were great navigators. Here was the age of trade, and they were the best traders of Spain. Here was the great age of world politics, and—where were their statesmen?

For Spain, after all, was not governed by the king, even under Charles V or Philip II. Spain was governed by men, ecclesiastics and lawyers for the most part and some soldiers and grandees. Two of the most powerful secretaries of Philip II, Gonzalo

Pérez and his son, Antonio Pérez, were Aragonese. If Aragonese could rise to the government of the empire, why not Catalans? If the Catalans were then what some Catalanists claim them to be now, the most forward, enlightened and European men of the Peninsula, why did they not try to run the immense empire instead of hopelessly watching the decadence of their old prosperity? The position would then have been similar to that of Scotland: first, an independent nation, at least as independent and historically important as Catalonia; then, after the union, a most powerful leaven in the British Empire and a mother of omnipresent statesmen and leaders of industry. It is true that Catalonia resisted all attempts of the crown to interfere with her liberties, be it said with all reservations which we shall have to make presently. Both Philip II and Philip III showed a wise restraint in their attempts at extending Castilian institutions to Catalonia. Philip IV, ill-advised by his minister, Olivares, brought about a rebellion during which the typical tendencies of Catalan separatism were observable. This rebellion was caused by general dissatisfaction owing to a number of things: taxes; the presence of non-Catalan troops on their way to foreign campaigns and their misbehavior while in Catalonia; the appointment of non-Catalans to Catalan posts; French intrigues with an eye on the recovery of Roussillon; the overbearing manner of Olivares, apt to be centralistic and impatient with Catalanist tendencies; last, but not least, the fear of the bigoted Catalan peasants lest so many foreign troops should corrupt their faith. The rebellion started in 1640 with cries of *"Visca la Iglesia; Visca'l Rey y muyra lo mal govern."* The Church and the king were the banners of these rebellious Catalans. The king sent a Catalan viceroy, the Duke of Cardona, to undo the evil caused by an inconsiderate Castilian viceroy. But the Barcelona authorities had had dealings with Richelieu; and while Olivares was secretly thinking of abolishing Catalan home rule Barcelona was hankering back to the republican idea, i.e. thinking in terms of Italian medievalism, while Olivares was thinking in terms of nineteenth-century nationhood. Two historical currents fought in this way and the hard fact which dominated the life of Catalonia, i.e. that she must be Spanish or become French, led the Barcelona authorities to recognize the sovereignty of Louis XIII. The war was long and wasteful. It lasted till 1652, not to count several further years during which troubles remained more or less endemic. Philip IV, however, though victorious, did not abolish the liberties of Catalonia.

The true crisis in the liberty of Catalonia came later. The rebellion under Philip IV was on a par with other movements which occurred in other parts of Spain: Aragon, where a conspiracy attempted to erect a separate kingdom under the Duke of Hijar; Andalusia, in which the Duke of Medina Sidonia tried to carve a kingdom for himself while his ally, the Marqués de Ayamonte, worked for a separate republic; the Basque Country, which rebelled in defense of the *fueros*. The rebellion at the end of the eighteenth century presents more typically Catalan features. Catalonia, or rather Barcelona, intervened in the War of the Spanish Succession with a policy of her own and widened the sphere of her international efforts, seeking again an independent republican status. Catalonia had been the staunchest Peninsular supporter of the archduke against Philip of Anjou, and was gradually, though reluctantly, abandoned by the Archduke after he assumed the imperial crown. When the termination of the war was being discussed in Utrecht, the Catalans hoped that, under the pressure of the emperor and of England, respect for their *fueros* would be stipulated in the treaty. Bolingbroke, however, had definite instructions to the effect that the liberty of Catalonia was of no special interest to England; an obvious fact, for Catalonia is on the east of Spain, tucked away in the northern corner of the Mediterranean; while the liberty of Portugal, as we shall see anon, was a different matter altogether, since Portugal is on the Atlantic Sea. Amnesty was all England asked on behalf of the Catalans, arguing—with the matter-of-fact common sense she was to apply in later years to her own northern neighbors, the Scots—that the Catalans would benefit more by the union and the consequent participation in the commercial privileges of the other Spaniards in America than by maintaining a separate establishment. The emperor then asked that

Catalonia should be made an independent republic under the protection of the allies and particularly of England (whose genius for chaperoning maiden nations was already beginning to be recognized the world over), but England modestly declined while gallantly offering a fleet to enable the empress (who as Queen of Spain had remained in Barcelona) to evacuate her temporary kingdom with dignity. The treaty signed in March 1713 in Utrecht left the matter of Catalan *fueros* untouched, a flaw which two of the emperor's delegates overlooked, but not the third, who refused to sign. This stickler for Catalan rights was a Castilian nobleman. In Article 13, Philip V granted them the same privileges which were enjoyed by . . . the Castilians. Catalonia meanwhile was occupied by Imperial troops. Starhemberg, the Emperor's viceroy, let her down gently and disappeared from the town with as little noise as possible. The Catalans were left to the tender mercies of a French king, born and bred in an absolutism which Spain had never known. The nobles and the churchmen of Barcelona were for compromise; the people voted for war and the nobles came over to their side. This, however, was Barcelona, for Catalonia as a whole was not responsive. The matter of Catalan liberties was again discussed in Rastatt while the Barcelona armies fought against the royal troops. A debate in the English House of Lords discussed the matter in a sense favorable to the Catalans. Philip V, however, was adamant. Barcelona, besieged, surrendered in September 1714. In the same month several Catalan institutions were suppressed (the Council of the Hundred, the General Deputation); the use of Catalan in the law courts as well as many other privileges of the Catalans disappeared by the *Decreto de Nueva Planta* in 1710. The Catalan Cortes had already been merged into the Cortes of the realm. All was not vindictiveness in this policy. Philip V and his French advisers were intent on unification on the French pattern, and the liberty of Aragon, Valencia, Galicia and the Basque provinces had already gone, in so far as these liberties meant differences from the Constitution which governed Castile. Catalonia was only tasting the kind of fate which would have been hers had she succeeded in her separatist tendencies, for such a success could only have meant leaving the Spanish pan to fall into the French fire.

The history of Catalonia does not really begin again until the nineteenth century. It is the history of her renascence, which had better be considered separately.

What, then, is the conclusion of this survey? The claim that Catalonia has a distinctive type within the Peninsular kingdoms is abundantly proved. This type shows itself in enterprise, war, law, commerce, art and literature. Catalonia is a definite national spirit, a culture, a civilization with characteristics of her own which one can recognize. The claim, however, that such a culture, such a national spirit, such a nation is a "Latin" nation like France and Italy, inherently independent from Spain, a nation whose development was frustrated by her union with Spain, is not, in our opinion, substantiated by historical facts. Historically, as psychologically, our conclusion is that Catalonia is one of the Spanish nations, profoundly linked up by nature and history (as she is by geography and economics) with the other nations of the Peninsula. We found a medieval state, a city of Barcelona, active and spirited from about 1000 to 1162; a city-state comparable with the more enterprising Italian republics and particularly with seafaring Venice, but evidently without a serious claim to compete in historical importance or in creative spirit with the Venetian republic. It is even arguable whether Catalonia can compare in historical importance with Scotland, Burgundy, or even Savoy. But, even if it were admitted, as indeed may be, that Catalonia was at one time a nation with a European importance analogous to that of Scotland, Burgundy, Savoy or Venice, the separatist conclusion drawn by some contemporary Catalan historians from that fact would be rendered absurd in the face of the historical evolution which has obliterated all these one-time typically independent European nations, or, rather, integrated them into higher units which, while absorbing their history, have developed and increased their significance for the history of mankind. We found this State of Barcelona, or Catalonia, following a similar evolution to that of the others we have mentioned; amalgamating first with the kingdom of Aragon, then with Castile, i.e. seeking with a kind of historical instinct, the fulfillment of her Spanish destinies. In the Catalan-Aragonese federation, precisely when known to all the world as Aragon, Catalonia reached her maximum splendor, no longer a county of Barcelona, but a clearly Spanish nation inseparable from Aragon. It was then, and particularly when governed not by the Catalan but by the Castilian dynasty, that Catalonia reached the crest of her culture. But of this culture an English scholar says: "His works [Vives'] however, when not in Latin, were written in Castilian, and the works of Lull, Eximeniç, Roïç de Corella and others owed their wide circulation to the Castilian and sometimes French translations in which they were diffused through Europe. Ancient Catalan literature is strictly medieval. It never adapted itself to the spirit of the renaissance, and remained bound to the old Provençal forms when the current of general taste was leading in a very different direction. Its death was due more to inanition than to political causes, for though Catalonia suffered a loss of prestige in the union with Castile, it only lost national independence in 1714, after the Wars of the Spanish Succession."[2] For Catalonia was a medieval creation, and, therefore, as a separate entity she died with the Middle Ages. During the period of the Spanish Empire Catalonia remained absorbed despite the hardships entailed by the discovery of America. The Catalan language, the only specific feature of the region, died as a language of culture early in the sixteenth century. Catalonia defended her liberties now and then against the king just as did other parts of Spain, but with the added zest of national consciousness that remembered its tendency toward a republican status. But her culture was Castilian; so was her language.

We observe, therefore, in the history of Catalonia a national consciousness which manifests itself in particularistic and negative, rather than in cooperative and positive, ways. It is but natural that the strong individualism of the Catalans, stronger, as we know, than that of their co-Spaniards, should have mani-

[2] Professor J. B. Trend in *A Picture of Modern Spain.*

fested itself in the national sphere by making Catalonia self-centered and so to speak centrifugal. Her history shows how devoid of any fundamental principle of foreign policy she found herself as soon as she tried to resist the only natural historical law which governed her life. She now sought help in France, now in the Emperor, now even in England. But it was obvious *a priori,* and it was proved by events that of all these nations France alone was in a position to help her, but not to her advantage—for the help of France meant either the absorption of the whole of Catalonia, or at least the loss of that part which she claimed as hers, and which lies north of the Pyrenees. The phase of negative nationalism in Catalonia must be considered, therefore, as a natural outcome of her psychology. We are about to see that her rebirth in the nineteenth and twentieth centuries had still to live down a long phase of negative nationalism before some of her more distinguished sons evolved a political philosophy truly worthy of a nation with such a glorious past and so splendid a future.

CHAPTER 17

THE CATALAN QUESTION

THE ORIGINS OF THE PRESENT POSITION

At the beginning of the nineteenth century Catalonia as a national spirit was as good as dead. The language was spoken by illiterate peasants and a kind of corruption of it by the rabble of the towns. The newspapers, which, under the brief French occupation in 1810, were printed in Catalan by the French invaders, went back to Castilian in order to be read at all as soon as the French turned tail. The Spanish government, now under the liberal but dogmatic and centralistic inspiration of the Cortes de Cádiz, now under the absolutist inspiration of the crown, completed the work left unachieved by Philip V and deprived Catalonia of her forgotten and unused liberties. The nineteenth century resounded to the hammerings of the government hammer driving nail after nail into the coffin of Catalonia: her penal law went in 1822; her right to use Catalan

214

in schools in 1825; her commercial law in 1829; her special tribunals in 1834; her coinage in 1837; her regional administration in 1845. Down went the hammer on the coffin. The body was well held under the lid—yes, but the spirit was free. And, at that very moment Catalonia was resuscitating.

Obscure efforts date from the end of the previous century. An association had been created for the purpose of Catalan being spoken by its members. Other signs here and there appeared to the wary eye. But the dramatic move occurred in 1833 when a Catalan bank clerk, Aribau, who lived in Madrid, wishing to celebrate the birthday of his employer, also a Catalan, struck the idea of writing an ode to the fatherland in the Catalan language. The poem was published in a Barcelona paper quaintly called *El Vapor*. This progressive paper, as its name showed, and the review *El Europeo,* both, of course, published in Castilian, were the organs of the Catalan romantics, all of whom dreamed of a *renaixença* of Catalan culture; but none of whom, save a scholar, Rubio y Ors, dared believe in the possibility of raising the Catalan language from the gutter. Rubio y Ors did it, however, single-handed. History works in such strange ways that this man who, by giving Catalan a new distinction for purely intellectual reasons, did more than anyone to set in motion the political rebirth of Catalan nationalism, never took part in the political movement itself; nor is it certain that he approved it. In 1859 the Municipal Council of Barcelona called back to life the old festivity known as the *jochs florals,* or floral games, a kind of poetic tournament in Catalan. A French saying has it that in France everything ends in song. In Catalonia everything begins in a poem, and experience shows that the custom is not so bad at all. The Catalan press began its career a few years later represented with appropriate modesty by a newspaper with the name of *Un Troç de Paper* (a bit of paper), followed by a literary review, *Lo Gay Saber.* The Catalan theater dates from the same epoch, with Federico Soler.

The time was ripe for political nationalism to emerge. The first feeling of some kind of local desire for freedom appears in Pi y Margall's federalism. Pi, who was one of the four presidents whom the Spanish Republic successively tried in one year, held federal opinions of a somewhat theoretical kind. In his idea the extreme variety of regional life in Spain required some form of devolution, and he, as a Catalan, would have been content with such a formula. He conceived political life as a regular hierarchy of covenants between individuals to form the city, between cities to form the region, between regions to form the nation. He organized the Spanish Republican Federal Party. One of his followers, Almirall, laid the foundations of republican Catalanism in his *Lo Catalanisme* (1886), a doctrine which seceded from Pi y Margall's because, according to Almirall, Pi was too theoretical and understood Catalanism not in itself, but merely as one of the by-products of constitutional thinking about Spain. Almirall is thus the creator of what might be described as Left-Wing Catalanism. The eminent Bishop of Vich, Torras y Bagés, with his *Tradició Catalana,* became the authority for Catholic or Right-Wing Catalanism. (This symmetry, Republican Left and Clerical Right, is indispensable in Spain. It is the first of a long list of typically Spanish characteristics of Catalanism.)

It will be noticed that Catalanism, born in poetry, was still in the domain of pure intellectualism with Almirall and Torras y Bagés. These two authors each in his way tried to define the personality of Catalonia within the framework of Spain. They differ, of course, in that for the one Catalonia means "Progress," free-thinking and democracy, while, for the other, Catalonia means faith, order, and, above all, tradition. So far, however, neither had clearly seen Catalonia as a nation.

This step was to be taken by the master and leader of Catalan nationalism, Enric Prat de la Riba. For him Catalonia was a nation and not merely a regional form of Spanish life. Prat de la Riba was a noble thinker, and there was in him more statesmanship than in any other leader of Catalan life, with the single exception of his disciple and political heir, Cambó. Prat saw that the resurrection of a medieval Catalonia could not take place as if nothing had occurred since 1492; he realized not only that Spain could not be dismembered in order to please a few philologists, but that Catalonia could not revolutionize her whole life in order to adapt herself to a new political conception, however pleasing to the Catalan historical imagination. Prat saw things in a big scale—but as a Catalan and as a Spaniard. His ideal for Catalonia was a federation of all the Catalan-speaking lands, Valencia, the Balearic Islands and Catalonia proper; nor did he always omit the Catalan territories belonging to the French republic, for there was in him that dash of romantic imagination which is nearly always to be found even in the most practical and hard-headed of Catalans. For Spain, his ideal was an Iberian Federation including Great Catalonia, Castile and Portugal. Prat was the undisputed intellectual leader of Catalonia until his premature death.

This rapid evolution from apparent extinction to vigorous rebirth took place in this realm of thought. The fact is sometimes used as an argument to minimize the *renaixença* by those for whom thought does not matter at all. Certain peculiar defects of Catalan thought, notably a kind of airy tendency to forget the hard bones of reality, lend authority to this shortsighted and cynical view. In our opinion, thought blossoms out of the blood of men and nations and we cannot behold without respect and admiration this wonderful re-creation of a national spirit achieved by the faith, the devotion and the ability of a handful of men. Coming after pages—perhaps too many—in which the arguments of Catalan political thinkers on the problem have been strictly scrutinized, these words should be read as a spontaneous homage to the substance of the Catalan claim no matter how flimsy some of the arguments, historical and psychological, used on its behalf may be. *In our opinion Catalonia is a nation, if a Spanish nation.* She has a spirit of her own with every title to the full manifestation of her genius and culture and to the full enjoyment of her own life. That she owes her rebirth to but a few of her sons is only a further proof that the national spirit which they called back to life, though dormant, was ready to hover again over the waters of history. We are going to follow its first, somewhat awkward, steps as it tried to descend from the pure heights of idealism to the dismal and troubled spheres of politics.

But, as we approach practical politics, the beautiful order and symmetry of political principles begins to be blurred. The question whether Catalonia is going to live as a nation or not presented itself in Catalonian life as only one of the several problems at issue. A part of Spain in practice, Catalonia felt her life-blood circulating in a body politic which was Spain's, not merely hers. And Catalan politics are governed by at least three movements of almost equal value: the nationalist movement with its antagonistic reaction—centralism—in Castile and also in Catalonia; the labor movement; and the action of economic interests.

We have already made acquaintance with both the nationalist and the labor movements. The matter of economic interests is very complex indeed. Centralistic writers, whether Catalan or Castilian, have not failed to lay stress on the economic solidarity which binds Catalonia to the Peninsula. This solidarity is obvious and its consequences all important. Much harm, however, has been done to the cause of good understanding between Madrid and Barcelona by presenting it as if the connection were all to the advantage of Catalonia. It is true that the Catalans were the first, and the most persistent, advocates of that excessive protectionism which prevented Spain from taking full advantage of her excellent economic opportunities and of the high gold reserves which she then possessed. It is also true that, up to a point, Catalan protectionism is devised in order to enable the industry of Catalonia to produce in the uneconomic conditions dictated by excessive Catalan individualism. The claim of some Castilian writers that Spain as a whole has to pay for Catalan individualism and industrial indiscipline by raising her tariffs against cheap foreign goods is not altogether unfounded. But the Catalans can counter it by pointing out that, if they were allowed to get foreign food by sea instead of having to buy expensive Spanish grain and meat transported through the hilliest country in Europe, they would be able to produce cheaper cloth. To which, of course, the Castilian farmer retorts that he cannot produce cheap grain when he has to buy his cloth from the Catalan and his tools from the Basque at fantastic prices.

Let us turn a French dictum upside-down and sum up by saying that when everybody is right everybody is wrong. The common-sense view is that Spanish economic life is moving in that vicious circle—or rather vicious spiral—into which protection is apt to launch nations if engaged in without due moderation as to time and as to the industries selected for protection. Who began first, the farmer or the industrialist? Moreover, the matter is not merely one of tariffs. Obsolete machinery, workers reluctant to sacrifice comfort and leisure to gain, defective agrarian laws, unnecessarily harsh employers, the selfish policy of foreign capitalism, a complex knot of circumstances, handicap Spanish production. Hence protection. The addition of political influences explains overprotection, and then things become too difficult for anyone to apportion the rights and the wrongs. We shall not follow the Castilian school in attributing to the Catalans the responsibility for protection, much as Prat de la Riba himself tempts us to do so when he says in his *Nacionalisme,* "The economic point of view [*criteri*] of the Catalans in tariff matters has prevailed [in Spain] for years." We refuse even to accept the view that Catalonia benefits by the situation any more than the rest of Spain. We limit our position to this moderate but indisputable ground: that the economic argument establishes beyond doubt the closest possible solidarity between Catalonia and the rest of Spain.

As for the political side of economics, we would go a little further. It is obvious to any student of Spanish contemporary history that the Catalan sector of Spanish politics has always been particularly alive to tariff matters and that it has nearly always succeeded in carrying the rest of the nation over to its view. The words just quoted from one of the most eminent leaders of Catalonia would suffice to establish the point. Some observers have even suggested that Catalan nationalism has often been ready to barter political demands in exchange for tariff favors. Politics is a strange art, and it would be difficult for

Catalans to deny that such things have ever occurred at all. Indeed, a tinge of regret at their occurrence does now and then appear in the writings of some of the more disinterested intellectual leaders of Catalanism. It would, however, be a profound mistake to jump to the conclusion that the leaders of the Catalan movement were bluffing the Spanish government with a nationalistic ghost in order to extract economic advantages from a reluctant nation. No. Catalanism is a deep spiritual faith, sincerely held, powerfully felt. And in so far as it is one of the truly profound emotions in Spanish political life it is, we are convinced, one of the few factors which are contributing to the true political rebirth of the whole Peninsula.

The nationalist emotion is therefore cooled down, controlled and made as practical as possible by the Catalan sense of business. It is also complicated by the dualism which afflicts Catalonia, like the rest of Spain, in matters of religious politics. Clericals and anti-clericals, Catholics and free-thinkers, men of the Right and men of the Left, pessimists and optimists, reactionaries and liberals, men hankering back to absolutism and men yearning for a republic—such is the line of cleavage which cuts across Catalanism as across every other form of Spanish political life. We know that in the realm of Catalanist theory these two ways of thinking are represented respectively by Bishop Torras y Bagés and by Almirall. The cleavage stands for much that is complicated and even obscure in Catalan politics, for such political enmities, simple enough in ordinary public life, become blurred and confused in the presence of a nationalist "previous question" which, by forcing the political world to a kind of sacred union, drives differences underground and makes them dark and distorted. As if further to complicate matters, the labor movement long professed to ignore nationalist questions, being interested only in economic and class struggles, while the whole process of Catalanism was dominated by the ferment of individualism, and by a tendency to uncompromising dispersion due to the Spanish psychology of the Catalan.

Strictly speaking, the political movement is an offshoot of federalism. The first period of Catalan nationalism is dominated by the figure of Valentí Almirall, whose first newspaper (1869), written in Castilian, was significantly styled *El Estado Catalán.* Thus the movement from its birth revealed its will to be before the very instrument for its being—the language—was entrusted with the duties of political life. But, in 1879, Almirall founded the *Diari Catalá* and, in 1882, he created the first strong Catalanist institution, the *Centre Catalá,* professedly a home of Catalanism independently of the political ideas of its members on other subjects. This first attempt to unite Catalans exclusively on the field of nationalism failed, and the moderate elements of the association (moderate not precisely in Catalanism but in other matters along the Right-Left line) seceded and founded the *Lliga de Cataluñya* (1887), and a newspaper, *La Renaixença.* The *Lliga* ultimately was to become the leading organ of Catalanism. The dramatic touch had not been neglected by these Mediterraneans, some of whom, like Guimerá, one of the founders of the *Lliga,* were excellent dramatists. In 1885 Almirall submitted to the king a *Memoria en Defensa de los Intereses Morales y Materiales de Cataluña,* which, typically enough, was prompted by the negotiations then begun toward commercial treaties with France and England as well as by the attempts of the government to standardize civil law in the Peninsula. In 1888 the *Lliga* addressed a message to the queen regent on her visit to the Barcelona Exhibition, when Menéndez y Pelayo, the great Castilian philologist, extolled the beauty and glory of the Catalan language in a speech pronounced before Her Majesty. The movement gathered strength and led to the Assembly of Manresa (1892), in which a program of Catalan requirements was drafted which became famous in Spanish politics under the name of *Las Bases de Manresa.*

The task of appraising this document is no easy one. It would be unfair to describe it as a reactionary charter, since it aimed at securing the freedom of a whole people to evolve along its own lines. And yet the philosophy which underlies it is not particularly liberal. It is rather that philosophy of nationalism under which the rights and welfare of individuals are apt to be forgotten, or even deliberately sacrificed, for the sake of the rights of the community. The *Bases de Manresa* sought to reorganize Spain on a federal basis which would secure for Catalonia the control of all matters of internal administration, including coinage and the manner in which she would contribute to national defense, while reserving for the federal government matters concerning more than one of the several regions or states, defense, foreign affairs, interstate communications and customs. The document reflects that particularism which under Almirall passed from the realm of subconscious character (where we found it), to that of political theory—to the point of excluding non-Catalans from public offices in Catalonia even when such offices depended on the federal government.[1] The Assembly of Manresa was followed by those of Reus (1893), Balaguer (1894), Olot (1895), all of which discussed schemes of action, or theoretical questions bearing on the program, not in the least troubled by the fact that the application of them was out of the question in the circumstances. This may seem curious to positive and practical minds. Yet the method was perhaps instinctively wise, and its value as a process of direct education cannot be disputed.

Two sets of events came deeply to trouble the evolution of Catalanism. The first was the wave of terrorism which plunged Barcelona in chaos between 1892, date of the attempt on the life of Marshal Martínez Campos, and the disorders of Monjuich in 1896. This period was the first of a series of anarchist outbreaks to which Barcelona was doomed owing to the peculiar forces acting at the head of, and more often lurking behind, Catalan labor. Simultaneously Cuban events were going from bad to worse, and it became apparent that Spain was heading toward a catastrophe there. Catalanist opinion was not sympathetic. Particularism played a definite part in the situation, though in the responsibility for Spain's failure in Cuba, Catalonia had at least her fair share with the rest of Spain. When the Treaty of Paris closed this chapter of Spanish history, Catalanism

[1] This was an immemorial bee in the Spanish bonnet. Petitions to that effect were addressed by the several "kingdoms" to the Kings of Spain at all times. Llorente gives some curious examples. *Noticias Históricas* (Vol. II). See note, p. 467.

received a powerful accession of strength—a typically particularistic one. Let us quote that noble, if narrow-minded, exponent of the doctrine, Señor Rovira y Virgili: "This general movement of protest led towards decentralizing and regionalistic points of view a considerable number of elements, particularly from industry and commerce, which in actual fact lacked all Catalanist spirit. This was the cause of the great strength which Catalanism suddenly acquired during the last years of the nineteenth century, and also the cause of the internal weakness of the movement." This movement, curiously enough, coincided with the first serious attempt on the part of Madrid to meet Catalan aspirations. It was made by a Cabinet presided over by Silvela, but inspired in these matters by a general who, though returned from the Philippine Islands at the head of a defeated army, tried to play the part of savior of Spain, for which he lacked every quality, including mental ability. Castile had been "saved" so often by incapable generals that she did not mind watching in silence, but Catalonia, with that ever rising optimism of the Mediterranean sun, gave credit to "the Christian soldier," for such was the quaint name which his clerical admirers gave to General Polavieja. Failure came from both sides. Polavieja's program met with opposition among certain Madrid diehards, and the Catalans protested against the wise and statesmanlike measures which the Minister of Finance, Villaverde, adopted in order to extricate Spain from a difficult financial postwar situation. This example is typical of contemporary Catalan history. Wrongs always on both sides: narrow-mindedness toward Catalan home rule on the part of Madrid and toward sound financial and economic policy on the part of Catalonia.

New leaders arose almost with the new century and, faithful even in this detail to the law of contemporary Spanish events, Catalonia turned the corner of her history toward 1900. In 1901 the two organizations, *Centre Nacional Catalá* (nationalist), and *Unió Regionalista* combined, won a famous victory at the polls. These were soon afterward amalgamated under the name of *Lliga Regionalista*. Prat de la Riba was the leader of this powerful organism of Catalan nationalism, and it was then that, by his side, there appeared in Catalan politics a precocious political leader and lawyer, Cambó. But the field was not clear. In Catalonia, particularly in Barcelona, there was a mass of Left opinion, radicals, anti-clericals, republicans, for whom these ideas, independently of all nationalism, were more important than the Catalan question. This mass found a leader in Don Alejandro Lerroux, who led them to a remarkable victory in 1903, when the nationalists were beaten. This result was hailed by centralist monarchists as a victory, though their own candidates were also defeated, for the elected deputies were all republicans. Catalanist politicians have always since then suspected Señor Lerroux of being in actual fact an agent of centralistic politics.

From that moment until the present day the Catalan movement becomes so intimately connected with the other events of the period that separate treatment is impossible. A discussion of its possibilities, its future evolution and the final solution which all well-meaning Spaniards should strive for must be left for a later occasion. This much may, however, be suggested here: that the nineteenth and twentieth centuries in the history of Catalan nationalism show it to be a Spanish, all too Spanish, phenomenon. Why did it appear just then? Because it was precisely then that all Spain awakened to a new sense of nationhood; and it was therefore only natural that Catalonia should wake up as Catalonia. The main obstacles in the way of the solution came precisely from the strong Spanish character of the Catalans. Spaniards settled in the Mediterranean, we have found them to be. In later years they have evolved an abundant crop of doctrines and schools, centers and leagues which melted and dissociated, grouped themselves and fell out and recombined kaleidoscopically, at times exalted to a point of stridency (to use a now established term in Spanish Catalan politics), at times ready to hear the alluring voice of this or that ally, Spanish or foreign; while the main thing, the art of persuading and gaining the confidence of the main partner, was sadly neglected. Why? Because of another Spanish feature, the Catalan individualistic sense of dispersion which we have observed in our historical survey and detected in our psychological analysis. As a matter of course, national consciousness implies a sense of difference, but not necessarily a political or constitutional separation. This last tendency, with which the majority of Catalonists disagree nowadays, has been unwisely aired by some Catalanists, coupled with a cordial separation, a kind of cutting of the knot of solidarity. The attempts to shake off all responsibility for Cuban affairs, for instance, were misguided both on the score of fact and on that of feeling. A tendency to wound has been too much in evidence in Catalan nationalism. And—need we say it?—it has been admirably reciprocated in Madrid. Nor is it necessary to waste time in idle discussion as to who began this tiresome process of mutual irritation.

There are other difficulties. The reader will have noticed the predominant position which Barcelona occupies in the history of Catalonia. This, the chief factor in past history, remains the most important in present politics. Catalanism is, above all, a Barcelona affair. It was created in Barcelona, developed there, talked of there, organized there, and it is there it lives. And yet Barcelona is not and can never be wholly Catalan. Her *hinterland* extends far up into the Peninsula. Even if Greater Catalonia were given her to satisfy her political ambitions, Valencia, with the great town of the same name and the harbor of El Grao, will always be a natural rival of Barcelona, needing a *hinterland* of her own. A Catalan republic is an economic impossibility, even if it were feasible politically. Barcelona, then, the main cause of Catalanism, is at the same time the origin of the main forces working for Spanish union. Moreover, Barcelona contains a high proportion of non-Catalanist inhabitants (both Catalans and non-Catalans), enough at times to put Catalanists in a minority. Thus, despite the remarkable progress made in recent years by the Catalan press written in Catalan, the biggest newspapers in Barcelona are still printed in Castilian. Last, but not least, experience has shown that the labor situation in Barcelona is of so grave a character that, though often mismanaged by the central government, an exclusively Catalan government would probably be too weak to handle some of its more serious aspects.

All these factors combine to render Catalanism a difficult

problem. None perhaps more so than that all-or-nothing attitude of the Spaniard, as typical of the Catalan as of the Castilian. An admirable case in point is the career of the most statesman-like political genius which Catalonia and possibly Spain has produced in the twentieth century. The difficulties with which Señor Cambó had to contend in his own country spring from his spirit of compromise, from his readiness to take what the day can give and wait for more to come from the morrow. Such an evidently wise attitude for a political leader was constantly mis-interpreted both in Catalonia and in Castile as an actual moral weakness. Another form of the same difficulty is the sense of hurry, the lack of political patience which afflicts most Cata-lanists. Having slept for three centuries in the bosom of Spain, they now wake up and want Spain to let go the work of centuries in one generation. Castile is slow, terribly slow. But she is mov-ing. She is moving in many ways, thanks to the fact among others that Catalonia herself has awakened. And in this observa-tion we may find hope that the Catalan question may still be solved in mutual happiness.

CHAPTER 18

THE BASQUE AND GALLEGAN QUESTIONS

THE BASQUE QUESTION

The linguistic element is a guiding light in Catalanism; it is a less trustworthy factor in the Basque question. The Basque language is a mystery which has baffled both history and philology. Some similarity has been found between its pronouns and those of Hebrew; between its marvelously complicated verbs and those of certain American-Indian languages, such as the Dakota and the Aztec; its vocabulary is a thing in itself; its numerical system an eclectic combination of the decimal and the vigesimal. The language is receding in Spain more even than in France to the point that in Spain it is not spoken in any of the big towns in the Basco-Navarrese region, which was once its undisputed domain. Of the four provinces, Alava, Biscay, Guipúzcoa and Navarra, the third only has remained entirely faithful to it—with the exception of San Sebastián. It has lost most of Alava, including the capital, Vitoria; the west of Biscay, including Bilbao; the southern half of Navarra, including Pamplona: in France it is not spoken in Bayonne. There is a school which holds that the Basque was orginally spoken by the Iberian pre-Roman population of Spain. The idea, first put forward by Humboldt, has been restored to the scientific dignity which it had lost by the authority of that brilliant expert, Dr. Hugo Schuchardt. It seems a natural conclusion to adopt, for, otherwise, it would be very difficult to explain the subsistence of such a philological curiosity in that corner of Europe.

Needless to say, if the Humboldt-Schuchardt theory held the field finally, the claims of Basque extremists would be deprived of their main basis, which is linguistic. For, unless the linguistic argument starting from a difference of languages leads to a difference in nationality, it has but little use in home rule matters. Now it is evident that if Basque were the general language of Spain before her Romanization, the remnant of it is but a philogogical curiosity without much historical significance; it merely shows that the Basque-speaking Spaniards were left, somehow or other, out of the Romanizing process.[1]

This is an excellent peg on which to hang a claim to separatism, the tendency to "get away," to "break loose," being of course the more vigorous in the Basque for this very circumstance which left untouched the deepest Iberian characteristics in him. His language is an excellent proof of the fact, for in the small area of the Three Provinces and Navarra, Prince Bonaparte, an expert, was able to classify no less than twenty-five dialects. Strictly speaking, a Basque language does not exist. And needless to say, there is no Basque literature whatsoever outside folklore. The Basque country itself as a unit is a modern creation for history only knows three provinces: Alava, Gui-

---

[1] More recent history provides an argument to the same effect. It is now evident to Spanish medievalists that Castile was, for a relatively long period during the Arabic occupation, a kind of desert no-man's land between Christians and Moslems, and that it was repopulated by Navarrese and Basque settlers. Thus the fundamental unity of Castile and the Basque country is historically ascertained.

púzcoa and Biscay; and a kingdom: Navarra; as well as three linguistically connected regions over the French border—La Basse Navarre, La Soule and Le Labourd. *Euzkadi* is a word of contemporary invention.

This lack of a real cultural Basque nucleus, the non-existence of any true Basque civilization throughout history outside whatever civilization (Roman, Visigothic or European) Spain had, is perhaps the real origin of the complexities and varieties of the Basque languages. There never was one conscious, logically built, systematic Basque mind, to stand as a light behind the several dispersive linguistic forms, as it does for instance between, *am, is, be, ain't, aren't,* in English; so that every Basque village or individual speaks out of a local family tradition, and the result is a maze of forms. It explains also the lack of interest for the Basque language evinced by all the great creative Basques without exception, Unamuno, Maeztu, Baroja.[2]

In the dispersive, fiercely individualistic tendency of this people, deeply embedded in their soul with a peculiar vigor of its own, we recognize the core of the Iberian character. And in point of fact, the Basques are the core of Spain. Spain is like a tree which stands erect on the trunk of Castile, and spreads in graceful foliage over Galicia and Portugal, in plastic, luminous forms over Catalonia, in odorous and colorful flowers over Andalusia—but its sinewy roots are Basque. The greatest Basque of all times, with the exception of Ignatius Loyola, Miguel de Unamuno, saw it clearly when he spoke of the Basque as "the "alkaloid of the Spaniard." In the composite nature of Spanish psychology, the Basque brings in a particular hard, dour quality, without which the blue Mediterranean and the delights of El Andalus might have turned Spain into a soft, pleasure-loving country. Of all the Spaniards, the Basque is the most inclined

[2] Unamuno, as a member of the Constituent Assembly of 1931-33, presented an amendment to the Draft Constitution—in the following terms:

"The Spanish language is the official language of the Republic. All Spanish citizens have the duty to know it and the right to speak it. In each region the language of the majority of its inhabitants may be declared co-official. No one will be bound to use any regional language."

to action, the least endowed with aesthetic sense. His awkwardness in aesthetic affairs is the cause of much good-humored amusement on the part of his fellow Spaniards, who, more richly endowed in grace, are apt to smile at his uncouth ways. There is always something primitive, elementary, peasantlike and perhaps too simple in the Basque. His sense of action is born of his natural vigor rather than of a particularly developed sense of things and men, such as the English possess. Indeed, the Basque has none of the natural complexities of the Englishman, though he reminds one of the Englishman in his disinclination toward speculative thought.

As a compensation, the Basque brings to life an upright, earnest nature not unlike that of the Scot. Indeed, the Scot, particularly the dark-haired type of high cheekbones and set, narrow perhaps but straight principles, is the human type which the Basque resembles most clearly—and to the body politic of Spain the Basque provinces contribute essences and virtues similar to those which the Scotch bring to bear on the British body politic. Their local administration is the best in Spain—in a curious contrast with the Catalans, who are not, as a rule, good managers of their own public affairs.

A similar observation may be made in other aspects of Spanish life less related to politics. Thus, for instance, the peculiar epic-dramatic character of the central part of Spain (the Basque-Castilian-Andalusian) can no doubt be traced to the strong Basque element in this part of the Spanish population. The sturdy, blunt aspect of Castilian letters (later modified by Andalusian poets under the influence of Italy) is rooted in the primitive strength of the Basques who form the substratum of the population of Castile. And even to this day, the Basques who have illustrated Castilian letters and the Spanish arts reveal this, somewhat narrow, but always admirably vigorous, spirit. Unamuno, Baroja, Maeztu, are men of more vigor than grace, defective in sense of form—all three uncouth though virile writers. Zuloaga's pictures are the masterpieces of a Basque peasant.

On this background, the strong attachment of the Basques to

the Roman Catholic faith can be easily explained. Here, again, they reveal themselves as the core of Spain. If in the course of centuries Spain has assumed the part of the Soldier of Christ in world history, the vigor and the perseverance of this endeavor are in a high degree due to the Basque element in her life. They are no great mystics. Mysticism is a subtler flower of the spirit than the Basques can give forth unaided. In Spain it flourished best in the Castilian tablelands, accessible to both influences— that of the hard Basque spirit, which gave strength for ascetic self-denials; and that of the luminous Andalus which gave grace for divine love. But the Basques gave Spain great leaders of Church life and activity, a host of monks, bishops and mission- aries, whose prototypes are two great Basque saints and knights- errant of the Church Militant: St. Ignatius Loyola and St. Francis Xavier.

These great men worked in an age of unity which sought still greater unity. We live nowadays in an age of anarchy which seeks more anarchy. Many Basques are now endeavoring to build up a Basque nation either within a Spanish federation or even independently of the rest of Spain. We have no right to be surprised. We know that this dispersive and disruptive tendency is a typical feature of the Spanish character, and we have found the Basque to be the quintessence of the Spaniard. Our discussion of the Catalan problem has revealed that the historical, literary and other intellectual constructions put for- ward to justify many of the Catalan claims are but intellectual superstructures erected in order to rationalize a primitive dis- persive instinct. No better proof could be provided of this asser- tion than the Basque case. For here in the Basque country there is no Ramón Lull, there are no primitive painters, there is no separate history, no literature, no culture outside Spanish culture —there is nothing but a group of twenty-five archaic languages. What are then the forces which explain the strength of the Basque movement?

We take for granted the root-force of it all: the dispersive nature of the Spanish character. With the Basques, it manifests mainly in two political tendencies: religious fanaticism and a stubborn tradition of local rights or *fueros*, which right up to the Civil War had secured for the Three Provinces a high measure of home rule.

Religious fanaticism is a logical consequence of Basque primitive strength. These simple, sturdy mountaineers and fisherman look askance at the imported habits of less austere men. The Basque clergy were ever jealous to keep the purity of their flock intact by keeping nearly closed the chief pass which led to the outside world—the Castilian language. Basque nationalism is but the extreme form of this solicitude of the Basque priests to keep unpolluted by liberalism, socialism . . . and the rest, by far the most reactionary region of Spain. This explains the strong part taken by the clergy in Basque nationalism, as well as the fact that the historical roots of Basque nationalism should be found in Carlism.

During the nineteenth century the chief strongholds of Carlism were the Catalan countryside and the high, narrow valleys of Biscay and Guipúzcoa. Carlism was, of course, a much deeper movement than a mere dynastic dispute. The Carlists represented the forces of religious and political authority against the liberals, whose stronghold was Madrid backed by a few Andalusian towns. The chief hero of this uncompromising anti-liberal spirit was the Basque Carlist chief Zumalacárregui. The Basque beret was right through the nineteenth century the symbol of clerical reaction against free thinking and of absolutism against parliamentary liberalism. But even within the Basque country the dour reactionaries who fought for the past did not have it all their way. The chief towns, with their more mixed population, were liberal and Bilbao, the modern capital of Biscay, fought heroically for freedom against the spiritual ancestors of our contemporary Basque nationalists, the reactionary Carlists who besieged her twice, in 1835 and in 1874. The chief liberal club of Bilbao is known as *El Sitio,* The Siege.

This attitude toward religion and progress on the part of the liberal big towns on the one hand and the Carlist and nationalist countryside on the other was bound to create a rift in the Basque population. The other force behind Basque nationalism offered better possibilities for union between Basque and Basque. This was a tradition of local freedom which had crystallized in legislation separate from that of the rest of Spain, notably in financial affairs. Thus for instance the citizens of the Basque provinces were not taxed direct by the state. The three provinces, in virtue of their *Concierto Económico* with the state, were taxed an agreed total sum which they raised among their citizens as they thought fit. The historical foundations for such a tradition of home rule, stubborn and ancient as it is, have proved to be a tissue of misquotations, imaginary battles and fake documents by no less an authority than Llorente, the very man who wrote the Annals of the Inquisition.[3] In a scholarly treatise in three volumes, published in Madrid in 1806, Llorente scrutinizes every bit of historical evidence adduced as a proof of the original independence and republican system of the Three Basque Provinces, and of their alleged entry into the Spanish Monarchy by a kind of treaty of agreement. His analysis is devastating. And his conclusions are:

1. Alava, Guipúzcoa and Biscay were never free, sovereign, independent republics; they were territories subjected like the other territories of Spain by conquest, inheritance or particular treaties between the kings of Asturias, León, Castile and Navarra.

2. The *fueros* or local rights are either Castilian rights, better preserved in the Basque country owing to the smaller area of its communities, or special concessions graciously granted by the kings.

[3] It is not by mere hazard that we find Llorente, the anti-clerical priest and scholarly denouncer of the Inquisition, demonstrating the inanity of the Basque claims. For these claims have always been put forward by men of anti-liberal and clerical principles. Even in his time, he was fiercely attacked for having taken up this cause, *being a priest. Noticias Históricas de las Tres Provincias Vascongadas,* by Dr. Don Juan Antonio Llorente. Madrid. 1806-7. Tome III, p. xxiii.

3. The form of government of the three Basque provinces is modern. Until the fourteenth century, they were in no way different from the Castilian provinces and knew no provincial laws.

As for Navarra, it is well known, of course, that it was a separate kingdom which after many vicissitudes finally fell to the Spanish Crown by the marriage of Ferdinand V, widower of Isabel of Castile, to Germaine de Foix (1505).

This utter lack of a cultural, historical, political and above all racial basis for a Basque nationalism is of course no obstacle to its vigor. Nationalism is a state of mind. And in the distinctive characteristics which separate him from his brother Basques diluted with other human bloods and transplanted to other soils, whom we know as Castilians, the Basque nationalist finds ample reason for turning his face away from the rest of Spain. The founder of the movement was a half-educated *bilbaino,* Sabino Arana Goiri, born in 1865, of course in a family of ardent Carlists. A Carlist himself, he saw new and bolder horizons when his elder brother Luis explained to him the nationalist doctrine which he had in fact invented and expounded in his book *Formulario de los Principios Esenciales del Primitivo Nacionalismo Vasco.* Carlism was concerned with keeping the whole of Spain under the undisputed authority of king and priest. Why the whole of Spain? By concentrating on the Basque country the problem could be more easily solved. At sixteen, Sabino Arana Goiri became a nationalist. He was sent to read law at the University of Barcelona, where his Basque nationalism was strengthened by contact with Catalan nationalists—for both movements felt a natural mutual attraction explicable since they are both branches of the same root-force, the dispersive tendency of primeval Spain. Upon his return, he set about to learn the Basque language, which he did not know, and later, to endeavor to purify it of the numerous Castilian, Latin and other words it had borrowed to adapt itself to modern ways.

In 1893, Arana Goiri founded *The Bizkaitarra,* a nationalist newspaper, and a review, the name of which, *Euzkadi,* was to become the new name for a new thing—the unified Basque nation which had never to this day existed. His motto was JAUNGOIKOA ETA LAGI ZARRA, "God and our old Laws," in which we find a trace of the two forces of the movement— Roman Catholic Carlism and the pseudo-historical tradition of local *fueros.* The title of the pamphlet in which Arana Goiri put forward his views is in itself typical of their empirical and improvised character: *Bizcaya por su independencia.* It is in Castilian, of course, like all Basque writing, and it refers to "Biscay," for "Euzkadi" had not yet been invented. In those days, Sabino Arana Goiri would have the other two provinces, Guipúzcoa and Alava, as independent of Biscay as Biscay of the rest of Spain. His attitude toward outsiders was also typical of the hermetic spirit which Basque nationalism inherited from its progenitor Carlism; for Arana Goiri wished to keep the Basque country and language for the Basques and was wholly inimical to any influx of foreign influences or people.

This spirit prevailed in the Bizkaitarra party or movement which right through the Restoration was ever on the side of clerical reaction. As the country as a whole evolved toward the Left, this divergence in matters of general political outlook stimulated the separatist tendency inherent in Bizkaitarrism; priests and Carlists flocked to its growing ranks; and in their turn the parties of the Left, entrenched in the industrial towns, Bilbao and Eibar, in particular, took a more pronounced anti-home-rule position. The elements of a local civil war were therefore taking shape, and now and then blood was spilled.

THE GALLEGAN QUESTION

There is also a Gallegan question. It is a curious movement, if only because it shows how different Spanish questions can be from one point to another of the map. One thing is certain: in so far as the Gallegan movement has any political importance at all, it is a reflection of the Catalan movement, which has stimulated all the awakenings of local feelings to be observed in Spain today. The language is, here again, the basis for the movement. Gallegan is a language far more akin to Portuguese than to Castilian. It was the language in which the Castilian poets wrote when they felt in a genuine lyrical mood. As late as the fifteenth century there were still lyrical poems written in Gallegan by Castilian poets. Then, as in the case of Catalonia, Gallegan poetry, practically the only literature which Galicia ever had, all but died out. The language fell, as Catalan had fallen, to become the exclusive appanage of the humbler classes. In the nineteenth century the big towns such as Coruña and Vigo spoke Castilian. They are still overwhelmingly Castilian. And yet the best poetry written in Spain in the nineteenth century was—with that of Maragall in Catalan—that of Rosalía Castro, the admirable poetess who, though she wrote also in Castilian, was at her best in her native Gallegan.

Rosalía Castro, Curros Enríquez and other less known poets, were read in Galicia even by those who disdained to speak the language. But under an obscure poltical inspiration, societies known as *Irmandades da Fala* (language confraternities) appeared toward the beginning of the twentieth century endeavoring to resuscitate Gallegan as a cultivated language and to fight by example against the prejudice which exiled it to the lower strata of society. A *Seminario de Estudios Gallegos* has been created since. Galicia, though densely populated and suffering from want at the lower end of the social scale, has an upper and middle class in fair prosperity, and the historic university in the old city of Santiago de Compostela is considered by some Gallegan leaders as the future center for the rebirth of her culture. Galicia has the makings of a rich local spiritual life.

But there is Portugal; and obviously the more Galicia becomes herself the more her inherent likeness to Portugal will become apparent. We see how the future of the Gallegan movement opens out perspectives of what should be fruitful collaboration but might also be—who knows?—misunderstanding and strife.

CONCLUSION

This outline of three home-rule movements of Spain should have gone a long way to illustrate their chief characteristics. The positive aspect of these local nationalisms is the very richness of the Spanish nature, which in the relative small compass of the Peninsula gives forth such wonderful varieties, so full of salt and flavor, of color and music, as the Andalusian and the Basque, the Gallegan and the Castilian, and which even within the boundaries of the Catalan-speaking lands can create three varieties as conscious of their differences as the Catalan, the Valencian and the Balearic. Yet, when all is said for these local forms of Spanish life, nothing justifies the setting of the Catalan, the Basque or the Gallegan case in a different category from the Welsh or Scotch case in Great Britain or from the Breton, Basque or Provençal case in France—nothing but the Spanish character giving vent to its dispersion no less in the three local— indeed more in the three local—than in the general environments of the nation. The vigor with which these local spirits reappear in the life of the nation is due to a set of circumstances usually described by the parties as if they were sticks with but one end. But there are always two ends to the stick—and the local one is not the less important of the two. Local cases of centralist oppression there were against Catalonia (not against the Basques), but it cannot for one moment be doubted that, in comparison with France, the centralizing spirit of Spain was very mild; indeed had it been less mild, Spain might have gotten rid of her home-rule problems as France had done.

The next circumstance is lack of historical success. Had Spain continued to be a historical success, such as she was for three centuries, Catalonia and the Basques would have remained in a quiescent enjoyment of her imperial plums. But, as we say in Castilian, "Where there is no flour, every mood is sour." This is confirmed, by the fact that the Catalan and Basque problems began to turn acid when the last vestiges of the Spanish Empire went by the board in 1898.

The prominent part taken in modern times by Catalan and

Basque capitalists in the exploitation of the economic advantages of this empire is common knowledge. The benefits of the collaboration were often due to state aid. The Transatlantic Shipping Company, mostly Catalan, was strongly subsidized by the state (and politically backed by the Jesuits); while to this day a (mainly Catalan) Spanish company, the *Compañía de Tabacos de Filipinas,* still retains in the Philippines a position of power and privilege which it owed for a good part to state backing. As for the Basques, the financial standby of the separatists, the notorious Don Ramón de la Sota, was one of the most reactionary capitalists Spain ever knew.

Much of the uncompromising and intransigent character of these home-rule problems, their tendency to separatism, far from being justified by their more or less solid arguments as "differences," turn out to be the outcome of an *identity* of character between Catalans, Basques and other Spaniards. *The more separatist a Catalan or a Basque is the more Spanish he reveals himself to be.* Just as the Anarcho-Syndicalist is a separatist from the Socialist, and the Right from the Left, and the Church from progress, and the army from the people, and everything from everything else in Spanish political life, so the Catalans and Basques tend toward separatism from the rest of Spain. Separatism is the first impulse of the politically inexperienced Spaniard. Violence moreover in Spanish character and history is at least as often Basque or Catalan as Castilian. The dour ways of the Basque Carlists have left a permanent trace in the nineteenth century and most of the bombs thrown at statesmen and kings were hurled by Catalan quixotic hotheads. Morral, who threw the bomb at the king and queen on their wedding day, Casanelles and Mateu, who killed Dato,[4] Rull and others of the same type were Catalan dreamers, self-taught doctrinaires with more drive and imagination than experience and sense. This must be recorded when incompetent would-be experts in Spanish affairs endeavor to represent Basques and Catalans as more advanced, more European (European, indeed!) than the rest of the Spaniards, a grotesque distortion of the facts.

[4] There was a third man, who was not a Catalan.

All these considerations should be borne in mind in order to appraise the attitude of certain Basques and Catalans both with regard to past history and to contemporary events, which curiously dismisses the political and historical responsibilities of the regions themselves in the common task, surely no other than the building of Spain as a modern nation. They curse Castile and some of their hotheads would even break loose from Castile—from Spain as they say—with a madness not without its method; for it would be, or so at any rate they imagine it, the easiest and the laziest road. But the high road, though the harder, is to build up Spain in a common endeavor. Differences of spirit, of turn of mind, of character within a nation are tensions which enrich the inner life of the whole body politic. Spain is rich in these tensions. Are the local forms of life known as Catalonia, the Basque country, Galicia, to understand their vivifying function within the nation? Or, following the example of Portugal, are they going to seek a secession which is bound to reduce them to the rank of political curiosities or of mere pawns on the European chessboard?

CHAPTER 19

PORTUGAL

The relations between Spain and Portugal are no exception to
the rule prevailing among the Peninsular peoples. A double
wall of pride bristling, on the Portuguese side, with mistrust of
Spanish ambitions prevents a clear understanding of a reality
which in its essentials is simple enough. So simple, indeed, as
to amount to a repetition of the Catalan reality: the Portuguese
is a Spaniard with his back to Castile and his eyes on the Atlantic Ocean.

The symmetry of the position has been described in the chapter on Catalonia. Political and literary history confirm at every
turn the description there given. If we take it as correct, relying
on the following pages for further proofs of the main ideas
which it embodies, we shall find in it the root cause of the permanent separation between Spain and Portugal: the identity
of temperament between these two varieties of Iberian stock.
Here, as in the case of Catalonia, arguments, theories, history,

240

geography, and what not, are to a considerable extent the intellectual puppets of a radical emotion which is no other than the dispersive force of the Iberian people. No doubt geographical factors exert some kind of influence. Just as Catalonia may be explained by her trans-Ebrian position in the margin, so to speak, of the Castilian tableland, so Portugal finds a geographical basis for her separate existence in the geological accident that caused the sinking of the western territory, cutting it off from the tableland. But reasons remain to be found for the difference between the destinies of Catalonia and those of Portugal, for the one remained attached to Castile while the other, but for a brief period of sixty years in the sixteenth century, succeeded in maintaining a separate historical development to this date.

As was to be expected, the reasons are numerous and closely interwoven by history. Let us begin by pointing out that the symmetry between the two cases is not geometrically perfect; in a north-south direction the Peninsula is symmetrical, with Portugal on the left, and Catalonia on the right, of Castile; but from east to west the symmetry is inverted, or in other words the figure before us is not an M but an N, a remark which applies to both geography and history. As for geography, Catalonia is out of the way behind the high ranges which limit the tableland toward the northeast, while it is easily accessible by the plains of La Mancha and the southern end of the Valencian kingdom in a line running from south to north along the coast. Moreover, the Catalan-Valencian region has its main nucleus to the north in Barcelona, and a secondary one, not so important, further south in Valencia. Portugal, on the other hand, has her great port to the south in Lisbon and a second port further north in Oporto, therefore in an inverse position from that of the two sea cities of the Catalan-Valencian region. Moreover, though access is fairly easy from Madrid southward toward Lisbon, this line of approach was under Moorish occupation at the period when Spanish nationalities were being formed, while the movement of reconquest naturally took place from the north. We know, moreover, the important role played by the Castilian tableland as a center of attraction, and how the

Christian effort, born in Galicia and in Asturias, concentrated later in the kingdom of León, to settle finally in Castile. This obviously determines for the Christian reconquest a line of advance in a diagonal direction from Galicia toward Murcia and Alicante, i.e. a northwest=southeast line, being the middle line of the letter N which schematizes these medieval movements.

These obvious facts determine, also, other not less significant events in early Peninsular history. Catalonia was born in her own capital. She began as Barcelona, and this metropolis remained so predominant in her history that, to the present day, the King of Spain's title to sovereignty over the Catalan region is that of Count of Barcelona. Starting from her base, Catalonia cannot, therefore, spread in the Peninsula without moving away from it, and therefore without moving toward the Castilian magnet, whether through Aragon or through Valencia. The enterprises of the Catalans in France, in Italy, in Africa, were gallant attempts at escaping their fate. But the county of Barcelona was not a sufficient base of operations for wide expansion abroad. The Aragonese Confederation and the conquest of Valencia were inevitable events in the history of Catalonia, and we know that, once federated with Aragon, the political attraction of Castile was to prove too strong for the independence of Catalonia. The very reverse is the case of Portugal. The main base of what was to be Portugal, Lisbon, was in the hands of the Moors. Portugal became a mere feudal affair, a gift of Alfonso VI to one of his sisters, who had married a turbulent Frenchman of the House of Burgundy. This first Count of Portugal worked for his own ends and he contributed in a most spirited manner to the anarchy which followed the death of Alfonso, trying to round off his Atlantic estate with typically Castilian lands and actually occupying the Galician territories of Orense and Tuy. His son, Alfonso Enríquez, came to trouble with the King of Castile, Alfonso VII, who laid great stress on his imperial title and did not trifle with his rights over the other princes of the Peninsula. That is perhaps why, although he had beaten Alfonso Enríquez, he granted him the title of king under his suzerainty in 1143. It is clear that Portugal was born without a base and Catalonia with, and on, her base. This explains, also, why Portugal should have been born with a historical tendency to secede from, while Catalonia was born with a historical tendency to accede to, the Spanish-Castilian unity, particularly if it be noticed that, while the expansion of Castile, as we have pointed out, had to follow the diagonal line northwest→ Castile→southeast, the Portuguese line of advance was inevitably drawn dead south toward Lisbon, thereby creating a natural divergence; while the Catalan line of advance being also dead south along the coast (following the line of lowlands and to avoid as far as possible the attraction of Castile) was bound to meet Castile all the same where it actually met it, in Murcia—hence the agreement between the King-Count of Aragon-Barcelona and the King of Castile as to the conquest of Murcia. Thus the N shape, which we found convenient to explain the characteristics of the literature and culture of the Peninsula, accounts also for the movements of her early history. While Catalonia, through Aragon, falls into the Castilian basket, Portugal remains hanging outside it.

Efforts were, no doubt, made to bring her in, both from the Portuguese and from the Castilian side. In the thirteenth century John I of Spain, having married the Portuguese Doña Beatriz, came by the throne of Portugal, which he was, however, unable to conquer owing to a revolt of the Portuguese, led by the Master of the Order of Avis, who became king under the name of John I of Portugal. In a sense, the duel between Isabel the Catholic and her niece, Juana La Beltraneja, for the succession to the Castilian throne, implied a choice between union with Aragon-Catalonia on the one hand and union with Portugal on the other; for Doña Juana, daughter of the Portuguese princess, would have carried the kingdom of Portugal with her had she been successful in securing her father's throne for herself. The choice had already been made by Isabel, for when after her brother, Henry IV, father of Doña Juana, had disinherited his daughter and recognized Isabel as his heir to the throne, he expressed his wish that she should marry the king of Portugal. Isabel, however, preferred Ferdinand, the heir of Aragon. The Portuguese were undoubtedly then under the subtle influence of the Castilian "magnet," for the tendency toward union came at least as strongly from Alfonso V of Portugal as from the Castilian court. Yet Castile could not marry both east and west at a time; and Isabel probably thought that the great Aragonese-Catalan-Valencian federation, so strong on the Mediterranean, was worth having first unless, being a woman after all, she preferred Ferdinand's looks to Alfonso's, for of such things, also, history is made. That she did not forget Spanish unity she was to prove in later years. Ferdinand and Isabel, the two most efficient nation-builders that Spain has known, tried to enmesh Portugal when casting far and wide their matrimonial nets. Nor was Portugal the obstacle in this case. The obstacle was Fate, through her chief steward, Death. Fate seems to have made up her mind that Portugal was to remain a separate unit in the Peninsula. In 1479 Ferdinand and Isabel arranged that their heir, Don Juan, should marry Juana La Beltraneja (who as the daughter of a Portuguese princess might bring in Portuguese rights eventually), while their daughter Isabel would marry a Portuguese prince. The first marriage failed because Juana entered a convent, and the second came to nothing because the Portuguese prince died untimely; and this was the first time that Death cut the nets of Ferdinand and Isabel. Nothing daunted, they married young Isabel to the Duke of Beja, heir to the Portuguese throne, and Don Miguel, issue of this match, had the chance of being king of a united Spain by the death of Prince Juan of Castile and Aragon. This chance Don Miguel threw away by dying, and, as if Death meant to dot the *i's* and cross the *t's,* she also took Don Miguel's mother, Princess Isabel. The Castilian royal couple persisted in their policy and married her Portuguese widower to another of their daughters, Mary, whom Death also took away, then with yet another, Doña Leonor.

But Death was not the only factor working for separation. The era of discovery which sealed the fate of Catalonia by binding her to Castile gave a new impetus to the separate existence of Portugal. Let us remember our definitions. The Catalan is a Spaniard on the shores of the Mediterranean; the Portuguese is a Spaniard on the shores of the Atlantic. A historical wind blowing westward was bound to have dramatically opposite effects on Catalonia and on Portugal. The seafaring activities of the Catalans withered when history's stage shifted from the mere Mediterranean to the vast Atlantic and to the mysterious Pacific. The seafaring activities of the Portuguese gained a great impetus thereby. It mattered little to them that the Queen of Castile forbade their trade with the newly discovered empires. They sailed forth magnificently; indeed, they went on sailing forth, for, as good Atlantians, they had begun before the Castilians, they, the dauntless forerunners of all sea daring and discovery, and Christopher Columbus gave them but a wider scope to do

> Mais do que prometia a força humana
> Por mares nunca de antes navegados.

The Portuguese historian, Oliveira Martins, has dramatically described the emotions of the Portuguese discoverers of the eastward way to the Pacific when, to their amazement, they found on these far-off waters the ensign of the Castilian king flown by the boats of Magellan, after the discovery of the Straits; and Magellan himself, writing to a friend in India, expressed the hope that he would meet him some day, when he would come back to Europe either by "the Portuguese way" (i.e. the eastern way), or by "the Castilian way" (the Magellan Straits). The world was small in those days for Castile and Portugal. The Pope had to be brought in to carve it between them, giving Portugal all the lands lying east of a line which he defined so vaguely as to enable every kind of conflict to flourish right and left of it. Ferdinand did not hesitate to organize armed resistance against the Portuguese on his newly acquired domains; and this rivalry and colonizing activity did, of course, much to strengthen the historical vigor of Portugal.

Both Charles V and Philip II married Portuguese princesses, and married their sisters to Portuguese princes. Charles V's mar-

riage was the cause of the union with Portugal which lasted from
1580 to 1668, for the throne of Portugal fell vacant and Philip
II was the candidate with the best legal title and also with the
strongest army at his disposal, a combination generally irresistible. The period during which Portugal was ruled by Spanish
kings is by no means a period of Spanish rule. In fact, a detached
study of these sixty years of Portuguese history goes a long way
to upset a number of prejudices and yet to confirm the essential
features of the common psychology of both Castilians and Portuguese. Philip II's reputation has been made on his Netherlands
record, but since his record there was due to the stern faith
which he held, it is to be expected that his dealings with a nation
so devoutly orthodox as Portugal was then would differ considerably. In fact, though the Dutch, hopelessly heretical as they
appeared to him, were bound to force the king to actions which
show him in an intolerant light, Philip was no maniac of intolerance. As monarchs went in that period he was, on the whole, a
moderate ruler, even in religious matters, as shown by his efforts
to damp the Inquisitional zeal of Mary Tudor. The Spanish
period of Portugal is a case in point. It was, on the whole, brief;
and the reader, knowing all about Alba and Egmont, says: "No
wonder." But what did actually happen during those sixty years?
Philip appointed not a single Castilian to a Portuguese post; laid
hands on not a single Portuguese institution; respected every Portuguese liberty. His only difficulty from the very beginning was in
the lower clergy, many of whose members he had to punish for
their violent attacks against him. The old court remained unmo-
lested in the full possession of its dignities and privileges, a leniency which was to be ill repaid in later days; the political and
commercial organization of the colonies was respected, and Lisbon lost neither materially nor morally by the personal union;
no military, naval or financial help was exacted for the king's
Spanish activities abroad; customs barriers between Spain and
Portugal were abolished; public works were prepared in order to
increase the navigation value of the Tagus, which flows past
Toledo and Lisbon without really linking the old imperial capital
of Spain and the wonderful sea capital of Portugal; legislation

and administration were improved; the aristocracy, the commercial and liberal professions were contented and felt self-
governed—but there was the lower clergy and there were the
Jesuits, who thorougly disliked Philip II, a feeling which the
king heartily reciprocated. And the Jesuits, the lower clergy
and the ambitions of a Spanish woman broke the union as soon
as an unwise Spanish Minister of State gave them an opportunity
therefor.

The trouble came because the King of Spain wanted fair play
for the Jews. Spanish history is full of unexpectedness. Philip III
first, then Philip IV, tried to soften the condition of the Portuguese Jews—oh, ever so little!—for they were too pious themselves to go too far in this dangerous direction. They merely
suggested that, when the Jew made up his mind to emigrate
toward freer lands, he might be allowed to sell his property.
The lower clergy of Portugal and the masses whom they led
were shocked at these winds of heresy coming from Madrid,
and the mood of Portugal was ready for secession. Then Olivares, Philip IV's minister, thought fit to advise his sovereign
to go now and then to Portugal, to appoint some Portuguese
nobility as ambassadors, viceroys and high dignitaries of his
household and service, and to send Castilians to Portugal also
in order to promote an interchange of the higher staff of the
monarchy. And this again raised a wind of fury in the separatist
Iberian. Finally, the worst of mistakes came from Madrid, for,
breaking away from the wise policy of Philip II, taxes were laid
on the Portuguese people to further the king's policy in Europe.
Olivares first tried to get rid of the Duke of Braganza, who as
a scion of the royal house might dangerously personify the
separatist tendency, by making him Viceroy of Naples, an honor
which the Portuguese prince declined; then, taking the bull by
the horns, the Spanish minister entrusted the duke with the
command of the military forces of the Portuguese realm. The
duke, a man of honor, was thus placed in a position of trust
from which he would not spontaneously have felt inclined to
strike a disloyal blow. But Olivares forgot the duchess. She
was a Spanish woman, an Andalusian, a sister of that duke of

Medina Sidonia who was to make his name famous by organizing a separatist move in Andalusia, and, unable to resist the sight of a queenly crown so close to her, she drove the duke to rebellion and had him proclaimed king in 1641.

He had but to look round the map of Europe to see prospective friends. French, Dutch and English help was forthcoming. The Spanish armies were fortunate at first, but after a protracted war which Philip IV fought but halfheartedly, having too many conflicts on his hands already, the secession of Portugal was consolidated in the Battle of Villaviciosa, in 1665, with no other loss to Portugal than that of some colonies which one of her allies, the Dutch, had taken from her during the crisis.

There was, however, a further and more lasting and important loss. Portugal lost her independence. English help was given her only under conditions which bound her destinies to those of the rising star of the North. Not by her two treaties (1654 with Cromwell, 1661 with Charles II), but by the new system of forces which her secession created was her dependence on England sealed for centuries. Portugal became the fulcrum of England's lever against the might of Spain. By then, of course, Spain was no longer Philip II's, but that ghostly empire which a half-witted king ruled with a hesitating hand; half a century later, during the War of Succession, England was to conquer her second fulcrum on Spanish territory—the invaluable Rock. But the secession of Portugal was the most important of downward events in Spanish history and, in a truer sense than the superficial one usually applied to it, of Portuguese history also. English political domination over Portugal is the last and perhaps the most important factor tending to separate Portugal from Spain. The political reasons which explain this fact are so obvious that they need no elaboration. With a weakening Spain and a rising England strong at sea and conscious of the value of a division between Spain and Portugal for her policy, Spanish efforts toward re-union by means of dynastic family arrangements had no longer any sense.[1] But the existence of this

[1] War attempts, of course, still less so, but then it is a curious fact of Spanish history that though there were numerous civil wars between

strong English interest in Portugal acted against the union in at least two other ways, more far-reaching than mere politics.

Politics, after all, is but the moving surface of the waters, and we cannot claim more than superficial knowledge when we stop at political events. In the case of Spain and Portugal a survey of the relations between them in literary history is indispensable. One of the most important documents in the history of Spanish letters is the epistle which the Marqués de Santillana sent to Don Pedro, the Constable of Portugal, with a gift of his works, in 1449. Don Pedro, a prince of the royal house, following the traditions of his family, was a poet, and the first Portuguese who wrote Castilian prose and verse. The Marqués having referred in his letter to the ancients, then the French, the Italians, the Catalans, the Valencians, "and even a few of the kingdom of Aragon," reminds his Portuguese friend that the *Arte mayor* was discovered "in the kingdoms of Galicia and Portugal in which there is no doubt that the exercise of these sciences [of poetry] is more customary than in any other region or province of Spain, to such an extent that not long ago all reciters and *trouvères* of these parts, whether Castilians, Andalusians or of Estremadura, composed their works in the Gallegan or Portuguese language." It remained Gallegan-Portuguese (to the point that the King of Castile himself, Alfonso X, wrote his poems in that language) as long as it remained lyrical. Then the mood of the Peninsula changed and from lyrical it became epic. The tide had turned. The people were no longer a race of Christians expelled from their country by the Moors; they were a race which had reconquered the land and was full of the marvelous vigor that, not very much later, was to expand European civilization beyond the dreams of the boldest medieval imagination. Spain (including Portugal) became epic and dramatic. She had to express herself in Castilian. It was not—we saw it with Catalan—it was not the political connection which

Christians, the aggrandizement of Christian states by war against other Christian states was never attempted; wars between Christian states did take place in order to avoid separation, but never in order to bring about union, with the single exception of Navarra.

preceded the linguistic conquest; it was the language which unified Spanish culture before any conception of political unity had appeared. Portugal did not become politically united under Philip II until 1580. Don Pedro began to write Castilian poems and prose in 1449. Castilian became a normal means of expression for the Portuguese as Portuguese had been earlier for the Castilians. The *Catálogo Razonado,* issued in 1890 by Domingo García in Madrid, contains upward of six hundred names of Portuguese authors who wrote in Castilian. The most efficient instrument of Castilian penetration was the *romance,* that swift-moving poem of eight syllables in assonance, so admirably adapted to the popular genius of Spain that, to this day, the Spanish Jews expelled from Spain in the fifteenth century still know *romances* by heart and sing them from Asia Minor to Colombia and from Tangier to Amsterdam. The Castilian *romance* caught on in Portugal as much as the lyrical *cántigas* of Portugal had caught on in Castile. Indeed, more deeply, for the Portuguese lyrical poetry was adopted, as Santillana says, by *decidores y trovadores,* while the Castilian *romances* were adopted by the Portuguese people as well.Their popularity in Portugal is attested by the number of *romanceros* or collections of them which appeared in Lisbon. Moreover, long before any *romance* had been published in Portugal, Spanish *romances* in Castilian appeared on the Portuguese stage on the lips of popular characters. A typical case in point is that of Gil Vicente, that truly magnificent poet, one of the most gifted of Europe, the creator of the Portuguese theater, whose work is, in form as in substance, a link between the two nations, a garland of poetical flowers uniting in spirit Castile and Portugal.

On June 6, 1502—Portugal had been an independent kingdom for four centuries and Philip II was not to be her king till seventy-eight years later—a prince was born in the Portuguese court, he who was to be John III. The next day, Gil Vicente, the Portuguese poet, put his muse at the service of his patriotic heart and, disguised as a shepherd, celebrated the birth of the *infante* in a kind of pastoral monologue, a dramatic sketch *written in Castilian.* Twelve years earlier, in a tournament celebrated in Evora on the occasion of a royal marriage, all but one of the mottoes of the knights participating in the festivity were written in Castilian. Castilian became so deeply ingrained a language in the Portuguese court that the word king, *rei,* to the present day does not take in correct Portuguese the Portuguese article, but must be used with the Castilian article: *el rei.* Gil Vicente, in many ways a poet of the court, used the two languages indiscriminately, writing plays now entirely in Portuguese, now using both languages in the same play; as when he makes a nurse in a play written in Portuguese sing a *romance* in Castilian. Nor was he a Peninsular author in language only, for the very spirit of his work, ranging from his sacred *autos* to his merry and satirical *comedias* and *farsas,* brings to mind the typical features of the Castilian theater. He stands in the line of great Peninsular dramatists, a successor and pupil of the Spanish Encina (far surpassing his master), and the predecessor of Lope and Calderón. Yet with this difference, that he possessed that marvelous gift for lyrical poetry which, in the Peninsula, we know to be the privilege of the Gallegan-Portuguese West.

The vicissitudes of Castilian influence over Portuguese literature do not concern us here. All we need remark is that the greatest Portuguese poets used both languages of their own free will out of the sheer wealth of impressions and inspirations which they wished to manifest. While men of mere talent, however refined, more imitative and cultivated than creative and spontaneous, men such as Sa de Miranda or Antonio Ferreira, severely denied themselves the use of Castilian, Gil Vicente used it freely, and Camões, the Portuguese poet *par excellence,* wrote in Castilian with such splendor that he deserves to count as one of the best poets of the Castilian language. An edition of Camões' songs and *canções* passes without warning from Portuguese to Castilian, from Castilian to Portuguese. And this simple fact is eloquent. For both Gil Vicente and Camões were ardent patriots, and no one can claim that the practice which these two poets followed could be prejudicial to either the development of Portuguese genius and culture or to the respect which Portuguese sovereignty and independence deserve. The two great poets felt that the spirit which moved Peninsular inspiration could equally well emerge in either of the two languages (as it can in the east in either Catalan or Castilian), for it all depends on the mood of the poem itself. They had two means of expression at their disposal, just as the painter has oil and water colors, and being rich in things to say, they quietly assumed the right to use whichever means was more adequate to the aim in view.

For, in fact, Castilian and Portuguese literature cannot be studied separately—any more than Castilian and Catalan. When the compiler of *romances* prints an anthology he does not know how many of his flowers were grown on Portuguese soil. *The Oxford Book of Portuguese Verse* contains a fair number of Spaniards belonging to all periods from the very earliest down to the nineteenth century. *The Oxford Book of Spanish Verse* also contains a good number of Portuguese poets. The fact is that there is an inherent unity underlying all Iberian differences which makes these two cultures in these two nations two aspects of one and the same spirit.

The political union under Philip II was not particularly favorable to the manifestation of this inherent harmony. The golden age of Spanish-Portuguese collaboration in the realms of the spirit is precisely that in which the two nations, though united in culture, are politically apart. In the sixteenth century Spain and Portugal were two separate kingdoms thinking more or less vaguely of union, their kings even scheming for it, and, at the same time, curiously linked up by a subconscious feeling of common Spanishness which somehow or other underlies all Peninsular life at that time. The direct political connection under Philip II did much to weaken that feeling. Camões died in the year when Philip II became King of Portugal. The period which then began was closed in the following century with the War of Secession and Portugal's treaties with England.

These treaties and what they implied account for the phase of mutual neglect and isolation which then set in. The magnet was no longer Castile, but England. In Portugal this change brought about deep spiritual effects. Philip II's rule was not the best historically to be wished for Portugal, though, of course, no other was available at the time in the divine imagination. This fact, combined with the dispersive tendency which the Portuguese share with the remaining Iberians, was bound to lead to secession. But there is little doubt that ultimately the interests of Portugal would have been better served had she remained a Spanish kingdom, even at the risk of falling under the Bourbon absolutism of Philip V. The mistake which Catalonia tried to commit several times in her history Portugal committed in 1662. Psychology, geography and history pointed to an Iberian evolution for Portugal. She chose a precarious life in the English alliance, forgetting that there is no alliance between the very weak and the very strong. And though England has been a good friend and even a generous one, and though Portugal, unlike Spain, has not lost her colonies, she has been melancholy ever since. For Portugal, three centuries of common life in Spain, even though cut about by civil wars, would have been more invigorating than peace and a nominal independence underpinned from abroad.

From the point of view of Spain the new historical phase determined a kind of inhibition from Portuguese affairs. The almost total indifference toward Portugal, the ignorance of Portuguese life, the almost complete annihilation of Portugal in the Spanish mind, has often been observed. Not so often the fact that it dates precisely from the period when England took charge. It is an example of a feature of Spanish psychology which may be observed in many other cases—the tendency to give up all interest and to withdraw within the tent of silence and passivity when actions and words are useless. Let us recall the dignified withdrawal of Katherine of Aragon from the tribunal of the two papal legates who were to examine the legitimacy of her marriage to King Henry VIII, or, again, the wholesale inhibition of the Spanish political intelligentsia under the Primo de Rivera dictatorship. The case of Portugal is of the same kind. England is there. Very well. Let England do it. And Spain turned away from Portugal.

The tradition of the unity of old remained perhaps fairly alive among scholars. No one could look back on the fifteenth and sixteenth centuries without finding there such eloquent testimonies of it as the close cooperation between the scholars of Coimbra and Salamanca universities in the early sixteenth century, the period before political union, a time when Portuguese names abound in every walk of Spanish scholarship. Moreover, the matter of a political union or federation was never quite dormant, least of all in the nineteenth century when political thought became more general. Curiously enough, Portugal was the keener of the two, for the change it would imply looms larger in her future than in that of Spain. Some enlightened Portuguese realized that Portugal must be either an autonomous limb of the Iberian body or a disguised and hardly more autonomous limb of the British Empire. One of the most eloquent voices to call Spain back to life, that Spain which includes Catalonia as it includes Portugal, was a Portuguese historian, Oliveira Martins. In his *History of Iberian Civilization,* dedicated to the Spanish novelist and critic Juan Valera, Oliveira Martins endeavors to delve under historical details in order to draw out the essential unity of the Iberian civilization. He had the courage to write such things as "Those differences are but aspects separating our nations without destroying the unity of thought, of character and of action which make Spain one though her modern history has constituted her under a régime of political dualism." He asserted his faith in a "future Spain more noble and illustrious even than that of the sixteenth century," but he wisely pointed out: "In many ways our present-day history repeats the past; and if we meditate on it thoroughly, we, the men of the Peninsula, may still discover an inner and permanent force which, by liberating us from the imitation of foreign forms, may give the work of organic reconstitution of society a distinctive turn, more lasting as resting on the nature of our race, more efficient as better answering the requirements of the work itself." One of Portugal's greatest scholars, Teófilo Braga, in his *As Modernas Ideias da Literatura Portuguesa,* enumerates the efforts made by the Portuguese through all their history to bring about a dynastic union; from those of John IV at the death of Charles II to the several attempts during the nineteenth century, including the endeavors of Luis I to obtain from Napoleon III the crown of Spain which Prim ultimately offered to Amadeo of Savoy after the Revolution of 1868.

On the Spanish side there have been no dynastic attempts in modern times, but the matter seems to have come up now and then, from the time when Campuzano, the Spanish ambassador in London, discussed it with Canning till 1844, when Queen Isabel and her younger sister were considered as possible brides for the Portuguese heir and his brother. Ideas more in keeping with modern times began to appear toward the middle of the century. Union receded on the horizon and a kind of federation emerged in the mind of Peninsular enthusiasts. Works such as the *Estudos Sobre A Reforma Em Portugal* (1851), by the Portuguese, Henriques Nogueira, advocated this solution as corresponding to the inherent unity of the two peoples, and a pamphlet entitled *A Iberia. Memoria em que se provam as vantagems políticas, económicas e sociaes da união das duas monarquías peninsulares em uma só naçao,* though still hankering after a dynastic union, rather fostered the ideas of federation. As in most Spanish questions, however, a split occurred between the Right and the Left, the clerical Right in both countries being for union and the republican or anti-clerical Left being for federation. Discussion became so heated that, in 1853, the Spanish government forbade all reference to it in the papers. In 1854 no less a person than the future leader of Spanish politics, Cánovas, proposed a dynastic union in a pamphlet called *El Recuerdo*.

The Revolution of 1868 did not help matters because the revolutionary government needed all the help it could get from foreign countries and it was thought prudent not to offend British susceptibilities. A certain amount of anti-federation work was done at this time, notably by Teixeira de Vasconcellos, who went so far as to assert in a Portuguese paper that Spain was preparing the conquest of Portugal; but federal hopes were not forgotten by Ruiz Zorrilla, the Spanish republican leader, when, in exile after the Restoration, he issued his Brussels manifesto, and there was a sensational republican campaign in Spain, led by both Spaniards and Portuguese, which culminated in an Iberian-Republican Congress held in Badajoz in 1889.

During the same period ideas similar to those which guided the Portuguese federationists of the Oliveira Martins school began to germinate in Catalonia. The West and the East were feeling their way toward the new ideal of Peninsular reconstruction. As was to be expected, the idea progressed at a quicker pace in the East than in the West. Oliveira Martins had but little following. His Iberian views, in fact, had injured his popularity with his countrymen. The fear of a rigid political interpretation of the union is, in many a Portuguese soul, combined with the more concrete fear of actual Spanish conquest and occupation. The unintelligent attitude of some Castilian politicians and newspapers toward Catalonia does little to remove this feeling in Portugal. In Castile, however, no man in his senses would hesitate for a second to declare that whatever happens must be the result of the free and inner convictions of all concerned. The work of cultural and material approximation has still a long way to go. And if Portugal were never to wish for a more intimate association with the rest of the Peninsula, why should Spain? Ganivet, on the eve of King Alfonso XIII's accession, summed up the matter with his admirable common sense:

> The problem of Iberian unity is not European but Spanish: as the very words show, it is Peninsular or Iberian. Though some European nations may be interested in maintaining the Peninsula divided, it does not follow that the question is European: if all nations tolerated that we should constitute such a happy unity that would not justify us in committing an aggression thereto; there would be no one in Spain, whatever may be thought on the matter, capable of such a thing. On the other hand, if Spain and Portugal of their own free will were to agree to bring about such a union no one in Europe would oppose an objection to an agreement which would not affect the continental political balance. The union must be the exclusive work of those

who are to be united; it is an internal affair about which it is dangerous to seek outside help.

Similarly I have never understood the Iberian union as a purely Spanish question. . . . For a long time I was saddened by the sight of two different colors on the map of the Peninsula. But I have seen so many artificial unions that my opinions have changed: if we were to be united like England and Ireland, or Sweden and Norway, or Austria and Hungary, we might just as well remain separate and let that separation serve at any rate to foster feelings of confraternity incompatible with a system of violent union. The union of several nationalities in one single nation can only have as a useful and human aim the bringing together of different civilizations in order that a spiritual stimulation may come from their mutual influence; and this aim may possibly be brought about without any material political domination.

CHAPTER 20

MOROCCO

There is an episode within an episode in Don Quixote which throws more light on the historical roots of Spanish-Moroccan policy than all the expert literature written since. The "captive" is telling his new friends, in the hospitable inn where so many things happen, how he escaped from captivity in Algiers with the beautiful Moorish girl who had fallen in love with him. After a series of dramatic episodes, the party land at last on the deserted shore on the southern coast of Spain and walk on in search of human beings. Suddenly they are much elated to see a young shepherd and his flock. But the shepherd, seeing first the Moorish girl and the renegade guide, also in Moorish attire, runs away shouting: "Moors. Moors in the land. To arms, to arms." And presently the little band sees a troop of about fifty knights coming toward them, armed to defend their country against the invader. This was supposed to happen more than a

258

hundred years after the last Moorish king had wept on the hill which was to block Granada forever from his eyes.

For eight centuries Spain had been the battleground of two peoples, one of which, the southern, had northern Africa as its base. Whenever things went wrong in the Peninsula, the Spanish Moors called for help from their Moroccan friends. The idea of retaliating, of carrying the war from Spain into Morocco was but the natural reaction to expect once the Moor had been expelled from the Peninsula. It occurs early in Christian Spain as soon as a man strong enough to incarnate it appears in the Christian host. Such a man was El Cid. His Homer, the unknown author of the *Poema del Cid,* wrote (*circa* 1140) after one of El Cid's victories over the King of Morocco before Valencia, that the Moors in Morocco, "where the mosques are," feared that the Spanish champion might fall upon them one night. El Cid was a cautious soldier and a shrewd politician. His faithful interpreter makes him say: "This they may fear but I think it not. I shall not go to fetch them. I shall stay in Valencia. They will pay me tribute with the help of the Creator." For the idea of crossing over to Morocco when more than half the Peninsula was still occupied by the Moors was premature by about three centuries. But the fact that we find it attributed to El Cid by his earliest interpreter shows that the idea was not merely political but national as well; it was not merely a knightly thought but a popular instinct.

As soon as the Spaniards obtained command of the Spanish coast on the Straits free expeditions began. The late fifteenth century, an epoch in which Spanish energy, repressed at home by the stern energy of Ferdinand and Isabel, overflowed in the four directions of the compass, witnessed numerous adventures of a private character for settling on the southern side of the Straits. The most important of them was that led by Don Pedro Estopiñán, who, with the private fleet of the Duke of Medina Sidonia, a magnate holding feudal rights over the African coast granted him by the Castilian King John II in 1449, took Melilla and held it for the king and duke.

Ferdinand and Isabel let their subjects go toward Africa, the importance of which they fully realized. For Isabel, the center of interest was in Morocco, for many of the Moslems who had been bound to leave Spain in 1492 lived there and might reasonably be expected to work toward a new invasion of the Spanish coast. For Ferdinand, Tunis was important, since he was also King of Naples and of Sicily, and, in fact, of the whole coast between Tangier and Tripoli, if only because piracy was a pest which afflicted particularly his Catalan subjects. Nothing, not even that discovery of America which was so violently to deflect Spanish history, could make Castile forget altogether—though it did make her at times neglect—the importance of Moroccan policy. When, after the death of the queen and the brief regency of Philip the Handsome, King Ferdinand took over the Castilian regency, Cardinal Cisneros, who had been Isabel's confessor, did not hesitate to carry on the queen's African policy at his own personal expense, while King Ferdinand was busy over his European affairs. The spirited churchman conquered Peñón de la Gomera, Orán, Bougie and Tripoli and made the Moorish kings of Tunis, Algiers and Tlemcen vassals of Ferdinand. The connection between Spain and the African coast became thus one of the permanent factors in the network of activities which harassed the head and heart of Spanish monarchs. With the appearance of Barbarossa the Corsair, backed by the sultan from Constantinople and by the King of Algiers, the situation of Catalan and Valencian merchants and the safety of the Balearic Islands and of the sea communications between the Spanish and the Italian dominions of the crown became precarious—so precarious that as late as 1575 Spain was in danger of losing the most precious of her sons before he had given his best to the world when Cervantes was caught and made a slave by Algerian pirates while sailing home from Italy, a wounded, ambitious young soldier. Charles V tried to put an end to this state of affairs by attacking the corsair in Tunis (1535), an expedition which gave the emperor considerable prestige as the champion of Christendom. Yet the fight against the Moor was an ever recurring one. After Philip II,

in the person of his half-brother Don Juan of Austria, had won
the famous battle of Lepanto (1571), in which Cervantes was
wounded and lost the use of his left hand, Don Juan had to
take Tunis again and leave in it a Spanish garrison. Signs of
activity appear again under Philip III. Some of them, such as
the Duke of Osuna's expeditions to Morocco, where he took
Larache from the pirates, were offshoots of private initiative.
African piracy seems to have stimulated international cooperation, for in 1619 France, England and Spain negotiated an
agreement for common action in this field. This cooperation in
the face of the common enemy did not last long. Louis XIV
in his period of anti-Spanish policy attacked the Spanish-African
posts. The Africans needed no such stimulus. In 1666 Larache
was nearly lost to a pirate; in 1667 and 1672 Orán was in
danger of falling to the Turkish Viceroy of Algiers. The French
ambassador wrote that many people in Spain feared a return
of the Moorish invasion if Orán were lost. This clearly shows
the persistence of the traditional "frontier" feeling prevailing in
Andalusia, where even to this day, Jerez (where sherry comes
from) is officially known as *Jerez de la Frontera*. Larache was
lost in 1684 and Ceuta just saved in 1694. It was evident that
Spain had not followed up the line of obvious expansion which
she would have adopted had America remained undiscovered
and had Charles V been less solicitous for the salvation of the
Dutch. But Madrid thought of nothing but the gold of America
and the soul of the Netherlands, and Africa remained a raw
problem for later centuries.

When Spain stirred again in these quarters the most important
change in the Straits had occurred; Admiral Rooke on behalf
of the Archduke Charles, who considered himself King of Spain,
had taken Gibraltar (1704), and English diplomacy had kept
it for England in Utrecht (1713). Nevertheless, a minimum of
activity in Morocco, a kind of defensive-offensive, was maintained as a matter of course by all successive governments. That
this policy was indispensable is shown by the fact that Moroccan
activity was the only foreign action which that most enlightened
of Spanish monarchs, Ferdinand VI, undertook during his reign.

By then, it had been discovered that a million pesos spent in naval armaments against the corsairs paid better than a similar sum doled out in ransom to redeem slaves, a method which resulted in whetting the corsairs' appetite for more slave raiding. In 1767, the Emperor of Morocco signed a treaty with Charles III of Spain on the basis of no corsairs and free commerce. This did not prevent His Shereefian Majesty from declaring war on Spain in 1774, and besieging Melilla for a few months. Spain retaliated by an attack on Algiers which, though begun with vigor and power, ended in disaster through incompetence. A new expedition was organized in 1783-84. Algiers thought better of it, and, having been bombarded twice, signed an agreement in 1786 whereby Spanish consuls were admitted, trade allowed, corsairs forbidden, and the Spanish granted the free exercise of their religion. Tunis followed the good example of Algiers. The next fit of African activity took place in the following century when, under the O'Donnell Ministry, Spain declared war on Morocco in order to obtain some respite from incessant attacks on her settlements there. O'Donnell himself took charge of the operations and, after a campaign more spectacular than technically brilliant, took Tetuán. An indemnity, a moderate enlargement of her zone of influence round Ceuta, and the consolidation of an old claim on Santa Cruz de la Mar Pequeña was all Spain obtained from this affair, which was extremely popular at the time and in which particular distinction was won by a body of Catalan volunteers commanded by General Prim. That this expedition led to no permanent results was evident already at the time. But possibly for the first time the fault was not all on the side of Spain. Further trouble arose in 1893 when, in the vicinity of Melilla, General Margallo perished in an attempt to subject the unruly tribes to some kind of peaceful neighborly behavior. The incident was settled without further bloodshed, thanks to the firm but able negotiations led by General Martínez Campos.

It will be seen, then, that Spain never actually forgot Africa, yet never actually took up there the position which history, geography and inherent destiny seemed obviously to suggest.

Other tasks called her to far-off parts of the world while the main task at her gates remained unfulfilled. Yet, in a quiet non-political way, her people had penetrated far into the life of northern Africa. She was settled for a long time in Orán; she had frequent intercourse with the most unfriendly centers of Tunis and Algiers through the regular flow of captives who came in by the door of piracy and left duly shorn by the door of charity—a circulation which, in its lucrative effects and in its permanency, would suggest piracy as an occupation somewhat akin to banking. She had, moreover, by expelling her Jews across the Straits, spread a leaven of Hispanification all over Morocco so that, until quite recently, the language of business and the coinage in the Shereefian Empire were Spanish. Moreover, by a kind of historical tradition which the victory of Charles V had endowed with a certain brilliance and majesty, the Spanish nation maintained a specially privileged position in Morocco till the nineteenth century.

Yet, passing from imponderabilia to hard facts, the main forces which determined the Moroccan position in the nineteenth century were: first of all, Spain's own political weakness, implying as it did a certain fitfulness, a lack of continuity in her policy as well as the lack of sufficient power to carry it out in the face of other rivals; then, the fact that she had no intention of actually settling in northern Africa, for all her activity there seems to have limited itself to establishing a sufficient number of coastal settlements as a guarantee against possible trouble from the south; further, the fact that, having lost Gibraltar to England, the question of Straits strategy could not arise. Some French authors have accused her of having neglected the wonderful possibilities of Ceuta as a stronghold on the Straits opposite Gibraltar. But, surely, given the respective naval and economic forces of Spain and England, the transformation of Ceuta into another Gibraltar could only have been made either against England or as second fiddle to her. The first would have been mad, and the second foolish. As a matter of fact, the loss of Gibraltar must have produced deep changes in the subconscious attitude of Spain toward Africa. Before England settled in the

Straits there was no "foreign body" blocking Spanish imagination on its way southward. The Spanish people, in periods of peaceful overflow of their energies, might have penetrated gradually into Morocco, forcing the state finally to intervene and give an official status to the popular colonization of the country. Let us remember that, as a colonizer, Spain always came after the Spaniards (another feature which brings back to the mind that haunting yet deceptive subject of Spain's likeness to England). Given the inherent similarity of racial basis, Morocco might thus have become a mere prolongation of Spain, a Spain beyond the Straits. But Gibraltar stood in the way, a wedge of foreign spirit drawn in between two peoples who, for eight centuries, had mingled together in peace and war; and those subtle spiritual currents which fecundate the meadows of history found themselves powerfully deflected in this case so that Spain lost the zest of old and turned herself inward.

Meanwhile France had attained a phase when colonial expansion was to become a necessity for her. In this "solar" country, deeply possessed of the value of Paris as a center, and therefore of the need of an adequate circumference for such a center fully to irradiate, Paris found herself blocked by the growth of a knot of dour resistance in that Germanic mass till then so plastic under her sway. It is generally recognized that when, in 1830, the French sent a strong expedition to punish the Dey of Algiers for his time-honored predatory habits, they did not mean to stay thirty years and transform Algiers into three French departments. But the fact is significant that the French did turn their minds towards Africa *then,* whether to punish or to stay, and also that their minds once turned there stayed there. Bismarck, who knew how history is made out of the stuff of life, encouraged France to settle in Tunis, for the French had by then discovered that what was wrong with them was colonial ambition, and they pursued their aims with that intelligent determination which makes of their foreign policy an art as scientific and as aggressive as the art of war. Both France and England prevented O'Donnell from gathering territorial fruits from his exploits of 1859, the first time perhaps the three nations met—if only to differ—on the question of Moroccan destinies. From that day on Spain could do little more than defend the *status quo,* i. e. range herself on the side of England, also favorable to leaving the knotty problem in abeyance.

And yet it was indirectly through English action that the *status quo* became so precarious as to lose every right to the name. For in 1856 the British government obtained the right of protection for all persons who placed themselves under her flag in Morocco, a fact which led, of course, to equal concessions to every other nation. Consular agents were thus enabled to put Moroccan subjects or foreigners under their nation's protection. The difficulties produced by this practice and the malpractices into which it degenerated led, however, to an important step. An international conference met in Madrid in 1880, attended by representatives of Austria-Hungary, Belgium, France, Germany, Great Britain, Italy, Morocco, the Netherlands, Norway, Portugal, Spain, Sweden and the United States of America. If it did not do much to cure the evils of "protection" it inaugurated an era perhaps too hastily closed—that during which Moroccan questions were a matter of international concern.

When King Alfonso attained his majority the Moroccan question was ripe for European ambitions. France was led by a stubborn foreign secretary anxious to carve for himself a reputation worthy of a successor of Richelieu. She found Morocco an appetizing prey after the excellent meal she had made of Algiers and Tunis. She was rich, she was powerful. True, she had fears concerning the East, but that was the more reason for widening the basis of her wealth and of her manpower. Spain, on the other hand, had just returned from Cuba and the Philippines, beaten by the United States. The last remnants of her empire had gone. Her ports had seen the soldiers back from the fight, emaciated by fevers and privations. Spain was in no mood for further adventures. She dreamed of a few years without telegrams about dead and wounded and "glorious victories" in her newspapers. She wanted to rest from emotional life, to work and put her house in order. Above all, she felt that every man is well off where he is and should not be bothered with foreign rule, the white man's burden, the standards of civilization and the light of Christianity. Spain was in the mood of Don Quixote after the last battle, or perhaps better still in that of Sancho retiring disillusioned and alone from his experiment as a governor: "Naked I was born, naked I am. I have not lost, I have not won."

But Morocco was there to the south; France there to the north; and England in Gibraltar still a mystery.

CHAPTER 21

SPANISH-AMERICANISM

The relations between Spain and the Spanish-American nations
evolved during the nineteenth and twentieth centuries far more
quickly than during the three preceding ones. At the beginning
of this period the Spanish-American nations still belonged to
the Spanish Crown. The Cortes de Cádiz which studied and
voted the Constitution of 1812 were under the spell of the
Americanos, i.e. the representatives of the Spanish-American
constituencies. Most of them, enlightened readers of political
thought, had followed the history of the rising United States
with keen enthusiasm and generous idealism and tried, not without success, to instill some of the political principles of the
young republic into the Spanish Constitution. Their position,
however, could not be more illogical. The peoples at home took
a more consistent attitude. The Spanish dependencies had been
conquered by the Spaniards for the king. In law, as well as in
that inner law which is the core of all Spanish political philos-

267

ophy and instinct, these territories were not Spanish dominions; they were, just as Spain was, dominions of the King of Spain in so far as the King of Spain incarnated the commonwealth, i.e. each and every one of the separate commonwealths. The union was, therefore, merely a personal union between all the crowns of the king. And when Ferdinand VII abandoned the throne, the only link which kept together his European and his American dominions was destroyed.

The revolts in America began in the name of the king. Sooner or later it was realized by the *Americanos,* who significantly called themselves *patriotas,* that the king was no longer necessary as a symbol of a commonwealth which, by assuming its own defense, had assumed its own separate existence. Essentially, therefore, the Wars of Emancipation were not wars of the Spanish-Americans against Spain, but wars between the Spanish-American peoples and the Spanish state, identical with the wars between the Spanish people and the Spanish state when such a state ruled by a foreign king was disowned by the Spaniards. It is true that when Ferdinand VII returned he attempted to repress the revolt in America by force of arms, but here again the Spanish state was behaving in its American dominions exactly as it behaved in its European territory, with this difference: that in the first case it failed, mostly owing to distance, while in the second case the war lasted right through the nineteenth century and is not yet perhaps altogether over.

The Wars of Emancipation did much to embitter feelings between Spaniards and *Americanos.* The war was carried on in some cases with grim determination. The Spanish state was very slow to bow before the inevitable, and it was not till 1836 that the law authorizing the government to recognize the independent sovereignty of the American nations was passed. There followed a period in which relations between Spain and her former dependencies evolved awkwardly and, perhaps unconsciously, toward a final adjustment. Spain still intervened in America, not always wisely. In 1862 she participated in a Mexican expedition organized in agreement with France and England, ostensibly to secure fair treatment for their respective nationals in Mexico. The

Spanish commander, Prim, was not long, however, in realizing that both England and Spain were in Mexico as the mere pawns of Napoleon III, and backed out as soon as possible partly owing to this discovery, partly to his wish to keep a closer eye on political events in Madrid; for, like most Spanish generals, he was more interested in politics than in war. Toward the same period, Santo Domingo having decided of her own accord to put herself under Spanish sovereignty in 1861 and then to sever the connection again in 1863, O'Donnell was unwise enough to attempt a military repression which the nation was too busy at home to maintain with sufficient vigor. Finally, the same bellicose general managed to entangle Spain in a war with Peru, Chile, Bolivia and Ecuador, when Méndez Núñez with a Spanish fleet bombarded the port of Callao (May 2, 1866) and passed down to history as the admiral who coined the saying: "Better honor without ships than ships without honor." He managed, however, to keep both, though he did not end the war, which, as a purely platonic manifestation, lasted on paper till 1871, when an armistice was signed, treaties being slowly evolved in successive years.

Spain had only Cuba and Puerto Rico left under her sovereignty. Both revolted in 1868 at the moment when the mother country was busy with her own revolution. The events of Puerto Rico were not of so grave a character as those of Cuba, where the rebellion was serious and protracted, owing to the help the Cuban insurgents were able to draw from the United States. Puerto Rico benefited by peace, for a government of advanced views abolished slavery in the island (1873). The war in Cuba lasted through the period of revolutionary troubles in Spain. The man who was to bring it to an end was that general, Martínez Campos, who had taken upon himself to proclaim Alfonso XII King of Spain and thus close the revolutionary period in the mother country. He was sent to Cuba as soon as he could be spared from Spain, and he ended the war with the Agreement of Zanjón (1878). In the following year slavery was abolished in the island.

All these activties of Spain in the American continent contributed to maintain the anti-Spanish tradition which the Wars of Emancipation had established. To this period belong the two masterpieces of Argentine literature, *Martín Fierro,* by Hernández, and *Facundo,* by Sarmiento, this last with a definitely anti-Spanish bias. Yet the natural attraction resulting from a community of origin and civilization was gradually working its way into the spirit of the Spanish-American nations and the enormous growth of the United States was also acting in the same direction. The Monroe Doctrine, hailed at first by the nations of Spanish-America as a guarantee of their independence, was slowly evolving away from that. Several attempts which they made to transform it into a multilateral declaration had conspicuously failed. Not a few of their suggestions for its application, such as the two cases in which the Argentine Republic claimed help under the Doctrine when England occupied the Falkland Islands, had disappointed public opinion in the whole continent as to its actual value for the Spanish-American world. Successive declarations by American presidents made it clear that the United States meant to keep complete control over the definition, interpretation and application of the Doctrine. In 1889 the first Pan-American Conference took place and the foundations of the Pan-American Union were laid. There is no question that this new factor has been highly beneficial in bringing about a closer union between the Spanish-American nations, for it acted as a kind of outside pressure counteracting the dispersive tendency which the Spanish-Americans had inherited from the Spanish-Europeans. It is significant that the first date in the history of Spanish-Americanism occurs three years after the first Pan-American Conference (1889). The date, of course, could not be more suggestive: 1892, the fourth centenary of the discovery of America. The Spanish government, then already fairly stabilized, organized a number of events all planned on a Spanish-American basis, invitations for official representation having been sent to all the Spanish-American nations and accepted by them. Spanish-American congresses were held on a number of subjects and the 12th of October was declared a national holiday in Spain. No definite tendencies could as yet be discerned in this movement. It was a mere affective drawing-together without any political aim, the almost physical reaction manifesting the obvious fact that the Spanish-American nations were sisters *in* Spain (as mystics are brothers in God). That and no more.

Yet two factors stood in the way. The first was the as yet insufficient prestige of Spanish culture in South America. The Spanish-American peoples were born to freedom in an atmosphere of keen intellectual activity. Most of the leaders of the Wars of Emancipation were eager readers of European books. The influence of eighteenth-century French encyclopedic thought has no doubt been much exaggerated, and the more deeply the great American figures of the time are studied the more striking is the unmistakably Spanish originality of their thought. Bolívar is the most brilliant case in point—Bolívar who fought Spain with a magnificent Spanish temperament. All these men, however, lived in an age when psychology did not delve so deep. Not till the twentieth century was a distinguished Venezuelan historian, Señor Parra Pérez, to remark that free Spanish-America has never produced a generation so brilliant as that which liberated her, which was raised under Spanish rule. The times were inclined to simple generalizations, and it was decided that Spain was the backward country and that light and thought came from Paris. Paris spoke in French, and French is an easy language for Spaniards and Spanish-Americans to read, at any rate. The nineteenth century was, therefore, in Spanish-America the French century *par excellence*. Both as a reaction against Spanish domination and as a revelation to minds till then shut off from foreign books, French culture impressed Spanish-Americans deeply. True, the shrewder minds among them realized that ultimately culture is but the flower of blood, and that Spanish-America could not go on, in the somewhat naïve words of a Spanish-American delegate in Europe to a French journalist, "Feeling and speaking in Spanish and thinking in French." (There was but a moderate amount of thought in that statement.) But before the Spanish-American nations could again feel drawn toward

Spanish culture, this culture had to evolve out of the phase of foreign subservience which it was itself undergoing in the Peninsula.

The second obstacle to the growth of genuine feelings of mutual affection and confidence between Spain and her former colonies was the situation in Cuba and Puerto Rico. The movement in favor of Cuban independence had never entirely abated. During Alfonso XII's reign and during the regency of his widow, Queen María Cristina, the Cuban patriots were active over the whole continent enlisting help in the United States and sympathy in the nations of the Spanish-speaking world. Cuban propaganda was bound to produce a deeply anti-Spanish effect on Spanish-American countries, first by recalling the past and stirring in every Spanish-American nation emotions similar to those of her own emancipation days, and then by presenting Spain for propaganda purposes under an unfavorable light.

This obstacle to Spanish-American understanding with Spain disappeared with the loss of Cuba and Puerto Rico in 1898. At the same time the United States of America, who had gained sympathy among Spanish-Americans owing to her advocacy of the Cuban cause, rapidly lost her ground on her decision to retain Puerto Rico and to impose on the promised independence of Cuba the serious limitations implied in the Platt Amendment. In 1900 the frigate *Presidente Sarmiento,* of the Argentine navy, paid a visit to Barcelona. The Argentine naval officers were warmly received in Spain and Argentina decided to omit from her national anthem two stanzas reminiscent of the War of Emancipation. When the king came of age in 1902, the way was clear for a truly cordial gathering of the Spanish-American nations around their old spiritual home. The progress of Spanish-Americanism was made easier by that of Spanish culture which set in then. Thus everything contributed to making the last years of the century a turning point in this aspect of Spanish life.

CHAPTER 22

FOREIGN AFFAIRS

A glance at a map suffices to show that Spain's natural strategic advantages are such that, if strong, she must play a first-rank role in the world, and, if weak, she must be the constant object of close attention on the part of the strong. The main natural advantage of the Peninsula lies in the control of the Straits of Gibraltar. This situation makes her the *prima facie* adversary of whichever nation controls the seas and, therefore, it determines her relations with England. It makes her also an indispensable element in the peace and safety of France, since at any moment Spain can block the sea communications between the French Mediterranean and Atlantic coasts. As, moreover, Spain shares with France the longest frontier of this nation, placed at the rear of any European trouble which France may develop, it follows that Spain is a nation which France cannot afford to see strong. This brief and elementary survey leads to the obvious

273

conclusion that Spain has two natural adversaries in the world: France and England.

History confirms what observation detects. England and France have been the traditional adversaries of Spain ever since the three nations attained their maturity, which they did at approximately the same time. The relations between Henry VIII, Charles V and Francis I symbolize the curious situation created by the fact that France and England, though both adversaries of Spain, are not necessarily allied. The brief spell of Anglo-Spanish alliance which brought about the marriage of Philip II with Mary Tudor was but a makeshift whereby Philip II tried to secure his sea communications with Flanders. But Flanders, though for centuries the well into which Castilian energies were sunk, had nothing to do with Spain's true interests. With the advent of Elizabeth the instinctive rivalry between Spain and England set in, not to flag again until England had deprived Spain of her rank as a Great Power, first at the Peace of Utrecht, then at the Congress of Vienna.

It is doubtful whether a true Spanish policy, i.e. the inherent policy arising out of her geographical situation and of the creative possibilities and consequent requirements of her soul and people, has ever existed. It came as near existence as it ever did in the statesmanlike imagination of Ferdinand and Isabel. Two strokes of destiny deflected Spain from her true course: one was the discovery of America; the other the election of King Charles I to the imperial throne, a stroke for which, by a curious irony of history, Spain helped to pay by enabling Charles to bribe his electors with Spanish gold.

America, in Spanish history, was a white elephant. To be sure, Spain decorated it wonderfully and reaped a considerable amount of prestige from the possession of so immense and picturesque an animal. No doubt, moreover, the discovery made Spain a universal nation before any other European power, and to a degree unequaled even by Great Britain later. But the greatness of Spain, in so far as it came from the discovery and colonization of America, had something abnormal and almost monstrous about it. It was more in the nature of a diseased growth than in that of organic development and it contributed greatly to prevent the normal evolution of a foreign policy adequately adapted to the requirements of the nation.

The imperial connection was no better calculated to lead to such a policy. Under Charles V Spain was the base of operations for European schemes in which the emperor sought to create unity of Christendom conceived in his mind, of which Spain was but a part. Charles, who was his own foreign secretary, never saw Spanish foreign policy as such; he saw Christendom, of which he was the political chief, and, if he was gradually won over from his father's to his mother's country to the point of dying in a Spanish monastery, he never was able to see Spain and her future as his grandmother, Queen Isabel, had seen them. When he died his hopes of European union had been shattered by the Lutheran Reformation, and Philip II was left with the comparatively simple task of saving Spain from heresy. But even then Spain was to be sacrificed to the dynastic loyalty of the monarchs of the House of Austria toward the spiritual welfare of their northern subjects as they understood it. The Low Countries, which should have gone to Ferdinand, went to Philip, and the energies of Spain had to concentrate on the hopeless and entirely disinterested, if odious, task of keeping the Dutch within the fold. This, of course, had no connection whatsoever with true Spanish policy.

It is difficult to estimate to what an extent these two mighty events, the discovery of America and the imperial connection with its sequel of religious wars, by working themselves deeply into the Spainsh soul, have prevented it from acquiring a conscious or subconscious sense of foreign policy such as England and France evolved from a relatively early date. Every opinion is possible: from that which sees Spain as the tragic victim of two mighty and somewhat quixotic enterprises, to that which considers her as naturally disinclined to conceive and apply a systematic conception of her own history. Truth lies, probably, in a combination of all the intermediate views, the recipe of which must remain a divine secret particularly inaccessible to historians. The results, however, are only too clear. Under the lesser Austrias the policy of Spain was an imitation of that of Charles and Philip, combined with a new difficulty which arose out of the necessity of keeping together the two branches of the House of Austria against the French. Under the Bourbons the policy was what the king wanted it to be, which, more often than not, meant what the queen wished. The only king of that period who seems to have had a truly autonomous sense of an inherent Spanish policy was Ferdinand VI. He stuck to peace and reconstruction with that quiet determination which is the mark of true enlightened and meditated opinion, and even his one exception to the rule of peace, his Moroccan activity, is but a brilliant confirmation of the intelligent attention which underlay his policy. But both his predecessors and successors in his dynasty squandered away Spanish energies in futile and misguided attempts to meddle with events in which Spanish vital interests were unaffected, inspired nearly always by a patrimonial and personal conception of thrones and territories which they considered as family estates.

The lack of a central line of foreign policy was, in a sense, but the natural result of the sudden accession of power which befell Spain immediately after she attained full nationhood. A full-grown nation in 1492, she was a full-grown empire in 1519, predominant in Europe, ruling over America and the Pacific Sea. The natural attitude in such a case was defensive. There was no need for a line of expansion. This passivity and this absence of a definite principle of action in foreign affairs were to turn to the advantage of Spain's adversaries. England had for centuries, as the main principle of her foreign policy, the gradual weakening of the Spanish Empire and its ultimate destruction, with the seizure of every point of vantage which fell to her in the process. France found Spain most inconvenient on the flank of her traditional duel with the House of Austria, even after she had recovered from the Spanish crown the considerable territories, potentially French, which had been handed down to Spain from the House of Burgundy. And during the eighteenth century France made Spain an ally in her own exclusive interests, through the *Pacte de Famille,* the very name of which reveals the purely personal outlook of the diplomacy which inspired it.

When the Spanish people emerged out of the monarchical shell to take a direct responsibility in their destinies after the War of Independence (*anglice* Peninsular War), the situation was far from rosy. England had succeeded in maiming Spain in her three most vulnerable places: her American Empire was gone; her reunion with Portugal was made impossible; her control over the Straits was lost; and, what was worse, England had set foot on her soil in Gibraltar, the very name of which rings with an echo of the Moorish Conquest. France had ruined the Spanish navy by forcing an incapable monarch to put it at the disposal of an incapable French admiral, who led it to defeat at Trafalgar. She had tried to erect Spain into a French kingdom; she had led Spain to a disastrous civil war, the more disastrous as it contributed to lend the noble and convincing colors of patriotism to the most reactionary and isolationist passions of the Spanish people. In foreign, as in home affairs, Spain had to start the nineteenth century from the bare ground. There was nothing.

The century began with both France and England on Spanish soil. The two adversaries were not necessarily allies. Spain, too weak to play an independent role, as she had done under Charles and Philip, was nevertheless mixed up in their quarrels, so that, while she fought with France against England at Trafalgar, she fought her War of Independence with England against France. Nor was this change merely capricious. The Spain that fought at Trafalgar was the state; the Spain that fought at Bailén was the people. England went over to fight on the side of the Spanish people. Wellington, of course, was not so much fighting *for* Spanish independence as *against* Napoleon, and, so far as England was concerned, the Spanish War of Independence was merely the Peninsular War. This contrast, which moved the generous mind of Wordsworth to write his spirited pamphlet on the Convention of Cintra and inspired him with many a fine sonnet in praise of the people of Spain, was, however, inevitable in the circumstances and at the time. The main lesson that emerges from that war, when England contributed powerfully to the independence of Spain while fighting her own duel with France, is that neither England nor France can go to extremes in their policy with Spain without coming into conflict with one another.

The basic rule of the nineteenth-century foreign policy of Spain was thus evolved from experience. When England and France agree, seek agreement with both; when they disagree, abstain, following Sancho's wise dictum: do not put your thumbs between two millstones. So far as Spain was concerned that was the only rule of the game. The stakes were mostly of a conservative character. Often they could not go beyond ensuring foreign respect, or even mere recognition, of this or that precarious form of government, for the nineteenth century was spent in constitutional strife. Rare was the government which did not have to solicit favors from London, and more frequently from Paris, with regard to the close watch which it had to keep on its political exiles and would-be conspirators. This source of internal weakness made itself felt also in the colonial field, for Spain had often to conciliate foreign interests while dealing with the colonial troubles in what remained of the overseas empires. African preoccupations were, of course, a matter of frequent discussion. Spain protested rather platonically when France occupied Algiers; she had to bow before the joint opposition of France and England to her reaping any territorial advantages from General O'Donnell's victory in Morocco in 1860. Her throne was twice at least an apple of discord in European politics, first when Palmerston and Louis Philippe played rather sharp chess with the marriage of Isabel II; then when Prim made the round of Europe in search of a king after Isabel II's expulsion, and Prussia tried to secure the throne for a Hohenzollern.

Toward the middle of the century, in spite of the terrible waste of an almost chronic civil war, Spain had attained sufficient economic development to sharpen the political competition of her two intimate and faithful adversaries with a material edge. A land of great mineral wealth, hedged round with fertile fruit orchards, it attracted the industrial and commercial attention of

Englishmen and Frenchmen alike. Capital began to flow in. Through competition these two adversaries of Spain became the most efficient artisans of her economic development. Railways were built in the North and East mostly by French, in the South and West mostly by English, enterprise. Mines were likewise developed, with roughly the same geographical distribution as to the nationality of the capital and expert management. Simultaneously, both France and England reached the summit of their world power, and thus became the most important customers of Spain. The picture was now complete. Spain became closely linked up by ties of interest with the two nations with which she had constantly had to contend on the fields of history.

When Alfonso XII felt himself safely in harness he began his foreign policy from the beginning. He tried to secure for Spain the predominant position in Morocco which was traditionally thought necessary. The Conference of Madrid (1880) showed the Spanish government that Morocco was one of those rare, yet essential, points of Spanish policy which had the virtue of bringing France and England together in a united front against her. Cánovas, who was a historian and a politician, bowed before the laws of power. But the young king was not of so philosophical a disposition, and he then began to widen the diplomatic area in which Spain had so far moved. Anxious to provide the throne with good dynastic props in foreign countries, Cánovas (after a short-lived love match into which the king had entered against his advice) had succeeded in marrying the king to María Cristina of Hapsburg, a princess of the strongest Roman Catholic court available in Europe at the time. Alfonso followed up this hint possibly beyond what Cánovas would have wished and moved toward Germany, Austria-Hungary and Italy with a view to securing, either from them or from the balance between them and the Western Powers, better treatment in Morocco and the restoration of Spain's position in Europe as a Great Power. In 1883, Alfonso accepted the Kaiser's invitation to visit him in Berlin and was made a colonel of Uhlans. The King of Spain held to his previous public decision to return to Spain via Paris.

He faced an imposing demonstration of popular disfavor in the French capital, which he met with dignified calm, received with cold demeanor the apologies of the French president at the Spanish Embassy, and returned to Spain more than ever convinced of the wisdom of his policy. Two years later he was rudely shaken out of his assurance by the Caroline Islands incident provoked by Germany, who with characteristic directness sent a German squadron to occupy a port in the archipelago without the slightest consideration for the undisputed Spanish sovereignty there. The populace in Madrid got out of hand and burned the scutcheon of the German Embassy in the Puerta del Sol. Alfonso and his Cabinet succeeded in solving this grave incident satisfactorily by suggesting that it should be entrusted to the arbitration of the Pope, who gave an award in favor of Spain. The king died less than a year later, and Spain had again to seek the good will of all foreign powers on behalf of a young widowed queen and a child who was born a king. Foreign nations responded with every kind of helpful and sympathetic assurance, but Spain was reduced thereby to a policy of strict passivity while there was reason to fear for the stability of the throne.

This prudence did not save Spain from trouble. So long as Cuba remained under the Spanish flag there was an inherent source of conflict with the United States of America. The old puritan and peace-loving republic of Washington and Jefferson had gradually developed appetite as it developed strength. Most of its acquisitions, the very territories on which it expanded westward, had taken place at the expense of Spain. As late as 1800 Spain possessed a much larger proportion of what is now the United States than did the United States herself. Louisiana, illegally ceded by Napoleon, was Spanish when the United States received it from the French emperor who did not possess it, and Spain's protests were of no avail. Florida had to go, under threats of force which Spain was not then in a condition to face. Several times during the nineteenth century Spain observed the tendency to help or even stimulate Cuban rebellion on the part of the United States, and at least once she made representations to that effect in Paris and London. The rebellion in 1883 was followed with keen interest in the United States. A still closer attention was bestowed on that of 1895. The events of this rebellion and the war with America which ensued have been dealt with in a previous chapter. Here we are concerned only with the international aspects of it. Writing to his friend, F. C. Moore, on February 9, 1898, Theodore Roosevelt said:

> I should myself like to shape our foreign policy with a purpose ultimately of driving off this continent every European Power. I would begin with Spain, and in the end would take all other European nations, including England. It is even more important to prevent any new nation from getting a foothold. Germany as a republic would very possibly be a friendly nation, but under the present despotism she is much more bitterly and outspokenly hostile to us than is England.

Yet it was but natural that England should take the side she took in the juncture. When, through the Pope and the Austrian Court, Spain sought the mediation of the European Powers, England's attitude chilled an impulse which, to be candid, had not shown signs of much warmth. And when the German squadron present in Manila evinced a tendency to intervene against the American fleet (possibly with an eye on valuable territorial spoils), Admiral Chichester made it clear that England was resolved to prevent all interference between the United States and Spain. Her action was the natural sequel to both her traditional policy toward the Spanish Empire and the ties of racial kinship with the United States. In Spain the events of 1898 did much to revive the old historical consciousness of antagonism with England which the War of Independence had helped to abate. France was sympathetic. While England took over American diplomatic interests in Spain, France took over Spanish interests in America. Negotiations for peace were started by her ambassadors and a treaty was signed in Paris.

With her evacuation of the seas and continents which had seen her rise and fall, Spain turned her eyes again to the natural line of her foreign policy: the Straits and Africa beyond. On June 29, 1900, Don Fernando de León y Castillo, the Spanish ambassador in Paris, signed an agreement with the French government whereby Spain acquired important territories in El Muni. The South became at last the point on which Spanish attention was to concentrate for the years to come. The coming reign was to tackle these problems partly because no other enterprises remained to distract the country from her true course, partly because, as fate would have it, the Moroccan question was then ripe for international action, whether Spain was ready for it or not. What was the mood in which Spain approached the problem? First, with a deep consciousness of the fact that the two nations which, together, controlled, and separately, paralyzed, all Spanish action were, at the same time, her natural adversaries and her best customers, as well as the two peoples most stimulating to her life and culture. Then, with that kind of philosophical acceptance of inevitable facts which the full knowledge of a situation brings about in men and, particularly, in Spaniards. It is part of their stoic dignity that they do not abuse or criticize or even refuse recognition and praise to those who have wronged them. This sober view of the position which Spain occupies in international life was admirably expressed by Ganivet, writing, precisely, at the close of the nineteenth century:

> There is no humiliation nor dishonor in the recognition of the adversary's superiority: it is more than obvious that England exerts supremacy over the seas of the world; few nations have been free from her abuse of power favored by disunion on the Continent. And against such abuse the wisest policy is to make oneself strong and to inspire respect. Facts of force, such as the occupation of Gibraltar, are not without practical utility, for they act as regulators of national energies and prevent overconfident people from shouting too loudly. Gibraltar is a force for England so long as Spain is weak; but if Spain were strong it would become a vulnerable point and would lose its *raison d'être*.

Among all the nations of Europe Spain is, after Italy, the nation most interested in the preservation of the naval supremacy of Great Britain for a long time to come. We are in this case very much as that ruined gentleman who on no account would part with an old steward of his, not particularly honest. "Not for any love that I may feel for you," said the poor man, "but because I fear that your successor will leave me a beggar." And if some of those who feel irritated at the affront of Gibraltar do not find this idea elevated enough, let them bear in mind that it has been suggested to me by the wise Sancho Panza, who was as Spanish and as Manchegan as Don Quixote.

England has two advantages on her side: the first, that she has no immediate connection with the Continent and still less with the Mediterranean shores; the second, that she has attained the fullness of her development and feels already bound to take shelter under a defensive policy. Her power, therefore, would be useful for Europe if, shorn of her aggressive possibilities, she succeeded in maintaining herself as the agent of international public order.[1]

Gibraltar is a permanent offense which we in part deserve for our lack of good government; but it does not hinder the normal development of our nation and is not a sufficient cause for us to sacrifice other more valuable interests in order to anticipate (on the most advantageous hypothesis) a fact which must come about as the restoration of our nationality evolves towards its logical conclusion. It seems absurd at first sight that our interests should be linked up with those of the only nation toward whom we have motives of real resentment, but in recognizing and accepting such absurdities lies at times the deepest wisdom.

[1] This was written in 1896, twenty-eight years before the Geneva Protocol was discussed.

PART 4

THE REIGN OF

ALFONSO XIII

PRE-WAR

On May 17, 1902, a youth who had that day attained his sixteenth year made ready to take over his royal duties from the devoted and cautious hands of his mother. Count Romanones, then a minister in the Sagasta Cabinet, has given us a striking picture of that historic day. A luminous morning such as Madrid can enjoy in the Castilian spring which, for vigor and warmth, deserves the name of summer. The Cabinet were waiting on the stone steps of the Congress of Deputies, a group of black and gold uniforms the diplomatic monotony of which was broken by the naval uniform of the Minister of Marine, the Duke of Veragua (who, though a civilian, was admiral of the fleet by birthright as the lineal descendant of Christopher Columbus) and by the military uniform of General Weyler, a small, determined and taciturn figure famous for his resolute ways in Cuba, then Minister of War. Sagasta, who feared for the future the dangers he had experienced in the past as a parliamentary politician, had amended Moret's draft of the king's message to his people, inserting in it the following significant passage: "The education which I have received makes me see that from this first moment duties weigh on me which I accept without hesitation as without hesitation I have sworn the Constitution and the laws, conscious of all that is implied in the solemn engagement contracted thereby before God and before the nation." He had, moreover, resolved that the ceremony of the king's oath before the Cortes should be as solemn as possible, "in order," says Count Romanones, "that the monarch and the people should fully realize all its transcendental importance." The people were represented by an innumerable crowd covering with its waves the Carrera de San Jerónimo and the Plaza de la Cibeles, all agog with excitement and sunshine. The procession of stately carriages of the picturesque Spanish court, drawn by magnificent horses in gorgeous harness, aroused powerful waves of enthusiasm. The senators and deputies in the House were no less enthusiastic when the boy king, followed by the queen regent, entered the Hall of Assembly. The President of the Cortes, the old Marqués de la Vega de Armijo, who had been a Cabinet minister under Isabel II (the king's grandmother whose pranks with the Constitution had cost her the crown), was to administer the oath, or rather, as Count Romanones puts it, was to pronounce the formal words for the purpose, for the king takes the oath spontaneously and is not asked to swear by anyone. So the stately marqués bent deferentially toward the royal youth and, in a voice which trembled a little, said: "Sir, the Cortes convened by your august mother have met to receive from Your Majesty the oath which, in accordance with Article 45 of the Constitution of the state, Your Majesty comes to pronounce, to the effect that Your Majesty will observe the Constitution and the laws."

Amidst tense silence, the king, laying his right hand on the Gospels open on the table, with clear, ringing voice said: "I swear by the Lord on the holy Gospels that I will observe the Constitution and the laws. If I do so, let God reward me, and if not, let Him call me to account."

These words were received with a loud ovation by senators

and deputies; the moving ceremony was over and the official world headed by the new effective chief of the state went to the old church of St. Francis for a Thanksgiving service. When the king and his ministers at last reached the royal palace the Cabinet, encased in their uncomfortable uniforms, were exhausted with heat, excitement and responsibility. They formally resigned. The king formally reinstated them, and the ministers felt then free to go and change and have a rest, most of all Sagasta, who was old and asthmatic and, in fact, within a year of his death. But the king was neither old nor asthmatic nor near his death and he loved uniforms and the political game, so he suddenly sprang upon his ministers the proposal that there should be a Cabinet meeting at once. In Spain the king presides over Cabinet meetings. The queen regent had made the king attend the meetings in the period preceding his actual accession. There was nothing for the Cabinet to do but to acquiesce.

That historic meeting, the first Cabinet Council held by Alfonso XIII, has been described by Count Romanones with enough detail to make us wish for more. The king took the chair at the head of the long walnut table and, after a few words of salutation spoken by Sagasta with tired gesture and voice, "the king, as if he had never done anything but preside over ministers all his life and with great coolness, addressing the war secretary in an imperious voice, submitting him to a close examination with regard to the causes of the recent decree shutting down the military colleges. [The army was then hopelessly overstaffed as the result of the Cuban and Spanish-American wars.] Ample explanations, ample for his wonted laconism, were given by General Weyler—Don Alfonso was not satisfied and held that the colleges should be reopened. General Weyler replied with respectful firmness and, when the argument was taking a dangerous turn, Sagasta cut in, making the king's view his own and thereby defeating his war minister. After a brief pause, the king with the text of the Constitution in his hand read Case 8 of Article 55 [the king makes all appointments to civil posts and grants honors and distinctions of all kinds] and, by way of comment, said: 'As you have just heard, the Constitution confers

upon me the granting of honors, titles and grandeeships; that
is why I warn you that I reserve for myself entirely the exercise
of this right.' We heard these words with great surprise. The
Duke of Veragua, a scion of one of the most illustrious lines of
Spanish nobility, and a man of proven Liberal spirit, met the
king's words with a simple reply: having asked his leave, he
read paragraph 2 of Article 49, which says: 'No order of the
king can be put into operation unless it be countersigned by a
minister.'" Sagasta, who attached no importance to honors and
decorations, did not trouble to intervene. The lesson of constitutional law was lost, and Count Romanones winds up his
narrative in typical fashion: "Ah! if the day had not been so hot
perhaps the fate of the Constitution would have been different
from what it is. Solomon in his Book of Proverbs already said:
*Train up a child in the way he should go and when he is old
he will not depart from it.*"

Such was the tone in which the reign began. This scene already reveals the main features of Spanish politics in later years:
personal power, based on the army and on the husbanding of
royal favor, on the part of the monarch; weakness and vacillation
in the royal palace, on the part of the political personnel. There
were in this situation some of the elements which might have
made a truly great reign: a masterful personality on the throne,
served by intelligent, though pliable, instruments of his will,
might have been able to build up a peaceful and vigorous nation
even in the face of the grave problems outlined in the preceding
pages. Unfortunately, the master's will was not led by a mind
trained for its tremendous responsibilities. Quick this mind certainly was, but it had no vision beyond a sincere and ardent
patriotism; and, in the place of general principles and of a
mental-moral culture, all the youthful king could bring to the
government of the state was a knot of narrow prejudices of a
frankly anti-democratic and anti-parliamentary tradition. "It was
a pity," writes Count Romanones, "that the opportunity afforded
by the last months of the Regency should not have been seized
to send the monarch to travel abroad and make him familiar
particularly with those nations which have mastered the practice

of the parliamentary system. Motherly affection won, and the queen had not the courage to part with her son." The count may be right, yet the trouble was older. In 1900, Canalejas made a sensational anti-clerical speech on the occasion of the marriage of the king's elder sister (then heir to the throne) to the Count of Caserta, of obviously Carlist and clerical leanings. He was violently attacked in the leading clerical newspaper by a priest, Father Montaña, who boldly signed his article though he was the confessor and tutor of the king. The queen dismissed him instantly, but the king thus shriven and tutored began effectively to reign within two years.

The fact is that while the two parties which, with varying fortunes but equally sincere efforts, were endeavoring to guide Spain toward a peaceful parliamentary regime fought each other, ousted each other from power and solved or left unsolved more or less doctrinaire questions, the three factors which were to shape the destinies of Spain in the early twentieth century were left to themselves and no one troubled as to how they were being educated. The army, the Church and the king—all three estimable in many ways and particularly as raw material—had not been adequately educated for the fulfillment of their responsible functions. The army, the Church and the king killed the parliamentary system.

Troubles poured in from every quarter at a time in the general effervescence caused by the liquidation of the war. The movement of the *Unión Nacional,* led by Joaquín Costa, with the enterprising Aragonese businessman, Basilio Paraïso, and a young Castilian barrister, Santiago Alba, was a forerunner of later events which were to shake the confidence wherewith the two old parties held the wheels of the state machine. The parties themselves were gradually disintegrating now that the two great chiefs had gone. Sagasta died in 1903, leaving a party unable to agree on a leader. The Conservatives took office in December 1902, and fell in July 1905. In this brief period they went through five prime ministers (Silvela, Villaverde, Maura, Azcárraga, Villaverde again), and sixty-six new ministers. Count Romanones' comment on this fact deserves quotation. It took place, he says, "as a logical consequence of the weakening of the parties and owing to the initiative of the king, who, no doubt anxious to find out the most competent, did not cease changing, rather did he seem to enjoy frequent changing of the persons in whom he deposited, more or less completely, his confidence."

And yet all the questions of Spanish political life were waiting for the attention and considerate thought which only a stable government could devote to them. Catalanism was entering a perilous phase during which all the nationalistic forces united against the radical centralists led by Lerroux, and a tension of fierce political hatred was thus artificially created. Clericalism, which had forced the Sagasta government to abandon its efforts to limit the number of religious houses, had forced Maura to appoint an unpopular monk, Father Nozaleda, as Archbishop of Valencia. It was also responsible for his proposal, (to a nation which had just met a crushing war debt and submitted to Villaverde's severe financial measures) that a loan should be raised to compensate religious orders for the damage done during the Revolution of 1868. The anti-dynastic ferment seething in the towns was provoking serious riots in Salamanca, Madrid and Barcelona, and, in the general election of April 1903, in which Maura tried to reform the evil ways of past home secretaries, the big towns, Madrid in particular, had elected Republican deputies. In December 1904, a serious situation developed in Andalusia, where the farm laborers suffered from unemployment and famine. This period, however, was fertile in constructive ideas, mostly under Maura's administration. The prime minister tried to deal at the same time with the Catalan situation and with electoral corruption, by a Local Government Bill reforming the administration of the country and granting a certain amount of devolution. In this period also the *Instituto de Reformas Sociales* was created, a statesmanlike experiment which was to prove fully successful in the study of industrial questions and their peaceful solution. The Moroccan question had sprung forward in 1900, when León y Castillo, from the Spanish Embassy in Paris, had called the attention of the government to the instability of the *status quo,* and in 1901, when Silvela had anonymously published in *La Lectura* a sensational article urging negotiations with France to meet possible developments there. This was precisely what the Duke of Almodóvar del Río, Sagasta's foreign secretary, was doing at the time with Monsieur Delcassé. But when Silvela took office in 1902 he refused to sanction the favorable treaty which had been negotiated because, in his opinion, nothing should be done in Morocco without consulting England—perhaps also because he thought the treaty laid too heavy obligations on Spain. In the circumstances it is to be regretted that England should have agreed to negotiate with France in 1904 in the absence of Spain. England's refusal to negotiate separately behind the back of the nation most directly interested in Morocco would have been but the just recognition of the correct attitude of Spain in the matter, and would have saved France the loss of sympathy and confidence she underwent when, in later years, she again applied the 1904 method by treating alone with Germany and turning to Spain with a *fait accompli*. The agreement of April 8, 1904, between France and England paved the way for the Franco-Spanish Treaty of November 1904. This treaty, in the good old way, declared publicly that France and Spain agreed as to the terms of the Anglo-French Treaty concerning Morocco, i.e. the integrity of the Shereefian Empire, its independence and its sovereignty, matters in which France and Spain were recognized to have a special interest. This done, the treaty went on behind the veil to the effect that, things remaining as they were, Spain and France might, nevertheless, exercise certain specified actions under certain specified conditions, each in a certain specified zone; and that should the sultan's sovereignty vanish, France and Spain would enter into practically full possession of such respective zones. The treaty defined the zones, granting Spain a considerably larger part than that now left to her.

The government, which had borne the responsibility for these important negotiations and which should have been left in peace to ripen the consequences thereof, a government led by one of the two statesmen who Spain had then to spare, the same Maura who, a year earlier, while accompanying the king to Barcelona, had been wounded by a fanatical enemy of the regime, had to leave office in circumstances which throw much light on the true origins of the fall of the monarchy. The Cabinet decided to appoint a certain general as Chief of Staff. The king had other views. The Cabinet could and should have insisted on its right to govern under the Constitution. The king held his ground and Maura resigned. The clearest symptom of the new and grave disease which was to sap the system, and maybe the very regime, was that a Cabinet was formed under General Azcárraga merely in order to endorse the king's signature for his candidate's appointment. This Cabinet was so unstable that it fell within a few weeks.

The combination of internal party bickerings and royal policy on the one hand, and the pressure of public problems on the other, had worn out the Conservative Party before the Liberals had had time to recover from the death of their last leader—a recovery which could not be achieved until another man of sufficient standing was ripe for leadership. The party possessed such a man in Canalejas, but between him and power there were three obstacles: two men with better party claims, i.e. Montero Ríos and Moret, and Canalejas' own radical opinions on the clerical problem. Montero Ríos took office and the general election gave him a comfortable majority. A liberal phase lasted from the summer of 1905 till January 1907. This short period saw seven Cabinets with four prime ministers (Montero Ríos, Moret, López Domínguez, and Vega de Armijo). The country meanwhile was seething with political and social troubles. Catalonia led the van. The pendulum between Catalanists and Radical Centralists which, in a country such as England, would have led to political stability by stately swinging, began to rock wildly, threatening to break the machinery altogether with its inordinate movements. The 1905 election was a triumph for the nationalist *Lliga*. A caricature offensive to the Spanish army, published on this occasion by a satirical paper (an incident described in a previous chapter), led to the Law of Jurisdictions, which did more toward providing the heat necessary for the hothouse cultivation of Catalanism than all the hot air of Catalan orators. The two problems, Catalanism and Militarism, became thus hopelessly entangled. All the Spanish garrisons, particularly those of Madrid and Seville, backed the garrison in Barcelona. The Cabinet decided to deprive the three captains-general (Madrid, Barcelona and Seville) of their commands, but the war secretary, General Weyler, demurred, knowing the strength of the forces against the step, among which he probably counted the king's opposition. The Cortes were aroused against the military by the Republican minority; those members who had not forgotten 1873, when General Pavia had dispersed the Cortes with his soldiers, came to the sittings armed with revolvers; and Canalejas, with the true statesman's eye on realities, had a quiet talk with the officer commanding the Civil Guards in charge of the protection of Parliament House, who frankly answered his inquiries by announcing that the guard would do nothing to prevent an attack from the Madrid garrison. The attack did not take place, because the king negotiated with the "army" on the basis of the Law of Jurisdictions. Montero Ríos refused to put his signature to the treaty and made way for the more pliable Moret.

Before taking office the new government had capitulated to such an extent that the new war minister was General Luque, the same who, as Captain-General of Seville, had incurred the wrath of the previous government by sending an enthusiastic telegram to the Captain-General of Barcelona. Luque from the first, and, given the circumstances, not unnaturally, considered himself as the representative of the army in the Cabinet. The army had its law and became a state within the state, but it had tasted blood, and neither the Cortes nor the king was ever to recover from this disastrous surrender before what was at worst a serious crisis and, more likely, a mere bogy which would have collapsed at the first sign of real energy on the part of the king, the Cabinet or Parliament.

The first result of the law was the conclusion of the *Solidaridad Catalana* proclaimed in the Gerona Meeting (1906) by delegates

of the Regionalist, Republican, Federal, Integrist, Left, Nationalist and Catalan Union (for such was the number of Catalan
parties) on the basis of Catalanist interests. On May 20 the
Solidarity celebrated a feast in Barcelona in honor of the parliamentarians who had fought against the Law of Jurisdictions. In
October another imposing meeting of protest took place. The
most dramatic event of the new movement was the conversion
to Catalanism of the ex-President of the Spanish Republic, Salmerón, till then a convinced Centralist. The arm had been forged
which would thereafter lead Catalonia to the polls.

While such grave events were occurring in home politics the
government had to lend close attention to foreign affairs. In
May 1905, under the Villaverde (Conservative) Cabinet, the
king had paid an official visit to the President of the French
Republic, M. Loubet, during which he had undergone his first
ordeal at the hands of anarchists, who threw a bomb at his
carriage as he came out of the theater in the Rue de Rohan.
The king gained much popularity by the cool courage which he
showed in danger. As soon as Montero Ríos took office, he
endeavored to draw the political conclusions which this journey
seemed to imply in anticipation of the impending visit of M.
Loubet to Spain. He went to San Sebastián to negotiate with
M. Cambon on Tangier, where Spain desired an exceptional
position in recognition of her exceptional historical and geographical claims. Nothing came of this effort, which perhaps
accounted for the somewhat cold reception which M. Loubet
met in Spain. Leading statesmen in Spain were beginning to
experience the peculiar indifference to Spanish interests which
France evinces whenever she feels on good terms with England.
In November 1906, scarcely one month after M. Loubet's visit,
the king went on an official visit to the courts of Austria-Hungary
and Germany. This visit does not seem to have had any political
effects, though it cannot have failed to encourage the young
king to persevere in his policy as head of the army, after having
seen the chief artist in that kind of tragicomedy in Berlin. Good
observers, however, did not believe that the Kaiser impressed

the Spanish king as a very attractive person—two actor-managers are hardly comfortable on the same stage together.[1]

William II was then at the top of his form. Earlier in the year he had made his dramatic visit to Tangier which led to the Conference of Algeciras (April 1906). At this conference the effects of the Franco-British Agreement of 1904 were obvious, and Great Britain stood loyally by France. The meeting led to a somewhat obscure situation in which the integrity of Morocco was once again proclaimed and encroached upon, and France and Spain were granted special privileges such as the police of the ports and specified shares in the organization of the Moroccan State Bank. The Prime Minister (Moret) was then in the throes of the militaristic difficulty and, at the same time, within a few weeks of settling that English royal marriage which had been his constant endeavor for some time. Moret's liberalism was strongly colored with English ideas, for he was in the line of those Spanish statesmen who had been won over by the wisdom of English institutions, the most typical of whom had been Olózaga. Nature was good enough to help him, and for some time before the news was official the king rejoiced in a swift-sailing boat which he had named *Queen* * * *, the three stars representing Ena, the name under which the future Queen of Spain was known until her marriage. Things were not, however, as easy as they might seem, and the cloud of "blacks" which swarmed in the royal palace was humming with dissatisfaction. The Pope was helpful and gave the newly christened queen the Golden Rose, but the clericals were not appeased, particularly when they read the comments of the liberal wing of

[1] Count Romanones records a scene which says much for the wit and presence of mind of King Alfonso. The speeches for the state banquet at the royal palace in Berlin had been agreed upon and written beforehand in polished and meaningless French. The Kaiser rose, however, and without a glance at his paper waxed eloquent in free and untutored German. King Alfonso quickly perceived the possibilities for misunderstanding which the situation afforded and immediately devised a happy escape therefrom: he waxed eloquent in a Spanish at once so swift and obscure that honor and policy were both comfortably safe.

the press in which hopes were expressed of an enlightened education for the coming royal generation. The wedding took place on May 31, the young queen conquering her new country at once by the simple yet rare method of looking every inch a queen. The day was marred by an attempt on the lives of the royal couple from which they escaped unhurt, but which cost the life of about a dozen soldiers and civilians. The bomb had been thrown by a Catalan anarchist of good family, who had absorbed his misguided doctrines in the *Escuela Moderna,* held in Barcelona by a narrow-minded reformer, known as Ferrer, who was to become famous three years later.

Soon after the wedding Moret had to resign on the king's refusal to dissolve the Cortes, for it was the royal policy not to grant this privilege twice in succession to the same party, and in this case he was backed by a strong letter which he had received from Maura. General López Domínguez took office with a strong anti-clerical program—strong, that is, for Spain. Violent protests were raised by the episcopate, but the Cabinet was short-lived, for Moret, apparently shaken in his anti-clerical convictions by a conversation with M. Clemenceau in Paris, opposed the anti-clerical policy of his successor and of his own party, and wrote to the king to that effect. He had to take office again in the teeth of his own party's opposition, fell and was succeeded by the veteran Marqués de la Vega de Armijo, who revived the anti-clerical program of López Domínguez. A typical situation, combining in a nutshell all the faults of that disappointing period: Canalejas, firm both in vetoing Moret's candidates for the Cabinet and in demanding that the Law of Associations, which was the backbone of the anti-clerical program, should be passed; the clergy, insolently rebellious to such a point that the Cardinal Archbishop of Toledo, in an official telegram addressed to the government, accused it of cowardice and hypocrisy, with complete immunity; the king, congratulating the prime minister on his anti-clerical policy in an affectionate private letter: "for that is the right way, your ever, Alfonso"; Count Romanones working against the bill provoking the crisis by informing his prime minister that Canalejas no longer supported the Cabinet owing to its vacillating policy in anti-clerical matters. Thus King Alfonso saved at once the Church and his Liberal reputation by playing on the ready keyboard of his political personnel.

It was now time to call in the Conservatives again. This time, however, the party had a man at its head. Don Antonio Maura had the necessary qualifications of mind and will to be a strong and respected leader, and though he made mistakes, some of them serious, he was not easily maneuvered. His first mistake was the choice of Señor La Cierva as home secretary. A fanatic of force and, though a successful barrister, a man with an inelastic and incurious mind, Señor La Cierva organized a general election which was to undo in advance by example all the good which Maura's plans were meant to do in reconstruction and organization. All his resolute methods did not prevent the triumph of a strong anti-dynastic minority and the sweeping victory of the Catalan Solidarity in Catalonia, forty-one seats out of the forty-four assigned to the region having fallen to its candidates. This success was partly due to the emotion produced by a criminal attempt on the life of Señor Cambó a few days before the election. In striking contrast with his home secretary's methods, Maura introduced his Local Government Bill, the most efficient attempt yet made to cope with the power of *caciques* and to purify the roots of political life. The bill met with strong opposition from the Liberal Centralists owing to its regionalistic tendencies, and did not reach the statute book.

Maura's government was particularly active in foreign affairs. It negotiated the Cartagena Agreements on the occasion of King Edward's visit to Cartagena, whereby Spain, France and England acknowledged a common interest in the *status quo* in the Mediterranean and agreed to consult each other whenever circumstances should arise which might alter it. In order to provide the country with the necessary means to carry out his bolder foreign policy, Señor Maura reorganized the navy and initiated the policy of reconstruction of the Spanish naval strength, much depleted since the war, by a certain number of contracts with English firms which laid the foundations not only of the Spanish strength on the water, but of the renewal of the Spanish naval building industry in the Peninsula itself. These efforts did not particularly help the popularity of the government, which was suspected of capitalistic leanings, and public opinion was inclined to criticize its naval policy on the strength of the generous terms which it granted to capital and to certain heavy industries. The government, moreover, was soon brought back from external to home events by a campaign of anarchist outrages which broke out in Barcelona. These anarchist outbursts in Barcelona have always had somewhat mysterious features. The claim made by the Catalanists that, as they occurred always when Catalan nationalism gave signs of special vitality and as they always led to repressive measures which reacted against Catalan nationalist interests, the question *cui prodest?* suggested uncomfortable answers, never was adequately met. Nor was the absolute quiescence of Barcelona anarchism under the Dictatorship of Primo de Rivera a phenomenon likely to allay Catalanist suspicions. At the time, at any rate, the series of outrages in Barcelona influenced Maura to introduce a bill for the repression of terrorism, which aroused storms of protest in the Liberal sectors of Spanish public opinion all over the Peninsula. The hard and tactless mind of his home secretary had been obviously at work in this bill, and the campaign then started was to prepare the atmosphere of public excitement which ultimately brought about the downfall of the government as a sensational world event. The bill had to be dropped, but the home secretary was enabled to leave at least one good trace of his passage in office, i.e. a sound reorganization of the police.

Despite so many obstacles, Maura's qualities would have enabled him to remain in office for a long term and to mature a number of reforms which he had at heart, but for Moroccan events, which drew out his peculiar weakness, an unyielding sense of government authority, even when in the wrong. An attack by Riff tribesmen on the railway line linking up Melilla with Spanish iron mines upcountry made the sending of reinforcements imperative. The war secretary, General Linares, struck on the worst possible idea: calling up the Catalan Reserves. A general strike followed (July 26, 1909), quickly transformed by the revolutionary ferment ever present in Barcelona into a violent riot against convents and monasteries. Three days of street fighting ensued and a period of stern military rule all over Spain. A theoretician of anarchism and anti-clericalism, Francisco Ferrer, a narrow-minded intellectual but an honest person, was sentenced to death by a military tribunal, in spite of a brilliant and convincing defense by his legal counsel, a captain of Royal Engineers. There is little doubt that he was technically, and probably also morally, innocent. Even if legally guilty his death would have been a political blunder. He was shot. The emotion in Spain and abroad was profound and the Cabinet fell, having against it not merely the dynastic opposition but also the Liberal Party, whose leader, Moret, headed the popular demonstration against the government in Madrid.

Moret became prime minister on October 22, 1909, but had to resign on February 9, 1910, for the king, who had not forgiven him his pro-Ferrer activities, refused to grant him the dissolution decree, on the ground that he had mismanaged his party affairs. (An intrigue had been organized against him by Count Romanones.) Canalejas took office. He was the only Liberal statesman capable of holding his party together by sheer superiority. His rule lasted till he was murdered on November 12, 1912. He came to power determined to tackle the preliminary problem without the solution of which Spain's free development cannot take place, i.e. the emancipation of the state from the control of the Church. Count Romanones records the effect of his appointment in the royal palace. The veil of his story is not so thick as to prevent us from guessing that it was the queen mother herself who said to the count, in anguished tones: "For Heaven's sake, Romanones, we rely on you." But Canalejas was no fire-eating radical, as his term of office was to show. He was, in fact, a sincere and devout Catholic, but, like the Catholics of sixteenth-century Spain, he declined to admit that loyalty to his faith, and even to his Church, implied submission to the Vatican and a free license for religious orders to remain above the law. Moreover, his integrity, his firm moderation and his intellectual distinction had succeeded where most of his predecessors had failed: in obtaining real ascendancy over the king.

He tackled the work at once with an order for the coercion of all religious houses which had disregarded previous laws and decrees with regard to registration and payment of taxes when engaging in industrial and commercial enterprises. Furthermore, he made the king declare, in the royal speech at the opening of the Cortes (June 16, 1910), that there would be a check on the growth of religious orders and that Article 11 of the Constitution would henceforth be interpreted in accordance with the spirit of liberty of conscience prevailing everywhere. Simultaneously he announced compulsory service and the abolition of the municipal food tax *(consumos)*. These measures were intended to propitiate the Republican wing of public opinion, which looked askance at his Cabinet, believing it to have been born in a dark palatine intrigue to get rid of Moret as a punishment against Moret's opposition to the execution of Ferrer. This episode is also typical of the complexity of Spanish political problems. When the progressive parties had at last found a man capable of carrying out a constructive program of liberalism, whose sincerity and ability were beyond doubt, they launched a discussion on the somewhat obscure and even shady origins of his political power, thereby playing into the hands of the crown, which, with consummate ability, divided the enemies of clericalism at the very moment when they seemed to have attained power.

While he had to defend himself against his own kith and kin, Canalejas was withstanding the onslaught of an infuriated Vatican, which was enlisting against him practically all the bishops of Spain. The prime minister countered with his famous Padlock Bill, which closed the frontier to further religious congregations until negotiations with the Vatican should finally establish a new regime. The Vatican objected and asked for the withdrawal of this and other precautionary measures before opening negotiations at all. Canalejas resolved to withdraw his ambassador in Rome. The Vatican, with its usual methods of *Realpolitik,* second in nothing but sincerity to those of the hardest period of Bismarck, tried the effect of the Carlist ghost on the royal palace. Meanwhile, the storm raised in Spain had impressed the necessity of conciliation on the prime minister himself, and a formula, which revealed the Jesuitical upbringing of its ingenious contriver, was found by the Marqués de Comillas: the law was passed for two years unless, in the interval, a new law of association should be voted. The Marqués de Comillas knew his Spain. The king stood by his prime minister while contributing powerfully to water down his anti-clerical wine. But he seized the first opportunity available to put himself right with the Pope. Just when Canalejas introduced his bill for regulating the right of association a Eucharistic congress was taking place in Madrid. The prime minister succeeded, not without difficulty, in dissuading the king from taking the chair at the opening meeting, but the king arranged that the closing ceremony should be an imposing religious procession which, after circulating in the main streets of the capital, ascended the grand stairs of the royal palace and ended in depositing the Sacrament in the throne room, while the Cardinal Archbishop of Toledo blessed the royal family with the utmost solemnity.

The Spanish prime minister's attention had then to turn to foreign affairs. He was beginning to realize that, unless Spain took prompt action, all was over with the Spanish position in Morocco, not through any danger from the infidel, but owing to the irrepressible civilizing zeal of the French Republic. The "colonial" party in Paris was growing impatient and, as usual in such cases, obliging disorders occurred in the region of Fez. The prime minister, who had observed signs of French vitality in those quarters, warned the French government that, should French troops occupy Fez or Tazza, Spanish troops would follow their example in a few picked spots of the zone reserved to Spain. A French column under Major Brémond entered Fez and, on June 3, 1911, despite an unfavorable public opinion at home, Spanish troops landed in Larache and took Alcázar and Arcila. Canalejas was safe in defying public opinion, for he knew that his step in Morocco would unchain a French storm, which would

justify him at once in Spain. At this juncture the German government chose to send a cruiser, the *Panther,* to Agadir (July 1),
and much capital was made in the French press of the coincidence between the Spanish and the German actions. Nevertheless, the key to the decision of the Spanish government was to
be revealed in later years to Count Romanones by "a person
to whom the utmost authority is granted on Moroccan affairs" in
France. This mysterious person declared to the count that, had
Canalejas' orders been delayed by a few hours, the Spanish
troops which landed in Larache would have found that the
French had preceded them there. Such is the generous eagerness
wherewith Christian nations vie with one another in their anxiety
to spread civilization amongst the unruly and uncooperative
tribes of the Black Continent.

These events required a readjustment of the Moroccan position. What had happened? France had alienated the confidence
of Spain to such an extent that the Spanish army sent to Larache
was convinced that the Moors whom they met on the River
Kert were provided with French arms and ammunition. This
state of mind, whether justified or not, is explicable in the light
of the following words of M. Tardieu:

Often for lack of a synthetic policy both governments
adjusted their actions to that of their local agents whose
patriotic zeal underestimated the strength of common interests and of mutual obligations. If we were to survey the
grievances on either side we would conclude, no doubt, that
in this excess of zeal the Spanish agents went farther than
ours. [M. Tardieu may be right. On the other hand, as he is
a Frenchman himself, this opinion may be a pure effect of
perspective.] But how could we deny, on the other hand,
that the French government of 1909, by keeping Spain out
of its negotiation with Germany, and, later, by allowing the
Franco-Spanish negotiations on Morocco, whether financial
or of another kind, to drag on either intentionally or by
negligence, had not remained sufficiently within the spirit
of the initial agreements and had diminished the credit

which it was necessary to maintain in Madrid in order to obtain from the Spanish government a treatment of good neighborhood?[2]

This is an admirable summary of the psychological situation. In her dealings on Moroccan affairs with England, as well as with Germany, France always treated Spain with scant courtesy. In her direct dealings with Spain she resorted to a policy of obvious procrastination and ill will, the shortsightedness of which events were soon to demonstrate. France bought Germany off in her 1911 negotiations, then once more went alone to Fez and signed the Franco-Moroccan Treaty of March 1912, establishing what amounted to a French protectorate; having thus secured a predominant and isolated position in Morocco, while Spain remained out in the cold, she turned to Spain and claimed from her a share of her zone as part price of what she had had to pay in Berlin for freedom of action in this sphere. Spain stuck to the treaty of 1904, but, by force of circumstances, negotiations had to be reopened and, after laborious discussions embittered by a press campaign of unusual violence on both sides of the Pyrenees, the treaty of November 27, 1912, was concluded, mostly at the expense of Spain, whose zone was further reduced for the third time in twelve years. The Spanish zone was at last limited to an area of 18,300 square miles, while France secured 460,000. Tangier remained a thorny problem to be solved later. Much responsibility for these events was attributed in Spain to the policy of the British government.

[2] *Souvent, faute de vues d'ensemble, les deux gouvernements ont emboîté le pas à des agents locaux, dont le zèle patriotique appréciait trop peu la communauté des intérêts généraux et de l'obligation des transactions. S'il fallait reviser les griefs, on trouverait sans doute que, dans ces excès de zèle, les agents espagnols ont été plus loin que les nôtres. Mais comment nier, d'autre part, que le gouvernement français de 1909, en excluant l'Espagne de la négociation avec l'Allemagne, en laissant ensuite par système ou par négligence traîner toutes les négociations franco-espagnoles, financières ou autres, relatives au Maroc, s'était mal inspiré des accords initiaux et avait diminué le crédit qui lui était nécessaire à Madrid pour obtenir du gouvernement espagnol des procédés de bon voisinage?*

Home affairs revealed in Canalejas a good grasp of realities combined with genuine idealism. His stand against the power of Rome has been described. Militarism did not make him retreat. When Congress debated the Ferrer Case retrospectively, it was obvious that the prime minister was not endeavoring to go beyond a perfunctory defense of the military tribunal concerned. His war secretary felt offended at this attitude and resigned, but Canalejas let him go with equanimity. In this enlightened man Catalonia soon perceived a mind capable of understanding her grievances. Being led then by a statesman of equal breadth of view, Prat de la Riba, the Catalanists tried to come to terms. The prime minister received them cordially and met them by introducing a bill, *De Mancomunidades y Delegaciones,* which enabled the four Catalan provincial councils *(diputaciones)* to combine in one *mancomunidad,* to which the state granted a fair measure of devolution. The bill was, of course, freely attacked by many Liberals and Conservatives, yet provided the basis for a decree granted in later years by Count Romanones, which enabled Catalonia to make a first and promising home rule experiment till 1923.

Such sympathy and understanding did not come from any weakness in the prime minister's character. When in September 1912 a general railway strike threatened to plunge the country into anarchy, Canalejas decided to call up the railwaymen of military age and made them serve as soldiers in their railway posts, a measure which, though fiercely attacked by the parties of the Left, was undoubtedly at the time an indispensable act of state defense. But, though firm, he was not harsh. Far from it. No Spanish prime minister ever took more to heart the responsibilities of life and death which power implies. His advice was always for leniency. In one particular case, when after terrible scenes of disorder in Valencia a few men were sentenced to death, he advised the king to reprieve all but one of them. The king reprieved all without exception, and Canalejas, anxious that the king should reap the full benefit of this generosity, formally resigned. This dramatic gesture greatly enhanced the popularity of the monarch. Never, neither before nor after this period, was King Alfonso's popularity more general and genuine than when Canalejas was able to tender his generous and liberal advice on public affairs. The democratic current, which had set in as the reaction from the execution of Ferrer, had impressed on many dynastic Liberals the necessity of absorbing the Republican Left by enlarging the monarchical program in that direction. Moret had tried, somewhat prematurely, to attract to the government men such as Azcárate and Don Melquíades Alvarez, leaders of moderate republicanism. The revolution in Portugal which resulted in the expulsion of the Braganza dynasty and the setting up of a republic helped this evolution of the monarchists. Canalejas' policy had the same aim, even though he tried to secure it by more direct methods, and the king seemed to be wholeheartedly convinced by his prime minister. In 1912, Don Melquíades Alvarez, whose gifts of eloquence made him a powerful leader with the urban republican masses, responded to these efforts from the monarchical field by initiating an evolution towards monarchism which the enlightened policy of the prime minister enabled him to pursue. The moment seemed propitious for a gradual change of heart. There was, however, no lack of symptoms that the usual shady political intrigue was beginning to be woven round the great prime minister. Count Romanones, who more than once, moved by personal ambition, had taken steps which it was difficult not to connect with palatine tendencies, was beginning to show signs of premature appetite for power. Maura had a somewhat sensational meeting with Moret. This time, however, the dismal crisis which seemed to be in preparation in the back yard of the palace was spared to the nation and the prime minister. Canalejas fell. He fell dead, shot through the head by an anarchist while he was looking at the books in a bookshop window in the Puerta del Sol.

The only ruler which Spain had evolved during the reign of Alfonso XIII had been destroyed by fate. Had Canalejas lived, it is almost certain that the forces which were disrupting the system which had been slowly evolving from the Restoration would have been controlled by his masterly hand and keen intellect. The petty party intrigues, above which he had not always been able to remain, would have been met by frank exposure and attack, and the help which they were apt to meet with in the royal palace energetically checked. The progressive forces of the nation would have been absorbed into active partnership; the army and the Church reduced to obedience by a moderate, yet firm, handling of their preposterous claims; and foreign affairs conducted with tactful vigor. But Canalejas was killed by an irresponsible fanatic and the Liberal Party found itself without a head. Señor García Prieto was no more than a well-meaning gentleman, and Count Romanones was the prototype of the Spanish politician and nothing more. Count Romanones became prime minister and began by endeavoring to consolidate the absorption of the moderate wing of the Republican Party by having Azcárate and some of his friends called to the royal palace to advise the king on the crisis. The king heard, then, some of the best men of Spain. They spoke to him with loyal sincerity; some of them, it is said on excellent authority, moved him to deep emotion. But, while he looked toward the Left, Maura from the Right thundered "implacable hostility" to the parties which had precipitated his fall on the occasion of the Ferrer trial. Romanones, who was trying to conciliate these parties over to monarchical ground, felt thus excommunicated by the man who normally was to be his collaborator in carrying on the king's government, and finally resigned (October 25), immediately after the visit which the French president, M. Poincaré, paid to Madrid as a return for the visit which King Alfonso had paid to Paris to celebrate the Franco-Spanish Treaty on Morocco. The obvious choice was Maura. But at his name there was a regular revolt in the Republican and Socialist ranks. *Maura no* was the motto. This campaign of ostracism was so intense that the king bowed before it and called in the next Conservative leader available. Dato, who took office with a Cabinet of Conservatives, thought it well to revive the old name of the party: Liberal-Conservative. The political parties were thereby thoroughly disorganized both on the Right and on the Left. While the Liberals had lost their leader by assassination, the Conservatives had lost theirs by

ostracism and by that kind of political *hara-kiri* which Maura
was now and then led to commit, under the influence of his
intractable pride. The system inaugurated by Cánovas and
Sagasta in the pact of El Pardo was thus coming to an end.

One afternoon in the month of March 1914 a youthful man
with a heavy forehead, expressive eyes and an attractive, if self-
conscious, smile, came forward on the stage of the theater of
La Comedia in Madrid and began to speak with quiet assurance,
elegant gesture and a finely modulated voice to a crowded house
which listened eagerly, and now and then interrupted with vigorous ovations. He was the already famous professor of meta-
physics of the University of Madrid, José Ortega y Gasset. But
what he was explaining to this packed theater was no meta-
physical question; it was the grief of his generation at the sight
of what their elders had done with Spain. "Our generation,"
he said. "has never negotiated with the topics of patriotism,
and when it hears the word Spain it does not think of Calderón
and Lepanto, it does not remember the victories of The Cross,
it does not call forth the vision of a blue sky, and under it a
splendor—it merely feels, and that which it feels is grief." He
poured scorn on what he called "Official Spain." "Official Spain
consists, as it were, in ghostly parties upholding ghosts of ideas
which, backed by the shadows of newspapers, keep going Cabinets of hallucination." Yet he was careful not to let the blame
fall on the political world alone. "I hold a point of view which
is harder as a judgment on the past, but more optimistic as
to the future. The old Spain—with its governing and its governed
classes, with its abuses and its usages—is now dying." The Restoration, he held, was the period when all Spain was subordinated
to peace, and peace to the monarchy. The Republicans were
no better, for, in their turn, by putting the Republican ideal
above peace they also forgot Spain. For him it was necessary
to kill the Restoration, since, he added, "the dead must be thoroughly killed." And he concluded that it was high time that
everything in Spain was nationalized and liberalized: the army,
the Crown, the clergy, the workers, and even, he pleasantly
added, the ladies who now and then sign petitions without realiz-

ing their essentially anti-national import—a dart, this, at the clerical ladies of the aristocracy who, without realizing the gravity of their step, were always found on the side of the Vatican against the true interests of the nation.

This memorable day was the beginning of a movement of real leadership in Spanish politics. The spring tapped by Don Francisco Giner and fed by the devoted efforts of the *Junta,* or Committee for the Development of Studies, had by now become a strong and clear river of intelligent opinion flowing into the troubled and muddy waters of Spanish politics. Great hopes were raised when this body of new men, uncontaminated by the responsibilities of the past and the intrigues of the present, declared their intention to take part in public life and to raise the tone and the substance of Spanish politics. But four months after this day an Austrian prince was killed in Sarajevo, and Europe went mad.

CHAPTER 24

THE FIRST WORLD WAR

The Cartagena Agreements signed in 1907 and the conversations held in 1913 between M. Poincaré and Count Romanones stipulated that, "should new circumstances arise tending to alter the territorial *status quo*" in the Mediterranean or on the African and European coasts of the Atlantic, the governments of England, France and Spain would "enter into communication" with a view to adopting the measures required by the new situation. The declaration of war could no doubt be fairly interpreted as falling within the purview of these provisions, and it is almost certain that the Spanish government expected some sort of "communication" to be made to it. Nothing, however, was forthcoming, and Dato lost no time in declaring Spain a neutral. On the face of it Spain might—almost should—have been drawn into the vortex. Situated on two of the three main seas on which the conflict was raging; touching war on her three frontiers, France, Portugal and Gibraltar; intimately connected by her

311

foreign policy with the two leaders of the Allied group, France and England—how could she remain a neutral? The reasons are to be found in both domestic and foreign conditions. At home the nation split in two. Roughly the liberal, anti-clerical, progressive Left was pro-Ally; the reactionary, clerical Right, pro-German. But strictly speaking, there were in Spain neither pro-Germans nor pro-Allies, but only mental and emotional attitudes toward national, historical and philosophical problems which might be more or less adequately represented by these two convenient and popular labels.

The so-called pro-Ally side was led by the liberal and progressive intellectuals. It would be difficult to find a case in which the intellectual leaders of a country gave better proof of their capacity for rising above shortsighted national views and feelings than that which the Spanish elite gave in 1914 when they sided with France and England. The men who took up the cudgels for the Allies knew the historical role which these two nations had played in the downfall of the Austrian dynasty and in the destruction of the power of Spain which Ferdinand VI and Charles III had built up again after the War of Succession. They were aware of England's share in the disruption of the Spanish Empire from Canning to Salisbury; of France's ways in Morocco. Yet they did not hesitate. For them France and England were fighting their own battles, but incidentally they were fighting for liberalism, i.e. for the political school of thought which sees in the individual the true aim of the state and not a mere tool in the state's hands. They were not so much pro-Ally as anti-Prussian, and in this term they did not in the least condemn the Prussian people, but the political system which, for good or ill, was identified with Prussia at the time. Unlike the generation of the middle of the nineteenth century, most of them owed more perhaps to Germany than to France, and felt far more in sympathy with German than with French culture, philosophy and letters. Several of them had to master their feelings, which would have led them naturally to espouse the cause of Germany, because their mind pointed clearly the other way even from the point of view of the best interests of Germany. And for many

the open advocacy of the Western cause implied a painful sacrifice of friendships and memories dear to them from their student
days beyond the Rhine.

The line of cleavage which the best minds of the nation had
discerned from the beginning cut across public opinion and
proved to be the real frontier, irrespective of political party lines
or other considerations. At bottom the issue was one between
the liberal and the imperious temperaments. Behind the intellectual leaders and the liberal temperaments in the political world
(which were not all of them necessarily in the Liberal Party)
there were a fair proportion, perhaps the majority, of the professions, and practically the whole of the organized working
classes, a substantial minority of the army and a handful of
enlightened clergy. The peasantry was for the most part indifferent. The upper middle classes, the clerical world, the majority
of the army and the reactionary politicians were pro-German.
Business was, on the whole, pro-Ally, even though heart and
temperament inclined it to Prussianism, as is often the case in
the best-regulated industries; but then the winds of prosperity
blew unmistakably from the West. The Court was divided. The
king, with his unrivaled skill and exceptional opportunities,
managed to conceal his true sentiments right through the war,
and it would be a bold man who would even now venture to
express a definite opinion as to the side to which he was more
attached. The queen was English; the queen-mother was Austrian. The court had always been a quiet but ardent battleground
between the clerical and the reactionary elements entrenched on
the queen mother's wing of the palace and the liberals (of course
with moderation) who clustered round the young queen. The
former were probably stronger and certainly more vocal. Shortly
after the death in action of Prince Maurice of Battenberg, brother
of the Queen of Spain, Señor Vázquez de Mella, the Carlist
leader, addressed a pro-German meeting crowded with wealthy
aristocrats. In a highfalutin style, which went by the name of
eloquence among his enthusiastic supporters, he sang his admiration for mighty Germany, cried his pity for "poor France,"
and shouted his historical hatred of perfidious Albion. A bright

array of court ladies attended the meeting and ostentatiously
applauded the speaker, whose feet they covered with flowers
while he declaimed a passionate *finale*.

It is obvious that a nation so deeply cleft in twain by the
war issue could not be an active belligerent on either side.
Moreover, both sections of public opinion were agreed that the
war was not Spain's business, and this for at least two reasons:
the first, a kind of underlying skepticism born of a long historical
experience which the Treaty of Versailles was later to justify;
the second, an intimate conviction that no vital Spanish interest
was at stake or could be benefited by Spain joining in the fray.

This second reason, at any rate, was no doubt reciprocated
by France and England, who do not appear to have shown any
eagerness to recruit Spain's belligerent help. Both France and
England well knew that Spain could not enlist without putting
Gibraltar and Morocco on the tray of the war stakes. On the
other hand, Spain was an admirable war factory, for the Peninsula produces practically every mineral, animal and vegetable
raw material, except rubber and mineral oil, and she could also
provide abundant labor and a fair amount of technical skill and
even of capital. The choice for the Allies was, therefore, not
doubtful. And as the obvious interests of all concerned could
be served best by neutrality, Spain remained a neutral.

The war, nevertheless, produced deep effects on Spain. They
may be summed up in one sentence: the war drove a powerful
current of foreign vitality right into the inmost recesses of the
nation. The current was as muddy and impure as it was impetuous. It carried much gold and much poison along with the
vivifying ferments of a new life. And it came further to complete
and render acute practically every one of the problems which
beset Spanish governments. In the intenser atmosphere of the
war and through the din of the constant debate between pro-Ally
and pro-German advocates, the now familiar processes of Spanish politics evolved apace with grave international difficulties
arising out of the German submarine campaign.

Developments during this period include:

The gradual disintegration of the two political parties, in part through their own internal weakness, in part through the peculiar policy of the king.

The definite alignment of the king in favor of coalition ministries which was bound to accelerate the downfall of the party system.

The gradual emancipation of the electorate, which, in the end, made it impossible for the government that "made" the general election to be sure of a majority.

The revolt of the army, i.e. of the officers' soviet, and its usurpation of the powers of both king and Parliament.

The swift development of syndicalist, communist and anarchist movements, partly under the financial stimulus of German agents, and later, under the political stimulus of the Russian Revolution.

The endeavors of certain Catalanists to obtain the help now of Germany, now of France, for setting up a separate nationhood.

The picture was black enough. But it began rosy. Orders from the Allies were plentiful and money flowed into the nation, which enabled the government to lay the foundations for the repatriation of the foreign debt. The peseta rose in a gratifying manner and the nation seemed to be settling down to its work as an Allied war factory, when a debate on military reforms forced Dato to resign (December 1915). Count Romanones took office in rather difficult circumstances. Military operations were being carried out in Morocco, where public opinion suspected him of being financially interested in the mines which it was the predominant intention of the operations to safeguard from Moorish attack, and German submarines were carrying on a brisk campaign against Spanish ships, while the prime minister was also suspected of wanting Spain to join the Allied battalion. He took his responsibilities bravely in the teeth of a campaign against him in the pro-German press, as ruthless as the submarine campaign of Germany against the Spanish ships; and while news of heavy fighting arrived from Ceuta he was making strong representations in Berlin. At the same time he had to face a general railway strike in the summer of 1916 and, in September, a violent campaign against his finance minister, Don Santiago Alba, for the heinous crime of introducing a bill to make the Treasury participate in the handsome war profits which businessmen were reaping at the time. Spain had by then lost close upon 40,000 tons of shipping, and, when Germany sent in her note of absolute blockade of the Allied coasts, Count Romanones decided to test public opinion by answering it in stiff and spirited terms (February 6, 1917). Public opinion was by then not only divided on this important issue of foreign policy, but profoundly disturbed by no less than three movements of a revolutionary character, hereafter described, and Count Romanones decided to leave power on April 19.

There was more than met the eye in this resignation. In point of fact, Count Romanones knew that a serious military revolt was brewing and he preferred to be out of reach when it broke out. This revolt was a curious after-effect of syndicalism acting on the permanent state of semi-rebellion of the Spanish officers. The syndicalist idea, preached in Barcelona by a few disciples of Sorel, had fallen on particularly favorable soil in Spain. The tenets of particularist association, abstention from politics and direct action, spoke but too eloquently to the individualistic Spanish soul; they were revolutionizing the labor movement in Barcelona where a syndicalist *Confederación Nacional del Trabajo* had been set up against the socialist *Unión General de Trabajadores* in Madrid. In a curious indirect way, they were at the same time influencing the medium in which such influence was least to be expected. The committees of defense, organized by the army officers with a conscientiousness, a discipline and a foresight which might have produced far-reaching effects if applied to the army's proper purposes, arose partly as a kind of irritated reaction against the more objectionable forms of "antipatriotic" Catalanism, partly as an instrument of internal solidarity and with a view to removing the evil effects of favoritism in the ranks of officers, but mostly in order to break down the power of the *Casa Militar,* or military house of the king, a kind of palatine war office which administered the king's pleasure in military matters. Their official aims were "moderation in rewards, justice in promotions, respect for seniority, reorganization of the medical corps and the commissariat, improvement of staff and material conditions and exclusion of military forces from civilian conflicts in order to avoid dangerous strife between the people and the army." The ostensible aims were perfect. The methods were, of course, inadmissible. All confabulations of officers were illegal, but, moreover, the committees, though theoretically a secret organization, soon started to threaten and bully cabinets and even the crown.

And yet the crown continued its policy of whittling down and destroying its political parties. García Prieto, always a willing tool in the king's hands, had organized a Cabinet of Liberals into which, at the king's request, he had admitted the Conservative Admiral Miranda as Minister of Marine. But soon after he had taken office, and while social troubles were threatening on the horizon, the Committees of Defense initiated their attack on the institutions. General Aguilera, the war secretary, ordered the arrest of the leaders. The committees sent an ultimatum to the government. Pressure, it is believed, from the crown did the rest. The Cabinet resigned and the committees won.

Curiously enough, the nation was with the officers, a fact which admits of two explanations, both true. There is no doubt that a man or body of men who succeed in carrying their point through sheer will power, manfully facing all obstacles, is sure to appeal to the Spanish people, whose dramatic sense is the most keen of their political reactions. The Committees of Defense were popular because they beat the king; not on account of any enmity against the king as a person, or as an institution, but merely because a king takes some beating. Then it was felt that the committees were bringing a renovating element to Spanish political life. The old "ghostly" system was going; realities were coming in. Renovation was in the air. "Renovation" became the watchword of a new hope. It became the motto of the new daily, *El Sol,* a clean, intelligent, wide and generous organ of opinion,

free from bonds or prejudices, just created under the same inspiration by an enterprising businessman and intellectual, Don
Nicolas María Urgoiti. With uncompromising independence of
the past, *El Sol* led public opinion, over which it had quickly
acquired considerable command, to the view that, through the
somewhat revolutionary action of the Committees of Defense,
the old system would be forced to acquire a new spirit and
organize the life of Spain on a new basis. The crisis was hailed,
not as what it was—the triumph of a rebellious body of army
officers over Crown, Cabinet and Parliament—but as the turning
point in the history of the Restoration; the moment when new
men and new ideas would have to be called to the government
of Spain. The king gave office to Dato and to the most orthodox
of Conservative Cabinets.

The disappointment was keen. Catalonia in particular, where
the nationalist ferment, then stirring in all Europe from Ireland
to Macedonia, had stimulated the old cause, felt defrauded of
the high expectations which the "Renovation" movement had
made her conceive. A meeting of Catalan members of Parliament
took place in Barcelona, and decided to ask the government to
call a session of Cortes, failing which the Catalan members would
call all Spanish parliamentarians willing to meet them to hold
an assembly. The government was not in the least anxious to
add to its difficulties by a series of stormy sittings in which the
king's and its own surrender before the military would have to
be discussed. It declared that the Assembly would be considered
as factious and took the somewhat unwise step of discrediting
the movement in Castile by tainting it with Catalanist colors.
The Assembly met on July 19, attended by seventy-one members
of both Houses (out of 760). It decided to consider itself as
permanently constituted and set up three commissions: one on
constitution, one on army and justice, and one on national economy. These commissions were to prepare reports to be submitted
to a later meeting in another town. The Assembly was thoroughly
popular in the whole country; the municipalities of Barcelona,
Málaga, Oviedo, Salamanca, Zaragoza and the Basque Provinces
expressed their approval of the movement, and the support which

it received from the other provinces, where the political machinery held official bodies in silence or in opposition to it, was nevertheless considerable. The movement aimed at a non-party ministry and a general election under guarantees of respect for the popular vote with a view to a constituent Assembly.

This movement might have been the true salvation of Spain and, in particular, of the monarchical system, had the crown been more convinced of the advantages of a parliamentary form of government and had the hot-heads of the labor movement been less convinced of the advantages of revolution. As it happened, the moderate but bold and statesmanlike action of the Parliamentary Assembly fell flat under a combined attack coming from the extremists of the Right and of the Left. A movement toward direct action and violence had begun a few years earlier in Barcelona. The roots of it were to be found in that proclivity to anarchist outrages which is a permanent disease in the Catalan capital. Later, toward 1910, the more enterprising of the followers of Lerroux could with difficulty be distinguished from political guerrillas. The royalist bands known in Paris as *Camelots du Roy* were imitated in Barcelona by the Carlist party, which organized so-called *Requetés*, or bands of young men ready to fight at any moment for their cause. The radicals of Lerroux then countered with similar bands, significantly styled *Jóvenes Bárbaros*. All this ferment of violence and agitation helped, in an indirect way, the cause of syndicalism, which aimed at influencing events by organized force and in contempt of political institutions. Add to the picture the deplorable example of anarchy given by the army itself, and over it all the exhilarating reports, just then arriving, of the brand-new Russian Revolution. On August 10, 1917, six days before the day chosen for the second meeting of the Assembly, a revolutionary general strike was declared. The moderate *Unión* of Madrid, in order not to be outdone by the hot-headed *Confederación* of Barcelona, had taken the lead. The aim was political as well as social: a socialist democratic republic. The strike spread over the whole country: Madrid, Barcelona, Bilbao, Oviedo. The industrial districts of Valencia, Catalonia, Aragón and Andalusia were paralyzed.

Trains, tramways, bakeries, the building trades, came to a standstill. But the army was intact. Machine guns and artillery swept the barricaded streets of Madrid and Barcelona. Three days sufficed to put down the disorder. The revolution left behind two thousand prisoners, several hundred victims, dead and wounded, and the Constitution dead. The Labor hot-heads had delivered the nation and its hopeful Assembly into the hands of the only force that remained: the army.

On August 10 the Cabinet had passed a credit for military expenses. But on August 19 the army had "saved the nation," and mere credits would not satisfy them. The representatives of the Committees of Defense had called on the king as well as on several important personages, and found in La Cierva (the resolute man who had insisted that Ferrer should be shot) a man to their liking. A message, which was an ultimatum, had been sent to the palace, as a consequence of which the king suggested to Dato that he might, perhaps, resign. A new Cabinet had to be built around the war secretary whom the committees imposed: La Cierva. The only man ready to accept such a condition was Garcia Prieto. He became prime minister. The crisis took place while the Assembly was holding a session in Madrid. By a movement not yet fully explained the constitution of the new Cabinet deprived the Assembly of its main strength by securing the cooperation of Señor Cambó, who allowed two of his collaborators to enter the ministry. Thus, by a mixture of stupidity in labor, astuteness in the older institutions, firmness in the Dato government, and vacillation and disunion in the Assembly, the grave but hopeful crisis of 1917 went by without leaving behind beneficial results of any importance.

The inroads on the political system of what was now the past had been so deep that no one was surprised to see in office a Cabinet composed of Maurists, Catalanists and Liberals. The true dictator of the Ministry was La Cierva. The first difficulty he had to weather was a movement among the non-commissioned officers, who, not without logic, had formed committees of defense and tried to imitate the methods of their superior officers. They were ruthlessly reduced to discipline by the war secretary, who had been put in office by indiscipline. This happened at the beginning of 1918. But a kind of fever of syndicalism had by then seized all the corporations of the realm, from the postal workers to the members of the nobility, who organized themselves and issued a manifesto. The movement came to a head when, the telegraph officers having declared a strike, La Cierva tried to apply his resolute ways to the conflict and plunged the country into chaos. This event, coming on top of a general election, as a result of which the four leaders of the 1917 revolution (sentenced to death and reprieved with life sentences) were elected members to Parliament by Madrid, Barcelona and Valencia, brought about the downfall of the government. After days of painful negotiations the king called a meeting of ex–prime ministers at the palace at midnight on March 21. It is generally believed that he threatened abdication if his suggestion were not accepted. It was. Maura became prime minister of a Cabinet in which all the ex–prime ministers were included, along with a few outstanding political leaders, notably Señor Cambó, who became Minister of Finance, and Señor Alba, who became Minister of Education. The constitution of this Cabinet was extremely popular, for it was a dramatic stroke and it ostracized La Cierva. It took, moreover, a bold and wise, though strictly, perhaps, an illegal, measure: it validated the election of the four Socialist members of Parliament, who passed from prison to Parliament. The Cabinet, nevertheless, was of short duration. Internal dissensions, probably due to political antagonism between Señor Alba (a Castilian Centralist) and Señor Cambó, led to its disintegration. It fell on November 6. A new crisis was negotiated under the shadow cast by foreign events. The Kaiser fled, and every day brought news of a fresh abdication. The falling of thrones is contagious, and the fear of contagion is a source of caution in the boldest hearts. A Liberal government was the order of the day. The first attempt, under García Prieto, was not successful. Count Romanones took office on December 3, 1918, and immediately left for Paris to interview President Wilson.

Caught in the throes of such grave internal events, Spanish

governments had been hard put to it to maintain Spain's neutrality free from the dangers which beset it. The German government, in its plight, had concentrated its efforts on war requirements without regard for other considerations. Its secret and propaganda services in Spain had unlimited means at their disposal and a remarkable freedom from prejudice as to the ways of using them. Anarchists and Left Wing syndicalists were enabled to organize themselves and strikes were always sure of support. Strange Teutonic types were active, at times on the labor, at times on the employer, side, and always in a manner which fostered dissatisfaction, unrest, strife and even bloodshed. Barcelona knew no peace. Troubles spread also to other industrial centers. Submarines frequented the Spanish coasts, not always in vain. The pro-German press, with a deplorable lack of national spirit, took the side of Germany to the bitter end. The government had to steer clear of action which might be misrepresented by the pro-German papers as a disguised attempt to launch Spain into the war. In 1917 a submarine entered Cádiz and was interned on parole, yet broke its word and fled. Trade became practically the monopoly of the Allies, and Spain, in protecting her trade, had of necessity to protect Allied trade. Toward the end of 1917 an agreement was negotiated to that effect with the British government. But Spanish shipping losses became heavier and heavier, and the government had just obtained from Germany the recognition of the principle of ton-for-ton indemnity when the war came to an end. Spain had lost 65 ships and 140,000 tons.

What had she won? First, a considerable amount of capital. Her trade balance had, of course, changed its sign during the war, so that between 1915 and 1919, both inclusive, official figures show a balance in her favor of 768,000,000 pesetas. But the influx of capital was much bigger, and, as a result of it, Spain was able to acquire a considerable proportion of her foreign industrial debt and practically all her national debt. Her railways, in particular, became practically her own. The clearest indication of this change in her economic condition may be seen in the affairs of the Bank of Spain and particularly in its gold reserves. The gold held by the Bank of Spain amounted to 567,000,000 pesetas ($110,224,800) in 1914. In 1918 it had risen to 2,223,000,000 pesetas ($422,370,000). At the same time the basis of trade expanded, as the table on the next page will show.

The most typical feature of this change was a considerable increase in the trade with America, both North and South, and particularly of both imports and exports with Spanish-America and of imports from the United States.

Much of this rise in the commercial activity of Spain was due to the industrial and commercial stimulus arising out of the necessity to work under exacting conditions of time and quality during the war. Many industries which were founded during the war disappeared with the abnormal conditions which had given them birth, but a number remained and much permanent improvement of old plant and conditions was effected, notably in the iron and steel plants of the Basque country and in the new establishments of the same trade on the eastern coast.

The working classes went through a period of high salaries which did much to ripen their views and to make them at the same time more exacting in their aims and more moderate and constructive in their methods. Though much trouble was still to come from the unruly elements which disturb the evolution of labor in Spain—both on the labor and on the employer side— the gain was permanent and was to show its effects in due time. The importance of big-scale efforts in industry and generally in public life was driven home to the imagination of the country and, along with it, the fundamental role of machinery. This period saw the beginning of the influence of American life in Spain. Spain was then invaded by all kinds of refugees from Europe, not a few of those stray human beings living their own isolated life with no concern for the events of history—but also many undesirable types, floating between spying and drug addiction, white slave traffic and gambling, fraudulent finance and shoplifting. Madrid and Barcelona were constellated with cabarets and the jewelers, perfume shops and travel agencies minted money. Along with this internationalism of a lower kind Spain

Spanish Trade with Foreign Countries	1914				1920			
	Imports in Pesetas	Per Cent of Total	Exports in Pesetas	Per Cent of Total	Imports in Pesetas	Per Cent of Total	Exports in Pesetas	Per Cent of Total
Europe	708,786,634	65.19	697,251,646	75.94	730,880,894	49.79	700,449,370	66.64
Asia	78,601,471	7.20	7,764,949	0.84	91,576,896	6.24	3,560,510	0.33
Africa	19,824,235	1.83	19,349,856	2.10	26,784,757	1.83	30,134,127	2.85
South America	97,920,988	9.01	126,884,661	13.82	264,176,256	17.99	238,675,120	22.73
North America	154,813,522	14.26	65,664,740	7.15	345,840,071	23.55	78,782,456	7.44
Oceania	27,228,598	2.51	1,420,668	0.15	8,742,050	0.60	69,352	0.01
Total	1,087,175,448	100.00	918,336,520	100.00	1,468,000,924	100.00	1,051,670,935	100.00

had then to intervene in foreign affairs both at home and abroad. Madrid was the most important European neutral city, and many matters of finance and general policy found a convenient soil and atmosphere there. The king had organized an efficient system of information and help whereby the cases of missing soldiers of both camps were investigated and many of them handled with the utmost care and devotion. The official diplomatic service of the country had to take over a growing number of embassies and legations as the area of belligerency enlarged, and there came a time when the Spanish ambassador in Berlin represented nearly every nation there. Spanish doctors had to travel in Allied hospital ships to guarantee their *bona fide* character to the irate commanders of German submarines; Spanish military officers had to inspect prisoners' camps to ensure the welfare of the prisoners. All these duties of world collaboration acted as powerful stimuli to the Spanish mind, and, in the aggregate, it may be said that Spain lived then an international life such as she had not known since the days when in the sixteenth and seventeenth centuries her statesmen, generals, churchmen and ambassadors were paramount in the affairs of Europe.

CHAPTER 25

FROM THE END OF THE FIRST WORLD WAR
TO THE END OF THE CONSTITUTION

When peace broke out a wind of liberalism blew over the country. The government was, of course, in liberal hands—at least, in the safely liberal hands of Count Romanones. He had a clean record in international matters. He had always been as favorable to the Allies as was possible in Spain. He went to Paris, saw Wilson, and returned with a seat for Spain on the Council of the League of Nations. Grave events awaited him at home. The Catalans, stimulated by the nationalist movements of Europe, called on him and asked for a further measure of home rule. In the debates in Congress Señor Cambó, their leader, boldly asserted Catalonia's claim to nationhood. The count had, moreover, been able to find in Paris traces of Catalan efforts to bring the case of Catalonia before the Peace Conference. Meanwhile, Barcelona was brewing another of her anarchist-militaristic crises. The permanent state of industrial war there was being handled with lenient tact by a progressive civil governor, Montañés, with the cooperation of a brilliant lawyer, Doval, who had courageously taken over the arduous duties of chief of the Barcelona police. A dualism had begun to manifest itself amongst the authorities of Barcelona. The civil governor was inclined to arbitration and conciliation and usually found ready help in the more moderate leaders of labor as well as in a small, but not very influential, group of intelligent employers. The bulk of the employers, however, were of a more resolute and reactionary temperament and gravitated toward the offices of the captain-general, in the military atmosphere of which they found ready sympathy for their breezy methods. The complexity of the situations may be gathered from the fact that, while the industrial labor leaders in cooperation with the liberal civil governor were indifferent, or lukewarm, to the regionalistic issue, to which the civil politicians were on the whole sympathetic; the reactionary employers, so friendly with the military authorities, were adepts of Catalanism, a doctrine heretical and infamous to army men. With such hopelessly entangled relationships were Catalan politics then being woven. Doval found his work handicapped by the more than shady activities of one Bravo Portillo, an ex-chief of police who had been expelled by the civilian authorities on being found guilty of espionage on behalf of Germany, and who was, nevertheless, in the employ of the captain-general's office. Matters between the civil and the military authorities went from bad to worse, and one evening both the governor and the chief of police were faced with an ultimatum to leave town at once, which they did to avoid worse dangers. The Cabinet, unable to vindicate civil authority, resigned.

By then the whole Peninsula was being rapidly overrun with Bolshevik measles. The infection began, of course, in Barcelona, where the *Confederación Nacional del Trabajo* was actively organizing a campaign for the *Sindicato Unico,* or One Big Union. This campaign bore fruit in Andalusia, where the *Federación Nacional de Agricultores,* founded by the Congress of Córdoba in 1913, lent a ready ear to the new ideas on revolutionary tactics which their Catalan comrades advocated. A congress of the regionalist (Andalusian) syndicalist federations had taken place in 1918, and since then a wave of disorders, strikes and even crimes had swept over the small townships and fields of Andalusia—the tragic expiation of a past full of shortsighted mistakes and even of cynical brutality on the part of many a callous landlord. The situation was equally bad in Barcelona. The employers had taken a leaf from the labor book and sought strength in association. In 1914, the first Congress of Employers' Federations had taken place in Madrid. A second congress met in Barcelona in 1919. Between the dates of these two congresses the Employers' League had set up a general secretariat in Madrid, and had launched a policy of uncompromising opposition to labor claims and to government concessions to labor, which was to lead to disastrous results.

Such were the circumstances in which, on Count Romanones' resignation, Maura was called to power by the king. It should be noticed that Maura was not then the chief of the Conservative Party. The party had moved away from him owing precisely to a disagreement on the resolute methods of La Cierva which Maura had adopted. Dato, the new Conservative chief, prided himself on being the pioneer of government reform on social and industrial questions in a sense sympathetic to labor's moderate claims. The king's choice in the circumstances was interpreted as a definite preference for the strong way, coupled with indifference to the claims of his main dynastic party. But disapproval of his step rose to a pitch of indignation when the king granted Maura the coveted dissolution decree, although it is believed by well-informed Conservative leaders that His Majesty first convinced Dato of the advisability, or, at any rate, the inevitability, of this decision. Maura, in that general election which he controlled, destroyed all the reputation which he had acquired as a sincere respecter of the suffrage in years past. His methods brought back the style of party electioneering to the worst period of the Regency. And yet in spite of his ruthless and unscrupulous methods, he failed to bring more than a handful of government candidates to the House. The *suffrage was beginning to work in Spain.* This failure in the field of politics was paralleled in the field of social unrest. Confronted with a serious situation in the South and in Catalonia, he met it with force and nothing but force. He suspended the guarantees of the Constitution, he imprisoned and expelled labor leaders, closed labor associations and clubs, applied a strict censorship, used, in fact, all the paraphernalia of lazy and violent governments. A general was sent to Andalusia to deal with the revolting agrarian workers as if they were an army of enemy invaders, when all might have been pacified with a state guarantee of steady work through the year. This deplorable government fell on July 20.

Every effort was made, however, to persevere in the resolute policy which had brought it to its end, and, consequently, to obstruct the obvious and constitutional solution, a Conservative government, because the men who then led the party were committed to a conciliatory policy with labor and such a policy was opposed by the military authorities in Barcelona and by the crown. No doubt, dissatisfied with the king's attitude and in indifferent health at the time, Dato had advised the king to form a government of Conservatives under Sánchez Toca, and the king had agreed, a fact which Dato had announced to his party. To their surprise, however, the summons was sent not to Sánchez Toca, but to Maura; and serious and strenuous efforts were made to induce the Conservative leaders to accept this preposterous solution. These efforts included a visit of Marshal Primo de Rivera (uncle of the future dictator), who threatened the Conservatives with an extreme Left ministry under the ex-Republican leader, Don Melquíades Alvarez, if they did not accept the king's solution, and, later, a visit of La Cierva himself, who failed to carry conviction. Even at this late hour the king persisted, and the task of forming a Cabinet was entrusted to Admiral Miranda. At long last the enlightened wing of the Conservative Party had its way and Sánchez Toca was asked to form a ministry—a mandate which he accepted only after persistent efforts made by his chief, Dato; for by this time Señor Sánchez Toca was indignant at the king's obduracy and cavalier treatment of his old advisers.

The history of this crisis is all-important because the Sánchez

Toca ministry went far to prove that most of the criticisms leveled against Spanish democracy by those who never made a sincere effort to trust it, in combination with those who made persistent efforts to betray it, are baseless. The Sánchez Toca ministry was a government of Conservatives, in fact some of its members would be considered as die-hard reactionaries in France or England. Its home secretary, Burgos y Mazo, was a devout Catholic, and as distant from Socialism as Lord Baldwin or President Coolidge. But this ministry came to office determined to do its best to solve industrial problems with common sense, tact, firmness and prudence, and above all with a high sense of impartiality and justice. No one who reads the remarkable book writtten by Burgos y Mazo, under the significant title of *The Summer of 1919 at the Home Office,* can fail to be impressed by its transparent honesty and convinced by the abundant documents which it contains, ranging from diagrams of the German secret service system in Spain to confidential police notes and transcripts of telephone conversations. The general conclusions to be drawn from this study are an indispensable basis for judging subsequent events.

First, the government vindicated its enlightened policy in every way by repeated successes every time it was allowed the unhampered use of its methods; thus it weathered grave strikes and revolts in Valencia and Málaga without bloodshed in the teeth of the stubborn and unenlightened behavior on the part of the Málaga employers; and it dismissed the civil governor of Zaragoza for having expelled some labor leaders without reason, thereby provoking a general strike.

Second, even in Barcelona, where its policy was to be held in check by the dark forces at work there, the government succeeded in eliminating the worst cancer from which the town suffered: assassination. This is a point that must be emphasized. *Political and industrial murders were at their lowest in Barcelona while the Sánchez Toca authorities were in charge of affairs,* and it is therefore not true to say that exceptional measures other than the ordinary application of intelligence and justice were indispensable to bring peace to this much-tried capital.

Third, the main obstacle to the statesmanlike policy of the government came from precisely those who claimed to represent law and order, and, in particular, from a more or less avowed combination of the political and press interests connected with La Cierva, the Employers' Federation, and the military authorities. The story and, what is more to the point, the documents, printed by Burgos y Mazo, go far to show the singular methods of this reactionary combination. The head of the Barcelona Employers' Federation is clearly shown working for a break and a lockout even after committting himself to a solution on the basis of arbitration which he himself had put forward. A curious correspondence shows how General Milans del Bosch, a Catalan, took it as a matter of course that, while the civil governor would deal with the labor representatives, he, the captain-general, would negotiate with the employers: a suggestion, or rather an assumption, which the Home Secretary rightly corrected at once. The negotiations may be followed step by step in the complete and impartial record of the Home Secretary. They show treasures of patience on the part of the government and of the moderate leaders of labor, then clearly in control of their rank and file, but they also show a determination on the part of the Employers' Federation to fight at all costs or, to put it in their favorite words, "to give the battle" (*dar la batalla*). The matter came to a deadlock when the military, in complete agreement with the Employers' Federation, threatened to repeat their exploit of the days of the Romanones government and expel the civil governor.

But the crisis which caused the fall of the government did not come from militarism meddling with social questions. It came from militarism pure and simple. A number of captains studying in the *Escuela Superior de Guerra* (Staff College) had refused to submit to the illegal and vexatious conditions which the Committees of Defense required from all officers. They were accordingly asked to resign. They refused. They were brought before a court of honor and sentenced to resign from the school. This incident created a profound impression, and public opinion was shocked at the monstrous injustice done to these men whose very stand implied high qualities of character. The Cabinet resolved that a new court should hear the case and that no solution should be made final without first referring to the Supreme Council of War (a military court of justice). Contrary to his explicit undertaking to that effect General Tovar, the war secretary, approved the decision of the second court, unfavorable to the captains, without referring the matter to the Supreme Council. He had been the object of strong military pressure. The government resigned. A pliable man was sought to take charge, and an inconspicuous Conservative, Allende Salazar, answered the purpose. The lockout, so much desired by the employers, was launched in Barcelona. It quickly degenerated into a campaign of sporadic murder which cost victims on both sides and which, therefore, may not unfairly be traced to both sides. By a kind of contagion a military rebellion occurred in the lower ranks in Zaragoza, and was ruthlessly repressed, of course. This unfortunate government had to take political responsibility for an unpleasant incident which occurred in Barcelona on the occasion of Marshal Joffre's visit. After the French victory the more enthusiastic Catalanists had suddenly realized that Marshal Joffre was a French Catalan, and the visit was made the occasion for exhibiting rather violent Catalanist passions with so little tact that the visitor had to leave before his appointed time. The country could not live through such difficult days under so gray a government. Dato took office in May, and soon after his accession Count Salvatierra, the "strong" governor of Barcelona, appointed by the previous Cabinet to please the employers, fell a victim to that ruthless social strife which he had, unwittingly perhaps, helped to promote. Dato appointed as civil governor a division general with a reputation for energy, General Martínez Anido. From that moment the attention of the government became concentrated on two problems: the general election and the social strife in Barcelona. The first was a complete fiasco for the government (177 members out of 405), but a brilliant vindication of the view that, despite the imperfections of the electoral law deliberately maintained in order the better to juggle with the votes, the suffrage was rapidly becoming effective. As for the events in Barcelona, General Martínez Anido obtained some kind of peace, but by methods which it would be difficult to describe. He himself declared in conversation with an interviewer that "he was but a surgeon, and a doctor would have to take charge at a later stage." The upshot of it all was that Dato was assassinated on March 8, 1921.

The king tried to bring back Maura, but Maura had by now become a convinced advocate of coalition governments and found no support for his ideas in either Liberals or Conservatives. The king called on Allende Salazar again. A deplorable choice, if only because His Majesty had by then come to a stage when, more than ever, he needed strong and independent advice. The scene of grave events shifted from Barcelona, where one general was sowing seeds of future storms, to Morocco, where another general was ready for his harvest of disasters. The high commissioner, General Berenguer, was an able and distinguished officer, a man of cool judgment, forbearance, knowledge of Morocco and of his people, technical skill and general ability, yet sinning, as who did not in those days, in excessive weakness toward the constant encroachments of the crown in the management of affairs. Two years earlier, under the Sánchez Toca ministry, General Berenguer had won great success by taking over from the tribes the strong vantage point of El Fondak. Since then his ability and quiet methods had enabled the Spanish cause to progress morally and territorially more effectively than it had under any of his predecessors and at a much smaller cost in blood and treasure. But one of his subordinate officers, General Silvestre, in charge of the Melilla division, whose cavalry soul felt afflicted at so much civilian skill and at so little military dash, decided to strike a blow. His plan was evidently approved by the king, who sent him warm telegraphic encouragement couched in friendly and familiar language. It is not clear to what extent it was approved, or even actually known in all its importance, by General Berenguer, his military chief. General Silvestre went gaily on, placed himself in an absurdly dangerous position, overlooking the strong armament of the enemy, and suffered a severe defeat (July 21, 1921). In a few hours the Spanish troops lost all the eastern zone which had been gradually taken from the enemy since 1909, thousands of dead, wounded and prisoners, and a considerable amount of war material. Moreover, this defeat created a deep impression in Morocco, and greatly enhanced the prestige of Abd-el Krim, the leader of the rebellion. General Silvestre committed suicide.

The effect in Spain was, of course, profound. It brought down the government, and Maura was called to meet the emergency with exceptional measures. The nation was generous in men and money, and an army of 140,000 was put at the disposal of the high commissioner. But the nation was also wrathful and wanted guarantees that the responsibility for what had happened should be investigated and exacted. The situation immediately took an unpleasant turn owing to the interference of the Committees of Defense. Maura had asked La Cierva to take over the War Office on a strong hint from somewhere; and, though he personally was averse to the military committees, his war secretary liked to consider himself as their man. Maura, who realized that the situation was fraught with danger, tried to get them on his side; but public excitement, far from abating, was constantly rising—partly under the effect of further revelations made by special press envoys, partly under such provocations as a bill submitted to Parliament by La Cierva, granting rewards to generals and officers on account of the very events pending investigation, or the somewhat ostentatious welcome wherewith the king received General Berenguer in Madrid. Public opinion became so insistent that Maura gave way and appointed General Picasso as a special investigator. The general presented a courageous and outspoken report. The military committees were incensed. Maura tried to put down their insolent protests and, exhausted by the effort, resigned his mandate to the king. "Let those who prevent government govern," he exclaimed. The time had not yet come.

The king had by now unwillingly to accept the collaboration of the Liberal-Conservative party, the new chief of which, Sánchez Guerra, took office in March 1922. Sánchez Guerra had distinguished himself as the Home Secretary who, in 1917, had put down the revolutionary general strike. He was known for his somewhat old-fashioned methods in electioneering, but events were to show that he had learned from experience and had adopted the more enlightened views on social questions which had been applied by the Sánchez Toca ministry in 1919. He was also known to be a firm upholder of civil authority against the Committees of Defense. The committees were by then holding an Assembly which had been authorized under the previous ministry, and they had voted a strict syndicalist discipline for their members. The movement became so threatening that the king referred to it in a sensational speech which he delivered in Barcelona (June 1922) and which called forth much criticism, for, though the advice was good, the manner and circumstances were unconstitutional. Meanwhile, the campaign for "responsibilities" proceeded, under the stimulus of further revelations on Moroccan irregularities. The counterattack of the military committees had widened the campaign to include civil, i.e. political, responsibility as well. Sánchez Guerra had by then gained some authority over public opinion by curtly dismissing General Martínez Anido from his Barcelona governorship and by issuing a decree prohibiting military officers from joining associations connected with their service. With these moral assets he faced a heated debate on responsibilities in Congress. The parliamentary committee appointed to study the Picasso report and hear witnesses had led to three different reports: the Conservative members concluded that the disaster had been due to causes beyond human control; the Liberal members that the government in office at the time deserved a vote of censure; the Labor members that definite responsibilities attached to definite named persons. The debate in the House proved beyond doubt that the matter was too explosive for so slender an institution to handle. The government resigned.

A coalition composed of all the branches of the Liberal Party and of the reformists took office with signal courage (December 1922). Not content with the knot of thorny problems which it inherited, it announced that it would amend Article 2 of the Constitution (on tolerance of other than Catholic worships) in a liberal sense. The bishops shouted anathema: the prime minister, García Prieto, immediately beat a retreat, and thereupon the reformist Minister of Finance, Pedregal, withdrew on grounds of principle. This shelved the religious question for the time being, but there remained enough problems to destroy many a government. The general election produced remarkable results: a majority for the government and a cluster of five Socialists (out of seven seats) as members for Madrid. This event confirmed the prevailing impression that the parliamentary system was rapidly ceasing to be a puppet show, and brought home to the wire-pullers the imminent danger of unemployment which threatened them.

Unfortunately, as the parliamentary system began to be a reality, it began also to commit real blunders. The worst blunder in politics is to forget the actual forces in existence, for politics might be defined as the mechanics of moral forces. Signs of coming trouble had not been lacking. Social unrest in Barcelona had abated since strong methods had been abandoned by more enlightened Cabinets, but Moroccan affairs were still in a grave state and hopelessly intertwined with the quarrel between the military and the civil power. The government was strongly imbued with the necessity of asserting civil authority. The Moroccan enterprise was becoming more and more expensive. Thus the average yearly expenditure, which had been 75 million pesetas in 1909-13, had risen to 146 yearly in 1913-19, and to 358 yearly in 1919-23. The government had broken with the tradition which entrusted the leading posts overseas to military men and sent a Conservative ex-minister, Don Luis Silvela, as high commissioner. The foreign secretary responsible for Moroccan affairs in the Cabinet was Don Santiago Alba, well known for his policy of friendly negotiation with the Riffs. This attitude of the government was keenly resented by the military. The government should have taken heed, for disquieting signs of a dangerous convergence of anti-parliamentary forces were becoming more frequent and ominous. Generel Martínez Anido, who, since his dismissal had remained in obscurity, was suddenly brought back and forced on the government as the head of the Melilla command, from which post he endeavored in every way to cross the policy of the foreign secretary. Soon after this appointment an important Moorish businessman, Dris Ben Said, who had been the chief link between Señor Alba and the Riffs with a view to peaceful action and the liberation of prisoners, was killed in somewhat mysterous circumstances. Meanwhile, the Supreme Court of Military Justice had taken a strong line in the matter of responsibilities, and in the army the word "dictator" had begun to enter discussion.

Why a dictator? The question would be difficult to answer in a simple way. No less than four historical currents converged toward a dictatorship. The army officers were carried toward it by the inner logic of their own professional temperament. Once in the political business—and they had been in the thick of it since 1917—it was but natural that they should apply the technique of the barracks to politics. There was a substratum of dictatorial opinion lying dormant in the national temperament and very much awake in the parties and papers of the extreme Right, whose big man and champion was Señor La Cierva; there was the inexperience of the liberal opinion of the country, which, with characteristic courage but also with characteristic lack of political sense, was then carrying the inquiry over responsibilities to the bitter end, undeterred by the fact that such action led inevitably to a kind or sacred union between all the threatened parties and, notably, between the army and the crown; and, last but not least, there was the natural inclination of the crown itself.

The idea of a military government was old and tenacious in King Alfonso's mind. Canalejas had already referred to this fact in a famous speech. Count Romanones had heard a suggestion about a government of colonels headed by a general. In more recent years the idea had become an obsession and it had begun to figure prominently in the royal conversation, and even in those public speeches wherewith the king was loosening the screws and bolts of the constitutional machinery before breaking it altogether. In his speech delivered in Córdoba, on May 23, 1921, the king had gone as far as he possibly could in his denunciation of Parliament:

At this moment my government has submitted to Parliament a most important bill on the question of communications. Now, the king is no absolute monarch and therefore does no more than authorize with his signature the bills that his governments wish to submit to Parliament. He can do nothing to certify that these bills come out of Parliament duly approved . . . yet it is hard that things which we are all interested in furthering should not prosper owing to the smaller side of politics. One of my governments will submit a bill. The bill will be fought against and the government will fall. The ministers who succeed the fallen ones cannot do better for the bill since the former ones have become the opposition and avenge themselves. How could they help those who are responsible for their political death? There may be some who think that, in speaking as I am speaking, I overstep my constitutional duties; but my answer is that, having reigned for nineteen years, during which I have risked my life more than once, I am not likely to be caught in a constitutional mistake. I believe that the provinces should initiate a movement in support of their king and of the bills which are beneficial to them, and then Parliament will remember that they are the mere mandatories of the people, for that is the meaning of the vote you give them at the polls.

Good observers were already beginning to realize that the king's hankering was hardening into a policy. The king had gone so far as to express the desirability of a military government to Salvatella, a Catalan who was Minister of Education in the Cabinet, in the course of a conversation during a railway journey. His movements, and those of his friends, suggested the action which was being contemplated. When, in the early months of 1923, the government came to difficulties with General Primo de Rivera, then Captain-General of Catalonia, and decided to recall him, the king withheld his signature and the government remained silent for reasons as yet unexplained. A definite move was difficult so long as the War Office was in the hands of a civilian, for the Liberals, breaking with tradition here also, had appointed a lawyer, Señor Alcalá Zamora, as war secretary. Though a civilian, he had been brought over by his military advisers to a view on Moroccan affairs more consonant with military opinion than with the views of his colleague, the foreign secretary, and when the two ministers joined issue the king sided with the foreign secretary, Señor Alba. Señor Alcalá Zamora thereupon resigned and the Liberal government, forgetting its principles or else yielding to royal pressure, appointed a military war secretary, General Aizpuru, who, as his future behavior was to show, was to be no obstacle to any plans against the Constitution.

From that moment all efforts were concentrated on the foreign secretary, the strongest personality in the ministry and in the party. According to custom, Señor Alba was the government representative in the summer residence of the king, San Sebastián. The government, however, remained in Madrid. It is asserted by some students of this period that the prime minister, García Prieto, had clear indications as to what was being prepared in a few important garrisons, and that he kept all such information from his colleagues for reasons as yet obscure. Señor Alba, however, knew that General Primo de Rivera harbored strong feelings against him, and that there was much criticism of his attitude in the army. He did not know that the *coup d'état* was ready for September 14, but he did know that General Martínez Anido, one of its chief organizers, was in San Sebastián, keeping him under close observation. The foreign secretary had, moreover, received confidential information that a manifesto had been printed in Zaragoza by the conspirators in which he, Señor Alba, was pointed out to the Spanish people as a depraved and cynical minister who would be prosecuted by the new government. On September 12 he tendered his resignation to the prime minister and to the king in order, he said, to permit of a legal solution of the difficulty. But Señor Alba, who had tapped the wires, preferred the protection of the frontier. At three o'clock in the afternoon of the 13th he left his office in his private car, ostensibly for a ride in the country. He did not return.

On that day General Primo de Rivera decided to strike his blow, twenty-four hours before the appointed time. The Cabinet behaved with the utmost lack of vigor. Instead of taking appropriate measures, which in the divided and hesitating state of the army would probably have been successful, they decided to await the arrival of the king, whom they summoned to Madrid. The king demurred. It is believed by some students of those curious days that he spent the time motoring between San Sebastián, Burgos and Zaragoza, to keep in touch with his garrisons while allowing things to ripen. He arrived in Madrid on the morning of the 14th. Till then, though the garrisons of Barcelona and Zaragoza were in rebellion, the garrison of Valencia had expressed its loyalty to the government, most of the others were passive, and that of Madrid was deliberately awaiting the king's orders. The final word which swept away the regime came from the king's own lips, and the definite move came from his own will. The prime minister asked leave to recall the captains-general of Barcelona and Zaragoza and to open the Cortes on the following Tuesday. The king answered that such measures needed time for reflection. The prime minister resigned and the king accepted his resignation.

Thus ended the Constitution which had been framed for his father by Cánovas and Sagasta, and under which his mother had saved his crown during the longest regency which Spain had known. With undaunted courage the king removed the very foundations of the Restoration. A devout Catholic, he made the sacrifice of his oath on the Gospels; a king, he broke his royal word. For such valuable hostages given to fortune, what were his expectations? "Since I was born a king let me govern," he had said. The king wanted to govern.

CHAPTER 26

THE DICTATORSHIP

Governing is no easy art for a king. Alfonso XIII would have preferred to remain in control of the new situation. He was going to try government by the army, and the army's chief is the king. Things, however, proved less smooth than he had expected. The generals who had directed the movement in Madrid were all known for their palatine leanings, yet, when the king, half an hour after he had dismissed the last civil government of his reign, signified to the Captain-General of Madrid that he approved Primo de Rivera's step and would hear his views, but that he would have to think over the crisis and its solution, the rebellious generals of Madrid objected so hotly that they had to be received in a body that very morning at the palace and, after a protracted scene, they emerged with the right to announce to the press that General Primo de Rivera would be asked to form a government. Who was Primo de Rivera?

The fact that he called himself a dictator led to not a little

341

confusion, due to the tendency to associate his regime with Fascism. Unfriendly wits, Spanish perhaps more than Italian, coined a quip to celebrate the general's visit to Rome: *"Primo de Rivera, ma secondo di Mussolini."* A mere quip. Though Fascism did stimulate him to "cut through the middle street," as the Spanish saying goes, General Primo de Rivera was second to no one—to no foreign dictator at any rate. He was in the true Spanish tradition. The ambition of every Spanish general is to save his country by becoming her ruler.

This ambition is not limited to such Spaniards as happen to be generals. It is, on the contrary, passionately felt by every Spaniard, military or civilian, high or low. Your Englishman, German, Frenchman, when he thinks of public affairs, is quite content with joining the party organization, hospital fund committee, county council administration, United Nations Association branch, or other such collective institution, private or public, which he may find handy. His patriotism is modest and humdrum. The Spaniard sees the country and sees it whole. He wants to pluck out all the ills of the country at once by pulling out the root which feeds them all. He is always ready to explain what he would do if he were in office to any person who cares to listen to his views in club, café, railway carriage, or government office. If he is a general, he is tempted to use his soldiers in order to make a short cut between government and himself. Fundamentally, if General Primo de Rivera differed from the *político de café* it was not in nature but in quality. He was a genius of the species, but the species is genuinely national. This was the true cause of his popularity with a considerable proportion of the urban population of the country.

He was a truly representative man, resembling the mass sufficiently for the people to recognize themselves in him, but rising above them enough to carry the burden of representation—spontaneous, intuitive, uninformed, impatient of all delay, imaginative, intensely patriotic, apt to take simple views of things, to cut Gordian knots, to solve intricate problems with Arcadian simplicity, to judge in equity and to think in common sense, to act, think, and feel only from his own point of view.

Above these features, which stamped him one of the many, there were qualities which made him one above the mass. First, his courage, both physical and moral, a courage at times bordering on audacity, as in his excursions on the field of intellect, at times rising to high statesmanship, as in his Moroccan successes, political and military. Then, his generosity, for this dictator was a truly generous man and bore no grudge either against those that wronged him or against those he had wronged—the last, a difficult kind of generosity, which irony without humor seems unable to understand. His heart was not only in the right place, but it beat in harmony with his sense. An Andalusian, he was shrewd and, as the saying goes, *fino*. Some of his master strokes elicited the unwilling admiration of many an "old gang" artist driven by him to unemployment. Thus when, as a punishment for his alleged connivance in a plot to upset the government, he fined Count Romanones five hundred thousand pesetas, he knew he would have with him all the Spaniards who can see a capital joke—and there are enough of them to make a man popular.

His generosity was the positive agent in the disarming sincerity with which he could alter his views. His appearance on the political stage as the knight who was to rescue the Dulcinea of politics from the old regime Malandrins was in itself a startling change, for no more typical representative of the old system could perhaps have been found in the field of Spanish politics than General Primo de Rivera. The Spanish people do not feel that incurable horror of sin in others which afflicts some races, so the general's enemies wasted their time in recalling, through the chinks of the censorship, that this contemner of nepotism owed his exceptionally rapid military career not to military talents—which he undoubtedly had—but to the fact that he happened to be the nephew of Marshal Primo de Rivera, one of the political generals of the Restoration. That weakness in his history made him more human, more representative, and even more convincing in his appeal for a change of heart. His was the first heart to change.

General Primo de Rivera worked by instinct and inspiration. His system was: Wish the best, work for the best, hope for the best. His motto: "Country, Religion, Monarchy." He was very particular as to the order in which the three deities were to be worshiped. His political ideas burst up through a mind unfettered by any philosophy or political theory. The Spanish cadet, when he was one, could win his officer star with but little mental exertion. His intuition and his experience could work such miracles that there does not seem to be any reason why he should plod and look up precedents. This explains the true originality of some of his views, as well as the arbitrary manner in which he was apt to solve the difficulties on his path. Note again the difference with the Italian dictator. Though the Spanish dictator had no grim chapter in his history, he was more arbitrary than the Italian because less systematic and less objective. In fact, Signor Mussolini tried to be a statesman and General Primo de Rivera was a man. Even though his conscious ideal were Signor Mussolini (which is by no means certain) his subconscious model would rather be Haroun-al-Raschid—after all, a not unnatural model for an Andalusian. He was the good sultan from whose hands fall the honey of good government on high and low, particularly the low; he sat under the porch of his palace and administered justice to all according to their deserts, turning from a decree granting millions of pounds for a new naval program to a letter thanking and rewarding two fisherman for having caught a rare specimen of a turtle and rescued it for the Zoological Museum; a ruler who, having closed the nation's accounts on an excess of income over expenses, decides to devote part of it to rescuing from pawn garments pledged by poor families in need.

He believed himself to be the leader of a new Spanish order, but he was representative not of the "old regime," i.e. of the Restoration, but of the "very old regime," i.e. the era of pronunciamentos, which covers practically the middle third of the nineteenth century. He belonged to the dynasty which gave Spain Riego, Espartero, O'Donnell, Narváez, Prim, Pavia, Martínez Campos. No doubt he was a man of his century in many ways, but he descended from that line, just as King Alfonso, also a man of his century, descended from the line which gave Spain

Ferdinand VII and Isabel II. With his usual insight and courage he absorbed the twentieth-century elements from the atmosphere of his day. But if the foliage was in our age, the roots were in that middle nineteenth century. His originality lay in that he could not be easily classed either as a liberal or as a reactionary leader. The century is rather eclectic in politics, and General Primo de Rivera was of his century. Thus we shall see him a liberal in municipal affairs, a socialist of sorts in labor matters, a conservative in constitutional ideas, a reactionary in education, an opportunist (with but scanty opportunities) in military administration, a truly spirited leader in Moroccan affairs, and an indifferent amateur in foreign policy.

One thing was certain. The new ruler meant to rule. On arriving in Madrid he reconstituted the directorate, dismissed all the men who had prepared the ground for it (though seeing to it that they received adequate compensation), and organized a directorate composed of a brigadier-general from every military region and of a rear admiral to associate the navy with the enterprise. The admiral, the Marqués de Magaz, had seniority over all generals except Primo de Rivera, and thus the dictator made sure that no question of seniority should threaten his control of affairs. He also arranged that, while the directorate, as a collegiate body, would have powers similar to those of the Council of Ministers, he would be the sole minister, the other directors being not in charge of ministerial departments, but entrusted with such questions as might from time to time be handed over to them by the directorate as a whole. The departments were left in charge of under-secretary-generals, practically all permanent officials. As a significant exception to this rule, the under-secretary for the Home Office was General Martínez Anido. After two years of this organization the dictator altered the form of his government, raised most of his under-secretaries to the status of ministers, dismissed his military colleagues and made General Martínez Anido vice-president of the Council and home secretary.

So much for organization. As for policy, General Primo de Rivera's beginnings were frankly bad. He dismissed Don Luis

Silvela, the civilian high commissioner in Morocco, and appointed in his stead General Aizpuru, the war secretary of the Cabinet which he had displaced—an appointment which was a singularly candid comment on the general's loyalty to his former colleagues. He dismissed the Cortes and secured the files of the Commission on Responsibilities. This is the moment to observe the date of the *coup d'état*, September 13, 1923. On September 15, after the summer recess, the Supreme Council of Military Justice was to reopen and hear the case against the military chiefs responsible for Moroccan affairs; on September 20 the Commission on Responsibilities was to meet again. On October 1 the Cortes were to discuss its report. It was evident that the *coup d'état* had for its main object the silencing of the Commission and of Parliament on a question which, above all others, threatened to expose the incompetence of many generals and officers and the unconstitutional action of the crown. This vice of origin was to be the main cause of the failure of the dictatorship to achieve any essential change in Spanish political life. It bound the king and the dictator to a policy of censorship, which was to prevent the rise of a new political opinion and of new political institutions to replace those which had been destroyed.

In its main lines the dictatorship was a regime founded on force rather than on authority, with a strong centralistic tendency, relying on the army, favorable to the Clerical Party and the Church, aristocratic and friendly to big landowners and sympathetic to socialism as opposed to syndicalism.

I believe it was Cavour who once said, "Any fool can govern with a press censorship." The dictator was no fool, but the proof thereof must not be sought in his treatment of the press. Nothing was printed that did not suit the government. In suppressing free discussion the dictator was but carrying to its logical conclusion the action he had taken with regard to Parliament. In point of fact, the press had become a kind of third House of Parliament, rather more powerful than the other two as an organ of publicity and criticism. General Primo de Rivera periodically sought to justify his policy in this connection by accusing the Spanish press of all kinds of misdeeds, but the press was able to answer all accusations by the simplest yet most effective of methods: under a dictatorship disposing of all the springs of power and patronage, ninety per cent of the press of the country, according to the dictator's own statement, persisted in a dignified and independent opposition. No more eloquent proof of disinterestedness and loyalty to ideals could be given. The fact is that the censorship was not due to any defects of the Spanish press, but to the inherent necessities of the dictatorship. Dictators rely on physical force and are, therefore, afraid of the moral forces that would be unchained by free criticism, and this dictator, moreover, had reason to fear free investigation into the origins and causes of the system which he had installed.

Next to the censorship, the dictator relied on the support of the army, the Church and business; the Socialists were neutral. Finally, the crown was the object of every possible outward deference, but it was allowed little or no influence on events. The king was soon able to realize the consequences of his action. His mistakes in the past fell on his ministers; the mistakes of his chosen dictator fell now on the king. On November 13, 1923, the president of the Senate, Count Romanones, and the president of the Congress of Deputies, Don Melquíades Alvarez, formally called on the king. They came to remind him that Article 32 of the Constitution laid on the king in person the obligation to convene the Cortes of the Realm within three months of their dissolution and that this article had always been scrupulously respected since 1876. The king received them standing and dismissed them within five minutes. When walking down the grand staircase of the Palace, Count Romanones may well have remembered the day when, arriving for the first time as president of the Lower House, to submit to the king the laws passed by the legislature, he had in the ardor of his newly acquired parliamentary majesty suggested to the president of the Senate, who accompanied him, that the custom of receiving two presidents with the "March of Infantes" (a kind of second-class national anthem), was not a sufficient recognition of the sovereignty of the Cortes, and that the *"Marcha Real"* should be played; to which the old president, Montero Ríos, had gruffly answered: "Leave music alone and be thankful for what you get, or a time may come when you will get none." The dictator, at any rate, promptly deprived Count Romanones and Don Melquíades Alvarez of their dignities and functions and announced that he would devote the two parliamentary buildings to some useful purpose in the future. The dictator won, but the king lost.

But, of course, the dictatorship did not limit itself to negative measures against the past. On the contrary, it relied for its political health on its vigor and activity. It would have been idle to look to the Spanish dictatorship for a consistent and coherent policy based on a definite philosophy such as is to be found in *Fascism*. Though unmistakably a chief, General Primo de Rivera was not a *Duce*. The activities of the government were good or bad according to whether the minister in charge was capable or incapable. In general, the record of the dictatorship was good in material reforms and bad in all that concerns the intellectual and spiritual life of the nation. That ubiquitous Englishman who was an enthusiastic *Fascist* because Signor Mussolini made trains arrive on time, found much to praise in "dictated-to" Spain. The roads were magnificent. They were described as the best in Europe by an English tourist writing to *The Times*. Railways progressed in length, quality and equipment, thanks to an arrangement whereby the government advanced capital in exchange for a considerable measure of control. After Moroccan affairs had taken a favorable turn and relieved the budget, the government launched an internal loan of 3,538,947,550 pesetas, a considerable proportion of which was devoted to public works in handsome yearly installments. Under this financial stimulation, helped by the period of peace which the government enforced on the nation, Spain settled down to a life of economic activity. The taste for large-scale enterprises developed. A contract granted by the government to the National Telephone Company of Spain, a branch of the International Telephone and Telegraph Corporation of New York, greatly improved the service in the country and bid fair to make Madrid the center of telephone and cable communications between Europe and

South America. The dictatorship turned its attention to the gasoline question and resolved to control supplies by means of a State monopoly. Strong encouragement was given to national and international aviation. In the beginning of 1926 sensational flights to Buenos Aires and Manila were made by Spanish aviators.

A vigorous economic nationalism inspired the regime. Every effort was made to foster home production and to limit unnecessary purchases abroad—an effort which, though at times misguided and at times resented by keen free-trading nations, was but natural in a country with a heavy adverse balance of trade. By a decree of 1927, coal consumers were required to use at least forty per cent of Spanish coal. In 1925 legislation was enacted compelling foreign insurance companies to deposit their statutory reserves in Spain and in specified Spanish securities. Aircraft manufacturing firms and airlines were made to become Spanish in capital, administration and equipment. All these efforts were marred by a return to the paternal policy handed down as a medieval tradition to the kings of old Spain, from which the nineteenth century had succeeded in liberating the country. A Commission for the Regulation of Industrial Production was empowered with authority to allow or refuse the settlement of new industries and even the enlargement and renovation of existing plant. Nevertheless, and despite this and other lines of criticism, the material or economic policy of the directorate was its strong point and, by attracting to it the sympathies of the business community, the cause of much of its stability.

As if, diverted from politics, the energies of the nation had sought an outlet in business, the commercial, industrial and agricultural life of the country seemed to move at a brisker pace. Money was plentiful and the government set up a special banking institution, the *Banco de Comercio Exterior,* in order to canalize investments abroad. As is the case every time the country enjoys a few years of uninterrupted peace, its prosperity rose rapidly and its vitality made itself immediately felt.

The dictatorship endeavored to apply statesmanlike principles to the social question. Its success was unequal in this field.

In agricultural matters it fostered agricultural credit by means of a *Banco de Crédito Agrario* which was a promising institution. The government's policy in the matter of land ownership, though well-meaning, was not so successful, partly because the aim in view, individual small ownership by the peasant, was not the best that can be devised for Spain, partly because the means, the breaking up of big estates, would have implied a heavy sacrifice on the part of landowners friendly to the government. But in the field of labor problems the dictatorship made a considerable advance. It took a regrettable step in abolishing the autonomy enjoyed by the *Instituto de Reformas Sociales,* turning it into a much simplified department of the Ministry of Labor, but it set up a comprehensive system of *Corporations* which, though suggested by an Italian experiment, had not a few original features, mostly an improvement on the Italian system.[1] This bold system of industrial organization met with the cordial approval of many of the leaders of the Socialist Party without incurring the active disapproval of the employer class.

[1] The Spanish organization may be described as follows. The trades and professions of the country were classified into 27 groups or *Corporaciones*. In each of them the organization comprised: locally a *comité paritario* composed of five employers and five men elected by their respective unions and a chairman appointed by the Government. These committees had power to regulate conditions of work, such as hours, rest, individual or collective labor contracts, to deal with conflicts, to organize labor exchanges and a trade census. Mixed commissions were also created locally in order to coordinate the work of the committees of connected trades. The competence of these commissions covered mostly matters of technical education, advice, study and reform. The mixed commissions, however, did not participate in the more general organization of the corporative system of the state. The corporation was defined as the sum total of all the *comités paritarios* of the same trade in the nation. Each of them was governed by a corporation council composed of eight employers and eight men elected by the committees. The council watched over national conditions in the industry covering the same ground locally entrusted to the committees. It was expected that they would also act as authoritative advisers to the government on matters concerning their industry and that they would engage in codifying the laws, by-laws, regulations and customs of their trade. At the apex of the organization the *Comisión Delegada de Consejos,* presided over by the Director-General of Labor, brought together delegates (one employer and one man) from all the Corporation Councils of the nation.

The most brilliant success of the dictatorship, however, was due to the dictator himself and in no less difficult a field than Morocco. General Primo de Rivera had always been a lukewarm supporter of the Moroccan adventure. In his early days as a young general he had even advocated the exchange of Ceuta for Gibraltar. When, after more than half a year of office, he realized the extent to which Moroccan expenses handicapped Spanish life, he resolved on a policy of retrenchment and withdrawal. Such a resolution spoke highly in his favor, for it meant adopting the very policy which Señor Alba had advocated and was, of course, in direct opposition to the wishes of the army in Africa. He was made aware of this second difficulty by the cold reception dispensed to him when he visited the army in Morocco—it is even said that his life was then in danger at the hands of a hot-headed captain unable to bear the thought that the Spanish army should give up avenging the affront of 1921. Nevertheless, he courageously decided to apply his policy in person, and appointed himself high commissioner in Morocco. In this capacity he conducted a skillful retreat from Xauen to Tetuán. These operations enabled the dictatorship to relieve the Spanish budget of some considerable expenditure. But they were destined to have more far-reaching effects. In the summer of 1925, Abd-el-Krim, somewhat encouraged by the retreat of the Spanish army, attacked the French zone with so much vigor that Paris was alarmed. This success of the Riffs immediately altered the tone and direction of French Moroccan Policy toward Spain. For years Spanish diplomacy had tried to bring about a cooperation between the two occupying nations, for, without it, neither could be sure of success in the work of establishing peace in Morocco. But the Quai d'Orsay demurred and played for time with a calm under which some Spaniards were led to suspect a certain amount of satisfaction. Meanwhile the Moors were always well armed, a fact which unfairly, but not unnaturally, Spaniards on the spot attributed to French help. As soon as Abd-el-Krim entered the French zone, the Quai d'Orsay became afire with the idea of cooperation between the two old "Latin sisters," and M. Malvy, followed by Marshal Pétain in person, was sent to Madrid to negotiate an agreement. The dictator, despite the fact that French requirements meant a complete reversal of his own policy, agreed to a combined effort—a decision as wise as that which he had taken in the reverse direction one year earlier. As a result of this collaboration, in the course of which General Primo de Rivera scored a brilliant success by landing in Alhucemas, Abd-el-Krim was beaten and surrendered. Primo de Rivera, however, was able to consolidate the advantages gained by an energetic policy of occupation and disarmament, and the Spanish zone has been quiet ever since.

The dictator was not equally succesful in his foreign policy. The first sign of activity was a visit to Rome. Both king and dictator, then in the honeymoon of dictatorship, had an opportunity to express their enthusiasm for Fascism, and used it to the full. In the Vatican the king delivered a speech which Charles V and even Philip II would have thought too filial to the Pope and which called forth unfavorable comment in Spain, not only for its excessive religious zeal, but for its indiscreet meddling with Spanish-American Church affairs; for the king went out of his way to ask that more cardinals' hats should be placed on Spanish-American heads. The outcome of the visit to the Quirinal was an Italo-Spanish treaty of arbitration, conciliation and peace. Though it was used at the time by the French press to whip up public opinion in favor of a French naval bill, this treaty had little theoretical, and less practical importance. No Spanish government would ever lead the Spanish people to a war between France and Italy, on whichever side of the contest it might try to involve them.

The next foreign adventure of the dictator was the Tangier Convention. Left over from the Moroccan treaties, Tangier had been the object of negotiations in 1941. They were resumed in 1923 and led to a solution which Spain accepted reluctantly (February 1924), since Great Britain had surrendered to the French claims for first place in the international administration of the town. Franco-Spanish rivalry was by no means appeased. A glance at the map shows that Tangier is the natural center and capital of the Spanish zone, as both Spain and Tangier found by experience; for, while Spain could not prevent the spying and smuggling of the Riffs in the town, the town suffered much hardship owing to war events in the Spanish zone. Nearly half of the population of Tangier, moreover, is Spanish, and for all practical purposes Tangier is a Spanish town, historically, geographically and racially. The matter was revived by General Primo de Rivera and his foreign secretary, Señor Yanguas, in 1927, simultaneously, if not in actual conjunction, with Spain's claim to a permanent seat in the Council of the League of Nations. Spain had belonged to the Council since its inception, being the only neutral nation mentioned in the text of the Covenant as one of the initial members of the Council. She had performed excellent services in it and her representative, Señor Quiñones de León, had succeeded in obtaining the confidence of the British, as well as the French, government, and had been the Council moderator in practically every grave conflict (Upper Silesia, Corfu, etc.). Senor Quiñones de León had received repeated assurances from all the governments represented on the Council that as soon as an opportunity arose Spain would be given a permanent seat. The entrance of Germany (with a permanent seat) afforded this opportunity. But Germany objected to any other claim but hers being considered at the time; and Brazil, then a member of the Council and a candidate for a permanent seat, blocked Germany's entrance. This led to the deadlock of March 1926. Spain had announced her intention to vote for Germany, though she certainly would have left the Council immediately afterward. A Council Reform Commission appointed to overhaul the position and report to the next session of the Assembly recommended that the number of Council members should be increased from ten to fourteen, that non-permanent members should sit for three years and not be eligible for readmission, and that a small number of seats should be created for nations which the Assembly, by a special vote, should wish to retain on the Council. A motion of the Commission, cordially endorsed by the Council of the Assembly, made it clear that this last measure aimed at ensuring the services of Spain. The Spanish government nevertheless gave notice of withdrawal. The dictator should have accepted the Council's offer there and then. He decided to leave only to return within two years on the same conditions. The rumor that he had been assured by Italy that she would follow Spain in her seceding move might make the action of the Spanish government more understandable, if not wiser—but so far there is no evidence to substantiate this rumor.

To make matters worse, General Primo de Rivera chose to connect the conflict over the League of Nations with a claim to complete control over Tangier. This question had to be discussed all over again. It led to but trifling changes, such as the replacing of the Belgian chief of police by a Spaniard and the admission of Italy to an equal share with England in the administration of the town. The solution adopted satisfied neither the requirements of Tangier nor those of Spain. Later France showed signs of aiming at an increase, rather than a decrease, of her influence there, and Tangier remained a point where conflicts were to be expected in the future.

Portuguese affairs were handled with more success. The setting up of a military dictatorship in Portugal was a favorable circumstance. On August 11, 1927, negotiations carried on in Lisbon with regard to the Douro water power reached a satisfactory conclusion. Spain retained the frontier waters below the Tormes and Portugal the frontier waters above it, giving respectively 339,000 h.p.s. to Spain and 285,000 to Portugal. In April 1928 a Hispano-Portuguese Commission on Economic Questions met in Lisbon and established a program of economic cooperation covering railways, roads, wire and wireless communications, passports, most-favored-nation clause, cooperation in the cork industry, etc. Some questions were left outstanding, among them those of air navigation and fisheries. In October 1929 the president of the Portuguese Republic visited Madrid to celebrate this new era of Iberian cooperation.

On the whole, therefore, the general policy of the dictatorship in material home affairs and in foreign relations compares not unfavorably with that of the constitutional period. Its adversaries were entitled to argue that the dictator benefited from stability and from the lack of military and clerical obstacles. But the

fact remains that the dictatorship made good use of these advantages. How is it, then, that public opinion remained hostile
to such an extent that censorship was indispensable to the regime
and that a constant watch had to be kept against revolutionary
attempts? The answer to this question is relatively simple. The
dictatorship made the nation pay too dearly for its material
progress and in a coin which is more precious to her than
wealth—liberty, justice and self-respect.

It is significant that the worst ministers of the dictatorship
were the Home Secretary, the Minister of Education and the
Minister of Justice. The Home Secretary's record in Barcelona
and Melilla would suffice to account for the nation's dissatisfaction had he neglected to give fresh cause for it in his new post.
Every measure of the bygone—and ever-recurring—days of
tyranny had been revived in the service of the dictatorship.
The censorship has already been mentioned. News carefully
filtered and views strictly limited to favorable comments mean
more than half the battle won. The opening of letters; imprisonment without limit, cause, explanation or guarantees; petty and
vexatious interference with the most innocent activities such as
after-dinner speeches; listening-in on telephonic and even oral
conversations; removal and coercion of civil servants—the
dictatorship went through the whole gamut in the hopeless task
of repressing the irrepressible. Liberal opinion did not surrender
easily, indeed did not surrender at all. Clubs and associations,
lecture halls, every possible means of communication and discussion of events was tied up to the government or destroyed.
For the first time in a long and illustrious life the Ateneo de
Madrid, a literary, scientific and artistic club to which all Spaniards with any claim to intellectual distinction made it a point
to belong, was closed. Driven underground, opposition became
revolutionary. The government, on its side, acted with the most
deplorable disregard for justice. By a kind of inverted selection
the judges and magistrates who took a strict view of their duties
were removed. This was the case, for instance, with the highest
dignitary of the Spanish judiciary, Don Buenaventura Muñoz,
president of the Supreme Court of Justice. Not content with

this grave interference with the judiciary, the government placed itself above the laws and applied penalties of its own invention, such as heavy fines, to citizens that displeased it. Plots succeeded plots and the best minds of the country were driven to an uncompromising opposition. Some of them had to suffer for it. Don Miguel de Unamuno had written a private letter, couched in violent terms, to a Spanish friend in Buenos Aires; the letter was published by an Argentine paper without consulting its author. For this fact Don Miguel de Unamuno was deprived of his Chair of Greek in Salamanca and confined in a small island of the Canary Archipelago. The Vera incident made a still more painful impression on the country. Early on November 7, 1924, on the French frontier near Vera, there was a shooting affray between a few unknown men and the civil guards. One of the men and two guards were killed. A handful of the unknown persons were apprehended and brought before a military court which gave a verdict of "Not guilty." The military officers who had acted as judges were imprisoned by order of the government and the public prosecutor (of the military legal corps) was deprived of his post for having refused to ask the court to punish the accused with the death penalty. A new court was set up. It was stated in print by the adversaries of the government that this court was induced to sentence the accused to death in order to placate the feelings of the Civil Guard Corps and on the understanding that they would be reprieved. The court gave a verdict of "Guilty" and the men were executed—all but one, who refused to suffer the ignominy and committed suicide in most dramatic circumstances. Don Miguel de Unamuno and Don Eduardo Ortega y Gasset, who led the opposition to the dictatorship on French territory, took responsibility for the statement that the whole affair had been arranged by the police under the Home Secretary. They provided details such as the number of the police car in which the police inspector, whose name was also given, arrived in Hendaye, the French side of the frontier, and bought a box of automatic pistols; and they printed in their paper a statement, which appeared also in the French press, in which Captain Cueto of the Anti-contraband

Guards (Carabineros) confirmed their version with a considerable amount of detail. Captain Cueto wrote letters to the same effect in a well-known Havana newspaper, *El Diario de la Marina*. He explained that he reported the whole matter to his chiefs, was imprisoned and told to recant, refused, and was set at liberty again. The censorship prevented the Spanish public from knowing this version of the affair, save those who read the paper edited in France by Don Eduardo Ortega, which circulated in Spain in a clandestine manner. The government gave no answer to the very precise accusations leveled against its adversaries abroad.

It is only fair to the dictator to put on record that this would be the worst instance of the use of force which could be brought against his regime, were we to accept as proved the case made by his adversaries. At the time Hendaye was the center of the opposition, a fact which would add plausibility to the incident as an attempt to justify a request to the French government for the expulsion of Don Miguel de Unamuno and his friends.

Next to the methods of the Home Office those of the Ministry of Education must be considered as one of the weakest spots in the dictatorship. The rule here was wholesale surrender to clerical claims. Under the pretext—not altogether ungrounded in fact—that a number of secondary teachers and university professors wrote textbooks to make money out of them, the government satisfied the dearest wish of the clerical reactionaries, i.e. the enforcing of a uniform textbook for the nation. The true aim of this measure was to secure a safe clerical point of view in controversial teachings such as history and philosophy. A frontal attack on the Committee for the Development of Studies failed, owing to the prestige of this institution, which had endeared itself to a vast number of middle-class families for its excellent educational centers. A more hypocritical move, however, succeeded in depriving it of its autonomous powers for selecting its governing body and forced it to accept government nominees who were chosen at once from uncompromising clericals. The teaching profession was put under the strictest pressure to bow before the Church, to go to Mass, whether they believed or not, and in every way to submit to clerical demands. The chief inspector of schools in Granada was deprived of his post for not being present at the official entrance of the cardinal archbishop into his diocese. The folly of such measures may be gauged by the opposition which they called forth in a nation jealous of its right to worship (or not) as it thinks fit. After a campaign of vexatious measures against university professors, which brought many of them to prison and others to resign their profession altogether, the trial of strength occurred in 1928-29, when, under pressure from the Jesuits, the minister prepared a decree whereby the two clerical colleges of Deusto (Jesuit) and El Escorial (Augustinian) were given the right to have their students examined by a jury composed of two tutors of their respective colleges and one professor of the university which was to grant the degree. The Advisory Assembly, though composed entirely of government nominees, rejected the proposal; the governing bodies of all the universities of the kingdom volunteered a strong expression of dissent. The National Student Federation was equally emphatic against this singular scheme by which the university seal was affixed to an education known to be inadequate. The Escorial College, by far the better of the two, waived the right proffered by the decree. The Jesuit College held to it in stubborn silence. The minister published the decree. There was a revolt in practically every university of the kingdom, led by that of Madrid, where some of the students shed their blood for the cause in street struggles with the police. The women students were prominent in the revolt. The dictator closed university after university. Four distinguished professors resigned their chairs. The dictator announced that he would allow the women students to take their examinations, but they refused until the men students had been put on the same footing. The government at last gave way, the decree was withdrawn and the universities reopened.

This incident is significant, particularly when put alongside the conflict between the government and the artillery officers. General Primo de Rivera wanted to reorganize the army in every way, but the army was full of officers and officers must live. He began by placing as many as he could in civilian jobs left vacant by the withdrawal of the political personnel of the old regime, and even by creating a considerable number of new posts of an entirely civilian nature in order to place more of his military friends. Try as he would he was unable to do much by way of retrenchment—partly through lack of a consistent policy of military reconstruction, but mostly owing to the fact that, after all, the army was the only force on which he could rely and it was unwise to interfere with it. In spite of these reasons it was perhaps in the army that the dictatorship effected its most far-reaching changes, though unfortunately more destructive than constructive. The dictator, an infantryman, tried to abolish the old tradition of the Artillery Corps whereby its members are pledged to refuse all promotion except on grounds of seniority (a tradition upheld as a defense against nepotism). This, General Primo de Rivera, the most famous nephew in the Spanish army, should have abstained from attacking. The artillery officers rebelled. There were several serious incidents, one of which caused the death of a young officer in Pamplona. But, owing, it is believed, to the personal intervention of the king, the officers gave up their rebellious attitude only to find that the government carried its measure over their heads and punished the leaders of the movement. Dissatisfaction simmered in the ranks of the Artillery Corps until, in January 1929, it found a leader in Señor Sánchez Guerra. But the rebellion led by the ex–prime minister was not the first in the field. In 1925 a plot was discovered in which several professors were implicated along with two well-known army leaders, General Aguilera and Field Marshal Weyler, whom it is wonderful to find leading a conspiracy at the ripe age of eighty-six, as he was then. Meanwhile, Primo de Rivera had been trying for some time to evolve a way out of the situation which he had created. As a transitional measure he had planned to summon a National Advisory Assembly composed almost entirely of government nominees with a handful of representatives from a certain number of institutions. Señor Sánchez Guerra, leader of the Conservative Party, had signified to the king that, disapproving as he did of all that had occurred since 1923, the royal assent to the calling of a National Assembly would mean for him that the king was determined to reign as an absolute monarch and that, therefore, the allegiance of the Conservative Party, based as it was on the constitutional principle, could no longer be due to him. The king hesitated for a long time before accepting his dictator's proposal, but in the end bowed before the inevitable, and Señor Sánchez Guerra went into voluntary exile and broke away from the king. He was a man of action and he decided to carry his convictions into practice at once. In January 1929 he landed in Valencia to put himself at the head of eighteen artillery garrisons ready to follow his lead. The plot failed owing to the hesitation of the Captain-General of Valencia, who had promised his support and changed his mind at the last moment, a move which won him favor with neither government nor conspirators. The tendency to get rid of the dictatorship was permanent and manifested itself in every possible form. For instance, though Señor Sánchez Guerra made it quite clear that his purpose in coming to Spain was seditious and whenever questioned by the authorities made a point of describing his activities in the very words of the Spanish code which define the crime of sedition and punish it with the death penalty, the government, after keeping him imprisoned in a warship[2] until October 1929, had to allow the law to take its course and bring him before a tribunal. A military court was chosen, and it is to be assumed that the government chose it carefully. It was composed of brigadier-generals. The court found Señor Sánchez Guerra "Not guilty," a decision which could only be interpreted as meaning that the dictatorship had lost the sympathies of the army.

[2] A significant precaution. No garrison was trusted to keep the dangerous prisoner.

CHAPTER 27

THE DEADLOCK

Let us now attempt an estimate of what the dictatorship represented in the history of contemporary Spain. To begin with, the dictatorship did not come to relieve Spain of a regime which was ruining or dishonoring her. Such views on the old system are melodramatic and false. That the system was incompetent and corrupt there is no question. But in what way, to what an extent, owing to what causes and with what compensating advantages? Finally, how much constructive work did it manage to perform in spite of its defects and what was the political progress of the nation under it?

The incompetence and the corruption of the old system did not extend to its political personnel save in a small proportion as to incompetence and political corruption, and in an almost negligible proportion as to moral corruption. This point must be made clear. The incompetence of the old system was due to the defective general and technical education of the civil service

361

and, during the Restoration, to the instability of tenure prevailing in the civil service as it prevails even nowadays in many states of the United States of America. The political staff met it in the only possible way by education and by organizing the civil services on a stable basis, and they were singularly successful in both these tasks. Progress, seen everywhere in this respect before the dictatorship, helped it considerably in its task. There were two exceptions to this progress in administrative education: the army and the Church, each governed by men of their own choice and enjoying a measure of excessive home rule which they proved unable to put to a good use.

The old regime was politically corrupt, i.e. state power was used by parties for political party aims. But this defect which it inherited from its founders, Cánovas and Sagasta, and which to a greater or lesser extent exists everywhere, was an indispensable substitute for the real parliamentary democracy which the Restoration professed to be, so long as this parliamentary democracy did not materialize. There were three ways toward this goal: agrarian reform, which the owning classes (backed by the army and the Church) opposed; education, which, as we know, the regime fostered with as much money as the army estimates and the Church allowed; and a natural process of evolution and education by experience, which actually brought about so much progress that the army and the king, frightened at the power of Parliament, destroyed it. It was, therefore, not as corrupt, but in so far as it was ceasing to be corrupt, that the regime perished.[1] Finally, when the old system is described as morally corrupt (the dictatorship was officially committed to that view) it must be made quite clear that, while on the outskirts of it there were, no doubt, men of dubious character, the higher political personnel was remarkably disinterested and honest. There are many ways of confirming this statement. Some

[1] It is a curious reflection on the dictator's strictures against the constitutional regime and on his claims to represent a purer form of government that one of his ministers had twice been refused his seat in the Congress of Deputies by the Supreme Court owing to illegal practices in his election. As it happened, he was one of the most efficient Cabinet ministers of the dictatorship.

of the men in politics were rich, heirs to large fortunes, such as Count Romanones, or self-made men, mostly through success in the Law, such as Don Santiago Alba, or through sheer financial genius, such as Señor Cambó. But the average Spanish politician was a modest man who lived in a middle-class moderate way, and who died in poverty. The most brilliant demonstration of the honor of the old system was to be made by the dictatorship itself. General Primo de Rivera, in his first manifesto, described Señor Alba, the last foreign secretary of the regime, as "a depraved and cynical minister who would meet with condign punishment at the Law Courts." His house was searched for proofs of his depravity, a specially selected judge worked long at his case, but all in vain; his honor had to be cleared by a magistrate trusted by a government which was strongly biased against him, and without his having taken any action whatsoever in the matter.

The main fault of the old system, that which caused its incompetence and most of its corruption, was its instability. The kaleidoscopic succession of prime ministers and Cabinets did not permit any political program to mature, any Cabinet minister to acquire command over the affairs of his department, any complicated and delicate reform to take root and benefit by experience. But what was the cause of such instability? Certainly, for a good part the petty jealousies and ambitions of the public men. But these defects would have been less prominent if they had been used by the monarch, not as the raw material for his policy of personal power, but as the elements whereby to construct a higher system of government. Let anyone who doubts compare the policy of King Alfonso with that of the queen regent, his mother. From November 1885 till May 1902, i.e. in sixteen years and five months, the queen had eleven ministries. Between May 1902 and September 1923, i.e. in twenty-one years and three months, the king had thirty-three ministries. The queen's Cabinets lasted, on an average, one year and six months; the king's average was just seven months and a half. Government is impossible in such circumstances.

When all is said against the political personnel of that fallen regime, it still remains that, taken in the aggregate, these men, who held ministerial posts under the Restoration, were among the best-meaning, the least selfish, the most enlightened and the most conscientious Spaniards of the epoch. They were weak toward the graft and jobbery of the lesser beasts of prey which prowl round the outskirts of the political city; weaker still toward the temptations which glittered for them in the royal palace. But they tried to govern to the best of their ability and some of them were very able indeed. They saw the importance of most of the fundamental problems Spain had to solve in the twentieth century; they rebuilt the economic life of the country within twenty years from the date of the American victory; they recast the system of education; they reconstructed the navy; they developed railways and ports; they evolved a sound, reasonable method of tackling industrial problems. They could have done more if they had been better men. But they would have done much more, such as they were, had the army and the Church allowed them, and had the crown sought to unite them by higher politics instead of dividing them by mingling in their intrigues and playing party politics with their petty quarrels. These men and the king were, after all, with a handful of intellectuals and of labor leaders, the only Spaniards who saw Spain as a historical problem and devoted their lives to it.

The old regime, moreover, had one saving quality in which it rises far above the dictatorship. *It knew it was bad.* It was self-critical and humble. And this precious moral quality proved highly creative. Spain owes to it some of her best institutions. The regime knew it was fettered by political ties and subject to the inconstancy of king and party politics and it evolved a fertile method for evading these defects. It entrusted important social and state functions to institutions of an autonomous character, financed by the state, but depending for their right working on the moral authority of their responsible leaders and ultimately on public opinion. This original and far-reaching method of government and administration has not received as much attention as it deserves from students of politics. It was justified by its signal success. The typical example of it was the Committee

for the Development of Studies to which reference has repeatedly
been made in this work. But other, no less remarkable institutions of this kind were also established under the constitutional
system, such as the *Junta para Ingenieros y Obreros,* a replica
of the Committee for the Development of Studies in the field
of technical education; the *Instituto Nacional de Previsión,* an
organization entrusted with the study and administration of
matters connected with social insurance; the *Junta de Colonización Interior,* in charge of agrarian problems, and above all,
the *Instituto de Reformas Sociales,* founded by a royal decree
of 1903, which, though signed by Silvela, was based on a plan
made by Canalejas.[2]

Some attention has had to be given to this curious side of the
constitutional regime because it is highly significant. Most of
the excellent institutions which it created had to come to life,

[2] The guiding principle of these institutions, i.e. that the men chosen
to control them should be selected on grounds of competence and not
of political allegiance, was brilliantly vindicated in this case. A Conservative government chose, as chairman of the Institute, Don Gumer-
sindo de Azcárate, one of the Republican leaders, a man universally
respected in Spain for his integrity and for the simplicity of his life, and
trusted by all for his moderate views. As members of the organizing
committee two specialists from the University of Oviedo, Professors
Buylla and Posada, were selected, despite their radical views, in collaboration with a retired military man, General Marvá, who had made a
reputation for himself in industrial affairs. The Institute consisted of a
collegiate body and a technical secretariat. The collegiate body was
composed of eighteen government nominees and six employer and six
labor representatives, chosen in each case by big industry, small industry
and agriculture, in equal parts, so that each category would be represented by two employers and two men. The government appointed its
eighteen nominees with a statesmanlike regard for all shades of opinion.
The very fact that the industrial members were to be elected acted as
a powerful stimulus to association both on the employers' and on the
men's side. The mandate of the institute comprised the study of social
and industrial conditions (what is known in America as a fact-finding
agency), the study and preparation of legislation and the inspection of
industrial life. In all these fields the Institute was eminently successful
and, until its character and independence were destroyed by the dictatorship, it acted as a powerful element of industrial peace even when
thwarted in its intelligent endeavors by the army, the reactionary employers and the anarchist and syndicalist hot-heads of labor.

in spite of Parliament, by the somewhat irregular procedure of royal decree legislation. The *Instituto de Reformas Sociales,* blocked in the Senate, was set up by royal decree. This, however, is not a condemnation of the parliamentary system, but rather of the undue weight which the unenlightened elements in the privileged classes were granted under the Constitution. We know that the parliamentary system, as understood by Cánovas and Sagasta, was a comedy; but we know that this comedy was fast becoming a reality in later years. Strictures against the Constitution miss the main point, i.e. that the political education of the Spanish people was being slowly matured by their having to live their Constitution, and that, though in all likelihood that Constitution would not have been workable in the end, some sort of a parliamentary system in harmony with Spanish character would have been evolved by the natural process of amendment had the Constitution been respected and loyally applied by those who had sworn to do so and had it not been torn to pieces by the sword paid to defend it.

It is evident, therefore, that, far from being a new factor in the life of Spain, the dictatorship represented the enthronement of the very forces which prevented a better progress under the regime which it came to displace. Though inefficient, corrupt, slow and weak, the old political system was the only constructive, statesmanlike, liberal and objective factor in the country struggling against the two forces—militarism and clericalism—which, with it, took complete possession of the field. The besetting sin of the dictatorship was that it glorified all that stands in the way of a better civilization for Spain. What is the essence of the Spanish trouble? It is the fanatical love of the Spaniard for personal liberty. But what is the method which the dictatorship brought to bear on this evil of the body politic? Dictatorship, i.e. the unrestricted use of liberty on the part of the government. There is a story told that one day, at the Cabinet Council, the youthful finance minister, Calvo Sotelo, drew the dictator's attention to the fact that a certain appointment which he wanted to make was contrary to the provincial and municipal statute which he, the finance minister, had drawn up a few

months earlier and published in two imposing volumes. The
prime minister turned to him and said: "Now, young man, do
you think that I have tossed the Constitution in the air in order
to bother about your two nice little pamphlets?" It may be fact
or it may be fancy, but this story is true to life. The dictator
governed the country with the best of good will, but with a
complete lack of any check on his impulses, good or bad, and
without the slightest suspicion of the spiritual harm which this
disregard for law produced in a nation of out-and-out individualists. Every day the twenty-two million Spaniards, every one
of whom was a potential dictator, and within the sphere of his
private and civil life an actual dictator so far as he was able,
received a splendid lesson of indiscipline and unrestrained
liberty, in fact, of anarchy, from this super-anarchist at the
head of the government. This is the greatest harm which the
dictator inflicted on the nation.

Though working for his popularity, up to a point, this situation nevertheless weakened and undermined it as well. The
dictator was popular when he succeeded in closing up a dismal
chapter of Moroccan history; but he squandered his popularity
in many ways, and particularly by disposing too freely of the
liberties, comforts and even prejudices of the people without
the backing which a statesman always finds in the dignity of
the established law. The Spanish people were, moreover, prevented from admiring the dictator in that dramatic way so typical
of them, i.e. as a man of action-in-itself, apart from any ethical
considerations, because they felt that the strict censorship which
the government applied was due to fear. The government was
afraid of public opinion, and the people, whose sense of power
is keen, guessed it. The censorship weakened the government
in other ways as well. Adversaries of the dictator and of his
colleagues were constantly publishing accusations of a serious
character against its actions and omissions. These accusations
were widely circulated abroad, and also in Spain despite the
efforts of the police. They were never discussed in the press.
The government, as a rule, was silent over them. This was
derogatory to the moral authority of the government, particu-

larly as some of the men who were carrying on this relentless campaign enjoyed a considerable prestige as austere and fearless Spaniards—for instance, Unamuno.

The dictatorship dragged on owing mainly to a number of reasons. The press was gagged. The masses, moreover, without whom it is difficult to organize a revolution, were largely socialist, and the Socialist Party, for tactical reasons, lay low and preferred to use this respite in order to strengthen its organization and to consolidate the trade union system. The liberal professions were on the whole against the government, but not numerous enough nor compact enough to fight. The army was the darkest factor. It was not pleased. It had been deeply disorganized by the measures of the dictatorship and disliked the part it was made to play. The two or three revolutionary attempts of the period had been made with the cooperation of considerable numbers of officers, and the Committees of Defense had turned Republican, if one is to believe a clandestine manifesto published in their name in 1929.

The dictatorship had shown evident signs of lassitude, and its desire to evolve towards a normal situation was obvious. But how was it to be done? Normal conditions mean publicity and justice for the wrongs committed, and there was a crowd of political figures determined to exact responsibilities for all that they and the nation had undergone. In the eyes of this opposition the dictatorship was but a system whereby the king and the prime minister were endeavoring to evade the reckoning. Three methods were tried—but all failed—to bring about a change without publicity or discussion of the past. The first was to attract the politicians back to the crown. All but a very few, however, maintained a dignified aloofness. Then the dictator endeavored to get rid of press and Parliament by legislation of a constitutional character, whereby parliament would be transformed into a kind of advisory council and the press put under severe supervision. By way of accustoming the nation to his ideas, the prime minister set up the National Advisory Assembly described above. But even this mild body seemed at times too wild for him. He entrusted it with the drafting of a Constitution which he would then have adopted by plebiscite. The draft was ready, but, though it put back the clock by several centuries, the dictator was so much afraid of it that he kept postponing the time when it was to be actually discussed by the Plenary Assembly, and particularly by the press.

The king, meanwhile, was a prisoner—a bitter experience for a spirited ruler whose ambition, in getting rid of Parliament, had been to rule. Efforts to supplant the dictator failed. The most notable of them was led by General Cavalcanti, who was then the head of the king's military household. This general had profited by General Primo de Rivera's absence in Morocco to weave a political combination in which he had tried, without success, to include some of the most respected and popular men of the progressive parties. The dictator heard of it, and with his usual promptness he appeared in Madrid, saw the king, and obtained from him a decree sending General Cavalcanti to study the organization of the armies of the Balkans. The position of the king had entirely changed. Under the old system he had a piano on which he could play any tune he pleased; now he had nothing but a clarion which, when played on, blared a note of its own. The king had no choice but to remain bound to the dictator whom he had chosen for himself. The old Spanish song applied with grim humor to his situation:

> *Esta sí que es calle calle*
> *Calle de valor y miedo.*
> *Quiero entrar y no me dejan;*
> *Quiero salir y no puedo.*[3]

And yet the dictator fell—which shows that General Primo de Rivera was not a dictator at all, but the mere figurehead of the system of forces which we have tried to describe. He fell because these forces abandoned him; in fact, because they began to feel uneasy as to the wisdom of prolonging the dictatorship.

The determining factor was the passive resistance of the

---

[3] Oh! what a street, what a street—a street of valor and fear. I want to get in and am not allowed, I want to get out and I can't.

nation which in the end impressed the forces in question with fear. The Church was afraid lest on the day of reckoning the angry crowds would make straight for convents and monasteries, as precedents led it to anticipate. The army, i.e. the officers, deeply dissatisfied and no longer able to bear the odium of a sterile dictatorship, made it obvious to all concerned that in its opinion the time for a change had arrived. Business at last awoke to the gravity of the financial situation, when seeing the peseta quoted at a price it had never touched since the blackest days of the Spanish-American War; the king, alarmed at the growth of republican feeling even in quarters till then traditionally safe, began to watch for an opportunity.

The opportunity was afforded him by the very exhaustion of the dictator. A revolt was brewing in a southern garrison. That this revolt was not altogether spontaneous is suspected by some on the ground that the general who was leading it in a republican direction became Under-Secretary of State for War in the royal government formed to supersede the dictator. The dictator, irritated by all these ever recurring movements in the ranks of officers, decided to consult the army through the regional commanders in a kind of military plebiscite. The king objected and asked him to resign.

On the day the dictator fell there were demonstrations in the main towns. The demonstrators, however, did not mention General Primo de Rivera at all. They shouted: "Down with the king." They knew perfectly well who was the main power behind the dictator. The new Cabinet was organized in the private house of Don Leopoldo Matos, a Conservative ex-minister and the legal counsel of the royal household. The prime minister was General Berenguer, the head of the military household; every other figure in it was a well-tried palatine friend.

Their task was extremely hard. It consisted in dissociating the king from the dictatorship, i.e. in solving what we have described as the deadlock. But was this deadlock soluble? The new administration made the deadlock but clearer. The irrelevancies of the old dictatorship—the figure of the general with his peculiar, picturesque ways of interpreting what government is, and the vexatious or ill-considered measures which weakened his rule—were eliminated; but the new government, composed on the whole of well-meaning and capable men, brought out the real issue into sharper relief. Whether he wanted it or not, General Berenguer was a dictator, or, better, he was the new instrument of the king's dictatorship.

General Berenguer endeavored to return to constitutional practices, and in so far as the preliminary measures thereto did not imply danger, he acted to that effect. Thus municipal and provincial councils were reorganized on a fair basis, and much hardship, both personal and political, caused by the deposed dictator was removed. But the key position was liberty of political discussion in the press and in public meetings. Here, the new regime had to walk cautiously. Every concession, however timid, showed that the country was ringing with Republican feeling. The reception granted in Salamanca to Don Miguel de Unamuno revealed the extent of the nation's enthusiasm for the Opposition. Sbert, the student exiled by General Primo de Rivera for his leadership of the anti-Jesuit campaign of 1928-29, was acclaimed by thousands on his return to Madrid. All this feeling pointed to the royal palace. Señor Sánchez Guerra, the king's Conservative prime minister of old, at last authorized to speak in Madrid, concentrated his attacks on the king and declared that he would never cooperate with him.

In vain did the government endeavor to screen the king. When the two heads of the two Houses of Parliament came to remind the crown that the calling together of Cortes three months after a dissolution was a duty which the Constitution laid on the king on person, the king had dismissed them within five minutes from the royal presence. The government was in a deadlock. If it advanced along the road to liberty, it freed the feeling which demanded the trial of those responsible for the dictatorship—the king's trial. If it resisted the evident wishes of public opinion it fell back on the dictatorship.

BOOK 2

THE REPUBLIC,
THE CIVIL WAR,
and AFTER

PART 1

THE REPUBLIC

CHAPTER 1

THE FALL OF THE MONARCHY

By the beginning of 1930, the Monarchy was in deadly peril. The king had unwisely come down to the arena of politics and taken sides in the daily strife of parties and opinions. His personal responsibility could not be concealed from the public. When on January 28, 1930, he dismissed Primo de Rivera, giving the premiership to General Berenguer with a civilian Cabinet, King Alfonso remained unscreened and exposed to public opinion as the responsible leader of political events over which the nation as a whole was critical and even resentful.

The death of Primo de Rivera in Paris (March 16, 1930) contributed—somewhat irrelevantly—to concentrate popular resentment on the king. Of the men who had served him in the past—all of whom nursed grievances against him—some chose to come out as his political enemies, others endeavored to save the Monarchy by leading it toward genuine constitutional ways. Don Francisco Cambó and Don Sàntiago Alba, in

377

particular, tried to liberalize the crown, and the king went all the way to Paris to see Alba, the very minister whom he had betrayed in 1923. More uncompromising, another liberal ex-minister of the crown, Don Niceto Alcalá Zamora, broke his link with the Monarchy, and appealed to the conservative, Catholic and moderate opinion of Spain to rally to the Republic. On July 14, 1930, the new party which Alcalá Zamora founded —the Liberal Republican Right—issued its Manifesto which was widely, though secretly, circulated. Miguel Maura (a son of Don Antonio Maura, who had led for years the Monarchist Conservative Party of Spain) was another of the founders of this party.

By this time, the Socialists, who under the opportunistic leadership of Largo Caballero, had "collaborated" with the dictatorship in conditions deeply resented by all liberals, had veered round and aligned themselves with the Opposition. The Republican movement had never covered so wide a sector of opinion. Clandestine committees were set up in every town and the Central Committee in Madrid comprised most of the names which were to lead the republic.

While the prime minister, General Berenguer, hesitated, the Committee organized its coup. Counting as it did on the working classes and on a strong part of the army, it decided to strike on December 15, 1930, the day on which the Republican regime would be proclaimed in the whole country. Mark this point. *The extreme Left betrayed the Left*. It is the law of Spanish progressive politics. Two officers revolted in Jaca on December 12. The Central Committee had sent them one of its members, Don Santiago Casares Quiroga, to bid them hold up their foolhardy plan. All in vain. The two desperadoes revolted, and carried their soldiers with them. They were beaten by the government troops. The two officers, Galán and García Hernández, were shot; the whole plot was brought to light; the Central Committee was imprisoned. A few young pilots flew over Madrid and dropped revolutionary leaflets. Their leader was a hothead: Ramón Franco. He had an elder brother whose head was cooler.

General Berenguer felt that his favorite tactics—playing for time—were but increasing the danger. He could no longer adjourn the general elections without risking an explosion. He could not yet grant freedom of the press and of meeting and discussion without exposing the crown to a devastating criticism. He decided to withhold the granting of these liberties till twenty days before polling day. The anti-monarchist parties announced that they would abstain from voting; that did not trouble the prime minister. But the royalist parties, later, also decided that in such conditions they would abstain. General Berenguer thereupon resigned.

The nation and the world then saw the strange spectacle of a monarch reduced to having to seek his Cabinet in prison. King Alfonso sent an emissary to offer the ministry to the Central Revolutionary Committee. The Committee refused. The king succeeded in forming some sort of a Cabinet—his last—under Admiral Aznar. This Cabinet embodied an idea, no doubt supplied by its ingenious foreign secretary, the veteran Count Romanones. There would be three successive elections: municipal first, provincial later, finally parliamentary. In any circumstances less deadly for the regime, the idea might have sufficed to squeeze it out of a tight corner. As it happened, it brought about the sudden, dramatic fall of the Monarchy.

The parties which had refused to stand for Parliament under a gagged opinion, shrewdly realizing that public opinion, gagged or not, was theirs, waived their objection on the ground that municipal elections were of an administrative character. A revolutionary wave swept the country. The government closed all the universities. Students and professors decided to carry on in private buildings. Three intellectual leaders, Don José Ortega y Gasset, Don Ramón Pérez de Ayala and Don Gregorio Marañón, founded the Group in the Service of the Republic. In March 1931, the Supreme Military Court heard the case against the Central Committee. The Counsel for the defense took their stand on the principal that the Committee could not be accused of rebellion because the Constitution had been violated by the king and without the Constitution there was no king. A number of members of the court, including the president, voted for the acquittal; the majority for a six months' sentence which the Committee had already served. The men were freed there and then and were received by an imposing crowd with unbounded enthusiasm.

On April 12, 1931, Spain elected its municipal councilors. It was a unique election both in its total absence of disorder and in its remarkable lack of interference on the part of the government. With the one exception of Cádiz, the whole of the capital cities of the fifty provinces of Spain voted for anti-king men. Public opinion insisted on immediate measures in harmony with this unexpected plebiscite. On April 13, Dr. Marañón, in close touch with both sides, warned Count Romanones of the danger of delay. The veteran statesman called on Alcalá Zamora (who had begun his career as a lawyer as Count Romanones' own assistant) and negotiated the change-over.

On April 14, 1931, the municipal councils of Barcelona, Oviedo, Seville, Valencia and other capital cities proclaimed the Republican regime. Alcalá Zamora insisted that the king should abdicate and leave the country before nightfall, so as to prevent bloodshed if the people came to suspect that they were being deceived. The decisive move came from General Sanjurjo, one of Primo de Rivera's chief accomplices in the conspiracy which had set up the dictatorship in 1923. He was in command of the *Guardia Civil,* a strongly militarized gendarmerie. He declared for the Republic. On hearing this news, the king abdicated and left by road for Cartagena, where at dawn he sailed away from the country he was never to see again.

He had left his wife and children in Madrid. The crowd covered the vast square in front of the royal palace, shouting with excitement and joy. About twenty-five hussars, discreetly hidden in an inner court, and about twenty-five halberdiers of the purely decorative guard, wandering forlorn and dispirited in the royal palace—that was all that stood between the queen and her children and that revolutionary crowd. But that crowd was not shouting death—it was shouting life—"Long live this" and "Long live that." The men in charge at the palace rang up the Home Office. Don Miguel Maura, who had taken charge as the Republican Home Secretary, promised to send "a force." He sent a number of citizens with red brassards and no weapons. They made a ring round the palace and ordered: "Citizens, go back five yards!" The order was instantly obeyed and gradually the crowd melted away.[1]

[1]My narrative is taken from that given in *A.B.C.*, the leading Monarchist paper in Spain. I hope it may nail to the counter the slanders one still reads even in the best regulated English monthlies by English polo-player politicians who will insist that the crowd "howled death" and so forth. The Madrid crowd behaved with the utmost chivalry to the queen.

CHAPTER 2

"THE PRETTY GIRL"

A joy like that of nature in spring—such was the mood of Spain in those glorious first days of the Republic. The revolution had been so clean, so untainted by any of the excesses which usually soil the dramatic moments of history, so free from military interference for or against, so clearly the outcome of an orderly expression of public opinion, that the first emotion aroused by their triumph in the breast of all Republicans was one of proud joy. Spain had shown the world that one of the oldest monarchies in Europe could be felled by a clean stroke of the mental axe of democracy without breaking as much as a window pane in the whole country. Truly, the Republic had come in smiling, fully deserving the quaint name her faithful conspirators used to give her throughout the nineteenth century: *La Niña Bonita,* The Pretty Girl.

There was wonder under the joy. Was it possible? Was Spain as republican as all that? And the minds who felt free enough

382

to observe events without political commitments, class prejudices or fears for their power and property were inclined to detect in this unexpected triumph of the Republic the signs of a wave of political passion rather than the features of a steady conviction. The very plebiscite which had been read as a Republican victory everywhere—even in the royal palace—was by no means as conclusive as it had seemed. The figures of municipal councilors (*concejales*) elected were: Republicans, 34,368; Socialists, 4,813; Communists, 67; total of anti-Monarchists, 39,248; Monarchists, 41,224. In other words the two trends were more or less balanced, with a slight advantage for the Monarchist vote. An objective analysis of the electoral system of the Monarchy would probably transform this Monarchist surplus of about 5 per cent into a deficit of as much as 20 per cent. Yet, when all is taken into account, it seems only fair to attribute to the Monarchy a voting strength of no less than 40 per cent—at the moment when it fell. The facts were soon to confirm this opinion. The Republican triumph of April 1931 was in fact, when adequately analyzed, no Republican triumph at all. An examination of the political map of Spain in the spring of 1931 will suffice to prove it.

The working classes voted for the combined "Republican" list. This list included Socialists and "Republicans," i.e. middle-class liberals. The vote of the working classes was split. The workers affiliated to the UGT (Socialists) voted for their men; but the Anarcho-Syndicalists, whose numbers were about as numerous, voted for the middle-class liberals. There were two reasons for this: the first was the unbridgeable enmity which separates socialists and syndicalists, due to their rival bid for the leadership of the working classes; the second was that as the Anarcho-syndicalists had always preached contempt for the suffrage, they had no political machinery of their own; so that, when it came to voting, which they did this time to help oust the Monarchy, they preferred to vote for the middle-class Republicans whose liberal views were more in harmony with the anti-Marxist ideas of the Spanish Syndicalists than with the orthodox and dogmatic tenets of the Socialists.

This is a most important point. It means that the syndicalists came to swell the votes of some middle-class mushroom formations without deep doctrinal or economic roots in the country, such as the so-called Radical-Socialist Party, whose members were led to make political hay while their sun shone, and to nurse their vote by demagogic demands. From the outset, therefore, the Republic found itself with its left flank exposed to the attacks of its own dangerous friends and allies. Needless to say, a Socialist political formation might and should have been one of the most solid foundations of the Republic; but the Spanish Socialist Party was deeply divided. Two out of its three leaders, Prieto and Besteiro, were for an evolutionary policy in cordial collaboration with the progressive and genuine liberals who followed Azaña. The third, however, Largo Caballero, had thrown to the winds the political wisdom of a lifetime, and, sowing his political wild oats at the time when people quietly eat the tasteless porridge of experience, he was leading the fiery socialist youth movement toward the proletarian revolution. It is characteristic of this period of Spanish history that the Socialists, and in particular those of Largo Caballero's branch, explicitly refused to be styled "Republicans"—an attitude which Léon Blum, for instance, would have found difficult to understand.

The mainstay of the Republic was the sector of public opinion which stood behind Azaña. Though his party—Republican Action—was not of course wholly free from dross, it was by far the most competent, intelligent, honest and well-meaning of the middle-class zone; the only bourgeois party progressive enough to want earnestly to lead Spain on to a new era, and conservative enough to do it effectively. It was, however, threatened in its central position by dangers coming both from the Right and from the Left. On the Left, the revolutionary wing of the Socialist Party, led by Largo Caballero; on the Right, the Radical party led by Lerroux and the extreme Right, a black patch into which nearly all the rich political palette of monarchical days had been compressed.

The Radical Party was a curious affair; its roots were most

honorable, and, through some of its oldest members, led back to the virtuous, ethical, anti-clerical, sometime atheistic, sometime theistic, freethinkers and freemasons one sees in Galdós' books conspiring against all tyrannies—of the king or of the Pope—(the tyranny of the employer was not actual yet in those days). From that picturesque epoch, the party had inherited a certain popularity with the anti-clerical sectors of opinion, a certain swing in its eloquence, and not a little unreality in its doctrine. Worse still, as most of its tenets had gradually become obsolete, either because the Monarchy had gradually adopted progressive reforms or because the Labor parties presented more substantial claims before public opinion, the Radical Party had grown used to a kind of merely formal opposition. It had become a tame lion kept by the Monarchy. Its leader, Don Alejandro Lerroux, roared perfectly and always in tune.

When the Monarchy fell, the Radical Party became the comfort and hope of those Monarchists of the Left and Republicans of the Right who were willing to go forward but neither too quickly nor very far. The party had, however, been deeply demoralized under its long spell of merely nominal opposition, a circumstance which was to prove fatal to the Republic. Nevertheless, the Radical Party, with all its defects and weaknesses, was sincerely progressive and its core had remained democratic. Had the circumstances, personal and others, hereafter analyzed, permitted a collaboration between Lerroux and Azaña, it seems evident that this undoubtedly republican force might have been restored to political health and made useful for the Republic, thereby sparing it the Civil War.[1]

To the right of it, Don Niceto Alcalá Zamora and Don Miguel Maura had formed a party of Republican Roman Catholics, which, at any rate on objective grounds, should have worked hand in hand with Azaña's Republican Action.

---

[1] This is confirmed by the secession of the Martínez Barrio-Lara group which went over to the left side of the political watershed when Señor Lerroux with the majority of the party entered into a political alliance with the Right.

Further to the right, other parties, either openly or covertly monarchist, grouped the land-owning, financial and clerical interests.

The picture was clear. The Republic and the country had before them two possible alternatives. Either a central core would be constituted, uniting moderate socialists and sincerely progressive Republicans in order to consolidate the regime and to defend it against the dangers which threatened it both from the Right and from the Left; or the several groups which might have constituted this center, unable to come together, would gravitate each in the direction of its proclivities. In the first case, the Republic would have steered a difficult, yet probably safe, course between the two extremes; in the second case, since nothing but the two extremes would be left, a civil war would be inevitable.

The history of the Republic is in its essence the history of this inner struggle—of the center, to exist; of the two extremes, to prevent it from gathering substance and momentum. In the end the extremes won and Spain was plunged into the most disastrous civil war of its history. The international importance which this war came to acquire, and the active intervention in it of two Fascist and one Communist states, have tended to obscure the fact that in its inception and in its essence the Civil War was above all Spanish. These Spanish origins and aspects of the Civil War must be stressed in order to understand it adequately even as an episode in the European civil war of which it was the prologue.

Why did the center fail—fail not merely to govern but even to be born? First and foremost because of the unyielding and absolute nature of the Spanish character. This is the psychological root cause of all Spanish troubles. It determines all that happens in Spain, and explains the periodical failures of parliamentary government and the periodical rises of dictators; as well as the separatist movements, whose leaders, be it Basques or Catalans, are blissfully unaware of the fact that the less tractable they are the more Spanish they reveal themselves to be. By nature the Spaniard gravitates to the farther end of his

thought, just as the Englishman gravitates to the near end of it
—for thoughts are tricky things, feels the Englishman. So, while
Englishmen who think differently are nevertheless always within
sight and hearing of each other and of the parting of their ways,
Spaniards are always out of each other's mental reach and must
shout to each other, and always run the risk of misinterpreting
a gesture of acquiescence or doubt as a gesture of threat, and of
mistaking a pipe for a revolver.

Quite apart from any objective factor, such a psychological
substratum was bound to strengthen the extremes to the detriment of the center. No one with direct experience of Spain will
underestimate its weight in the events which led to the rapid
deterioration and final undoing of the Republic.

Next to it, in order of importance must be placed personal
considerations, and in particular the natural antagonism between
the two leaders of the would-be center: Azaña and Lerroux.
They belonged to different epochs, to different orders of the
mind. Lerroux, the older of the two by a whole generation—if
not quite in point of age, certainly in point of activity and
political development—was a typical product of the late nineteenth century. A self-educated son of the people, he had begun
politics early in life, and decidedly with a demagogic, revolutionary tone. When the Republic triumphed in 1931, his days
as a popular leader, his sway over the crowds in Barcelona, his
triumphs as an anti-clerical orator inciting the workers to turn
nuns into mothers—were things of the past; but there remained
enough glamour in his name, and his Radical Party had enough
roots in many towns, to conquer for him one of the seats in the
provisional government. By then, Lerroux had become the hope
of the conservatives who thought the Republic inevitable. But
for the new generation Lerroux and his party sounded hollow,
and were suspect as tainted with the worst aspects of politics
in the worst sense this word might have in, say, the United
States two generations ago.

Differences in taste perhaps even more than in the ethical
approach to public life separated such a man from Manuel
Azaña, a fastidious intellectual of haughty character and re-

tiring ways who had devoted nearly all his life to the quiet discharge of his duties as a civil servant and to writing books of more literary merit than their actual success might indicate. Azaña had been educated in the Escorial College, an institution of Augustinian monks, and had then taken a law degree at the university. He was a man of great intellectual distinction, moral elevation and personal pride; not devoid, however, of a certain feminine side to his nature, which made him ultra-sensitive and led him to seek the sheltered atmosphere of a secluded number of friends—a hothouse environment apt to favor the growth of the thorns of resentment. "Beware of Azaña"—Unamuno used to say long before the fall of the Monarchy—"He is an author without readers. He would be capable of starting a revolution in order to be read." A mere taunt of Unamuno, which perhaps he himself would not have cared to take literally, yet one which reveals an important feature of the otherwise attractive and noble personality of Azaña.

For Azaña, Lerroux was unbearably coarse, vulgar, and indifferent to moral elegance in public affairs. On strictly political grounds there was little to choose between the programs of Azaña's *Acción Republicana* and of Lerroux's Radical Party. Lerroux, moreover, would almost certainly have swallowed any changes in his views to come to terms with Azaña, for while his own party had a certain amount of popular following, especially in the lower middle classes, it had no prestige, whereas most of the prominent men in the intellectual life of the nation had gathered round Azaña, whether they officially belonged to his party or not. But Azaña was unable to conquer his aversion toward Lerroux, whom he considered as "a mortgage on the Republic," and so Lerroux, rejected on his left, was gradually led to gravitate more and more to the right, while Azaña himself leaned more and more toward the Socialists. Even as a big river can be traced back to a slender brook, so the Spanish Civil War may be said to begin on that day when Azaña made up his mind that he could not go hand-in-hand with the Radical Party. This decision is easy to understand and was perhaps inevitable. Yet two conclusions impose themselves on the mind.

The first is that Azaña took a course fraught with heavy dangers for the Republic, on considerations of personal taste; and the second, that, in taking it, he revealed a disastrous lack of confidence in his own powers and in those of his friends to absorb the Radical Party and to give it a new (and a purer) life—for all of which he was to pay heavily in acute agony and protracted sorrow till his death in exile.

And yet the beginning had been unimpeachable. Socialists, Republicans, Catalans, while conspiring against the Monarchy, had given each other and the nation an admirable proof of mutual tolerance and of political self-denial by putting at the head of the Revolutionary Committee (which was to be the Provisional Government) Don Niceto Alcalá Zamora, a bourgeois, a Monarchist but a year earlier, and at one time the most ardent opponent of Catalan home rule. Don Niceto Alcalá Zamora was an Andalusian lawyer who had acquired a precocious reputation both in the law courts and in Parliament as a fluent and passionate orator. Honest, shrewd, learned, patriotic, he had several times occupied cabinet posts in liberal ministries. A devout Catholic, he was, nevertheless, a man of liberal views. Yet, despite his sterling qualities, it was a misfortune that this well-meaning man should have been maneuvered by fate into a position of eminence and responsibility for which he was not fitted. Extremely shortsighted, he was—perhaps owing to that infirmity—inclined to see enemies everywhere; and as a man in public life is never wholly without them, Señor Alcalá Zamora was often the victim of his own suspicions and of resentment. He had suffered petty persecutions from the dictator, and the evolution which relatively late in life led him to the Republic cannot be said to have been entirely determined by objective considerations.

The men who, coming from the different sectors of Spanish progressive life, concluded the Pact of San Sebastián (August 1930), put Alcalá Zamora at their head precisely because he was a Catholic and a recent Monarchist. In so doing, they meant to say to the more conservative sectors of Spanish opinion: "Do not be frightened. We bring you freedom; we bring you a quickening of Spain's political evolution; but we do not bring you a violent upheaval of your way of life."

This was admirable statesmanship—if it was sincere. But was it sincere? The events which were soon to mar the clean record of the newborn Republic might tempt one to answer in the negative. Yet, it is more likely that at the time the leaders who signed the Pact of San Sebastián were honestly thinking of nothing more subversive than a brisk evolution of Spain's political and social order. This wisdom was, however, against the grain, and so was unable to withstand the onslaught of the two extremes. On May 7, 1931, the Cardinal-Archbishop of Toledo issued a pastoral letter accepting the new regime with less good grace and more suspicion than he might have done. On May 10 disorders broke out in Madrid under the windows of the Monarchist Club—whether provoked by the club members or by the crowd it is now difficult to say. The crowd dispersed, but later assaulted the offices of the Royalist paper *A.B.C.* and tried to burn them. The government closed down the paper's offices and arrested the editor. The crowd was not calmed. It was obvious to those who knew the town that some revolutionary action was deliberately at work. Churches began to burn and reg flags appeared. Disturbances of an identical character, the chief feature of which was the burning of churches, broke out simultaneously in Seville, Alicante, Zaragoza, Murcia, Córdoba, Granada, worst of all Málaga. It is too soon to say whether the trouble came from Communists, extreme Socialists, Anarchists, or paid agents of the Monarchists . . . or, what is most likely, of a mixture of all those elements. One thing was certain. These disorders had nothing to do with a genuine state of mind of the people. Communism, an unimportant factor in those days, began to appear in the news. The joyful mood of the first days began to give place to a more concerned state of mind.

But the Republic felt still full of youth, vigor and hope. In the midst of troubles of all kinds, provoked by the impatient, the extremists, and the reactionaries, the Provisional Government went on patiently and courageously building up a new progressive state. An epidemic of strikes afflicted the country;

some provoked by employers with anti-Republican political aims; others, and in particular, a number of general strikes (of all trades and services) in a few towns, called for political reasons by the Anarcho-Syndicalists. A general strike in the telephone service was launched during the week which should have been devoted to the general election. The Church was restive over the case of Cardinal Segura, the aggressive Archbishop of Toledo, who on June 14 had been expelled by the government. Intolerance? By no means. The archbishop was "impossible," but, moreover, the Vatican had on May 24 refused its diplomatic *placet* to Don Luis Zulueta as the Spanish ambassador—a truly incomprehensible step, for Don Luis Zulueta, a distinguished scholar with a truly religious mind, albeit not an orthodox Catholic, was an admirable choice for this post, and one which revealed in the utmost consideration on the part of the Provisional Government for the Vatican. The Army was also restive. Azaña, who had carefully prepared himself for years for his duties as Minister of War, had disbanded thirty-seven infantry and seventeen cavalry regiments, reducing the army's peace strength to eight divisions, which meant the dethronement of eight regional commanders from their all but vice-regal splendor. There were obvious signs that the reactionary forces in Spain had enlisted the discreet collaboration of international financial forces, which, leaning heavily on any disquieting signs coming from Spain, made a strong attack on the peseta: from 48 to the pound at the height of the crisis of the Monarchy it fell to 50, 57 and even 62 (June 7). On June 28, a young, unruly airman with extreme-left leanings and hot ambitions led a revolt of extremist air officers in the aerodrome of Tablada, near Seville. His name was Ramón Franco. His elder brother, General Francisco Franco, of monarchist leanings, had rallied to the Republic.

CHAPTER 3

IDEALISTS AND UNREALISTS

On July 14, 1931, the Constituent Assembly met in Madrid. It had been elected on June 28, on a basis of one member for every 50,000 of population, and universal suffrage. Its membership was remarkable in many ways. It included two women and a few priests, more young men than the old Cortes, fewer members with political experience and fewer still with any experience in government. Its composition revealed the multiplicity of views and parties usual in Spain as in most countries of Central and Southern Europe. There were, from Left to Right: 116 Socialists; 60 Radical-Socialists; 30 members of Republican Action (Azaña); 17 Federalists; 90 Radicals (Lerroux); 22 Progressives (Alcalá Zamora and Maura); 60 Right (Agrarians, Basques and others). Alongside these parties, there were 43 Catalans and 16 Gallegans who usually voted with the Party of Republican Action led by Azaña. The Constituent Cortes elected as its president Don Julián Besteiro, the veteran leader of the Socialist Party whose intellectual and political distinction lent a special dignity to the new Assembly.

Its first duty was to prepare a Constitution. But most of its members, new to public life, came animated with too eager a desire for retribution to rest content with looking forward and building the future. They were intent on thoroughly demolishing the past and on seeking responsibilities. This Assembly gave public opinion the first opportunity to make itself heard since 1923. The impetus, the passion, with which the Constituent Assembly legislated *against* the past rather than *for* the future were the logical outcome of eight years of an arbitrary if comparatively mild dictatorship. Since human beings are moved and swayed by their temperament rather than by logic, the very tendencies of the dictatorship reappeared in the ranks of its fierce opponents. The bill setting up a commission with judiciary powers to sit in judgment over the case of those responsible for the dictatorship provided that the usual guarantees which protect the accused in the Code of Criminal Procedure should be dispensed with. This proposal was successfully opposed, but that it should have been officially put forward is a curious illustration of the way temperament may undermine the best-grounded political convictions.

The majority of the Assembly members were new to parliamentary life, and a considerable number of them were men with a doctrinarian turn of mind. This circumstance was extremely unfortunate, for it led to a Constitution which made it impossible for the Republic to thrive. The three chief defects of the Constitution were the weakness of the Executive, the lack of a Senate and the disestablishment of the Church. The President of the Republic was looked upon as an uncrowned heir of the monarch, and therefore with a kind of posthumous distrust which hemmed in his powers in every possible way. Of all these powers, the most coveted (and dreaded) was that of dissolving Parliament. The president was to be allowed to use it but once during his term of office. If he used it twice, the Parliament elected immediately afterward had to devote its first debate to an examination of this second dissolution and approve

or disapprove it. This incredible provision of the Constitution
was to be applied in 1936 in an even more incredible fashion.
The government, moreover, saw its powers of preventive arrest
and other similar weapons for keeping order severely curtailed,
on grounds theoretically unimpeachable, as a reaction against
the arbitrary ways of the dictator. The Republic, under the
leadership of the Left, had to "protect" itself against its own
Constitution by laws of exception known as the Law for the
Defense of the Republic and the Public Order Law, which,
though difficult to conciliate with the wide principles laid down
by the Constitution, proved insufficient to hold the effervescence
of the violent-minded. "Next Tuesday," said a home secretary
of the Left one day in his office at the Puerta del Sol to a Spanish
ambassador who, happening to be in Madrid, had called on
him, "Parliament reassembles. I have about one hundred Anarchists in jail in Zaragoza. I must release them on Monday; I
will have no trouble in Parliament on Tuesday. And there will
be bloodshed in Zaragoza on Wednesday." For once, he was a
prophet.

The Commission of Jurists appointed by the Provisional government to prepare a Draft Constitution had recommended two
houses of Parliament: a Congress of Deputies elected by universal
suffrage and a Senate of 240 members, elected in equal parts
by (1) the liberal professions, (2) the Universities and other
cultural and religious institutions, (3) the workers, and (4) the
employers. It was, in a more modern form, a Senate very much
on the original lines of the old monarchical Upper House. The
idea was abandoned owing to the uncompromising opposition of
the Socialists. By thus giving up a second chamber, as time was
to show, the Republic threw away one of the strongest guarantees
against the violent movements of opinion which were to disrupt
its whole frame.

Finally, in its constitutional measures with regard to the
Church, the Republic made one of its worst blunders. Had it
chosen to live under the then ruling concordat, it would have
inherited the unique privileges which the Spanish state had con-

quered over Rome in the course of centuries, while by merely insisting on the strict application of the somewhat stiff conditions of this remarkable instrument, it would have freed the country of three-quarters of the superfluous religious orders. But the Assembly was committed to disestablishment and gave the world the spectacle of a state which divests itself of its own privileges at the moment it needs them most. Priests were deprived of their salaries, although the clerical proletariat, in opposition to the wealthy bishops, might have been won over to the Republic; while religious orders, though shorn of many of their privileges, remained both powerful and inimical. The Jesuit Order was dissolved. The argument against this purely theoretical policy could be summed up in a dilemma: either the Assembly did not realize that bishops and priests held a spiritual power over the country comparable to that of the press—and if so, they lived in a fool's paradise—or they did realize it—and if so, they were behaving as a state which gives a foreign government the power to appoint all its editors and journalists. Advice was not lacking which—if advice ever could—might have spared the error. Yet, such was the strength of the prejudice that the anti-clerical articles of the Constitution were passed even at the cost of a serious crisis in the Assembly and in the Provisional Government. The Basque deputies withdrew in a body, offended in their religious feelings by the anti-clerical bigotry of Republicans and Socialists. The President of the Provisional Government (Señor Alcalá Zamora) and the Home Secretary (Don Miguel Maura), the two leaders of the Republican Catholics, withdrew, and the chief anti-clerical leader, Señor Azaña, took charge (October 13-14, 1931).

By the side of these three capital mistakes, the remaining provisions of the Constitution present little more than an academic importance. Most of them were of an equalitarian, generous and popular character; some, like the Divorce Law, long due; others like feminine suffrage, risky though liberal experiments; others again, like the detailed and elaborate promises made to the workers, more well-meant than practical or even possible.

The Constitution was ratified on December 9, 1931. Don Niceto Alcalá Zamora was elected President of the Republic on the following day. Azaña took office as prime minister. And the Republic started on its stormy crossing toward the Civil War.

The Constitution was born on December 9, 1931. It died on July 18, 1936, with the suspension of Spain's independence. In these four and a half years, Spain lived under three leaderships: Left (December 9, 1931–December 3, 1933), Right (December 3, 1933–February 16, 1936), and Left (February 16–July 18, 1936). During the first period, the Left in office had to meet an armed revolt of the Right (August 1932). During the second period, the Right in office had to meet an armed revolt of the Left (October 6, 1934). During the third period, the Left in office had to meet an armed revolt from the Right —and the Republic, giddy with these wild swings, died of them.

The rest is words.

Let us now look at things as they might have appeared to a well-informed, realistic but disinterested observer, at the beginning of Spain's free constitutional life. In the foreground, the familiar problems shone with a clearer light, now that the veil thrown over them by the Monarchy and by the dictatorship had been torn aside by the nation. The Catalan problem could be tackled with a generous common sense without fear of kingly frowns or military oaths. The clerical Gordian knot had been cut. Education could be fostered with complete freedom from monarchical and clerical interference. The Army could be reduced to its strictly technical function. Labor could rest assured that its interests were in the safekeeping of one of its veteran leaders. Agrarian reform was at last to be tackled in earnest. In foreign affairs, Spain was determined to be a model member of the parliament of nations. There was no reason why the Spanish Republic should not have succeeded in building up a prosperous, contented and progressive Spain.

Beneath this clear picture, however, there lurked the two constant, the two only real problems of Spanish political life: a civil general staff, inadequate to modern needs both in quantity and in quality (coupled with the lack of internal peace to develop it); and the weakness of the collective instincts of citizenship in the Spanish psychology.

First, the inadequacy of a general staff. Every nation needs a number of thousands of men—it may be ten thousand or it may be a thousand thousand—to lead its public life: political and permanent heads of its Departments of State, leaders of its educational, scientific, artistic, commercial, technical and labor institutions, specialists of the numerous specialities which make up modern life. The collapse of Spain's framework at the beginning of the nineteenth century made it imperative for Spain to begin her reconstruction from scratch. Here and there, efforts of the highest quality were made by private individuals, sometimes even by the government of the time, to create or develop this leading tissue in the body politic. These efforts were invariably ground to dust again by constantly recurring civil wars. The last of these creative endeavors, that which owes its origin to Don Francisco Giner de los Rios, was the most successful of all.[1] Thanks to the protracted internal peace which Spain owed to the Bourbon Restoration (1876-1931) this effort had time to gather some momentum, and as the country is rich in vigor and in creative gifts, the reign of Alfonso XIII will count in the history of Spanish culture as, at least, a silver era. The chief task of the Republic, therefore, should have been to ensure the continuation of this peace till the development of "leading tissue" in the body politic enabled it to tackle the burning problems over which its public opinion was divided. The leaders of the Republic should have conceived it as their first duty to reduce their respective, conflicting claims to a bare minimum, not merely within the walls of the Republican citadel (within which the number of factions was considerable), but even with their adversaries outside, who, in the first days of the Republican triumph, were too frightened to have been very exacting. But though the triumph of the Republic was evident, the number,

---

[1] See Book I, chapter 7.

strength and power of its enemies was formidable enough to arouse reasonable concern as to what might happen if they were goaded into rebellion. Now rebellion, from whichever quarter, no matter by whose fault, meant infinitely more for Spain than a merely political issue; it meant a biological issue: the arrest of the creative process within her body politic, without which merely political changes could have no significance and merely administrative changes no practical effect.

The psychological conditions in which the Republic was born might have made some such moderation possible on the part of the Republic. The wise decision of the Monarchists and the king to avoid a civil war might have eased the pressure of political passions accumulated by eight years of a dictatorship which, oppressive and unintelligent though it was, seems singularly mild in the lurid light of a later experience. But though the Republic might have been moderate, it simply was not. The impetus of eight years of bottled-up energy and the pressure of eight years of political dreaming were too much for the men in charge of the ship of state, and they steered her full steam ahead against the immutable rocks of Spanish obduracy.

Harassed by the constant incidents and minor or major revolts which its own partisanship had stimulated, the government was never able—if it ever thought of it—to undertake the political education of the people. No. I am not thinking of the percentage of people in Spain who can read the Spanish equivalent for the *Daily Blank* or release their criminal instincts by saturating their minds with murder mysteries. It is more complex than that. What was wanted in 1931 was an organization to drive the elementary truths of collective life into the consciousness of the nation, as effectively and as quickly as possible, and in particular to impress upon public opinion that the success of the Republic depended on every citizen performing his private and public duties to the best of his ability. More often than not, the kernel of a problem turned out to be less political than psychological—namely a dereliction of duty on the part of a considerable class or section of the citizens. These discoveries, however, were not palatable, and remained discreetly hidden in the wings of the political stage. They were, nevertheless, the symptoms of the profound trouble which afflicted the country, and the fact that they were not heeded, the fact that the whole-sale education of the country to raise it to self-government was not attempted, must be counted as one of the chief causes of the downfall of the Republic.

CHAPTER 4

THE FIRST ROUND—LEFT

HOME-RULE MATTERS

The Catalan Question

Barcelona had preceded Madrid in its eagerness to proclaim the Republic. One of the new *concejales,* Don Lluis Companys, elected on April 12, took the initiative. He hoisted the flags of Catalonia and of Republican Spain from the noble building of the Town Hall. On the same day (April 14) the leader of the Catalan Left, Colonel Maciá, was "elected" President of the Catalan Republic, and he addressed the enthusiastic crowds in the following words:

"In the name of the people of Catalonia, I proclaim the Catalan State, under the regime of a Catalan Republic, which freely and in all cordiality seeks and asks the collaboration of the other brother peoples of Spain in order to create a confederation of Iberian peoples, offering them, by whatever means, to liberate them from the Bourbon Monarchy. At this moment we reach out with our voice to all the peoples of the world in the name of freedom, of justice and of the peace of the peoples."

Thus on this first day of the new era of Spain's hopes did the Catalans assert the typical features of their character: their republican spirit; their autonomous ways; their romantic nature. The voice of Colonel Maciá was no longer that cautious, well-tuned, well-controlled whisper of the diplomatic leaders of the Lliga—the league of the conservative home-rulers; it was the romantic, generous, somewhat sentimental voice of the Catalan middle class. He spoke as a Catalan, in Catalan, and putting forward first the claims of Catalonia. But almost in the same breath he spoke as a Spaniard, and called to the "brother peoples of Spain" to create a federation of all Iberians; and eventually of the whole world for universal peace.

His words were drowned in the enthusiastic cheers of the crowd; and a second wave of enthusiasm thrilled the capital of the new Catalan state when the news reached it of the proclamation of the Republic in Madrid. The Provisional Government in Madrid was nevertheless somewhat concerned at this event. One of their number, Señor Nicolau d'Olwer, a classical scholar, represented in their midst all that Colonel Maciá and his friends stood for. The utmost friendliness and the best spirit prevailed throughout, but the men in Madrid were the trustees of a tradition—which, through Hispano-Roman and Visigothic times, Austrian and Bourbon dynasties, had endeavored to perform the historical function of keeping Spain one. These men knew that they could go a long way in devolving home-rule powers on the Catalan government; but that, if they were to accept a self-born Catalan republic, freely federated to other peoples of Spain who were not organized into local states, whose organization into local states was indeed impossible, they would plunge the nation into a war of secession. The Provisional Government could not play at the same time the parts of Washington and of Lincoln, drive out the king and fight for union.

They had, moreover, a pledged word on their side. The Pact of San Sebastián did not bind them to more than a home-rule regime to be discussed and voted by the Constituent Assembly of the Spanish Republic. The matter was settled by negotiation. The *Estat Catalá* became the *Generalitat,* an old Catalan word rich in historical associations, meaning "Commonwealth"; and a constitutional procedure fair to both sides was agreed upon. The Constitution allowed for local statutes to be adopted by the several regions within the general Constitution of the Spanish State, whereby the local governments would hold powers specifically granted them by the Spanish State. On August 2, 1931, Catalonia voted on its Statute, which was approved by a nearly unanimous vote. It was discussed by the Constitutional Cortes during the summer of 1932 and finally passed, though with a number of amendments which the Catalans, masters of bargaining, took with some disappointment but with a good grace. The sore points were language, education and police. The difficulties in the situation have not always been correctly appreciated. Briefly put, the Catalans were less alive then the rest of the Spaniards to the necessity of maintaining the Castilian language as an actual living force throughout the whole nation, for two reasons at least: political unity and expediency. Thus, the Statute made Catalan the official language of the Generalitat, Castilian to be used by the Generalitat in its relations with the government of the Republic. The Cortes obtained that the Generalitat should be officially bilingual, which was the obvious solution if one bears in mind the high percentage of non-Catalan-speaking Spaniards who live in Catalonia. In education, the Generalitat sought a kind of monopoly; the Republic, a condominium, or a free field for both the Republican and the Catalan governments. Here, however, the Republic agreed to grant a privileged position to the Generalitat, even though less than the Catalans wanted. Thus, for instance, the Republic would have preferred to set up in Barcelona a Catalan-speaking university under the Generalitat and a Castilian-speaking university under the Republic, but the Catalans objected to this proposal, and in the end the University of Barcelona became practically a Catalan-controlled institution, though supported by both governments.

The Catalan Statute aroused considerable opposition in Spain.

Some of it was sincere. Most of it was probably due to a camouflaged anti-Republican feeling which found a convenient outlet in this issue. This conflict gave Azaña one of his great opportunities for leadership. He was always at his best as a parliamentary debater. Without his powerful advocacy the Catalan Statute might have been lost. He secured its triumph, and on September 9, 1931, the Cortes having ratified the Statute by 314 votes to 24, Catalonia was at last able to enter on her own career as an autonomous state. On September 25, 1931, Azaña in person went to Barcelona to deliver their new Statute to the Catalans. He addressed the crowd, who gave him a well-deserved ovation. *"Ahora sois de la República,"* he said three times, in a ringing voice which asserted yet asked as well. And three times the enthusiastic crowd gave him back a sonorous *"Sí."*

The Basque Question

An early, hastily improvised imitation of the proclamation of the Catalan State made in Barcelona on April 14, 1931, had been staged by a few Basque nationalists in Guernica, close to the time-honored oak of that historical place, on April 17. It was not a success. But, under the stimulus of the Catalans in whose wake the Basques have traveled ever since Sabino Arana Goiri transplanted the seeds of nationalism[1] from Barcelona to Biscayan soil, the Basques went on with their plans for a Statute. The conference of Estella, an old Carlist town, gathered Basques and Navarrese of all colors except Socialists and leftist Republicans. There were Carlists, Monarchists and Nationalists as well as Conservative Republicans; but no men of the Left. The fact was that the movement was still smarting under the resentment caused in its ranks by the anti-clerical attitude of the Republic, which had made the Basque Nationalist members of Parliament withdraw as a body from the Constituent Assembly (again in typical Spanish style). The celebrations announced to commemorate the anniversary of the Pact of San Sebastián (August 17)

[1] See Book I, chapter 18.

had been cancelled owing to this state of unrest. Twelve newspapers had been suspended in the Basque provinces for publishing incitements to civil war in the interests of religion (August
27, 1931). On September 17, 1931, Basque Republicans and
Basque Nationalists came to blows. There were one dead and
two wounded. The police closed the headquarters of the *Juventud
Vasca* (Basque Youth, a nationalist organization), and later the
government closed all the Basque Nationalist centers, not because of their advocacy of home rule, which was the official
policy of the Republic, but because of their anti-Republican
attitude. This led to further disorders in Bilbao. In this atmosphere, the drafting of the Statute was laborious, owing mainly
to the religious question; realizing that, otherwise, the Statute
would have no chance whatever of being ratified by the Constituent Assembly, the draftsmen agreed to leave religious matters
to the central government, despite strong opposition on the part
of many Guipúzcoan municipal councils, which desired a separate concordat with Rome; when the draft was put to the vote
in Pamplona (June 1932) the Navarrese turned it down by
123 to 109; the Three Provinces, however—Alava, Biscay,
Guipúzcoa—accepted it by 245 to 14. Thus approved, though
limited to the Three Provinces, the Draft Statute of Basque
Home Rule was confirmed by plebiscite in Guipúzcoa, Biscay
and Alava by a vote of 87, 89 and 50 per cent respectively.
The lukewarm attitude of Alava, the opposition of Navarra
and pressure of other work held up its progress in the Constituent Assembly.

The Gallegan Question

The most important party in Galicia, to judge by the number
of its members in the Assembly, was the ORGA (*Organización
Regional Gallega Autónoma*) whose leader was Don Santiago
Casares Quiroga, the scion of an old Republican family of La
Coruña. It was a home-rule party. It organized the drafting and
the voting of a local Statute in the now approved fashion, amidst

but lukewarm interest, for the Gallegan is subtle and practical and less addicted to theoretical and constitutional issues than either Basque or Catalan. Still, a draft was ready and duly voted upon by December 1932. But no one was in a special hurry to press it through in Parliament. And so it waited patiently for better days.

The Religious Question

It is a now well-established fact that the trouble with the Catholic Church in Spain was its intolerance rather than its power. Politically the Church was a force. It could intrigue in palace and ministries, and up to a point influence public opinion. But it had all but abandoned its spiritual and cultural field. Had the Republic left it alone, the mere creative work of the new regime in the field of letters, arts and sciences would have more than sufficed to reduce the Church to political impotence, for the Church had a tendency to fall owing to its own weight.

This was not, however, the policy of the passionate, new rulers. They were intent on a frontal attack. Some of the measures which they introduced were indeed inevitable. The divorce law, for instance, was demanded by the spirit of the times, and so much overdue that there was a long line of ill-assorted couples waiting for the day when the courts would at last be empowered to grant them their longed-for liberty. Even here, the Republic went from one extreme to the other, and made the country pass from a marriage which only death could dissolve to one which the two conjoints might dissolve by mutual consent after a paltry two years of conjugal experience. The Church was of course indignant. It should be added that, at the time, a brisk business in dissolution of marriages had been set up by the Diocese of Paris, to which—the Church being universal—Spanish couples with French francs to spare could apply. Still, these are temporal infirmities which a spiritual power can outlive with dignity; and the fact remains that even in this matter of divorce, in which the Republic stood on strong ground, it might have acted with more moderation.

In January 1932, the Order of the Jesuits was dissolved and its property confiscated by the State. This measure was popular but gave rise to a curious situation. Article 26, par. 4, of the Constitution had forbidden educational activities to religious orders. The Jesuits had therefore to close their establishments. On the dissolution of the order they ceased to be Jesuits and could carry on teaching. This was not to be the last case of legislative incoherence in the history of the Republic.

As prescribed by this same Article 26 (one of the gravediggers of the Republic) the "special law providing for the wiping out of the budget for the clergy within a maximum delay of two years" was passed and this budget was reduced by one-third in 1932 and abolished in 1933. It amounted to about 35 million pesetas, or around $4,000,000. The policy here should have been clear: to increase the budget, instead of abolishing it, so as to raise the miserable standard of living of the village priest, whom it would have been easy to win over to the Republic; and to re-incorporate the education of priests into the universities, from which it had been unfortunately severed by the 1868 revolutionists.[2]

This spirit of petty, almost vindictive anti-clericalism reached its climax in a matter as theoretical and unimportant as that of burials. The Church had always kept a close watch on burials. Efforts—not always dignified—were often made to bury with religious rites persons of note who had left clear instructions to the contrary. In every town, the *Cementerio Civil* was set aside for the obdurate who refused to pass the Gates in the prescribed style. Then came the Republic, and some of us thought that this tug of war would at least respect the bones of the dead. But the bigots and priests of the Holy Anti-clerical Church were watching, and when so many things, and so urgent, were still undone, the new rulers of Spain found time to decree that all cemeteries should be secularized, while religious burial was

[2] See Castillejo: *War of Ideas in Spain*, London, 1937, p. 87.

prohibited unless provided for in the will of the deceased—
which, in a country in which nine out of ten persons die without
troubling to put on paper their last decisions, was little short
of oppressive.

The fact was and is that, while atheism is rapidly spreading
in the working classes, more rapidly among the men than among
the women, the peasant and middle classes are deeply Catholic.
This widely diffused and not very militant Catholic opinion
would have tolerated, indeed welcomed, the anti-clerical measures which were needed in order to reduce the Church to its
true function within the state. But the petty and vindictive aspects
evinced by the anti-clerical policy of the Republic gave the
core of militant, reactionary Catholics the opportunity they were
looking for to appeal to a wider circle than their own.

Two fighting organizations appeared in the political arena
toward the summer of 1932: *Acción Católica,* a Union of Catholics professing to abstain from politics and to be exclusively
concerned with the defense of the Church; and *Acción Popular,*
its avowedly political counterpart. In June 1933, the law on
religious orders was promulgated. It confiscated their property,
and prohibited them all industrial, commercial and educational
activities. The Pope issued an encyclical letter condemning this
law, and the bishops of Spain a pastoral forbidding their faithful
to send their children to the state schools.

The Military Question

Its frequent interventions in the political life of the country
during the nineteenth century had made of the Spanish Army—
by which is generally meant the body of its officers—a kind of
political party. It had its press, one or two dailies, its members
of Parliament—some senators and deputies who happened to be
officers and openly spoke as representatives of the Army—and
its minister, for with trifling exceptions the war secretary was a
general and considered himself as the spokesman of the Army.
Though the remnants of the Spanish Empire had gone, the

Army could still count on a number of plums. The high commissioner in Morocco was nearly always a general; decorative and comfortable sinecures such as the Directorates General of the *Guardia Civil,* the *Carabineros* (Frontier Customs Guards), and even the Corps of Invalided Soldiers, were reserved for generals, and finally at the head of the eight military regions there were eight captains general who enjoyed a not very strenuous life full of honors and of political influence. The Army, moreover, had secured for itself in the Law of Jurisdictions an exorbitant privilege. It sat in judgment over all those who attacked the fatherland or its fundamental institutions, which in practice amounted to all those who attacked the Army. It was, in fact, a state within the state, rather touchy and apt to be ill-tempered.

During his years as a Republican conspirator, Azaña had made a special study of military matters, and he came to power ready to put order into what, despite appearances, was the most anarchical administration of the state. He took the War Office, and kept it even when he had to take the premiership.

He began by abolishing the Law of Jurisdictions, whereby military courts had invaded the sphere of strictly civil life. He then abolished the Supreme Council of War and the Navy, a supreme court for dealing with military cases, entirely composed of military and naval men, thus bringing military and naval citizens within the jurisdiction of the ordinary courts. To meet objections based on technical grounds, he set up a special chamber in the Supreme Court, provided with military advisers for dealing with military cases. He abolished the eight captains general and in fact all ranks above that of division general. He gave all officers the choice of swearing allegiance to the Republic or resigning and, more generous than wise, decreed that those who chose to resign would receive full pay. And finally, he actively prepared for the technical and thorough training and equipment as an efficient weapon of defense of what had previously been mostly inefficient and idle in this respect, and only too active as a political force.

Azaña was right in his aims. But a high percentage of officers had chosen to retire on full pay. Some of them went over to

civilian professions or business, underselling their rivals owing
to the material advantages provided by their pensions. Others,
the majority of them, made use of the leisure paid them by the
Republic to conspire against it. Gradually the ranks of disgruntled and discontented officers grew thicker in a union for
conspiracy such as had developed in the Spanish Army during
the nineteenth century, more often than not at the instigation
of impatient politicians, now of the Right, now of the Left. The
Republic had made another enemy—the one whose case was
the least justified of all, yet perhaps the most dangerous.

The Land Question

The land question was only acute in a wide southern and
southwestern area, i.e. in Andalusia and Estremadura. In these
regions there were but few landlords, owning huge estates, surrounded by a landless proletariat whose very subsistence depended on the day-to-day caprice of the landlord stewards.

This was the chief evil which the Republic set about to cure
with its agrarian reform. The Agrarian Law was studied through
the summer of 1932 and passed in September of that year. A
whole year was provided for a study of the lands and a census
of the workers. This study as well as the actual carrying out of
the law was entrusted to an Institute of Agrarian Reform, endowed with fifty million pesetas a year. The law was to apply
to fourteen provinces—i.e. the eight provinces of Andalusia,
the two provinces of Estremadura, three Castilian provinces
(Ciudad Real, Toledo, Salamanca), and Albacete (which belongs
to the kingdom of Murcia)—but large estates would be similarly
expropriated even if located elsewhere. Feudal estates would be
taken over without compensation; other lands would be paid
for by capitalizing the farm income shown on the tax registers.
This was a clever stroke, since tax evasion was considerable.
The lands thus secured would remain the property of the state,
which would distribute it either to independent farmers or to
collective farming associations. Unable to make up its mind

between individual and collective farming, the Assembly passed on the problem to the local municipalities, which it empowered to decide the problem on a majority vote. The Institute was to foster cooperative societies for the supply of food, fertilizers and machinery as well as credit. A number of feudal payments which still lingered here and there, notably in Galicia, were abolished.

This reform was on the whole well-meant and statesmanlike, with the exception of one or two articles bearing signs of a vindictive and confiscatory character. It failed, however, because of the slow pace at which it was undertaken, owing in part to the difficulties of the problem itself, in part to the initial defect of the Spanish state, to which Azaña, though a civil servant by profession, paid no attention—the inefficiency of the Civil Service. In this particular case, Azaña himself gave a deplorable example, appointing as general secretary of the all-important Agrarian Institute a lighthearted and irresponsible journalist with no experience whatever in either land or administrative questions.

The Labor Question

The Second Republic was born under a political constellation far more deeply influenced by the working classes than the first. This difference was to be impressed into its Constitution not directly by the working classes themselves but through a number of Socialist intellectuals and of intellectualized labor leaders. These labor prophets drafted and made the Assembly vote their masterpice, Article 46 of the Constitution, which reads as follows:

> Work, in its several forms, is a social duty and will enjoy the protection of the law.
>
> The Republic will guarantee to every worker the necessary conditions for a dignified existence. Its social legislation will regulate: cases of sickness, accident, unemployment, old age, infirmity and life insurance; the labor of women and children, and in particular, the protection of motherhood; the working day and minimum

and family wages; yearly paid vacations; the conditions of Spanish workers abroad; cooperative institutions; the economic-juridical relations among the several factors which make up production; the participation of the workers in the management, administration and profits of businesses, and all that concerns the welfare of the workers.

This text clearly shows that the doctrinaires and the demagogues were determined to put all their wares in the window from the first day of the fair. No attempt was made to tackle the problem of Spain's economy as an organic whole, in order to bring it back gradually to a normal, healthy life, in tune with the life of her neighbors. Yet, without such a general plan in mind, the measures ambitiously described in Article 46 were doomed to remain as standards of failure rather than as goals for success. As it happened, the labor policy of the Republic was most effective and so to speak tangible in two directions, one of which dated from the dictatorship while the other one hailed back to the Middle Ages. The first was the Law of Mixed Juries, whereby juries of six workers and six employers in each kind of industry were empowered to decide all disputes arising between capital and labor. These mixed juries differed in little but detail from the *Comités Paritarios* set up under Primo de Rivera. But though the letter was the same, the music was different. And in this case, the music was dictated by the president of each particular jury. When in agreement, the twelve jurymen elected the president; but this was rare. When the twelve jurymen could not agree, the president was appointed by the Ministry of Labor. This, given the circumstances, was bound to lead to a kind of social warfare, disguised as justice.

The other measure, introduced by Largo Caballero as Minister of Labor, went much further back than the dictatorship for its inspiration: it went to the Middle Ages. The Law of Municipal Boundaries *(Ley de Términos Municipales)* forbade the importation of workers from one municipality into another until every one of the local workers of the same trade had been employed. This law was the all too natural consequence of the vexations, the callous practices, the infamies even, to which the existence of a poverty-stricken land proletariat had given rise, notably in the South and Southwest. But an explanation is not a defense.

In many other ways, however, Señor Largo Caballero's leadership of the Ministry of Labor was creative and statesmanlike. The Law of Labor Contracts was a welcome, stabilizing factor in industry, for it provided the workers with a legal basis for enforcing collective bargaining. The government took over all labor exchanges. A law regulated labor associations, under the supervision of the Ministry of Labor, represented in every province by a labor delegate. An unemployment insurance fund was established. The Accident Insurance Law was amended so as to replace the old lump sum by a kind of accident and age insurance-benefit varying from 9 to 75 per cent of the wages, and applied also to land laborers; maternity insurance was made compulsory; and an ambitious program of public works was set in motion to keep down unemployment.

This spirited policy was the more necessary for reasons which may be plainly described as competitive. The Socialists were in office. The Syndicalists watched. It was necessary to prove to the Spanish working classes that the Socialists were right; that the political-democratic way was the way to victory. The triumph of the Republic had stimulated the old feud between the two branches of labor. This feud was to provoke numerous violent incidents which were to make particularly rough and dangerous the first two years of the Republic.

Education

The Republic took up educational matters with the utmost enthusiasm, and resolved to spend freely in this department. The trouble, however, was that in such matters money is not enough and time is essential. The problem in itself had, moreover, been rendered even more difficult by the anti-clerical policy of the Constituent Assembly whereby the confessional schools were closed, thus increasing the liabilities of the Ministry of Education by anything between 350,000 and 700,000 children. Plans were ambitious. The first Minister of Education of the Republic, Don Marcelino Domingo, a Catalan teacher, created 7000 schools on paper, about 3000 in fact. The second, Don Fernando de los Ríos, a nephew of Giner de los Ríos, raised this number to 10,000. Salaries were increased. Pedagogic missions were organized to convey the joys of knowledge and the arts to the out-of-the-way communities which abound in mountainous Spain. They were composed of small bands of teachers and students traveling with enough material to give their audiences plays, films, music, picture-reproductions and books. This truly creative experiment was a great success, mostly because it was confined within the limits of its manpower possibilities. A number of secondary schools were also developed. But here, as in the sudden expansion of primary schools, the Republic was heavily handicapped by the very depth of the evil itself. Spain developed in the twentieth century (and even in the nineteenth) under the Monarchy (and even under the Primo de Rivera dictatorship) some of the most interesting educational institutions in Europe. But this could only be done in a small and slow way, at the pace of the organic growth of men and institutions. The Republic, spurred by the competition of the Church, which it wished to oust from the educational field, made the mistake of relying upon figures. Schools as buildings were often shockingly bad; and a building policy, such as was adopted by the Republic, was a welcome change. But the tendency to assume that a school-building was a school spread with disastrous results. When in the spring of 1934 the author of this book was allowed to occupy the Ministry of Education for a period of five weeks, he discovered that there were in Spain about 10,500 schoolmasters without a school, and about 10,500 schools without a schoolmaster. In one word, the schoolmaster class, like every other class of public servants in Spain, carried an overwhelming deadweight of time-servers and salary-hunters. The problem therefore was less how to educate the children than how to educate the educators.

Political Events

These two years were beset with dangers arising from a number of quarters: the Right; the Left; the government; Parliament; the president; or in one word, *all* the "quarters" available.

In January 1932 the miners of Figols, in Catalonia, revolted against the state and proclaimed libertarian Communism, to celebrate which they declared a general strike in the busy valley of the Llobregat River. "What does 'to proclaim libertarian Communism' mean?" asks the reader. Exactly. What does that mean? And here your Anglo-Saxon journalist or "pink" intellectual will wax eloquent about the illiteracy and lack of education and whatnot of the Spanish working classes, ignorant himself of the fact that these libertarians who, in a Quixote-like spirit, were trying to drive into immediate reality their cherished dreams can and often do read books, but find them less interesting than the ideas they can spin for themselves out of their fertile brains. They live their ideas in a curious, earnest, vigorous, consistent, religious way; never marry in either Church or registry office, give their children symbolic names like *Libertad,* and are as certain of bringing about peace and prosperity to the world once the state has been abolished as a mystic nun is of eternal bliss. "More education!" will be argued. It takes a lot to educate faith out of an illuminated man.

On May 1, 1933, toward 9 A.M., I arrived in Madrid. The station-yard was deserted and the passengers stood at the curb nonplused and helpless, with their bags at their feet. No taxis. No buses. No trolleys. One single car, with two gold-braided attendants, obviously the official Foreign Office car, awaiting me. On the window pane, a label: "Official and Urgent Business." "What is the matter?" I asked. And the driver answered: "Labor Day." Not a single vehicle was to be seen in the whole town.

I lunched next day at the French Embassy, where I met several Socialist members of the government, notably Don Indalecio Prieto. I had gathered some information in the interval. "Prieto," I said, "we are heading straight for civil war." The minister looked up. "Yes. Do you remember in the old mon-

archical days, how irritated we all were with the tyrannical way
in which the Church paralyzed the city on Good Friday?
Well, that was nothing. Trolleys could circulate, and buses, and
the underground railway. But on May first, the workers have
vexatiously and tyrannically tabooed all public transport, including taxis, which is pretty stiff for a city of one million people,
but might pass; all private cars driven by paid drivers, which is
stiffer still, but, let it pass; and finally all private cars driven by
owner-drivers, which is downright tyranny. This country will
never stand it. And you, the government, should have put your
foot down."

So much for the spirit with which the Left understood power.
"But what about the Right?" it will be asked. Why ask? The
Right was bound to be moved by the same spirit; first because
it was the Right and that spirit of command and of repression
is what it incarnates; and then because, being as Spanish as the
Left, it obviously had to yield to the same temptation to mistake
power for arbitrary caprice. We must therefore take for granted
that the only reason why the Right did not make an oppressive
use of power at this stage is because it had no power to make
any use of—good or bad. But the point is that the Left, which
ought to have known better, as this symbolic detail shows, was
unable to use power with statesmanship and moderation.

On August 10, 1932, a *Putsch* skillfully organized by some
retired Army officers was launched in combination with a military revolt in Seville. The two immediate aims of the rebels in
Madrid were the General Post Office first, then the War Office,
opposite. There was some street fighting, but the *Putsch* was
finally beaten off within the day. The rising in Seville had as its
leader General Sanjurjo, the very man who as head of the Civil
Guard had declared for the Republic on April 14, 1931, thus
sparing Spain a civil war. He had been restive, in truth like
many Spaniards more staunch Republicans than he could be
expected to be; but at the first attempt to use this general's name
to agitate public opinion, Azaña had removed him from his command, and, not without irony, given him the command of the
Customs Guards. He led an attack on Seville which degenerated

into a tripartite fight; for, while the government fought the military rebels, the Syndicalists let loose on the town their pent-up revolutionary energies. Sanjurjo was beaten, fled, and was caught on his way to the sea. Azaña weathered this crisis with dignity and calm. Sanjurjo was sentenced to death by the Supreme Court; but Azaña sided with a sector of public opinion (probably the most numerous though the least vociferous) and had him reprieved. He was, however, adamant as to the treatment the rebel general was to receive in jail, and General Sanjurjo had to don the usual prisoner's uniform.

Sanjurjo was a brave soldier, with no brains and no political talent. He was still to be a thorn in the flesh of the Republic. But for the time being the crisis was over, save that a shipload of Monarchists, guilty of the Madrid *Putsch,* was sent in exile to Villa Cisneros, in Spanish West Africa.

The government which had to face these serious difficulties was weakened by internal discussions. Its very birth in December 1931 had marked the beginning of that rift between Lerroux and Azaña which was to be fatal for the Republic. Lerroux had insisted on a reduction of the Socialist contingent in the government as a condition for accepting a share in it. Azaña refused. This gave Lerroux his opportunity to set his party up as the Parliamentary Opposition and heir presumptive to the coalition in power. It led also to a feud between Socialists and Radicals which made the task of both Government and Parliament singularly difficult.

On July 17, 1932, about a month before Sanjurjo's revolt, the Socialist Party issued a manifesto in which they foreshadowed the policy which was to lead them to the disaster of 1934. They accused the Radical Party of dictatorial designs and announced that they would oppose such attempts "by the most violent means." "The revolutionary movement initiated with the downfall of the Monarchy is not over yet," they tactfully went on to say. Meanwhile the government indefinitely suspended the newspapers *A.B.C., El Debate* and *Informaciones* (the first of which remained gagged for one hundred and twelve days) and, as if further to increase the area of its enemies, it organized an ill-advised purge of the diplomatic service which, on the whole, had behaved with impartial patriotism and served the Republic to the best of its ability. Parliament, as undisciplined as the rest, wasted its time in passionate debates, wholly unregulated, on the mistaken assumption that discipline in the Cortes was tantamount to tyranny; so it debated on the antediluvian responsibilities of King Alfonso or of Primo de Rivera, while burning problems waited outside. To crown it all, the Extreme Left, always ready to betray the Left, entered the lists at the beginning of 1933. A ferment of revolution and violence was abroad, mainly in the Barcelona-Valencia-Murcia-Seville arc, that eastern and southeastern sector in which the old Iberian anarchism had been spurred to action by Bakhunin and Sorel. Libertarian Communism proclaimed, attacks on the Civil Guard, seizure of lands and houses, and strikes kept going for the sake of social war in the manner recommended by Sorel in his *Réflexions Sur La Violence* were frequent features in these outbreaks, which kept the government and the nation on the alert and prevented Parliament from calming down and getting to business. The movement reached its climax on January 11, 1933, when an exceptionally spirited outbreak flared up in the village of Casas Viejas, on the edge of an estate of the Duke of Medinaceli that was on the point of being distributed to the peasants. The peasants, however, had not initiated and did not lead the rising, which was under Anarcho-Syndicalist inspiration, and well armed with revolvers and explosives. The small Guardia Civil garrison was besieged; the sergeant in command refused to surrender. Three of his comrades fell mortally wounded. But, after reinforcements had reached him, the rebellion was quenched—all but a house in which an old anarchist, Seisdedos, with his daughter Libertaria and six other militants, fought undaunted till the end. Captain Rojas, of the Storm Troops, who had taken command, bombed and set fire to the house.

There was an outcry in the country, and the government was hotly accused of cruel and inhuman ways, and of "murdering the people." Azaña and his home secretary Casares Quiroga were the butt of the indignation—of whom? There is the rub.

Of course, the Anarcho-Syndicalists were hot in their denunciations of a government which had met force by force. But the loudest cries came from the Right; and from the *A.B.C.,* the paper of the Monarchists, to the Radicals of Lerroux (not excluding Señor Martínez Barrio, who was later to cross over from Center Right to Center Left), all the Right was aflame against Azaña's government.

As usual in political matters, there was a kernel of fact to justify some dissatisfaction over the incident. Captain Rojas was perhaps too spirited in attack and too callous after his victory; and the home secretary might perhaps have blended some caution and patience with the energy which he instilled into his instructions. But the hard fact was that the Right, the so-called party of law and order, made party politics of the incident and saw in it a good opportunity to unchain on Azaña the passions which his own dry, hard policy had aroused in many a breast. Azaña won the vote in the Parliamentary debate (though only by a majority of forty-three), but had to consent to a Commission of Inquiry, which undoubtedly weakened his standing in Parliament and in the nation.

The results of the election of April 23 were expected by many as an indication of this fact. It was a limited and peculiar election to elect municipal councilors in the place of the 29,804 who in several parts of Spain had taken office in 1931 under Article 29 of the old electoral law whereby an unopposed candidate was *ipso facto* declared elected. The result was hailed everywhere as a government defeat. It was of course nothing of the kind. In 1931 the figures had been roughly 50 per cent Left and 50 per cent Monarchist. In 1933, they were if anything more favorable to the Left; and in any case the Monarchist vote had been considerably reduced, a clear victory for the government in office, which the Republicans of the Right, and particularly the Radical Party, should have generously acknowledged, since they were those who benefited most from it. Azaña met the demand that he should resign with a less able—though possibly a truer—argument: the districts were rotten boroughs. (He actually took this leaf out of the book of English parliamentary history.) He therefore announced that he would remain in office till he had completed his task—the passing of a number of laws to supplement the Constitution. Now, to the average non-Spaniard, this sounds pretty innocent. And to the average Spaniard too. I confess I saw nothing sinful at the time in this desire of a well-meaning, supremely intelligent, and, within the weaknesses of human nature, competent statesman, to complete his creative task before surrendering the seals of office. But your Spanish politician is no average Spaniard, and when Azaña made his famous declaration everyone shook his head either with gloom or with glee, according to the way the light fell on his face.

The light came from the presidential palace. For though it is easy to kill the form of things, their essence is of a tougher nature; and though the king had gone, the habit of turning to the palace in order to get rid of a government had remained deeply rooted in Spanish political life. The uncrowned King of the Spanish Republic, Don Niceto Alcalá Zamora, born and bred under monarchical ways, was no less jealous of his prerogative than King Alfonso had been; and this prerogative consisted of dismissing Cabinets on equal terms with the Cortes. In short, a Cabinet had to carry on not on one but on two wheels—Parliament and the crown—I mean, the president. And when Azaña said "I shall carry on" merely because he had a majority in Parliament, he sealed his fate at the palace. The Opposition led by Lerroux adopted obstruction as a protest, and the Law of Confessions and Congregations was held up for months. There are reasons for thinking that the signal to begin obstruction came from the presidential palace.

The distracted government of a country in which so many difficult problems awaited solution had therefore to face an inimical president, an opposition in open parliamentary civil war, and an uninterrupted string of strikes, all of a revolutionary and political nature, which paralyzed creative life and threw into bloody turmoil city after city: Barcelona, Zaragoza, Oviedo, Coruña, Seville. The sparks of civil war fired the University, where reactionary students and the FUE (*Federación Universi-*

taria de Estudiantes) of Left tendency came to grips. On May 17, 1933, the Law of Confessions and Congregations was voted by 278 to 50 and sent to the palace for signature. Señor Alcalá Zamora kept it the entire fifteen days which the Constitution allowed him—a unique action on his part—during which time the bishops issued a pastoral condemning it—also a unique case of rather undignified moral pressure. Señor Alcalá Zamora signed the law on the last day, June 2. And on June 9 he dismissed the government—just as King Alfonso would have done.

He tried other men, but of course had to take back Azaña. During this second term of office, Azaña passed the law setting up the Tribunal of Constitutional Guarantees, and the Law of Public Order to replace the unpopular Law for the Defense of the Republic. Strikes and local risings continued unabated. The opposition was tired of what Lerroux had picturesquely described as their march through the desert—a desert with none of those famous plum trees which give forth the plums of office —and the same Lerroux threatened obstruction again. Azaña resigned (September 13, 1933). After a brief ministerial existence, Lerroux resigned in the face of a hostile House (October 3, 1933). His lieutenant, Señor Martínez Barrio, took office to organize a general election.

CHAPTER 5

THE SECOND ROUND—RIGHT

The forces of the Right, under the stimulus which the mistakes
of the Left had given them during two years, had grown and
united under the leadership of a young Roman Catholic professor, Don José María Gil Robles, who, well provided with
funds, had set up the *Confederación Española de Derechas Au-
tónomas,* known by its initials as CEDA. Its nucleus was the
Acción Popular, a Roman Catholic political organization.

When the country was consulted (November 19 and December
3, 1933) the choice before it was somewhat bewildering, for
there were no less than nineteen parties in the lists, not to speak
of the powerful Anarcho-Syndicalist Confederation, too contemptuous of politics to stand as such, though its members
usually voted, if they voted at all, for the parties of the Left.
These nineteen parties were grouped for electoral purposes into
three alliances, Right, Center and Left, even though a serious
rift was beginning to appear in the Left owing to the revolu-

421

tionary impulsion which Largo Caballero was driving into the Socialist Party. Two new factors came further to complicate this general election: for the first time women voted in Spain, adding six million votes to the electorate. The electoral law voted by Azaña's party presented a number of odd features which made it an even darker horse than the feminine vote. Thus, it favored big parties well supplied with money by providing for very large constituencies which no single man could cover. This meant that the only parties which could fight on equal terms were the Conservatives, backed by capitalist money, and the Socialists, backed by trade-union funds; while the moderate liberals could not vie with either; the law, moreover, insured a few seats to the minority by stipulating that the citizen should vote for no more than four candidates for every five seats, but it granted a premium on the party which obtained a relative majority of votes, which made it theoretically possible for a party to win the election although its total number of votes in the country was smaller than those of its adversary. This theoretical possibility became an actual fact in the two general elections held under the law, in 1933 and in 1936. The Anarcho-Syndicalists, moreover, were divided: a majority had advised abstention, while a powerful minority had left their followers free to vote as they pleased, which of course meant voting for the Left. Finally, there was that disastrous decision of the Constituent Assembly: to do without a Senate.

The result was the rout of the Left and a success of the Right which not even its most sanguine adherents had expected. The Right returned 207 members, the Center 167 and the Left 99. The composition of each of these figures was no less instructive than its total. The Right comprised 62 *Acción Popular,* i.e. reactionary Catholics; 86 Agrarians representing the landed interests not already covered by the Catholics; 14 Basque Nationalists; 43 Navarrese and other Traditionalists along with some Alfonsine Monarchists; finally 2 Independents.

The Center included 104 Radicals (Señor Lerroux thus becoming the head of the biggest single party in the new House, though Señor Gil Robles was the head of the biggest coalition);

18 Conservatives, i.e., open-minded Catholics; 25 *Lliga Regionalista* or Conservative Catalan Home Rulers; 9 Liberal Democrats; 3 Progressivists; and 8 Independents. The Left consisted of 2 Federalists; 19 Esquerra (Catalan Left); 6 O.R.G.A. (Gallegan Left); 5 Radical Socialists (split into two groups of 1 and 4 respectively, separated by the subtlest of differences); 5 *Acción Republicana;* 3 Catalan Socialists; 58 Socialists; and 1 Communist.

A number of facts leap to the eye and in particular the wiping out of the two chief non-Socialist parties of Azaña's Parliament as well as the halving of the Socialist Party itself. If we compare the figures of the Left coalition in the first and in the second Parliament, the parallel is striking:

Parties	1931	1933
Socialists	116	59
Radical Socialists	60	5
Acción Republicana (Azaña)	30	5
O.R.G.A.	16	6
Esquerra	43	19
Federalists	17	2
Total,	282	96

This result fully confirmed the fears of those who had seen in the first electoral triumph of the Republic a wave of emotion rather than a firm stand of conviction. There were, moreover, many signs to show that the defeat of the Left had been something more than a mere fall in the emotional fever of 1931. For while the coalition which had been governing the country from 1931 to 1933 dropped from 282 to 96, the Radical Party rose from 90 to 104 and the coalition of the Right went up from 60 to 217. The pendulum had swung wildly and there was no Senate to moderate its frantic movements. Moreover, a significant detail, Besteiro, the head of the moderate wing of the Socialist Party, came up to the top of the list, while Largo Caballero, the leader of the revolutionary here-and-now fraction of the party, for the first time in his political life, dropped to thirteenth. The country could not more clearly signify its longing for moderation. In the next general election it was to speak with equal clarity in favor of moderation.

Lerroux became the arbiter of the new House. The Left, restive at Señor Gil Robles's success, was beginning to threaten open rebellion through the energetic and always respected voice of Largo Caballero. The president thereupon called on Lerroux to put together a Cabinet of Center-Right tendencies. For a man who obviously had to lean on the Right, Lerroux was extremely cautious and took on board only one man from the coalition which after all was the biggest by far in the House, an Agrarian whom he balanced, moreover, with a member of the Left, a Gallegan Home-Ruler. He then entered the narrow path which was left him between a powerful and resentful Right which dominated the Cortes and a powerful and resentful Left which its own parliamentary failure had driven to attempt to dominate the street.

The outstanding features of this period were Lerroux's endeavors to absorb the forces of the Right into the Republic and the increase of the power of the president as a consequence of the weakness of the parties in the Cortes. The first aggravated the dangers to which the government was exposed; the second weakened the government and indeed the whole regime, which gradually returned to the practices of King Alfonso's reign, when men and parties took their cue from the palace rather than from Parliament.

The outbreak of strikes and violent disorders which began on December 8, 1933, was not particularly connected with the change of government. It was due to the revolutionary impetus of the Anarcho-Syndicalists, for whom such things were good in themselves. Barcelona saw its street flower booths replaced by machine-gun nests; and disorders broke out in La Coruña, Zaragoza, Huesca, Barbastro, Calatayud and Granada, where convents and churches were attacked and destroyed by fire. The Barcelona-Seville express was derailed by deliberate action. Nineteen passengers were killed.

This state of affairs only served to increase the popularity of Lerroux, an old politician much below Azaña in intellectual distinction and in the way he looked on politics, its rights and obligations for a public man, but much above him in his knowledge of the actual face, muscle and sinews of Spanish politics. Being fully aware of the strength existing in both the Army and the Church, Lerroux set about to reconquer these two forces of state, possibly to buy them back. Yet, with a difference. He had been anti-clerical all his life and the older generation had not forgotten his outspoken, indeed profane, speeches against the Church and even the faith. His wooing of the Church was wholly opportunistic. But for the Army there was always a warm spot in his heart, for in his youth he had been a private and a corporal, and in his old age he still kept the bearing of one who had been trained under the flag. In his youth, moreover, the Army had still a liberal reputation, and the names of the liberal generals, Serrano and Prim, still stayed in the political atmosphere of the country. Lerroux was too much of an old hand not to realize that a general must be shot or befriended—but never hurt. One such general he distinguished above the others. He appointed him head of the General Military College. His name was Don Francisco Franco. He also granted amnesty to General Sanjurjo, though at the cost of a ministerial crisis which lost him his premiership.

These somewhat symbolic gestures calmed the feelings of the Army for the time being. As for the Church, hints and even acts or omissions were soon to justify the view that the new administration did not intend to carry out the anti-clerical measures of the Constitution with any particular eagerness. Such a state of affairs had always been good enough for the Spanish Church, whose policy was not unlike that implied in the gypsy's prayer: "Oh Lord, I do not ask for money, I ask to be put where there is some!" For money substitute "power" and it fits the Church in Spain as to the manner born. The Jesuits went on teaching; Azaña's plans for replacing religious education with newly created lay institutions were shelved; and a law was passed granting the priests two-thirds of their salaries for the year 1934 as a gracious act of the Republic, politically wise in itself perhaps, yet of more than doubtful fidelity to the Constitution. Moreover, in order to negotiate with the Vatican, the somewhat unusual step was taken of appointing the foreign secretary, Señor Pita Romero, Ambassador Extraordinary to the Vatican while allowing him to retain his portfolio.

On the political stage, Señor Lerroux's policy was meant to reconquer Señor Gil Robles and his CEDA. Señor Gil Robles was no easy man to conquer. He knew his strength and was endowed with a truly exceptional gift for political maneuver, and with a remarkable control over manner and speech. Fully a match for the best parliamentarian of the Republic (probably Azaña), he had set his course toward full acceptance of the Republican regime, including the Constitution of 1931 (with which he strongly disagreed) until at any rate he had reformed it; but he progressed on this course with a cautious step, so as to carry with him his slowest followers and also to obtain the maximum yield for every concession. Señor Lerroux, an old hand at this game, let him do with the patience of old age; but the fiery Left were much incensed and hotly accused the young leader of *Acción Popular* of harboring dark designs against the Republic. Time was to vindicate Señor Gil Robles, but meanwhile this fear of anti-Republican action by the CEDA leader, partly genuine in the leaders of the Left, partly cultivated by them to excuse and justify their rash schemes, was to plunge the Republic into the 1934 rebellion, the prelude to the Civil War.

While the politicians kept their eyes on the parliamentary stage, however, graver movements were taking place in the country. The gravest of all was the shift of power in the institutions regulating labor as a result of the change in personnel. The mixed juries took on a different political color and their awards tended to be as unfair to labor as they had been unfair to the employers during the previous period. Simultaneously, the new administration starved the Institute of Agrarian Reform, thus depriving it of its fuel, and put many brakes as well on its activities. Seen from the countryside, in terms of actual lived facts, of bread on the table for the land-worker's family, the change was disastrous. Many, too many, landlords, had forgotten nothing and learned nothing, and their callous and shortsighted policy of old had been sharpened by a tooth of vindictiveness for insults and injuries received while the Left had ruled—not very wisely perhaps. The land-worker saw his wages drop again to famine levels, the security of his employment disappear, his hope of land vanish. These facts, thousands and millions of them hidden away in villages, dales and hills of the center, south and southeast of Spain, were some of the most potent seeds of the Civil War which two years later was to tear asunder the vitals of the country.

While this ferment worked its way into the countryside, the towns were flooded with literature on Russia. The Comintern need not be dragged in to explain this fact. The Russian revolution had appealed to the working classes and to the intellectuals in Spain at least as much as in any other land. It set ablaze the messianic imagination of the Spaniard and raised such a curiosity over Russian affairs in the nation that any book about Russia, good or bad, for or against, was sure of a good sale. The Communist Party, till then a negligible quantity in Spain, began to grow and would almost certainly have achieved its most dramatic triumph in Spain but for the Moscow trials and the growing feeling that there was too much Czardom in Stalindom and too much Czarist secret police in the GPU. Nevertheless, Communism appealed to the young because of its "here and now."

The leaders of the Socialist Party were not all of a mettle to withstand the fears for their own position which this situation aroused in them. The oldest, most trusted leader of Spanish Socialist labor, Don Francisco Largo Caballero, lost his head and rapidly evolved toward a rebellious attitude in his desire to outdo the Communists. As a political mast to which to nail his red flag he took the pro-Right policy of Lerroux, and he announced that if Señor Gil Robles or his followers were allowed in the Cabinet, the people, i.e. he and his friends, would rise in arms.

What arms? Spain was rapidly learning the disastrous lesson taught Europe by Mussolini in the arts of violence as weapons of internal politics. These arts were by no means unknown in Spain, for Barcelona had already a long experience of both reactionary *Requetés* and radical *Jóvenes Bárbaros*. All they had to learn from the Duce was the use of the shirt. A son of Primo de Rivera, José Antonio, was leader of Falange Española, a Fascist organization. He was a brave, intelligent and idealistic young man, utterly disqualified for dictatorship by an irrepressible sense of humor, but he held that Communism was inevitable and that therefore it was best to travel toward it by way of an authoritarian system such as Fascism. This view suffices to show that José Antonio (as he is nowadays styled), unlike the immense majority of his followers, was no fool, since Fascism has been shown to possess as strong a tendency toward Communism in economics as Communism to Fascism in politics. At any rate in Spain, both Fascism and Communism went in for shirts. And, of course, Largo Caballero's Socialist Youths displayed their shirts also.

The two poles of the coming Civil War were thus raising each other's pitch, heat, electricity. The wholesale murder of Socialists organized by Dollfuss in Vienna (February 12, 1934) had moved the Spanish Socialists to a combative mood. Further, Largo Caballero did not conceal his intention to lead his people against the Republic, which in his view had betrayed them. The government felt the danger so imminent that it was necessary for the premier officially to deny that he had the intention of declaring the Socialists an illegal party. Señor Gil Robles had visited Vienna in the summer and organized a muster of his followers in the Nazi style in the Escorial. In Barcelona, where Lluis Companys, a lawyer with Anarcho-Syndicalist connections, had succeeded Maciá as President of the Generalitat, Doctor Dencás, his Councilor for Home Affairs, was organizing the Escamots, a colored-shirt corps which it was difficult to distinguish from a Fascist organization. The whole country was rapidly moving toward civil war.

In such a situation, courageous and magnanimous measures were required. Unfortunately, President Alcalá Zamora was a shortsighted lawyer and no more. Instead of building up a strong

Cabinet, he yielded to his tendency to surround himself with yes-men, and therefore with men without moral authority. It is easy to understand that he should have hesitated to call on Señor Gil Robles, and this much must be said for him, that the parties of the Left were singularly ungrateful to him considering the bias (for so it must be described in strict democratic justice) with which he kept at bay the leader of the strongest party in the House merely because this leader was a reactionary. By leaving the leader of the biggest party out in the cold, President Alcalá Zamora strengthened Señor Gil Robles and enabled him to threaten every government and to exact a kind of political blackmail from every Cabinet. In the summer of 1934, the Republic should have been governed by a Lerroux-Gil Robles coalition, binding both men under a joint declaration of respect for civil authority and for constitutional ways.

Instead, President Alcalá Zamora called on Señor Samper to form a Cabinet. Who was Señor Samper? He was one of the most undistinguished followers of Lerroux. No thinker, no speaker, no man to be put at the head of a government. And it was Señor Samper who had to face the storms of the summer, forerunners of the October blitz Civil War.

Two conflicts of a regionalist nature came to complicate the situation. The provinces of Biscay and Guipúzcoa protested against certain new taxes which, they asserted, ran contrary to the economic agreement between the Basque provinces and the state. This kind of thing may happen in the best regulated nations and is easily solved in a few weeks. In Spain it raged for months and gave rise to much bad blood, let alone trouble and expense. The provinces decided to elect representatives in each municipality to uphold the agreement. The government declared these elections illegal. They were held in the teeth of the government decision. Many mayors were arrested, though merely as a formality, and in the end the excitement subsided with the arrival of the summer months and the absence of most of the leaders at the seaside.

Earlier in the summer, trouble of a more serious character arose in Catalonia. It was no longer the Catalonia of Francesc

Maciá. In a brief span of time, there had been in fact three Catalonias: of the Lliga, of Maciá, and of Companys-Dencás. The first was Center-Right both in religious and in economic matters. It was led by intelligent, cold, wealthy lawyer-financiers, such as Cambó and Ventosa. "Monarchy or Republic?—Catalonia!" This famous utterance of Cambó might do for their motto. The Catalonia led by the Lliga was animated by a cold, efficient, European, "modern" capitalistic spirit. It had some popular following, but limited to the lower middle classes and to the rural countryside, particularly devout in Catalonia. It worried and defied Madrid in public, but was on excellent terms with it in private. The second Catalonia, that of Maciá, had dared to be itself and to cut itself loose from the politics of Madrid. Yet Catalonia had never been more Spanish than under Maciá. He himself was in body as well as in spirit the truest incarnation of Don Quixote Spain had ever known, with the possible exception of the Basque Ignatius of Loyola. And he had found in Señor Gassol the truest incarnation of Sancho Panza. For years, whether in Spain or in exile, Francesc Maciá and Ventura Gassol had been the Knight and the Squire of a Dulcinea which was Free Catalonia—both idealistic (for Sancho Panza was also an idealist, though not in Don Quixote's way.) When Maciá, in whom no cold, mere common-sense Catalan could believe, achieved his triumph against and above common sense and became the President of the Generalitat, Gassol became his Councilor of Education. The learned Catalans who in *Acció Catalana* had been endeavoring to build up by reason what Maciá had created by faith, were too slow in providing him with intellectual help—exactly what he needed—and when they bethought themselves of it they found the Knight of Free Catalonia surrounded by all the minor adventurers of politics, chief among whom was Dr. Dencás, an ambitious medical practitioner of clerical reactionary origins who was then finding his way by exploiting extreme Catalanist aims allied to Fascist methods. When Maciá, who was an old man in his hour of triumph, died, Catalonia hesitated between Gassol and Companys, the municipal councilor who had declared the Catalan state on April 14, 1931. The true successor should have been Gassol, for obviously no one but Sancho could succeed Don Quixote, Sancho who was a closer relative to Don Quixote than any of the knight's own family. But Lluis Companys was preferred owing perhaps to the fact that he was a less pronounced Catalanist who had always written in Castilian and had a large following among the Anarcho-Syndicalist masses, indifferent or even hostile to Catalanism. Companys was a demagogue. He needed the vote of the small man and courted it.

Under his inspiration the Generalitat voted a Catalan law regulating disputes between landlords and farmers (*rabassaires*) in a manner which the Catalan landlords concerned found unjust and even oppressive. The landlords succeeded in making a *prima facie* case for referring the law to the Tribunal of Constitutional Guarantees which, though only by a small majority, quashed the law on the ground that the Catalan Parliament was incompetent to legislate on such a matter. Catalan public opinion was split, for the *Lliga* strongly supported the view of the Tribunal; but Lluis Companys, who was, according to the Constitution, not only the President of the Catalan Government but also the Trustee of the Republican authority in Catalonia and therefore the guardian of the decisions of the Tribunal of Constitutional Guarantees on Catalan affairs, ostentatiously ratified and promulgated the law which had been quashed by the highest tribunal of the land.

The two conflicts, the Basque and the Catalan, sprang again to the foreground in September (as people came back from the seaside). There was a general resignation of municipalities in the Basque country, where the demand for home rule became universal, and in Madrid a general strike penalized the whole population as a protest against an assembly held there by the Catalan landlords. In the whole country the old Spanish separatism rose to a fever. Lluis Companys, unable to resist the wine of popularity at its frothiest, made speech upon speech threatening Spain with a separate Catalan nationality. The Basques made chorus. Largo Caballero went up and down the country announcing the dictatorship of the proletariat as the only remedy for Spain's troubles, i.e. "separating" from the Republic. Arms were discovered here and there by the police, now in Fascist cellars, now in Socialist housetops. On July 11, 1934, bombs and poison gas were discovered in the cellars of a house where a Fascist meeting was being held, and José Antonio Primo de Rivera was arrested and prosecuted after the Cortes had given the required authority (for he was a member of Parliament). In September about one hundred youths were arrested for drilling with rifles under the Monarchist flag in Olesa (Catalonia) and documents were found on them with plans for a Monarchist rising in October. In Asturias arms were found landed somewhat mysteriously from a ship coming from a southern port in Spain the origin and destination of which were not clear. They were part of a vast scheme for arming the Left, particularly the mining districts, toward a rising also to take place in October. The Catalan government and the Socialists had been preparing a rising for the autumn, and though, mainly for lack of funds, the Generalitat had not been able to arm as well as it wished, the Socialists had more money and better agents abroad. On September 26 Señor Carner, a Catalan industrialist who had been a Minister of Finance with Azaña, died in Barcelona, and several of his former colleagues went from Madrid to the funeral. On the train, Azaña and Largo Caballero discussed the outlook and Azaña wisely pointed out to Largo Caballero the dangers to which the rebellious attitude of the Socialist leader exposed the Republic. Largo Caballero held his ground and in the end, short of arguments, but still rich in stubbornness, he blurted out: "It must be, for I am committed to it before my followers, and let me add, Don Manuel, that I am already jeopardizing my prestige by merely talking with you so freely." He meant that the company of a mere bourgeois like Azaña, was no longer politically healthy for him. Azaña, with his dry, pungent scorn, retorted: "Very well, Don Francisco. You need all the prestige you have, and I shall not impair it any longer"—and he broke off the conversation.

A few days after this scene, on October 1, 1934, the Cortes met. Señor Gil Robles, whose support was indispensable for any Cabinet, announced that he withdrew his vote from Señor Samper. The Cabinet fell. It was obvious from previous statements made by Señor Gil Robles in his most emphatic style that he meant to ask for the lion's share of any new government, as indeed, under a dispassionate parliamentary stystem, he had every right to do. But the combined efforts of the president and of Lerroux succeeded in buying him off with three portfolios (Agriculture, Justice and Labor), important in themselves yet by no means dangerous from the point of view of those who, from the Left, professed to believe that the CEDA leader was preparing an imminent attack on the Republican regime.

As soon as the news was known, the Left launched its long-prepared revolt. A general strike paralyzed Madrid, Barcelona, Valencia, Seville, Córdoba, San Sebastián, Bilbao and Santander. The rebellion soon revealed three centers: Oviedo, Barcelona, Madrid. In Madrid, where the leader was Largo Caballero, it collapsed quickly, and Largo Caballero was caught on October 14. In Oviedo it was led by Señor González Peña, a Socialist member of Parliament belonging to Prieto's group, who, with all this group, had been lukewarm about the whole plan while it was being debated by the Socialists, but who, once in the fray, stood his ground resolutely. The workers in Asturias fought stubbornly. They were well-armed with armored cars, machine guns and vast quantities of dynamite, a substance for which miners feel all the contempt bred by familiarity. They callously persecuted men of the highest private and public character, and they tried to set up a rough-and-ready form of Communism. The rebellion developed into a short but fierce civil war in which General López Ochoa, an officer well known for his long-standing Republican opinions, had to fight his way from Avilés to rescue the hard-pressed garrison in Oviedo. This fine old town suffered terribly from the fierceness of the fights. The miners had turned the University, a fine old building, into a dynamite dump, and when they saw the game was up, they blew up the University with many surrounding blocks of houses. In the middle of the central quadrangle, the sole immune survivor of the appalling havoc, the Inquisitor General Valdés, founder of the University, sat, a bronze figure on his bronze chair. The contrast was too much for Unamuno's pungent wit, and with inconsolable bitterness he used to say: "There he sat, admonishing us with his finger: 'I told you so!' "

I shall not dwell on atrocities. Both sides flooded Spain and even foreign countries with harrowing tales, both unfortunately true though both possibly exaggerated.

The Barcelona rebellion was a curious and obscure affair. Companys, fully aware that his Catalanist history was not too strong, in an eloquent proclamation to the crowd from the balcony of the Generalitat building reasserted the loyalty of Catalonia to the Spanish Republic, but boldly violated the Constitution, whose guardian in Catalonia he was, by declaring that he took over all public powers and proclaiming the Catalan state within the Spanish Federal Republic, inviting "the leaders of the general protest against Fascism . . . to establish the Provisional Government of the Republic in Catalonia." These words were generously meant, yet unwise in the extreme, for they compromised Azaña, who happened to be in Barcelona at the time and was by no means in agreement with the revolt.

The troops in Barcelona were commanded by General Batet who, on declaring martial law the day before, had expressed his hope "as a Catalan, a Spaniard and a man" that there would be no fighting. But the Catalan government refused to surrender and General Batet attacked them in their fortified palace during the night of October 6-7. At dawn, the fight was over and the Government of Catalonia was in jail—all but Dr. Dencás, who fled through the sewer.

The revolt of 1934 is unpardonable. The decision of the president in calling the CEDA to share in the government was not only unimpeachable, not only unavoidable, but long overdue. The argument that Señor Gil Robles intended to bring in Fascism was both hypocritical and demonstrably untrue. It was hypocritical because everybody knew that the Socialists of Largo Caballero were dragging the other Socialists to a rebellion and in the teeth of Azaña's opposition to such a desperate course; demonstrably untrue because, had Señor Gil Robles meant to destroy the Constitution by violent means, the defeat of the rebellion of 1934 gave him a golden opportunity to do so—and he did not take it. In fact, Señor Gil Robles was a convinced parliamentarian too deeply committed to a Republican-Parliamentarian mode of life to be in any way acceptable to Fascism or susceptible to it. As for the Asturian miners, their revolt was entirely due to doctrinarian and theoretical prepossessions. Had the hungry Andalusian peasants risen in revolt, what could one do but sympathize with their despair? But the Asturian miners were well paid, and, in fact, the whole industry, by a collusion between employers and workers, was kept working at an artificial level by state subsidies beyond what many of the seams deserved in a sound economy. Lastly the Catalan case was no more justified. True, the policy of the government of Madrid was not very intelligent. It should not have allowed itself to be maneuvered by the Catalan landlords and the Lliga to the point of having to make the Tribunal of Constitutional Guarantees a pawn in internal Catalan quarrels. But the Catalan government should never have violated the Constitution merely because the Tribunal of Guarantees had given as its legal opinion one which happened to suit the Catalan opposition. That they sinned against the light is obvious, for Azaña was at great pains to explain the position to them with the utmost lucidity. Moreover, as events were to show and we shall see presently, the CEDA had no evil intentions against the Catalan Statute. This incident therefore comes to confirm the view here maintained throughout, i.e. that Catalonians and Basques are typically Spanish types and present in a no less acute form than other Spaniards the typically Spanish political failures. The Catalan Right sought outside help in their internal feud against their own Left. The Catalan Left broke off the game as soon as one of its rules happened to work against them. Both all too frequent features in Spanish political life.

With the rebellion of 1934, the Left lost every shred of moral authority to condemn the rebellion of 1936.

The period which extends from October 1934, when the Left tried to seize power by violent methods and failed, till February

1936, when it tried to seize power by democratic methods and succeeded, was obviously one during which Spain was governed almost without opposition by the Right. This period ended in its discomfiture mainly because the margin of power in Spain —whether for the Right or for the Left—does not allow for so many mistakes as Right or Left are apt to make when in office —and the Right this time surpassed itself.

Three sets of facts should be distinguished: (1) punishment, repression and political action as the aftermath of the revolt; (2) reforms contemplated in the Constitution; and (3) current affairs. The government found itself with a number of Left leaders in prison—including Largo Caballero and Azaña—and a free hand to get rid of political opponents everywhere, which it of course did with alacrity. The nondescript mass of the easily swayed was flocking to the "parties of order," which meant not merely the CEDA (after all a party with some claims to the name) but the Falange or Fascists, a party which, of course, under its show of order and authority, was that of the monopoly of disorder. The whole country remained for two months under martial law. There was a relative calm through the winter.

From the point of view of the winners, the keynote was what a dispassionate observer might have foretold: petty vindictive politics, in which the personal note was paramount; repression, at first unnecessarily harsh while under the sole control of the military, later tempered by prudence as the civil authorities reasserted their rights; exploitation of the revolt of the Left to extract from it political advantages for the Right; but no upsetting of the Republican institutions.

The persecution of Azaña was a sad enough example of the first. Azaña behaved throughout this crisis in an unimpeachable manner. He was nevertheless illegally detained in violation of the Constitutional privileges of the members of the Cortes, and the country was flooded with most disingenuous reports on his alleged share in the revolt, which, coming as they undoubtedly did from the fountain of authority, were bound to disconcert public opinion.

As an example of the second, the record of the repression in

Asturias should suffice. Governing requires a certain minimum of human obligations. These the government did not satisfy during the first period of the repression. Moreover, the military authorities, strong in their victory, were ruthless in their punishment. Even then, after some time, decency prevailed mostly through the courageous insistence of President Alcalá Zamora, backed by the radical members of the Cabinet. Let us, moreover, keep our sense of proportion. When the shortsightedness, the pettiness, the personal limitations, the cruelty of the first days are all set down on record, the fact remains that this government of Conservatives and clericals who stood for authority and were supposed to be dangerous enough for the liberties of Spain to justify an armed revolt of the Left, did not take one single life of the leaders of the revolt. Azaña's death as a result of this revolt would have been monstrous. However, the *prima facie* case against Largo Caballero and Companys was no less strong than that against General Sanjurjo had been in 1932. While Sanjurjo was sentenced to death (though reprieved), Largo Caballero was let off easily after a none too dignified defense on his part, and Companys was sentenced to a long term of imprisonment, which in a country as rich in amnesties as Spain meant very little indeed. This is the time for recording that Companys did not betray Spain at all as was most unfairly said at the time. He was a Spanish patriot, who in a tight corner acted in good faith, to the best of his ability. He stood for Catalonia and Spain together. But he did break his oath to the Constitution and he challenged the regularly constituted government in a way in which the government had a perfect right to see high treason. I am of course far from arguing that either he or Largo Caballero should have been more severely punished. I am arguing, in all fairness to a government as distant from my way of thinking as any can be, that its acts at this moment did not correspond to the description of it on which the Left attempted to justify its rebellion. If a better proof were needed of a difference between a government merely dubbed Fascist and a truly Fascist government, I may point out that while the Gil Robles-Lerroux government let off Largo Caballero and

Companys, though guilty, the nationalist government of General Franco executed Companys, though this time, in law, Companys was right and it was wrong.

In fact, even of the thirty death sentences which the courts pronounced as the outcome of the 1934 Civil War two only were carried out, one of which was that of Sergeant Vázquez, a soldier who was of course court-martialed for military rebellion and whom the military did not let go. Eight were commuted straightway in January 1935. The remaining twenty were the object of a discussion in the Cabinet, the Radicals being for reprieve, the CEDA for execution; and although thereby he caused the fall of the Cabinet, the president signed the reprieve.

A similar spirit prevailed with regard to Catalonia. The case of the Generalitat was very poor indeed. Its president (Companys) was in the terms of the Catalan Statute both head of the local government and representative of the central government in Catalonia. This was a signal proof of trust on the part of the Republic. Companys had failed to live up to it. No doubt he had had his reasons, or rather his emotions, fears, ambitions for taking the course he took on October 6, 1934. But the fact was that the very ground on which the Generalitat had revolted —namely to forestall an attack on Catalan liberties—proved false when the Right, having the Catalan revolt as an invaluable asset to strengthen them in their alleged intention of destroying the liberties of Catalonia, did nothing of the kind. To be sure they could not be expected to put the Statute back into operation the day after, as if nothing had happened, but the fact is that though a temporary system of government through a Governor General was set up, the Statute remained the fundamental law of Catalonia and a number of home rule services was devolved on the Catalan authorities as early as April 1935. No doubt the Catalans were not pleased. No one claims that the Lerroux-CEDA government was a liberal combination. But no one in his senses would say that such measures as a suspension of the Catalan Statute till things had cooled off, and the devolution of nearly all home-rule powers but public order, were oppressive, nor that a government which at the height of its might behaved in this way was committed to crush the liberties of the Catalans. It should be added that nearly every Cabinet of 1935 till the advent of the Popular Front included a prominent Catalan home-ruler, though of course of the Conservative Lliga.

As for Fascism and the betrayal of the Constitution, events also went far to show that the outcry of the Left to justify their revolt on this account was based on a biased view of events which distorted them out of all recognition. The disappointment and the bitterness of the Left and of the Center-Left on seeing the reins of power in the hands of a tanned, old skeptical Republican like Lerroux and of a Clerical reactionary like Gil Robles was only too natural. But the fact was that these men had been put in office by the regular working of a Republican Constitution and of an electoral law voted by the Left. The democratic attitude could be no other than to bow to the will of the people and to wait till the Right and the Center-Right had made enough mistakes in office to bring about another change in favor of the Left. Instead of this, the Left began to declare that it could not admit a government of Gil Robles's followers because they meant to upset the regime by violence; and so, in order to forestall this hypothetical and, as events were to show, non-existent violent action against the regime, it launched its own violent action against the regime. What are the facts? To begin with, Lerroux was able to crush the Civil War in Asturias mainly through the collaboration of Generals Franco and Goded, the future leaders of the 1936 revolt, who took charge of the technical leadership of the operations from the War Office; and yet, even when the army leaders were in such demand, these two generals were unable to force the government to accept their views on things of such grave import as death sentences. With their usual appetite for sensation, pressmen, home and foreign, swarmed round Gil Robles humming "Dictatorship?" The CEDA leader was final: "No dictatorship. We shall not allow any tampering with the parliamentary system," and he meant it.

The proof of the pudding is in the eating. When the Lerroux Cabinet fell on May 3, 1935, it was universally believed that this time the president would call on Señor Gil Robles, who was leader of the biggest coalition in the House. His time was long overdue. And yet his time did not come. Lerroux succeeded himself, though giving five portfolios to the CEDA, including the War Office, which Gil Robles took in person. This was then a second opportunity for Gil Robles to upset the Republic by force. But the leader of the CEDA was not thinking of blood. He was thinking of ink. He wanted to amend the Constitution.

Are we to blame him? At the beginning of the year, President Alcalá Zamora himself had devoted three Cabinet meetings to a three-day study course of the Constitution for the benefit of his Cabinet, in which he had examined the working of the fundamental laws in the light of his experience. He also had concluded that the Constitution should be amended. Are we to blame him too? We know two things: the Constitution of 1931 had not been drafted so as to seek a maximum agreement among all Spaniards; and it had not been drafted as a practical instrument of government for any nation, let alone one so spirited, original and individualistic as Spain. Theoretically at least it was desirable to amend the Constitution.

Was it wise? Should a Spain already so unsettled remove the foundations when the house itself was tottering? That is an open question. But this must be said: that a government which proposed to reform the Constitution of 1931 through the procedure set down in Article 125 of the Constitution itself could by no stretch of imagination be described as a Fascist government. Moreover, what were its proposals? The chief points which were recommended for amendment were: powers of the president (Article 76); a second Chamber (Article 51); attenuation of the drastic powers of expropriation of private property granted to the Cortes by Article 44; religious matters (Articles 19, 20) and divorce (Article 43); and changes in articles 12, 14, 15, on home rule, though without in any way seeking to abolish autonomy. It would be a waste of time to discuss these amendments in detail. The chief point is that they were all arguable, some of them highly desirable, and in any case that not one of them was outside the jurisdiction of a reasonably understood Republican system.

As to current affairs, they had to take a back seat in a Spain too bent on drama to remember plain and simple life. And yet the material life of the Republic was none too easy. The strong Socialist wind raised by the Left in 1931, though in reality amounting to little more than hot air, had driven away a good deal of capital in search of safer political climates, and the peseta had fallen from about 8 to 10.34 to the dollar. On the advent of the Republic the total debt was 29,000 million pesetas, most of it, however, owed within the country. The deficit had been 417 million in 1925 and 924 in 1929. (So much for the administration of Primo de Rivera.) The Republic (Left) meant to save much superfluous expense, but to increase its budget on education, agrarian reform and social services. It was singularly unfortunate that world conditions were so unfavorable at the time of its advent. The economic crisis through which world trade was passing hit Spain hard and most of her staple products (olive oil, wine, cork, oranges, flax, metals) fell in price. From nearly 2300 million pesetas in 1930, exports fell to 990 in 1931 and 742 in 1932. Nevertheless the budget steadily rose. In 1930, the dictatorship estimated its budget and deficit respectively at 4012 million and 158 million, while the corresponding figures for 1933 were 4711 and 783, and the deficits for 1931 and 1932 had been 509 and 712 million pesetas respectively. The public debt, of course, had to rise. Meanwhile constant strikes, launched more often than not for political reasons, made it difficult for the country's economy to keep apace with its requirements.

No budget had been studied or prepared since the Right had taken office, and the Republic lived from hand to mouth. Financial affairs did not begin to be seriously considered till two specialists were brought into the Cabinet: Señor Marraco, an Aragonese Radical banker, who became finance secretary on October 4, 1934; and Don Joaquín Chapaprieta, who took charge of the department on May 8, 1935. Chapaprieta was a specialist who had served as Under Secretary for Finance under the Monarchy. He was a man of strong will and short temper. He came to office determined to put some order into the Civil Service and to effect considerable economies thereby. He introduced a "law of restrictions" which drove a ruthless axe into the thick though by no means virgin forest of Spanish administration. The law was passed, not without arousing a deep resentment in the ranks of the numerous poor families which in Spain (as in many other countries) looked upon the state budget as the Cow-Goddess dispenser of the milk and cream of daily life. Chapaprieta knew full well that it would be indispensable to balance these sacrifices that he had exacted from the poor with at least equal sacrifices from the rich. Meantime a minor crisis over devolution of further powers to Catalonia had brought down the Cabinet (September 25, 1935) and Chapaprieta himself had become prime minister—for the President still kept Gil Robles at bay. The foreign secretary in the new Cabinet was Señor Lerroux, who, however, had to resign on October 30, as a result of an affair over a gambling operation in which Don Aurelio Lerroux, nephew and adoptive son of the Radical leader, was heavily implicated. Unperturbed by these incidents, Chapaprieta proceeded with his financial plans. He introduced reforms of a relatively mild character but this time aiming at the moneybags of the country. The reaction was such as might have been expected of the shortsighted selfishness of the Conservatives. The CEDA had already given the measure of its folly by hounding out of office their best man, Professor Jiménez Fernández, for the crime of having taken his Catholic faith in earnest and having appealed to his co-religionists as a Minister of Agriculture, begging them to be Christian toward the land-dispossessed peasants. As he quoted the Pope to his officially militant "Catholic" co-religionists, one of them, not precisely of the rank and file, shouted back: "If the Pope has said that, I will turn Protestant." These worthy representatives of the moneyed interests protested hotly against Chapaprieta's plans—they who had assented with glee to the bleeding of the poor civil servants, although the Prime Minister's proposals were but trifling increases in taxes, for after all Chapaprieta was no Red. These blind Conservatives, unable to conserve themselves, preferred to bring down the Cabinet—a crash which was to entail their own downfall as well, before long—rather than open their miserly purses (December 17, 1935).

President Alcalá Zamora, after many arduous labors in the course of which he tried to set up a government of Republican concord under Don Miguel Maura, a Left Catholic, entrusted the Premiership to Señor Portela—an ex-Monarchist also—granting him the decree dissolving the Cortes, since it was no longer possible to resist the pressure of public opinion which demanded a general election.

The second round had ended like the first, in the self-defeat of the side which for the time being seemed to be the stronger.

CHAPTER 6

THE THIRD ROUND—LEFT

Public opinion was changing, yet, as time was to show, it was
not changing very much—despite appearances. Throughout the
giddy swings of politics the mass of the nation had remained
very much the same, but the middle opinion was apt to lean
now on the Right, now on the Left, and as Parliamentary majorities had adopted the obnoxious and dangerous habit of governing as if the opposition did not count, a small shift in numbers
was enough to determine dramatic changes in the nation.

When it became known that President Alcalá Zamora had
granted Portela the decree of dissolution of the Cortes (January 7, 1936)—that decree which was still under the Republic,
as it had been under the Monarch, the manna of all Spanish
politicians—both sides cleared the decks for action. The Right
had set up an anti-Marxist alliance; the Left constituted the
Frente Popular, based on a pact signed and published on
January 15, 1936, between all the parties of the Left, including

444

a section of the Radical Party, led by Señor Martínez Barrio, which had seceded from Lerroux. This document was little more than a statement of what the several parties allied for electoral purposes meant to do with their victory, and could hardly be described as an agreement, since on some points, such as nationalization of land and others, it limited itself to stating: "The Republicans do not accept" what the Socialists defined as desirable. It has often been argued that this pact was a most moderate document, untainted by Communism. Things, however, were not quite as simple as that. The general election took place on February 16. The results were for practical purposes a complete victory for the Left. Here are the figures:

Parties	Votes	Deputies	Votes per Deputy
Popular Front	4,206,156	258	16,300
Center	681,047	62	10,987
Right	3,783,601	152	24,900

After the House had met a revision of these figures began that, in the words of President Alcalá Zamora whom no one would suspect of excessive sympathy toward Gil Robles, cut down the figures of the Right with a strong partisan bias.[1]

Let us then consider these figures again. Popular Front, 258. Centre, 62. Right, 152. A victory, but not such a victory as to wipe out the opposition, i.e. "the other Spain," particularly if it be borne in mind that the Left this time included the Basque Nationalists who, despite their clerical convictions, had crossed the line of Spanish politics as a matter of home-rule tactics.

A number of observations must be made on these figures. The first is that, within the Left, the extreme Left had been beaten by the Center Left. The bourgeois non-Marxist parties of the Left had returned 148 deputies against 110 to the Marxists. Let us then note that the number of votes per member in

[1] The revised figures were:

Parties	Votes	Deputies	Votes per Deputy
Popular Front	4,838,449	277	17,140
Center	449,320	32	14,040
Right	3,996,931	132	30,279

this election of February 16, 1936, was 10,987 for the Center, 16,300 for the Left and 24,980 for the Right. It follows that the electoral law had worked in this case most unfairly for the Right, most favorably for the Center, and about midway between the two for the Left. If, therefore, we are to reason on a sound basis we must go back to the actual votes cast by the nation and not to the number of members returned for each party. We then find, in round numbers:

Left:

Socialists and Communists	1,793,000	
Left Center (Azaña)	2,413,200	
Total Left		4,206,200
Right Center		681,000
Right		3,783,600

These figures may be interpreted in different ways according to the color under which the Center is seen, I mean the zone of Spanish opinion not over-happily represented by Lerroux. If we first take the view of the Left, namely, that Lerroux and his lot were a pack of masked reactionaries, we have to group the Center Right with the Right. Then we find that the general election of February 16, 1936, was a triumph for the Right, to wit:

Popular Front	4,206,200
Right	4,464,600

This conclusion, which flows inevitably from the attitude of the Left toward the Center Right, is in my opinion untenable, and I must defend the Left against itself. The man of February 16, 1936, was not Largo Caballero; it was Azaña. He was the idol of the nation. Why? Because he was known to combine these two qualities: undoubted loyalty and even enthusiasm for the Republic of 1931 and common sense which had led him to oppose the mad adventures in revolution which Largo Caballero dreamed. As the winter of 1934-35 and the summer of 1935 allowed the nation to realize how calumniated Azaña had been with regard to the events of October 1934, and as the nation saw more and more clearly how unimpeachable his attitude had been during those events, everyone said in Spain: "This is the man we want." Azaña was at the head of the polls wherever he stood and his party brought 82 members as compared to 89 Socialists and 14 Communists—which for a new party, without trade-union funds and with practically no local organization, was a triumph of sheer opinion. If, moreover, as we have every right to do, we add to Azaña's party the members of the Catalan Esquerra, which was of an identical political color, we find that Azaña was in the new House at the head of 103 deputies, exactly as many as composed the Marxist group.

The votes cast for the Center Right were obviously of the same climate of Spanish politics, though more conservative than the party of Azaña. They were votes of people who disagreed with the Right—Freemasons, for instance—most of whom had followed Lerroux from the first day of his career, and although they were opposed to Socialism and looked askance at Azaña's commitments to the Socialists, they could by no stretch of imagination be counted as men of the Right without doing violence to the most permanent rules of Spanish politics, those which draw the line at free thinking. The logical thing to do with them in this analysis is therefore to group the figures of the Center Right and of the Center Left not according to the splits caused by tactical mistakes and personal feuds but on objective political standards. Thus considered, the figures of February 16, 1936, must be classified in the following manner:

MARXIST LEFT
    (i.e. Anti-Clerical, Anti-Militaristic)   1,793,000 votes

NON-MARXIST LEFT
    (i.e. Anti-Clerical, Anti-Militaristic)   3,193,000 votes

PARLIAMENTARY RIGHT
    (i.e. Anti-Marxist, Clerical,
    Non-Militaristic)   3,783,000 votes

ANTI-PARLIAMENTARY RIGHT
    (i.e. Anti-Marxist, Non-Clerical,
    Militaristic)   a few thousand

All parties thus defined might have been able to put forward this or that objection to this or that point relating to the above figures. For the purposes of our argument, however, it is best to grant all the benefit of the doubt not merely to the Left, but to the Marxist Left. To that effect, let us go as far as granting it nearly double the amount of votes which it actually received in the general election, raising its figure to 3.3 million. Let us also raise to 3.3 millions the 3.1 of the Non-Marxist Left. Let us finally reduce to 3.3 the 3.7 million obtained by the Right.[2] We must, moreover, bear in mind that within the Marxist group not more than one in three were for an immediate revolution. In this guise, to which the Left will not object as ungenerous to them, the result of the famous Popular Front election would be that Spain pronounced herself:

1. By two to one against Marxism;
2. By two to one against Clericals and Militarists;
3. By eight to one against a Socialist revolution;
4. Almost unanimously against a military rebellion.

These, however, were the results in depth which cool analysis reveals after the event. In the emotional days which followed the election, the figures were read as what they officially were, in virtue of the tactical alliance of the evolutionary Left with the revolutionary Left. It was a triumph for Azaña. Now Azaña was, far more even than Socialists and Communists, the

[2] We are entitled to this rearrangement of votes although it implies an increase of about .3 million votes in the aggregate, because there were about 2 million voters who did not vote. It has often been argued that the abstainers were the Anarcho-Syndicalists. This is not true. The CNT instructed its members to vote for the Left. (Private information, Letter of President Alcalá Zamora to *Journal de Genève,* Charles A. Thompson, who writes: "Even the Anarcho-Syndicalists overcame their traditional aversion to political action and went to the polls, hoping to secure amnesty for their imprisoned comrades through a Popular Front victory.")— Foreign policy reports, January 1, 1937, p. 254. Mr. Borkenau, a good observer, also agrees that the Anarcho-Syndicalists did not abstain and voted for the Left—*The Spanish Cockpit* (pp. 58-59).

arch-enemy of the Army. And we know now that when the figures of the election were known, General Franco called on the prime minister to offer him the backing of the Army so as to enable him to refuse to hand over the reins of office to the Left. "It was not only Señor Portela who courageously refused to abet the overthrow of the electoral results"—writes one of the most outspoken advocates of the Spanish Left—"but also Don José Maria Gil Robles, who alternated between moves which were disastrous for the regime and good turns to it. He saved the Republic after the October revolt of 1934 by definitely opposing the menacing attitude adopted by officers belonging to the clique to which Generals Mola, Sanjurjo, Franco, Goded and many other senior and junior officers belonged. Now he once again set his face against a dictatorship."

It is therefore evident that from the black CEDA to the reddish Prieto, passing through the dark-brown Lerroux and the pink Azaña, practically everybody was agreed on the fundamentals of the regime, and in particular on a parliamentary system. The regime was, however, attacked by two extremist movements, two pronunciamentos in fact: one, frankly outside it, the military pronunciamento of the generals, organized by Mola and led by Generals Sanjurjo, Goded and Franco; the other, both in and out of it, the trade-union pronunciamento of the revolutionary workers led by Largo Caballero. None but the biased bigots of either side could see any fundamental difference between these two threats. A union leader who takes advantage of the discipline of his rank and file and of their strategic situation within the state to revolt against the freely expressed opinion of his fellow citizens differs in no way from a general who takes advantage of the discipline of his rank and file and of their strategic situation within the state to revolt against the freely expressed opinion of his fellow citizens. The two cases are identical, and in 1936 Largo Caballero and General Franco played exactly the same part in Spanish history. Both stabbed the Republic, the one on the left, the other one on the right.

Unfortunately, whatever were the discreet doings of those on whom the generals relied for their coup, the doings of Largo Caballero were noisy and reached the public ear first. The conversion of Largo Caballero from his opportunistic and conservative tactics under Primo de Rivera, when he had been a collaborationist, over to the tactics of violence and revolution which he now preached up and down the country, was bound to have deep effects, for he was an upright and sincere man, of transparent honesty and a lifelong and devoted servant of the labor and socialist movements in Spain, a man with whom one could disagree but who commands one's respect and even affection. This conversion was due to a number of causes: disappointment in the Republic, fear of Gil Robles's intentions; fear of being outbidden by the Communists; belated ambition, perhaps; but possibly above all a change in his Intellectual in Ordinary. As a man of action, Largo Caballero had at an early stage in his career evolved the habit of having at his elbow an intellectual adviser, a kind of bookish chaplain and keeper of his conscience. This position had been for many years filled by an empirical, positive, practical Catalan socialist, Señor Fabra Ribas, an old friend of Albert Thomas, who represented the International Labor Office in Madrid. Then came the Republic and Fabra Ribas became a Spanish politician. Harold Butler, as head of the ILO, asked him to choose between Spanish politics and League service. He chose League service—wise man! And Largo Caballero had to look around for another Intellectual in Ordinary. He found two: Luis Araquistain and Julio Alvarez del Vayo. Their intellectual relations were then closer than they were to become later, but they differed considerably, for while Araquistain's center of gravity is in the brain, Vayo's is in the heart. And while Araquistain is a Socialist in the Western sense of the word, Vayo is a Communist, though like many Communists active in other parties—including conservative parties—he does not wear the red star on the lapel. These two men turned Largo Caballero's head and made him believe he was predestined to be the Spanish Lenin. "The initiative in the use of this title," writes Araquistain, "came from Moscow."

Largo Caballero had been preaching a here-and-now Socialism to the working classes and throwing to the winds all allegiance not merely to the Republic but to freedom as well. "Freedom for what?" he asked in his speeches. The crowd, the Spanish crowd, always messianic and ever ready to take short-cuts, was only too eager to listen to this hot gospel. The temperature of the nation rose rapidly. Riots, occupation of farms, of private houses, of factories and mills, became the disorder of the day. Frightened at the look of things, Portela's Cabinet resigned[3] (February 19, 1936) and President Alcalá Zamora called on Azaña, who at the moment when he should have summoned all the political strength he could muster to control the crowd on the one hand and the Army on the other, was reduced to forming a Cabinet composed exclusively of his own followers, without a single Socialist to share his power and responsibility. It was obvious that he had been trapped by the Extreme Left into the Popular Front which, sheltering behind his popular name, had rushed into power but shirked its responsibilities. Largo Caballero continued his propaganda in fiery speeches calling for the dictatorship of the proletariat. Gil Robles issued a statement on behalf of his party, bowing before the will of the nation, asking for equal treatment for all parties and offering his party's cooperation in maintaining public order. Azaña addressed a statesman-like appeal to the nation in a broadcast on February 20. He announced his program as: no reprisals, no persecution; liberty, prosperity and justice for all. A hasty amnesty was decreed, thousands of prisoners were set free . . . and alas! disorders and violence increased tenfold at once and the smoke from churches and convents rose again toward the blue skies—the only serene feature left in the Spanish landscape. Land riots continued, the houses of landowners were invaded, their cattle destroyed, their crops burned. Azaña settled 75,000 peasants in Estremadura by a decree of more than doubtful legal basis, yet fully justified

---

[3] Colonel Casado may be right in his surmise that this resignation was due less to fear of street disorders than to fear of a military *coup d'état.*
—*The Last Days of Madrid,* Colonel Casado, p. 33.

in the circumstances.[4] The riots, however, continued, for the country was overrun with revolutionary agents much less interested in land reform than in revolution. Strikes everywhere, murders of political personages of local importance, the political color of the victim clearly showing in every case whether the criminal had been black or red, at times attempts on a national figure. Señor Jiménez Asúa, a Socialist lawyer, president of the commission which had prepared the 1931 Constitution, was shot at and escaped unhurt in March 1936. A few days later Doctor Alfredo Martínez, a Liberal Democrat (i.e. a member of a party which all Spain had thought enlightened and progressive till 1931), who had been a Cabinet minister with Portela, was assassinated. On his deathbed he made a pathetic request: that no inquiry should be made on the cause of his death since punishment of the murderer could but increase the country's unrest. The palace of Gandia in Madrid was occupied by a Left Wing organization and the red flag hoisted over it. The country had entered into a plainly revolutionary phase. Neither life nor property was safe anywhere. It is sheer prejudice to try to explain matters with parrot cries on variations of the word "feudal." It was not only the owner of thousands of acres

---

[4] *B.S.S.*, Vol. xiii, p. 133, says between forty and fifty thousand. My figure comes from Azaña in person, who told me the last time I saw him. "That makes," he added, "anything between four and five hundred thousand persons who will eat on credit from now on. And you may ask me, why don't you do the same in Andalusia and the agrarian problem will be solved? But you see, if I give land to the Andalusians without careful legislation, they will sell it to go to the next bullfight."

The following quotation from the Royal Institute of International Affairs *Survey*, 1938, p. 296n, may be of use in this connection: "The difficulty of the problem is illustrated by the following comments by an Englishman who was living in Spain at the time of the outbreak of the war:

"Agrarian unrest has been ended in other parts of Europe by breaking up the large estates and settling peasants in individual holdings on them. This was the Republican solution in Spain. But it happens that in dry-farming districts, i.e. in the whole of the center and south of Spain, except in those few areas where there is irrigation, the small peasant farmer cannot live, because he cannot get through the bad years. Further, in Andalusia, the campesinos are accustomed to wages and have no land-hunger."

granted his ancestors by King So-and-so whose house was invaded and whose cattle were left bleeding with broken legs on the smoking fields of his lands. It was the modest Madrid doctor or lawyer who had a villa of four rooms and bath and a garden as big as three handkerchiefs, who saw his house occupied by land-workers, by no means houseless and by no means hungry, who came to harvest his crop: ten men to do the work of one, and to stay in his house till they had finished. It was the secretary of the local gardeners' union who came to threaten the young girl watering her roses that all watering had to be done by union men; it was a movement to prohibit owner-drivers from driving their own cars and to force them to accept a union driver. It was a strike of the building trades, which dragged on and on until even some of the most preposterous demands were conceded. When the Socialist union had agreed to come back to work, two men from the Syndicalist union accosted the keeper of one of the houses being built and asked him: "Are you married?" "Yes." "Have you any children?" "Yes." "Then go for a walk, for we have a bit of a job here." And when the keeper came back the dynamite had done its work. Strikes and more strikes, occupation of factories . . . and meanwhile the House of Parliament playing the most incredible political tragicomedy which the wildest imagination could conceive: the deposition of the President of the Republic.

President Alcalá Zamora had done his best not to dissolve the Cortes. And rightly so. It is obvious that a dissolution of Parliament is an action which should only be taken under the stress of abnormal and imperious circumstances, and that a parliamentary body should be normally allowed to live through its full term. But over and above this general rule of common sense there was a special and grave reason why the Parliament elected in 1933 should not be dissolved, namely that it would be the second time President Alcalá Zamora would use his powers to that effect and therefore, according to Article 81 of the Constitution, the two following consequences would inevitably result: (1) he would not be able to dissolve the next Parliament at all whatever happened; and (2) it would be the first duty of the new Parliament "to examine and decide whether the decree dissolving the previous Cortes had been necessary. An adverse vote by an absolute majority of the Cortes implies the deposition of the President."

Now this Parliament which owed its existence to the presidential decree, a decree which turned a majority of the Right into a majority of the Left and which therefore proved, at any rate to the satisfaction of the Left, that the nation had changed its opinion radically and that therefore the previous Parliament no longer represented the will of the nation at the time when it was dissolved, this Parliament officially declared by 238 votes to 5 (the Right abstaining) that the dissolution had not been necessary. That is, it did not hesitate to show the world that the Spanish Republic was incapable of keeping its first president in office for more than half his term, and in order to satisfy its vindictiveness (though it is not easy to find out for what) it committed itself to the most glaring denial of logic the history of a free nation can show.

This singular event was, however, but one of the tactical moves in the Civil War then raging within the Socialist Party. The mover of the resolution which in practice aimed at deposing the president was Don Indalecio Prieto, a Socialist leader in close touch with Azaña. The feud between Don Indalecio Prieto, and Don Francisco Largo Caballero had become acute. Each of the two leaders had his own cure for the chief danger which threatened the Socialist Party—the infiltration of Communism. Vayo, the chief Communist agent inside the Socialist Party, in cooperation with Codovila, alias Medina, the agent of the Comintern in Spain, had succeeded in unifying the Communist Youths and the Socialist Youths, the two Marxist organizations built up in imitation of the Fascists even down—or up—to the shirts (blue with a red tie for the Communists, red with a red tie for the Socialists). Largo Caballero meant to meet the danger by rushing ahead of it. His line was a kind of national Communism independent of Moscow but doing for Spain within Spain what Bolshevism did for Russia within Russia. He advocated the dictatorship of the proletariat. Señor Prieto, on the other hand, had come back from Paris (where he had sought refuge after the 1934 revolt) converted to the policy of the Popular Front. He wanted to govern as prime minister with a team of all the parties of the Popular Front without exception, including the Communists. His plan was to hoist Azaña to the presidency and to launch the Republic on six steady years of brisk yet not disorderly Left policy under his own leadership. It was a good plan both from the point of view of the aims of policy and from that of the two men who would have been in charge of it, for Azaña and Prieto made a good team, each completing the other in a most happy manner and both genuine democrats having the good of the Republic at heart. Had this plan succeeded, Prieto and Azaña would probably have spared Spain the Civil War.

What made the Spanish Civil War inevitable was the Civil War within the Socialist Party. This is no exaggeration. The Largo Caballero group had founded a paper, *Claridad,* edited by Don Luis Araquistain. The Prieto group had kept control over *El Socialista,* the traditional party paper, under the editorship of a Basque Socialist, Señor Zugazagoitia, who carried to Socialism that fanatical narrowness which often afflicts our Basque countrymen. The pen fights between these two brother enemies of the party press became one of the chief features of the political arena of those days. "Where does the money come from?" daily asked *El Socialista,* which was run on party funds. And the ever-repeated question did but increase the heat of the controversy. Nor did the fight stop at pen and ink. On May 10, 1936, Azaña was elected President of the Republic. The election took place in the Crystal Palace of the Retiro, the only building big enough to hold the 911 electors required.[5] Araquistain and

---

[5] The electors were all the members of the Cortes plus an equal number of specially elected representatives who had no other function than this one and were dismissed and sent back home as soon as the president had been elected. This was one of the most absurd articles of a Constitution rich in absurdities. As I unsuccesfully pointed out at the time, either these *ad hoc* electors reproduced the political image of the Cortes or they did not. In the first case they only doubled the trouble and

Zugazagoitia met in the corridors. "Met" is not the word. They collided and had to be separated before Socialism caused Socialism one or perhaps two losses amongst its most spirited advocates. Señor Prieto meanwhile tried to put his case before his party followers. It was not easy, particularly when, as in a meeting of Egea de los Caballeros, his arguments were met with volleys of stones. In the company of González Peña, the leader of the Asturian rising in 1934 for which he had been sentenced to death (and amnestied)—as good a blazon as any for a Socialist gathering—he arrived on a day in May before a big crowd of Socialists in the Andalusian town of Ecija. Mark the fact, they were Socialists. No Fascists in Ecija, no Clericals, no bourgeois, whether of the Right or of the Left, no Communists, no Anarcho-Syndicalists. Just plain Socialists of Prieto's own party. And now let us listen to Prieto's own version: "In Ecija neither González Peña back from jail nor Belarmino Tomás nor I back from exile was allowed to speak. We three Socialists were hounded out of Ecija at the point of the revolver by our own co-religionists shooting at us hard. . . . The Seville police officer Saez and the head of the Municipal Guard of Carmona, revolver in hand, standing on the footboard of my car, covering the windows with their bodies, succeeded in breaking through toward the road to Córdoba, while youths from my mechanized guard, with their backs to the wall of the bull ring, protected my retreat with the fire of their machine pistols." All that because Don Indalecio Prieto had committed the crime of wishing to form a Popular Front Cabinet which Don Francisco Largo Caballero found objectionable. And in consequence thereof the Socialists of the second shot death at the Socialists of the first.

Such was the state of Spain in May 1936. It was not the clash between Right and Left, not the rising of that "feudalism" so dear to the political adolescents of all ages who invaded Spain in 1936 with their typewriters and saw in her whatever they brought in their own romantic eyes. It was a stampede of the

considerably increased the expense; in the second case they destroyed the authority of the members of the Cortes at the moment when it was most needed.

Largo Caballero faction of the Socialist Party in violent opposition to the will of the country as recorded in the general election —the non-revolutionary, steady-headed and legal stand of all Republican leaders, from Indalecio Prieto to Gil Robles; the opinion of a considerable portion of his own party which was not allowed to listen in peace to its leaders and whose meetings were dissolved by bands of gunmen who were Socialists—that and not the artificial picture painted by passion, ignorance and prejudice, was the keynote of those days.

No wonder Fascism grew. Let no one argue that it was Fascist violence which developed Socialist violence, for leaving aside the fact that a Socialist democracy should have been able to conquer violence not with violence but with the massive power of a nation standing fast on the law, it was not at the Fascists that Largo Caballero's gunmen shot but at their brother Socialists whose crime was that they wanted a Popular Front government. Much ink has been wasted in discussing whether a rising of the Extreme Left was being prepared when the Army officers rebelled against the State. Largo Caballero never made a mystery of it. It was his avowed, nay, his proclaimed policy to rush Spain on to the dictatorship of the proletariat. Thus pushed on the road to violence, the nation, always prone to it, became more violent than ever. This suited the Fascists admirably, for they are nothing if not lovers and adepts of violence. They also proclaimed their faith in force. Prominent men, now of the Right, now of the Left, fell wounded or dead. Churches, convents were burned. A judge who had given a sentence of thirty years (mild punishment in a country of amnesties) to a Fascist for the murder of a Socialist newpaper boy was shot dead in Madrid on April 13. On April 14, during a parade to celebrate the anniversary of the Republic, a lieutenant of the Civil Guard was shot dead by Socialists. His funeral was considered by the Fascists as an excellent opportunity for retaliation and developed into a battle between Socialists and Fascists in the very center of Madrid, through which the funeral was passing in defiance of government orders. A lieutenant of the *Guardias de Asalto,* or Government shock troops police, a man with Communist sympathies, distinguished himself by his valor and eagerness in attacking the Fascists. His name was Castillo. We shall hear of him again.

The reaction to these events on the part of the Extreme, anti-Republic Right was threefold. First, street-fights in which the Fascists were at times the aggressors, at times however the attacked. Then, a parliamentary struggle led by a distinguished Monarchist leader who, though not technically a member of the Fascist Party, voiced their views in the Cortes, particularly after the government decided to imprison the Fascist leader José Antonio Primo de Rivera. This Monarchist deputy was Señor Calvo Sotelo, a former finance minister under General Primo de Rivera. Finally, conspiracy. But in their eagerness to justify their own revolt, the Extreme Left have lumped together in their description of the Right trends of reaction which must be kept distinctly separate. It is clear already, and later events will make it still clearer, that the Gil Robles group had nothing to do with the violent turns which events were taking. The CEDA had been challenged in the democratic field—elections, parliamentary debates, majorities, Cabinet-making—and in this field the CEDA were confident that they could at least hold their own and even now and then, helped mostly by their adversaries' mistakes rather than by their own merits, reach power. In my opinion they were right in this. But whether right or wrong, they were too confident of their democratic strength to wish to upset the Republic; and, though among the rank and file confusion of thought and motives led to a good deal of collaboration between the CEDA and the Fascists, the set policy of the party and the consistent attitude of its leaders was against the use of violence in the conduct of political affairs.

This was precisely the chief cause of the rivalry between Gil Robles and Calvo Sotelo. The ex-finance minister of Primo de Rivera was still a relatively young man in 1936. He had returned from exile upon his election as member of the Cortes in February of that year and his forcible temperament and eloquence had at once conquered a leading position for him in the House. He was less attractive but had more driving power than the fastidious and at bottom skeptical José Antonio (Primo de Rivera junior) and his powerful voice rang through the ranks of Fascism like a call to arms.

Finally there was the Army. The Azaña reforms had bitten deeply into the once powerful officer class and, save for a relatively small minority of Republicans, most of them were determined to continue their now century-long history of conspiracies and pronunciamentos. Allies, of sorts, of the Fascists, they looked askance on those intruders in the field of armed politics which they had so far exploited undisturbed, and secretly planning to make short shrift of them once the business had been completed; they took them for the time being into their counsels as a regular army takes volunteers in case of need. The fact remains, however, that for the Army officers no assault on the state was worth considering unless it were launched in the already established fashion—by a wholesale revolt of the garrisons prepared and led by a secret conspiracy of the officers. The secret society *Unión Militar Española* had been in existence for some time. Its leader was General Mola, a literary general who had been head of the police under the Monarchy and was at the time Military Governor of Pamplona.[6]

On June 16, 1936, Señor Gil Robles made a speech in the Cortes in which he indicted the government for its leniency with regard to the prevailing violence and crime: 160 churches totally destroyed and 251 set on fire or otherwise attacked; 269 persons murdered and 1287 injured; 69 political premises destroyed; 113 general strikes and 228 partial strikes, as well as many cases of other forms of violence. Calvo Sotelo followed him with a strong speech, not in itself beyond what his right as a member of Parliament warranted, yet unwise in the extreme for

[6] In the course of a speech delivered on July 28, 1938, General Franco revealed that as the crisis of 1934 was coming to a head, he received a letter from José Antonio Primo de Rivera appealing to him to save the country. General Franco added: "My instructions were 'to wait watchfully without losing faith in the Army,' and when the moment came and the revolution broke out, to report to the military authorities in the certainty that their services would be welcome." This confirms all the analysis that precedes.

a man of his views in those heated days. As he sat down, Dolores Ibárruri, better known as *La Pasionaria,* a Communist member of Parliament, shouted at him: "That is your last speech!" It was.

On July 12, as Lieutenant Castillo left his home in the Calle de Fuencarral, at twelve o'clock midday, he fell on the pavement. Three Fascists had shot him dead. That night Calvo Sotelo happened to be sleeping in his own house for the first time after weeks of changing beds for safety. At 3 A.M. a number of *guardias de asalto* in uniform entered his bedroom and told him to dress and surrender, a prisoner. He claimed Parliamentary immunity. The leader of the intruders, later identified as Captain Moreno, in brusque, commanding tones, exacted obedience. Calvo Sotelo reached for the telephone to ring up the home secretary. "Useless. We have cut the wires." Calvo Sotelo dressed and went downstairs with his captors, who after all were government police in uniform. They took him into a police-truck, number 17. Their deed done, they drove to the cemetery and woke up the keeper. "Here," said one of the guards, "take this body. You will get the papers tomorrow morning." "As it sometimes happened that I received the bodies of dead people at night and the whole thing was regularized the next day," explained the keeper to the authorities later, "and as they were in uniform, I did not object."

The government jailed the ninety men of the company of the *guardias de asalto* to which Lieutenant Castillo belonged, but did no more about it. Five days later the army of Morocco revolted and the Civil War began.

It was a civil war. Up to now we have had to refer in no way whatever to the international feud which was to take hold of Spain and open wide the wound of her Civil War making her bleed for causes and interests other than her own. We are about to study the foreign intervention in this Civil War, not without first describing the foreign policy of the Republic. But meanwhile let us not lose sight of this all-important fact. The Spanish Civil War began as a purely Spanish affair, grown out of the Spanish soil in the old Spanish way. It was the outcome of the typical combination of the two predominant political passions of the Spaniard: dictatorship and separatism. It came from the scarcity of water and the excess of fire in the Spanish tempera- ment. When the ardent sun of Spain dries up the land—not particularly rich in water at that—the parched earth splits open. The well-meaning foreigner, set ablaze himself by Spanish pas- sions, says: "This earth here on the right . . . " or else "The earth here on the left is responsible."

But there is but one earth.

CHAPTER 7

THE FOREIGN POLICY
OF THE REPUBLIC

The first intimation of the attitude of the Republic to foreign affairs was that, in the Provisional Government, the Foreign Office was entrusted to Don Alejandro Lerroux. A curious choice. Lerroux, though a Spaniard of distant French descent, spoke very little French, understood it less still and had no knowledge of any other foreign language. He had never given to foreign affairs more attention than was usual on the part of middle-class citizens in Spain. His designation to that post was merely due to the fact that the majority of his colleagues in the Revolutionary Committee (which later became the Provisional Government) had come to a more or less tacit agreement to elbow him out of any of the ministerial departments having to do with home affairs. And that was that.

The next move in the field of foreign affairs was the appointment of a number of men of letters for the chief embassies abroad. This was not, as might have been imagined at first, an attempt at cultural window-dressing. It was an intelligent plan to replace the professional ambassadors of the Monarchy by men who were good—or at least passable—linguists; and the obvious choice was a group of men who had made their name in the letters of the country. One of them had had the privilege of sharing in the work of Geneva as a civil servant of the League. He is in the awkward position of being unable to write this chapter without now and then falling into the odious first person singular. I was appointed Ambassador in Washington in May 1931 and reluctantly had to leave the service of the Republic on July 9, 1936. The fact that I remained throughout these five years the *de facto* (I never was *de jure*) permanent representative of Spain in Geneva was one of the circumstances which contributed to whatever stability the foreign policy of the Republic had during its normal life. Other contributory factors were the relative indifference to foreign affairs on the part of parties and persons distracted by home feuds and the inertia of the problem itself, i.e. the permanent geographical, political and economic conditions which restricted the field of alternative policies.

This frame within which Spain was bound to determine her foreign policy was outlined by the following facts:

Internal: Need of peace for reconstruction; need of devoting expenditure preferably to social and economic purposes, and therefore, a limited part of the budget only available for re-armament, a matter of national interest; opinion divided in its sympathies as to the several European groups which led policy, though perhaps on balance slightly tipped in favor of France and Great Britain.

External: Geographical and economic considerations advised a policy of collaboration with France and Great Britain. Trend of opinion pointed to a good working understanding with the neutral powers in Geneva and of course to the closest and most cordial relations with the Spanish American countries.

Over and above these objective realities which determined Spanish policy there arose an opportunity to incorporate the true and complete League principles into the positive foreign policy of a reborn European nation. Some of us endeavored to make the Spanish Republic espouse this cause worthy of her national tradition. And so the lines along which the new Republic launched forth into the outer world might be laid down as follows:

1. Spain was to put into a modern idiom the leading ideas of her great theologian-jurists of the sixteenth century, particularly of Vitoria, therefore:

2. Spain was not merely to adhere to the League of Nations but was also to try to instill a true and sincere world community spirit into it.

3. In so doing Spain was not going to abandon the two chief claims to which she thought herself entitled: the restoration of Gibraltar and an agreement with the two Americas whereby her language and culture should be respected in the new world—without prejudice of course to the action of time and to whatever changes the free evolution of the Spanish-American nations might bring about.

4. Spain would endeavor to live in a fraternal friendship with Portugal.

5. Finally, as for tactics, Spain would follow in Geneva a policy of collaboration with the democratic small nations; while neutral in the struggle for power endemically going on in Europe, would keep a closer collaboration with France and Great Britain than with the other powers; and while claiming no leadership whatever, would remain in permanent touch with the nations of her language and culture in the parliament of nations.

The theoretical principles of this policy were embodied in the Constitution.

These principles of the young Republic were put to the test at once. Hardly had Lerroux announced them to the world in a speech read before the Assembly of the League, when, before that Assembly had dispersed, Japan started the ill-fated Manchurian aggression with a wanton and premeditated "incident." The Spanish delegate, by a strange coincidence, happened to be acting president of the Council. In the company of

Don Julio López Oliván, then Secretary General of our delegation, I called that very morning at the Hotel Metropole to ask Mr. Yoshisawa, the Japanese delegate, for explanations. This is not, of course, the place in which to relate the Manchurian affair. During the whole of it, with rare eclipses, due to occasional visits of the Spanish foreign secretary, it fell to my lot to handle it on behalf of Spain. I tried to conduct it as nearly on the principles of the Covenant as circumstances and my ability allowed. It was not always easy, for in so doing, the Spanish delegate had to incur the displeasure of the powers which wished things transacted on a more empirical plane.

But while the Spanish advocacy of the rights of China was apt to appear indiscreet to the French and to the British and positively obnoxious to the Germans and to the Italians, it won for Spain a strong position in the Assembly, particularly in two sectors of League or world opinion: Spanish America and the European "neutrals." Spain began then that move toward collaboration with the Scandinavian states, Switzerland, Holland, Belgium, and Czechoslovakia, which should count in history as one of the clearest cases of policy based on disinterested principles.

As to Spanish America the advent of the Republic had removed the last hindrance to a sound brotherly understanding. The Spanish-Americans are all republicans. True the political and social landscape there was and is complex, but in many ways, indeed in all but the peculiar problems arising out of racial tensions in some Spanish-American republics with a strong Indian population, the ups and downs of the Spanish-American political map were not unlike those of Spain, so that Spanish affairs were apt to be understood and felt more deeply in Spanish America than anywhere else in the world. The first administration of the Republic (Left) had sent Señor Alvarez del Vayo as Ambassador to Mexico. His work there was open-minded and generous. In 1935, the second administration (Right) sent a special embassy to Uruguay, Argentina, Chile and Peru to present decorations to the four presidents. At least two of the presidents concerned were wielding self-granted dictatorial powers. Spanish America was of course undergoing a political fermentation not unlike that of Spain. The oscillations of the Spanish pendulum were followed there with a keen interest. In Geneva there grew up a closer intimacy between the Spanish and the Spanish-American delegations than under the Monarchy.

The Disarmament Conference began in February 1932. I had been in charge of disarmament affairs in the League Secretariat from 1922 till 1928, a year in which I had published my views on the subject. The Spanish government gave me a free hand to organize the Spanish delegation and entrusted me with the task of defining its policy. I advised Azaña, then Prime Minister and Minister of War, to appoint himself as head of the delegation, which he did. I had by then been transferred from the Washington to the Paris Embassy. He wrote to me in terms which showed his sincere intention of attending the conference and in which his enlightened, clear and concrete mind shone at every line, asking to be instructed as how best to fulfill his task. To my deep regret he was prevented from coming by internal politics. I had looked forward with the keenest anticipation both to his success in Geneva—of which I was certain—and to the salutary effect which the international atmosphere of the League would have had on a first-rate man whose only limitations were due to the somewhat confined environment of petty friendships in which he vegetated.

I tried to draw as many men as possible to the delegation, Socialists like Luis Araquistain, Left Republicans such as Gabriel Franco and Américo Castro. Gradually however things proved too protracted and technical for most of the political delegates and I was left practically alone with the invaluable Señor López Oliván and the military experts. I had been elected president of the Air Disarmament Committee. Ever since 1928 I had insisted on the crucial importance of air disarmament and pointed out that the only way, if not to reach it, at any rate to endeavor to reach it, was the organization of world air transport under an international authority. Though idealistic, the Spanish policy on disarmament had never been unrealistic. Our argument was: "We must disarm or perish, either in peace under crushing taxes or in war under crashing bombs. We cannot disarm unless we pool policy. We must therefore set up world institutions of government and administration. If we are not able or willing to do so, then *we must rearm*." That last warning will be found in nearly all our utterances, especially when referring to naval affairs.

In accordance with this policy we introduced our air disarmament proposals and as their indispensable prerequisite we suggested an international air authority to take over all civil flying thus preventing its eventual use for military purposes by any aggressive nation. We were accused of being utopians. We were the only people in that Assembly who were realists, for we were the only ones who tried to meet the challenge of our age. When M. Pierre Cot became air minister in France he took over our scheme and proposed it at Geneva as his own (with our consent), adding to it an international air police force. (A police force is the most persistent bee in Marianne's Phrygian bonnet, perhaps a bee from the mantle of Napoleon.) The Spanish delegation of course supported the French proposals.

The Spaniards felt as keen an interest in European peace as any nation at the Conference—if only for internal reasons. But they felt that disarmament in itself was a meaningless word and that no security could be obtained by steel alone. Their aim was to strengthen the League as a world government, not precisely by adding to its police force but by invigorating its faith.

Hence our persistent campaign to strengthen—the *international* as people then still said, the *world* as we prefer to say —spirit of the League Secretariat. Well started, at least as well as might be expected in the circumstances, the Secretariat had begun to deteriorate after the visit paid by Sir Eric Drummond (later the Earl of Perth) to Mussolini in 1925. The Italian undersecretary general of the League was allowed to display the Fascist colors on his lapel in official gatherings without the secretary general or anyone else turning a hair, and even to transform his office into a regular branch of the Fascist Party in all but name within the League. This unseemly sight had demoralized the international civil service. The Spanish delegation took the view that the Balfour report of 1921 meant what it said, namely that the members of the Secretariat owed their allegiance to the collegiate bodies of the League, Council, Assembly, Court and their respective emanations, but to no national government. We obtained in spite of much passive opposition that all members of the Secretariat from the secretary general down should take an oath to that effect. We also broke down the well-guarded fortress which the big powers had built around the leading posts of the Secretariat by having it put on record that one of the two deputy secretaryships of the League should be reserved for a citizen of a small power.[1]

This spirit of world patriotism was also to animate the work of our delegation in two Spanish American disputes. They need not detain us at length. The conflict between Bolivia and Paraguay over the Chaco and that between Colombia and Peru over some disputed territories present a curious contrast. The first took years to settle and cost a long war to the two nations concerned. The second was settled with relative ease—as these things go. Why the difference? Because in the conflict between Peru and Colombia League procedures began at an early stage and were consistently adhered to by Colombia, while in the Chaco dispute both Pan-American and League procedures were engaged in at the same time, let alone other efforts carried out at several stages either jointly or separately by several other South American republics. The Chaco affair became a paradise

Pablo de Azcárate, to this post. This, however, in no way reflected on the moral authority of the Spanish delegation whom everybody knew to have had nothing to do with this rather unexpected appointment. Leaving aside the person concerned (the only argument that could be used with some force in favor of Sir Eric Drummond's decision), the Spanish delegation thought the appointment somewhat unfortunate since its aim had been to dissociate the high posts of the Secretariat from the nations permanently represented at the Council; and Spain while not theoretically permanent, had acquired in practice what amounted to a permanent seat. This matter of the Secretariat of the League will be found discussed at some length in my book, *The World's Design*, London, 1940. It is not quite accurately dealt with in the otherwise admirable *History of the League of Nations*, by Frank Walters.

for diplomats and Nobel Prize hunters. The Spanish delegation
was responsible for an energetic reassertion of the duties of the
League Council in the matter. But the old meshes caught the
fish again and after years of arguing and meeting, postponing,
dispersing and meeting again, the matter came to be settled in
Buenos Aires under the aegis of the Argentine foreign secretary
Doctor Saavedra Lamas.

In 1933 Spain and the Soviet Republic came to an agreement
whereby they mutually recognized each other and exchanged
diplomatic representatives. Lunatcharsky, who had been People's
Commissar for Education, was appointed Ambassador to Spain.
Lunatcharsky died without having gone to Spain and meanwhile
the Azaña administration had given place to one led by Lerroux.
The new foreign secretary felt that his predecessor had been too
lighthearted in agreeing to a mutual recognition without defining
any prophylactic measures against propaganda. The Spanish
delegate in Geneva was asked to negotiate a new agreement with
M. Litvinov regulating in detail the numbers of diplomatic
establishments and personnel to be admitted to each country.
All was ready for an exchange of ambassadors when the Left
revolted on October 4, 1934, and the matter was left in abeyance.

At the beginning of November 1932 Edouard Herriot, then
French prime minister, paid a three-day visit to Madrid. This visit
was what migh be described as a premeditated improvisation.
Lunching with Herriot at Geneva one day during the 1932
Assembly, I had suddenly asked him: "When are you coming to
Madrid to confer the Grand Cross of the Legion of Honor on
President Alcalá Zamora?" There had never been any question of
such a distinction before, and I thought that the decoration and

¹ Sir Eric Drummond, a master at chess, appointed a Spaniard, Don

the visit were in themselves desirable for a relatively young republic. Herriot was as usual charming and friendly. "As soon as
you like," he answered. He was laboring under the fears which
oppressed all Frenchmen before the rising power of Germany.
He evidently hoped to find help in Spain, whose geographical
position between France and her African colonies was so strategic from the French point of view. I thought it for my part
worth while to try the possibilities of a closer alliance between

the two republics. Spain after all had signed the Covenant and was bound to help France under Article 16 if France were attacked.

Herriot had a huge personal success with the people. Unfortunately Azaña chose to dodge a private meeting with him and of course was successful. Herriot was feted and in every way made at home, but he was kept politically starved during the three days he enjoyed our hospitality. On the third day the crowd which assembled at the station to see him off was so thick that fully a quarter of an hour was necessary to cross the few yards which separated the railway station from the carriage, and as the train began to move, Herriot, not without deep emotion, was able to hear the "Marseillaise" sung by thousands of friends of his country. Yet he left Spain a disappointed man. At the French frontier we parted, for he cut across to Toulouse where, on November 5 (1932), he had to address the Congress of the Radical Socialist Party. He spoke little of Spain and, somewhat too much in a hurry perhaps, he extended his hand, empty of Spanish friendship, to Mussolini. The Duce did not grasp it. He already had other views.

The star of Hitler was rising on the northern horizon and Mussolini was thinking furiously—always a painful process for a dictator whose stand is on brawn rather than brain. With or against? That was the problem. If imitation is the best form of flattery, Hitler was flattering Mussolini heavily, even to the point of inflicting shirts on his followers in a climate where to go about in shirt sleeves would appear to be unwise. The Duce was bound, however, to reflect that if it came to blows (and to what else could Fascist policy come outside Italy?) his northern disciple would be in a stronger position to make his blows effective than he had ever been or could ever hope to be. To keep the new threat at bay, France and Great Britain had granted Germany concession after concession. Mussolini was cynically meddling in the Danube, arming Fascism in Austria and in Hungary as the notorious Hirtenberg affair (January 8, 1933) had revealed. M. Paul Boncour who had succeeded Herriot as prime minister and foreign secretary, swallowing his strong anti-fascist feelings, had sent M. de Jouvenel to Rome as a special ambassador to try to tame the Fascist lion.

These movements, and in particular the rapid rise of Hitler, had also caused deep heart searchings in Moscow. The Soviet dictator was brewing a change of tactics which was to bring him gradually to collaborate with as many parties as possible both in foreign affairs and in internal politics. The first was to lead him to Geneva and to the International Peace Campaign, a League of Nations Union hallowed with the spirit of Communism; the second to the Popular Front. This change of tactics manifested itself without delay: on November 29, 1932, Herriot's government signed a pact of non-aggression with the Soviet Union; on February 6, 1933, speaking at the Disarmament Conference in Geneva, Litvinov fully endorsed the French thesis that security was the basis for all disarmament.

Mussolini, who at first had received de Jouvenel with dignified aloofness, later put forward his scheme. It consisted, of course, in a dictatorship: that of the four powers, Germany, France, Italy and Great Britain. This would have implied a return to secret diplomacy and to power politics and the abolition of the League of Nations as a clearing house of public opinion —far and away the most important function of the League. Spain with its associated powers declared against this plan.

Far from being weakened by these threats the League was growing stronger in people's minds and even the Soviet Union began rapidly to evolve toward it. The Spanish delegate was fortunate in sponsoring the entry into the fold of Geneva of no less than three important powers—the Soviet Union, Turkey and Mexico—thus contributing to that universality of the Commonwealth of Nations which was a tradition of the best Spanish political thought.

But other forces were at work which, temporarily at any rate, were to win. In January 1935 Laval paid a visit to Mussolini. Upon his return he was good enough to receive the Spanish delegate in Geneva and to read him the papers which were the outcome of that historical meeting. The Spanish delegate was struck by the lack of balance between what President Laval had obtained from the Duce and what he had given in exchange. "Is that all?" he asked President Laval. The answer was a repeated assurance that that was all. The Duce began to prepare his attack on Ethiopia. Meanwhile Hitler decided to increase the Reichswehr to 550,000 and to restore conscription, thus challenging the Treaty of Versailles openly. France, Great Britain and Italy, who had so far tolerated many a discreet breach of the treaty even in this highly dangerous field of German rearmament, had to react, and a meeting was held at Stresa between the prime ministers and the foreign secretaries of the three countries. No mention was made of Ethiopia at that meeting.

Before leaving Stresa, Ramsay MacDonald announced to the press that he meant to ask the Spanish delegate in Geneva to be *rapporteur* before the Council. Both Ramsay MacDonald and Laval requested me to act in this capacity a few days later in Geneva. The Spanish government would not of course allow their representative to act alone in such delicate matters, and it was decided that the Danish and the Chilean members of the Council act with the Spanish member. The changes which we introduced into the draft report which the three powers had brought from Stresa were unacceptable to Laval. We declined to proceed with the report.

During the year the Abyssinian dispute rapidly deteriorated. I was in a curious position about it, for I no longer held any official post within the Spanish state and was an off-and-on representative appointed only if and when and for the time when there were important gatherings in Geneva. Reasoning therefore more or less *a priori,* i.e. by deductive logic based on (1) the declared policy of the British people, (2) British interests, (3) the commitments of the British government both with their electorate and abroad, I consistently reported to my government that Great Britain meant business and that therefore Signor Mussolini would have to climb down or be beaten by the concerted action of the League Powers under Article 16. But Don Ramón Pérez de Ayala, who was Spanish ambassador in London and had become a close friend of Sir Robert Vansittart (as he was then), no less consistently reported that nothing whatever would happen and that the Spanish government need not worry about Abyssinia. There is no question that Sir Robert Vansittart knew best which of us was right.

The negotiations with Mussolini were of two kinds: public and private. The Spanish delegate was the nominal head of the public negotiations, for it was by then recognized that Spain stood for the League and nothing but the League. But things happened in the soft light and padded atmosphere of the big chancelleries and the Spanish delegate had no illusions about it. Right at the apex of the League formal power as chairman of the Committee of Five, composed, beside himself, of the Foreign Secretaries of Great Britain, France, Poland, and Turkey, he knew full well that his authority was only symbolic and his power but that which his nation, and possibly also his personal advocacy of League ideals, might allow him to wield over public opinion. In his League ardor, he was moreover no less limited by national considerations than were other delegates. After all Spain was on this hard earth, very much so indeed, and while collective security, and all that, was very noble and beautiful, anyone but a fool could see that France and Great Britain were carrying on a game of power politics in which League moral forces were but another wing of their economic and military armies, while we, the other nations, had nothing to fall back upon if sanctions failed, i.e. if they no longer suited Great Britain or France. At one stage in the proceedings Great Britain sent letters to the Mediterranean powers asking them whether they would cooperate with England on the basis of Article 16 assuming that naval sanctions had to be applied to Italy. This question was not put to Spain at the same time as it was put to the other powers, but a good deal later. When it came, Spain answered that her forces would always side with those of the League.

Nevertheless, a doubt was bound to linger in the minds of those Spaniards who carried on the work of the League as to the actual strength of the roots which the decision to stand by the League had in the country. We knew only too well how

shallow and uninformed the interest taken in foreign affairs
was apt to be in a country torn asunder by deep internal feuds.
Don Fernando de los Ríos, one of the few competent foreign
secretaries the Republic possessed, had set up a Permanent Committee of Foreign Affairs composed of all present and past
holders of the posts of President of the Republic, President of
the Cortes, Prime Minister and Minister of Foreign Affairs. It
was an admirable idea. Señor Azaña refused to attend while
he was in the Opposition, even, be it noticed, before the unseemly persecution of which he was the victim after October
1934, which might have justified such an action. Besteiro and
Don Fernando de los Ríos himself were deprived of any possibility of attending since they had too much common sense to
acquiesce in a preposterous demand of the Socialist Party to
the effect that they report the proceedings of the Foreign Affairs
Committee to the party. Policy and decisions arising out of it
were constantly at the mercy of the arbitrary ideas of the politician who happened to be Foreign Secretary. While the Foreign
Office was in charge of Señor Lerroux or of one of his appointees, whose interest and knowledge of foreign affairs was
but moderate, a certain continuity could be maintained. Even
then policy was apt to be at the mercy of an enterprising under
secretary. This happened for instance during the five weeks
(March-April 1934) during which I was Minister of Education,
when the policy of close touch with the ex-neutrals plus Belgium
and Czechoslovakia was altered by excluding these two nations
from the group. In my view the basis for the group should have
been a common faith in democratic ideas rather than a common
legacy of attitudes from the First World War. For both these
reasons it was therefore necessary to keep Belgium and Czechoslovakia in the group. But when, temporarily absorbed in the
affairs of another Department of State, I had to let go whatever
hold I had on foreign affairs, a young undersecretary of State,
a diplomat of pro-German leanings, succeeded in giving the
necessary push to pre-existing tendencies within the group, and
Belgium and Czechoslovakia ceased to receive invitations to our
meetings.

Shortly before the fall of the last Cabinet of the Right administration of the Republic, that presided over by Señor Chapaprieta, I thought it necessary to warn our Foreign Office that sanctions were growing more and more effective and that it might come to shooting against Italy. Since I had always maintained in Geneva an attitude favorable to sanctions I wanted to be sure that I carried my government with me. The prime minister himself, an ex-Monarchist who had never to my knowledge expressed his Republican faith in particularly forcible terms, answered: "Well, we have signed the Covenant, haven't we? Then, let us go ahead." There came a change, *the* change. And the Popular Front took office. Azaña was at the helm. I was in New York. When I arrived in Madrid I called on him, for I had been informed that my services were required for Geneva. (I had held no official post since April 1934.) The first thing Azaña said to me was: "You must get me rid of Article 16. I will have nothing to do with it." This was his official language. His unofficial language was: "What do I care for the Negus?"

These details must be given because they provide the necessary corrective for our tendency to take too rigid a view of life. Those who have drawn lines as straight as steel rails, inserting Spain in a Fascist-anti-Fascist plot, are mistaken. Spain is mysterious, elusive and nearly always unexpected. Señor Chapaprieta, the ex-Monarchist, the head of a reactionary ministry which all the Left branded as Fascist, was ready to shoot at Fascist Italy in defense of Abyssinia and of the Covenant of the League. Azaña, the pure spirit of the Spanish Republic at the head of a Popular Front Cabinet and Parliament, was anxious to forget all about Article 16 and declared that the Negus' interests were of no interest to him. These are the facts, and we have to make what we can of them. Despite appearances and a certain "café" style in his "to hell with the Negus," there was at least as intelligent an attitude in his reserve about Article 16 as in Señor Chapaprieta's resignation over it. For Azaña Article 16 was something which called forth guns in the Balearic Islands which he had not yet installed, munitions for the army which he had not yet bought, aircraft which he did not possess. He was right. It so happened that within the group of neutral states in Geneva conversations had been going on for some time over the failure of the League in the Abyssinian dispute. They were by no means definite negotiations; just collective searchings of heart. We nations without a world policy or ambition other than peace were called upon to share the dangers of the policy of the Big Powers when it went wrong but not in the councils of the Big Powers when this policy was being devised, and still less in the benefits of it when the policy went well. This fact seemed to me an inherent injustice in the working of the League. The utter inability of Switzerland to share in the sanctions against Italy was a lesson of reality to us all, and we Spaniards could not forget how powerless Spain had felt when the question of sanctions against Paraguay had been raised. The Soviet Union, moreover, had by then developed a keen interest in the League and M. Litvinov was brooding over the peace indivisible. Yet for some of the states of our democratic group this enthusiasm of the Bolshevik neophyte was at least as suspect as that of France. They felt that the Soviet Union wanted to work *through* rather than *for* the League; to turn the League into a barrier against the German danger, rather than to see in the League the portals to a new world of real peace. This was particularly true of the Netherlands and Switzerland, states which had always refused to recognize the Soviet Union.

I discussed these matters several times with both Azaña and Don Augusto Barcia, his foreign secretary. In these conversations I had endeavored to put the requirements of Spain into technical League terms, and when I was ready, with the foreign secretary's agreement, we called a meeting of the neutrals in Geneva. At the request of the Dutch foreign secretary I circulated among the neutrals of the group a note summing up our points as follows:

1. The Covenant must be revised to make it more practical.

2. No textual amendment either needed or desirable.

3. Nations to reserve their rights to limit their general obliga-

tions under Article 16 as long as (a) the League was not universal, (b) Article 8 (disarmament) had not been applied.

4. Express acceptance of the obligations of Article 16 for concrete political and geographical zones defined by the states concerned.

5. Simplified Covenant reduced to Article 11 for such states as wished to remain outside the League.

6. Abolition of the unanimity rule in the application of Articles 10 and 11.

7. Stress to be put on preventive rather than punitive procedure.

8. No collective security without collective policy.

These proposals were presented on May 9 and their text sent to Madrid the same day. They were of course confidential, and as a matter of diplomatic manners had been put forward as my personal suggestions, though of course they corresponded exactly to the wishes of Azaña and to the views of his foreign secretary and I believe were beneficial both to the true interests of Spain and to those of the League itself. Under circumstances which are obscure the memorandum leaked out and at once gave rise to a press campaign against the Spanish delegate, in the papers not merely of the Socialist Party but of Azaña's party as well. On July 9 I published a statement declaring that I was no longer at the disposal of the government. I could not resign because I had nothing to resign from. The move was part of the clearing of the decks in which the Left was engaged at the time in order to prepare for the coming Civil War. The revolutionaries needed another man in Geneva.

PART 2

THE CIVIL WAR

CHAPTER 8

THE BATTLE OF
THE THREE FRANCISCOS

The controversy which raged in the West over the Civil War was largely obscured by the fact that most foreign disputants minimized or ignored the genuine Spanish nature of the conflict and stressed its international aspect. They were sedulously misled and encouraged thereto by the two parties to the dispute, for each, powerfully interested in securing foreign help, sought to win it by declaring its enemy strongly Fascist or strongly Communist. This double maneuver was met by a double barrage of counter-propaganda, tending to show that there was no such things as Communism in the Left or as Fascism in the Right, and incidentally that neither Communism nor Fascism had anything to do with the outbreak, while Fascism or Communism had everything to do with the outbreak on the other side.

In these matters, however, the denial had more strength than the assertion. Though both Russian Communism and German-

481

Italian Fascism had shown a marked interest in the Spanish Civil War for some time before it actually broke out, it is a fact that the actual outbreak was the combined effect of two typically Spanish pronunciamentos: that of Don Francisco Largo Caballero, Commander-in-Chief of the revolutionary wing of the General Union of Workers (UGT), which was not Communist, and that of Don Francisco Franco, Commander-in-Chief of the rebellious General Union of Officers (UME), which was not Fascist. In July 1936 these two men incarnated the Spanish tradition of violent interference in internal affairs. We are to see that Azaña belatedly thought of incarnating the other Spanish tradition, that of reasonable compromise and mutual understanding so admirably cultivated in Spain by Don Francisco Giner. In this battle of the three Franciscos the true, the great, the creative Francisco, the hope of Spain, was crushed out of action by the other two. And yet though still too weak and too inchoate to assert itself, it was the spirit of Don Francisco Giner which the majority of Spain preferred.

Those are right therefore who claim that Russia had no direct responsibility in the Spanish Civil War. They are, however, wrong when they refuse to recognize the fact that Italy and Germany had no direct responsibility either. The Civil War was a strictly Spanish event and its two initial protagonists were two men of the truest Spanish character at the head of two institutions which in the truest Spanish tradition revolted against the state through sheer inability to resist the temptations of the power which they happened to possess. Neither Communism, Russian or otherwise, nor Nazi-Fascism, German or otherwise, had the slightest possibility of provoking a Spanish Civil War in 1936, even if they had tried, which they did not. Such a power was exclusively in the hands of the Army officers and of the union workers.

This does not mean that Russian Communism had been idle, or that German-Italian Fascism had held aloof. Far from it. The hopes raised in Lenin, Trotsky and other Communist leaders by Spain as the second Russia of Europe are a commonplace of Bolshevik literature. The Third International had followed, and probably "preceded" the Asturias revolt of 1934 with the utmost interest. During the Eighth Congress of the Communist International which took place in Moscow in August 1935, the Trojan Horse policy to be adopted by the Comintern from then on was formulated and expounded by Comrade Dimitrov. This was the policy which led Russia to Geneva, to the International Peace Campaign and to the Popular Front. The chief agent for that policy in Spain was to be Señor Alvarez del Vayo, the stronger and more efficient for his remaining officially a Socialist. His trips to Moscow had begun in 1930, a year before the fall of the Spanish Monarchy. In April 1936, a party of over a hundred Spaniards and pseudo-Spaniards who had been living in Moscow passed through Paris and were sent on to Spain with every possible care and attention by the Spanish Embassy. The mayor of Getafe, a small township close to Madrid, the seat of one of the capital's chief military airfields, was in July 1936 a man known as *El Ruso,* for no one knew his real name but everybody knew his views and where he had got them. *Viva Rusia* and *Viva Thaelmann* were to be read on all walls, and people greeted passers-by in town and country with the clenched fist. Youths collected money in theatres, cinema halls and cafés or from cars halted for the purpose on the road, offering as a receipt little squares of white paper with a red clenched fist and the words: "Socorro Rojo" (Red Help). The feeling that Russia was behind the storm was universal.

And yet M. Litvinov was probably sincere when during the May council meeting in London he said to the Spanish delegate: "I wish your Socialists would keep quiet!" It did not suit the Comintern, it did not at any rate suit Litvinov's policy to have a violent shake-up in Spain at that time. The policy of the Trojan Horse requires a wooden horse and not a live colt which kicks and neighs and plays unexpected pranks. Soviet Russia was as interested in a Spanish revolution as Don Francisco Largo Caballero, but not at the same time nor in the same manner, and in point of fact, though it was Moscow which had dubbed Largo Caballero "the Spanish Lenin," Moscow was beginning to find him rather a nuisance.

This view tallies perfectly with the fierce duels which were being fought at the time within Spanish Socialism for or against a Popular Front Cabinet. In those days the man who advocated full collaboration with the Spanish Communist Party was not the Left Socialist leader Largo Caballero but the Center Socialist leader Don Indalecio Prieto, and the shots in Ecija were fired for or against an all-in Popular Front Cabinet with Señor Prieto as its head. The setting up of such a Cabinet was known to be the policy of President Azaña who, not unnaturally, wished to load all his wild horses with an equal load of governmental responsibility. The Communists, however, were not very keen to embark on such a venture. They preferred the game their French comrades played with M. Blum—criticism and overbidding from the ranks of the parliamentary majority—but they let Largo Caballero oppose the scheme for them.

From a confidence made by Gil Robles to a foreign ambassador and from another confidence made by Azaña to a common friend, I am in a position to assert that neither side expected a victory at the polls in February. There is ample evidence, some of it private but reliable, to justify the belief that while from Señor Prieto to Señor Gil Robles, both inclusive, all sectors of Spanish political life would have accepted parliamentary defeat in a sporting spirit, neither the Left Socialists nor the military would take a popular verdict unsavory to them without violence; and that therefore the next election was bound, one way or another, to lead the country to a civil war. The extreme Right, and in particular the officers, were convinced that a plot against them was being brewed by the Revolutionists, and on both sides lists of names of the men marked for assassination were known to circulate.

How far had the connivance with the two Fascist states gone? The answer is not easy. Here again, as on the other side, a good deal of propaganda has been built up on a case which is not as big as the paper it has inked over. The most substantial piece which has been exhibited, a record of an interview with Signor Mussolini and Balbo in Rome on March 31, 1934, can only be exploited as a proof of the origin of the Italian help to the

Falange by people without sufficient knowledge of Spanish politics. It is signed by four Monarchists, three of whom happen to be Basques,[1] and it merely states that the Duce will provide arms and money to restore the Monarchy in Spain. The very poverty of these documents suggests that, here as with the Communists, what happened was that Hitler and Mussolini, in fact Germany and Italy, had been spreading their nets in Spain to suit their own ends of military and economic espionage very much as every big power does in a greater or lesser degree everywhere, and at any rate so far as Germany is concerned with tremendous power and efficiency;[2] but that definite plans for a Fascist rising had not been established at all despite a number of journeys of military and Falange leaders to Germany and Italy.

In discussing this matter, the extent of responsibility which attaches to Soviet Russia on the one hand and to Nazi Germany and Fascist Italy on the other, in the Spanish Civil War, both sides seem to forget that oncoming events seldom bear any resemblance whatsoever to what they turn out to be after they have run their course. For Moscow a Spanish revolution probably looked like a seething caldron of conflicting workers' unions ending after a series of mutual terrors in the dictatorship of a particular "Stalinez"; and when Spanish generals or Falangists visited Mussolini asking for help, they certainly would recall to his mind the bon-vivant, debonair, big-hearted, naive Primo de Rivera, and he would certainly think that a matter of a week would be all the new men—be it Sanjurjo, Goded or Franco —would need to be firmly established on the saddle of a new

[1] Note in passing that this Monarchist paper of purely Spanish general politics having nothing to do with local Basque politics throws up three Basques out of four protagonists. This shows how heavily weighted with Basque influence was and is the Spanish Right. This document will be seen in G. T. Garratt's, *Mussolini's Roman Empire*, p. 37. Other publications against Italy and Germany as instigators of the Spanish Civil War are: Louis Fischer, *Why Spain Fights On*, U.D.C., London. *The Nazi Conspiracy in Spain*, London, 1937.

[2] A most impressive account of these German infiltrators in Spain was issued in June 1938, in Barcelona, by the Office of Foreign Propaganda of the Anarcho-Syndicalists under the title *El Nazismo al Desnudo*.

dictatorship. Plans? Did anyone make plans for the most cruel and destructive civil war even Spain has known? These matters are all too often discussed in the spirit of the famous chorus of steel-clad knights who stepped forward on the stage during a historical play singing: "We are off for the thirty years' war!"

On July 17 in the afternoon the garrison of Melilla revolted. On the same day General Franco,[3] having obtained full command for his cause over the Canary Islands where he was Division General and Commander-in-Chief for the Republic, flew over to Morocco where he was a popular figure with the troops, the Spanish Tercio (a professional unit) and the Moors, owing to his personal courage, and put himself at the head of the rebels. On the 18th many Peninsular garrisons went over to the pronunciamento. Señor Casares Quiroga, the prime minister, who had made light of the coming trouble a few days earlier, resigned that night; and President Azaña sought to return to the middle of the path (from which he should never have strayed) by forming a Cabinet under Señor Martínez Barrio with his own men and with the collaboration of Don Felipe Sánchez Román (a Left Republican who had not accepted the Popular Front Pact). This move was in the right direction, but while to all appearances the rebel Right found it was too late, the revolutionary Left countered it even more violently with a pronunciamento of their own "general": Don Francisco Largo Caballero, at the head of the "army" of workers, declared that he would prevent such a solution if necessary by force of arms. Señor Martinez Barrio's Cabinet ceased to exist after three hours. A Ministry under Don José Giral, which in practice meant under President Azaña and entirely made up of Azaña's friends, took charge.

It found itself powerless to act. The rebels had won nearly everywhere except in the East and on a strip of territory on the northern coast. These two exceptions were not due to the same cause. In the first case, the center of Republican resistance, Barcelona, had been stoutly defended by an able military commander loyal to the established authority, who with Civil Guards

[3] A biographical sketch of General Franco will be found in Arthur F. Loveday's *World War in Spain,* London, 1939, chapter 16.

and Storm Guards prevented the several forces of the rebellious garrison from coming together and beat them separately. The soldiers, moreover, when free from the drugged drinks administered to them to induce them to fight, realized the game and refused. General Goded, who commanded in Majorca and who, leaving it in the hands of the rebels, had flown over to Barcelona to take charge of the rising there, was caught and shot. (Since General Sanjurjo had been killed in an air accident as he flew from Lisbon to put himself at the head of the rebellion, this left Generals Franco and Mola as the only leaders.) In Madrid the rebel commander General Fanjul procrastinated, and when he struck, the workers' unions, armed by the government, overpowered him on July 20 and stormed the barracks of La Montaña.

When this first wave of events subsided both sides realized that the plot had neither failed nor succeeded and that they were in for a civil war. The situation was confused in the extreme.

From the point of view of territory: The government held Madrid, the whole eastern coast, the Mancha, New Castile and an important band of Estremadura which cut the rebel territory into two. They were, however, cut off from the northern territories which had remained under the Republican authority, Guipúzcoa, Biscay and Santander. Beyond Santander, Asturias was cut about by civil war and in Oviedo, General Aranda, gone over to the Rebels with his garrison, was besieged. The rest of the country had gone over to the Rebels.

From the point of military strength: With few exceptions, it may be said that every army officer who was free to do so joined the rebels. Of the officers who sided with the Government, only a minority did so out of personal conviction. The majority would have joined their comrades had they been in a position to do so; they often tried and at times succeeded in crossing the line. The rank and file of the regular army was honeycombed with a minority of Government sympathizers, but there is little evidence to substantiate the view that they were unreliable for the Rebel generals in the western territory as they had been in some big towns. A glance at the figures of the general election of 1936 will show that left opinions were not in Spain by any means as popular as it is sometimes maintained, and in general, the North and the West of Spain, apart from industrial districts, has never shown much sympathy for revolution, a fact which need not be accounted for by calling this part of Spain such names as feudal or illiterate or medieval. The *Guardia Civil* (about 34,000 strong) were nearly unanimously for the Rebels, though everywhere their first impulse was to side with authority (which explains the Barcelona success). The Storm Guard or *Guardias de Asalto* (about 6,500) sided with the Government nearly everywhere. The Rebels counted on the Moorish troops, known as *Regulares,* a well-organized force about 11,000 strong, and with the *Tercio* or Legion (composed of professional soldiers, most of them Spanish) rather less than 5,000 strong, but excellent fighters. There was no lack of free-lances on the fringes of the rebel force, whether of the new school (Falange) or of the old (Carlists and *requetés*). The Air Force split about half and half. Many airmen, by a kind of natural selection, were of extreme Left views. But being extreme is a matter of temperament, while being Right or Left is often a matter of mere hazard. So there were many pilots with Falange sympathies too. As for the Navy, it would have gone over to the Rebels altogether but for the Communist cells which had been set up in many ships. In these ships the crews promptly murdered their officers and seized command. A battleship *(España),* the two new 10,000-ton cruisers *Baleares* and *Canarias,* as well as two smaller ones, *República* and *Almirante Cervera,* with smaller craft and the bases of Ferrol and Cádiz, were all that remained to the Rebels.

The Government had practically no regular troops and hardly any officers. The storm troops were its stand-by at the outset, but they were a handful of men, albeit resolute. The militias and irregular formations of the several unions were well-armed for the relatively small affrays in which they used to indulge, but their armament was no match for the Rebel forces even after the Government had opened the state arsenals to them. Worse still, the workers were handicapped by the mutual separatism of their unions and by indiscipline within their ranks. Separatism between Anarcho-Syndicalists and Socialists, between Socialists and Communists and even within Socialists, led to setting up a number of politically colored military units. In the Anarcho-Syndicalist units, commanding officers were unknown and there was complete equality. These units moreover fought where and when they pleased, left the front when they pleased and served under their own flag.

At sea the Republican Government kept control of one battle-ship (*Jaime I*), three cruisers, fifty destroyers and ten submarines, with the naval base of Cartagena. Few officers remained in the service and still fewer after the murder of their comrades and the setting up of sailors' committees to lead the ships. The Republican Navy rapidly lost its efficiency and power and its submarines were practically useless. (It may well be, however, that the state of the submarines was not of the best even before the murder of the officers.)

From the political point of view: The rebel side was first and foremost a military dictatorship. Here again it is important to remember that things did not look then as they turned out to be later. The Army had rebelled. Well. What of it? It had done so before. And in its view, the Army would soon have wiped out the "four desperadoes" who opposed it. There was therefore no necessity to set up a complicated government or to seek the help of any public opinion, national or foreign. The revolt of 1936 had little to do with Fascism. To be sure Falange and Requeté volunteers were welcome, but they hardly counted, while the generals felt certain of winning without their help. Sanjurjo's death on July 29 had left but two leaders in the field. General Cabanellas, an old republican, by the way, set up a kind of governing junta in orthodox military fashion: five generals (including himself) and two colonels—as perfect a government as could be dreamed of in any barracks. The two aces of the Army in revolt were members of it: General Mola, who commanded in the North; and General Franco who commanded in the Southwest. There is no doubt that General Mola had a better claim than General Franco to lead this junta; yet, through the operation of forces still obscure, it was General Franco who on October 1, 1936, became generalissimo and head of the Spanish State.

This appointment may well have been the first sign of the evolution which gradually turned a military, Spanish-born, into a Fascist, foreign-inspired movement. There are signs to warrant the belief that in the summer of 1936 both Italy and Germany expected to see a more or less conservative parliamentary, representative or perhaps corporative monarchy in Spain. When General Franco occupied the seat where the throne should have been, it began to be doubtful whether the views of the preceding summer had resisted the wear and tear of over two months of Civil War.

On the Republican side, the Giral Cabinet ceased to count the moment it handed the weapons over to the unions. The ministers lived the first days of the war inside the Ministry of the Navy, barricaded against their own followers. The country gave itself over to the two ruling passions of the Spaniards: dictatorship and separatism. Every region, town, province and village had its own government; every working-class organization also. Some attention was paid to the Civil War, but more to the proletarian revolution. Schemes for taking over lands, factories, houses, were not merely discussed but put into operation forthwith by dictatorial authority in every one of the thousand and one totalitarian states into which Spain had split. The cooler and more experienced minds of the country saw the disaster toward which Spain was fast traveling along this road of anarchy, and in order to diminish the distance between the Government and the revolution it was decided to put in office the very man who had let loose the hurricane. Don Francisco Largo Caballero became prime minister (September 4, 1936). There was a surprise in the composition of his Cabinet. His foreign secretary was not Don Luis Araquistain but Don Julio Alvarez del Vayo. This was a clear sign of the rising power of Moscow in Spanish affairs. Another one was the inclusion of Don Indalecio Prieto, the exponent of the Popular Front, as

Minister for the Navy and Air Force. There was a new figure in the Cabinet—the Minister of Finance, Don Juan Negrín. In the Left as in the Right, under the pressure of the war and the need of foreign help, the genuine Spanish element, the pronunciamento of the working-class army leader, was gradually giving place to the foreign-inspired product: in this case, Communism.

Catalonia had had to meet similar difficulties. Dictatorship and separatism developed in her body politic with no less force, indeed with more force, than in the rest of Spain. The Committee of Fifteen which, in Barcelona, took upon itself to lead the people against the Rebels included a number of government representatives, as a concession, but rarely if ever stopped to think that there was a regular government over there in the building of the *Generalitat*. In August 1936 a committee was set up to supervise the collectivization of industry, trade and agriculture. But this collectivization was carried out thoroughly by the innumerable governments, juntas and committees which had sprung up in every town, province and village and were all carrying out their ideas to the bitter end on the particular piece of territory which had fallen to their lot, rejoicing in being separated not in the least from the rest of Spain, but from the next town or village, which of course made it the easier for them to govern dictatorially.

Cutting across this fermentation of dictatorship and separatism, the most vigorous exponent of both these Spanish passions, the National Confederation of Labor (CNT), was organizing them both for its own enjoyment and satisfaction, strong in the possession of the best stock of arms in the country. The CNT owed this advantage partly to its traditional attachment to lethal weapons, partly to its quick and efficient action on the day the state arsenals were thrown open to the people. It gradually organized a militia while the more spirited of its followers put an unbounded energy in sending flying columns right into the country to impress the peasants with the urgency of revolution. This meant killing the prominent people, burning the church and destroying the land registration office. The chief leaders of this organization were a number of Anarchists and Syndicalists, two of whom, both Catalans, were to be in later days members of the Government: García Oliver and Federica Monseny. This group was less interested in the war—passionately interested in it though it was—than in the establishment of libertarian Communism in towns and villages so as to pave the way for the abolition of the state.

The Socialist Party had never been strong in Catalonia, for their optimistic temperament made Catalan workers more addicted to anarchism. Dire experience made the Catalans less optimistic and so the PSUC (*Partido Socialista Unificado de Cataluña*) came into being, under the aegis of the Third International, as a relatively conservative force not merely in the field of revolution (which it wanted, if not put off, at least subordinated to the war), but also in the field of the war itself, for the PSUC advocated a People's Force, disciplined, uniformed and technically led. These ideas, so obvious to us, had a revolutionary air in the picturesque anarchy of the revolutionists. There were overwhelming reasons for this policy, yet the Anarcho-Syndicalists looked askance on it, not merely out of their attachment for freer and more spontaneous ways, but because they feared that behind it there lurked the danger of a Communist dictatorship when none but Russian arms, tanks and airplanes would be available. The Anarcho-Syndicalists, however, were not alone in their opposition to the Communist variety of Marxism. The POUM (*Partido Obrero Unificado Marxista*) was also on the field fighting for the true doctrines of Marxism as incarnated in Trotsky.

Sitting on the stormy clouds above so many separatisms, the government of the Generalitat itself would not be left behind either in dictatorship or in separatism. It found, however, more facilities for the latter than for the former, and so, profiting by the exceptional circumstances in which the country had been plunged by the rebellion of the Right and the revolution of the Left, it tore a few leaves from the Constitution and from the Catalan Statute. It appointed a Minister of Defense (August 1936); issued legislation openly beyond its powers, notably in matters of collectivization of the land; founded a Catalan Army; printed money and appointed a Councilor for Foreign Relations.

In the Basque country opinion was deeply divided. Navarra had gone over wholeheartedly to the Rebels, had indeed supplied them with some of their hardiest and most enthusiastic troops, the Requetés, the backbone of traditionalist opinion, than whom in Spanish politics no one could be more to the Right. Alava is deeply religious, the most devout Roman Catholic province in Spain[4] and one in which Basque Nationalism was not less developed than in Guipúzcoa or Biscay. The outbreak of the Civil War put the three provinces in a terrible predicament. Industrial centers, big or small (Bilbao or Eibar, for instance) were of course with the Republic, but on the other hand were by no means hot on Basque nationalism. The memories and traditions of political and social strife were clear for them on that point. For the workers of Bilbao or Eibar, Basque Nationalism meant priests and employers, not freedom and high salaries. On the other hand, the military Rebels who were soon also to adopt the battle name of "Nationalists" (though of course, Nationalists of the whole Spanish nation) looked askance on Basque Nationalism. It seems, though the point is not yet certain, that the Rebels tried to win over the Basque Nationalists as they had done the Basque Monarchists (both Alfonsine and Carlist). At any rate, in August 1936, the bishops of Vitoria and Pamplona exhorted the Basques to separate their cause from that of Communists and Anarchists. But by that time, the Basque Nationalists were already setting their hopes on the Revolutionary Government in the hope of obtaining a better price in terms of home rule, and in the end, on October 10, 1936, the Cortes of the Republic voted the Basque Statute and the three provinces threw in their lot with the Left.

It was a strange combination, for the fact that the Church

[4] Those simple minds who think religious devotion and even bigotry incompatible with "education" measured by indexes of literacy might take note that Alava is the second-best province in Spain in the scale of literacy. Its figure yields only to that of Santander, a province of Old Castile. Cf. similar observations on Palencia, Book I, chapter 15.

was being ruthlessly persecuted by the revolutionists can only be disputed or contested by ignorant or prejudiced critics. Whether the number of priests murdered was 16,000 or 1600 time will say. But that for months, years perhaps, the mere fact of being a priest was tantamount to a capital sentence, and the fact that no Catholic worship was allowed at all till the end of the war or very nearly, and that churches and cathedrals were used as markets and thoroughfares for animal-driven vehicles cannot be disputed. The Basque Nationalists could hardly appease their conscience with the thought that many of their priests had been imprisoned, some shot and others ill-treated by the Rebels for their Basque-Nationalist views; for there is a far cry from ill-treating or even killing a man, though a priest, for political reasons to a systematic persecution and wholesale murder of priests *qua* priests and the prohibition of worship and the desecration of churches. It was a clear case of inward separatism even from their faith.

Yet while the mind recoils in horror before these events, and while the heartless persecution of the Church and its ministers was undoubtedly one of the most unpardonable mistakes of the revolutionists, it is necessary to bear in mind a number of points. The Church had sadly neglected its chief duty in Spain. No institution in any country had at its disposal assets as splendid as those the Catholic Church had in Spain to keep its hold on the people, for Spanish Catholic culture is exceptionally rich in all that which most easily touches the soul, and particularly the Spanish soul: the arts. Whether in architecture, sculpture, painting, customs and traditions (processions, *romerías, etc.*), the dramatic arts or music, Spain stands at the head of Catholic culture. What use had the Church made of this spiritual treasure? None whatever. The "flowery and starry autos of Calderón" (as Shelley admirably describes them) were often staged on the porches of cathedrals . . . in Switzerland. The Spanish priests and bishops do not read them. The noble music of Victoria, Cabezón, Salinas, is never heard in our religious services and the fine Gothic buildings have gradually emptied themselves of all national and religious significance and degenerated into show-pieces of a vast museum for guide-book readers. This was the worst crime of the Spanish Church, for it has let the spirit of the Spanish people lie fallow, ready for other seeds. This is the crime for which it had to pay in 1936-39.

There were others, however, and in particular that the Church almost infallibly espoused the worst causes in our national life. Always on the side of the powerful, the rich, the oppressive authority, the priest had to become the object of general aversion. "The Reds have destroyed our churches," sadly said one of the finest priests of the Catalan Church on board ship in Barcelona ready to leave for a long exile, "but we priests had first destroyed the Church!" [5]

This was no exception. When the Civil War broke out, the Spanish Church ought to have opened out its arms like its Leader, to the Right and to the Left. It ought to have opened its breast and heart to both sides in a gesture of peace and union, to have fought for peace and union and died for it. But no. From the outset it was with one side, the side of military force. To be sure, there was something to be said for that side in those days. No man is entirely and hopelessly wrong. But it was not for the Church to say it. And on July 10, 1937, the Spanish Episcopate published a collective Pastoral siding officially with Rebel Nationalists.

When the Civil War broke out the country was full of rumors about the armament which had been stored up in churches, convents and monasteries. Cases of fortified religious houses there certainly were, nor can we entirely blame the Church for it since for three or four years violent acts against religious buildings had been recurring with growing frequency. Cases in which the crowd succeeded in persuading itself that it was being shot at from church tower windows which on inspection were found to be completely inaccessible must also have been frequent, for I know of one myself. But in the tension of the circumstances it was inevitable that the combination of three forces—the anti-

---

[5] He was one of the many priests courageously saved by Companys from the terror of the first days. I know of no effort by the Church to save Companys.

clerical passion of the extremists, the anti-clerical feeling of the vast majority of the urban popular classes, and the spirited rather than spiritual attitude of the priests themselves—should give rise to deplorable events.

The more so as during the first days the prisons had been thrown open under the uncontrolled frenzy for freedom which seized hold of the Extreme Left.[6] Emptied months earlier of their political prisoners by Azaña's amnesty law, they could only disgorge common criminals. The judge of the Criminal Court suddenly found in his private apartment the thief and criminal whom he had recently sentenced to thirty years' hard labor transmogrified into a militiaman who, after demanding all the silver and gold objects of the household and tying them into a linen sheet, shot him dead in the presence of his wife and daughter. Thus was a revolution being dishonored when even in its most extreme elements it was not lacking in cleanliness. An American citizen who visited the cruiser *Miguel de Cervantes* in August 1936 talked with the sailors who had formed themselves into a committee for commanding her. He saw the cabins of the murdered officers sealed. He was surprised. "Don't you need the space for yourselves?" he asked. "Why, yes," they answered. They could use that space, but they had a reason for keeping it empty. They were killers, they explained, but they were not thieves. "In those cabins there was money. There was clothing. There were jewelery and watches and personal property. They were not going to have any looting. As a favor they broke the seal on the Admiral's cabin and let me go in. Everything was untouched; there was a nice clock on the table and pretty things here and there. The Admiral's chair stood in front of his desk just as it was when he used it, except that the back and seat was sticky with blood and there were bullet holes through the cushion."

There are two sides to this story. It shows the admirable honesty of the revolution. It shows also the systematic nature, nay, the political nature, of the murders. Too much stress has been laid on the anarchical, irregular and irresponsible nature

[6] This frenzy went so far as to opening lepers' houses in some cases.

of the terror which shook Spain at the beginning of the Civil War. An objective examination of the facts shows that there was a good deal of method under the madness. Thousands of persons perished by authority of the workers' revolutionary committees. Toward the end of August the Government tried to canalize terrorism—suppress it, they could not—by setting up People's Tribunals composed of three legal judges and fifteen representatives of the several political and labor organizations which composed the Popular Front.

But the idea that such things could happen on one side without occurring on the other was purely romantic nonsense. And, of course, the tale of terror is equally bad on both sides. All attempts at distinction are futile. The usual line is for the Rebels to deny or minimize the quantity of their acts of terror; for the revolutionists to excuse theirs on the ground that their government at first lacked police and military forces to stop them and did stop them in course of time. Let those with a bias choose their bias. But it is all one and the same. Terrorism on both sides was rife, systematic and prolonged. In a sense it was inevitable and irrelevant.

Impartial information proved after the event that both sides sinned equally. A moment of reflection shows it was bound to be so. There are at least two reasons: both sides were in a hopeless minority within their borders, therefore both were bound to be oppressive and violent out of fear; and, moreover, the deepest reason of all: there is but one earth, the same Spanish earth on both sides.

In this atmosphere of violence the life of the mind could not thrive. At the beginning of the war, under the most severe coercion, the intellectual leaders of the country had been made to sign a manifesto in favor of "the Republic," i.e., the revolution which paraded abroad under the Republican mask. The three leaders who had founded the Association in the Service of the Republic in 1931, Don José Ortega y Gasset, Dr. Marañón and Don Ramón Pérez de Ayala, repudiated this manifesto as soon as they found themselves freed by exile, and it may well be that this unsavory experience contributed to the regrettable attitude in favor of the other side which they were inclined to take since. Other men of rank in Spanish culture had equally tragic experiences. That great Spanish mind Don Miguel de Unamuno had felt so much alienated by the errors of the Republic that he had enthusiastically hailed General Franco's rebellion; but when he saw the Germans heavily trampling on the soil of his beloved Salamanca he died of grief. Don Pío Baroja fled from Rebel Spain after having fled from Revolutionary Spain. And the majority of men of thought of the Liberal Left, including Cabinet ministers and members of Parliament of the Popular Front, left the country oppressed by the revolutionists as soon as they were able to do so.

This is perhaps the moment to say that the much advertised salvage of the Prado pictures, far from being such a salvage, was one of the worst crimes against culture committed by the Revolutionary Government in the teeth of the determined opposition of that magnificent museum keeper Señor Sánchez Cantón. Madrid possessed an up-to-date underground chamber for the protection of such art treasures, recently built and fitted with the best technical appliances ninety feet below the cellars of the Bank of Spain. The English experts who visited the country to investigate this matter were made to believe that this chamber was not technically safe. I was at the time chairman of the International Office of Museums of the League of Nations and am in a position to declare that there was no foundation whatever other than political smallness for exposing the inestimable treasures of the Prado to the risks to which they were exposed, with deplorable effects.

To offset this heavy responsibility, the Revolutionary Government has to its credit the excellent work performed in salvaging books and works of art from private houses during the days of revolutionary anarchy and of Rebel bombardment in Madrid; while the Rebel Government can hardly claim to pass muster unscathed since it is responsible for the destruction of the beautiful Palace del Infantado in Guadalajara and its followers bear the shame of having murdered the poet García Lorca, one of the brightest hopes of Spain.

CHAPTER 9

THE FIRST TWO PHASES
OF THE CIVIL WAR

THE NATIONAL PHASE

The purely national phase of the Spanish Civil War begins on
July 17-19, 1936, with the military rising in Morocco and it
ends on November 8, 1936, with the dramatic appearance of
the International Brigade in the streets of Madrid. It may seem
at first paradoxical to classify as national the phase which begins
with the collaboration of Italian airplanes in General Franco's
operations and ends with the arrival of the International Brigade;
but the fact is that during this period the war is a purely Spanish
affair which the Italians on the one hand and the French on the
other supply with a number of aircraft, without as yet coloring
or determining to a considerable degree the political or military
leadership of the war.

Italian help began at the start of the rebellion. On July 30,

1936, three Italian airplanes made a forced landing in Algeria. The French inquiry established that they were part of an airforce put at General Franco's disposal by the Duce. These reinforcements tipped the balance in favor of the Rebels at a critical moment in the war. General Franco drove his advantage home, and by means of airborne troops took Algeciras and La Linea while the Revolutionary Fleet still held the mastery over the Straits. By the end of the month, however, after a battle off Cape Espartel, the control of the Straits changed hands and General Franco was able to count on Morocco as a relatively safe base for his operations. Between July and September his forces operating in Andalusia gradually took every important town except Málaga and Almería as well as the valuable mining districts of Río Tinto and Peñarroya which provided him with important means for obtaining foreign currency, and gave the English and the French financial concerns interested in these two districts some food for thought about the issues of the Civil War. The fall of Mérida (August 9) and of Badajoz (August 15) allowed him to join hands with General Mola whose armies were operating in the North.

General Mola with but a slight curtain of troops on the Sierra covering his rear from the somewhat casual and spasmodic attacks of the inexperienced militias of Madrid, concentrated his efforts on Irún, so as to win for his side the vital railway communication with France. He took it on September 5 and he took San Sebastián on September 13. His offenxive against Bilbao and Santander, however, lost its impetus after a few weeks, probably through lack of material, for General Franco needed all available forces for his attack on Madrid.

This attack was launched up the valley of the Tagus with about 4,200 soldiers of the Tercio and 2,000 Moors, not to speak of more or less efficient Falangists. This force took Oropesa on August 29 and Talavera on September 3. The chief military interest should have been Madrid. Sentiment, however, ruled otherwise. From the first week of the war, Toledo had revolted against the Government, then had been recovered by the Government not without a stubborn aerial bombardment.

About 1,000 men (Civil Guards, regular soldiers, cadets of the Infantry Military School and volunteers) had resisted in the Alcázar a siege which was followed everywhere for its dramatic interest. Shelled, bombed, mined, the besieged refused to surrender, and when on September 22 the forces of General Franco reached Maqueda, forty-six miles from Madrid, instead of marching on to take the capital and finish the war, they turned southeast to relieve the Alcázar. The troops there were freed after a seventy-day siege. It is doubtful whether the gain in spirit and enthusiasm fully compensated the Rebels for the loss of time which this romantic episode entailed.

General Franco took supreme command of the Rebel forces and made it his chief task to take Madrid. On November 4 the Rebels were already within seven miles of Madrid and the whole bend of the Manzanares was invested by their eager troops. General Franco was then evidently sure of taking the town and had adopted a number of measures in anticipation of his victory, with regard for instance to public order, political arrangements, food and even, it is said, material for triumphal arches.

While the Rebels advanced under the aegis of dictatorship, the Revolutionists were indulging in an orgy of separatism. Every political formation was developing its own militia. There was no common flag, and Catalonia was trying to conquer Majorca as in the medieval days of James the Conqueror. Fighting was heroic, costly in human lives, sporadic and futile. The rapid advance of the Rebels brought about a healthy reaction. Señor Giral's Cabinet resigned to give room for a frankly proletarian ministry presided over of course by Largo Caballero. His first decision was to call back the Catalan expedition which was trying to conquer Majorca. The Rebels occupied all the Balearic Islands save Minorca by the end of September, but Don Francisco Largo Caballero thought that the islands could wait while the fate of Madrid hung in the balance. He was determined to create a real army out of the several militias which the uncontrolled enthusiasm of the proletariat had improvised, and he began by appointing a General Staff—for, strange to say, it did not exist yet. Such an army did eventually come into being and the achievement must count as one of the great feats of creative improvisation for which the Spanish people are justly famous. At the outbreak of the Civil War, the Republic had been left with twenty-five staff officers (i.e., men having gone through the regular courses of the General Staff College) and with about five hundred professional officers of several arms. This mother cell developed into an army of 1,500,000 men and 40,000 officers. But it took time. Meanwhile the enemy was at the gates of Madrid and the new ministry had but a handful of soldiers, a handful of weapons and no discipline.

No wonder General Franco was sure of taking Madrid. He had surrounded it, leaving, however, a generous opening toward the southeast and east to allow the Revolutionists to escape, for as the Spanish saying goes, a fleeing enemy should have a bridge of silver. On October 19 the President of the Republic and those of his ministers who were closest to his way of thinking left Madrid for the eastern fronts. On November 5, a manifesto was issued by the ministry to the effect that Madrid would be defended to the bitter end. The ministry, however, left for Valencia the next night leaving Madrid in the hands of General Miaja with an advisory committee composed of representatives of every one of the political colors of the Popular Front rainbow. Four columns of Rebels were converging on Madrid. It was then that General Mola coined a phrase which has had the fortune of becoming familiar in every language of the world: he had, he said, a fifth column inside Madrid. This moment was the high-water mark of the Rebel hopes. On the 8th of November these hopes were dashed to the ground. The first battalion of the International Brigade had arrived.

THE PHASE OF FOREIGN INFILTRATION

This event marks the end of the Spanish phase of the Civil War. To be sure, foreign help was available from the beginning. The Italian aircraft caught in the act on July 30 had been followed by many airplanes, both German and Italian. By the middle of August, General Franco was credited with twenty Junker transport planes, five German fighters and seven Italian (Caproni) bombers, while a number of Italian and German pilots and instructors were serving with the Rebels wearing the uniform of the Tercio. Monsieur Pierre Cot was sending as many airplanes as he could to Barcelona. "Cot tells me," writes one of the chief exponents of Dr. Negrín's policy, "that he was instrumental in sending one hundred French airplanes to the Loyalists. Seventy of these went in 1936, thirty in 1937. Of the seventy, fifty were sold by private French companies with the consent of the French Government. Thirty-five of these were new pursuit planes and fifteen were good bombers and reconnaissance machines. The other twenty were old and were sold unofficially to André Malraux. . . . Here André Malraux performed an invaluable, historic service. His Foreign Legion of the Air, which he recruited abroad, and which flew the planes which he purchased abroad, disputed the Fascists' mastery of the air and reinforced Loyalist resistance at a time when it might otherwise have collapsed in August, 1936." [1]

Italian whippet tanks appear in the Rebel Army as early as the second half of October. By October 29 the revolutionists were using Russian tanks and their Air Force was observed to have grown stronger. Still, so far both sides were at the phase of material help, and personal aid was limited to a number of pilots, flying instructors and mechanics as well as tank experts which Italy and Germany had sent the Rebels and to a number of Russian generals and staff officers who appeared in Madrid in September 1936.

The military rebellion had not been a walk-over. The revolutionary rising against the generals (and against the Republic in the process) had not been a walk-over. Neither side had succeeded in walking over the great majority of the nation which lay helpless and disarmed between them and which they were both trampling underfoot to satisfy their intransigent, absolute political passions. Each side had therefore felt bound to appeal

[1] Louis Fischer: *Men and Politics,* Jonathan Cape, London, 1941.

to its foreign friends. And at the same time these foreign friends were beginning to wonder what was going to happen in Spain.

This is the moment when international Communism took over the Spanish Civil War. This and no earlier. Let us remember that the Third International was then in that "Trojan Horse" phase under which it had developed the tactics of the Popular Front for internal affairs and of the International Peace Campaign for foreign affairs, that is, in both cases the tactics of collaboration not merely with the other Socialist parties but with any party ready to collaborate with it—even the Roman Catholics. In Spain the Communists had protested against the fierce anti-clerical onslaughts of the revolutionists of other labels. The Communists all over the world took up the cudgels for the Left, for the Spanish Republic, for the Loyalists, in whose government, they and their liberal friends loudly protested, there was not a single Communist. Not a word about the thoroughgoing social revolution which was driving a coach and four through the Constitution of 1931. The enthusiasm which seized nearly every man, woman and student for this cause was due to Communist endeavors to an extent which can only be realized by comparing its heat and effects with the attitude of the Left of the world (both Marxist and Liberal) during the phase of the Second World War previous to June 22, 1941, in all non-belligerent countries and, so far as the Communists were concerned, even in the belligerent countries. If International Brigades were put together and students in American universities enlisted and died to rescue the Spanish Left on the ground that it fought for democracy, what less than international divisions or armies should have been recruited for England when she stood alone in the world for democracy after Dunkirk? But no. The Communists were not in the business and there was no enthusiasm for England in the world, none even among the English Communists themselves. "When these Internationals marched through Madrid," writes Louis Fischer, "the civilians greeted them with *'Viva Rusia.'* " Everybody knew who had sent them, though most of them were actually French.

The International Brigades were organized in France, of

course, with the tacit approval of the French government. The first impulse of this government was to help the Spanish Republic, and there is little doubt that they would have done so but for two factors: the swift transformation of the Civil War into a social revolution, with which the relatively conservative mass of the French people felt out of sympathy,[2] and the general state of affairs in Europe, which made it unwise for France to launch into European adventures without careful stocktaking of her military resources.

The true originator of the policy of non-intervention was M. Alexis Léger, the permanent undersecretary at the Quai d'Orsay. The last word was pronounced on a direct question put by President Lebrun to the war secretary, M. Daladier, who had remained silent throughout the whole discussion during the Cabinet meeting which debated it. "Will the war secretary take responsibility for sending war material out of France at this moment?" The war secretary answered "No." That settled the matter.

But the wider problem has not always been discussed as realistically as it might have been had the passions raised by the Spanish Civil War in most other countries permitted it. Agreements are only a part of international life. In actual fact, much depends on the percentage of their efficiency. The non-intervention agreement served its purpose in so far as it drove underground a double set of activities which, had it been given free course on the surface of European life, would have precipitated the crisis disastrously early—how disastrously we know today better still than we knew then. While the two Fascist powers were cynical in the way they interpreted the agreement, none but England could withstand a scrutinizing gaze from the Angel Guardian of non-intervention, and as Mr. Winston Churchill tersely wrote at the end of a year of Civil War, France was neutral and England strictly neutral.

[2] This was typified in the attitude of the French ambassador, M. Herbette, who had been the staunchest friend of the Republic, particularly during its Leftist administrations, and who strongly advised his government to exert the utmost caution as soon as the Civil War began.

The very definition of the agreement owed its most important weakness and the one best exploited by the totalitarians to the liberal and generous scruples of the French government. France suggested non-intervention merely in matters related to the supply of war material. When her original proposals were made to the British and Italian governments first, then (on England's suggestion) to Russia, Germany and Portugal as well, the two Fascist powers countered with a super-proposal to the effect that volunteers were to be prohibited as well. This could not be swallowed by French public opinion, and M. Blum stood for the right of any man to volunteer for any cause. He did not realize what an opportunity he was giving to the countries in which all the will to volunteer was concentrated in one man. The six powers had come to a final agreement on non-intervention by August 24. On September 9 the first meeting of the Non-Intervention Committee took place in London. On November 8 the First International Brigade organized in France saved Madrid. They were 1,900 men, among them the cream and flower of the most generous souls ready to die for freedom in the countries of the West. On November 14 the Second International Brigade, commanded by Lukacs, reached the front. As they increased in quantity, their average standard deteriorated in quality. But that came later. At the War Office, from the end of September on, sat a Russian General Staff headed by General Goriev.

About the beginning of December Italian infantry detachments began to arrive in Spain soon to be withdrawn again after a short period of service.[3] The stream of "volunteers" from Italy began again later and kept pace with that of the Communist contingents which reached Spain from France. These contingents have been variously estimated on both sides. Some estimates put the maximum of Italians at 100,000 and that of Germans at 6,000 to 10,000; while the International Brigades were, I happen to know, at one given moment exactly 22,200. The contingent of Russian experts has been generally estimated

[3] Royal Institute of International Affairs: *Survey,* 1937, Vol. II, p. 47.

as 6,000, but it does not appear that more than 500 were ever in Spain at a time.[4] The *Survey of International Affairs 1938* asserts that Italian help must have amounted to at least 100,000 men, 4,370 vehicles, 40,000 tons of material and 750 guns. As for the Germans, they began to provide air support on July 31, 1936, and twenty of their Junkers' were used for transporting Moroccan troops to Spain. The Kondor Legion was dispatched in November. Air, sea and land, signal, artillery and other specialists were also sent to train Spanish personnel. In both cases the authorities for these data are German and Italian.

Figures, however, are not the main factor in such things. From the point of view of the conflict itself the intervention of volunteers was graver still than that of war material. It determined the growing dependence of both sides on the powers which acted as supply bases for them. Both parties tried to dramatize the issue. We were told that the Left of Spain was falling into the claws of Russian Communism, but as Russia was very far away, it did not sound convincing. On the other hand, the Communist-bamboozled Left of the Western Powers grew anxious about a Spain permanently occupied by Hitler and Mussolini, and refused to believe that Mussolini would evacuate the Balearic Islands after the war. While the London *Times* published a solemn article reminding the world that Spain had never tolerated the foreigner to keep an inch of her soil after any civil war (clean forgetting Gibraltar), British Communists complained of the indifference of their Conservative countrymen to the dangers arising for the British Empire out of the policy of non-intervention. Passion had gone to everybody's head and Englishmen and Americans were unable to talk sense, or to hear it, as soon as Spain was mentioned.

Everybody became passionately interested in Spain. British Laborites who had always lived in blissful indifference toward the exploitation of Spanish workers by British capitalists and

---

[4] According to Mr. Fischer, who recruited for the International Brigade: "About 40,000 foreigners entered Spain during the war to join the International Brigade, of those, no less than 3,000 were from the United States." Op. cit.

who stoutly resisted the Popular Front tactics inside Great Britain, suddenly waxed eloquent about the misery of the Spanish land proletariat and paraded before Spanish crowds raising their clenched fists. English Liberals who, a few years before, could not bear the idea that Danzig was not German, and had never had any qualms about Gibraltar being English, could not swallow the idea that Mussolini might keep Ibiza, of whose existence some of them had only just read. It was well-nigh impossible to talk sense in this atmosphere without being branded as a traitor by both sides and darkly suspected of wishing to sit on the fence—as if the fence between the two parties were a safe place on which to sit during a civil war.

Small wonder that, caught in this atmosphere, the men at the helm in France and in Great Britain, whether Socialists like M. Blum or Conservatives like Mr. Eden, should have found it difficult to steer a steady course. Daily the encroachments of the three Totalitarian Powers increased. On November 18, Germany and Italy recognized General Franco's government, a few days (as they thought), two and a half years (as it turned out) before he took Madrid. On the initiative of the Spanish government the Spanish Civil War was discussed by the League Council at its December (1936) meeting, as an event likely to endanger the peace of the world. The resolution adopted by the Council reflected the fears then universally entertained about the territorial integrity of Spain, for it recalled the obligation of all states to respect each other's territorial integrity and to abstain from intervention and the efforts which were then being made by France and Great Britain to end the conflict by mediation.

As for territorial integrity, both sides protested too much, but the facts condemned them both. Though no doubt exaggerated, the reports of German activity in Spanish Morocco toward the end of 1936 and the beginning of 1937 were true, and had it not been for the energy with which the French government spoke and acted at the time, this activity might have led to the establishment of German air and army bases in Spanish Africa. As it was it led to assurances of respect for the integrity of

Spanish territory by Hitler himself to M. François Poncet (January 1, 1937). On the other hand, the revolutionists on February 19 sent a note to the British and the French governments offering territorial changes in North Africa to France and Britain, to the detriment of Spain, in exchange for help in the Civil War. Great Britain replied in the negative on March 20.[5]

The efforts toward mediation made by France and England (December 4, 1936) were of course doomed to fail. The only point on which both sides were in complete agreement was that there was to be a Civil War. Simultaneously France and Great Britain were endeavoring to put a stop to the arrival of volunteers, whether of the free, the compulsory or the mercenary variety, which in the end they succeeded in doing, at any rate on paper, in February 1937. The plan included a system of frontier and coast control which had to be amended in view of the opposition to it on the part of both sides of the Spanish Civil War. This as a matter of fact was another of the points on which both sides thought alike: they wanted no control. By the end of April 1937 the corps of observers was working on the frontiers outside Spain.

This plan, part of the general scheme for localizing the war, nearly made it flare up over the whole of Europe. Italy and Germany were supposed to patrol the eastern coast of Spain. On May 24, 1937, an Italian patrol ship was bombed off Palma de Mallorca by Spanish revolutionist airplanes, with the loss of several Italian sailors. The incident did not lead to grave consequences. But on May 29, 1937, the *Deutschland,* in patrol service off Ibiza, was also bombed by Spanish Revolutionist airplanes, with fatal German losses. Both these incidents were the outcome of individual action and lack of discipline within the air force. But Nazi Germany reacted with typical brutality, and as a reprisal, Almería, an open harbor, was bombarded by German ships on May 29. The two Totalitarian Powers seized this opportunity to withdraw from patrol service and from the Non-Intervention Committee until adequate guarantees had been

[5] R.I.I.A., *Survey,* 1937, vol. ii, p. 283.

provided against the recurrence of such incidents. The agreement reached on June 12, 1937, was strained by still another naval incident, the alleged attack on the German cruiser *Leipzig* by a submarine. Germany and Italy withdrew from the naval patrol altogether.

After much bickering, the British government presented proposals on July 14 providing that when substantial progress had been made in the withdrawal of volunteers the two sides should be given belligerent rights. Matters had by then become acute owing to a campaign of mysterious sinking of ships which the brisk trade in arms and ammunition then being practiced at the expense of Spain's blood and treasure professed to find most inconvenient—though in actual fact it evidently raised its profits. The campaign was due to another of Signor Mussolini's cynical tricks. On the initiative of the British Foreign Office the nine states interested in the repression of this new form of piracy met at Nyon (September 10, 1937) and took strong decisions. Any submarine found in suspicious circumstances by the warships of these powers was to be attacked forthwith. Piracy ceased instantly, particularly when Signor Mussolini adhered to the Nyon decisions, and as Mr. Churchill pointed out in an unforgettable speech, never since the days of Caesar had the fiat of Rome more instantly pacified the Mediterranean.

CHAPTER 10

THE PHASE OF FOREIGN CONTROL

The difficulties which both sides were encountering in the struggle raised the importance of foreign help, and therefore this phase of the war sees the rise of the Communist Party and of Russian help on the Left and the rise of the Falange and of Italo-German help on the Right.

The influence of the Russian General Staff on the War Office increased. Russian advice often prevailed over that of the Spanish experts, who, though few, were competent and resented what for them was a political rather than a technical conception of strategy. The Russians stood firmly for a unified army under a unified command, which in itself was mere common sense, but which nevertheless carried little conviction since at the same time they retained complete control through the Spanish Communist Party over the Fifth Regiment, a Communist army in itself. The true aim of this campaign for a unified army and command was not merely technical but political as well. The

511

Communists felt that if the Army could be unified, it could be put more efficiently under their complete control, owing to their hold on supplies, and once in possession of the Army, they would be in possession of Spain.

The technical idea of the Russians was the mixed brigade, which, under pressure from them, was adopted as the tactical unit of the Revolutionary army very much against the opinion of the Spanish technicians. The mixed brigade was a kind of miniature army in itself, endowed with small units (usually a company) of all the auxiliary arms and services round a nucleus of four rifle battalions. The Revolutionary Government under Señor Largo Caballero set up six of these mixed brigades, as well as two international brigades in Albacete. Of these eight brigades, five were given militant Communists as commanders. The tank and aircraft services were kept under separate control by the Russians, to such an extent that secret airfields existed which were unknown even to the Spanish General Staff, to the Army commanders in whose territory the airfields were established and to the war secretary who happened then to be prime minister as well.

How could such a thing be possible? By that time, the Soviet Union was officially represented in Spain by Comrade Marcel Rosenberg. He attended the Councils of Ministers and meddled in Spanish affairs with the authority of the man who delivers the goods. He made a mistake: he did not read Señor Largo Caballero's character aright. Don Francisco Largo Caballero was at that time as much of a revolutionist as—indeed more so than—Comrade Stalin. He was governing very much like a dictator himself within the sphere of his actual power, and showed an utter disregard for President Azaña whom he did not even take the trouble to protect against occasional—more or less staged—accesses of so-called popular fury. But with all his defects, Señor Largo Caballero, a proud man, was not the kind of person to allow himself to be driven by anyone. This is what Comrade Rosenberg forgot. The Soviet ambassador used to call on the prime minister with an array of experts, generally to insist on appointments of Communists to key posts within the state. As he spoke no Spanish, Comrade Rosenberg used to take Señor Alvarez del Vayo with him so that the foreign secretary should be his interpreter. Señor Alvarez del Vayo was moreover at the time General Commissar for the Army, a point which should be noted since he had been for years the chief agent of Bolshevism in Spain.

Every effort was made at the time to bring D. Francisco Largo Caballero under the fold of the Muscovite orthodoxy—not excluding a (Red) Papal Brief. On December 21, 1936, Pope Stalin and two of his Cardinals, Molotov and Voroshilov, wrote to Comrade Largo Caballero a letter brought from Moscow by Comrade Rosenberg in which promises and advice were skillfully blended with discreet warnings. This letter is most illuminating, particularly as an illustration of the care bestowed upon tactics by the Bolsheviks. It will be remembered that at the time these tactics had become moderate, liberal, democratic. So, here is Comrade Stalin's advice to Comrade Largo Caballero:

> The Spanish Revolution[1] strikes out its own line, different in many ways from that followed by Russia. This results from the difference in the social, historic and geographic conditions, *and from the necessities of the international situation.* It may well be that the parliamentary way will prove to be a more effective instrument for revolutionary development than in Russia. . . . Here are four friendly pieces of advice which we put before you: (1) Due attention should be paid to the peasants, whose importance for an agrarian country such as Spain is considerable. It would be advisable to issue decrees on land matters and taxes meeting the peasants' wishes. Also to attract the peasants to the Army and to set up military units of partisans behind the Fascist lines. Decrees in favor of the peasants would

---

[1] As between comrades, there was no need to mince words, for after all Stalin was not writing to a liberal newspaper in England. So, no word here about defending the Spanish Republic against Fascism. For Stalin what Comrade Largo Caballero was leading was *the* Spanish (Marxist) Revolution. And of course, so it was.

pave the way for this. (2) It would be advisable to draw to the Government the lower and middle bourgeoisie of the towns or in any case to enable them to remain neutral and favorable to the Government, by protecting them against all attempts at confiscation, and by securing for them, so far as possible, freedom of commerce, for otherwise these groups will follow Fascism. (3) The heads of the Republican Party must not be alienated, but on the contrary, attracted and drawn closer to the Government, harnessed to the common task of the Government. It is above all necessary to secure for the Government the support of Azaña and his group, doing all that might be needed to help them to conquer their hesitations. This is necessary to prevent the enemies of Spain from looking upon her as a Communist Republic. (4) An opportunity might be found to declare in the press that the Spanish Government will not tolerate attempts against the property and legitimate interests of foreigners in Spain who are citizens of the countries which do not support the Rebels.

Such was the advice Comrade Stalin gave Comrade Largo Caballero. Note the turn of mind of the autocrat who can please his peasants by merely issuing decrees forgetting the Spanish Parliament altogether; the economic prejudice of the Marxist who imagines that the Spanish peasants who fought on Franco's side would shoot him in the back in exchange for lower taxes and rents, and other curious irrelevancies revealing his not unnatural ignorance of Spanish affairs; the whole of it blended with an admirable common sense on the basis of his ambassador's reports about Señor Largo Caballero's ways—thus particularly his advice about treating Azaña with more deference than the Socialist dictatorial prime minister was evincing at the time.

But Don Francisco Largo Caballero was not the man to receive advice patiently. Gradually this Communist atmosphere was stifling the Spaniard and making him feel more and more irritated. Moscow was getting disquieting reports about his lack of flexibility. Matters came to a head owing to Commissar-

General Alvarez del Vayo's high-handed action in appointing hundreds of commissars to the Army over the head of the prime minister and war secretary. Needless to say most of these commissars were Communists. The Russians began to look around for another man. Señor Alvarez del Vayo himelf was no solution, for it would have shown the game too clearly. They needed a Socialist without any specific ties with Communism.

The man was there in the Ministry of Finance. Doctor Negrín was a relatively new arrival to Socialist politics. A bourgeois right through, a keen mind, professor of physiology at the University of Madrid, he had never taken an active part in political life and therefore possessed all the advantages required for the Communists: no strong political color in home politics, a comfortable bourgeois with polished manners who (to recall the words of Stalin in his letter to Largo Caballero) was not likely to expose Spain to the danger of being looked upon as a Communist Republic, and a good linguist—all valuable assets for presentation abroad; finally no political future but that which the Communists could give him. "From my observation post at the Embassy in Paris," writes Don Luis Araquistain, "I was able to observe with some surprise that, as far back as the first months of 1937, some London liberal newspapers which allowed themselves to be inspired more or less consciously by Communists or sympathizers with Communism, began to publish portraits and general praise of Dr. Negrín, then the Finance Minister, without any visible motive. The hidden motive was that Moscow had elected him as Largo Caballero's successor." [2]

The Soviet Union had taken the best possible precautions to secure Dr. Negrín with the stoutest chains. On October 25, 1936, 7,500 boxes of gold left Cartagena for Odessa. Dr. Negrin was Minister of Finance. Don Francisco Largo Caballero was prime

[2] Luis Araquistain: *El Comunismo y la Guerra de España,* 1939, p. 12. A typical example of how Communist propaganda managed to manufacture and destroy a reputation is that of General Miaja, an estimable officer of modest parts and achievements, turned into a national and world hero till he refused to follow the *fiat* of the party, when he was promptly dropped back into obscurity.

minister and war secretary. Don Indalecio Prieto was Minister of the Navy and Air. Don Julio Alvarez del Vayo was foreign secretary. Don Indalecio Prieto, one of the two Socialists who has told the story,[3] says that he only knew by accident that it had been shipped. We are assured that Señor Largo Caballero "never gave his signature to any operations on the gold deposited in Russia." Whatever we may think about those who did not know while in the Cabinet what happened to the Spanish gold, no one can deny that the direct responsibility lies with Dr. Negrín. The amount of gold sent to Moscow was 510,079,592 grams.The gold was deposited in the name of Dr. Negrín, Señor Largo Caballero and Señor Prieto. It had gone to Moscow in the custody of four officials of the Bank of Spain who thought they were sailing for France. On November 6, 1936, they arrived in Moscow. The counting and testing of the Spanish gold by the officials of the Gosbank lasted a lifetime. The Spanish officials were nonplused, till they came to realize that it was all part of a plan to keep them in Russia as long as possible. But even when after a stay of two years they were allowed to leave, they were dispersed all over the world: one was dumped in Stockholm, one in Buenos Aires, one in Washington and one in Mexico, while the high Soviet dignitaries who had transacted the business with them, including the Commissar for Finance, disappeared in several directions.

On January 20, 1937, Dr. Negrín issued a semi-official note denying that the Spanish reserves of gold had been shipped abroad at all.[4]

---

[3] In a preface to the second edition of his pamphlet already quoted. The other Socialist is Don Luis Araquistain in the pamphlet also quoted, from which I borrow the following data.

[4] See chapter 16 for an account of Dr. Negrín's return of the receipt for this gold to the Franco government at his death. Among the many articles published on this occasion, two of Don Indalecio Prieto in *El Socialista* (published at Toulouse) bring fresh news. One is that he knows nothing about Señor Araquistain's story that the gold had been deposited in the name of the four men mentioned above; and the other to the effect that: "the number of cases was not merely 7,800 but 13,000 weighing roughly 851½ tons, not counting packing; for not all the gold that went to Cartagena was sent to Odessa. The 340½ remaining tons

These events explain in part why the Government, which had started the Civil War with about $447,381,000 (2,258,569,908 pesetas, nearly 70 per cent of which was in gold sovereigns) while the Rebels started with nothing, found itself with its peseta quoted at about half the Rebel peseta by the beginning of 1937. Needless to say there were other forces at work. The financial and banking world was with the Rebels, but the inference that this was one hundred per cent the fault of the banks would appear to overlook a number of events which had taken place in Madrid. Private safes in the Bank of Spain and in private banks had been opened with blowtorches and untold wealth had been piled into sacks and taken into government custody without either compensation or even adequate safeguards that the wealth would actually reach the government cellars. That is not the kind of thing which helps the quotation of one's currency abroad.

The Rebel side, on the other hand, no doubt relied on a good deal of discreet and powerful help. It is likely that it never lacked credits for either arms and ammunition or oil and that it need not have restricted its hopes on this account to the capitalists of the Totalitarian Powers. A strict control on exports which secured for the Rebel Government all the benefit of the foreign exchange, pegged at an arbitrary value, strengthened the treasury of the Rebel cause. This and other measures were taken on the advice of Señor Ventosa, a Catalan financier, who had several times occupied the Ministry of Finance under the Monarchy. His advice, however, was tendered from afar, for there seems to have been no love lost between the Falange and the man to whose talent they owed the singular success of the Rebel finances.

Not that the Rebel side had a very considerable advantage over the Revolutionary as regards the natural wealth of their respective territories. A close examination might indeed show that the advantage was on the Revolutionary side. The Rebels,

were divided into two equal parts: one was sent to Marseilles before the Odessa lot sailed; the other one was sent much later to Barcelona." Señor Prieto says no more. It is a pity he has not disclosed what became of those two consignments.

however, possessed from the beginning the iron ore of the Riff and the pyrites of Río Tinto; while from 1937 onward they were able to draw upon the coal measures of Léon and Asturias and upon the mines and metallurgical establishments of Bilbao and Santander, including the valuable armament factory of Reinosa. This enabled them to manufacture their own armament and munitions and to tighten their grip over their exchange which they pegged at 42 pesetas to the pound for exports and at 52 for imports, when the real free value would have been in the vicinity of one hundred.

In spite of these financial successes and of a certain amount of military centralization, the Rebels were still a motley force with far divergent views. The Requetés fought for a return to the sixteenth century under a Carlist prince; the Alfonsists wanted Don Juan III with General Franco as his Mussolini; but the Falangists were not interested in this matter and, imbued with the revolutionary spirit of Nazism and Fascism, characteristically styled themselves National Syndicalists. In the spring of 1937 there were conspiracies against General Franco's rule in Málaga and Morocco. He crushed them ruthlessly and then tried to compress the ramshackle mass of his followers into at least an external unity, by setting up the *Falange Española Tradicionalista y de las JONS,* very much as if the President of the United States organized the Republican-Democratic-Socialist-Communist-League-of-the-Daughters-of-the-American-Revolution in the hope of unifying American politics. This magnificent harlequin was to be ruled by a National Council and a political junta (April 19, 1937).

General Franco was not then as strong as he was to become later, for as a matter of fact his most spectacular move, the campaign against Madrid, had failed. He had tried to storm the city in November and December 1936, then in January 1937. He tried again on February 6, in an attempt to cut the Madrid-Valencia road, when he won some ground in the Jarama valley, but failed again. These offensives were all made in the good old way, by means of waves of frontal attacks very costly in human lives. Why moreover they were tried at all instead of falling down on Madrid from the Sierra, cutting the two water supplies (Lozoya and Santillana) both of which were during nearly the whole war almost within arm's reach of the Rebels, is one of the mysteries of this war, for no one in his senses could consider an attack from the riverside as anything but the worst possible scheme for a military commander.

It would appear that in the short and successful campaign which led to the fall of Málaga (February 8, 1937) the Italians had begun to adumbrate the possibilities of a new use of the tank. This new idea, which was later developed into the *Blitzkrieg,* consisted in running ahead with a strong force of tanks followed by motorized troops and backed by low-flying planes. The new tactics were put in operation at Brihuega, northeast of Madrid, at the beginning of March. On March 8, 1937, two Italian divisions advanced at full speed along the Zaragoza-Madrid road. The Revolutionary army did not seek to stop them simply because they were utterly unable to do so. They let them pass. The Italians aimed at Guadalajara, and beyond at Alcalá. But "it pleased the Lord" that on the 11th there was a heavy fall of rain. The airplanes could not rise from their muddy improvised airfields to back the Italian tanks, and the Revolutionary army which stood by, somewhat nonplused, on both sides of the road, fell on the Italian soldiers, who, panic-stricken, fled and abandoned most of the ground they had overrun.

This victory of his Spanish adversaries over his Italian friends greatly strengthened General Franco's (and the Army's) position against the Falangists—for of such unexpected combinations is the cloth of history woven. Further attacks on Madrid were given up for the time being and General Mola found himself with a free hand to clear the North. The Revolutionists and the Basques in an unholy combination mustered about 70,000 troops against about half their number of Rebels, but General Mola had a stronger airforce and much better artillery. On April 26, 1937, German airmen destroyed Guernica, a historical town of the Basques. This was a clear case of German frightfulness, the psychological consequences of which must have been unsavory to General Franco and his associates. On June 19, 1937, Bilbao fell. On August 25, Santander. October 21, Gijón fell, this time to Spanish forces unhindered by any Fascist collaboration.

These military events had a profound influence on the political situation on both sides. The pressure of Comrade Rosenberg on Señor Largo Caballero increased to such an extent that people in the anteroom of the prime minister's office at least once heard Señor Largo Caballero requesting the Soviet ambassador in vociferous terms to leave his presence straightaway. Not much later, at the prime minister's suggestion, he was recalled and replaced by Comrade Gaikis. It was a pyrrhic victory for the veteran trade-union leader. He was then in sympathy, if not in actual alliance, with the Anarcho-Syndicalists, but when he found that the CNT controlled the key telephone stations between Barcelona and Valencia through their men he decided not to brook interference even from his friends, and on May 30 had the Barcelona telephone exchange raided by the police to expel the Anarcho-Syndicalist garrison. This started a minor civil war between two of the most united groups behind the Government, and though this civil war within the Civil War spread like wildfire through the whole Catalan territory, it was quickly put out, not without considerable loss of life. The Government profited by it to tighten up its grip on Catalonia which was by then indulging in a curious mixture of separatism, dictatorship, anarchy and a certain cooling off of interest toward the Civil War.

And yet this victory again was a pyrrhic one, for behind it all stood the fact that Moscow had declared Señor Largo Caballero's political life at an end. The occasion for his fall was a military operation which failed before it ever was engaged. The Spanish General Staff had carefully studied an offensive on the least defended Rebel front, that of Estremadura, with the object of capturing Mérida and Badajoz, which would have cut the northern from the southern territories, held by the adversary. The Central Army, under Communist influence, was opposed to this idea. Largo Caballero had his authority vindicated against this force which, though Communist, was after all Spanish. But at this moment, the Russians came out into the open and intimated that for such an operation there would be no aircraft.

Simultaneously, the two Communist Cabinet ministers resigned, for the plan was to bring down Largo Caballero in order to install Don Juan Negrín. After some skirmishing, during which the part played by Don Indalecio Prieto is not clear, the Largo Caballero Cabinet fell and Dr. Negrín took office (May 17, 1937) with a Cabinet in which Señor Alvarez del Vayo was not at the Foreign Office—an excellent alibi. But it is not certain whether at this early stage Dr. Negrín himself was aware of the part for which he was being coached by the Communists nor even whether he would have acquiesced in it if he had known it. After all, the sending of the gold to Moscow, though injudicious, was one of the solutions which could be envisaged in the circumstances, and it does not seem evident that it had been done so completely behind the back of Señor Largo Caballero and of Señor Prieto as the friends of these two Socialist leaders maintain. It may still be found on closer scrutiny that in ousting Señor Largo Caballero, the Communists, both Russian and Spanish, were the only actors who knew the script of the whole play, while Don Indalecio Prieto and Dr. Negrín knew little more than some cues and the hard fact that they were getting rid of their rival in the Socialist Party. That in the mind of Dr. Negrín the new Cabinet meant a move to the Right, to authority, order and centralization, was obvious. He gave the Foreign Office to Señor Giral, a friend of President Azaña, with the hope either of conquering British and French opinion or of initiating some peace move or both.

True the new combination was unable to prevent the ill-fated battle of Brunete, fought in the teeth of Spanish technical opposition. It cost 15,000 dead and brought no advantages to anyone but the Rebels. True the POUM was savagely persecuted and its leader Andrés Nin assassinated by order of the Cheka which was by then active in Barcelona and strong enough to flout the well-meaning but powerless efforts of the Minister of Justice D. Manuel Irujo to put some order and some humanity in the social warfare which was going on under the name of justice.[5] Yet there is no doubt that, possibly for the rest of the year 1937, the leader of the Cabinet was Don Indalecio Prieto as much as the prime minister, and that his policy was by no means pliable to the Communists. On November 18 he removed Señor Alvarez del Vayo from his post as chief of the political Commissars of the Army and abolished the system of commissars altogether. This was a staggering blow to Communist propaganda in the armed forces.

The Russians immediately countered by reducing their supplies. They had always kept the Spanish revolutionists on short commons so as to have them well in hand. Dr. Negrín seems to have realized the position at this moment. Gradually Don Indalecio Prieto was found pessimistic and too much of a defeatist. The fact was that his orders bearing directly on the war, such as bombing of certain objectives—were simply disobeyed by the Russian pilots and air staff chiefs; while his reluctance to give over to the Russians a Messerschmidt and a Heinkel which happened to fall intact into Spanish hands was most unwelcome to his Soviet "advisers." Dr. Negrín's part in this incident as told by Don Indalecio Prieto himself shows that by then the prime minister had gone a long way toward accepting the part cut out for him by the Third International.[6]

These deep cleavages in the Revolutionary front were bound to strengthen the hands of the Rebel commander and what he still represented: the Army as against the Falange. But General Franco is a Gallegan, and the Gallegan is the only European who can beat the Englishman at the number of things he can think at a time. The Englishman can carry on two lines of thought; the Gallegan at least three and there is usually a fourth at the back of his head. Moreover, like the Englishman, he seldom looks or speaks cleverly. His way of dominating the Falange was not merely to repress them—though he did a certain

[5] See a pamphlet, by Mr. John McGovern, M.P., *Terror in Spain*, published after a visit to Barcelona.

[6] Indalecio Prieto: *Cómo y por qué salí del Ministerio de Defensa Nacional*, Paris, 1939.

amount of repression—but to put himself at their head. On August 4, 1937, he decided that all officers and non-commissioned officers of the Army would automatically be members of the *Falange Española Tradicionalista y de las JONS*. The thing became as unwieldy as its name. The National Council was to be chosen entirely by him. He allowed himself to be described as *El Caudillo,* which means "The Chief."

On January 30, 1938, General Franco completed this evolution by setting up a regular Cabinet of Ministers (three generals and eight civilians) presided over by himself. The Minister of Public Order was an old hand at repression, General Martínez Anido, a fixture inherited from the first dictatorship, that of Primo de Rivera. Unsavory police methods and the encouragement of private denunciation, even anonymous, were the result, for which General Martínez Anido had no need of the help or advice of the Gestapo. The Minister of the Interior was a new man, the Caudillo's brother-in-law Don Ramón Serrano Suñer, an ex-member of Señor Gil Robles's party, a lawyer educated in Italy, an admirer of the Duce. The Cabinet was carefully balanced, but undoubtedly the politico-military tendency of pure Spanish tradition predominated in it. It was represented not merely by the Caudillo himself but by his vice prime minister and foreign Secretary, General Jordana.

Why this difference between the progress of Communism on one side and of Nazi-Fascism on the other? Partly perhaps because of the play of European international relations; partly also because of a difference in the tactical aims of the powers which were meddling in the Spanish war. The year had gone by in long and complicated wrangles over non-intervention, mainly on the basis of a British plan linking together the withdrawal of volunteers with the granting of belligerent rights. But whatever energy the anti-Fascist tendency in the Committee of Non-Intervention might evince, it was being undermined by the desire of the majority of the British Conservative Party to come to terms with Signor Mussolini in order to stop Hitler on the road to Vienna on which it was expected the Führer would start soon. A resolution presented to the League Assembly on

October 2, 1937, to the effect that non-intervention would cease unless all nations respected their obligations under it, was accepted by all but Albania and Portugal and believed in by none. On October 18 the Italian government issued a semi-official statement estimating at 40,000 the Italian volunteers who were in Spain. On November 16, Sir Robert Hodgson was appointed British agent in Nationalist Spain and on November 22 it was announced that the Duke of Alba would be his opposite number in London. On February 20, 1938, Mr. Eden resigned precisely on the issue of Italy's intervention in Spain. Mussolini and Hitler were both represented at Burgos, where the Rebel Caudillo had established its capital after a brief stay in Salamanca. The two dictators were proceeding in Spanish affairs with the leisure of men who feel sure of their victory.

Stalin, on the other hand, was beginning to wonder whether the Litvinov policy of collaboration with the Western Democracies through the International Peace Campaign and the Popular Front tactics was to succeed or to fail. The horizon was darkening both over Europe and over the Pacific and he was not ready. In either case, whether he fought Hitler under the flag of Geneva or ran quicker than Chamberlain to hold Hitler's hand in a gesture of friendship to prevent the unpredictable Führer from grasping his revolver, it was imperative that he should be strong in Spain. Whatever we may think as Spaniards of the effect of Stalin's policy on Spain, whatever we may think of those of our countrymen who allowed themselves to become his tools in Spain, we have to look at the matter from the point of view of Mr. Stalin, both as the head of the Russian State, i.e., as a Russian patriot, and as the Pope of the Communist faith. His aims in Spain were essentially the same as those of the two Fascist dictators, though of course for opposite reasons: to secure a Western outpost for his side against the dangers which were lurking ever larger on the European horizon. But while all Hitler and Mussolini need do to secure a relatively strong and friendly Spain was to let General Franco win, allowing him to organize his victory, the side in which Stalin was interested had no such unity. It was a true revolutionary hydra with a

Syndicalist, an Anarchist, two Communist and three Socialist heads, furiously biting at each other, and it was necessary for Stalin to master this monster and tame it in order to hold his own in the West.

It was therefore indispensable for Stalin to gain time to allow for the internal evolution of the Spanish Revolution, which in his eyes could only mean the gradual devouring of all the other heads of the hydra by the orthodox Communist head. Meanwhile he would be both preparing for the coming war, if war there was to be, and seeking an agreement with Hitler which would enable him either to ward off the Soviet-German war for good and all or to gain more time still for his tanks and airplanes. In terms of Spain this meant carrying on the Spanish war as long as possible while strengthening his position there while the war lasted. The first added to his time for negotiating with Hitler; the second raised the value of his assets in the negotiation.

Hence this remarkable difference in the evolution of the two sides of the Spanish Civil War. It was, however, merely a tactical difference. The political leadership of the Rebel State remained Spanish and military. But under cover of the war many German and to a lesser extent Italian experts were gradually infiltrating themselves into the country, in preparation for future campaigns of greater import. At the beginning of 1938 the number of Germans encased in the nooks and corners of the Spanish administration must have been high.[7] They were of course Nazis and bound to encourage the Falange as against the Army in the delicate balance of forces which prevailed on the Rebel side. As to the Revolutionary side, the government was to fall gradually into the firm but Communist-led hands of Dr. Negrín.

Strengthened by his political reconstruction, the Caudillo of the Nationalists began to prepare a fresh offensive against Guadalajara. The Revolutionists, however, forestalled him with an offensive on Teruel, the spearhead of a dangerous salient into

[7] It was put by some observers at 10,000.

their eastern lines, which they took between December 15, 1937, and January 7, 1938. This reverse, the first which the Rebels had undergone, forced General Franco to divert his forces to Teruel, which, mostly for reasons of prestige, he would not leave in the hands of the Revolutionists, and after a long and sanguinary battle, the city, though destroyed in the process, was recaptured by the Rebels on February 22. As a consolation the Revolutionists sank the *Baleares,* the best cruiser of the Rebel fleet, on March 6. As for Spain herself, to whom belonged the old city and the new warship, she had no consolation whatsoever.

On March 9, 1938, the Rebels were enabled to launch their Aragon offensive. The advance was swift. On March 17 they captured Caspe, headquarters of the Revolutionary Army of Aragon, then turning northward took Lérida (April 3, 1938), thus opening the way for a general attack on Catalonia. During this offensive Dr. Negrín flew to Paris to seek the help of the French government, for the Revolutionists had neither enough aircraft nor enough munitions, nor enough food either. And this last item tells a tale. Why should revolutionary Spain go hungry? Truth must be stated. All the lack of munitions and armaments was not due to the ill will of the foreign powers In fact the non-intervention arrangements had never been so tight that a brisk trade in armaments could not be made. Some day this unsavory aspect of the Spanish Civil War will have to be studied and it will not be the least sad of all. The arrangements for the purchase and transport of armaments and munitions for the Revolutionists were a model of anarchy, to such an extent that at least one cargo has been known to have been bought by the Revolutionists in the north of Europe and to have been delivered to the Rebels in Spain. Don Indalecio Prieto, who ought to know, writes: "I could reveal nothing to the French Government because the French Government knew. . . . Thirdly that the French Communist Party had administered two thousand five hundred million francs given them by Negrin to buy war material, without any control whatsoever from any official of the Spanish State. Fourthly that the French Communist Party had withdrawn for itself, possibly as middleman rights, considerable quantities of the money put at their disposal by Negrín. . . . Eighthly that the fleet of twelve ships belonging to the Company "France Navigation" was the property of Spain, since the ships had been bought with Spanish money, despite which the French Communists who were its administrators refused to return them and considered them their own."[8]

The arrangements for making armaments in Spain were no less anarchical. Internal strife for securing control over this or that factory in which armaments, munitions or explosives were made was rife between the several parties as well as between the Catalan and the central government; more or less successful experiments in collectivization and management by workers' committees, Russian interference and class-struggle persecution of technicians complicated matters even further. The food situation suffered from the same ills. There was no reason why Revolutionary Spain should have lacked food and yet it was pathetically hungry. The soil was rich and there was money in the treasury, but the people starved. The very arrangements made abroad by charitable souls to help the Spanish starving people were turned into foreign currency-making machinery by the Government. It was for instance officially decided that persons desirous of sending parcels of food to Spain might instead pay in the money at a Spanish consulate abroad and the Spanish government would deliver a parcel of food to the person in Spain for whom it was intended—which obviously amounted to a confession that people went hungry in Spain through no lack of food in the hands of the Government.

This period saw one of the most ruthless campaigns ever launched by a nation against itself. The bombing campaign had begun of course with the destructive air raids against Madrid launched on October 29, 1936, as a reprisal against raids on Seville, Cáceres and Granada the day before.[9] In November of

---

[8] Preface to the second edition of Don Indalecio Prieto's *Cómo y por qué salí del Ministerio de Defensa Nacional*, Mexico, 1940.

[9] As a matter of fact I believe the first time a Spanish airplane bombed a Spanish town was on July 20 at Toledo, where Don Francisco Largo Caballero had the city bombed at regular intervals for three days in the hope of regaining it from the Rebels.

the same year Madrid underwent twenty-three raids, the casualties of which were estimated for the week of the 10th-17th at 500 killed and 1200 wounded. About one year later, on November 2, the Rebels bombed Lérida with a toll of 225 victims, including 50 children. As reprisals, Salamanca and Seville were bombed on January 21 and 27, 1937, and Valladolid also, though this last town was raided by the Communists in the teeth of definite orders from the air minister, Don Indalecio Prieto.[10] On January 28, 1938, Señor Prieto offered to stop bombing the distant rearguard towns if the Rebels ceased their air raids. On February 6 the Rebels answered they would continue to bomb Barcelona unless its industries were evacuated. Heavy raids followed on the handsome city with much loss of life and destructive effects. The Germans were training their pilots and trying new bombs.

These events paved the way for the third political step taken by the Communists to seize hold of power. The first had been the formation of Señor Largo Caballero's Cabinet with their own henchman, Señor Alvarez del Vayo, at the Foreign Office. The second, the expulsion of the same Señor Largo Caballero found too impervious to Communist suggestions. The third was the expulsion of Don Indalecio Prieto, who so far had walked along with them for his own ends, but who would not consent to walk behind them for their ends. One of his two Communist ministerial colleagues, Jesús Hernández, had suggested to him at the outset that he would be ready "to call on me every morning to put before me the suggestions, ideas or views of the Political Bureau of the Communist Party on war affairs." Don Indalecio Prieto retorted that the place to bring these ideas was the Council of Ministers. Toward the end of March 1938 matters came to a head. A change in the government was inevitable, and as usual in such cases, supplies from Moscow began to dwindle, so as to make the matter clearer still.

Dr. Negrín took the hint and in an interview with Azaña he tried for the first time the high-handed methods which he was

[10] *Cómo y por qué salí del Ministerio de Defensa Nacional* (first edition), p. 74.

fully to develop six months later. He succeeded, for by then Azaña was resigned to his position as a prisoner of the Revolutionists and realized the gravity of a situation so dependent on Russian supplies. Dr. Negrín was able to form a government to the satisfaction of the Communists. He took over with the premiership the Ministry of National Defense, putting the three departments of War, Navy and Air in charge of three Communist under secretaries; he gave the Foreign Office to Señor Alvarez del Vayo who appointed a Communist under secretary and in general turned over the Foreign Office to the Communists; and although he failed in his purpose of appointing the Communist Jesús Hernández as General Commissar for the Army, he gave him the General Commissariat of the Army of the Center, which amounted to about four-fifths of the whole (April 5, 1938).

With clockwork precision, supplies began to flow again. A few weeks after Don Indalecio Prieto had been expelled from the Cabinet, Barcelona, undefended against recent German raids, witnessed an impressive flight of Russian airplanes.

While the several heads of the Revolutionary hydra bit each other hard, the Rebels pressed on towards the Mediterranean. Thwarted in their thrust at Tortosa, they succeeded in reaching the sea at Vinaroz (April 15, 1938). On June 15, 1938, they took the important city of Castellón de la Plana, on the Mediterranean. With their troops in control of the fastnesses of the Western Catalan Pyrenees, including the power station of Tremp and the whole southern bank of the Ebro, which meant Catalonia all but paralyzed for lack of electrical current, and cut off from the rest of Spain, it looked as if the Rebels should have been able to win the war soon. At any rate, on July 24 the Revolutionists gave the Rebels an unpleasant surprise: they crossed the river Ebro and shook them out of their complacency by a most brilliant and daring operation which secured for them the command of the southern bank of the river. Despite heavy land and air counter-attacks they held their ground during the whole summer, with a disregard for human life somewhat out of proportion with the actual strategic value of their operation. Not till November 16, 1938, did they lose their last bridgehead.

Their gallant sacrifice had cost the Rebels four months, yet had no other effective result than that of wasting Spanish life and treasure to that extent.

In Barcelona the game of politics continued. There was a tug of war between Dr. Negrín and the Generalitat over their respective powers, in which the Catalans were not merely struggling to preserve their local powers from the centralistic inroads of the prime minister but also to uphold the principles of justice and human decency against the terrorism of the numerous Chekas which had sprung up everywhere in the country. The number of political murders (many committed by the SIM or Service of Military Investigation, an organization of military police which was entirely under Communist control) rose rapidly; the number of people sentenced to death in a more regular way and whose sentences awaited the decision of the Council of Ministers had risen to fifty-eight by the end of July. The Minister of Justice, Don Manuel Irujo, one of the Basque leaders, had resigned as a protest against the institution of the *Tribunales de Guardia*, or Courts of Urgency, set up by Dr. Negrín in which Señor Irujo and his Catalan friends, as well as most enlightened Republicans, saw a dangerous reaction toward an oppressive administration of so-called justice. These courts and the Court for the Repression of Spying (*Tribunal de Espionaje*) were spreading terror by their hasty sentences and President Companys had written officially to Dr. Negrín protesting against concrete cases of shocking injustice and police murders.

Simultaneously, a strong movement of opinion was coming to a head advocating peace by negotiation. Azaña was favorable to this movement. Dr. Negrín was against it and he decided this time to strike at the president. No other interpretation at any rate can be ascribed to the strange crisis of August 1938. He wanted a change in the Cabinet in order to reassert his authority over that of the president. He must have a crisis. So he proposed that the Council of Ministers should approve the fifty-eight pending death sentences. As he no doubt had expected, this brought down the Cabinet. Dr. Negrín called on President Companys to suggest to him that the Catalan leader should form a Cabinet since he was the chief of the opposition. It seems that President Azaña was considering a Cabinet led by Don Julián Besteiro with a view to negotiating a peace. Dr. Negrín had his paper *La Vanguardia* publish a list of ministers in which his name was mentioned in one of the minor posts, and managed to have it generally known that he was leaving Spain for a considerable length of time. This brought about a prearranged shower of telegrams from all the military units commanded by Communists, putting themselves at the disposal of Dr. Negrín, and the Russian-controlled tanks and airplanes paraded in the streets and over the skies of Barcelona. After this show of military power, never equaled even in the most militaristic moments of King Alfonso's Monarchy, Dr. Negrín went to see Azaña merely to collect a formal acquiescence to his list. He was henceforward the dictator of Revolutionary Spain (August 16, 1938).[11]

Toward the end of the year General Franco made up his mind to strike at Catalonia, the seat of the revolutionary power. An army of 350,000 men (including 16,315 Italians) were pitted against the Revolutionists with better artillery and air force than their adversaries. While the armies of the Center were still intact though badly armed, the armies of Catalonia had suffered severe losses in Teruel and worse still at the Ebro where the casualties amounted to 60,000. The Rebel offensive began on December 23 along the rivers Segre and Noguera Pallaresa. Artesa was taken on January 4 and Borjas Blancas, which had resisted the attacks of the unaided Italian corps, fell to the combined onslaughts of Italians and Navarrese on January 5. On January 11 the Rebels reached Montblanch, at the confluence of the Artesa-Tarragona and Lérida-Tarragona roads. The second line of defense had gone. On January 25 Tarragona was occupied. The third line was broken by the fall of Igulada on January 22. Though the Government of course loudly proclaimed its intention to defend Barcelona, the mood was by no means that of Madrid in November 1936. On January 26, 1939, the Re-

---

[11] In his correspondence with Señor Prieto (see chapter 14 below) Dr. Negrín vehemently denies this military bullying. I have carefully weighed the evidence, and it tells against him.

quetés and the Moorish troops entered the capital, closely followed by the Tercio and the Arrow Mixed (Italian-Spanish) Division. The political staffs of both the Central and the Catalan governments had left the city and gone northward, but the administrative staff had remained, most of them ready to go over to the Rebels.

Nothing remained but to declare the war at an end and a government truly free to put Spain above party would have made the best of a deplorable situation and resigned itself to negotiate at once. But Dr. Negrín was not free. He was attached to Moscow by a chain of gold. His Socialist adversaries, who are his co-religionists, have accused him of having adapted himself to Stalin's policy, thereby prolonging the war. It may well be, however, that the motives of Dr. Negrín at this juncture were more complex, as human motives are apt to be. He may well have entertained hopes of a European conflagration which, so he and his friends had the right to think at the time, would have saved him and his side from defeat. The policy of Stalin at that moment was moreover far from clear. The events of those days were of such dramatic nature, and the stakes, both national and personal, were so high, that the several viewpoints are apt to confront each other with more heat than light. The one clear fact is that no one but the Communists and Dr. Negrín was for continuing the fight. Dr. Negrín's adversaries have counted it as a crime. He, on the other hand, maintains that his attitude was purely tactical. He was just fighting a kind of delaying action on the diplomatic field to secure from the other side a promise of no reprisals, and to allow time for the evacuation of as many Left Spaniards as possible before General Franco's troops overran the territory. This is a perfectly valid reason. One thing is certain: at that moment, none but Dr. Negrín and the Communists were in favor of fighting. It is obvious that the Communists had instructions to carry on the war and to hold fast to Dr. Negrín. On these two points the evidence is overwhelming. Every single man around Dr. Negrín during these last hours around the last airplane, when by the natural selection of loyalties numbers dwindled to a minimum, was a Communist. The reason could not be that Stalin wished to prolong the war thinking he was going to win it, for he was too well informed to believe that such a thing was possible. Evidently Stalin saw two possibilities, for both of which it was useful to hold off General Franco's inevitable victory: either a general European conflagration or a pact with Hitler for which his hand in Spain was still an asset.

In any case, whatever the reasons for his policy and for that of the Communists, no one should deny Dr. Negrín and Señor Alvarez del Vayo the courage and determination with which they faced those last days, nor the Communists their loyalty to the two men they had chosen to govern Spain for them. It is also a fact that although they constantly spoke of fighting they sincerely endeavored to negotiate.[12]

[12] Dr. Negrín's statement to the Permanent Committee of the Cortes on March 31, 1939, is indispensable for the study of this period.

CHAPTER 11

THE END OF THE CIVIL WAR

The idea of mediation had begun almost with the war. In the confused atmosphere of those days it was bound to be often misunderstood. Two closely interrelated factors contributed to this confusion: the first was that the propaganda of the two militant sides of the Spanish Civil War had succeeded in bamboozling world public opinion in such a way that all the Center and Left parties in the world believed that the "Loyalists" and "Republicans," as they were styled, were the true Spain trodden by the tyranny of the Rebels; while in fact the true Spain lay gagged and trodden equally by the two tyrannies which fought the war over her body; and the other factor was the duel which was already taking place between the Nazi-Fascist powers and the democracies and which some leaders in the democracies were endeavoring to exorcise by "appeasement." The combination of these two factors fatally led to a confusion between mediation and appeasement, i.e., to interpreting mediation as one of the

534

forms of appeasement. But there was no parity whatever between the two and it may be safely asserted that not one in a thousand of the Spaniards who sought the end of the Civil War by mediation thought it advisable or possible to tame the Nazi tiger and the Fascist vulture. What mediation aimed at was the end of an insane and meaningless civil war between Spaniards after due elimination of the two foreign elements which complicated it.

This is borne out by the fact that the spirit of mediation was latent under the clatter and the blood from the first day of the Civil War and even before.[1] For it was nothing else but a restatement of the political position of the real Spain, that of Don Francisco Giner, the Spain of peace and patience, as against the two Spains of violence led by Don Francisco Largo Caballero and Don Francisco Franco. On August 18, 1936, I wrote to Mr. Eden a private letter in which I developed this idea, which I quote from its first paragraph: "The right policy *now* . . . is no longer one of non-intervention in war but one of intervention for peace." [2] From the very first days of the outbreak Don Indalecio Prieto, whose faith in the victory of his side was never staunch, spoke to the country through the broadcasting stations in tones which every trained ear could understand as appeals for the Rebels to overhear and understand. The government of Uruguay had suggested a joint *démarche* to all the nations of the Pan-American Union (August 16, 1936), but with little success in Washington, for American public opinion was too set and too disposed to identify mediation with appeasement. This initiative, however, led to negotiations in St. Jean de Luz under the aegis of Señor Mansilla, the Argentine Ambassador to Madrid, but the negotiations were fruitless, for at the time both sides had an exaggerated idea of their chances to win the war. A similar fate overtook the Anglo-French effort of Decem-

---

[1] I may be forgiven for recalling here that the first Spanish edition of my book *Anarchy or Hierarchy,* published in 1935, began with a twenty-page preface entirely devoted to a critical study of the spirit of Civil War and to concrete proposals for placating it.

[2] *See* "A Personal Memoir," Appendix II, for further efforts made on this line right to the end of the war.

ber 1936, though this time the two Western Powers had taken the precaution of appealing first to the respective European backers of the two Spanish parties. In those days the policy of Moscow was still that of M. Litvinov and therefore its interest was to put a stop to the Spanish war. The Soviet government was the only one which declared itself ready to cooperate in the Anglo-French effort; while those of Germany, Italy and Portugal turned down the proposal—most unwisely it would seem at any rate on the part of Portugal. On March 2, 1937, Mr. Eden was led to report to the House of Commons that there was "no indication so far that either party was prepared to consider mediation."

What he, however, did not say was that neither party was Spain and Spain had been ready, indeed, longing for mediation all the time, and that the powers of the group France-Great Britain-United States, had they been resolute, might perhaps have forced the two intruders, the Revolutionists and the Rebels, to evacuate the field of war and to allow Spain to speak and live.

In September 1937, Dr. Koth, Norwegian foreign secretary, proposed to the League Assembly that the League should invite the two belligerents to agree to an armistice during which a referendum would be taken under League auspices to settle the form of government of the country. He met with no support. A similar proposal emanating from Cuba failed owing mostly to the opposition of the United States.

Nevertheless, negotiations for peace, at any rate between the Rebels and the Basques, had taken place in Bilbao and Paris from February to May 1937 through the good offices of Señor de la Barra, a Mexican ex-president who lived in Paris, Cardinal Gomá, Archbishop of Toledo, and Monsignor Valerio Valeri, the Papal Nuncio in Paris. Arms were quicker than tongues and Bilbao fell to the Rebels before the parleys could succeed.[3]

---

[3] *See* article by J. de Bivort de la Saudrée in *Revue des Deux Mondes,* Paris, February 13, 1940. The negotiations failed owing to the separatist tendency of the Spaniard which of course flourishes in the Basque to a high degree. The Basques insisted on having General Franco's promises guaranteed by a foreign power.

In May 1937 President Azaña, a member of that middle Spain gagged and jailed by the extremists, seized the unique opportunity of Señor Besteiro's journey to London to represent Spain at the coronation to make his voice heard in favor of mediation. D. Julián Besteiro had been all along, more consistently even than Azaña, a genuine representative of that common-sense Spain. He was entrusted by President Azaña with the task of putting before the British government a plan for peace in Spain. A prominent exponent of Dr. Negrín's policy describes the proposal as follows: "A truce between the Government and the Rebels was to be declared. All foreign troops and volunteers serving on both sides would then be withdrawn from the country. During the truce no battlelines would be shifted. England, France, Germany, Italy and the Soviet Union would thereupon devise a scheme, which the Republic promised in advance to accept, whereby the will of the entire Spanish nation on its political future would be ascertained." [4] Apparently President Azaña received no answer from Mr. Eden.

Don Indalecio Prieto has related a curious scene which reveals how near the end, and how close to peace negotiations had matters come by March 1938: he is arguing with Dr. Negrín in the course of an exchange of letters between the two rival leaders in the summer of 1938, and starts with the show of military power with which Dr. Negrín coerced the President of the Republic in August 1938.

> This ignominious parade of military forces had had a precedent a few months earlier, which put me on the track of many things. I am referring to that demonstration which, headed by Guardias de Asalto, arrived one March afternoon at Pedralbes Palace from the center of Barcelona and flooded tumultuously the gardens of the official residence of the president of the republic while the Council of Ministers was meeting under his chairmanship. The demonstration was organized by emptying theaters and cinemas

---

[4] Louis Fischer: *Men and Politics.*

so that willy-nilly all spectators should come to swell it, and the same was done with passengers in omnibuses and tramways, the circulation of which was suspended. What were the posters and the shouts saying? "Down with treacherous ministers! Down with the Minister of National Defense!" Let us remember what happened that afternoon in the Palace of Pedralbes in order to find its relation with what happened outside. Before the meeting of the Council, you called apart the two Socialist Ministers, Zugazagoitia and me, and begged us to back your refusal if anyone in the coming meeting suggested negotiations for peace. We both promised to do so, as it was our duty to do, for how could we weaken, with a different attitude, that of the Chief of the government, who was responsible for the leadership of our policy?

. . . Before meeting under Señor Azaña, we had a preliminary gathering of the ministers. You brought with you a suspicion that someone was to ask for peace negotiations, but that "someone" did not turn up. One after the other, all the ministers agreed with the prime minister. The foreign secretary, Señor Giral, reported that Monsieur Labonne, the French ambassador, had called on him, to offer, as all the help he was ready to tender, in the name of the French government, that the government of the Republic, in case of need, should take refuge in the French embassy, and that our fleet should sail for Toulon or Bizerte where it would be neutralized and would not add its numbers to the naval forces in the Mediterranean which were hostile to France. . . . This was the answer which France gave to our urgent requests for war material and to my plan— which needed but small and hidden help on the French coast—to reconquer the Basque country. Such an answer made us all indignant, and me in particular. The ministers with equal unanimity agreed with the proposal that if France were to mediate for peace, as Labonne had suggested, she was to do so on her own account, but without the assent of the Spanish government, an assent which at that moment, might have weakened us greatly.

After you had gathered our way of thinking, we entered the president's room, and soon after, the rumors of the street tumult began to reach us and to grow. You went out to parley with the organizers of the demonstration. From the Council room, I heard the Pasionaria haranguing the masses. As a matter of fact, I did not realize the character of the demonstration. As I left Pedralbes, the chief of my escorts asked leave to enter my car, and then got his machine-gun at the ready. And it was he who ordered the driver to take an out-of-the-way route in order to dodge the demonstrators. . . . The boys of my escort gathered the true meaning of the demonstration from the subversive shouts and the comments heard from the demonstrators in the palace gardens. The procession had been organized in order to protest against the intention attributed to some of the ministers to propose that afternoon to the Council the opening of peace negotiations.

It may well be that the decision of Dr. Negrín's government to withdraw all non-Spanish volunteers as a unilateral act, announced by Señor Alvarez del Vayo to the League Council on September 30, 1938, was in itself an indirect move toward peace. "Let us get rid of the foreigner on both sides and talk." That way and only that way was—or rather had been—salvation. By September 1938 it was too late. The League Council appointed an International Military Commission to report on this withdrawal and to make arrangements for feeding the numberless refugees who by then had gathered in Catalonia. The withdrawal actually began on November 13. Three days later, the Republican troops withdrew from their quixotic adventure on the Ebro and soon after the last Rebel offensive on Catalonia began.

On May 1, 1938, Dr. Negrín announced to the world his thirteen points, which had an air of an offer of peace and were

so considered by the world. They were unimpeachable so far
as they went, but as far removed from the facts and practices
of his government as words have ever been, and therefore could
inspire no confidence whatever in those who knew whence they
came. "The maintenance of the independence of Spain and its
deliverance from invasion and economic penetration," said the
man who had delivered Spain to the Russians; "the determination of the legal and social form of the new Republic by the
national will expressed in a free plebiscite," said the man who
had forced Azaña to swallow his Cabinet with a flourish of
Russian tanks and airplanes; "respect for regional liberties," said
the man who had taken from the Catalans, and for that matter
from the rest of the Spaniards as well, every vestige of a guarantee of objective justice; "an assurance of the free exercise of
religious beliefs," said the man who could not protect the life of
the priests nor the exercise of the Catholic worship in his territory; "the property of foreigners who had not assisted the
Nationalists would be respected," said the man who had read
that very sentence in the letter of advice sent by Stalin to Largo
Caballero. Every item called forth in the Spanish reader on
both sides, but more so in the vast majority of neither side, an
echo of experience which belied it.[5]

It does not follow, however, that Dr. Negrín was insincere
in his desire for some compromise, for there are many signs to

[5] If we are to believe Mr. Louis Fischer, than whom no more eloquent
advocate of Dr. Negrín could be found, the genesis of the 13 points is
the following: "Throughout my stay in Barcelona, I visited the Foreign
Office every day, and every day I saw Ivor Montagu sitting in del Vayo's
ante-chamber still waiting for permission from the War Department to
take moving pictures at the front. Frequently I found Ivor reading
Puschkin's poems in English translation. Once he said to me, 'You know,
it seems to me that the Loyalist Government ought to enunciate its war
aims, a sort of Fourteen Points program like Woodrow Wilson's.'
"'Wonderful idea,' I said, 'why has it never occurred to anybody?' I
passed the idea on to del Vayo. '*Stupendo*,'*he exclaimed. He talked to
Negrín. Negrín said, 'We must have 13 to show that we are not superstitious,' and he added three himself. The Thirteen Points were published

---

* Italics Mr. Fischer's. Spanish also.

point that by then he knew he could not win the war. When on leaving office, Señor Prieto conceived the idea of sounding the Rebel Government on the possibilities of ending the war and consulted the Prime Minister. Dr. Negrín, though advising caution, did not object. "How could I consider such steps as indiscreet," he wrote later to Señor Prieto, "when from July or August 1937, I have been in direct or indirect touch with the enemy: Spanish, German, Italian and neutral [*sic*] adversaries?"

Meanwhile things came to a head with the defeat of the Revolutionary Government in Barcelona and the disastrous ex-

on May 1, 1938, and became the cardinal principles of the Republic. Negrín frequently referred to them in speeches. They were communicated officially to foreign governments, and pro-Loyalist propaganda abroad often took them as its text."—*Men in Politics.*

Mr. Fischer was, of course, well informed as to Dr. Negrín's propaganda, for we know through Don Indalecio Prieto that he was the chief agent of this propaganda abroad. In a letter addressed by Señor Prieto to Don Juan Negrín (Mexico, July 3, 1939) he writes: "Considerable sums—this time in foreign currency and not in pesetas—were also spent in journalistic propaganda abroad. I admit the legitimacy of this expense, particularly in time of war. What I do not admit is that such propaganda, paid with State funds, should be blended with attacks on the President of the Republic to bring out the praises of the head of the Government. That is what, on one occasion, your friend Mr. Fischer, chief agent of the said propaganda and probable financial manager of it, to judge by the big sums you handed him, did." (*Epistolario, P.* iv, 1939).

Cf. "I had obtained considerable sums of money for the transportation of volunteers to Spain" (Mr. Fischer, which would appear to show that Mr. Fischer had enjoyed the utmost confidence on the part of Dr. Negrín. This undoubtedly adds weight to his utterances.)

When the English edition of Mr. Fischer's book appeared in London, I found that the thirteen-point episode has been touched up to adapt it, no doubt, to English tastes. Here it is in its new form: "For some time, the Loyalist leaders had considered the advisability of announcing their social peace aims. They hoped they would undermine morale in Franco territory and reinforce sympathy for Loyalist Spain in foreign countries. Del Vayo and Negrín drafted most of the war aims and they were finally approved at a solemn session of the Cabinet. They were incorporated into the now famous Thirteen Points. The Thirteen Points were published on May 1, 1938, and became the cardinal principles of the Republic. Negrín frequently referred to them in speeches. They were communicated officially to foreign Governments, and pro-Loyalist propaganda abroad often took them as its text" (p. 465). "At a solemn session of the Cabinet" is good.

odus which followed. The eighth Pan-American Conference at Lima considered a proposal for mediation, this time put forward by the three nations more in sympathy with the Left: Cuba, Haiti and Mexico. But the remaining Spanish-American nations were passive, and the United States, all along rather reluctant to take any action on either side in Spanish affairs, voted with the majority. On February 1, Dr. Negrín had called together a skeleton meeting of the Cortes in the cellar of the fortress at Figueras. He then expounded his views as to peace terms: independence and integrity of Spain; no persecution after the war; right of the people to choose its government. Instructions were sent to the Spanish ambassador in London to solicit the good offices of the British government so that these points could be put to the nationalists as coming from England. By then, of course, the Rebels were no longer ready to negotiate.

Belgium had left the Non-Intervention Committee on November 29, 1938, and sent a representative to Burgos. France herself was beginning to feel her way toward the winning side. General Franco having informed London that he would rather take Minorca without German or Italian help, the British government had lent the cruiser *Devonshire* to negotiate this delicate operation, which was thoroughly successful but for an irrational outburst of Italian anger which took the form of an air raid on Mahon. The Revolutionists were still in possession of a considerable part of the territory, from Sagunto on the eastern coast to Almadén (including its invaluable mercury mines), southwest of Madrid; they still had several thousand men and some war material. But whom would they be fighting for if they fought? The President of the Republic was abroad. After protracted negotiations with Señor Alvarez del Vayo in Paris (February 15-18) Azaña had given it as his opinion that all resistance was useless (February 21) and he resigned on the 28th, as soon as he heard that France and Great Britain had recognized the Rebels. The presidents of the Catalan and Basque governments, Señor Companys and Señor Aguirre, were in Paris. Señor Martínez Barrio, President of the Cortes and the highest authority of the Republic since Azaña's resignation, was in Paris. Whom did Dr. Negrín, whom did Señor Alvarez del Vayo represent?[6]

No one in Spain. With Catalonia had gone seventy per cent of the war industries, a disastrous proportion of the armed forces, the only land communication with the rest of Europe. In Madrid there remained provisions for two days at the rate (which had prevailed for the last fourteen months) of 150 grams of bread and 100 grams of other foods per person per day. While outside, the Rebels had thirty-two divisions, abundant tanks and artillery and six hundred aircraft. When Colonel Casado who commanded the Central Army put these facts before Dr. Negrín on March 1, the prime minister answered that the Government had ten thousand machine guns, six hundred airplanes and five hundred guns waiting in France.[7]

A few days later the prime minister called a meeting of the Army commanders at Los Llanos Aerodrome, near Albacete. After hearing a two-hour speech by the prime minister in favor of resistance, the Army commanders, all but one, were unanimous for immediate negotiation with General Franco. As for Admiral Buiza, he notified the meeting that the Navy would leave Spanish waters if peace was not negotiated, for a committee representing the crews had called on him to report that they considered the war as lost and were not ready to continue exposed to air bombing without aircraft. The air commander, Colonel Camacho, explained he had only five squadrons of Russian bombers and about twenty-five fighters. He also proposed peace negotiations. One more general, the Military Governor of Cartagena, energetically asked for immediate peace, adding that disastrous events might otherwise happen in the Cartagena naval base—which was prophetic enough. At last spoke the excep-

---

[6] In his book *Freedom's Battle*, p. 282, Señor Alvarez del Vayo insinuates that Azaña's refusal to return to Spain was due to cowardice. It should now be clear after the data herewith provided that Señor Azaña had been the prisoner successively of Señor Largo Caballero and of Dr. Negrín and therefore not only could not trust them to respect his personal safety but consequently could not be expected to return of his own free will to the part of constitutional puppet which he had been made to play right through the Civil War.

[7] Casado: *The Last Days of Madrid*, pp. 107 *et seq.*

tional voice: General Miaja, who was Commander in Chief of
the Spanish forces of land, sea and air, advocated resistance at
all costs. This seems to have been the last time he allowed himself to act as a military loudspeaker for the Communist Party,
as events were to show. Dr. Negrín summed up the debate but
maintained his attitude: resistance.

The only party in Spain which was of his opinion was the
Communist Party. Dr. Negrín decided to recall Colonel Casado
and to entrust the command of the Central Army to Colonel
Modesto, a Communist-improvised commander thrown up by
the war. The emotion which the news, though as yet unofficial,
aroused in Madrid, led him to withhold his decision for some
days. But by then Colonel Casado had begun his conversations
with all the components of the Popular Front except the Communists, and with his colleagues in the Army to eliminate from
public authority Dr. Negrín and Señor del Vayo, remnants of
an unburied yet definitely dead government.

On March 5, 1939, the Fleet revolted in Cartagena and took
to sea. The Government appointed Lieutenant-Colonel Galán to
command the naval base.[8] In the afternoon the six ministers who
were then in Madrid left for Yuste where Dr. Negrín had taken
refuge. Colonel Casado and General Miaja, despite repeated
orders from Dr. Negrín, had refused to attend the meeting, feeling certain Dr. Negrín meant to have them arrested. Dr. Negrín
had entertained similar fears in his turn and keenly suspected
Colonel Casado of evil designs on his person.[9] Evidently by then
General Miaja had changed his mind. Next morning Colonel
Casado transferred his headquarters to the old, solid granite-

[8] Though sometimes described as Fascist, this revolt of Cartagena
was a complex affair. There was a fifth column; there was also an anti-
Negrín, anti-Fascist rising. The Fleet seems to have revolted against Dr.
Negrín and in favor of the Council of Defense. What induced Admiral
Buiza to take it to Algiers is not clear. It happened on exactly the same
day that the Council of Defense under Colonel Casado was set up. *See*
del Vayo's *Freedom's Battle*, p. 292, on the one hand, and Colonel
Casado's *The Last Days of Madrid*, p. 155, on the other.

[9] As related by Dr. Negrín to the Permanent Committee of the Cortes,
March 31, 1939.

walled Ministry of Finance in the Calle de Alcalá and called together the members of the Council of Defense he had set up in defiance of the Negrín–del Vayo–Communist Party combination. All the parties (but the Communist) which in 1936 had come together in the Popular Front were represented on this Council and Señor Besteiro had consented to be a member of it, though he had refused to be its chairman on the ground that the situation required a military leadership. Colonel Casado accepted the responsibility, as he explained, because there was no longer a President of the Republic, but he later put General Miaja in his place. There is no question that the greatest moral authority came from Don Julián Besteiro, whose fidelity to Madrid, which he had not left during the whole war, had made him the most popular and respected figure in the capital.[10]

That night Besteiro and Colonel Casado addressed the nation by radio. The gist of their speeches was: "We must lose, but honorably." It is sheer prejudice to stigmatize this courageous action as a rebellion against a constituted authority. Dr. Negrín was no longer anything whatsoever in Spain since there was neither a President of the Republic nor a Parliament, the two indispensable bases for ministerial authority in the Republic. The full political composition of the Council of Defense was a guarantee that public opinion, in so far as it could be ascertained at the time, was genuinely embodied in the new leaders.

The Army Corps commanded by Communists thereupon opened hostilities against the Council of Defense. After some hard fighting the Communists were beaten and by the morning of the 12th the Council was able to relieve all the commanders and commissars of the Communist persuasion.[11]

[10] As related above, Señor Besteiro was in London to represent the Republic at the Coronation, but he returned immediately to Madrid and was therefore one of the rare Spaniards of the Left without official duties who did not take an opportunity to go abroad in order to stay abroad. This of course increased his popularity with the tried inhabitants of Madrid.

[11] One Communist commander, Lieutenant-Colonel Barceló, and one commissar, Conesa, were shot. It has been charged against the Council of Defense. They were accused of common-law crimes.

Peace negotiations began at once. The conditions laid down by the Council of Defense were: No intervention of foreign powers; guarantees of (a) national independence and integrity; (b) expatriation for all who wish to leave; (c) no reprisals. On March 11, 1939, a statement to that effect was approved by the Council of Defense. The next day it was known to the leaders of the Fifth Column in Madrid, who coolly called on Colonel Casado to offer their good services in the cause of peace. When he had recovered from his surprise and mastered his first impulse to have them arrested, Colonel Casado accepted their proposal. The two Fifth Columnists told Colonel Casado that General Franco would require an unconditional surrender, whereupon the leader of the Council of Defense reported that in that case Madrid would fight to the end. They then produced a list of "concessions" which General Franco would make, based on "generosity" and "pardon" to all those who were not guilty of murders and who had been misled into the Civil War.

Very unfavorably impressed by this document, the Council of Defense secretly prepared a plan for the evacuation of Madrid while waiting for General Franco's official answer (March 13-19, 1939). To the Council's surprise the answer to a request for conversations was in the affirmative, and though the only subject declared acceptable for such a conversation was that of the details of the surrender, the Council took it as a good sign. Two officers, Lieutenant Colonel Garijo and Lieutenant Colonel Ortega, were sent to Burgos on March 23. They took with them a number of suggestions mostly on how to evacuate those wishing to leave and how to supply the needs of those who would remain. Upon their return the same evening they reported: German photographers at the airdrome; coldness in their comrades in arms, Colonels Gonzalo and Ungría, who represented General Franco; and counter-proposals for immediate surrender. No pact and no signature; assurances of best intentions and of cordial feelings on the part of General Franco. The Council insisted on a document being signed and the next day, in the course of another meeting at Burgos, the two delegates obtained this concession from the victorious Rebels. As Colonel Garijo was drafting it, however, a message came from General Franco that since the surrender of the Air Force (one of his initial conditions) had not been accepted, all negotiations were to be broken off at once. An offensive began the next day, though not close to Madrid. The Council decided to take the people into its confidence and put before them the whole history of the negotiations. This was done in a broadcast at 10 P.M. on March 26, 1939. That afternoon the Rebel radio had broadcast their conditions, ably cast in a language which sounded safe enough to the officers of the Revolutionary Army. Their troops were allowed to disband and most of them went home.

The Civil War was over.

Why had the Rebels won? The lazy answer, and the passionate, is: "Because they had the help of Germany and Italy." This answer will not do. Important though it was, this help was not crucial, and no honest and well-informed student of Spanish affairs would dare be dogmatic as to what would have happened if no foreign help whatsoever had accrued to either side. The chief reason for the failure of the Revolutionaries was the Revolution itself. When the Rebels rose, the Revolutionaries found that most of the springs of public force had gone over to the Rebel side. This in itself was due to the weakness which the Government had evinced for some time in matters of public order. Two alternatives remained for the leaders of the Republic: to get out of the way and let the military take charge, or to arm the people. The first would have been similar to the course King Alfonso had taken in 1931, when, faced with a popular rebuff, he was wise and patriotic enough to prefer his own exile to a civil war which he could have launched with much better chances of winning it than the Republican Government ever had. Had the Republican leaders imitated him, though this time the challenge was an illegitimate and rebellious one, they would have spared the country the horrors of the Civil War and the state of beggary and prostration in which she finds herself today. Moreover, they would have prevented the German and Italian inroads into Spain. In the end, military rule is never lasting in Spain, and experience shows that it always leads to further endeavors to establish parliamentary democracy. However, that did not happen. The leaders of the Republic chose the other alternative: they armed "the people," a hopelessly romantic conception dating from the French Revolution, which in actual fact meant arming a number of fiercely rival workers' unions, and chaos.

From that moment on the Civil War became a duel between a fairly well-held army and state under military discipline and an ill-assorted, loose group of tribes known as the UGT, the FAI, the POUM, the PSUC, the Communist Party, the Generalitat, Euzkadi, and several others, each pulling its way. This ill-assorted crowd could by no means be described as an alliance. They lived in a constant state of civil war, by which no mere metaphor is intended, for it is a matter-of-fact description of reality, with its battles and casualties and plans of campaign. The very aim of these tribes was not—as one might have thought —to win the war against the Rebels. For most of them it was to achieve a proletarian revolution, though not the same, for each tribe had a revolution of its own to achieve and one wholly incompatible with that of its adversaries; while others of these tribes, like the Catalans or the Basques, dreamed of achieving their own political statehood under cover of the war.

Every now and then wisdom moved the heart of this or that tribe. The Communists became wise, constructive and moderate; or the Syndicalist CNT shook off the chains of the Anarchist FAI and went on the road of reasonableness as far as to consent to take a share in the political government of the country; the Socialists made peace within themselves (no mean feat); the Catalans generously gave their men and munitions and swallowed the centralistic and dictatorial tendencies of Dr. Negrín for the sake of Spain; the Basques showed a fine sense of collaboration by sending their government back to Catalonia after their own territory had been overrun by the Rebels, and by remaining on Spanish soil right to the last; the Central Government endeavored to pull everything and everybody into shape and to regulate disorder when it was unable to stamp it out. But these strains of wisdom touched this or that party or political force at different moments in the Civil War, so that right through the struggle the keynote was one of internal strife and anarchy.

This and no other is the deepest cause of the downfall of the Republic: its inability to coordinate and harmonize the dispersive tendencies of the energetic and at times violent Spaniard; its failure to kindle a high national passion strong enough to absorb into a national unity the two negative passions of the Spaniard: dictatorship and separatism.

PART 3

BETWEEN THE

CIVIL WAR and

THE WORLD WAR

CHAPTER 12

INTERNAL AFFAIRS

Three were the aspects of the task which General Franco found
before him when he became the Spanish dictator: to rebuild
the nation's soul; to reinvigorate her body; to steer a dangerous
course through the stormiest waters which the foreign policy of
Spain had known for centuries. He failed in the first; he did
what he could, and it was not much, in the second; he showed
himself a shrewd and patient diplomat in the third.

When the Civil War came to a close the nation longed for
peace, had been longing for peace on both sides for a very long
time, which, of course, in the case of the majority of the Spaniards, went as far back as the first days of the hostilities. True,
the excesses to which the Civil War had given rise had woven
an appalling net of hate and counter-hate.[1] But there is another

[1] "Murders and executions are put by some observers at 800,000
(probably a low estimate) and military losses at 400,000."—Figures from
the London *Times,* January 3, 1940.

side to the picture which, though less well known, is equally important. Right through the war there was a good deal of fraternizing across the trenches. In the University City lines a man would throw a box of sardines to the hungry Revolutionary trench from the better-provided Rebel side with a request that it be sent to his aged mother, giving street and number, and the food would get there. Regular open-air meetings were held for months every afternoon between the men on both sides of a front near Talavera, and an abstruse political discussion was once broken off at one of these open-air meetings held in no man's land because a rumor went from the Rebel over to the Revolutionary side to the effect that El Estudiante, a famous torero, had been performing in Salamanca, and everyone wanted to hear all about it. Finally, during the Ebro battle, the chaplain of a Navarrese regiment was one evening surprised to observe a "strike," at prayer time when, having in the usual fashion led a prayer "for our dead," no one answered. "What is the matter?" he asked. And a soldier answered: "We want 'a prayer for our dead and for those of our brothers opposite.' "

This was the Spain which at the beginning of April 1939 looked to General Franco as the man who would forge a united nation in the crucible of grief. He was all-powerful. He was the undisputed leader of the victorious side and had the Army behind him. A great and noble voice leading the country to union and to unity would have called out a deep echo in every heart. The hates and counter-hates would have withered in the new climate, and, though poor and bled white, at least Spain might have been reborn.

God knows how long Spain will still have to suffer because General Franco failed in this his highest task. God knows why the Church, which claims to speak in His name, chose to remain silent in this great hour. The murdered priests could not in her case be a motive for worldly vengeance, but a call to duty and an inspiration for charity which would have turned them from political victims into religious martyrs. The Church chose to remain silent and vindictive like just another trade union, say of sacristy workers. And so the leader of the New Spain, for lack of both political and religious inspiration, failed in his supreme task.

To be sure the task was not easy. The score of criminal responsibilities, by no means confined to the Revolutionary side, put the authorities under the dilemma of either filling the jails with prisoners and the execution yards with dead, or leaving tens of thousands of Spaniards with a sense of grievance which might tempt them to take justice into their hands. But easy tasks require no dictators. It is possible that if General Franco had been content to remain on the somewhat simple and expeditious plane which his Andalusian predecessor, General Primo de Rivera, had never abandoned, the plane of a general who comes as a surgeon to extirpate political evils pending a cure and a return to normal, he would have been able to solve this, the most important because the only fundamental part of his duties. Unfortunately he was misled into assuming the part of a political philosopher and creative statesman by the deplorable examples of Hitler and Mussolini. Spain began to hear from the *Caudillo* (a word, by the way, which is but a poor translation of *Führer* and *Duce,* and, if feelings had any logic, should therefore be repugnant to people who call themselves Nationalists) that she owed all her ordeals to that liberalism which, said General Franco, had arrived in Spain astride the encyclopedia; Freemasons and Jews were thrown in to spice this lamentably weak stock, and the upshot of it all was that, "as the author of the historic regime whereby Spain has acquired the possibility of realizing her destiny, the leader assumes absolute authority. He is responsible only to God and to history."

Both God and history are patient. But men are not. The Falange Española, which in its own eyes is a mixture of history and of God, became in virtue of the decree to which the above phrase belongs the basis of the new state (July 31, 1939). A further concession to the two foreign sponsors of General Franco's cause, no doubt. Yet, in the very words in which the decree defines the task of the Falange can be detected the dour resistance of Spanish individualism: "to establish an economic regime overriding the interests of individual group or class . . .

to multiply wealth in the service of the state, of social justice and of the Christian liberty of the individual." These last words would have been out of tune in a Fascist, and unthinkable in a Nazi text.

This decree sets up a state within the state, in imitation of the Fascist and Nazi regimes, the so-called one-party system, in itself an imitation of Bolshevism. Its organs of power are the Caudillo, the National Council, the Political Junta (with a president and a secretary general), and a number of local delegates. The party has three main emanations: military (the Militia); economic (the Syndicates); and feminine, with which may be connected the activities of the *Auxilio Social,* an organization similar to, but not identical with, the *Winterhilfe.*

The increased hold of the Falange over the state, undoubtedly due to German and Italian influences, was not easy to establish. The newcomer was a threat to the two previous occupiers of the field of Spanish politics: the Army and the Church. In its essence, the new regime was and has remained in unsteady equilibrium between these three ill-assorted forces. The duel between the Falange and the army in particular is permanent and, if it ever came to a trial of strength, it is bound to end in favor of the army.

General Franco's policy, it would appear, is to avoid this trial of strength. In the summer of 1939 he put his own brother-in-law, Don Ramón Serrano Suñer, at the head of the Falange Council, giving to a General (Muñoz Grandes) the general secretaryship of the party, with a genuine Falangist as his second. General Franco's intention was then clear: to sit on, rather than allow himself to be sat upon by, the Falange. In August 1939 he reconstructed his Cabinet. His gradual evolution away from the Monarchy was shown in the elimination of General Jordana, who had been his vice-president of the Council and foreign secretary. The movement did not necessarily mean, however, a step toward Germany and Italy, for the Foreign Office was given to Colonel Beigbeder, a Staff Officer who had had a long and distinguished career as Military Attaché in Berlin. As for the Church, General Franco had sent Señor Serrano Suñer to Rome to ascertain from the highest source the best way for an agreement with the Vatican. Señor Serrano Suñer is a devout Catholic, but Spaniards have a way of wearing their devotion with a difference, and as far back as the sixteenth century the Vatican had already begun to suspect that every Spaniard is apt to think of himself as a Pope.

The Church was at times shocked by the Falangist tendency to discriminate between Catholicism and Vaticanism—an attitude against which Cardinal Gomá, the Archbishop of Toledo, had protested as early as January 1938. The solemn procession transferring the ashes of José Antonio Primo de Rivera from Alicante to El Escorial across Spain brought Spain's thoughts back to the days of the long funeral procession of Queen Isabel the Catholic. But the burial of José Antonio's ashes at the foot of the main altar in the Escorial Chapel was too bold for the Church and evinced a new spirit not very respectful of traditional values. General Franco, however, endeavored to restore the Church to the position it occupied before the Republican days. On May 3, 1938, the Society of Jesus had been restored to its previous position in the country, and in the same year diplomatic relations were renewed with the Vatican. The Crucifix reappeared in law courts and schools, the divorce law was cancelled and the budget for the Clergy inscribed again in the state budget, while conversations began to return to the Concordat of 1851. On October 12, 1939 (anniversary of the discovery of America) the Caudillo broadcast to Spanish America thanking the Virgin of the Pillar for his victory. A certain touch of popular and traditional superstition became the fashion and, notably in Spanish-American matters, the new State tried to identify the spirit of Spain with the Roman Catholic faith.

The two autonomous regions, Catalonia and Euzkadi, were deprived of their Home Rule. On April 5, 1938, the Catalonia Statute Law was abolished. As for the three Basque provinces, they had been "punished" with centralistic measures as soon as the Nationalists had conquered them. No attempts were made to discriminate between constructive home rule and separatism in either the Basque provinces or Catalonia.

As for reprisals, they were led by the Government itself. On February 13, 1939, General Franco, in order, it was claimed, to forestall an outbreak of private reprisals, issued a decree on the treatment of political offenders. It applied to all persons "guilty of subversive activities" from October 1, 1934, to July 18, 1936, as well as to all those who since then had "opposed the national movement in fact or by grave passivity." This wide definition covered most of the Spanish Left, Freemasons, separatists and absentees abroad during or after the Civil War. It did not, however cover trade-union members as such. A special Tribunal of Political Responsibilities was set up on March 14, 1939. Penalties included confiscation of property, fines, loss of civic rights, exile and imprisonment up to fifteen years.

As a symbol of shortsighted partisanship the victors sentenced Don Julián Besteiro to thirty years' imprisonment. He was well treated in his monastery prison, where he lived with a number of Basque priests imprisoned as Basque Nationalists, but died in 1940, no doubt heartbroken.[2] After the collapse of France, the Vichy Government began freely to deliver Spanish political leaders to the Spanish Nationalist Government. Many of them lost their lives after trial by court martial which, in the circumstances, organized by officers of the rebellious Army, must strike all fair minds as monstrous. So died, among others, Señor Zugazagoitia, who had been a close collaborator of both Don Indalecio Prieto and Dr. Negrín, and Don Luis Companys, President of the Catalan Generalitat, executed in October 1940.

This was not the way to bring back peace to the country. Executions in many cases, it is true, punished criminal acts. Too often, however, these were merely the political "crime" of having shared in the Civil War on the other side. It is doubtful whether this vindictive and repressive attitude can be solely ascribed to the narrow-minded and violent ways of the Falange. "The steady toll of life taken by the tribunals set up in many of the principal towns," wrote The *Times* Hendaye correspondent on August 5, 1939, "is driving to desperation the Republican

[2] He died of a tuberculous meningitis. The Government refused him pain-alleviating drugs.

militiamen who have hitherto succeeded in avoiding capture or have escaped from concentration camps." No doubt there were many Revolutionists with a heavy score, men like José Puig Lázaro, an anarchist stone mason, later a captain in the militia, who as head of the Cheka, which operated in the Fine Arts Club in Madrid, had sentenced to death six hundred persons. Yet there is something revolting in the spectacle of military officers, who, after all, whatever their reasons, had risen in rebellion against the State, sentencing people to death for rebellion.

There were whole zones of the country which were not at peace, notably in the fastnesses of Asturias, where thousands of miners had taken to the woods; and the new Cabinet, in the statement issued in Burgos on August 12, 1939, stated that "a period of austere sacrifices must be imposed, sacrifices which the persistence of treacherous attacks in which the enemy is exhausting a sterile offensive will render more severe."

This violence, however, was but the symptom of a deeper evil. The nation was not on its way to convalescence. Through the tragic failure of the Caudillo to find the right tone, the new attitude, the true voice, the gash in the nation's soul was not being healed and the spirit of the Civil War was still at large over the country.

How could the body of Spain be healed when her soul was still cut in two? This was the hopeless task which the Caudillo set before himself, doomed, of course, to failure. The capital of the country had been thrown into the furnace of the Civil War and there destroyed, with equal recklessness by both sides. The gold was in Moscow; the cattle had been decimated; the railway rolling stock halved; the motor vehicles reduced to one-third; the roads and bridges broken up; thousands of houses, streets, public buildings were in ruins; the merchant navy had been all but wiped out; and, to complete the picture, Europe was heading straight for a war and the very foreign policy which nationalist Spain was bound to follow put credits out of the question.

The cost of the Civil War to the country is still unknown and to a large extent incalculable. Leaving, it would appear, out of account the loss to the nation on the Revolutionary side, General

Franco's Ministry of Finance issued some figures on August 5, 1940, summing up expenditure on the Rebel side. Between July 1936 and July 1939 expenditure had amounted to 12,000,000,-000 gold pesetas, i.e. about $2,257,488,000. As in the same period the national revenue had been 3,700 million gold pesetas, the deficit had been 8,300 million, met mostly by advances from the Bank of Spain. The Ministry estimated at 5,000 million lire (£56 million) Spain's debt to Italy, repayable within twenty-five years from 1942, interest to be at rates increasing from one-quarter to four per cent; over and above this debt to the Italian State, Spain owed 300 million lire to the Syndicate of Italian Banks and commercial credits to the value of £3,200,000, 12 million Swiss francs and 50 million Portuguese escudos. Total national indebtedness was estimated at 1,200 million gold pesetas. During the Civil War the Bank of Spain financed both sides, it may be surmised, with unequal alacrity. The Rebels received advances to the amount of 7,600 million and the Revolutionists 23,000 million of their respective, very much inflated, currency.

So much for things. How about men? Spain is a country rich in skilled workers, but the oppression and persecution which the victors had thought fit to inflict deprived them of this invaluable asset. Many of these workers were in exile, and a hard exile at that. They would no doubt have returned had they not heard of the fate of those of their comrades who had remained in the country and were falling under the firing squads, or remained behind the barbed wire of concentration camps or were working on the roads in the *batallones penales*. As for the technicians of all kinds, an appalling proportion of them had fallen during the red terror of the first half-year of the Civil War; many of the best were in exile, kept there both by the fear of execution and by the defensive measures against their return taken by their less able colleagues entrenched by the strong hand of the Falange in the positions the exiles once occupied. Add to this that Germany, obviously determined to reserve for the Herrenvolk the profitable exploitation of industry in Europe, was doing her best to sabotage the rebirth of Spanish industry.

The definitely Socialistic hue of the Falange impressed itself on the new state in the principles of the Labor Charter promulgated on March 9, 1938. This Charter professed to be something entirely original. It is doubtful, however, whether it goes very much farther than codifying the pre-existing ideas for the protection of labor and small farmers, some of which had already been embodied in the Republican and even in the Monarchical laws, while others were already commonly accepted as overdue. If there is anything new in the Charter it is its authoritarian and somewhat simplified idea of the relations of labor and the state. A national organization of "vertical" syndicates built on a compulsory basis provided the administrative machinery for these laws.

Spain is rich in raw materials and can normally live on her own better than most people. But to start the wheels of peaceful creative work after the Civil War was no easy task when the bare necessities of food and clothing were the first which cried for satisfaction. Money itself was scarce, as the victors had refused to honor the notes issued by the vanquished. Toward the end of 1939, a general amnesty for the less important offenses committed by "the Marxists" was granted by the government. It did not carry enough conviction to set up a repatriation movement which the hardships of the exiles in France would have sufficed to encourage. The loan offered to the public in the autumn, 2,000 million pesetas in Treasury Bonds at 3 per cent redeemable in three years (September 29, 1939), was oversubscribed, the public asking for 5,582,585,000. This encouraged the government to effect several conversions, all successful, and government stock went up. A considerable amount of work was undertaken on roads and railways. Wheat was at the time obtained from France in exchange for ore on a barter basis.

Soon after his victory, on June 5, 1939, in the course of a speech to the National Council of the Falange, General Franco drew attention to the chief economic disease of Spain: un unfavorable balance of payments, which even under the shrunken trade volume caused by the world crisis had reached an average deficit of 250 million pesetas in the Republican days, and he rightly announced that the chief aim of the government should be to wipe out this commercial deficit. His method, however, which he outlined in the same speech, was rather Spartan: to develop production and exports, to cut down imports, and to do without foreign credits.

Nothing daunted by these handicaps, General Franco launched forth on his work of reconstruction. Salaries of civil servants were increased by from 10 to 40 per cent (which still left them at the pretty low level of 3,500 pesetas minimum to 17,500 maximum); a plan of public works was announced under which 1,500 million pesetas would be devoted to the roads, another 1,500 million would be spent on hydraulic works and 1,200 million on harbors. The rebuilding of Madrid was to take 157 million. Treaties of commerce were signed with Portugal in December 1939 and with Argentina in January 1940 respectively, and exports of fruit and other land produce began to flow, particularly toward Great Britain. A trade mission was sent to England in November 1939, presumably to counterbalance the economic influence of the two Totalitarian Powers. The budget for 1940 rose to 5,960,245,337 pesetas, of which 1,156 million were absorbed by the public debt and 1,283 million by the armed services, while 379 went to education, 450 to public works and the Falange took a tip of 9.5 million. Revenue from the end of the Civil War to December 1939 had reached nearly 2,500 million gold pesetas. Though the Republican Bank notes had been cancelled, the note circulation had risen to 9,000 million in 1939 as against 5,000 in 1936.

Commercial statistics began to reappear after years of eclipse. Foreign trade for the period April-December 1939 amounted to 207.7 million exports and 317.7 million imports (gold pesetas) with an adverse balance of 110 million. The four chief nations in the list are Germany (59E and 44I), Argentina (5E and 96I), Great Britain (61E and 17I) and the U.S.A. (24E and 48I). This unfavorable balance could not be considered as disastrous after such a war. In 1935 it had been as high as 285 million on a total trade of 1,462. And yet in those pre-Civil War days Spain was practically self-supporting as to food. With the exception of dried cod and eggs and a small amount of beans of all kinds,

Spain needed to import no food other than about 10 per cent of her usual wheat crop every three or four years. After the Civil War, however, the situation was quite different and the country was actually hungry.

In spite of General Franco's attitude of proud independence with regard to foreign loans, an Anglo-Spanish trade and payments agreement was signed in Madrid on March 18, 1940, providing for a loan not to exceed £2,000,000. Though the conditions could not be described as other than strictly business-like, there was an undoubted element of open-minded statesmanship in them so far as England was concerned, since at the time, under the lee of a Spanish-German so-called "cultural" agreement (January 25, 1939) public opinion in Spain was being treated to a severe anti-British campaign.

Material conditions, however, made it imperative for General Franco to treat with Great Britain. On January 15, 1941, bread rationing was reintroduced. The population was divided into three categories according to their dependence on bread; and their rations were fixed at 80, 125 and 175 grams respectively. Important purchases of wheat, meat and cotton were made in Argentina at the beginning of 1941, and to a much lesser extent wheat was also bought in Canada. In February and April 1941 cargoes of wheat, clothing, flour, milk and medical supplies were sent to Spain by the American Red Cross. A curious tripartite arrangement through an exchange of notes was made in Lisbon between Great Britain, Portugal and Spain, whereby purchases of wheat and of Portuguese colonial products were made by Spain through facilities for payment supplied by Great Britain. An arrangement was also concluded to certify all shipments of oil to Spain within quantities closely calculated so as to prevent any leakage from reaching the Totalitarian Powers. Mercury and oranges were bought by England in the spring of 1941, thus enabling Spain to purchase wheat and rubber in the sterling market, and on April 7, Señor Serrano Suñer and Sir Samuel Hoare signed an agreement for a loan of £2,500,000 for purchases of raw materials and foodstuffs.

Evidently General Franco did not mean to remain adamant

in his refusal to accept loans from the democracies, whose financial advances, moreover, were carefully measured according to the state of public opinion and policy in Spain. In his finances, as in the rest of his foreign policy, General Franco seems to have been led by a "skillfully prudent" opportunism.

CHAPTER 13

FOREIGN POLICY

General Franco's foreign policy has been less bad than his home policy. The reason is not far to seek. In home affairs General Franco, though by no means all-powerful, was closer to omnipotence. In international affairs he was governed to a considerable extent by formidable outside forces which were bound to stimulate his judgment and challenge his native prudence.

Some of the old-time Liberals and Republicans whom the follies of the Republic had driven to sympathizing with the Rebels, when challenged by us, the middle-of-the-way diehards, as to General Franco's foreign friends, met our criticism with this shrewd remark: "If Spain came out of the Civil War tied to France and Great Britain, no one would be able to deliver her; but when she comes out of the Civil War tied to Germany and Italy, there will be France and Great Britain to set her free."

There is little doubt that this thought, freely expressed by Spanish residents abroad, must have lain hidden in many a Nationalist breast as the Nazis stamped and the Fascists strutted over the soil of Spain. The repeated soundings made by France and England about Spain's intention in foreign affairs, about the integrity of her territory and policy and similar matters, invariably drew from the Nationalist government an uncompromising answer, outwardly, at any rate, satisfactory. In March 1938, the British government had received oral, later confirmed by written, assurances that no alienation of Spanish territory would be entertained after the war and no permission given to either Italy or Germany to set up bases in Spain. In a note addressed to the Non-Intervention Committee on August 16, 1938, General Franco reaffirmed his determination never to assent to the slightest mortgage upon the soil or the economic life of Spain. The British government was inclined to accept these assurances and to recognize the Nationalist government as soon as the occupation of Catalonia by the troops of General Franco had made it clear that the Rebels had won the war. The French government, whose position in Nationalist Spain was much worse owing to their less neutral attitude during the Civil War, and who had, moreover, more direct fears on the score of German or Italian forces in Spain, decided to subordinate recognition to a number of conditions relating to the new government's foreign policy. As early as September 27, 1938, General Franco had declared that Spain would remain neutral in case of a European war. On the other hand, his power over his friends had not sufficed to prevent the notorious Minorca incident, when Italian planes from a Majorca station bombed Mahon at the time H.M.S. *Devonshire* was meditating for its surrender to General Franco (February 9, 1939). The injudicious action of the Italian authorities in Majorca made it plain to the whole world that, at any rate in Majorca and at the time, General Franco could not call himself master in his own house. The French government therefore decided to send a negotiator to Spain.

The person chosen was Senator Bérard, a Conservative with strong Spanish intellectual interest and many friends in Spain. Senator Bérard went first to Burgos as an unofficial agent and diplomatic explorer. He found courtesy without much warmth. On matters such as the revival of communications and the reabsorption of the host of refugees which were invading France there seemed to be little difficulty; but General Jordana was stiff as to the conditions which the French wished to attach to their recognition. The Nationalists considered recognition their due. Nevertheless, even here, Senator Berard was given the impression that France had nothing to fear from Nationalist Spain, and the Nationalist government invited three French generals to see for themselves that the story of fortifications on the French frontier was a fabrication.

Monsieur Bérard returned to Burgos as an official representative after a brief stay in Paris to report progress, and during the week of February 18-26 was able to negotiate the so-called Bérard-Jordana agreement which embodied the recognition of General Franco's government. The two governments expressed their intention to live in amity and as good neighbors, to cooperate loyally in Morocco and to prevent all activities directed against the peace and security of the other party. The French government undertook to use all the means in its power to ensure that Spanish property, and in particular the goods which had passed on to French territory against the wishes of their rightful owners, was returned. This included first and foremost £8,000,000 of gold deposited in Mont de Marsan in 1931 as security for a loan and which, although the loan had been fully reimbursed, the French government had refused to pay back to the Revolutionaries; it covered also war material on its way to Spain, Revolutionary Spain of course, and war material brought out to France after the Catalonian disaster; cattle; merchant and fishing vessels; works of art and jewels; title deeds and documents and vehicles of all kinds. Attempts at securing some form of compensation for French expenses arising out of the Spanish exodus were foiled by the Nationalist government—a success due in part to the fact that the British government had decided on February 15 to recognize General Franco without further delay. This decision was conveyed to the French government immediately and on February 27 the two governments recognized the Nationalist government simultaneously (though M. Daladier had announced his decision on February 24).

While Senator Bérard negotiated in Burgos some Spanish-American nations had suggested common American action on the matter of recognition, but the Government of the United States could not afford to be rushed, for its public opinion had been more strenuously agitated over the Spanish war than any other in the world; and after every other Spanish-American state but Mexico had recognized General Franco, the American Government announced its decision to follow suit following the surrender of Madrid, on April 1, 1939.

When toward the middle of March, Marshal Pétain arrived in Burgos as the first French Ambassador he found a colder reception than his highly decorative figure might have led him to expect, and General Franco made him wait for a week before granting him his first audience. One of the chief difficulties for better relations between France and Spain is that France will always insist on bargaining and on holding fast to her assets. Therefore none of the conditions of the Bérard-Jordana agreement had been fulfilled. The French public were told so twice in blunt and somewhat unusual terms by the Spanish Ambassador, Don José Félix Lequerica, a Basque supporter of the Nationalist movement, in Embassy communiques somewhat devoid of amenity. The French government gradually let go its pawns, and in particular the gold deposited in Mont de Marsan, as well as Ł60 million held in La Rochelle, where it had been brought by the Basque autonomous government after the fall of their territory.

The next difficulty arose with regard to the evacuation of German and Italian forces. Europe was living at the time through dramatic events. Hitler had just seized what remained of Czechoslovakia (March 15, 1939) and statesmen and generals looked with some anxiety toward the Peninsula, where a number, not accurately known, of Italians and the German Kondor Legion still lingered. Signor Mussolini had signed an agreement with England on April 16, 1938, pledging himself to withdraw his troops (the same troops which he had previously pledged himself not to send to Spain), as soon as the war was over. The war had been declared at an end on April 1, 1939, and the Italian troops were still there, which was all normal if repetition is the hallmark of norm. On April 7, Signor Mussolini had criminally entered Albania and the world was informed that Spain had adhered to the anti-Comintern pact on March 27. This sounded bad enough. Two days later, however, Count Ciano informed Lord Perth, the British ambassador in Rome, that the Italians were staying in Spain merely to take part in the victory parade. The victory parade was postponed week after week and the German government announced that the spring maneuvers of their fleet would take place off the coast of Spain. Flesh-creeping rumors ran all over Europe of German and Italian preparations in Spain, against the Pyrenees, against Gibraltar. The technique of the war of nerves was being tried for the first time. Why, it is not clear. On May 17, 1939, the German fleet was back in Kiel; on May 19 the victory parade took place in Madrid and the Italians began to get ready to leave the Spanish shores. On May 26 the Germans of the Kondor Legion left in five transports which sailed from Vigo to Hamburg. Twenty thousand Italians sailed from Cádiz on May 31. Experts, airmen, sick and wounded kept flocking back home during the summer, but the evacuation of personnel to both Germany and Italy was complete.

Three more aspects of this liquidation of German and Italian help to the Rebels remained to be cleared up: material, bases, policy.

The Italians left a good deal of war material in Spain. Though this was another breach of the Anglo-Italian agreement of April 16, 1938, it was not in itself serious; it might in fact be thought an advantage from the point of view of a Spain intent on recovering her freedom of action. As for bases, one fact is certain: the lugubrious prophesies made during the war about the Balearics becoming Italian and whatnot did not materialize. Neither Germany nor Italy kept in Spain anything to compare with the base of Guantánamo which the United States kept in Cuba after 1898. Not an inch of Spanish sovereignty has been given away nor an inch of Spanish territory. That is the legal position, without prejudice to the uses and abuses which for all we know may have been going on.

In matters of policy the Nationalist government found itself in unstable equilibrium: with a debt of gratitude toward the two Totalitarian Powers yet fully aware of the strong geographical, political and economic ties which linked the country to the West. This situation was reflected in the composition of the Cabinet whose head, General Franco, endeavored to keep an even keel in fact if not always in words, while his foreign secretary, General Jordana, leaned toward the West and his home secretary, Señor Serrano Suñer, to the Central Powers. The position of Portugal further complicated matters. Now that the two Peninsular nations were under similar (though by no means identical) regimes a closer cooperation could be arranged, and on March 31, 1939, ratifications were exchanged for a treaty whereby each nation undertook to respect the other nation's frontiers and peace and to give no assistance, still less to allow the use of its territory, for any aggression against the other.

It seems natural to conclude, in view of all happenings up to the end of 1941, that General Franco's set course in foreign affairs was to play both sides against each other, France and Great Britain against Germany and Italy, within the orbit of his power and in the shaky framework of the foreign events themselves. It explains, among other reasons, the stiff attitude taken by the Spanish government toward various attempts made by Anglo-Franco-American capitalism to catch Nationalist Spain in the nets of a big reconstruction loan. In May 1939 a group of banks—ostensibly Dutch, Belgian and French; probably, however, with strong Anglo-Saxon backing—tried an operation which, at any rate for the public, seemed to be led by M. van Zeeland, a former Belgian prime minister, head of the Belgian State Bank. General Franco made it clear that he did not wish to have financial help. This meant untold hardship for a country paralyzed by lack of capital. The decision could therefore have been dictated only by higher considerations of national policy.

On the other side a German commission was at the time studying the possibilities of German collaboration in the economic reconstruction of the country, and Italy was putting forward joint plans with Spain for the rebuilding of railways and roads. It stands to reason that, since by then the two dictators knew that their war was coming, these so-called economic studies and plans must have been at least in part camouflages for military studies and preparations which might some day mature. General Franco on the other hand seems to have been quite clear in his mind that his first duty was to keep out of the war.

The Germans seemed then to be well on the way to oust the Italians at the moment of garnering in the harvest of their common illicit intervention in Spain. Señor Serrano Suñer had gone to Italy to return his "volunteers" to Signor Mussolini with thanks, and on his way back had made a speech in Barcelona (June 14, 1939) to give vent to his pro-Italian feelings. Count Ciano returned the visit and landed in Barcelona on July 10. He had an interview with General Franco in San Sebastián on July 12 amidst scenes of reasonable enthusiasm. He visited Toledo and Madrid, flew to Seville and sailed back from Málaga to Italy, with nothing but bouquets of flowers of rhetoric in his hands; for, though his department in Rome made bold to depict Spain as in line with the Axis Powers against the democracies, the Spanish press kept an obstinate silence. Not in vain had General Franco said in his speech to the National Council (June 5, 1939): "The chief feature of our foreign policy is its *'hábil prudencia.'*"

Feeling against France was, however, general and not in the least counterbalanced, rather the reverse, by any gratitude on the part of the numberless members of the population who lived in sullen opposition to the victors. The French Consul in Madrid, Jacques Pigeonneau, was assaulted by some Spanish officers in a Madrid restaurant on July 9, 1939. The resumption of the patriotic celebration of May 2, in commemoration of the rising of Madrid against Napoleon, must be considered as definitely anti-French in intention. Nevertheless, the Cabinet reconstruction of August 1939 brought to the Foreign Office Colonel Beigbeder, a man with long experience of foreign affairs and a character by no means to be suspected of subservience to Germany, or for that matter to any foreign power. The signature of the Hitler-Stalin pact was received in National Spain with obvious astonishment. The Government and the party in office had to swallow it and so the press was hard at work to make it palatable to its readers under all kinds of specious reasons; yet, a party which had drenched the nation in blood and ruined it on the pretext (and, for many, a sincere reason) of a defense against Communism could hardly be turned overnight into an ally of Communism. When hostilities began it was evident that General Franco would be more than ever able to remain neutral. That enmity against Communism remained a strong feeling, stronger than any friendship the Nazis might inspire, was shown by the attitude of the (strictly controlled) press toward Finland during the Russo-Finnish war and by the thousands of letters of sympathy received by the Finnish minister in Madrid. The Spanish Red Cross sent supplies and volunteers to the Finnish Red Cross.

With the collapse of France in 1940 the wall behind which Spain might have hoped to shed the shackles of her new friends crashed to the ground. It may be safely asserted that the news of France's surrender and of the arrival of Germans at Hendaye must have been received in Madrid with mixed feelings. The effects of the mighty event were not long in coming. On September 16, 1940, Señor Serrano Suñer visited Berlin with an array of economic, political and military collaborators. He saw the Führer and Herr von Ribbentrop and declared that Spain's non-belligerency must not be interpreted as disinterestedness. No concrete military ties seem, however, to have been concluded.[1] From Berlin he went to Munich, then to Rome, where he saw the Duce and Count Ciano, both before and after the famous Brenner Pass meeting between the two dictators (October 4, 1940). He returned to Spain without calling at the Vatican, and on October 17 was transferred to the Foreign Office, where he inaugurated his tenure of office with a fierce speech under the

[1] True, an actual agreement seems to have been signed. (*See The Spanish Story* by Herbert Feis, New York, 1948.) But if so, it was not concrete enough to force the Spanish dictator to do anything whatsoever.

aggressive form of which could be discerned his fears lest the more experienced and competent members of the diplomatic service should not second his pro-Axis adventures.

Great Britain had appointed Sir Samuel Hoare as ambassador in Madrid in that darkest hour of the war when Winston Churchill took office as prime minister. But soon after Sir Samuel Hoare's arrival in Madrid the defeat of the Luftwaffe by the Royal Air Force inaugurated a new phase which allowed free scope to Sir Samuel Hoare's patience and skill. Spain had to steer a difficult course, the more so as the war was bound to be longer and its issue uncertain.

Spain was plunged again into a conflict of fierce passions, high and low, at the moment when she had no more ardent desire than to rebuild her own life. What were the chief ideas of the men in power at the outbreak of the Second World War? These men were first and foremost Nationalists, and that was the name they had chosen for themselves. Their ideal was defined in their motto: *Spain One Great and Free.* They believed in the ability to create such a Spain—if no one else did. They used many words to assert time and again and in most forcible terms that the time for words was past and the time for deeds had come. They sought to retemper the nation's faith in the contemplation of the glories of the past. Ferdinand and Isabel became the national figures and their "Yoke and Arrows" the symbol of the Falange. *Hispanidad* or Hispanity became the rallying cry. The word had been invented by Ramiro de Maeztu, the precursor of Falangism and even perhaps of all Fascism,[2] and sought to designate the spirit of the whole Spanish-speaking world, interpreting it somewhat anachronistically in terms of a faith which took no account of the deep spiritual changes undergone since the

---

[2] His *Authority, Liberty and Function in the Light of the War,* published in English in London during the last war and later in Spanish under the title *La Crisis del Humanismo,* would appear to be one of the earliest statements in favor of an authoritarian and functional state with any intellectual dignity. Maeztu was one of the numerous victims of the Red Terror in Madrid.

sixteenth century by the Spanish-speaking peoples on both sides of the Atlantic. A *Consejo de la Hispanidad* was set up on November 7, 1941, attached to the Ministry of Foreign Affairs. It was composed of leaders of Spanish thought and of the Church, the Spanish ambassadors in a number of Spanish-American republics and the Consul General in Manila. Ideas as to what this Council should do are not clear. We hear about race in accordance with the absurd tradition which designates as the "Day of the Race" the anniversary of the discovery of America by Christopher Columbus (October 12), though "race" hardly fits either the discoverer or the discovered or the result of the discovery.[3]

It became the fashion to speak of the Spanish Empire. The Falangists were not original in this. The harm done to many nations by the phrase "British Empire" is incalculable. Monsieur Daladier invented the French Empire a few years ago and Signor Mussolini dreamt the *Impero Italiano* till the Führer shook him out of his dreams and the *Imperator* awoke to find himself *Gauleiter* for Italy. The Spanish Empire is a Falangist invention. Spanish relations with America are, of course, mostly cultural and literary, and no one, not even a Falangist, thinks of them as anything else. But the fact that most of the chiefs of the Army had behind them a Moroccan career told in the foreign policy of Nationalist Spain, and imperial ambitions, now that the American cycle is closed, are apt to return to that African expansion from which the fantastic dreams of Columbus deflected them. One heard again of Queen Isabel's political testament and France was expected to return most, if not all, of the Moroccan territory which she gradually wrenched from Spain during the protracted negotiations of 1902-12.

This aspect of Nationalist foreign policy was the background of the Tangier events. In June 1940 Colonel Yuste, at the head of

[3] The Council of Hispanity, however, did not prevent General Franco's government from breaking relations with Chile (July 16, 1940) over the right Chile claimed to retain within the gates of its Madrid Embassy a number of refugees of the Left, much smaller than the number of refugees from the Right, which the Chilean *Chargé d'Affaires*, Señor Morla, saved from death by the same means during the Red Terror. Relations were restored in December 1940.

Spanish troops, entered the international city declaring his action to be due to the exceptional circumstances of the moment and in no way directed against the international regime of Tangier. On November 4, however, he issued a proclamation assuming the governorship of the town as delegate of the High Commissioner of Spanish Morocco. The Committee of Control and the Assembly were abolished. This, of course, radically altered the legal bases of the Government of Tangier under the international treaties in force. On December 13, British, French and Italian high officers of the city were deprived of their posts and the Spanish High Commissioner for Morocco took over all the services. There was a protest on the part of Sir Samuel Hoare in Madrid (December 15, 1940) and an American protest as well, but the Spanish Foreign Secretary argued that Spain's action in Tangier was a matter of natural right. It is evident that the Spanish government feared, or professed to fear, similar action by the French government, which they wished to forestall.[4] A conference of the British and Spanish Chambers of Commerce in Madrid (January 7, 1941) was assured that foreign financial and economic interests would be respected and that the system of exchange would remain untouched. The peseta, however, became the legal currency of the city.

Despite these assurances Great Britain grew uneasy. On December 3, 1940, the British Post Office had been wrecked by Italian rowdies without any action on the part of the Spanish authorities to enforce the law. Worse still, when two Italian submarines which had sought refuge in the port on November 3, 1940, lingered there till December 12, misgivings arose as to the use Nationalist Spain would make of Tangier. The British and Spanish governments came, however, to a temporary agreement (February 26, 1941) whereby Britain recognized the special rights of Spain in Tangier while reserving her own under the treaties in force, and the Spanish government gave an assurance that the zone would not be fortified and that British interests would be respected. On March 16, 1941, the Mendub, or Sul-

---

[4] *See* answer by Mr. Butler to Mr. Seymour Cocks in the House of Commons, January 29, 1941.

tan's representative (*de facto,* of course, a French-appointed authority), was ejected from power, and his residence, the former German Consulate, returned to the German authorities.

The Tangier episode was read abroad as one of the many German intrigues to secure a footing on the Straits and in North Africa. And so it was no doubt seen also in Berlin. In Spain, however, whose links with Tangier are many centuries old, it was read otherwise, and it would be a mistake to imagine that public opinion was as inimical to this as to other moves of the "Moroccan" generals who at the time commanded the foreign policy of the country.

The next feature of Nationalist foreign policy was its anti-Bolshevism. The Spanish signature to the anti-Comintern Pact was given in dead earnest and with a somewhat naive disregard for or ignorance of the cynical opportunism with which Nazis and Fascists viewed that instrument of their international intrigues. Señor Serrano Suñer's visit to Berlin in November 1940, when Herr von Ribbentrop offered him at lunch the champagne left over from the lunch given to M. Molotov a few days earlier, must have been galling to him. Nevertheless, the dictators held the field, though General Franco—this must be said to his credit —succeeded at any rate till the end of 1941 in *not* paying either dictator in their capitals the visits which they might, and may, have demanded on the score of gratitude. The Caudillo met the Führer on October 23, 1940, at the Spanish frontier, the longest distance from Berlin Hitler ever traveled to see anyone; and though the visit took place after a three-day stay of Himmler in Madrid, and although both von Ribbentrop and Señor Serrano Suñer were present, no very material results were seen to come out of the meeting up to the end of 1941. The Caudillo traveled as far as Bordighera to meet the Duce on February 12, 1941 —very generous on his part, for by then the first crop of laurels on the Roman Caesar's brow had been rudely plucked by General Wavell.

The attack on Russia by Hitler on June 22, 1941, despite its dastardly character, did much to simplify General Franco's diplomatic front. The dramatic successes of the first days gave rise to much flourish of pro-German feelings—or, at any rate, ut-terances—even on the part of the usually cautious Caudillo. On July 17, 1941, the fifth anniversary of the rising against the Republic, General Franco addressed the Falange in unusually aggressive terms, directed both to home and to foreign ears. He threatened all "internal enemies," whether "materialist Reds or frivolous bourgeoisie or foreign-influenced aristocrats." He bluntly reproached the United States with what he described as attempts at political shackling incompatible with our sovereignty and our dignity as a free nation," adding ominously: "It is illu-sory to think that the plutocracies dispose of gold to apply it to generous and noble enterprises. Nations, like individuals, become tainted through gold. This is eloquently shown in the exchange of fifty old destroyers for some pieces of an Empire." After claiming that the first battle for the new order had been won in Spain (the King Charles' head of both sides of the Spanish Civil War), he spoke in forcible terms against the United States enter-ing the war and boldly declared that the Allies had lost the war, which he very likely believed at the time, ending with a declara-tion of solidarity with the German Army which was fighting the battle "which Europe and Christianity have so long awaited."

On November 25, 1941, Señor Serrano Suñer attended the meeting of the anti-Comintern Powers in Berlin. It was a sub-stitute for the grandiose conference of the new order which Hitler had planned to call either in Vienna or in Moscow after the fall of the Bolshevik metropolis. Señor Serrano Suñer re-stated that Spain had fought the first battle for the new order, possibly with the object of limiting to one token division, the so-called Blue Division of so-called volunteers, the collaboration of Spain in the so-called crusade. Sent to fight on the Leningrad front in the thick of the Russian winter, the Blue Division lost eight thousand men out of fourteen thousand.

This was not the only help in manpower which Nationalist Spain rendered Germany. Señor Merino, the leader of the Falange labor organizations, went to Berlin in May 1941, as a result of which a treaty for the "exchange of producers and workers," i.e., the supply of Spanish labor for Germany, was concluded on August 25, and considerable numbers of skilled and unskilled workers were sent to Germany by the Nationalist government. Señor Serrano Suñer had been greatly elated by Hitler's declaration of war against Russia, which he had hailed as the saving of Europe. His relative and chief might well think that it was at any rate the saving of Spain, for General Franco, Champion of anti-Communism, found himself indebted to Russia for his deliverance from the impending threat of a German invasion which he would have been unable to prevent without the unexpected help of his arch-enemy Stalin. Life revels in such piquant ironies. To celebrate these mixed elations, a heroic attack on Sir Samuel Hoare's windows was made by a troop of Falangists supported by a battery of German cameramen and newsreelmen (June 24, 1941). After the usual assurances had been given to the British government, Señor Serrano Suñer felt free to raise the pitch of his utterances again; he declared to a correspondent of the *Messaggero* (end of July) that Spain could not remain indifferent in the event of an Anglo-American occupation of the Azores and Cape Verde Islands, and made bold to add that Eire, France and Portugal would be drawn into the war against Great Britain.

It was plain that in General Franco's orchestra his close relative and collaborator was in charge of the Axis big drum. It may be that the conductor turned a deaf ear to the noisy instrument, or that he did not dislike the tune after all. At any rate Señor Serrano Suñer was allowed to put the Spanish press and radio at the disposal of Axis propaganda and to grant an ample hospiltality to German and Italian agents, going even so far as to put the delicate machinery of Spanish diplomacy at the service of his Axis friends, whom he undertook to represent in the growing number of countries which broke with them. There was a field in which this ill-considered policy of the Spanish Fascist foreign secretary gave rise to situations singularly out of harmony with the professed intentions of the regime. In Spanish America opinion was rapidly gathering momentum in favor of a general break with the Axis Powers, and Spain, official Spain at any rate, found herself in the unenviable position of having to stand in the countries of her own language and culture as the only friend of their enemies.

Toward the end of the year this situation became acute owing to Japan's entry into the war and to Germany's declaration of war against the United States. On December 19 General Franco issued a decree, declaring Spain would remain non-belligerent. No mention of neutrality. The distinction seems to have been definite and substantial.

At this same time several Spanish and Portuguese ships were torpedoed in mysterious circumstances off the southeastern coast of Spain, in the neighborhood of Cartagena. This led to the suspicion that the Axis Powers were planning an attack on Gibraltar or North Africa through Spain. The year, however, came to an end and nothing had happened. From a still neutral Spain, General Franco silently watched the German Army, including his Blue Division, freeze to death on the snowy plains of Russia, the Japanese Air Force blast to the ground the monuments of *Hispanidad* respected by centuries and by the North Americans in Manila, and the whole of the American Continent gradually rise against his German and Japanese allies, while Señor Serrano Suñer's model, the Duce, fell into the most tragic impotence that history has ever witnessed.

CHAPTER 14

THE EXODUS

In a legal and figurative sense, an exodus had set in from the very outset in Madrid, for certain embassies had received under their technically foreign roof hundreds who fled from the anarchical terror of the first months. Some of these embassies, such as that of Chile in particular, and the Legations of Finland and of Poland, had rented blocks of flats for the purpose. On the other side, the exodus was more physical than legal and figurative. As early as the spring of 1938, France was being invaded by thousands of fugitives from Aragon. Those among them who had been combatants were made to return to Spain, though given the choice as to which side, and the majority went to Catalonia. Many non-combatants remained in France. But about a year later the problem became acute for France as the Catalan front collapsed and an exodus of unprecedented dimensions in modern times crashed the gates of the Franco-Spanish frontier. After fruitless negotiations with General Franco during which the

French government tried to set up a neutral zone on Spanish soil close to the French frontier, in which the refugees would be cared for by foreign agencies, the French government had felt unable to maintain their original refusal to admit able-bodied refugees. By January 28 thousands began to pour in, of all classes and ages, many with their belongings, often with their livestock. French troops, including many Senegalese, received them and shaped them into some kind of order, and the unfortunate exiles fell down the scale of human beings to the very lowest grade. The sufferings, both physical and moral, of these fugitives bear no description.

France has been most generous of her soil and hospitality during these barbarous years of European persecution and no nation in the world shows a cleaner record in this respect. The inrush of Spaniards, moreover, was of such vast proportions and so sudden that every allowance must be made for the shortcomings of the hastily arranged hospitality which the French government had to improvise. The picture, however, would not be complete if no mention were made of the appalling sufferings of the exiles in whose bleak camps, without food, warmth or sanitation, or often even housing, the recruiting sergeant and the white-slave-traffic dealer were more active than the social worker, the sister of charity, or the doctor. In their turn the newcomers can have been no welcome addition to the contented and happy countryside of France. Disease, disorder and at times crime smuggled themselves in their midst into the sunny Midi. Among the 500,000 refugees who had crossed the frontier, the French authorities reckoned that about 10,000 had committed crimes punishable by law in any country. The bulk of the refugees, moreover, had lived through two and a half years in highly abnormal circumstances. During these years the usual view on individual property had been somewhat blurred, if not altogether obliterated, while many brought animals which caused depredations on the well-cultivated fields of France. Finally, on securing treatment so far short of their expectations, at times almost like that of animals, they reacted violently and destroyed olive fields to warm themselves or ransacked farms to find food. Argelès,

Saint Cyprien, Le Boulon—names of these camps, are nightmare names for many Spanish exiles. Gradually things righted
themselves, however. Many refugees returned to Spain, prefer-
ring General Franco's fire to the pan of exile; early in March
1939, about 50,000 had been repatriated; 170,000 women and
children and 40,000 male civilians were still in several camps
and 1,000 sick and wounded were undergoing treatment in
various hospitals, while 220,000 soldiers and militiamen were
also in camps. General Menard was appointed by the French
government to coordinate all the services dealing with the
refugees.

The sums spent by the French government ran into millions.
Its efforts to share the burden with other governments were not
very successful. The Belgian government took between 2,000
and 3,000 children, but the British government was not willing
to accept any refugee immigration beyond a small number of
leaders[1] and the Russian government refused to take anybody
at all; both the Russian and the British governments, however,
contributed to the French effort with sums of money. The French
government found but small sympathy in their endeavors to
recover some of their expenses from the Spanish Nationalist
government; on the contrary, the Spanish government slowed
down the admission of the refugees who wished to return, evidently as a reprisal for the French reluctance to return the Spanish assets promised under the Berard-Jordana agreement.

Nevertheless the French government obtained compensation
to a certain extent by enlisting considerable numbers of Spanish
able-bodied men in labor battalions and of Spanish-trained
soldiers in the Foreign Legion. English officers bear witness that
during the worst moments in Flanders the Spanish Pioneer Battalions seized weapons which they found abandoned by French
units and held up the Germans; Spaniards fought at Dunkirk and
at Narvik and a handful of them were in British uniform in
England in 1941.

[1] A considerable number of children were housed in England when
the Basque provinces fell to General Franco. They were known as
"Basque" though many were not so. But in any case why not "Spanish"?

Meanwhile, what were the leaders doing? Most of them were free to move about in France, in particular nearly all the members of the Popular Front National Committee. No measures, however, seem to have been taken to collaborate with the French authorities in the protection of the refugees. There were still considerable resources at the disposal of Dr. Negrín; for the *Campsa-Gentibus,* a purchasing agency for the Revolutionary Government, had funds and cargoes of food in hand, while its fleet of ships, the Mid-Atlantic Company which obeyed Dr. Negrín's instructions, amounted to 150,000 tons. Yet the quantities of food put at the disposal of the refugees seem inconsiderable when compared with the tonnage of food sold for cash by order of the Minister of Finance, Señor Méndez Aspe.[2] A letter written to Dr. Negrín on March 28 by General Rojo, of his General Staff, provides some data as to the funds which had been put at the disposal of exiled officers and men till that date, as well as a measure of the irritation which the perhaps inevitable delays and disorders of those days was producing in the men. "From the first days of February," writes General Rojo, "we distrusted the behavior of some of our leaders of first and second rank, in spite of which we tried to abstain from an attitude of violence and vituperation and we endeavored to maintain the utmost discretion in our dealings, for we thought this to be in the best interests of Spaniards; but the way we have been treated recently forces us to let go the last remnants of respect and deference toward those who neither personally nor collectively evince them in their relations with our countrymen." General Rojo then goes on to criticize the plans evidently afoot to start big enterprises in Spanish America, in order, he says, to place a couple of thousand Spaniards, and to provide for a few prominent people, leaving the rank and file to their own resources.[3]

Though there is reason to believe that the plans thus criticized were carried out in Mexico and other parts of South America, this strong document emanating from one of the most respected

[2] *See* documents and figures in *The Last Days of Madrid* by Colonel Casado, p. 288.

[3] Text in *Crónica Obrera,* p. 14. London, December, 1941.

professional soldiers who remained faithful to the Left till the end seems to have brought about a closer consideration of the problem of the exiles in France. On March 29, 1939, one day after the date of General Rojo's letter, the Popular Front National Committee met in Paris to consider help to the refugees, and on March 31 it was decided to set up a *Servicio de Emigración para Republicanos Españoles* (SERE) in which all the parties and trade union movements of the Popular Front were represented. The leading committee of the SERE was assisted by a representative of the Mexican government. For its finances it relied on the funds belonging to the Spanish (Left) government which Dr. Negrín had succeeded in bringing over to France, as well as those which were deposited in several foreign banks in several ways which made them unclaimable by the Nationalist government. A scale of subsidies was arranged for, limited however to a number of relatively high categories of state, former heads of the government, ministers, undersecretaries, directors general, presidents of *Audiencias,* generals, colonels and General Staff officers. They were all to receive 1,500 French francs per month, plus 500 for a wife and 500 for each child.[4] As for the rest, they would be given facilities to emigrate.

The subsidies seem to have been suspended by the spring of 1940. The Mexican government had expressed its willingness to accept 50,000 refugees if the cost of transport was not a charge on its treasury. A first shipment was sent on May 24, 1939, on board the *Sinaia,* chartered by the British National Joint Committee for Spanish Relief. The 1,700 refugees who composed it were, however, selected by the SERE under strong Communist influence, as had been a previous group of 600 who had left on April 3. It is believed by many refugees that the Mexican government objected to the Communist selection of its immigrants, cooled off, and considerably moderated its original plans.

Matters were complicated by two sets of circumstances: the first was the utter lack of legal basis for Dr. Negrín's government, and therefore the lack of standing for his important financial

---

[4] I understand that the maximum subsidy was to be 2,500 French francs per month.

transactions; the second was the curious position in which Dr. Negrín and the SERE found themselves as a consequence of their close intimacy with the French Communist Party when this party, owing to the Stalin-Hitler Pact, took an anti-war attitude. One of the Paris pro-Communist papers, *Ce Soir,* had been founded with money provided from Barcelona by Dr. Negrín. The shipping company *France Navigation* was managed by the French Communist Party though the ships had been paid for by the Spanish Revolutionary Government. When President Daladier decided to suppress the Communist Party and to confiscate its property, *Ce Soir* was suspended, the fleet of *France Navigation* was confiscated, and finally the offices of SERE were raided.

Dr. Negrín's government meanwhile had ceased to exist. When on March 6, 1939, Dr. Negrín arrived in France, the *membra disjecta* of the Republican government were all in France. The President of the Republic had resigned. The Permanent Committee of the Cortes, an organ of state provided for by the Constitution of 1931, was in Paris. On March 7 it met and passed by ten to five the following resolution:

> In view of the latest events which have taken place in Spain, leading up to the exile[5] of Dr. Negrín and the setting up of another government in Madrid under General Miaja, the Permanent Committee of the Cortes declares that, since it is the standing representative of Parliament which in its turn is the only organism of the Republic with a popular character, it reserves for itself the right to demand from all Republican authorities, those who have resigned and those who remain, a report on their actions, and to express on them the opinion which it may think fit at the suitable place and moment.

Señor Martínez Barrio, President of the Cortes and therefore of the Permanent Committee, made it quite clear that while the resignation of the President of the Republic laid upon him the

[5] The Spanish word is *salida* and may, of course, mean also the cessation of Dr. Negrín's tenure of office.

duties of the presidency, this was limited to eight days during which he was to take measures to have a new president elected. The implication was that no such election of a new president could be justified in the circumstances and that therefore the office of President of the Spanish Republic became finally vacant.

The Permanent Committee of the Cortes met again on March 31 and April 1, this time to hear Dr. Negrín. The ousting of the Negrín government by the Casado-Besteiro Junta and the political tensions which had brought it about and which it had in turn set up could be felt in the meeting. Though Dr. Negrín had secured one of the Socialist members of the Committee, Señor Lamoneda, as his mouthpiece, the debates and the votes showed that his strength sprang from the Communists. The first day was spent in theoretical disquisitions over whether Dr. Negrín was prime minister or not and whether the Permanent Committee could have any status abroad. A working compromise was reached between Dr. Negrín and the Committee on the basis of admitting each other's existence, if only for the purpose of debate. But the mood of opposition with which he had been received by the Permanent Committee had stimulated Dr. Negrín's aggressiveness, and next day La Pasionaria delivered a scathing and offensive attack on her colleagues—an attack which some of them evidently attributed to Dr. Negrín's generalship. If such was the case, the style would have been that which can be observed in the doings of this able and executive man from the moment he rose to power: to bully and to woo almost in the same breath; for at the same sitting, forgetting his defiant attitude about the status of the Committee, he offered the exiled parliamentarians every deference for their Committee and every help for their need, in a masterly paragraph:

As for the regime to be adopted with regard to the gentlemen members of Parliament, that is a matter for your exclusive competence. The Government cannot define it. It is for you to do it, and I would even beg you not to do it in the presence of the head of the Government, for that would in effect run counter to the prestige and authority of the

Permanent Committee. It is for you to decide and to bear
the responsibility of your decision.

These words were meant to obtain the acquiescence of the
Committee for a shrewd solution to a complex situation. In Dr.
Negrín's view, no one could remove him from the office of prime
minister until a reborn free republic created its organs of state;
and no one could receive his accounts—whether political or
financial—or give him his quittance, till such a newborn republic
had started its machinery of state. He was therefore entitled to
remain sole administrator of the funds of the Spanish nation
available abroad. Yet, he was ready to admit the Permanent
Committee to some collaboration and even inspection of his
management, though not to any executive share in it. This was
his stand. And in the end, though only by ten votes to six and
four abstentions, this was the conclusion of the meeting.

There were among the Noes some of Dr. Negrín's passionate
adversaries. But the objective view was well represented. It was
voiced by the president of the Committee (and of the Cortes),
Señor Martínez Barrio. In his view, the Committee, being the
standing representative of the Cortes and therefore of the nation's sovereignty, could not accept the subordinate position Dr.
Negrín defined for it. Either it reserved its powers to retain or
dismiss Dr. Negrín or else, as the president had proposed in a
motion standing in his name, it left to Dr. Negrín the undivided
and unfettered responsibility of his stewardship.

There seems to have run throughout the proceedings (along
with a good deal of merely political passion) a not unnatural reluctance to share in financial responsibilities of an undefined
character over which, moreover, Dr. Negrín himself would
appear to have been somewhat lacking in candor. What had he
secured for the relief of the exiles and for other public services
abroad? Let us go to him for the answer.

First, to the Committee of the Cortes in Paris, April 1, 1939:

Señor Santaló asked: "Very well, and what are the means
to meet all that? Are there enough means?"—No. There

are not enough means. Everybody was astonished two years ago to find that we still had foreign currency to carry on the war; there are people who, a year and a half ago, carried on a defeatist campaign saying: "It is impossible that we still have money or foreign currencies." How could we have a treasure today? In the countries in which Franco has been recognized we can count on no means but those coming from international help.

Second, in a letter to Don Indalecio Prieto, Mexico, June 23, 1939:

> In March this year, when our Government was still recognized by France, England and the United States,[6] the minister of finance, in agreement with me, and following a carefully studied plan, prepared long in advance, tried to secure in countries or by such means that our rights over the assets of the Republican State could not run the risk of dangerous lawsuits, all the resources likely to remedy the misery of our emigrated countrymen as well as possible, without allowing us to be led astray by differences of class, cast or political color, still less of personal friendship or sympathy. Thanks to our foresight and exertion we were able to save such assets the amount of which could not have been dreamed of by those who two years ago asserted that the war was on the eve of ending through our lack of resources.

The obvious contradictions between these two texts suggest the kind of secretive art which some of the more dispassionate

[6] A lapse of memory of Dr. Negrín. General Franco was recognized by France and England on February 27-28. The narrative of the happenings at the sittings of the Permanent Committee, March 31-April 1, and the quotations come from a typescript copy of the proceedings of the Committee which I was able to consult. The letter to Señor Prieto comes from a collection of letters published by a group of Señor Prieto's friends in Paris: *Epistolario Prieto y Negrín. Puntos de vista sobre el desarrollo y consecuencias de la guerra civil española.* Imprimerie Nouvelle. Association Ouvrière, 53, Quai de la Seine. 1939.

members of the Permanent Committee must have felt in Dr. Negrín's now arrogant, now suave statements, and the lack of actual human effects behind the formal success of his parliamentary maneuver of March 31-April 1.

One of the chief items in this "treasure," the existence of which Dr. Negrín denied before the Permanent Committee and proudly described to Señor Prieto, was to be the object of a dramatic adventure. "Toward the end of 1938," writes one of Dr. Negrín's American friends, "the Spanish Republican Government rented a handsome villa in Deauville, one of the most fashionable seashore resorts in France. In the villa lived several well-dressed men and several beautiful Spanish ladies. They led the life of rich South Americans spending the season at the playground of Europe's high society." It is there that, as the Rebels advanced toward the Pyrenees, a few months later, Dr. Negrín had his treasure conveyed and in particular a considerable pile of valuable jewels. "One night in the second week of February 1939, the well-dressed inhabitants of the Deauville villa put on working clothes and carried huge cases filled with diamonds, sapphires, emeralds, pearls, and gold and platinum jewelry down to the sea and loaded them on the yacht *Vita*. The estimated value of the jewels was $50,000,000. The cargo also contained strongboxes packed tight with stocks and bonds." When the treasure arrived in Mexico, Don Indalecio Prieto, who happened to be there, seems to have had no difficulty in convincing President Cárdenas that he had a better claim than Dr. Negrín to the yachtful of jewels. This fact immediately gave Señor Prieto means for political action against his rival which he was not long in exploiting.

Dr. Negrín sailed for Mexico to try to rescue the valuable cargo. There developed between the two Socialists a duel over the ownership of the means of production for the manufacture of political power, a duel carried out mostly in the form of letters, some of them extremely lengthy. In the course of this correspondence. Dr. Negrín endeavored to recover the treasure even at the cost of setting up a management committee presided over by his rival; but Don Indalecio Prieto held the view that the valuables were public property while Dr. Negrín was just a private citizen, and that no one but the Permanent Committee of the Cortes had the right to take possession and administer that wealth. He invited the members of the Permanent Committee to come over to Mexico for that purpose, but in the end he sailed for Paris in the same boat with, though not in the company of, his rival, to attend a meeting of the Committee in the French capital.

This time the weapons were not equal; for while in point of the sinews of political war the two rivals were even, in point of eloquence and parliamentary strategy Don Indalecio Prieto was superior to Dr. Negrín. The Committee met on July 26, and passed a resolution favorable to Prieto.

This resolution marks the end of the Spanish Revolutionary Government as a juridical and political entity. *The Junta de Auxilio a los Republicanos Españoles* (JARE) was established within forty-eight hours. Its chairman was Don Luis Nicolau d'Olwer, a distinguished Catalan scholar who had been governor of the Bank of Spain for the Republican side till the last day of the war, a man with an excellent reputation and an upright character. Don Indalecio Prieto was vice chairman. Members of all the other parties and groups which had fought together against General Franco completed the Junta, with the exception of the Communists and the Basques. Dr. Negrín was not a member of it, either because he refused or because he was not asked to sit in it. This shows that the tension between the several rival groups had outlived the Civil War, or, in other words, that the civil war within the Socialist party, older than that between the Right and the Left, had survived it. It seemed only natural that Dr. Negrín, though not originally one of the prominent leaders of his party, should in virtue of his relatively long premiership have formed a part of the JARE. The Permanent Committee, however, decided otherwise and, as a consequence, instead of a harmonious and united leadership, the Spanish exiles were torn by separatism and dictatorship, just as if they had remained at home. While the JARE under the Permanent Committee of the Cortes upheld its claim to control the "national patrimony," i.e. the funds in one way or another at the disposal of the several exiled leaders, Dr. Negrín defied the Permanent Committee and chose to put the funds which he had taken out of Spain under his own separatist dictatorship.

The JARE had organized subsidies for the exiles and large sums of money were sent from Mexico to France to meet the expenses of the impoverished Spaniards there. In actual fact both the JARE and the SERE by the nature of things had become political instruments in the hands of Don Indalecio Prieto and Dr. Negrín respectively. The mass of emigrés settled mostly in France, Mexico, Argentina, and other Spanish-American Republics, the United States and England, followed world events with the keenness of people who realized that the outcome of the war—or even before that, a *faux pas* of General Franco—might put an end to their exile. The leaders of the Left had not succeeded in unifying exiled Spain any better than they had belligerent Revolutionary Spain. With the funds at their disposal, they might have set up a useful national administration which might have performed a number of invaluable services. As it is, the conclusion is inescapable that to a great extent the funds are either lying fallow or are being used for politics of a less than national scope by those who control them.

All, however, is not negative in this exile of hundreds of thousands of Spaniards. For many of them the experience acquired abroad will be invaluable. For the countries in which they are guests there is often a gain, for it happens that the Spaniard is creative and adaptive. Even the most advanced countries may find sometimes invaluable lessons in the experience of highly trained Spaniards with an inventive genius of their own.[7] Spanish America in particular has greatly benefited by Spanish immigration, and both Mexico and Buenos Aires owe to the immigrant

[7] I may be forgiven for quoting as an example the name of Dr. Trueta, the distinguished Catalan surgeon whose new technique for air-raid wounds, and wounds in general, has saved numberless lives and limbs in Great Britain.

Spaniard (as well as to the short-sighted policy of the Nationalist government) an unrivaled development of book production. Men of letters and of science are teaching in the universities of North and South America—teaching and learning. It may yet be that this exodus will determine the beginning of a change of character in Spain such as was observable at the beginning of the nineteenth century.

CHAPTER 15

THE DICTATOR SEES IT THROUGH

At the end of the Second World War, General Franco was in Spain the head of all that which lay dead on the ground; and outside of Spain, a pariah. Ten years later, he was in Spain the head of a strong regime (how really strong, it was difficult to say), and an ally and "favorite son" of the United States. This success he owed to his single-minded strategy, his able and unscrupulous tactics, and the so-called "realistic" diplomacy of the Anglo-Saxon powers.

General Franco's political strategy is as simple as a spear. Every action of his aims at only one achievement: to stay on. Under the most varied and even contradictory tactical appearances—peace, neutrality, warmongery, amnesty, persecution, monarchy, regency—General Franco has one and only one thought: General Franco.

His closest collaborators know, by now, that he will ever balance a tame liberal with a reactionary, a clerical with an anti-clerical, a Monarchist with an anti-Monarchist—thus keeping the boat nice and even for the skipper. This system, which he has carried to perfection in internal affairs, is the key to his foreign policy during the war. It consisted in making a fervent show of enthusiasm for the Axis, backed with considerable services, and balanced by enough betrayals of the Axis to reinsure himself in case the Allies won the war. He was brilliantly vindicated when the United States signed the three conventions of economic and military aid in 1954 with the war minister, General Vigón. This general, as air minister during the Second World War, had tried in vain to turn a Spanish air attaché in London into a spy for the Nazis and on the Spanish air officer's point-blank refusal, had hounded him out of the service.[1]

But long before the American surrender, General Franco had received high praise for his betrayal of Hitler from no less a person than Sir Winston Churchill. On May 25, 1944, the British prime minister opened a debate in the House of Commons with one of his masterly speeches. What he said about Spain in this speech filled with dismay not merely his true Spanish friends but the liberal world at large; for his praise of Franco was based on two stated or assumed rules: that a man is to be praised for betraying his friends when we profit by such a betrayal; and that the internal affairs of a country are none of our business so long as the nation concerned "leaves us alone." The first is untenable in ethics and the second is untenable in truly realistic international policy.

This speech did much to strengthen the dictatorship in the eyes of the Spanish people. Franco felt no longer a pariah—at worst he was a suspect. On November 4, 1949, he made a statement in plausible "liberal" terms, aimed at a seat at the Peace Conference. Premature though it was, it betrayed the evil effects of Sir Winston Churchill's unfortunate utterance. At about the same time, General Franco wrote a letter to Mr. Churchill pointing out that Spain, Great Britain and Germany were the only virile peoples left in Europe, and advocating that, after the

[1] The story has been told in a book by the officer in question. J. A. Ansaldo: *Para Qué?*

defeat of Germany, Britain and Spain should join to oppose "the Russian peril." Mr. Churchill sent this letter on to Stalin and Roosevelt and answered it declining the invitation. This was a failure, but one which at the time remained hidden behind the veil of diplomatic secrecy. Then came Franco's "excommunication" at Potsdam (July 17-August 2, 1945). Spain had been refused access to the United Nations Organization at the San Francisco Conference because of her regime. The Potsdam Declaration confirmed this exclusion. It stated:

> The three governments will support applications for membership from those States which have remained neutral during the war and which fulfill the qualifications set out above. They feel bound, however, to make it clear that they would not favor any application for membership put forward by the present Spanish government, which, having been founded with support of the Axis Powers, does not, in view of its origins, nature, record, and close association with the aggressor States, possess the qualifications necessary to justify such membership.

This text, like everything said and done about Spain in the official world in those days and since, carried a deadly internal contradiction: what was the UN? An association of states entering into an era of truly cooperative foreign policy, or the Victory Club ready to open its doors to mere neutrals provided they were found acceptable to the bosses? The UN, purporting to be an alliance against aggression, counted among its leading nations, governments and men that nation, the Soviet Union, that government, the Soviet government, those two men, Stalin and Molotov, who had been expelled by the League of Nations for a stark aggression on Finland. The Potsdam Declaration, therefore, lacked all moral authority to condemn or exclude anybody. It was one more stage in the process of debasement of key words which has been going on at an accelerated rate since 1918. Franco was kept out as a totalitarian and aggressor by Stalin, the arch-aggressor and arch-totalitarian.

Franco took the hint. On July 20, 1945, he reorganized his Cabinet and his new servants declared that it all meant "a further stage in Spain's spiritual and material reconstruction." Then he gave Spain the *Fuero de los Españoles,* a kind of Charter of Rights as remarkable for what it contains as for what it omits. Thus (Art. 13) "The State guarantees liberty of correspondence within the national territory," coolly reserves for the state the right to open your letters if you write to your friends abroad. Not that it matters. The Charter of Rights is the most mendacious document ever penned. It guarantees every right which the government tramples upon daily: freedom, when any man is at the mercy of any official and never knows whether his day will not end in jail; property, when any man's property may be confiscated and sold over his head at the behest of any official; honor, when any newspaper may insult any man without hope of redress on his part; justice, when none is administered unless it suits the regime; opinions, when none are allowed but those that please the dictator. There is not a single article of this Charter that is not in itself an insult to the nation whose daily experience gives it the lie. But the regime was in tune with the age. If Stalin was declared peace-loving in San Francisco and Potsdam, why shouldn't Franco be declared liberty-loving in Madrid?

The world, however, was not taken in. On December 14, 1945, the French government invited the British and American governments to a three-power talk on Spain. Mr. Bevin, then foreign secretary, had on December 5 declared in the House of Commons: "We detest the regime." The British and American governments accepted the French invitation, but with a certain reserve. London and Washington were beginning to detect in the anti-Franco campaigns of the day that touch of indignant insincerity which often betrays a Communist inspiration. This rift, just then emerging, was finally to benefit the Spanish dictatorship, a result neither unforeseen nor undesired by Moscow. For the time being, however, the Anglo-Saxon powers were still, outwardly at any rate, adversaries of the regime, and when the

American ambassador in Madrid, Mr. Norman Armour, resigned (November 11, 1945), no successor was appointed.

The execution of ten Republicans (February 20, 1946) raised another wave of anger in the free world. Let us keep the matter even. General Franco's repression was barbarous and unnecessarily cruel; but the world hardly ever heard of executions unless Communists were involved. Indignant insincerity again. On February 2, 1946, four more victims fell to the executioner in Barcelona. The French government closed the Spanish frontier on February 28. On March 4, the American, British and French governments issued a joint declaration to the effect that "so long as General Franco continues in control of Spain, the Spanish people cannot anticipate full and cordial association" with the victors over Hitler. The three governments expressed the hope that "leading patriotic and liberal-minded Spaniards may soon find the means to bring about a peaceful withdrawal of Franco." This sounded like a recipe of holy water to cure earthquakes; but the note tried to convey the impression that if the middle-of-the-road Spaniards could find some way out of the predicament, the three powers would be cooperative.

Then came the indictment of Spain before the Security Council on April 6. This was grotesque for more reasons than one: the accuser was Poland, a Soviet puppet state more totalitarian by far than Franco Spain; and the grounds for the indictment were that "the present regime in Spain is endangering international peace." Facing such ineptitude (or Machiavellian design?) in his enemies, Franco was able to answer his critics with equanimity. "How could he be accused of being a dictator," he asked the Cortes on May 14, "when the Cortes had approved so many important laws and their proceedings were public?" "Approved," he truthfully said, for that is all his Cortes can do, not being allowed to legislate; and as for the independence of their members, on February 22 he had dismissed six members (one of them the Duke of Alba) for having signed a message of greeting to the pretender to the throne. This pretender was in fact the only man who was not pretending. The Soviet group and the Government of France, then under Soviet influence, were pretending to be indignant at Franco; the two Anglo-Saxon powers were pretending to hope that liberal incantations would suffice to remove him; and General Franco was pretending to be the scion of the political marriage of Gladstone with Isabel the Catholic.

The imbroglio culminated in the resolution passed by the UN Assembly on December 12, 1946. This resolution, based on a mixture of motives, provided that Spain was to be debarred from representation in UN agencies and conferences, that if the internal situation in Spain had not changed within a reasonable time the Security Council was to "consider adequate measures," and that meanwhile all members of the UN were to recall their heads of missions from Madrid.

This step was *in itself* neither good nor bad. Much has been written about its effect in rallying Spain around the Caudillo. It did nothing of the kind. Demonstrations are easily arranged by dictatorships. If the resolution of the Assembly was to be deplored, the reasons are entirely different. They are three:

1. It lacked authority, owing to the leading part taken in it by nations such as Soviet Russia and Poland, which in point of totalitarianism were kettles to the Spanish pot.

2. It definitely showed the world that the United States and Britain were dragged into it instead of leading it.

3. It was what the French call a *coup d'épée dans l'eau,* a sword thrust into the water; an isolated gesture with no tomorrow.

General Franco must have realized that beneath its unpleasant surface the UN resolution conveyed what he most wanted to hear: that London and Washington were not to be feared as enemies and—who knew?—might even be valued, if not as friends, at any rate as "realist" partners. He chose this moment to pretend to move toward the Monarchy. On March 31, 1947, he made it known that a law soon to be enacted would declare Spain a monarchy again, but without a king while he lived. At his death, the Council of the Realm (a body set up by the law), jointly with the government, would propose to the Cortes the name of a prince of the blood to be king. The Cortes would have to approve the nomination by a two-thirds majority, and swear fidelity to the "fundamental laws," i.e., to the Fascist regime. The pretender spurned this law, which was as monarchist in its form as it was contrary to all monarchist doctrine and tradition in its substance. On June 8, 1947, the Cortes approved the law, by a unanimous vote of course; and the next day the dictator added ignominy to injury by issuing a decree providing for a referendum on the same law. This referendum was held on July 6, following the classic lines of such totalitarian farces, and led to unknown results. The government issued its own figures, for what they are worth: 12,628,983, yes; 643,501, no. 320,877 blank or void.

This pseudo-monarchist activity was a kind of homeopathic cure the regime was taking in advance against a possible under-standing between Socialists and Monarchists, toward fulfilling the conditions adumbrated by the three powers in their note of March 4, 1946. In September 1947 the Spanish Socialist Party in exile published a statement favorable to such an understanding. In October 1947, the Socialist leader, Don Indalecio Prieto and the Monarchist leader Don José María Gil Robles met in London and were received by Ernest Bevin (one of the few *earnest* enemies of the regime). This move was a success. A statement was prepared (end of August 1948) which answered the re-quirements of the three-power note of March 4, 1946, and of the UN resolution of December 12, 1946. This statement was forwarded by both Socialists and Monarchists to the governments of Belgium, the United States, France, Britain, Holland and Luxemburg. The agreement provided for a provisional govern-ment, a plebiscite to decide the form of government and the immediate incorporation of Spain in the Brussels Pact.

Why did this well-meaning effort miss fire? For a number of reasons. The Monarchists ran away from their success. Don José María Gil Robles laboriously explained to the press that he would never agree to the "March 4th formula"; an attitude some-times explained as due to pressure from the Portuguese govern-ment, sometimes as due to fear of being left alone with the "Reds" while his political troops ran to take cover under the regime. Then the regime took fierce counter-measures, and persecuted every Monarchist who showed the slightest inclination to "play." Then again, the Anglo-Saxon powers were by no means sound or eager on the issue. By the end of December a stream of American congressmen passed through Madrid, all anxious to talk to General Franco. On December 10, 1948, Mr. Churchill, during a debate on foreign policy, unbosomed his views on Spain in the House of Commons. "No Britons or Americans have been killed in Spain." "The way in which Hitler and Mussolini were treated by General Franco is a monumental example of ingratitude." Ergo, let us bring Spain into UN. Since on top of that Mr. Churchill admitted that at Potsdam he had agreed to exclude Spain only to induce Stalin to give the Charter "generous and friendly aid and support," a speech of the great English statesman was, for the second time, a powerful tonic for the regime which Spain was enduring. "Why should the Spaniards be treated as outcasts?"—asked Mr. Churchill, when he himself was treating them that way.

Confusion became worse confounded when it became known that the pretender had met General Franco off San Sebastián (August 25, 1948). It was a meeting of yachts, all rather fluid; but it bewildered and aggrieved many Monarchists, particularly when it was known that the young Don Juan Carlos, the pretender's son, was being sent to Spain for his education. On behalf of the pretender, his friends explained (but in private only) that the meeting had taken place on Franco's initiative; that the king had stood firm on his position, namely that he could only negotiate on the ways and means to transfer power from the dictatorship to a monarchy which would be constitutional; that he remained faithful to the Socialist-Monarchist document, and sole master of his son's education. Gravest of all, however, was their admission that the pretender on his followers' own showing, had agreed to talk with Franco because influential persons in both the United States and Great Britain strongly advised him to do so. This fact—for it is a fact—only shows how influential persons may at times misinterpret the most evident situations. Franco only wanted to "talk" in order to whittle down, to nibble, so to speak, the position which he knew to be strong, acquired by the pretender among the exiles. Which Franco effectively did.

The Monarchist-Socialist agreement, nevertheless, left behind at least two results: a liaison committee, working in Paris, and a certain "new look" in the relations between these two branches of Spanish politics, which enabled them to cooperate in other tasks. The European Congress which met at the Hague May 7-10, 1948, invited Señor Prieto and Señor Gil Robles to share in its work. I had also been invited because of my international activity. Gil Robles was unable to come owing to visa and passport restrictions. After patient negotiations, I succeeded in setting up a Spanish Federal Council of the European Movement, in which were represented all the non-totalitarian colors of the Spanish political palette: Monarchists, Republicans, Socialists, Basques and Catalans. This Council was living proof of the existence of a feeling of unanimity among the Spanish people on which to found a free Spain. It was, therefore, remarkable that even a statesman as friendly to Spanish aspirations as Mr. Acheson should have so oddly worded his May 11, 1949, statement to the press: "The U.N. decision of 1946 that ambassadors to the Franco Government should be withdrawn . . . was designed to convince the Spanish people that there must be a liberalization of their regime before their country can become a member of the community of free nations of Europe." As if the Spanish people were not convinced of the need of their own freedom! But the freedom of the Spanish people was the last thing that interested the congressmen and senators who daily called on General Franco and went back to sing his praises in Washington. This stream was organized by D. José Félix Lequerica, who had been Franco's ambassador to Pétain, then Franco's foreign secretary. Proposed by Spain as ambassador in the U.S., Lequerica had not been accepted by the latter nation because of his war record. However, General Franco forced the American government to receive him as Inspector of Embassies and Legations; and, once settled in the Spanish Embassy, he acted as

Spanish ambassador, generously "wining and dining" all Washington's Who's Who at the expense of the Spanish taxpayer. On December 27, 1950, he received his reward. He became officially the ambassador in Washington.

The veering around of official opinion, discreetly acting upon a public still strongly anti-Franco, had been favored and speeded up by events in Korea. Despite concrete warnings conveyed to the U.S. by the South Korean Assembly (November 21, 1948) that if American troops withdrew, the North Korean Communist Army would seek to unify all Korea under Communism by force of arms, the American Army was withdrawn (June 29, 1949). Exactly a year later, the North Korean Army crossed the 38th Parallel and took Seoul. President Truman acted boldly: he gave South Korea military support. Great Britain followed; and the operation was duly blessed by the UN high priests.

This was one of Stalin's worst blunders. The citizens of the United States had kept smiling till then, putting all their money into cars and refrigerators, and all their confidence in the peaceloving intentions of the Soviet Union. Rudely shaken by the North Korean aggression, they took matters in hand with a determination and a sense of responsibility most gratifying for those who had so often despaired of the United States in the days of the League of Nations.

But the new policy had its dangers; and one of them was that it increased the pull of the Pentagon on the State Department and the White House. When a group of Latin-American nations presented a resolution to the UN Assembly revoking the earlier resolution of December 12, 1946, advocating withdrawal of all heads of missions from Madrid, the U.S. voted for it, and the resolution was passed (November 5, 1950). At a press conference, President Truman declared it would be "a very, very long time" before he sent an ambassador to Madrid. He did so within seven weeks.

On July 16, 1951, Admiral Sherman, Chief of Naval Operations and member of the U.S. Joint Chiefs of Staff, arrived in Madrid, and called on General Franco on the same day. This visit began a series of negotiations which led to the adoption of three agreements between the two nations on September 26, 1952: on mutual defense, economic aid and again mutual defense.

What sort of a state was this Franco Spain with which the Pentagon was pushing the United States to form an alliance? To begin with: a military state at war with its people. This is not a figure of speech; it is a terse definition of the legal basis of the present Spanish state. On July 28, 1936, the Junta of Defense issued a *Bando* or order declaring the entire nation in a state of war. Most of the stipulations of this Bando have been re-enacted since in other "legal" texts and are so to speak doubly in force; for the Bando itself is still in force. The chief of the state succeeded the Junta as the sovereign power on September 29, 1936. Under a "law" of January 1, 1938, his decisions will carry the force of laws whenever they dwell on the organic structure of the state or constitute main rules for the legal organization of the state. The present Spanish state has no legal foundation; the power of its chief has no legal limit. He appoints and dismisses his ministers and seldom listens to their advice.

By virtue of the law of July 28, 1947, "Spain is a Catholic, social and representative state which, in accordance with its tradition, declares to form itself into a Kingdom." Article 2 of this law characteristically speaks of the command (not the headship nor the leadership) of the state; which Command "*belongs* to the Caudillo of Spain and of the Crusade, D. Francisco Franco Bahamonde." This law sets up the Council of Regency described above, a device to put off the return of the Monarchy until Franco's death.

The regime allows but one single political party: the Falange, which "holds the middle way between the community and the state" (so says a decree of April 19, 1937, so it must mean something). The Falange pays no taxes, but receives a handsome share of the budget (61 million pesetas in 1952). Its head is Franco. Its executive is appointed by Franco. The Cortes, as set up by the law of July 18, 1942, prepares laws which the Caudillo may or may not accept. It meets in a plenary sitting two or three times yearly when the president so decides. This president is appointed by Franco; who also appoints two-thirds of the *procuradores* (members), the remainder being elected by industrial, economic and municipal groups, under conditions which amount to being appointed by Franco's appointees. The plenary sittings are public only when the president so decides. There are no debates, but only votes on resolutions presented by the Commission.

The mayors are appointed by the home secretary. The municipal counselors, through a complicated system, are in fact, nominated by the government or by the Falange. The same applies to the Provincial Councils.

The Charter of Labor (March 3, 1937) allows no other syndicate (trade union) than those organized by the Falange, which took over and confiscated the assets of all Spanish trade unions. The Falange syndicates are government organizations, and their bosses (one could hardly call them leaders) are nominated by the government. All propagandizing or association of workers or employers outside this scheme is illegal and punishable by the courts. Strikes and lockouts are assimilated to sedition (Art. 222 of Penal Code).

After a period of terror which lasted from the beginning of the Civil War to the end of the Second World War, Franco Spain evolved a more discreet form of repression under the guise of justice. The chief instruments of this repression are a number of vindictive laws, the omnipotence of the military state and the subservience of the judicature to it; and the state monopoly of the press.

The law of political responsibilities of February 9, 1939 punishes (in some cases with death) every possible political activity the regime dislikes, going as far back as 1934; and is particularly aimed against persons who held posts under the Republic from the day the Civil War began. In practice, this restriction is waived whenever it suits the government.

The decree of June 9, 1943, makes provisions for disposition

of the booty which the victors just took from the vanquished as
the armies of the "Crusade" entered a city, and in the ensuing
years.

The law of April 13, 1945, abrogates that of political responsibilities (September 2, 1939), leaving, however, enough
loopholes to please the friends of the regime.

The law of April 18, 1947, ostensibly directed to the repression of "banditism and terrorism," is freely used to deal with
adversaries of the regime who can by no stretch of the imagination be described as either bandits or terrorists. Article 9 stipulates that military courts will be competent to administer this
law and their jurisdiction will be summary.

This "legal" framework is made even more oppressive by the
absolute hold the government keeps over the judicature. A judge
who does not submit has to go. It follows that the laws are only
a façade, bad enough, yet nothing like what goes on behind it.
Case after case could be quoted to show that one's life, property,
reputation, are at the mercy of the regime and its men. I can
assert that thrashings were in 1954 still recognized as a regular
feature of the regime.

Finally, there is the press. The press law (April 22, 1938)
lays it down that "the State has the sole authority to organize,
watch over and control the press as a national institution. In
this sense, its regulation is incumbent on the Minister in charge
of the "National Press Service." The minister appoints the editors
and the chief staff members of all newspapers; he dismisses them
when he so wishes. Legal texts of the utmost stringency subordinate the opinions expressed to the minister's way of thinking
under severe penalties (Article 18).

Over and above the sanctions which the minister can take if
displeased with any published material, the state exercises pre-
publication censorship over newspapers and reviews, books,
films, musical scores; all broadcasts. An order of September 16,
1937, set up commissions to search through all libraries belonging to clubs, colleges and academies, and destroy all printed
matter of a Marxist character or disrespectful to the dignity

of the Army, the unity of the nation, the Catholic religion or the aims of the national Crusade. No book can be printed or imported without the permission of the Home Office. Before publication or circulation in Spain a book must pass the censorship of the following authorities: Church, Director General of Propaganda, the three fighting Ministries, the General Staff, the Director General of Moroccan affairs. The only exceptions allowed are in favor of liturgical and Latin Catholic Church texts; Spanish literature prior to 1800; exclusively musical texts prior to 1900; technical and scientific books.

What passes for education in Franco-Spain is severely submitted to military discipline, to clerical influence and to Fascist indoctrination. This indoctrination begins in the primary school, where courses defined by the Falange are compulsory.

The universities are ruled by the law of July 29, 1943, which declares its aim to be "to make the University the most solid bastion of Falangism." It declares explicitly that all education shall be subordinated to the teaching of Catholic dogma and to the program of the Falange. There is only one Association of Students, the *Sindicato Español Universitario*, of course, a Falange-led organization. Acceptance of the fundamental principles of the state (i.e., Falangism), duly certified by the General Secretary of the Movement, is required of anyone, no matter how competent, who wishes to become a professor. Chairs of religion have been set up even in highly technical schools, and the professor of religion can, by blackballing a candidate, prevent the most brilliant man from obtaining his diploma.

In true military fashion, every measure, even the pettiest, is taken to repress Catalan and Basque cultural and linguistic life; a feature of the regime the more remarkable for the disproportionate share of Catalans and Basques to be found among its leaders.

The economic life of the country is at a low ebb. The destruction of capital wealth due to the Civil War was appalling. The nation groans under a large budget devoted for a considerable part to unproductive purposes with inflationary effects; and the absence of a free press combined with the assumption of almost every economic power of the State by the Falange has fostered corruption on an untold scale. The true budget for 1952 was calculated as follows by an expert:

Official budget	22,745	million pesetas
"Autonomous organizations"	7,153	" "
Tax on currencies	3,000	" "
Subsidies and public bodies	10,000	" "
Total	42,898	" "

As for the official budget, it might be divided into productive expenses (6,160 million) and unproductive and repressive (16,585). Between 1935 and 1952 the budget of the Home Office (police) had risen tenfold; that of the Department of Justice (prisons) thirteen times and that of the Armed Forces, twelve; while the Department of Industry rose three and a half; Agriculture, two and a half; Labor, three; and Education, six times.

A deficit is considered normal. The yearly average deficit for the period 1947-51 was 1,897 million pesetas. This deficit applies only to the official budget. The unofficial budget has no income. It caters for itself in the wildest and most chaotic way: as a mere example, it is reckoned that the contributions paid by the workers toward their Social Security and family allowances exceed by 55 million what they receive in subsidies. The public debt amounted to 19,392 at the end of the Civil War (1939), 19,776 million in 1950. It amounts today to 71,866.

According to the survey on the economic situation of Europe in 1953, published by the European Economic Commission (a branch of UN) the standard of living of workers and peasants in Spain was from 10 to 30 per cent lower than before the Civil War. Even after due allowance was made for social benefits. According to figures collected by the Archbishop of Valencia, the average salary was below 50 per cent of the minimum necessary for subsistence. The Economic Commission stated that land production did not reach the level of 1929 until 1951, when the population had increased by 20 per cent. Underemployment was reckoned at 35 per cent. Industrial development was both overcentralized and chaotic: aluminum works, for instance, had been built in Valladolid with no adequate provision for power to feed them. Constant industrial stoppages were caused by lack of electric power. The country lacks the administrative and technical framework needed to carry out the ambitious plans of an all-powerful and arrogant government that takes no advice and brooks no criticism from the public. The *Instituto Nacional de Industria,* a government organization established to foster mixed undertakings (private-public) has become a liability to the economic life of the country through its incompetence. As an example, its ill-conceived enterprise in the field of fibers has led to compulsory use of these unwanted fibers by textile manufacturers.

Is Franco Spain in spite of all this, important because of its military strength? The Army comprises ten Army corps (two of which are in Africa), each composed of two or of three divisions; a tank division composed of three brigades; a general artillery reserve; two autonomous commands (Balearic and Canary Islands); two cavalry divisions in the process of motorization; a few fortress regiments and seven mountain-infantry groups. The Navy comprises six ships of the line, the biggest of which measures 10,000 tons; and a modest number of smaller ships, nine of which are submarines, and all obsolete. The six hundred aircraft of the Spanish Air Force are of obsolete types. The pilots are excellent but untrained. The ground installations are poor. The Air Ministry building in Madrid is one of the best in the world.

On September 27, 1954, the governments of the United States and Franco Spain signed three executive agreements, on defense and economic aid, by virtue of which the United States acquired the use of a number of naval bases, notably Cartagena and Cádiz, as well as air bases, in particular, in Seville, Madrid and Zaragoza. Every formal satisfaction was given to General

Franco's desire to keep the Spanish flag flying in all three bases. Paragraph 2 of the Spanish Defense Agreement, however, is as vague and latitudinous as might be wished and might easily turn the whole of Spain into an American Gibraltar. An indiscretion on the part of U.S. Naval officials revealed that there are secret annexes to the agreement authorizing the use of Spanish bases for atomic warfare.

The change in Spanish foreign policy which these agreements imply is momentous. For the first time since the days of Napoleon the country steps out of its neutrality; and this, in itself neither good nor bad, is done by the will of one man, with no authority whatever to involve the country in such a fateful way. The consequences of such a fact when Spain regains her freedom may turn out to be incalculable.

Exactly two months earlier, the regime had scored a success in Rome: A contract was signed at the Vatican on July 27, 1954. In order to obtain this kind of Papal benediction General Franco gave away some of the most sacred rights of a state to manage its own affairs, and placed the clergy in a privileged position in respect to both justice and finance: they are exempt from military service, and cannot be prosecuted without authority from the bishop; all lands and property belonging to the Church are exempt from taxes. General Franco was made a Knight of the Order of Christ by the Pope. A Spanish Basque in exile sums up the two great successes of Franco in these pithy words: "He has sold the soul of Spain to the Vatican and her body to the United States." Yes. But what of the buyers?

The buyers are running frightful risks. As a result of the Civil War, Spain was well on the way to be cured of two of her worst political handicaps: anti-clericalism and a kind of proletarian extremism, as well as of any propensity to violence in politics. The backing of the Vatican and of the Pentagon of a regime not merely born of violence but living on it is acting as a poison on her body politic: *violence pays*. Moreover, the wrath of the people against the priest is mounting to a degree which only persons able to talk confidentially to Spaniards of all classes can gauge. Finally, while at the time of Hitler's fall Communism was on the run and Americans were popular, today Communism is making rapid progress in the working and intellectual classes and Americans are universally disliked. Sad to say, the Caudillo and the Pentagon are fast making of Spain a Communist-ridden country, like France and Italy.

CHAPTER 16

TURBULENCE IN THE NEW REGIME

The period stretching from that described in the previous chapter to the time of writing merely prolongs the story without in any way altering it. The country's political health deteriorates while a number of spectacular successes are paraded to keep the public mind away from stark realities.

As now established by custom, the dictator continued his tactics consisting in keeping home opinion interested in "coming" changes which never came.. The chief of these changes was the Restoration. On December 29, 1954, the pretender had a meeting with the usurper in a hunting lodge in Estremadura (Coto de las Cabezas) owned by a prominent Catalan monarchist, Count Ruiseñada, whose considerable shipping interests thrive under the wing of State protection. The pretender was accompanied by Count de los Andes, the recognized head of Spanish monarchists. The future of the Spanish Monarchy was discussed, and the only certain and visible result of the meeting was that

611

the pretender's heir, Don Juan Carlos, arrived in Madrid (January 18, 1955), there to remain for half a year under the tutorship of General Duke de la Torre to prepare for entering the Military Academy in Zaragoza.

This was in itself an unfortunate action. The Liberal, Republican and even Socialist sectors of Spanish public opinion had made some progress toward acceptance of a truly liberal and democratic restoration, in the manner of the progressive monarchies of Northern Europe. Spanish Liberals might have come to terms with a pretender who had known exile and who had undergone his military training in the liberal atmosphere of the British Navy. What were they to think, however, when they saw the education of the young prince being conducted exactly like that of his dethroned grandfather, under artillery officers and Jesuits, to prepare him for attendance at a military school the first director of which had been General Franco himself?

But worse still was to come. On January 23 and January 27, 1955, General Franco gave to the Fascist[1] newspaper *Arriba* two interviews in which he left the world in no doubt whatever about his intentions. In the first of them, he recalled that the Succession Law of 1947 provided for the restoration of the Monarchy after his death or in the event of his incapacity. He thought it wise, he said, in view of his age (then sixty-two), to provide for a smooth change-over. He then was asked (hardly a spontaneous question, it is safe to guess) whether the principles of the national revolution would be guaranteed in the event of a restoration, i.e., whether the Monarchy would respect the one-party system established by the dictatorship. His answer was: "This would definitely be the case." He declined to commit himself to an outspoken recognition of Don Juan Carlos as the heir to the Spanish throne. (This will become clearer anon.)

In his second interview, General Franco made it quite clear that for the restoration to take place, it was an "indispensable premise" that his successor should be "completely identified with

---

[1] All papers in Spain being gramophones of their master's voice, all may be said to be Fascist. But *Arriba* is the official organ of the Falange.

the national movement." He pointed out that after the monarchy had been restored, the Council of the Realm set up by the Succession Law would remain in power and would guarantee the continuation of the one-party system. This exorbitant claim reduced the future King of Spain to the rank of deputy secretary (not even secretary) of the Falange. Would the pretender accept his own forfeiture? He came very near to doing so when he declared (June 24, 1955) in an interview to the monarchist daily *A.B.C.* that the monarchy had always been in agreement with the ideals of the "nationalist movement," which, in fact, is far from being the case.

What was the dictator's aim in all this? Twofold. First, to keep people guessing, talking and expecting that "something which is going to happen next month"—the tactics he had so skillfully applied since the end of the Civil War; and, second, to discredit the pretender and rob him of any following he might have been gathering as the only way out from the dictatorship.

When this subject of gossip had been exhausted, a new one had to be found. The Falange were getting restive. At a party gathering in El Escorial, the Caudillo, who turned up in military and not in Falange uniform, was coldly, even discourteously, received. He dismissed the Falange secretary general, Raimundo Fernandez Cuesta, and reinstated José Luis Arrese, who had held the post from 1941 to 1945 (February 15, 1956). Señor Arrese, a convinced Fascist, began at once to prepare a set of "fundamental laws" aiming at putting the Falange at the apex of the Spanish state. These laws were announced to the public and outlined as the harbingers of a new era of political finality and stability, an era (so it was hinted rather than said) when the arbitrary and personal character of the dictatorship would yield to an objective and so to speak constitutional system.

This, however, was not to take place before the dictator's death. The super-Anarchist at the head of Spain would consent to no limitation to his powers. The most he would agree to was to hand over at his death to a Fascist Supreme Council the supreme powers he now exerts. Events were to show that such was the understanding, tacit or otherwise, between the dictator and Señor Arrese; but this aspect of the plan was given little if any prominence in the leakages, gossip and premature comments that were skillfully allowed free play during 1956.

So far, so good. People talked and, if they did not hope, they at least were led to expect. At last Señor Arrese presented his fundamental laws to the Council of Ministers (early November 1956); and the Council of Ministers did not like them at all. The Minister of Public Works, Count Vallellano, who represented the Monarchists in the Cabinet, wrote a severe report which eventually became known. The draft laws set up a National Council of the "Movement," i.e., a Falangist Party Council which would yield supreme powers. For instance:

The Cortes or Legislative Assembly (by no means democratically elected or even elected at all) would have to prepare their own bills in accordance with the reports of the National Council; the same provisions would apply to the decrees or decree-laws promulgated by the government. The National Council would be empowered to pass resolutions or prepare plans which the government would have to carry out. The National Council would be able to dismiss the government by means of three consecutive votes of censure. No wonder the Minister of Public Works concluded in his report that "the Arrese fundamental laws put the state and the community at the service of the Movement instead of the Movement at the service of the state and the community."

It is generally believed that the majority of the Cabinet, headed by Count Vallellano, the Minister of Foreign Affairs, Señor Martín Artajo, and the Minister of the Army, General Muñoz Grandes, uttered a spirited repulse of the scheme. Señor Arrese resigned (January 1957). General Franco neither backed him nor accepted his resignation.

The dictator obviously wished to discredit the Falange and make it patent that no institution in Spain, not even the Falange, can expect any deference or respect from the one and only power in the land.

The economic life of the country is precarious. Natural expansion is a positive force. Thus the population reached the figure of 28,638,977 according to the census of April 1955. American economic aid and the economic and financial consequences of the American alliance must also be counted as positive forces. They will be discussed later. On the negative side, improvisation, incompetence, state-centralization and corruption are the grave evils. They are discussed in the next chapter.

Spain is predominantly an agricultural country. The regime has endeavored to industrialize it, which in itself is, of course, right; but whether the industries, locations and methods chosen are the best, is another matter. In 1954, Spain produced 12,429,000 tons of coal to France's 54,405,000, and 1,097,000 of steel to France's 10,627,000.[2] The figures for Italy are: 1,074,000 for coal and 4,207,000 for steel. This shows how under-industrialized Spain is, since, in comparison with Italy, with ten times more home coal and a fine supply of iron ore it produces one-fourth of the steel.

According to officially approved figures production indexes for 1954 (using 100 for 1953) were: for agriculture, 107.1; for fisheries 100.9; for mining, 100.6; for industry, 105.1. As for the national income per citizen (all ages included), it was still less than $200 per annum in 1955.

Spain suffers from a chronic deficit in her balance of payments. The chaos of her present financial and economic administration is not the best remedy for it. During the first eight months of 1956 the deficit was 669 million pesetas or 223 million dollars (at the official rate). True, the year was bad and through an exceptionally severe February Spain lost the best of her olive oil and orange crops (and even plantations). But this disaster does not account for a deficit higher by 139.7 million than that of the corresponding period in the previous year. Moreover, the United States came to the rescue providing aid to the tune of 27 million dollars worth of agricultural

[2] Economic Commission for Europe.

products and 4 million dollars worth of war materials. The chief items in the excess of imports were metals, both as raw materials and in the form of machines and vehicles (including many luxurious cars) and chemical products.

This unfavorable economic situation is worsened by the many causes of inflation discussed in the next chapter, chief of which is a huge unproductive expenditure for armaments, police and inflated bureaucracy. From November 30, 1955, to November 30, 1956, banknote circulation increased by 6,875 million pesetas; from 44,379 million to 51,254. On December 31 it had reached 55,821 million. It was 26,471 at the end of 1948. Moreover on November 30, 1955, the Treasury had at the Bank of Spain a balance in its favor of 7,242 million; on November 30, 1956, the figure was 2,149 million. On December 31 it was 1,865 million.

This situation was forcibly put to a Council of Ministers by the Minister of Commerce, Señor Arburúa. It is characteristic of the present state of affairs in Spain that Cabinet ministers manage to give indirect yet authoritative publicity to their secret reports when they happen to be strongly critical of the regime to which they belong. Señor Arburúa's on the economic crisis was no exception. He expressed his anxiety for the economic stability of the country and among many other criticisms he pointed out that in 1955 investments reached a sum far in excess of the country's savings, 32,000 million pesetas of which, he remarks, 16,000 were government investments. He may well have glanced at the Minister of Labor who squandered away much of that sum in four monstrous and preposterous labor universities, or even at the Caudillo himself, who dissipated several thousand millions in a no less preposterous underground cathedral.

Meanwhile, according to a *New York Times* observer, writing in February 1957, the situation presented a number of disquieting features: banknote circulation up from 47,045 to 55,821 million; loans up by 6,000 million in December 1956; a rush to put money into shares at the three stock exchanges; the banks placing in loans and in other ways more money than they received on deposit accounts; the peseta falling from 47.5 to 54.3

to the dollar; harvests expected to be poor; the statistics of commerce becoming less favorable to Spain both for imports and exports.

The regime lives in hopes coming, curiously enough, from both Washington and Moscow. The newest hope has been aroused by an unexpected windfall. On the death of Dr. Juan Negrín (November 14, 1956) his heirs handed to the Spanish government the receipt for the Spanish gold deposited in Moscow (as related in Chapter 10, above). The details of this operation are obscure. None of Dr. Negrín's sons seems willing to own the deed itself and his own dissident Socialist group issued a statement (February 15, 1957) declaring they knew nothing about such a step and implicitly condemning it; but the fact is that, for the first time, the Spanish government is able to exhibit a document which it could brandish with some legal force before the Hague Court.[3]

The Soviet Union has studiously avoided recognizing any Spanish government at all. The Government-in-exile is recognized by all her satellites, which proves that Moscow's reluctance is due to the fact that once a Spanish government were recognized by Moscow a *prima facie* obligation would arise to return the gold to it. An indirect recognition of the Franco government is implied in the fact that the Soviet Union voted the admission of Spain to the United Nations Organization.

In these circumstances, a negotiation began between the Spanish and Soviet ambassadors in Paris (Count Casa-Rojas and

---

[3] According to the *New York Times* (Jan. 14, 1957) the documents delivered by Dr. Negrín's heirs to the Government of Franco Spain include: a decree (Sept. 13, 1936) signed by Azaña as president of the Republic and by Largo Caballero as prime minister, authorizing the Minister of Finance, Dr. Negrín, to export the gold to "wherever he would think it in safety"; an eight-page document in French, in four parts, enumerating the coins, ingots and other pieces received in Moscow by the GOKRAN, precious metals department of the Finance Commissariat; this document is signed by Dr. Marcelino Pascua, then Spanish ambassador in Moscow, G. F. Grinko, finance commissar, and N. N. Krestinsky, his deputy for foreign questions. Par. 2., Section 4 of this document stipulates that the Spanish government shall be able freely to re-export or dispose of the gold.

Professor Vinogradov)[4] with a view to the recovery of this considerable sum of gold. A slow but definite move toward better relations had been noticeable on both sides for some time. Soviet delegations had been admitted in Madrid to attend sundry non-political congresses; and it was an open secret that Spain was trading with Poland, Czechoslovakia and even the Soviet Union more or less indirectly; the Soviet Union had at long last agreed to release a number (though as yet by no means all) of the Spanish citizens which had been kept by force within her borders, some prisoners from the Blue Division and others grown-up Republican children whom their naive parents had sent to Russia (for safety!) during the Civil War.

Somewhat cooled by the events in Hungary (which hurt deeply the well-known liberty-loving feelings of the Spanish dictator), the issue will not be allowed to remain in abeyance for long; for the Spanish regime needs that gold to tide over its desperate financial and economic crisis; and the Soviet Union is anxious to build up in Madrid, under the roof of her embassy, a base from which to watch American activities, and to infiltrate the Spanish-speaking world with Communism.[5]

American aid to Spain began as early as 1951, a year in which Spain received loans totaling 120 million dollars, including

---

[4] The *New York Times,* Jan. 1, 1957.

[5] Things cannot have gone very smoothly for on April 5 the London *Times* carried a cable from Moscow to the effect that there was no Spanish gold left. *Pravda* described such reports of Spanish gold as "cock-and-bull stories" and went on to say:

Some foreign newspapers are publishing articles about the Spanish gold deposited 20 years ago in the Soviet Union, never mentioning all the expenditure of this gold made by the Spanish Republican Government, thus misleading public opinion by creating an impression that there are allegedly still some unused remnants of this gold.

The checking and weighing of the gold, on transfer to the Soviet authorities, was done jointly by Soviet and Spanish representatives. The Spanish Government stipulated that from the gold reserves deposited in the Soviet Union it would make payments for its orders abroad and make transfers of currency through the Soviet State Bank.

According to information received, the Spanish Government made numerous payments for its purchases abroad and gave instructions for transfer of currency abroad, which were executed by the Soviet government and private bank loans. In September 1953, the military and economic agreement was signed between the two countries. Under this agreement Spain received 50 million dollars in 1956. This is not, however, a present. The Spanish government must provide an equivalent amount in pesetas. Sixty per cent of this amount is spent in the construction of the American bases; ten per cent goes to pay American administrative expenses in Spain; and only the remaining thirty per cent is left for the Spanish government to spend, even this with two provisos: the expenditure to be approved by the American Aid Mission in Spain; and to be devoted to work bearing a fairly close relation to the common defense plans, such as railways, ports, roads and certain important industry.

The situation toward the end of 1956 was summed up as follows by an American observer:[6]

The construction program of the bases had been about 50 per cent carried out and it was expected to cost 400 million dollars. About 175 million dollars worth of war material to modernize the Spanish armed forces had been delivered and

State Bank. According to the data of the Soviet authorities, the Spanish Republican Government used up the gold deposited in the Soviet Union.

All the orders of the Spanish Republican Government were properly signed jointly by Francisco Largo Caballero, Spanish Republican Prime Minister, and Negrín, Finance Minister. Later, when Negrín became Prime Minister, he signed the orders as Prime Minister and Minister of Finance.

The last letter of Negrín, dated August 8, 1938, shows that the gold has been fully used up. The letter asks in the name of the Council of Ministers of the Spanish Republic to realize all the remaining Spanish gold in the Soviet Union. This has been done.

It is necessary to mention that the Soviet Government, at the request of the Spanish Republican Government, granted a credit of $85m., and only $35m. have been repaid. There remains, in consequence, a debt of $50m.

Negrín knew about it, as he signed all orders referring to the use of the gold and credit. No sums from the gold deposit were used for the upkeep of Spanish emigrants and children who found refuge in the Soviet Union. These expenses were met by the Soviet Union and Soviet social organizations, in particular the Soviet trade unions.

[6] Benjamin Welles in the *New York Times*.

about as much was still to be delivered. Congress had already granted economic aid considered as defense support to the tune of 280 million dollars. Sales of agricultural surpluses to Spain were to reach 176 million dollars. Finally, a free gift of 90,000 tons of alimentary products with 50 million dollars had already been sent to Spain. Moreover, on May 3, 1955, an agreement was announced in Madrid under which the United States undertakes to modernize the Spanish Fleet. No figures are given.

The Spanish newspapers often printed unfavorable comments on this program which they considered insufficient, as well as suggestions that this or that Cabinet minister was to be sent to Washington to ask for more. This aspect of the matter merges into the general relations between Spain and the United States.

Under the obvious if discreet leadership of the United States government, the maneuver to admit Spain into the United Nations grew apace during this period. On January 25, 1955, the Secretary General announced that Spain had been granted the status of permanent observer, pending full admission. This was achieved after strenuous debates in January 1956, when the deadlock between the Soviet Union and the West on admission of a number of nations, some vetoed by Moscow others by the West, was solved by the famous "package" resolution admitting them all except Mongolia and Japan. The Soviet Union did not veto nor did she abstain when the admission of Spain was voted with only Belgium and Mexico abstaining.

This victory for the dictator was a moral defeat for the United States. The Spanish nation realized the predominant part the United States had taken in the admission of Spain to an organization supposed to stand for freedom. The visit paid by the Secretary of State to Madrid on November 1, 1955, had left Spanish opinion in no doubt about what it could expect from the State Department. True, Mr. Dulles granted the dictator just five hours. He would not even stay a night; and the dictator, beggar of prestige that he is, demeaned himself by accepting this treatment for the sake of having his regime underwritten by the American government. The communiqué issued jointly after the meeting declared that the Secretary of State and the Spanish dictator had reviewed "the principal problems which affect the peace and security of the free nations." Having thus granted the police state he had visited a certificate of freedom, Mr. Dulles left Spain, possibly ruminating over yet another of his uplifting speeches about the need of moral principles in politics.

These spectacular successes the regime owed to the United States, 'as well as the expectations it had aroused of financial redemption through the Moscow-held gold, were somewhat spoiled by events in Morocco. When France was faced with an intransigent Moroccan nationalism, the Caudillo was unable to resist the temptation to help the Moroccans against the French. There were only two possible policies for Spain: to adopt a line in complete solidarity with that of France; or to lead in the granting of independence. The regime chose neither. It paid lip-service to the cause of Moroccan nationalism, being persuaded that France would not let go. When France did let go, the Spanish dictator found himself the prisoner of his own utterances and attitudes.

The French government did not make his path easy. The deposition of Sultan Mohammed ben Yusef (August 20, 1953) had been considered in Spain as the slight which it certainly would have been had the French government been the initiators of that strange measure. Spain continued to recognize the exiled sultan. Grave disorders on the French side of the Riff led to a stiff exchange of notes, Spain protesting against accusations of help being supplied to the rebels from Spanish territory. General Boyer de Latour (French Resident) declared (October 16, 1953) that "it was notorious that the Moroccan rebels had found help and refuge in the Spanish zone of Morocco"; and quoted a concrete example to which the Spanish Foreign Office replied: "The Resident-General complains that the Spanish position near the advanced post of Bou Zineb did not help that post when it was attacked by rebels. The French government, having violated treaties to depose the legitimate sultan, cannot now call upon Spain for assistance in military operations to suppress the discontent provoked by this obtuse policy." It is only fair to recall that Franco-Spanish cooperation in Morocco had seldom been harmonious; but at this juncture the point is that the Spanish dictator chose a policy which flattered Arab nationalism, without realizing that he was playing with fire.

France reversed her policy. The exiled sultan was brought back (October 31, 1955) and a statement explicitly defining French policy as working for the development of Morocco "as a modern, free and sovereign State" was issued at St.-Germain-en-Laye. By December 7 the sultan formed his first Cabinet; and even before the final agreement on independence had been signed by France (March 2, 1956), loud demands for independence began to be heard in the Spanish zone. A statement from the Unity and Independence Party (November 28, 1955) expressed the hope that "Spain, which has never ceased to give promises to the Moroccan people, will carry out those promises now that France has recognized the principle of Moroccan independence."

Two days later the Spanish dictator stated in an interview with some American journalists that it would be a grave error to introduce a democratic system in Morocco "as France was doing," and that it was much better to proceed gradually "as we are doing in our zone." He thought it best to wait till the Moroccans were ready to govern themselves. (This, coming from the man who does not allow the Spaniards to govern themselves, is a gem.) It was best, the dictator opined, to keep out of Morocco "the trickery and internal strife of political parties on the European model" and to avoid the risk of Communism implicit in democracy. And General García Valiño, the High Commissioner, while announcing that he would "increase the responsibilities of ministers of the native government and intensify the transfer of administrative powers to Morroccans," took care to add that there were "several long and complex stages" to be traversed before Morocco achieved complete unity and independence.

It is plain that General Franco had no idea of the actual situation and that he thought he was going to keep hold of the northern zone for a long time. On January 10, 1956, the French Resident (Dubois) and the Spanish High Commissioner (García Valiño) met at Palafito, in the Spanish zone, to discuss the situation. The chief Spanish aim was to obtain French acquiescence for a tripartite conference: France-Spain-Morocco. The French Resident refused to promise more than to keep Spain informed of Franco-Moroccan discussions. In the communiqué, after the usual platitudes, it was said that the High Commissioner had informed the French Resident of the Spanish government's intention to introduce "political reforms which will permit by a parallel development to secure the independence of Morocco while safeguarding the legitimate interests of the two Powers."

On January 18 a statement was issued by the Spanish government in the same paternal, leisurely and seemingly statesmanlike mood. But on March 2, the Spanish ambassador in Paris was informed by the Secretary General of the Quai d'Orsay of the Franco-Moroccan Agreement granting Morocco immediately full independence; and on March 4 and 5, 1956, nationalist demonstrations in the Spanish zone in celebration of the agreement led to serious clashes with the (Spanish-organized) police (Tetuán, Larache, El Ksar-el-Kebir), twenty people being killed and one hundred wounded. Anti-Spanish demonstrations took place in Rabat and Fez as well as in Tangier, and bombs were thrown at the Spanish Consulates in Casablanca and Meknés. The sultan stated that he had been "painfully surprised" and his government informed the Spanish government of "its strong reprobation" of the incidents. The Caudillo thought twice about it and conveyed to the sultan an invitation to visit Madrid.

He found himself at the confluence of two lines of policy: one aiming at safeguarding Spanish interests in Morocco across the Straits; the other endeavoring to secure a prominent if not a leading position in the Islamic world. His relations with the Arab states had been nursed; his foreign secretary had toured the Middle East. What was he to do with a sultan who was reaching full sovereign status and bade fair to become a leading figure in the Arab world and even in Islam!

With his full-sovereignty treaty signed by France in his pocket, the sultan went to Madrid on a state visit (April 4-9, 1956). The visit was showy, and bunting was only too abundant; but stark realities were discussed behind closed doors. The final meeting lasted thirteen hours. At dawn on April 7 the protocol was still unsigned, the sultan refusing to accept any reservation at all on the declaration of Moroccan independence. A threat to break off negotiations and leave Madrid brought about the final collapse of the empire-builder who on June 19, 1940, had claimed from Germany as his share in the spoils of Hitler's victory the whole of Morocco, Oran, and the coast from the mouth of the Niger to Cape Lopez. The independence of Morocco was recognized without any territorial reservations or guarantees. On April 9, 1956, the sultan flew from Madrid to Tetuán, which until that day had been the capital of the Spanish zone. He was acclaimed by a delirious crowd.

When he returned to Madrid in February 1957, he there met Ibn Saud on his return from his own official visit to the United States. The Spanish dictator, a sultan himself, was in his element. He had made some promises (which? how important?) to Colonel Nasser through an emissary, General Rafael Alvarez Serrano, and relations between Spain and Egypt had developed so rapidly that Egypt had bought some arms from Spain. That he found himself thus supplying weapons to the willing or unwilling stooge of the Soviets in the Arab world does not seem to have disturbed the Caudillo at all. During the Suez negotiations, his diplomacy steered as close as he dared to Colonel Nasser though as close as he must to Mr. Dulles. When President Nasser announced that the Canal Company had been nationalized (July 26, 1956) Spain (i.e., the Spanish government) backed Egypt and showed hostility to the Franco-British case. When the first London Conference was mooted, Spain was slow, if not reluctant, to join; and was the last to adhere to the proposal of the eighteen nations. In short, at every step, the Spanish dictator was careful to remain as favorable as he could to Colonel Nasser.

From the sultan, in this second visit, he obtained one of those diplomatic plums he likes to exhibit with all their sugar shining:

Spain was to represent Moroccan interests in all Spanish-
American States. This must have satisfied the sultans on both
sides of the Straits, since the one to the south asserted his diplomatic independence of France and the one to the north got some
of his own back after so many slights from Paris.

There is, however, more (if not much more) in all this Arab
activity about Madrid. The Spanish dictator dreams of a Mediterranean Pact which would be a kind of southern pendant to
NATO. It is not easy to imagine what this pact would contain
over and above the military provision already extant. Possibly it
is considered in Madrid as a way to bring about Franco-Spanish
entrance into NATO itself. More likely it is yet another of those
"somethings which are going to happen next month" which the
dictator launches now and then to keep tongues wagging and
years going by.

One of the by-products of the Moroccan independence has
been that the Spanish Moroccan Army is now unemployed. This
means mostly officers; for the men were for a good part Spanish-
trained Moroccans whom the sultan will find most handy. The
officers lose a good field for military activity, for higher salaries,
decorations and promotion. This influx of frustrated, spirited
men has considerably increased a discontent already rampant in
the ranks of officers other than the very top, for whom the dictator reserves the best plums of his state. These disgruntled officers
have organized themselves in *Juntas de Acción Patriótica* whose
ideas circulate in print (illegally, of course) and they are a serious
threat to the regime.

This circumstance has put some punch into an opposition so
far unable to impress a regime that respects naught but force.
Students' riots took place in February 1956. The students wanted
freedom of "thought, expression and corporate life." There were
riots on February 8, 9, and 10 in Madrid due to an invasion of
the University by Falange bullies who had nothing to do with
studies. A student who happened to be a Falangist was gravely
wounded in the head by a bullet, and anti-Fascist students were
accused of it, though none but the Falangists carried arms. The

Falange was ready to "execute" a number of prominent intellectuals if their student had died. The colonels of the Madrid garrison called on the Captain General and signified to him that they would not tolerate such a behavior. Nothing happened, except the dismissal of the Minister of Education and of the Secretary General of the Falange, who was replaced by a tougher one.

Similar events took place in November in Barcelona, where the civil governor (a general) had to storm the University by a military frontal attack. In 1957, under the leadership of the students both Barcelona and Madrid staged well-organized boycotts of the public transport system which by their "orchestration" and moderate behavior suggested a competent central leadership and organization. The regime is thus threatened from without, i.e., from Liberals and the Left. It is even more threatened from within, i.e., from its own former supporters. The Army is divided; the Church is at last beginning to grow restive lest her long backing of such an un-Christian state may sooner or later injure her spiritual interests; and even the Falange sees a considerable part of its members organizing themselves as a liberal opposition under the leadership of a dynamic personality: Dionisio Ridruejo. The regime seems unable to react in the brutal way it would have reacted in earlier days against all this almost public agitation.

Nevertheless, the prevailing unrest finally decided the dictator to "spring-clean" his political house. He dismissed his servants —all but six of them—and brought in a new team (February 25, 1957). The most remarkable changes were the dismissal of Señor Artajo and his replacement by a Falangist ex-Blue Division man, Señor Castiella; and the replacement of Sr. Blas Pérez, a flexible lawyer, by General Alonso Vega, a Civil Guard martinet, as Minister of the Interior (mostly Police). This is read by some observers as a return to the strong whip manner; but the political climate would appear unfavorable for such risks. At any rate, Señor Ridruejo was arrested shortly before Easter (April 1957), and it is known that a student of Barcelona University, Señor Masoliver, was brutally murdered by the so-called Franco Guard for having smashed a portrait of the dictator during a riot at the University in February 1957.

As against the real situation, in the country, the change of government has been compared to a pill to cure an earthquake. The most advertised features of the new Cabinet were the appointment of a Catalan economic expert, Señor Gual Villalbí, to liberalize the economic life of the country, i.e. to inject a minimum of sense into it; and that of an honest Minister of Commerce. Within a few days, the Minister of Industry had flatly contradicted a public utterance of the economic expert in a no less public utterance; and the honest Minister of Commerce had been driven to resignation—a resignation that was refused by the dictator. The situation remains tense and uncertain.

CHAPTER 17

SPAIN—THE ANOMALY

Spain is an anomaly in Europe. Leaving aside the nations overwhelmed by the Red Army, no other European country is under a dictatorship, except Yugoslavia, whose case is in a way parallel. In both Yugoslavia and Spain an ambitious man, having escaladed to power brandishing an ideological banner, remains there, banner or no banner. Yet one may discern in the Yugoslav dictator an ideological conviction which never troubles or hinders his Spanish counterpart. In non-Communist Europe, Spain remains an anachronism. England, Sweden, Norway, Denmark, Greece, Belgium, Holland and Luxemburg are liberal, constitutional monarchies; Switzerland, Austria, Iceland, France, Turkey, Italy and Ireland are liberal, constitutional republics. Solitary Spain is a kind of sultanate where the "Commander of the Faithful" exerts a wholly personal rule through a Cabinet of private secretaries decorated with the title of minister. What are the consequences of this state of affairs for Spain herself and for the world?

628

CONSEQUENCES AT HOME

For Spain herself the gravest consequence is twofold: it increases the national tendency to unruliness; and it prepares the country for Communism. This may sound at first paradoxical. Communism and anarchism are poles apart. Anarchy is centrifugal, and denies and defies command; Communism is centripetal and imposes command. Poor is, however, the psychology that does not see the possibility of two tendencies at first sight antagonistic being fostered simultaneously in a man or a people. The more so if, as in this case, they are at bottom complementary. A happy and free political life is only possible for a nation if the two tendencies, to liberty and to order, are in equilibrium. Let this equilibrium be broken, whether in favor of too much order or of too much liberty, and both liberty and order are impaired or actually vanish. It follows that nothing is more dangerous for a nation than to fall under a regime that wittingly or unwittingly fosters extremism and lack of balance.

Such is the disaster which has befallen the Spanish people, a people only too ready of its own bent to yield to extremism. The dictator may think himself the incarnation of discipline: he is the very opposite, a daily example, model and prototype of Spanish anarchism. Every one of his actions is tainted by irresponsibility. The very personal relations with his "ministers" are even to their details, shaped and colored by that sense of full independence from any law but his own will which is characteristic of General Franco. When Colonel Beigbeder, his Foreign Secretary, was replaced by Señor Serrano Suñer, he learned of his dismissal from the newspapers. When the philosopher José Ortega y Gasset wished to resume publication of his review, *La Revista de Occidente,* a rallying point of Spanish culture, the question was put to the Cabinet by the Minister of Education. The Minister of Agriculture pointed out that since his return to Spain from his voluntary exile, Ortega had not sought to call on the dictator. The dictator coldly let fall: *Exacto.* And that was the end of the matter.

This complete and absolute lack of any obligation, rule or respect is, of course, the ideal of every Spaniard. Nor would it do to deny that many of them enjoy, if vicariously, the sense of unfettered freedom their leader experiences, and like him the more for it. But the psychological consequences for a people only too prone to unruly ways are bound to be disastrous. From the apex of power a current of irresponsibility runs throughout the whole regime and permeates the nation.

Along with this daily lesson of anarchy, the regime is educating the people in the ways of Communism. It is the chief paradox of our day that Communism is fascist in politics while Fascism is communist in economics. We shall see anon to what an extent and in what sense. The point here is that this regime, led by a super-Anarchist, is in fact preparing Spain for Communism. To begin with, it successfully represses every political activity whatsoever. It is unfortunately the case that in the present Spanish regime the only efficient service is the secret police (organized by Himmler's men). By means of this police, the regime has so far succeeded in preventing every trace of political life to subsist for more than a few days. It follows that the only political activity left with any chance of survival is the Communist Party, an adept at undergound work. In this way, unwittingly and indirectly, but in no uncertain manner, the regime is fostering Communism in Spain.[1]

It does so moreover in several other ways. To begin with, since in politics Communism is fascist, many old Spanish Communists found themselves at home in the uniform of Falangists and in this disguise were able to infiltrate into the Falange. How many ex-Communists are ensconced in the Falange, how *many of them* are really "ex," how many there are to return to Communism when the regime falls, is everybody's guess.

Furthermore, the regime unwittingly acts as the best recruiting agent for Communism by dubbing as Communist every adversary it wishes to deprive of his liberty. This contributes in no small measure to popularize a party which owing to its excesses and crimes during the Civil War lost nearly all the ground it had won in Spain (it never was much).

---

[1] A number of prominent Communist exiles are returning and settling in Spain under the evidently contented eye of the government.

The alliance between the regime and the United States must be mentioned here in passing as another factor favorable to Communism; it will be dealt with anon when discussing world affairs. From the internal point of view here considered, one more item remains to be discussed—possibly the gravest of all. The present regime is training the Spaniards to obey orders blindly, depriving them of the government of their own affairs, accustoming them passively to acquiesce in whatever comes ready-made and decided from above. The nation is split into two parts, both irresponsible: a majority, irresponsible because it has no power; a minority, irresponsible, because it enjoys all the power there is. This is an ideal attitude in which to accept Communism.

It is now plain that the regime is simultaneously fostering two tendencies, at first sight antagonistic, yet by no means mutually excluding each other. Far from it. Insofar as it keeps the average citizen out of any effective share in public affairs, it encourages an indifference and an apathy which further lowers the already low level of public responsibility; this in its turn encourages anarchy. "Every man for himself" is the logical attitude of a people severed by the dictatorship from every contact with collective affairs. So that the country is at the same time disorganized and accustomed to obey; or, in other words, retrograded from the status of a society to that of a herd.

The assertion was made above that Fascism is communist in economics. This statement, however, must be retouched in that Communism, as practiced in the Soviet Union is *not* Communism but rather State Socialism. The present Spanish regime can be described as State Socialism tempered by the power of the big banks. But the collaboration between the big banks and the state is a complex affair. By and large, it may be said that the big banks bring to the work two chief assets: competence and continuity. The contribution of the state consists in improvisation and corruption. The INI (Instituto Nacional de Industria) is a byword of incompetence. Grandiose schemes, such as the Steel Works of Avilés, are launched with no particular inquiry into their financial, economic or commercial viability. A horde of public figures, with one leg on politics and the other on finance, cluster round councils and directorships, fostering all kinds of semi-public, semi-private enterprises. A complicated system of controls, regulations and inspectorates overlords capital issues, material supplies, labor questions, markets, quotas and tariffs; so that at every turn, a political sleight-of-hand becomes necessary in order to squeeze through all these bureaucratic toll gates. As all this happens behind the opaque curtain of paper raised by a "His Master's Voice" press, corruption is rife from top to bottom of the state.[2]

Here is an example. An American firm found that owing to some nonsensical regulations Spain had accumulated considerable stocks of molasses worth more thousands of dollars than she could spare. The firm was ready to acquire them and pay cash. This happened in 1956 when the peseta was falling hard in the international market. The Ministry of Agriculture and the Ministry of Commerce wrangled at length over which of the two was to grant the export license. Was each trying to shift the bore and the burden on to the other? Not at all. Moved by a nobly patriotic zeal they were vying to perform the service and would not yield to each other, no, even though the molasses was deteriorating and the dollars waiting. At last, the matter was on the point of being solved when the Ministry of Industry, arguing that molasses was a by-product of the manufacture of sugar, claimed its own right to license the export. The story does not record the language in which the agents of the American firm gave vent to their feelings of admiration for so much patriotism.

   [2] According to Señor Planell, Minister of Industry, investments made by the INI up to December 31, 1957, totaled 24,000 million pesetas. According to the report of INI itself up to December 31, 1955, the nominal capital of its many undertakings amounted to 15,362 million, and the capital actually paid up by it was 17,000 million. Twelve undertakings were wholly owned by INI with 8,826 million pesetas of nominal capital and 13,639 million actually paid up. There are twenty undertakings in which the INI share of capital is in a majority, with a total of 5,607 million pesetas nominal capital and 3,866 million pesetas of paid-up capital. In eight undertakings INI holds minority capital to the tune of 829 nominal and 129 paid up.

The visitor, unfamiliar with the ways of the country, is prone to dismiss the subject with a disdainful "Spanish ways!" This is most unfair to Spain. In the days of the Monarchy. and even in those of the Republic, when a whole class of people had hastily to be trained in the ways of power, corruption was certainly not unknown—where is it?—but it was by no means universal and scandalous as it is today in Spain; and it was unthinkable for ministers, ambassadors and generals even when in active service to make hay while the fair weather of their offices lasted. A glance at the preceding chapters, and in particular at that dealing with the dictatorship of Primo de Rivera, will suffice to show that the present regime has dragged the nation to the lowest level of public ethics it has ever known.

Those who bear the brunt of actual economic life in these conditions are convinced that this lowering of the ethical standards of everybody, officials and producers and even consumers, is deliberate. The experience of cotton textile manufacturers would appear to confirm this view. The Ministry fixes their selling prices, which turn out to be far below cost (in one case known to me they hardly covered the price of the cotton used in the garment). The manufacturers complain. They are told that, prices or no prices, they are all well off. They take the hint, sell twenty per cent of their output at legal prices and go into the black market with the rest. That is exactly the situation the state wants. The state can send inspectors who certify the infraction and either draw a nice income by selling their silence or land the manufacturer in jail or keep him wise and friendly to the dictatorship. In this astute way, the state turns the whole nation into a people of prisoners on parole; so that whenever any one of them ventures into even the mildest opposition, to prison he goes, on a perfectly legal charge.

The lack of a free press and the complete subservience of the Judiciary to the Command (for that is what "government" means in Spain under General Franco) amount in practice to the abolition of any objective justice. This means that the citizen has no redress against any abuse of power on the part of the ministers, the civil service, the police, or any of the local authorities. As an example of the kind of situation this state of affairs may lead to, the case may be quoted of the highly skilled workers of Bilbao who were selected for "punishment" after a strike there in 1953: they were exiled to rural districts where they had to earn their living in unskilled occupations.

The agents of the so-called Spanish government are therefore no more than the sergeants of a Spanish command. A civil governor, a police chief, can in fact, regardless of texts and theories, take any decision he wishes bearing on the life or property or residence or work of any citizen without fear of being traduced either before a court of law or before public opinion. There is in fact no real government in Spain, but only a kind of army of occupation which happens to be of the same nationality as the nation it occupies.

This system leads to a considerable expenditure of unproductive armaments, and therefore to inflation. The peseta has fallen continuously since the regime took charge. The certainty of its fall creates a feeling of instability, unfavorable to production. This in its turn aggravates inflation.

Two other causes lead to the same result. One is the strong tendency to State Socialism which, for the regime, is a kind of alibi for its lack of democracy and freedom. This tendency takes on many forms. Two are prominent: the setting up of huge enterprises (referred to above) and an ambitious welfare state. Neither of them need have been inflationary in its effects; but the fact that they had to develop in an atmosphere of corruption fostered by the lack of a free press makes them inflationary. State industries and state administrations under such a system require far more men, material and money than they would under a free regime able to watch and criticize its institutions and servants.

The third cause of inflation is corruption itself which necessitates huge sums to satisfy the unproductive (if not destructive) greed of the drones and locusts of the regime that are eating away the nation's patrimony. Millions of pesetas dubiously earned are leaving Spain daily for the safe haven of foreign currencies.

The upshot of it all is that the regime is chaining everybody to the state by chains of need. Spain was never conspicuous for a strong middle class. This class is now weaker than ever, owing to the inroads of State Socialism into the already feeble fields of private enterprise. The average son of his father in Spain seeks a government-sheltered post or some profession often leading to very much the same. Those who in the more enterprising regions venture into business are apt to find the deadening and corrupting hand of the State more and more deeply ensconced in everything they do. Discouragement and frustration follow, as well as separatism in one or two regions.

This policy is moreover having a disastrous effect in the field of technical progress. Here again, Spain was never conspicuous. The Spaniard is by temperament disinclined to technique. A laudable effort was made by the Monarchy and by the Republic to produce good technicians. There are some good and some brilliant ones. But the real test for a modern technician is free competition. Now one of the chief hindrances for genuine, national technical progress in Spain (as distinct from the growing influence of foreign technicians) has always been, even before this regime, the tendency to consider a diploma as a document entitling its owner to a government salary. Thus sheltered, the average Spanish technician does not go very far. It goes without saying that the State Socialist system favored by the Franco regime is by no means a cure for such an evil.

Emoluments are low. Often a man must carry on two or three professions or work in two or three different places to make both ends meet. And if he happens to be a civil servant, the temptation to irregular earnings will often prove too strong. This, of course, for reasons stated above suits the dictatorsrhip perfectly.

Similar conclusions apply to the working classes. Differences in currency and the rapid fall of the peseta detract from the value of figures as an index of level of life; but at the time when the dollar was (privately) quoted at 40 pesetas, the Archbishop of Valencia reckoned in a famous Pastoral (1953) that a man and his wife, with no children, needed about 48 pesetas a day for their necessary expenses counting nothing for smoking, drinking or going to the motion pictures. The average wages were then 17 to 20 pesetas. They are no higher in real value today. The worker, like the middle-class man, is often bound to work thirteen or even sixteen hours a day in two or even three jobs, merely to subsist. How his two or three employers can expect good work from him is a mystery. How they sometimes, indeed, get it is a deeper mystery.

Furthermore, agricultural salaries being more miserable still, heavy migration from the country to the cities is taking place. This is a pretty universal sociological feature of our day. In Spain it is made worse by the utter neglect of the villages and small townships, and the concentration of expenditure in show-pieces such as Madrid. An insane megalomania makes the regime waste away money in such useless luxuries as the so-called Labor Universities while making the working class more miserable by neglecting the countryside and drawing the peasant to the city. As the housing position is hopeless, the uprooted peasant settles in hovels and gasoline-can sheds in the vicinity of Madrid, Barcelona and other cities. These slums cheek by jowl with the insolent wealth of the cities are an excellent breeding ground for Communism.

CONSEQUENCES FOR THE WORLD

As for the world at large, the Spanish situation could not be more unfavorable. Its evil effects can be observed successively in the Spanish-speaking world; in the Arab world; in European affairs, and in what concerns the so-called East-West conflict.

In the Spanish-speaking world, the outward and material success of the dictator has acted as an example and a stimulus to all ambitious would-be dictators. The entire Perón episode was a direct consequence of the Spanish dictatorship. Likewise the majority of Spanish-speaking countries are today under the sway of imitators of the Spanish dictator, and in more than one case South American tyrants learned their trade in Spain.

This is a poor state of affairs for several reasons. The chief of them are two, both bearing on the general world outlook. The first is that (as it has been explained above in the case of Spain) dictatorships are the best introduction to Communism, everywhere, but above all in the countries of Spanish culture and tradition. The second is that there is abroad a widespread belief to the effect that the United States is quite happy with dictatorships, for they are more subservient and amenable than democratically ruled nations. Now, insofar as it impairs the moral authority of the United States, this situation prevents world peace and the ultimate victory of the West.

In the Arab world, the persistence of the Spanish dictatorship amounts to a twofold danger. The first is that it invigorates the innate tendency to personal rule in that all-important zone which stretches from Morocco to Pakistan; and the second that it enables General Franco to play at world politics with sultans and colonels in a manner and spirit by no means favorable to world peace. The policy of the Caudillo is neither nationalistic (nor even national) nor constructive. It is purely personal, swayed this way or that by considerations of prestige, vanity or necessity —as proved by the history of his recent relations with Morocco.

This unprincipled turbulence in one of the most strategic areas of the world keeps injecting an irrelevant and disturbing influence into matters of more import.

In European affairs, the Spanish dictatorship is a nuisance. Western Europe, on its way to federation, would have found its road easier if the Spanish Peninsula, its most strategic territory, had been ruled in ways less different from those of its other member states. France would have found it easier to run risks on her eastern frontiers had she felt safer to the south, as she would have been with a liberal-democratic Spain. And the economic integration of Spain into Europe would have been easier if Spain had not been brought to the edge of beggary by a reckless, incompetent and corrupt regime.

As for world affairs, it is meet to recall here that the regime is giving Communism a new lease of life in Spain. This in itself is grave enough, since Moscow is less interested in a war than in a political triumph of Communism everywhere. From the point of view of ideology, it may be said that the regimes of Moscow and Madrid are allies, as close allies as the two blades of a pair of scissors. Franco finds the existence of the Soviet system an excellent pretext for justifying his own existence (though the idea that the July 1936 uprising was prompted by the need to put down Communist menace in Spain is arrant nonsense); and the Soviet Union finds Franco invaluable as a blatant proof of the "fascist" nature of the West which relies on him as an ally.

Therefore: from the military point of view, while Spain is ruled by the dictator, there can be no true and complete NATO, for the nation that occupies by far the most strategic territory in the whole West will remain resentful and hostile.

From the point of view of the cold war or ideological war, while Spain is ruled by Franco the flag of the West is stained with a lie.

CHAPTER 18

ON THE EDGE OF THE FUTURE

What course will the life of Spain take beyond the storms and
the rapids of the present hour? It is idle to prophesy, idler still
to formulate programs, to lay down so-called historical laws, to
rationalize wishes and daydreams into theorems of sociology.
The life of Spain will flow as do all rivers along the meandering
lines which will result from the interaction between its own
biological impulse and the rock-facts of circumstances. All we
can usefully do is to outline a number of general observations
for the earnest consideration of those workers in the field of
world reconstruction, whether Spanish or foreign, who may have
to take on responsibilities bearing on Spanish affairs.

The first of these observations is of a negative character. Let
us drop narrow prejudices, half-baked notions and hasty information. Right and Left, "feudalism" and "the people," the
Church and freedom, yes; there is a certain amount in all that,
but only on the level of symptoms. Let us delve deeper, down

to the causes. And, for instance, let us by no means imagine
that when there is some backwardness or some injustice about,
the members of that particular section of the population which
we are inclined to consider as responsible are, as it were, foreigners who have invaded the country, instead of being what
they are, living limbs of it. In such cases, what has happened
is that the national tissue to which all classes belong, oppressors
as well as oppressed, has got into that unhealthy state, and it is
less important to condemn this or that section of the nation than
to seek the cause of the trouble which, though in appearance
only punishing one part of the population, does in reality afflict
the whole. When dealing with Spain in particular, precisely
because she is a country so apt to break into civil war, let us
all, Spaniards and non-Spaniards, bear in mind the importance
of this all-embracing point of view both as to diagnosis and as
to cure.

Seeking therefore the all-Spanish features behind the ills of
Spain, let us recall that "reduced to its essentials, we have already
defined the problem of Spanish politics as that of adapting the
national psychology to the conditions prevailing in the modern
world. This task can only be performed in peace and continuity;
but it also demands liberty. Now, the trouble comes from the
fact that the institutions in charge of peace do not seem able to
respect liberty. There is then a kind of preliminary problem to
be solved: how to secure the liberty of the country from the
fact that the institutions in charge of peace do not seem able to
respect liberty. There is then a kind of preliminary problem to
be solved: how to secure the liberty of the country from the
attacks of the Army and the Church." In these words the
Spanish problem has been stated in the first edition of the present
work (February 1930).

If we now apply to this definition the observation just made
above we are bound to conclude that neither the Spanish Army
nor the Spanish Church is a foreign conqueror in the country;
that neither the Church nor the Army has shown similar tendencies against the liberty of the people in Sweden or in Switzerland,
in England or in the United States. Therefore these tendencies

cannot be due to the fact that the Spanish Church is a Church and the Spanish Army is an Army, but to the fact that they are both Spanish. It follows that we are sure to find the same tendency in any other Spanish institution numerous enough, well-organized enough, and functionally powerful enough to bully the nation under the sway of the two Spanish political passions: separatism and dictatorship. And, of course, we find the organized working class yielding to dictatorship and separatism and bullying the nation; so that, as we have had occasion to show, Don Francisco Largo Caballero, Secretary General of the General Union of Workers, in 1934-36 played a part in Spanish politics undistinguishable from that of a general who leads the army into a pronunciamento. Thus we reach a truly objective and free view of Spanish political life, and we rediscover that the two chief political evils of the country are not the Army and the Church, are not Marxism or Anarchism either; they are Separatism and Dictatorship. All Spanish individuals and groups tend to tear themselves away from the rest in order to assert themselves in separation and to return no longer on the same level, but on top—as dictators. Dictatorship and separatism are in this way seen as two phases of the same movement.

But we can still delve deeper. The multiplication of acts and movements of dictatorship and separatism on the part of a large number of individuals and groups integrates itself into a general quality of the Spanish psychological stuff. The texture of the Spanish collective soul is thereby made dispersive and turbulent. It is a kind of ever-ebullient lava. Let us endeavor to visualize this all-embracing picture of Spanish life. Other nations flow placidly in a silky, continuous, horizontal movement, down the plain of time. The river of Spanish life is ever agitated by vertical movements surging from its rock bed, as if volcanic gases were constantly making it rise in turmoil. Struggle rather than collaboration is the state of mind and of affairs. The reason is a lack of balance between the social and the individual tendencies in man. I have elsewhere pointed out that Don Quixote and Hamlet may be interpreted as the symbols of the two opposite conflicts which an excess of the individual over the social and of the social over the individual tendency is bound to create. The Spaniard, through wealth of self and poverty of social self, tends to a desert, sandy nihilism which may be passive, and then it manifests itself in social barrenness; or active, and then it manifests itself in destruction. The recurrent civil wars of Spain may turn out to be politically rationalized outbursts of a pristine Spanish spirit of destruction, the volcanic protest of the self against the social self and all its creations. Hence such things as the cry of the Fascists: *Viva la Muerte!* or the cry of the Asturian miners: *Viva la dinamita!*

When, therefore, we approach Spain with our plans, charts, statistics and history manuals, let us bear in mind these natural facts which in a nation correspond to the physical and chemical indexes whereby we define metals and metalloids. No one expects mercury to behave like platinum, nor carbon like sulphur. And yet there are stubborn people who will have Spain behave like Sweden or like Wisconsin. Viewed with this almost physical impartiality, it might be argued that the Spaniard is the anti-type of the German. While the German rejoices in discipline and obedience, obedience and discipline are abhorrent to the Spaniard. It follows that dictatorship in Spain is due to reasons exactly opposite to those which cause it in Germany. While balanced nations like Great Britain or Switzerland may be compared to well-cemented granite walls, Germany is clay and Spain is a heap of rough-hewn granite blocks touching each other at as few points as possible and hurting each other as much as possible to the square inch of contact.

What is, then, the use of preaching liberty to Spain? Liberty comes naturally to the Spaniard. Let us preach liberty to the German, who does not know what it is. Nor will it do to argue that the Spanish "people" does not actually enjoy liberty, for in so far as this is true—and it is much less often and much less generally true than is usually imagined—this is due to the lack of order without which liberty cannot materialize, which lack of order in its turn is due to the exaggerated form liberty is apt to take in the ultra-individualistic Spanish environment. The chief need of the Spanish people, therefore, is to learn to create order, i.e., to grow and feed the social tissue of institutions.

What is the difficulty here? The same as everywhere in Spanish life: too much stress on the person; not enough stress on the thing. The Spaniard must be helped to lay stress on things, to develop cooperation, continuity, technique, method, the sense of growth, all the patient, humdrum virtues of everyday collective life. Now this effort is against the grain of his character. It is therefore unwise to make it more difficult than it already is by political and economic measures which are bound to work against it. The first positive need is to raise his standard of living and the density of population in which his life is set. If Don Quixote had not lived in a desert his imagination would not have carried him over the edge of common sense to perform actions which had no meaning for anyone but himself. Now Don Quixote is every Spaniard writ large. The Spaniard must be converted to collective life which at bottom he dislikes, if he does not altogether detest it.[1] The capitalistic nations which in the past viewed Spain mainly as a mine must alter their policy and develop her as a factory as well. This will be one of the most important steps towards stability.

The next should be an endeavor to mitigate the separatism of her several bodies of state. The chief organ for this should be the University. Priests, army officers, technicians and civil servants should all pass through the University together and mingle with the liberal professions in order to acquire a common national attitude before dispersing to the specialized schools which nowadays are only too apt to turn them into separate tribes. A system of working-class higher education should be devised to extend the benefit of this measure to the working classes and particularly to their leaders, for, contrary to what is generally believed, the trouble with the Spanish working classes is not so much igno-

---

[1] Let not the café habit be quoted against this view. The Spanish café is not a collective institution, it is but a cheap way of escaping from collective life, at best a tacit cooperative of deserts. Conversations in the café are not debates, but series of monologues in which the only hearer at any time is the speaker.

rance as a kind of self-assurance born of eagerly acquired and
ill-digested knowledge. Finally the film and broadcasting should
do much to extend the knowledge and better still the feeling of
collective life to all categories of the population, while the arts,
music and the theatre should be made accessible to all, for
the Spanish people are particularly sensitive to an aesthetic
education.

Under what political system? Who can tell? We are not the
masters of events. The most we can do is to establish conditional
relations: if this, then that. If Spain returns to the extreme Left
from the extreme Right, the wild swing of the pendulum will
continue, and presently she will have to return to the extreme
Right from the extreme Left. The destinies of Spain will then
be precarious and therefore also those of Europe, of which she
is an integral part, and those of America, in whose vast Spanish-
speaking territories the vibrations of the Spanish string reverber-
ate as in a sounding box. Politically Spain curiously resembles
Belgium in its shape though not in the quality of its metal. Like
Belgium it is composed of a Clerical-Catholic Right, a Liberal
Center and a Socialist Left.[2] It stands to reason that for Spain
as for Belgium the only possible government is one whose center
of gravity is in the liberal center. It may well be that the Civil
War will have curbed the tendency to extremism in the several
schools of working-class politics. There are labor leaders who
believe that as the outcome of the Civil War the several working-
class movements will converge into some kind of Spanish Socialism, and, if this be so, it would probably bear some resemblance
to guild Socialism rather than to Marxism. It may be, however,
that the dogmatic character of Marxism will still continue to
attract many Spanish minds. Whatever the case, the fact that
there is no hope for Spain but in a political line equidistant from
the Catholic Right and from the Socialist Left remains unshaken;
for it stands on the bedrock of facts, since only a central government can hope to conciliate enough opinion from the Right and
from the Left to bring about an indispensable minimum of con-

[2] This haunting likeness is completed by the fact that in Belgium as in
Spain there is a regionalist-separatist movement, the Flemish movement.

sent from public opinion and to prevent the concentration of powers of opposition strong enough to provoke a civil war. In broad outline, the Left must yield to the Right in religious matters and the Right to the Left in economic matters. (*Must* here does not mean, of course, a moral obligation, but merely that things *must* happen that way if we are to have a stable and orderly Spain.)

The Spanish case is one of those which will test the political acumen of the leaders of the coming world. If they insist in inflicting on Spain exactly the political institutions of other democracies of a quite different psychological metal, failure is certain. Universal direct suffrage is a case in point. Elections, representative executives and in general the machinery of the State should be contrived above all with an eye to order and continuity. All else should be subordinated to this supreme aim. If, on the other hand, in devising institutions to secure order and continuity no guarantees are taken to prevent that privileged and reactionary sectors of the country use them to obstruct progress toward economic democracy, order and continuity will go by the board again. The statesmen at the helm in the coming months and years would do well to concentrate on safeguarding the essentials of democracy rather than those details of its machinery which are still defended with bigoted stubbornness as indispensable everywhere although they have failed time and again in all but a limited number of countries. Respect for the person, freedom of thought and government by consent of the governed are points on which no compromise is possible. But all the rest is machinery and should be adapted to the metal in hand. As a suggestion to be considered, but no more, it may well be that the best system for ensuring the consent of the governed by representation in Spain may resemble that adopted by the Soviet Union until 1936 (plus freedom of the press, an important difference), rather than the somewhat primitive and rough-hewn direct representation adopted by the Anglo-Saxons.

Every facility should, of course, be given to the autonomous regions. No difficulty need be expected in this once the Nationalist regime has fallen. But if Catalonia and Euzkadi do not curb their all too Spanish tendency to separatism, a civil war is certain and one which for once would unite all Spain and would certainly be understood in the country of Lincoln.

There is, moreover, much that is obsolete in the Basque and Catalan nationalisms in these days of aviation. Their hankering is altogether medieval. The Second World War has ushered in the era of great families of nations. Let us think of this coming age when we approach the study of the kind of Spain we desire to see emerge from the ashes of the Civil and the World War.

The historical situation which evolved as the outcome of the Second World War is being shaped mainly by the West-Soviet schism. On its way toward a world organization, mankind finds itself divided by the deepest and yet simplest split in all its history. It goes toward one world; but what remains to be seen is whether this one world is to be Communist or free.

On this background, in itself rather simple and even elementary, shades and groups can be discerned which complicate the picture. The contrast of ideologies would appear to be lined with an economic grouping of nations, so that around each of the two poles, Moscow and Washington, a system of satellites, bound to move in orbits of economic subjection, are seen to gravitate. No doubt a distinction should be made between the Soviet system of satellites reduced to economic subjection by political and military power, and the American system of satellites, reduced to political subjection by economic and financial power; yet the resulting tensions are symmetrical, though by no means comparable.[3] Between the two worlds the British Commonwealth endeavors, not without success, to keep going a third system which, though less centralized, is not perhaps less solid.

This framework evinces features inherited from a past which is slowly fading out and others foreshadowing a future which is trying hard to become actuality. Toward the past, power policy grows paler, but does not die. The three systems—Soviet, American, British—amount to three empires in mutual opposition; and in the international space crossed by their lines of force, other

[3] A useful analysis of this symmetry will be found in Professor François Perroux's *Europe sans rivages,* Paris, 1954.

smaller empires move and set going forces of their own—the French, the Chinese, the Dutch, the Portuguese, the Belgian, not to speak of possible newcomers or *revenants* such as the Japanese.

Considered from the point of view of their situation within this system of forces, the nations of Europe fall into a number of groups. The largest and unhappiest of them is that of the nations now under Soviet occupation, which were directly or indirectly delivered into the hands of the Soviet tyrant by the Teheran, Yalta and Potsdam agreements. This group can do little more than suffer and hope. A second group might be made of the European nations (Switzerland and the Scandinavian states) whose one and only problem is how to resist Sovietization to save their souls. Finally, there is a group of nations which are on the one hand threatened by the power of the Soviets, and on the other attracted by power policy and the ambitions and satisfactions of empire. One might include in this group France, Germany, Italy, Spain, Belgium, Holland and Portugal.

This is the world that is due to die. But it does not die. It does not die because the three great powers, the United States, the Soviet Union and the British Commonwealth, carry on gaily their power policy game, and, therefore, are endowing this obsolete policy with a kind of borrowed vitality. Let anyone compare their language (particularly when in danger) with their deeds, and it will be patent that even the three great powers are fully aware of the fact that power policy is no longer acceptable to public opinion anywhere in the world; not even in their respective countries, so that when it comes to asking their men to sacrifice their lives, recourse has to be had to the other language, that of the future.

Such is the original lie which, in practice, has been all these years working in favor of the Soviet side in the cold war. For the Soviet Union can exhibit a perfect alibi to evade every accusation of imperialism. Its war aim is so clear and simple that the most untutored mind can understand it—the Sovietization of the whole earth. Thus every step the Soviet Union takes on the field of power politics appears to be dictated by its desire to free the proletariat, while the two great Western powers, whose sole real intention is to defend and if possible strengthen their empires, can only justify their policy by describing it as a crusade against Communism.

Now a crusade against Communism is not only a negative aim: it is also an aim lacking in clarity. Against Communism, you say? By all means. But why? Is it because Communism is a Marxist doctrine or because it is a totalitarian system? Or, in other words, is that crusade meant to defend the property of a few or the freedom of all? A crusade against Communism as a Marxist doctrine can hardly be the true aim of the West, since in our West, under the flags of that crusade, millions of Socialists are enlisted who feel themselves Marxists even though most of them may not have read Marx (just as millions of Catholics feel themselves Catholics without having read the Gospels). Then would it be that the Crusade is not out to defend property but freedom, and that it is anti-Communist because Communism is a totalitarian system? In that case how are we to understand the alliances with Tito and with Franco? For it is true that in time of danger one does not look too closely into the records of one's allies; but the two Western powers have not just resigned themselves to an association with Tito and Franco; they have taken them to their bosoms. In one word, they have sacrificed the strategy of the cold war, which is a fact, to the strategy (not well understood) of the hot war, which is a hypothesis.

And why? Because the cold war is a struggle where moral forces predominate, while the hot war is a struggle where physical forces predominate; and the two Western powers put much less faith in moral than in physical forces. In this way, they are making every day more certain of their victory in a hot war which the H-bomb makes less and less certain, while making every day more likely their defeat in a cold war which is actually swallowing us all in its turmoil.

This fondness for power policy which afflicts the two Western nations is having deplorable effects on the situation and sowing the seeds of future disasters. To begin with, it precludes the possibility of a true understanding, both as to feeling and as to action, between Britain and the United States; a fact only too obvious in a number of spots where the British and American lines of force meet at sharp angles, such as, for instance, China and Spain. It is plain that the policy of Peiping would have been much less petulant and dangerous for the West had Britain and the United States succeeded in striking a truly common policy in the Far East. And it is no less plain that the agreements signed by the United States with Franco (by no means with Spain) are just an episode in the struggle for supremacy between the two aero-naval powers of the West.

Another of the grave consequences of the power policy still adhered to by the two Anglo-Saxon states is the rebirth of German nationalism. The political evolution of Germany is determined by a fundamental feeling, an emulation of the British Empire. How blind are those British crowds and demagogues who loudly oppose the rearming of Germany for fear of a German nationalism which will be reborn the stronger precisely because of the mere existence of the British Empire and of the British obstinacy to remain aloof from all endeavors toward a genuine international integration.

There is at work in Madrid a center of German nationalism of black omen for Europe. This shoot of German imperialism, even in the wake of its second defeat within a generation, and such a frightful defeat, can be easily explained as the reaction of a tenacious and virile, though politically inept, people not precisely to the military victory of its adversaries but to their persistence in the imperial and arrogant attitude of times gone by.

The future of Europe depends then on Great Britain for two reasons: The more generally acknowledged of the two is that if Great Britain does not join a European federation the fears of France will obstruct the success of such a federation. But the less-mentioned reason is that, since Britain's refusal to join is mainly due to her traditional fondness for power policy, this attitude will strengthen the nationalistic forces in Germany whose return to power a third time would make the federation either impossible or most dangerous.

So much for the forces of the past still at work in the field of
international affairs. Other forces, however, are also at work
which tend to create a less absurd future. These forces aim at
expressing the obvious solidarity which unites all human beings
throughout the planet by means of institutions, rules and ways
of living. These were the forces which gave rise to the League
of Nations at the end of the First World War, and to the Organization of the United Nations at the end of the second. Though
in both cases the moving spirits meant well, in both their ideas
were far too simple. How could the whole world be governed by
means of an immense, unwieldy assembly, far more like the
Tower of Babel than like what such an organization should be, a
kind of family council sitting over the affairs of the family of
nations? And yet, the world had not altogether lacked sound
advice. In one of his great speeches, while the war was still on,
Sir Winston Churchill had proposed that Continental Councils
should be set up to preside over the affairs of Europe, Asia,
Africa and America with a coordinating council above them
all. The lack of this first "landing," so to speak, in the organization of world affairs undoubtedly is the chief cause of the
unwieldiness of the UNO. Four or five local federations should
be set up first, not all perhaps on a continental basis, and their
work should then be coordinated by a World Council, as suggested by Sir Winston.

In any case, note should be taken of the fact that by the side
of power policy of which they remain only too fond, the big
powers feel pushed by their public opinions to carry on a policy
not only different from but contrary to their usual line, a policy
aiming at federating the nations of the world *in a setting of
freedom*. This liberal aspect of the tendency is essential; for
there are in fact two rival tendencies afield, both aiming at a
world organization of all mankind: one, just described; the
other, led by Moscow. The first is a pure universalist tendency,
determining a deep movement of the human being (both individual and collective) in the direction of its natural evolution,
toward a state ever closer to the spirit. This movement is groping
toward a system of federations, from the federation of persons

in the family to the federation of nations in the world community. It is the liberal-humanist orientation.

We have seen how at present this evolution is hindered by nationalist and imperialist passions which hold man a prisoner of the beast in him, and by appealing to his gregarious instincts bring him back to the beast whenever he tries to evade its grasp. This reaction against the natural evolution of mankind is anti-universal, and turns its face toward the jungle. Left to itself, it would bring down mankind to the status of a pack of collective beasts of prey which would allow smaller beasts of prey to exist only in order to fatten on them.

On the other side, the natural, liberal evolution of man has to face another kind of reaction no less powerful and dangerous. This time the tendency is not contrary but favorable to universalism. Only, instead of reducing human communities to the status of herds, or collective beasts of prey, Communism grinds them into heaps of human sand, masses of beings all alike, with no access to thoughts, feelings or actions other than those determined from above. On one side, therefore, the animal reaction of imperialism—nationalism; on the other, the mineral reaction of Communism. And between the two, between the black and the red wing, the liberal-humanist movement toward a vital and natural organization of mankind on the planet.

Such is the field of forces in which Spain will have to move in the coming years. Her present regime belongs, of course, to the black wing, the animal reaction just described. It is, naturally, opposed to Communism, since the two reactions are rivals. Therefore, while this regime or a similar one rules over Spain, the incomparable strategic situation of the Peninsula is bound to remain in one way or another in the service of imperialist-nationalist interests and against humanist liberalism.

The strategic situation of Spain, yes, but by no means her people. By instinct the Spanish people side with the humanist universalism which inspires the liberal approach to world affairs. Strange as it may sound, this proclivity of the Spanish people to humanism and universalism may well be grounded in their

Catholic tradition. Does not the word *catholic,* after all, mean *universal?* In spite of some monstrous aberrations of Spanish Catholicism, such as the Inquisition, what really strikes the observer in the struggle between Spain and England in the sixteenth and seventeenth centuries, is the contrast between a universalist and a nationalist people. That is why the "black" or "animal" reaction has in Spain to seek the alliance of the Catholic Church to cover its nationalist nakedness with a universal flag.

As for the real reaction, Communism in Spain will never be but an impatient retort either toward the bad policy of some bad employer or toward a political blunder such as that committed by the United States in acquiring bases on Spanish territory while the country was not in a position to express her opinion and her wish. But by itself the Spanish working class will not take to Communism, for it fully realizes that Communism is deadly for the individual whom it grinds down to the status of an inert grain of mass.

Spain is, therefore, ready to accept the idea of a European federation. There are strong chances that, had Spain been mistress in her own house in 1952, the European Defense Community might have succeeded even without Great Britain; for then Spain would have helped balance the weight of Germany and allay the fears of France. Her entry into the European federation would have stabilized her own free regime, and all would have gained thereby. So that for all of us, who seek a political integration of Europe as the next natural phase in her evolution, the emancipation of Spain from the nationalist forces which control her destinies, becomes indispensable. A liberal-humanist Spain would fully share in the political, economic and cultural life of Europe, and very few years of peace would be required for her to give again to Europe and the world new proofs of her creative spirit.

NOTES AND APPENDICES

PART ONE

I. BIBLIOGRAPHY

BOOK ONE — PART ONE

Chapter 1

I have drawn chiefly from the excellent work of J. Dantin Cereceda: *Ensayo acerca de las Regiones Naturales de España*, tomo 1, Madrid, 1922, the cover of which carries the proudly Spanish sentence, "NO SE VENDE."

Other works on this subject which may be consulted are:

Lucas Mallada: *Explicación del Mapa Geológico de España*, 7 vols., 1895-1911.

E. H. del Villar: *Archivo Geográfico de la Península Ibérica*, Barcelona, 1916.

A. Blazquez: *España y Portugal*, Barcelona, 1914.

R. Beltrán Rózpide: *La Península Ibérica*, 1918.

L. Doporto: *Ensayo de Geografía general de España*, 1922.

In English, the best study available is that in the article "Spain," of the *Encyclopedia Britannica*. On the landscape, no

655

reader knowing Spanish should miss the admirable description
of Castile given by Unamuno in *En Torno al Casticismo,* of
which a French translation appeared in 1922, under the title
L'Essence de l'Espagne (Plon, Paris).

Chapter 2

As for the origins of the Spanish people, the choice is wider
than the knowledge which it brings. The more modern works are:

A. Schulten: *Hispania,* Barcelona, 1920.

P. Bosch Guimpera: *Ensayo de una Reconstrucción de
la Etnología Prehistórica de la Península Ibérica,* Santander, 1922.

E. Philipon: *Les Ibères,* Paris, 1909.

Pierre Paris: *Essai sur l'Art et l'Industrie de l'Espagne
Primitive,* 1903, 1904.

The ethnographical data in the chapter are from L. Hoyos
Sainz.

Other works that will be found useful are:

F. Oloriz: *Distribución Geográfica del Indice Cefálico en
España,* Madrid, 1894.

L. Sánchez Fernández: *El Hombre español útil para el
servicio de las armas y para el trabajo,* Madrid, 1913.

T. D. Aranzadi: *Antropología de España,* Barcelona, 1915.

I have slightly redrafted this chapter, having the benefit of *The
Iberians of Spain, their relations with the Aegean world,* by
Pierson Dixon, M.A., Oxford University Press, London, 1940.

On the psychology of the Spanish people by far the best interpretation is that given by Havelock Ellis in his *The Soul of
Spain.* Readers knowing Spanish have at their disposal:

Altamira: *Psicología del Pueblo Español,* Barcelona, 1917

Unamuno: *En Torno al Casticismo,* Madrid, 1916.

The views expressed in this chapter are, of course, identical
with those of my other works, *The Genius of Spain,* Oxford,
1923, and *Englishmen—Frenchmen—Spaniards,* Oxford, 1928.

Mr. J. B. Trend's book, *A Picture of Modern Spain,* London, 1921, is excellent from the point of view of land, people and events. *See also*:

> Maurice Legendre: *Portrait de l'Espagne,* Paris, 1923.
> Count Keyserling: *Europe,* 1928. The paragraph at the end of this book is quoted from the concluding words of Count Keyserling's essay on "Spain" in *Europe*.

Chapters 3-5

On the Spanish Empire the facts are well known. All that is wanted is perspective and interpretation. I have expressed my own views, much strengthened and confirmed by the two works of Professor Fernando de los Ríos mentioned in the preface. On Vitoria and his doctrines, *see* Vitoria: *De Indis et de Ivre Belli Relectiones,* published by the Carnegie Institution of Washington, 1917. There is also a useful treatise on Vitoria published in French by Professor Barcia Trelles, being a course of lectures at the Hague Institute of International Law.

On Spanish colonization:

From the well-meaning but passionate Las Casas, and by the well-known process of copying and enlarging errors to which we owe so much history, the legend of Spanish colonization as a short-lived and dismal failure has thrived. It flourishes even in works as modern as Cunningham's *An Essay on Western Civilization in its Economic Aspects, Medieval and Modern Times,* Cambridge, 1910, and Lord Bryce's *South America,* 1912. In his *Outline of History,* H. G. Wells deals with the whole history of the Spanish Empire, discovery, exploration and colonization, in a few paragraphs in which there is less room for facts than for errors. I have repeatedly drawn his attention to his responsibility in the matter, but without success. He did not know he was wrong when he wrote these preposterous paragraphs. He died unrepentant.

Leaving aside works by older Spanish writers which, though fairly reliable, are still too much influenced by the polemical atmosphere of Las Casas, the first scientific and dispassionate outlook is to be found in Alexander von Humboldt: *Voyage aux Régions Equinoxiales du Nouveau Continent,* published in 1809 as the result of first-hand observation, much wanted in the matter. There is an English edition, published in 1811. *See also* by the same author, *Essai Politique sur le Royaume de la Nouvelle Espagne,* Paris, 1827. In English there is a curious book, *Notes on Mexico made in the Autumn of 1822,* by an American citizen, J. R. Poinsett, member of Congress. He follows Humboldt, but adds his own shrewd observations. In more modern times L. S. Fisher: *Vice-regal Administration in the Spanish-American Colonies,* 1926; Bourne: *Spain in America,* New York, 1904.

On the discovery of America I have tried my hand at Columbus in *Christopher Columbus,* London and New York, 1939, in which will be found a bibliography on the subject. See also *The Spanish Conquistadores* by F. A. Kirkpatrick, London, 1934.

On the exploration of America by the Spaniards, Manuel Serrano y Sanz: *Orígenes de la Dominación Española en América,* Madrid, 1918. *The Spanish Main,* by Philip Ainsworth Means, New York, 1935, will be found most instructive, and it contains a rich bibliography. *See also* my *Hernán Cortés,* New York, 1941; London, 1942.

On Charles V and the Spanish Empire in Europe, *The Emperor Charles V,* by Professor Armstrong, Oxford, 2 vols., 1910, and *The Rise of the Spanish Empire in the Old World and the New,* 4 vols., New York, 1918-22, by R. B. Merriman.

The speech quoted on page 44 will be found in Professor de los Ríos booklet: *Religión y Estado en la España del Siglo XVI.*

"Philip II would require fresh treatment." So far my notes to the first edition. Since then, we have had, apart from other works of lesser import, *Philip II,* by William Thomas Walsh, London and New York, 1937, which is most useful and well informed, but falls perhaps too much on the Catholic side, a healthy reaction, however, against the all too frequent misrepresentation of this subject in Protestant culture; and the scholarly volume IV of Professor R. B. Merriman's monumental work quoted above, under the subtitle *Philip The Prudent*, New York, 1934.

On the Armada there is an interesting essay by Froude, inspired by the Spanish standard book: *La Armada Invencible*, by Fernández Duro.

There is an admirable description of Spanish culture in the sixteenth century in A. F. G. Bell: *Luis de León.*

On the dissolution of the Spanish Empire, and the meaning of the Wars of Emancipation, *see* Marius André: *La Fin de l'Empire Espagnol*, which, however, must be read remembering that the author holds strong opinions against the French Revolution. *Also* my *Fall of the Spanish American Empire*, New York, 1948.

L'Œuvre de l'Espagne en Amérique, by Carlos Pereyra, Paris, is a polemical work, but full of information, and useful to dispel many errors of fact.

See also F. A. Kirkpatrick: *Latin America: A Brief History in the Cambridge Series*, 1938. *South America with Mexico and Central America*, by J. B. Trend, Oxford, 1941, is a stimulating booklet with a short but useful bibliography, notable in particular for the tendency, frequent nowadays in the two Anglo-Saxon countries, to stress the native element in the history and culture of Spanish America.

Chapter 6

The best guides for the history of the nineteenth century are: Pi y Margall: *Historia de España en el Siglo XIX*, and Rafael Altamira: *Historia de la Civilización Española*, 1928. *See also* Blasco Ibáñez: *Historia de la Revolución Española*, 1808-74, Barcelona, 1890; S. Aguado: *Manual de Historia de España*, Bilbao, 1927-28. In English, Butler Clark: *Modern Spain*, 1815-98.

A useful monograph on the middle period of the century is that on *General Serrano*, by the Marques de Villaurrutia, Madrid, 1929. *See also* the interesting series: *Cartas de Conspiradores*, by V. Alvarez Villamil and Rodolfo Llopis, Madrid, 1929.

De la Revolución a la Restauración, by the Marqués de Lema, Madrid.

Apart from the above somewhat technical works an excellent approach to the knowledge of the nineteenth century is through the Spanish novel, chief amongst them the *Episodios Nacionales* of Galdós, the series *Ruedo Ibérico* by Valle-Inclán, and the series *Memorias de un Hombre de Acción* by Baroja.

War of Ideas in Spain, by Jose Castillejo, London, 1937, is excellent for some aspects of this century.

BOOK ONE — PART TWO

Chapter 7

On Don Francisco Giner, *see* an article in my *The Genius of Spain,* Oxford, 1923, and a monograph, *Mi Don Francisco Giner,* by J. Pijoan, San José de Costa Rica, 1927.

On education in Spain, *see* two articles in the Spanish Supplement of *The Times,* August 10, 1926; also L. Luzuriaga, *Documentos para la Historia Escolar de España,* Madrid, 1916.

> Rafael Altamira: *Problemas Urgentes de la Primera Enseñanza en España,* 1916.
>
> Manuel B. Cossío: *L'Enseignement en Espagne,* Madrid, 1908.

On the history of Spanish universities:

> Vicente de la Fuente: *Historia de las Universidades, Colegios, y demás establecimientos de Enseñanza de España,* Madrid, 1884.
>
> Francisco Giner de Los Ríos: *La Universidad Española,* Madrid, 1916.

Castillejo's *War of Ideas in Spain,* mentioned above, will be found most useful here also. For all this Part, *see also* J. B. Trend: *The Origins of Modern Spain,* 1934.

Chapter 8

On Galdós, *The Genius of Spain,* Oxford, 1923.

On the Generation of 1898, the books quoted in the text, and the following:

Ramiro de Maeztu: *Hacia otra España,* Madrid, 1899.

Luis Morote: *La Moral de la Derrota,* 1900.

Macias Picavea: *El Problema Nacional,* Madrid, 1897.

Angel Ganivet: *Idearium Español,* 1896.

Miguel de Unamuno: *En Torno al Casticismo,* 1902. (French translation, *L'Essence de l'Espagne.* Plon, Paris, 1922.)

Miguel de Unamuno and Angel Ganivet: *El Porvenir de España,* 1912. (A Collection of letters between Unamuno and Ganivet, published in 1897, in the newspaper *El Defensor de Granada.*)

José Ortega y Gasset: *España Invertebrada,* 1922. An incomplete English translation has come out in recent years: *Invertebrate Spain.*

José Ortega y Gasset: *Vieja y Nueva Política,* Madrid, 1914 (being the text of his lecture, quotations from which are given in the close of Chapter 23).

Chapter 9

General information may be gathered from Angel Marvaud: *L'Espagne au XXième Siècle,* Paris, 1915.

On agricultural matters:

Luis de Hoyos Sainz: *Riqueza Agrícola de España,* Madrid, 1926.

Luis de Hoyos Sainz: *Fertilidad de la Tierra,* Madrid, 1926.

J. Dantin Cereceda: *Dry-Farming Ibérico,* Guadalajara, 1916.

J. Brunhes: *L'Irrigation, ses conditions géographiques, ses modes et son organisation dans la Péninsule Ibérique et dans l'Afrique du Nord,* Paris, 1902.

A. Guillén: *El Tribunal de Aguas de Valencia y los modernos jurados de riego,* Valencia, 1920.

The Times, Spanish Supplement, August 10, 1926.

Antonio Flores de Lemus: *Algunos datos estadísticos sobre el estado actual de la economía Española.* (Articles appeared in *La Lectura,* Madrid, 1914. There is an English translation published in *The Times* Spanish Supplement, June 29, 1914, p. 15.)

Anuario estadístico de España.

Salvador Calderón: *Los minerales de España.*

José Marvá: *Ligero bosquejo de las industrias en España.*

Angel Marvaud: *L'Espagne au XXième Siècle,* Paris, 1915.

Luis Olariaga: *El problema ferroviario en España.*

A. N. Young: *Spanish Finance and Trade.*

BOOK ONE — PART THREE

Chapter 10

There are a number of books which apply to this entire Part, notably:

Soldevilla: *El Año Político,* Madrid yearly.

Count Romanones: *Las responsabilidades políticas del antiguo régimen,* Madrid, 1924.

Count Romanones: *El Ejército y la Política,* Madrid, 1920.

Count Romanones: *Notas de una Vida,* 1929.

Antonio Maura: *Treinta y cinco años de vida pública,* Madrid, 1917-18.

Santiago Alba: *Problemas de España,* Madrid, 1916.

Azorin: *El parlamentarismo Español,* Madrid, 1916.

Sánchez Toca: *La crisis de nuestro parlamentarismo,* Madrid, 1914.

Conde de la Mortera: *Historia crítica del reinado de Don Alfonso XIII,* Madrid, 1925.

On this and the following chapters, *Historia del Reinado de Don Alfonso XIII,* by Melchor Fernández Almagro, 1933.

Chapter 11

Barthe: *Las grandes propiedades rústicas en España,* Madrid, 1910.

Vizconde de Eza: *El problema agrario en España,* 1915.

Fernando de los Ríos: "The Agrarian Problem in Spain," in the *International Labor Review,* June 1925, p. 843.

Chapter 12

I am indebted for most of the information given in this chapter to the manuscript of an unpublished book by Don Leopoldo Palacios, on *Freedom of Labor Association.* Other useful works are:

Angel Marvaud: *L'Espagne au XXième Siècle,* Paris, 1915.

J. Uña: *Las asociaciones obreras en España,* Madrid, 1900.

Angel Marvaud: *La question sociale en Espagne,* Paris, 1910.

F. B. Deakin, *Spain To-day,* Londay, 1924.

A. Lorenzo: *El proletariado militante,* Barcelona.

J. J. Morato: *El partido socialista,* Madrid.

F. Largo Caballero: *Pasado, presente y futuro de la Unión General de Trabajadores,* Madrid.

Chapter 13

Francos Rodríguez: *La vida de Canalejas,* Madrid, 1918.

William Archer: *The Life, Trial and Death of Francisco Ferrer,* London, 1911.

J. Giron y Arcas: *La situación jurídica de la Iglesia Católica,* 1905.

This is a chapter on which the books of Count Romanones, already mentioned, repay reading. *See also* the articles in the Spanish Supplement of *The Times,* 1926, referred to in the notes for Chapter 7, under *Education.*

Spain, the Church and the Orders, E. Allison Peers, London, 1939.

Chapter 14

Here again Count Romanones is an excellent guide.

League of Nations Armament Yearbook.

A good chapter in the book of M. Marvaud, *L'Espagne au XXième Siècle.*
The works quoted under Chapter 20.

Chapter 15-17

A sympathetic and penetrating survey of the Catalan Question will be found in J. B. Trend: *A Picture of Modern Spain.* The Catalan historian quoted in the text is F. Valls-Taberner: *Historia de Catalunya,* Barcelona, 1922.

Quotations from Señor Rovira y Virgili are from his book, *El Nacionalismo Catalán,* Barcelona.

Other good documents are:

E. Prat de la Riba: *Nacionalisme,* Barcelona, 1918.

L. Nicolau d'Olwer: *Resum de Literatura Catalana,* Barcelona, 1927.

Francisco Curet: *El arte dramático en el resurgir de Cataluña,* Barcelona; *La Mancomunidad de Cataluña,* Barcelona, 1922.

A. Royo Villanova: *El Problema Catalán,* 1908.

F. Cambo: *Actuació Regionalista,* Barcelona, 1915.

Georges Dwelshauvers: *La Catalogne et le Problème Catalan,* Paris, 1926, unfortunately written, though by a Frenchman, from the point of view of the rash Catalan Nationalist.

The paragraph quoted on pages 189-90 is from a book, the mss. of which was placed at my disposal by its author, Don Francisco Cambó.

There are valuable opinions of contemporary Catalan writers in the following books:

J. Pijoan: *Mi Don Francisco Giner*, San José de Costa Rica, 1927.

J. Estelrich: *La Qüestió de les Minories Nacionals*, Barcelona, 1929.

See also *Historia de Cataluñya*, Ferran Soldevila, 1934-35 Barcelona. A really remarkable work.

Catalonia Infelix, E. Allison Peers, London, 1937.

Chapter 18

Noticias Históricas de las Tres Provincias Vascongadas, en que se procura investigar el estado civil antiguo de Alava, Guipúzcoa y Vizcaya y el orígen de sus Fueros, por el Dr. D. Juan Antonio Llorente, presbitero, canónigo de la Santa Iglesia Academia de la Historia. Tomo I. Madrid, en la Imprenta Real. Primada de Toledo. Academico Correspondiente de la Real Año de 1806. Tomo II, 1807. Tomo III, 1807.

A good article, "Basque," by Professor W. J. Entwistle, in *Bulletin of Spanish Studies*, vol. x, p. 71.

Le Problème Basque, by Dr. de Azpilikoeta, Paris, 1938, is a modern statement of the Basque Nationalist case.

On Galicia: *Una punta de Europa*, by V. Garcia Marti, Madrid, 1928,

Chapter 19

The bibliography for this chapter will be found in the chapter itself, where a number of books bearing on the matter are quoted. The concluding paragraphs are quoted from *Idearium Español*, by Ganivet.

Chapter 20

J. A. de Sangroniz: *Marruecos*, Madrid, 1921.

Conde de la Mortera: *La cuestión de Marruecos*, Madrid, 1915.

Angel Marvaud: *L'Espagne au XXième Siècle*, Paris, 1915.

André Tardieu: *La Conférence d'Algeciras*, Paris, 1915.

Gonzalo de Reparaz: *Política Española en Africa*, Barcelona, 1907.

Mariano Gómez González: *La penetración en Marruecos*, 1909.

Chapter 21

R. M. de Labra: *La orientación internacional de España*, Madrid, 1910.

Rafael Altamira: *Mi viaje a América*, Madrid, 1911.

R. M. de Labra: *Los Diputados Americanos en las Cortes de Cádiz*, 1911.

R. Cuneo-Vidal: *España. Impresiones de un Sudamericano.*

R. R. Zarate: *España y América,* Madrid, 1917.

An admirable statement of Spanish enlightened opinion on Spanish-Americanism will be found in:

José Pla: *La Misión internacional de la raza hispánica,* Madrid, 1929.

Chapter 22

R. M. de Labra: *La orientación internacional de España,* Madrid, 1910.

Marqués de Villaurrutia: *Relaciones entre España e Inglaterra durante la Guerra de la Independencia.*

A. Mousset: *La política exterior de España,* 1873-1918, Madrid, 1918.

F. de León y Castillo: *Mis Tiempos,* 1921.

R. Pinón: *L'Empire de la Méditerranée,* Paris, 1912.

J. Navarrete: *Las Llaves del Estrecho,* Madrid, 1881.

Colonel Jevenois: *El Túnel Submarino del Estrecho de Gibraltar.* Editorial, *Voluntad,* Madrid.

Article in *The Times,* Friday, October 25, 1929. The closing paragraphs are quoted from *Idearium Español,* by Ganivet.

BOOK ONE — PART FOUR

The general books quoted at the beginning of the notes for Part Three are indispensable here also.

Chapter 23

Salvador Canals: *Los sucesos de España de 1909*, Madrid, 1910.

J. Francos Rodríguez: *La vida de Canalejas*, Madrid, 1918.

Chapter 24

J. B. Trend: *A Picture of Modern Spain.*

A. Alcalá Galiano: *España ante el conflicto europeo*, Madrid, 1916.

A curious discussion on the political tendencies of the 1917 crisis, with some documents bearing on the period, will be found in *España en pie, por Un Diputado a Cortes*, published without date in Barcelona, Antonio López, Librero.

Chapter 25

The following work is a first-rate document for the study of this period:

Manuel de Burgos y Mazo: *El verano de 1919 en Gobernación, Cuenca*, 1921.

The following books bear on the setback of 1921 in Morocco:

A. Vivero: *El Derrumbamiento*, Madrid, 1922.

Dámaso Berenguer: *Campañas en el Rif*, 1923. (The High Commissioner and Commander-in-Chief's own story.)

V. Ruiz Albéniz: *Las Responsabilidades del Desastre*, 1922.

Chapter 26

The book *España Encadenada*, Paris, 1925, by Eduardo Ortega y Gasset, is strongly partisan, by an exile. The collection

Hojas Libres, published by Señor Ortega y Gasset on French territory, is also full of information. It must be handled with caution owing to the same partisan character which animates it. *Conde de La Mortera. Bosquejo Histórico de la Dictadura, Madrid,* 1930, is written with severity from a conservative point of view.

On the work of the Ministry of Labor:

> Victor González de Echavarri y Castañeda: *El Régimen Paritario,* Barcelona, 1927.
>
> Eduardo Aunós Pérez: *La Organización Corporativa del Trabajo,* Barcelona (without date).

Chapter 27

The general bibliography of Parts Three and Four.

BOOK TWO

For both the Republic and the Civil War, I have found the *Bulletin of Spanish Studies,* edited by Professor Allison Peers, an invaluable help, not only because it follows events week by week, thus recording them in the moral context in which they occur but because it gives a number of important documents in their original Spanish. I wish to record my indebtedness to this most useful publication. Professor Allison Peers' *The Spanish Tragedy* is a most useful storehouse of data for the period 1930-36, from which I have drawn freely, though not always in agreement with the author's views.

For the war period as well as for the Republic, I am also indebted to the excellent reports of the Foreign Policy Association of America, and in particular to the issues of December 20, 1933, January 1, 1937, January 15, 1937, April 1 and May 1, 1938. These reports are conscientious and objective, though they now and then need to be corrected by a better knowledge of Spanish life in order to set their merely factual accuracy in its living environment.

For the Civil War I have found many facts and data in the *Surveys* of the Royal Institute of International Affairs, usually recorded with admirable objectivity and industry. May I also express my indebtedness to them? It is a matter of regret to have to state that Professor Toynbee's theories on the Spanish background, as set forth in Part I of the *Survey* for 1937, are highly debatable and lead this distinguished scholar to conclusions of a most hazardous character which no well-informed Spanish authority would substantiate. Unfortunately, these theories are not without a certain influence on a number of aspects in the narrative of the Civil War, so that this work, otherwise so excellent, has to be read with reservations.

I cannot, of course, discuss here the library of books written on the Spanish Civil War, nor even all I have had to consult. *Life and Death of the Spanish Republic,* by Henry Buckley, London, 1940, is an honest and clear account by a man of Left sympathies. Other books of different tendencies (Casado, Alvarez del Vayo, etc.) are mentioned in the notes when consulted.

I must single out an exceptional book: *The Spanish Cockpit,* by Frank Borkenau, London, 1937. It comes so near to the deeper realities of the case that it is a pity it misses them. There are small inaccuracies, some of them perhaps due to lack of opportunities for a closer study of the local facts. I will quote some: His belief in the immunity of Bilbao (Prieto's stronghold) and of the Basque Country in general (the home of La Pasionaria) from Socialism, Communism and Anarchism, p. 10; his rash parallels between 1707, 1808 and 1873, which, even as he makes them, transform themselves into contrasts in his honest hands, pages 17-18; his assertion that during the administration of Lerroux-Gil Robles, "The Separation of Church and State was repealed," p. 51; that since 1925 "only members of the F.A.I. can hold positions of trust in the C.N.T.," p. 37; that Spaniards have "a strong sense of co-operation and of hierarchy," p. 21; alas! an undeserved compliment to the most uncooperative and anarchical people in the world, and several others. But to my mind, the chief failing of the book, and one somewhat surprising in so keen an observer is the romantic division of the

inhabitants of Spain into "people" and "upper classes." There is
but one earth, and the fight is not between classes or layers but
between the particles and the whole. It is a matter of texture of
a whole nation of which all classes and layers of society are but
tissues. Were it not for this failing, Mr. Borkenau's book would
have been the outstanding work of its kind on the Spanish War.
As it is, it remains the best I know.

Few subjects lead foreign writers on Spain so far astray as the
Church. Even Mr. Borkenau writes: "But it was impossible for
a régime based on the Army and the support of the Crown, and
shunning revolution, to enforce ideological conformity against
the Church; so it had to be enforced along the lines of the
Church. In other words, the Universities had to be muzzled. The
Ateneo, for the first time in its existence was closed." Mr. Borkenau is wide off the mark. He is discussing the regime of Primo de
Rivera and though some of the measures taken at the time aimed
at flattering the Church, those he mentions were purely political
repression. The dictator would have been delighted to see all the
Left of Spain indulge in an orgy of anti-clerical Voltairianism
provided he was left in undisturbed possession of the springs of
power. I give an example below.

The British and American public have been treated, I am
afraid, to a vast amount of ill-digested, in fact, ignorant, comment about Spain during the Civil War. I feel it my duty to
record a particularly bad case. On page 130 of a Penguin special,
Mussolini's Roman Empire, by G. T. Garratt, we read: "The
Catholic hierarchy were able to exercise an effective censorship
over all publications. . . ." There is not a single word of fact in
this statement. Books and pamphlets were, at the time Mr.
Garratt describes (Primo de Rivera's) and right through the
Restoration absolutely free from all censorship of the Church or
of the State; and though newspapers were in frequent periods of
unrest censored by the State, they were never either directly or
indirectly censored by the Church. Every man who knows Spain
will agree with me that even in the realm of subtle influences and
the unwritten law, the Church in Spain never had any power
over the printed word, except of course its own newspapers,

which were few. It is a fact that the English Church and what the Americans call the churches exert on the press of these two countries a bigger subtle influence than the Spanish Church on our press. Under Primo de Rivera I published on the front page of *El Sol*, which had then a position equivalent to that of the London *Times*, a somewhat irreverent and Voltairian sketch on the arrival of William Jennings Bryan in Heaven (it will be found in *Elysian Fields*, London and New York, 1937), which no English or American paper would have published for fear of offending its religious readers.

It is with deep regret I put these facts on record, but I must, for in view of the importance I attach to the adequate knowledge of Spanish affairs in the United States and Great Britain, I must say I am deeply concerned as to the lack of responsibility evinced by some writers who venture into this field without an adequate preparation for it.

I add now (1957) that *for the first time*, since Spain fell under Franco, the Church has been given powers of censorship.

II. TEXT OF COMRADE STALIN'S LETTER TO SEÑOR LARGO CABALLERO

Confidentiel

AU CAMARADE LARGO CABALLERO

Cher camarade,   *Valence*

Le camarade Rosenberg, notre représentant plénipotentiaire, nous a communiqué l'expression de vos sentiments fraternels. Il nous a aussi dit que vous êtes toujours animé d'une foi invariable en la victoire. Permettez de vous remercier fraternellement pour les sentiments exprimés et de vous dire que nous partageons votre foi en la victoire du peuple espagnol.

Nous avons considéré et nous considérons toujours comme notre devoir, dans la mesure de nos possibilités, de venir en aide au Gouvernement espagnol qui dirige la lutte de tous les travailleurs, de toute la démocratie espagnole contre la "clique militaire et fasciste, qui n'est qu'un instrument des forces fascistes internationales."

La révolution espagnole se trace ses chemins, distincts sous beaucoup des rapports du chemin traversé par la Russie. Ceci est déterminé par la différence des conditions sociales, historiques et géographiques, et par des nécessités de la situation internationale différentes de celles auxquelles avait à faire la révolution russe. Il est bien possible que le chemin parlementaire se montrera en Espagne comme un moyen de développement révolutionnaire plus efficace qu'en Russie.

Mais cela dit, nous croyons que notre expérience, surtout l'expérience de notre guerre civile, appliquée conformément aux conditions particulières de la lutte révolutionnaire espagnole, peut avoir pour l'Espagne une certaine importance. Partant de cela, nous avons consenti, sur vos demandes réitérées, qui nous avaient été transmises en son temps par le camarade Rosenberg, à envoyer un nombre de nos camarades militaires pour les mettre à votre disposition. Ces camarades ont reçu de nous les instructions de servir par leurs conseils dans le domaine militaire les chefs militaires espagnols auprès desquels vous les auriez envoyés pour les aider.

Il leur a été catégoriquement ordonné de ne point perdre de vue le fait, qu'avec toute la conscience de solidarité dont sont pénétrés à présent le peuple espagnol et les peuples de l'U.R.S.S., un camarade soviétique, étant un étranger en Espagne, ne peut être réellement utile qu'à condition de se tenir strictement aux fonctions d'un conseiller et d'un conseiller seulement.

Nous pensons que c'est précisément de cette manière que sont employés par vous nos camarades militaires.

Nous vous prions de nous informer, en ami, dans quelle mesure nos camarades militaires remplissent-ils avec succès les tâches dont vous les chargez, car, bien entendu, c'est seulement si vous jugez favorablement leur travail qu'il sera utile de les laisser continuer leur travail en Espagne.

Nous vous prions aussi de nous communiquer de façon directe et sans ambages votre avis sur le camarade Rosenberg: le Gouvernement espagnol, en est-il satisfait ou bien faut il le remplacer par un autre représentant?

Voice quatre conseils d'amis que nous vous soumettons:

(1) il faudrait prendre en considération les paysans qui sont d'une grande importance pour un pays agraire comme l'Espagne. Il serait bien de passer des décrets touchant les questions agraires et les questions des impôts, qui iraient au devant des intérêts des paysans. Il serait bien aussi d'attirer les paysans dans l'armée ou d'en créer des détachements de partisans à l'arrière des armées fascistes. Des décrets en faveur des paysans pourraient faciliter ceci.

(2) Il faudrait attirer du côté du Gouvernement la petite et moyenne bourgeoisie des villes, ou, en tout cas, leur donner la possibilité de prendre une position de neutralité, favorable au Gouvernement, en les protégeant contre les tentatives de confiscation et en leur assurant dans la mesure du possible la liberté du commerce, sinon ces groupes suivront le fascisme.

(3) Il ne faut pas repousser les chefs du parti républicain, mais, au contraire, il faut les attirer, les rapprocher du Gouvernement. Il est surtout nécessaire d'assurer au Gouvernement le soutien d'Azaña et de son groupe, en faisant tout ce qui est possible, pour les aider à vaincre leurs hésitations. Ceci est nécessaire pour empêcher les ennemis de l'Espagne de la considérer comme une république communiste, et pour avertir ainsi leur intervention ouverte, qui constitue le danger le plus grand pour l'Espagne républicaine.

(4) On pourrait trouver l'occasion de déclarer dans la presse que le Gouvernement de l'Espagne ne laissera personne porter atteinte à la propriété et aux intérêts légitimes des étrangers en Espagne, citoyens des pays qui ne soutiennent pas les rebelles.

Salut fraternel,
    Amis de l'Espagne républicaine

        (Signé) K. VOROSHILOV, N. MOLOTOV, J. STALIN

Moscou, le 21 décembre 1936.

III. A PERSONAL MEMOIR

The news of King Alfonso's abdication reached me in Mexico where I was holding a course as guest professor in the University. I had never served the Spanish State in my life,[1] and had lived abroad since 1916, i.e. for the last fifteen years. I had done nothing to bring about the Republic, partly because I felt the political problem of Spain was deeper than the issue Republic v. Monarchy, partly because even if I had felt convinced that the Republic was necessary, and even though I felt the Monarchy was in a bad way, I thought the change could not be actually brought about without the help of a military conspiracy, a remedy worse than the evil to my way of thinking. As it turned out I was wrong and the changeover in 1931 was the only one of any importance in the history of Spain which owed nothing to the active intervention of the military, although they did make it possible by their passive attitude of indifference.

[1] With the exception of a few weeks in the spring of 1921, as technical adviser to the Spanish Delegation to the League Transit Conference in Barcelona. Let this be stated, as we say in Spain, "so that the devil laugh not at my lie."

I held the Chair of Spanish Studies in Oxford, decorated with the name of King Alfonso by the grace of Colonel Bedford, the . . . well, not exactly founder, for he had not provided the funds, but the active recruiter of donors. King Alfonso had given no money for it, and it was a matter of regret, to me at any rate, that the name of Luis Vives, the Spanish scholar so closely connected with Oxford, had been passed over in favor of that of a king whose indifference to cultural values was notorious among us. I set this down because there have been people who have reproached me for my services to the Republic on the ground that I had been "King Alfonso XIII" Professor of Spanish Studies at Oxford. While on this note, I might as well add that neither the king nor his ministers had done anything—rather the reverse—to back me when I applied for a post as member of the League Secretariat. I have my reasons for thinking that the first time my name was mooted, the Spanish Ambassador in London vetoed it; while the second time, the Foreign Secretary, one of the best, by the way, Spain has had in recent times, Señor González Hontoria, gave his agreement when asked for it. But neither he nor any Spaniard, official or unofficial, took any initiative in the matter. The fact is that when the king fell I had no reasons whatever for attachment, gratitude or any feeling whatsoever for or against the Spanish State.

During the remaining fortnight of April, while I carried on my duties at the University of Mexico, news began to circulate to the effect that I was to be appointed Ambassador to Washington. The appointment of several of my literary friends to other embassies and legations lent some weight to the rumors, but as I had received no intimation from anyone in office, I left Mexico for Cuba at the end of April, feeling as free as when I had left Oxford a few months earlier. I had a month's lecturing engagement in Cuba. I had to cut it down to a week, for the papers carried the news that the American Secretary of State had given his agreement to my nomination as Ambassador. I had had no news from the Provisional Government or from anyone else either official or private. I had been appointed without anyone troubling to inquire whether I could or would accept the post.

On May 13 (1931) I landed in New York on my way to Spain. I rang up Don Fernando de los Ríos, the Minister of Education of the Republic in Madrid, the man in the new Cabinet with whom I was best acquainted. I had never met the new Foreign Secretary, Señor Lerroux. I expressed my astonishment and my embarrassment at the awkward situation in which I had been placed toward Oxford University, which had granted me leave for a year as professor, but not leave to take on an embassy while away. He explained that some allowance should be made in the case of a revolutionary government. I wrote to the vice-chancellor of the University explaining the position and resigning my chair, and I left for Madrid.

I found that the Gallegans were then organizing their home-rule party, the ORGA. I was not an out-and-out home-ruler, but I soon discovered that nearly all of the prominent members of the party, including its leader Don Santiago Casares Quiroga, were about as convinced as I was. I joined their party, closely allied with Azaña's, to stand as a candidate for my native town, La Coruña. I was elected a member of the Constituent Assembly without having visited my constituency, and while in New York, after I had presented my credentials, was informed by a United Press man who had come to interview me, that I had been elected Fourth Vice-President of the Assembly.

After a few weeks in Washington, I returned to Madrid to prepare the delegation to the League Assembly. During this Assembly, I had to "open" the League procedure over Manchuria, on behalf of the Foreign Secretary Señor Lerroux, Spain being at the time the occupant of the Council's chair. Frequent meetings were necessary throughout the winter and as it was out of the question that I should return to Washington while the Manchurian affair dragged on, I was transferred to Paris (January 1, 1932).

From that date till March 4, 1934, I was responsible for three whole-time posts: ambassador in Paris, *de facto* permanent delegate to the League Council and Assembly, at one of the most intense moments of activity the League has known; and *de facto* chief delegate to the Disarmament Conference. This period was closed when on March 4, 1934, I accepted the Ministry of Education in one of the many Cabinets Señor Lerroux had to put together.

It was the third time I had been offered a Cabinet post. While I was technically still Ambassador to Washington but already approved by Monsieur Briand as Ambassador to Paris, and when I happened to be in Paris engaged on League work, Azaña rang me up to offer me the Ministry of Finance (December 1931). I declined on grounds of incompetence—an unheard-of reason in the politics of Spain and of many other lands. A few days later, Azaña, still Cabinet-making, had to appoint a foreign secretary, and he passed me over. I never asked him or anyone else why, so I cannot explain it. Later, when Señor Lerroux had to build up his first Cabinet (September 1933) he rang me up to offer me the Foreign Office. I begged to consult my party (to which I belonged ever so little), and upon their somewhat luke-warm answer, I declined. The Cabinet ultimately formed did, however, include a member of my party. Señor Lerroux disliked my refusal to accept office under him.

I was myself rather inclined to leave the Paris Embassy. The physical strain was too heavy. I was no longer a member of Parliament. My parliamentary work, constantly interrupted by my calls abroad, had not gone beyond a couple of speeches during the autumn of 1931 while the Constitution was being debated; and one which I had to deliver while ambassador in Paris to answer a number of scurrilous attacks made against my diplomatic collaborators and myself by a demagogue of the Radical Socialist Party, Don Eduardo Ortega y Gasset, the brother of the distinguished philosopher. This man, who was venting his disappointment after the high hopes of personal success of which his years of exile under the dictatorship of Primo de Rivera had made him conceive, was not, however, the worst sinner in this respect. There was a kind of tacit agreement between the extreme Right and the extreme Left for slandering the men who had accepted service under the Republic. If only as an example of how it was done, let me say that a revolutionary journalist very active in Asturias, Javier Bueno, assiduously circulated among the workers lists of imaginary salaries alleged to be paid to prominent men, which had been prepared and given to the public in the course of a lecture in the Ateneo in Madrid by a reactionary lawyer, Don Joaquín del Moral. For example, in my case, the whole budget of the Embassy was written down as if it were my salary, to which were added impressive sums supposed to be paid me by the League (as if the League paid the national delegates) and by Oxford University as professor (for this Spanish reactionary and his revolutionary opposite number both took for granted that Oxford University followed the practice of Spanish universities, whereby professors who do not teach are paid their salaries). The total sum was, of course, of a size to raise the indignation of the working class.

But the fact was that, as a man without private means, I lived under constant fear of running into private debt, owing to the heavy cost of the Paris Embassy. I had resigned from Parliament and had not stood again in 1933, having grown skeptical as to the way the institution was then organized would work. When Señor Lerroux expressed to me his dissatisfaction at my refusal to serve in his first Cabinet, he had given me to understand that he would appeal to me again at the first opportunity. I thought it necessary to write him a letter defining the conditions under which I could collaborate. They were two: peace with the Socialists and no amnesty to General Sanjurjo. He had not answered my letter when a few weeks later he asked me to take the Ministry of Education, for, he said, he needed an impartial non-party man at the head of that much disputed department. I assumed my conditions were accepted and took office on March 4, 1934.

It was my only way to leave the Paris Embassy, and it may be that this circumstance led me to an over-optimistic appraisal of the situation with regard to those two conditions. I soon realized that I was something of an oddity in the Cabinet and that my ministerial life would not last. But I was resolved to do my best for the cause of collaboration and stability of all the moderate elements of the Republic, of the Right and of the Left, and therefore on no account to be instrumental in bringing about a crisis. Within a fortnight, Señor Lerroux intimated that he proposed to introduce an Amnesty Bill and made it clear that military prisoners would be among those to benefit by it. I put forward my objections and expressed doubts as to the possibility of my remaining in the Cabinet under such circumstances.

I was then particularly interested in the celebrations in honor of the anniversary of the Republic, April 14, which I wished to utilize in order to develop the sense of national unity above party, the lack of which seems to me at the root of all the evil in Spain. I had organized a national school festival to be held in the whole country at the same hour, provincial audiences to be connected by radio with the festival in Madrid. The chief items were: an address by the President (and it was admirable); the reading of a small number of selections of Spanish prose and verse, which were published in a booklet and printed by the million and distributed all over the country; folk songs in all the languages of the Peninsula, sung by individual singers and by choirs; and the last movement of Beethoven's ninth symphony. The program included also open-air shows of the best folk-dancing in all Spain, a sight of unimaginable beauty, and *El Alcalde de Zalamea* (the famous civic play of Calderón, which so boldly asserts the popular origin of authority and the primacy of the authority of the mayor, or the civil state, over that of the army), staged for the first time in a bull ring. Further to stress the national character of the celebrations, a new honor was inaugurated. On my initiative, the title of Citizen of Honor was created and surrounded with the highest moral, though not material, prerogatives. One such citizen was to be created every year on April 14. It was my intention to begin with two or three well-known men, of national prestige high above politics, and now and then to elect for the honor an unknown and humble-living person. That year Señor Cossío, the collaborator and spiritual heir of Don Francisco Giner, was the recipient.

While I was busy with these schemes of national union Señor Lerroux introduced his bill to amnesty all men guilty of political crimes committed before December 3, 1932. This meant the release of General Sanjurjo. I was trapped. If I stayed, I acted against my conviction; if I went, I gave an example of a public man unable to put into practice his own chief principle: tolerance and collaboration. I stayed. Meanwhile, the Minister of Justice suddenly had to resign, having given offense to the Left by referring to Galán and Hernández as rebels. All my colleagues, except the Minister of Labor, who was a doctor of medicine, were lawyers. It had been decided for reasons of internal politics to replace the Minister of Justice temporarily only, pending a ministerial reshuffle. This meant that if any of them took the portfolio, they would be automatically debarred from pursuing their legal profession for two years after they had occupied the post. They all begged me to take the portfolio. I took it, determined to make the Right pay for Sanjurjo's freedom by freeing as many Syndicalists as the Left would ask for, and for the rest of the debate my backbenchers had to bottle up their indignation while I yielded to Prieto's successive amendments to that effect.

The bill was voted. President Alcalá Zamora kept it on his desk as long as he could, was curt and even discourteous about it with us, and finally signed it with a long discourse in which he expounded legal disquisitions more learned than relevant. The Cabinet resigned. He chose as his next prime minister one of our colleagues in whom no one but President Alcalá Zamora could possibly have detected a budding prime minister, Señor Samper. When the new prime minister brought him his list of ministers, which differed in nothing from the previous Cabinet save that Señor Lerroux was not in it and that I was transferred to the Foreign Office, the president objected to my name on the ground, so I was told, that it would make it awkward for me to have to explain what had happened to the Amnesty Bill. It was therefore arranged that a *locum tenens* would be appointed till the debate on the crisis had been weathered, and then I would be retaken on board at the Foreign Office. As I left Madrid at the time for private reasons, I don't know how nor why the matter was quietly shelved, but I assume that the chief reasons were that Señor Samper wanted no trouble and the president wanted to be his own foreign secretary.

I was no professional politician and I had to earn my living. By then my literary profession enabled me to do so . . . on condition I was left free to follow it. This was not easy, for I had to be at hand at any time to attend League meetings in a variety of capacities. I asked that some facilities should be given to me. I had no office, no secretary, no information, no money for expenses. When I was in Geneva on government work, I was paid seventy Swiss francs a day for all personal and official expenses; when the League meeting ceased, all emoluments ceased. After months of delays a bill was introduced setting up the post of permanent delegate to the League of Nations on the Foreign Office budget with the salary of 25,000 (paper) pesetas a year. It was turned down by the Parliamentary Committee on Foreign Affairs on the motion of one of its members, by profession a member of the diplomatic service, who argued that everybody knew I was to be appointed to the post and that for such a post, which carried ambassadorial rank, I was not eligible since I had not passed the examinations for the diplomatic service.

I had been writing constantly in the newspapers of Madrid and Barcelona in favor of national union, trying to stem the current toward civil war which was taking possession of the nation. Radicals were hard at work to induce me to become a Radical, and assuring me that I would inherit the leadership of the party from Señor Lerroux. I refused to listen to these inducements for a number of reasons, and in particular because I had no private means to invest in such an expensive luxury as politics and my literary vocation was too strong to devote myself to an absorbing political life. My objectivity kept drawing me into difficult situations. Because I had agreed to work with Señor Lerroux, I became suspect to Azaña and his friends. Because I wrote an article asking respect, justice and deference for Azaña when the Right and the Radicals were attacking him, the Radicals were indignant. When the Popular Front triumphed on February 16, 1936, I was in New York. I returned to Madrid and explained to Azaña that, while I felt quite isolated in internal politics, my services for Geneva were at his disposal. The intrigue was already being prepared which has been told of in the text, but Azaña nevertheless appointed me to represent Spain in Geneva. His Foreign Secretary, Don Augusto Barcia, although unwittingly instrumental in bringing about my final separation from the government service, was a good friend and had always shown himself in complete agreement with my views and activities on foreign affairs in the frequent articles he devoted to them in the press.

I append a copy of the memorandum distributed to the neutrals, which was made the basis for the press campaign that led to my withdrawal.

NOTE SUR LA REVISION DE L'APPLICATION DU PACTE

Cette note confidentielle préparée par Monsieur de Madariaga, aux fins des études entreprises en commun par un certain nombre de pays membres de la Société des Nations, n'engage pas le Gouvernement espagnol. Ce Gouvernement est prêt à échanger des vues sur la question, avec les autres Gouvernements du groupe, sur la base ci-dessous ou sur toute autre base semblable.

1. De l'avis général, il y a lieu de revoir l'ensemble du Pacte, notamment en ce qui concerne l'efficace de ses stipulations à la lumière des seize années révolues. Les observations ci-dessous visent moins le perfectionnement du Pacte comme instrument juridique que la façon empirique de le rendre plus efficace du point de vue des nécessités politiques positives, telles que l'expérience de ces seize années les a révélées.

2. Il ne semble pas qu'il soit nécessaire de procéder par voie d'amendement. En principe, si les défauts observés

dans le fonctionnement du Pact peuvent être corrigés sans amendement de son texte, l'avantage de ne pas l'amender est évident puisque d'un côté il y a risque de détruire l'équilibre d'un document admirablement conçu, et que d'un autre côté la procédure de ratification est à tel point compliquée qu'il y aurait beaucoup trop d'optimisme à espérer que le nouveau Pacte ainsi établi entrerait en vigueur à une brève échéance. Du reste, il y a quelque intérêt à réserver l'intégrité du Pacte comme une borne nette vers laquelle doit tendre le développement de la Société.

3. Compte doit être tenu du fait que le Pacte ne peut agir à rendement plein que lorsque la Société sera universelle et que les circonstances politiques permettront que tous les articles soient également appliqués. Le défaut d'universalité est une cause suffisamment connue d'affaiblissement du Pacte pour exclure tout commentaire. Quant à l'équilibre de ses divers articles, il est évident que l'application pleine de l'article 8 est une nécessité politique et juridique qui détermine la vitalité de l'article 16. Il semble donc que les Etats membres de la Société seraient dans leur droit le plus strict en réservant au moyen d'une procédure à déterminer, leur obligation sur l'article 16 tant que l'universalité de la Société des Nations n'aura pas été atteinte et tant que les circonstances politiques n'auront pas permis l'application stricte de l'article 8.

Tout en laissant donc le texte du Pacte à l'état actuel, il serait l'objet d'une réserve générale qui délivrerait les Etats des responsabilités dérivant de cet article en ce qui concernerait les zones politiques et géographiques trop éloignées de la sphère de leurs intérêts; les Etats seraient libres de souscrire à nouveau les obligations pleines et entières de l'article 16 pour des zones politiques ou géographiques nettement définies par eux.

Cela permettrait de constituer à l'intérieur de Pacte des ententes régionales politiques d'assistance mutuelle efficace.

Il y a lieu de signaler les avantages que ce système présenterait à l'égard de la suppression pure et simple de l'article 16 d'un côté et des alliances ou ententes régionales de l'autre.

La disparition de l'article 16 ne saurait, dans l'état actuel des rapports politiques, que stimuler la création de groupes politico-militaires dont le danger est évident. Au contraire, le système de déclaration préalable d'application intégrale de l'article 16 pour des sanctions nettement définies soumettraient automatiquement l'action militaire éventuelle des groupes ainsi formés au conrôle du Conseil et de l'Assemblée, puisque le déclenchement de l'article 16 ne saurait se produire qu'après la mise en œuvre de la procédure des articles 12 à 15 ou la violation constatée de l'article 10. Le système pourrait être complété par un Pacte allégé de la plupart de ces articles et notamment des articles 10 et 16, *mais non de l'article II,* auquel pourraient être parties les Etats qui tiennent à rester en dehors du système de Genève.

5. Il y aurait lieu de revoir les pratiques jusqu'ici acceptées en matière d'unanimité en ce qui concerne les articles 10 et 11. L'usage de l'unanimité pour l'article 10 et, dans la plupart des cas, pour l'article 11 en fait des nonsens. L'opinion de la Société des Nations semble être déjà favorable à un changement dans les principes jusqu'ici maintenus par la majorité des juristes à cet égard.

6. Il faudrait remettre l'accent sur la partie préventive du Pacte, plutôt que sur son aspect punitif ou curatif. Tant que le Pacte est considéré surtout au point de vue des sanctions, il s'avère inefficace parce qu'il mène presque fatalement à des actes de guerre, alors qu'il est difficile de considérer la Société des Nations comme un instrument de guerre puisque son but est précisément de la prévenir. La politique préventive comprend au moins deux aspects importants:

a. Il ne peut y avoir de sécurité collective que pour autant qui'il y a politique collective. Il est inadmissible que les Etats membres de la Socièté soient appelés à leurs risques et périls à porter remède à des situations qui ont été créées sans eux. L'évolution de la solidarité sous l'article 16 doit être parallèle, non seulement à celle de la solidarité sous l'article 11, mais surtout à une solidarité d'action politique et diplomatique qui tout en n'étant pas définie dans aucun article du Pacte, en constitue l'esprit et s'exprime plus ou moins heureusement dans son préambule.

b. Il y a lieu de renforcer l'article 11 du Pacte, mais nullement en y attachant des sanctions, ce qui revient à en faire un second article 16.

La vraie méthode consiste à développer sous le bénéfice de cet article, l'idée des mesures conservatoires qui constitue la substance de la Convention sur les moyens de prévenir la guerre.

7. Procédure: il y a lieu de constater que les propositions ci-dessus exposées ne demandent point de procédures juridiques compliqués. *Sous réserve d'une étude juridique à faire par des personnes compétentes, elle semble tomber sous la sphère réservée à la souveraineté des Etats.* N'importe quel Etat ou groupe d'Etats pourrait par une déclaration écrite enrégistrée au Secrétariat général de la Société des Nations, mettre en vigueur l'état de choses ci-dessus esquissé sans autre forms de procès; une déclaration conjointe faite par un groupe d'Etats aurait naturellement plus d'autorité.

Genève, Mai 1936.

I was in London on private business in June 1936 when the campaign was started in the Spanish press against this document, stressing the point that it had been presented as a personal suggestion. It so happened that the foreign secretary, to whom I had given full notice and cognizance of the document in due time, no doubt under the stress of the grave preoccupations which then weighed on the government, forgot it, and to the pressing questions of journalists in the lobbies of the House of Parliament, answered that he knew nothing about it, thereby confirming the "personal" character of the paper. The Socialist Party issued a note in which they took as official and final this casual remark made by the foreign secretary to some journalists: "The facts go to show," they wrote in their official note, "that the Fascist systems are factors of war and in the midst of the growing tension which can be observed particularly in Europe, the Labor Socialist Party of Spain has seen with surprise the document which the permanent delegate of Spain to the League of Nations presented personally to the representatives of several states, a document which a month ago was being examined in the chancelleries owing to its bearing on peace. The Socialist Party notes with satisfaction that the Spanish government has rejected such a note and considers it neither as semi-official nor as official."

Published on June 6 in the Spanish press, this note of the Executive Committee of the Socialist Party unchained a passionate campaign of articles, notes, pin-pricks and caricatures, even in the press of the government I was serving. I was in London, blissfully unaware of it. On June 18 the Danish minister in London sent a Danish counter-proposal to my London residence at the request of his foreign secretary. "This proposal," he wrote, "embodies in some respects a somewhat closer development of the ideas contained in your memorandum, in other respects it deviates to some extent from it, and finally, certain other considerations have been added to it. We are thinking of using it as a basis of discussion, together with your memorandum, at a meeting which has been fixed for Thursday, 25 June, at Geneva."

I telegraphed this news to the foreign secretary and evidently my wire made him realize the error into which he had fallen. Why his staff was not able to point it out to him before, I am not in a position to say. He did his best to disentangle himself from the situation which his lapse of memory had created, without losing face; but of course he was bound to signify to the press that the position was not as simple as he and the Socialist note had so far led public opinion to believe. This did not prevent the campaign from continuing, particularly when, since I was *de jure* but a private individual, the government had to reappoint me to represent it at the meeting of the neutrals in Geneva and at that of the League Council as well, which they did on June 20. Although the foreign secretary, whom I saw in Geneva, paid a handsome tribute to my work in the private meeting of the neutral foreign secretaries, to undo whatever evil the campaign in Spain might have caused in their midst, and although the good faith of the foreign secretary was patent to me, I decided, in view of the press campaign, to withdraw from public service immediately after the Council meeting.

When I returned to Spain I drafted a note to the papers, the only answer I gave to the whole campaign, and after having read it to the foreign minister and the foreign secretary, I gave it to the press. Here is a translation of this note:

At the moment when I cease to consider myself at the service of the state, I beg the press to contribute, by publishing these lines, to inform the public on the circumstances in which I have come to this decision:

I. *The confidential note.*   Public opinion will understand that, although I discontinue my official duties, I am bound to keep the reserve which is indispensable in foreign affairs. I will therefore limit myself to putting on record that I hold at the disposal of the heads of all the parties the necessary documents to prove the following points:

1. The meeting of neutrals called for May 9 simultaneously by Spain and Denmark had precisely for its object the study of the reform, if not of the Covenant, of the League of Nations, and with that aim in view I had discussions with the then prime minister (Azaña) and the Minister of Foreign Affairs.

2. The verbal statement which, when my turn came, I made before my neutral colleagues, was strictly in line with these preparatory conversations.

3. The neutrals expressed their wish to have a written version of my statement.

4. I informed the Minister of Foreign Affairs of this wish and of my intention to satisfy it one day before beginning to work on my written note.

5. I drafted the note in the sense which flowed from my conversations in Madrid and from my telegram to the minister.

6. I sent five copies forthwith to Madrid by air, with a covering official note to which the Ministry of Foreign Affairs answered that they had taken note with interest.

7. By an elementary precaution, in view of the still rudimentary state of the discussions, I made the note my own, to allow the greatest possible liberty to the government.

8. It was distributed to the seven neutral powers and to a small number of delegations to which it could not be, in courtesy, refused, given the circumstances of each case.

9. I do not know when and how the text reached the agency which made it public.

II. The reaction of the press and of the Socialist Party rests therefore, so far as procedure is concerned, on no basis whatsoever, and therefore it does not affect me. As for the essence of the policy which the note implies, it is not for me to discuss it, but for the government. Nevertheless, I hold myself at the disposal of the heads of the parties if they should think my opinion useful to them.

It is not my wish, either, to express an opinion on the attacks which on this occasion have been leveled against me in the press of all shades of opinion. All I intend to do is to declare that in these circumstances I am not prepared to continue in the service of the state.

I had never served the state till the Republic was set up. I cease therefore after five years of service which I did not ask to render. In April 1931, I was professor of Spanish Studies in the University of Oxford and happened to be on leave holding a course of lectures in the University

of Mexico. I asked no post either directly or indirectly of
the Provisional Government. Without consulting me, they
appointed me Ambassador in Washington. On May 13,
from New York when the Republic was one month old but
for one day, I accepted the Embassy and resigned the Chair.
From April 1934 I have served continually as *de facto*
permanent delegate in Geneva. I have no appointment, no
post, no salary, no office, no secretary, no files. I have
nothing but my good will. I cannot even resign, for I have
nothing to resign from. I therefore renounce the only thing
I possess, the honor to serve the state of a nation which
was great and will be great again if all Spaniards are at one
to wish it.

I should only like to add that my faith is firmer than
ever in the League of Nations as the only form of international give-and-take capable of saving the world from
a catastrophe without precedent, and also to express my
gratitude to my collaborators of these five years among
whom I wish to single out the admirable López Oliván.

El Socialista, the paper which had attacked me most violently,
did not publish the note. Other papers which had also distinguished themselves for their violence published short extracts
with comments of their own as they thought fit. I withdrew to
a country cottage opposite Toledo where, at the urgent advice
of my physician, I planned to spend a month. Within a few days
government airplanes were flying over my roof to bomb the city
and force the Rebel garrison to surrender. I knew no one in
Toledo, for I had rarely been able to spend a free weekend
there. I then felt more than ever how detached and isolated I
was from the political forces of the country, but I did not
yet realize the full danger. I only felt the powerlessness of my
isolation, as I watched the black smoke of the bombs rising
between the Cathedral and the Alcázar and the flashes of the
Government artillery on the road to Madrid.

One evening, at dusk, five men armed with guns came to my
house. They explained that my sister in Madrid had put my car

at their disposal, for they were militiamen. This, by the way, was the only method to avoid the car's being taken by force. As she had heard them say that they had a mission in Toledo (I knew later that this mission was an innocent joy-ride), she had suggested they come and fetch me. I left with them. During the seventy-kilometer ride to Madrid we counted seventy-one abandoned cars. The password on the road was "Russia I." We were stopped at every village by armed guards to verify that we had not stolen anything; and at Villaverde, the last stop before Madrid, the village militiamen insisted on taking me into custody, mistaking me for a member of Parliament from Toledo, of Señor Gil Robles's Party, whose name happened to be Don Dimas Madariaga, no relation of mine. (He was shot dead shortly after this episode.) "Don't you see he is not the deputy, but the Ambassador?" asked the militiaman. "Is he?" retorted the militiaman on the road. "Then let us have him also." And to be sure, if I had been what the press this good man had been reading said I was, his zeal might have been justified. My five youths, however, took it as a matter of pride to assert their rights over my person and their responsibility for my safety. They left the militiaman grumbling on the road and drove away.

Madrid was then in the thick of the red terror. Every now and then, the sound of an automobile was heard. No one had cars but the Revolutionists. A car pulled up before a house; the bell rang. A man was taken away from his house and went to add to the heap of bodies in the Casa de Campo or any of several other places where a blind destructive force, not even furious, dumped its victims. A good-for-nothing who had drawn an unearned salary from the Spanish Embassy in Paris, and whom I had sent back for utter incompetence to the friends in Madrid who had recommended him, had suddenly emerged from obscurity and was filling the columns of the two Socialist papers of Madrid with poisonous articles against me, even though the two editors, Zugazagoitia and Araquistain, had both been given documentary proof of the value of their collaborator. I rang up the Minister of Foreign Affairs, who, with all his colleagues, was barricaded in the Ministry of the Navy. I offered my services to the government and added that if they were not taken it would be better if arrangements were made for me to go abroad, since no man, such as I was, without a trade-union or party ticket, was safe in Madrid. He gave me some papers and a detective and I left for France by rail, by way of Valencia and Barcelona.

I arrived in Geneva where I had left my wife and daughters, as well as a small secretariat, for I was then busy with my "World Foundation" activities. Within a month of the outbreak of the Civil War, I began actively to work to bring it to an end. On August 18 I wrote to Mr. Eden the letter to which I refer in the text and from that day on I kept in as close touch as I discreetly could with the British and the French Governments, always urging intervention for peace as well as, or rather than, non-intervention for war. This included some personal calls and a certain amount of correspondence which I would be glad to publish if it were within the bounds of discretion.

I need not say that this activity was deeply resented not only by those who had a vested interest, moral or otherwise, in the war, but also by many who ought to have kept their heads above the conflict. I cannot, of course, report all the attacks of which I was the victim here, but I do single out a particularly malevolent one from *Week,* the Communist newsletter, because, contrary to all traditions of British journalism, the editor did not print my answer.

I resisted every pressure to write or speak on the Civil War except an article I published in the *Observer* (October 11, 1936) in which I attempted to define the issue afresh for British public opinion. This article contained practically every fundamental idea which will be found developed in this volume. My silence on Spain was particularly trying in the United States where I spent three months that winter on a lecture tour and where my audiences, not unnaturally, found it difficult to understand that I should refuse to speak on the Civil War. My reasons were obvious: I could not speak for the Rebels, for they stood against all that I hold true; I could not speak for the Revolutionists, not only because I did not believe in their methods (nor, in the case of some of them, in their aims) but because they did not stand for what they said they stood for. They filled their mouths with democracy and liberty but allowed neither to live.

On Monday, July 19, 1937, the first anniversary of the Civil War, I published simultaneously in the London and New York *Times, Le Temps* and *La Nación* of Buenos Aires[1] the following letter:

> Sir,—In a few days Spain will enter upon the second year of the Civil War. I beg the hospitality of your columns to ask for peace. I am only too painfully aware of the difficulties that stand in the way. Let me first remove the humblest of them: that the request should come from a Spaniard who has throughout remained equally distant from both sides. May I ask both sides to bear with me? The hour is too grave, for Spain and for Europe, to stop at persons. Let them hear the message, if not the voice.
>
> Let each, moreover, forgive me my endeavor to understand the other—indeed, my endeavor to induce each to understand the other. Both fight for an ideal. But has not enough blood and treasure been sacrificed to such ideals, however high they may be? Both are moved by a noble patriotism, toward a better Spain—in their eyes. But, while fighting for an ideal Spain, are they not destroying that real Spain without which one cannot materialize their ideal? Both seek a victory. But they should see that moral victory —the one that matters—will not be theirs, whoever wins, since military victory will be due to the predominance of foreign war weapons—i.e. to a merely accidental and extraneous circumstance without any inherent meaning in the history of Spain. Thus the real Spain will not be committed to a victory which—whoever wins—will be a foreign victory. And so—whoever wins—Spain is defeated.
>
> Let the leaders on both sides forgive me if, as a fellow Spaniard, by no means wiser than they are, but who has over them the bitter advantage of exile and distance, I ask

[1] Owing to some technical difficulty, I believe the letter did not reach *La Nación* in time.

them to stand back in the solitude of their conscience, away from the fire and smoke of material and moral war; they will then realize that there is only one way for Spain to win this war—and that is precisely through a peace by reconciliation.

They are, on both sides, keen-eyed men. They cannot fail to delve below the enthusiasm—genuine though it is—which surrounds them. Human beings live at many levels, and true life seldom flows at the surface. To be sure, one side is fighting to free Spain from what it sees as tyranny, the other from what it sees as anarchy. But is there a worse anarchy and a worse tyranny than those implied in a civil war? Let them bear in mind the appalling host of the dead, the still more appalling host of the living forever spiritually maimed by what they have suffered, seen and, worst of all, *done*. Let them realize that, deep down, below the level of enthusiasm, what the Spanish people on both sides long for is peace. And, again, that whoever wins must govern with the good will of all Spaniards. And that good will cannot be enforced.

By a tragic coincidence, this war, essentially Spanish, has "caught on" abroad. Lured by somewhat shallow parallelisms, men, institutions, and even governments outside Spain have been adding fuel to the fire which is consuming our unhappy country. Spain is thus suffering vicariously the latent civil war which Europe is—so far—keeping in check. I earnestly hope that the more militant groups on both sides will realize that their activities are not merely dangerous—that they do see—but also sterile. Spain will never be either Communist or Fascist. Her foreign policy, determined by geopolitical and economic laws, will never vary fundamentally—whoever wins—and foreign help, known to have been given for something more than its own sake, is sure to call forth deep resentment after the war in Spain, in all Spain. Here again, the best policy, and the one most in harmony with the interests of all the nations concerned, is to agree to bring about a speedy end of the war through reconciliation.

Finally, I would ask both sides—in and out of Spain—to refrain from sacrificing to the satisfaction of their political passions the life and blood of a nation whose destinies and whose contribution to world life and culture are more precious than political theories, after all mere uncertain and ephemeral forms of our faltering human thought.

The British government did me the honor of associating themselves with the general tenor of this letter through Mr. Eden who quoted some of its paragraphs in the debate in the House of Commons of the same date. I was in Switzerland at the time and had not seen Mr. Eden or anybody at the Foreign Office for many months, but this spontaneous agreement which Mr. Eden made public may have given rise to a belief that something was afoot between His Majesty's Government and myself. On August 11, 1937, for instance, my old friend Senator de Brouckère, (now dead) wrote an article in *Le Peuple* of Brussels, commenting upon the rumors that were then abroad and which attributed to the British government, and especially to Sir Robert Vansittart (as he was then), the plan to put King Alfonso back on the throne in exchange for a number of political guarantees of which I would be the guarantor as prime minister, "placed by England close to the Monarch." I feel certain that Monsieur de Brouckère published the article knowing full well that, even if the British government had thought of such a complicated plan, I was not the man to be put anywhere by any government. In my answer to the paper I explained among other things that I had not seen King Alfonso since December 1927, and that it was through Monsieur de Brouckère's article I had learned the king was staying at the time close to Lausanne; that there was of course not the slightest foundation for the rumors which disquieted Monsieur de Brouckère; and finally, that I loved my country far too much to wish to govern it.

This was no phrase. I hold statesmanship to be the highest

of the fine arts, but I do not feel strongly drawn to politics. I had never before taken any part whatever in political life when I was "mobilized" by the Provisional Government in my forty-fifth year. Political categories are shoddy and rough; and in order to handle them one must do violence to life by oversimplification and overstatement. The rest of my life in exile has been spent in literary work; and in repeated endeavors to help bring about the end of the Civil War, particularly in collaboration with the *Comité de la Paix Civile* which was organized in Paris by Professor Menzidábal.

To close this brief sketch, I append two letters I wrote to the London *Times,* both of which explain themselves.

Sir,—There is a danger lest the Spanish state of war may be unduly prolonged under the influence of that ideological strife which did so much both to initiate and to feed its destructive fire for over two years. I am not merely thinking of the various pretexts now being raised to keep the Italian troops in Spain, but also of the reluctance shown by the Socialist and Liberal parties of Europe to evacute the Spanish field. There is a moral, as well as a physical, invasion, and both are injuring Spain badly. Recent events would appear to show that General Franco may be trusted to deal with the first. But it may be that the Liberal and Socialist parties of several European countries do not fully realize that the time has come for them to withdraw from Spain.

A few hard facts may help:

(1) The number of people who are dying of hunger in Madrid a week is between 40 and 500. No one speaks for them. The future of Spain for them is a matter of life and death.

(2) There is no Spanish Republican Government left. According to the constitution of the Republic the authority of the Cabinet rests on the confidence of the President and of the Cortes. The President is in Paris and has not said a word as to the situation. If he

thought the war should go on he would be in Madrid. The Cortes of the Republic comprise 470 members of Parliament. The quorum of the last meeting, held in Figueras, was 62. I have no wish to disparage—or to praise—Dr. Negrín. The time has not come for that, and I am no judge. But when he says he wants to fight on, for whom does he speak?

(3) We are told that Spain must fight on till the foreigner goes. I am sure that the Liberal and Socialist parties of Europe will credit all Spaniards with at least as anxious a desire for that as they themselves feel. But who can seriously believe that the best way to liberate Spain from the foreigner is to carry on this senseless war?

(4) Every Spaniard who knows the facts will be grateful to Liberals and Socialists all over Europe, and in particular to those in this country, for all they intended to do in favor of Spain even if at times some of us may have differed as to what they actually did for Spain. But may we now ask them to ask themselves whether by encouraging Dr. Negrín and his colleagues to continue a war more senseless and useless than ever, though by no means less cruel, they are not shouldering a heavy responsibility?

The end of the war is not to their liking. It is not to the liking of many of us. But let there be peace and let Spain take care of herself and of her future undisturbed not only by Fascists, but also by Leftists.

February 13, 1939.

Sir,—Don Julián Besteiro, who has been court-martialled in Madrid and given a thirty-year—practically a life—sentence, though a prominent Marxist, was a consistent opponent of violent methods of opposition throughout the Republican days, and in the councils of the Socialist

Party he stood courageously against the hotheads who have brought the country to the present plight. His fidelity to Madrid, whose terrible sufferings he shared throughout the siege despite his years and indifferent health, his dignified silence under the scurrilous attacks of his extremist political enemies, and his constancy were the admiration of all impartial Spaniards. He was to surpass them by the heroic courage with which he chose to take office in order to put an end to a war which by then was but a heartless slaughter of misguided workers. In less harrowing times the whole civilized world would now be focusing its attention on the stoic figure, undoubtedly the noblest victim of the Spanish tragedy.

July 14, 1939.

INDEX

699